ANAÏS NIN

A Biography

ALSO BY DEIRDRE BAIR

Simone de Beauvoir: A Biography
Samuel Beckett: A Biography

ANAÏS NIN

A Biography

DEIRDRE BAIR

G. P. PUTNAM'S SONS · NEW YORK

The author thanks the Anaïs Nin Trust for use of the frontispiece photograph—Henry Miller's favorite picture of Anaïs Nin, it shows her standing in the garden at Louveciennes—as well as for the photographs on pages 124, 125, 156, 201, 225, 227 (two photographs), 263, 274, 291, 303, 329 (two photographs), 345, 354, 371, 385, 395, 407, 415, 443, 457, 459, 473 (photograph of Anaïs Nin), and 519; Joaquín Nin Culmell for the photographs on pages 7, 8, 19, 20, 33, 44 (two photographs), 45, 58, 59 (two photographs), 69, 79 (two photographs), 87, 88, 101, 115, 145, 175, 183, 384, and 489; Phyllis Grosskurth for photograph on page 191; Juste de Nin for drawing on page 217; UCLA for photographs on pages 250, 317, and 429; Gayle Nin Rosenkrantz for photograph on page 473; Rupert Pole for photograph on page 508; Joan Schwartz, courtesy Charles Ruas and Rob Wynn for photographs on pages 508 and 509; and Rochelle Lynn Holt for photograph on page 517.

Published by G. P. Putnam's Sons
200 Madison Avenue, New York, NY 10016
Published simultaneously in Canada

The text of this book is set in Garamond Book

Designed by MaryJane DiMassi

Library of Congress Cataloging-in-Publication Data

Bair, Deirdre.
Anaïs Nin, a biography / Deirdre Bair.
p. cm.
Includes bibliographical references and index
ISBN 0-399-13988-5
1. Nin, Anaïs, 1903–1977—Biography. 2. Women authors, American—20th century—Biography. I. Title.
PS3527.I865Z55 1995 94-28865 CIP
818'.5209—dc20
[B]

Printed in the United States of America
1 2 3 4 5 6 7 8 9 10

This book is printed on recycled paper.

For my sister and brother,
Linda B. Rankin and Vincent J. Bartolotta, Jr.

Contents

CONTENTS

Acknowledgments

THE PERSONS WHO KNEW Anaïs Nin best and loved her most made this book possible: Joaquín Nin-Culmell, John Ferrone, Rupert Pole, and Gunther Stuhlmann. They have allowed me to create the biographer's ideal working condition by giving me unparalleled access to written archives and personal memories while relinquishing all control of the final manuscript. I am enormously grateful for their unstinting generosity and for their friendships, which have sustained me.

Gayle Nin Rosenkrantz, Thorvald Nin's daughter, has provided a version of her family's history that has greatly enriched this book. She, too, has been generous with family archives and friendship I value.

The staff of the UCLA University Research Library provided every possible support and camaraderie during the many months I read Anaïs Nin's diaries there. I thank David S. Zeidberg, Anne Caiger, Lilace Hatayama, James Davis, Octavio Olivera, Jeffrey Rankin, Simon Elliot, Jaime Lara, Carol Turley, and Flora Ito.

Anaïs Nin was fortunate to have so many kind and caring friends. I wish space allowed me to do more than simply list the names of those who helped me here: Virginia Admiral, Frank Alberti, Daisy Aldan, Kenneth Anger, Don Bachardy, Bebe Barron, Wendy Beckett, Betty Berzon, Lili Bita, Frances Schiff Bolton, William Burford, Cameron, Richard Centing, William Claire, Anne Conover, Blanche Cooney, Samson De Brier, Renate Druks, Edwin Fancher, Pamela Fiori, Benjamin Franklin V, Nan Fuchs, Anne Geismar, Carter Harmon, Valerie Harms, Curtis Harrington, Jack and Caridad Sánchez Helm, James Leo Herlihy, Judith Hipskind, Rochelle Lynn Holt, Barbara Kraft, Victor Lipari, James Merrill,

Deena Metzger, Anna Crouse Murch, Nancy and Donald Newlove, Dorothy Norman, John Pierson, Tristine Rainer, Lila Rosenblum, Raymonde Olivera, Barbara Reis Poe, Charles Ruas, Martin Sameth, Martha J. Sattler, Duane Schneider, Alexandria Soteriou, Sharon Spencer, Daniel Stern, Barbara Stuhlmann, Kazuko Sugisaki, Lenore Tawney, Val Telberg, Gore Vidal, Beatrice Wood, Lori A. Wood, Rob Wynne, Marguerite Young, Robert Zaller, Harriet Zinnes.

For personal support and professional assistance, I wish to thank Greg Almquist, Digby and Jocelyn C. Baltzell, Mali BéLé, Mary Elizabeth and Craig Black, Diana Cavallo, Myra Chanin, Walter Clemons, John Cody, Larry Cohn, Marianna Costanza, Claude Courchay, James Devereux, Bettina Drew, Richard Elman, Pamela Emory, Helen W. Drutt English, Chriswell Gonzalez, Phyllis Grosskurth, Carolyn Heilbrun, Fred Hills, Carmen and Jairo Hinestroza, Temma Kaplan, Jascha and Julia Braun Kessler, Robert Kiely, Jane Kinney, Carol Klein, Elaine Lewis, E. James Lieberman, Patricia Louis, Nancy MacKnight, Alane Mason, Frances McCullough, Joan Mellen, Sylvia Molloy, Honor Moore, Inge Morath, Mary Perot Nichols, Gloria Orenstein, Winnifred Pasternack, Arthur Prager, Michael Rakosi, Paul Roazen, Elisabeth Roudinesco, Ricki and Wayne Rush, Peggy Sanday, Tom Schiller, Robert W. Schmitt, Claire Shapiro, James H. Silberman, Eileen Simpson, Michele Slung, Michael Tracy Smith, Allison Stokes, Rosemary Sullivan, Bob Tauber, Tom Thompson, Ann B. Toole, Helene Rank Veltfort, Robert Walters, Aileen Ward, Helen P. Wenck, Gail Woodley-Atella, Eugenia Zimmerman.

I thank the entire membership of the Women Writing Women's Lives Seminar for their interest during this book's long gestation, and the fellows of the New York Institute for the Humanities at New York University, who provided lively and thought-provoking dialogues during Friday lunches.

Elaine Markson is both friend and agent unparalleled, as are her associates, Sally Wofford Girand, Geri Thoma, Caomh Kavanagh, and Stephanie Hawkins.

I wish to thank Fred Sawyer for copyediting, Ann Spinelli for the book's splendid cover, and MaryJane DiMassi for its handsome design. Phyllis Grann has been an invaluable ally throughout the long publication process.

I owe special thanks to Keith B. Raskin, M.D., who put my shattered wrist back together; to Celia Vigliotta, O.T.R., who taught me how to regain the use of my arm; and to Larissa Baczyk and Gloria Espinosa, whose unfailing good cheer hastened my recovery.

Finally, I am deeply grateful to my family, who because of my arm had to live with this book a lot longer than they expected. For all their help,

ACKNOWLEDGMENTS

I thank Lavon H. Bair, Vonn Scott and Katney Bair, Niko Courtelis, John R. Rankin, Judith and Helen Bartolotta, Catherine Montecarlo, and Aldo, Armand, Leo, Agnes, Dora, Lorayne, and Joanne Bartolotta. Also, Leah and the late Bill Balliard.

I write this in every book and I truly mean it: one of my worst fears is that I will inadvertently omit naming persons who have helped make the book possible. If there are some whom I have not listed here, I apologize and beg them to believe that I did—and do—value their contribution.

DEIRDRE BAIR

New York
October 30, 1994

Introduction

"The idea of relativity makes many people fearful—the idea that you are one person with me today and another person with someone else later."[1] Anaïs Nin said this in a 1971 interview; I have been reminded of it every day since 1990, when I began to write this book. The quality of mutability was what intrigued me most as I struggled to interpret the facts and events of her life, for each morning, I was struck by how the Anaïs Nin I wrote about the previous day was fast becoming a different woman who required an altogether different approach and appraisal.

For my previous biographies (of Samuel Beckett and Simone de Beauvoir), I was fortunate that both were alive and willing to talk about (in some cases to argue) how the written versions of their lives should unfold. Unfortunately, this was not the case with Anaïs Nin, whom I never met, so I had to settle for the verbal testimony of those who had known her. I tried to talk to the many persons who figured throughout her life, and I was astonished at the range of their responses, especially how, in so many cases, the mere mention of her name provoked vehemence and outrage. I was puzzled, because the emotional expression seemed far greater than I thought appropriate. So a crucial issue became my trying to understand what there was about Anaïs Nin that made people react so strongly even though she had died more than a decade earlier.

The persons whose testimony I collected included those who had known her in varying degrees of friendship and intimacy, those who had merely read all or parts of her published diary (or "liary," as one called it), and those like the very young university students I addressed in far-off Australia who told me all they knew about her was that "Nin had a lot of sex and lied a lot."

Even the judgment of some of her so-called friends was that Anaïs Nin's life was less deserving of a biography than (to give the two examples I am best qualified to cite) Beckett's or Beauvoir's; that Nin did not "deserve" (the word I heard most frequently) a thorough, responsible, and scholarly biography, either by me, or for that matter, any other scholar.

When I pressed for their reasons, the answer was always simple and direct: Anaïs Nin "lied"; she "could not be trusted." Such a harsh appraisal made me think deeply about the evolution of Nin's many years and many variations of diary writing. When, I pondered, or where, or even why, was it decided that literature had to be founded on "truth" (whatever that concept stands for in this postmodern age)? And could we not apply the same appraisal—"she lied"—to any number of other writers, men and women alike?

What was there about Anaïs Nin and not about those other writers that provoked such vehement condemnation? Was it the teasing hint of sexuality that lies just beneath the textual surface of the published diaries? Was it because she was a woman who insisted upon "living out the dream" (her favorite expression) in so many shockingly different kinds of freedom long before others recognized, let alone identified, kinds of conduct and behavior that women throughout the world now take for granted?

In one form or another, this was what engaged me during the many months I sat poring over her original diaries in the UCLA library, hunting for clues that would allow me to present as unified a profile of this woman's personality as possible. I was frequently frustrated as I strove to express *my* view of *her* life in an objective and coherent manner, and this too, was intriguing. I have said elsewhere that the biographer's task is to remain skeptical of the subject's record of her life, both the written and the spoken. As a biographer in the postmodern age, I still believe in trying to capture what others may consider anachronistic—the impugned, much disputed concept of objectivity.

Because Anaïs Nin was not alive to argue her version of her life, I had to find other methods to allow her voice to be heard within the pages of my book. I tried to meld two separate processes here: first, to present her point of view as she expressed it in the diary and her many other writings, from fiction to correspondence; within this, I interspersed the memories and opinions, both oral and written, of the many others who were involved.

My starting point was Anaïs Nin's original diaries, the sixty-nine volumes of elegantly written prose, as well as the several hundred file folders compiled during the last thirty-some years of her life, into which she stuffed diary writings, letters from others and carbon copies of her own, or whatever else struck her fancy, from totally unrelated newspaper jottings to photographs of herself. I compared everything with the various typed versions of the diary that she prepared throughout her life, noting how time and distance made her change much in some instances and nothing at all in others. I checked her evolving texts against the documents that became the first seven volumes of her published diaries, the four volumes of the early diaries, and finally the series that is presently appearing as the "unexpurgated" diaries.

In every instance, I tried to collect written and spoken testimony from those who knew her, whether she wrote about them in the diary or not. Wherever it seemed appropriate, I presented the positions or points of view of those opposed in varying degrees to Nin's own.

Throughout this book, I tried to avoid labeling either Anaïs Nin or those persons who figured throughout her life, mostly because everyone I spoke to tried to do it for me. I tried to avoid all these labels, from the person who coined the term, "the liary," to the scholar who disrupted a lecture to insist that I apply a litany of clinical and pathological terms to Anaïs Nin's personality. I avoided attaching labels, terms, or clinical descriptions to her because my primary aim in this biography is to allow readers to form their own opinions about this woman I found so compellingly complex; also (and more important to me personally), because I believe in the biographical imperative that any given life must serve to present evidence for further scholarly inquiry.

This book is large, but it is, however, less than a third of the original manuscript and has been pared down to the extent that it sometimes merely touches on what I consider to be important about Anaïs Nin. I hope that it serves as the starting point for further critical and biographical inquiry, because a life as rich and full as Anaïs Nin's deserves further investigation if only to enable the rest of us to understand the chaotic century that is now winding down.

But why, many people asked, does a writer like Anaïs Nin, whose novels are seldom read these days, whose reputation has fallen into disrepute because of the "liary"—why does she need, indeed demand, biographical attention? I certainly agree with the view that Anaïs Nin will enter posterity as a minor writer, but I insist upon one distinction: that she must be judged a *major* minor writer.

The writer Cynthia Ozick made my point gracefully in an essay about the "neglected" novelist Alfred Chester.[2] Ozick argued that if we could agree upon and explain what constitutes a minor writer, it "would bring us a little nearer to defining a culture," for "the tone of a culture cannot depend only on the occasional genius, or the illusion of one; the prevailing temper of a society and a time is situated in its minor voices, in their variegated chorus." Ozick believes, and I agree, that "minor writers are the armature onto which the clay of greatness is thrown, pressed, prodded."

For me, Anaïs Nin was exactly that—the armature onto which the clay of greatness was thrown: sadly in her case, too haphazardly to create a uniform vessel. Perhaps it is equivocating to say that she was immensely talented even though not an original thinker, but yet she consistently discerned what was worthwhile in the literature and culture of her time. She was a shining exemplar of the modernist dictum "Make it new," for she was prescient enough to poise herself directly in the path of all that was fresh, exciting, and frequently controversial, from D. H. Lawrence to the Beat poets, and to embrace it willingly despite the consequences.

The twentieth century will be remembered for many concepts that brought sweeping societal change, and Anaïs Nin was among the pioneers who explored three of the most important: sex, the self, and psychoanalysis. When future generations seek to understand how these evolved in our time, Anaïs Nin will be the major minor writer whose work they must consult.

ANAÏS NIN

A Biography

1

A Most Unlikely Marriage

IN ALL OF CUBA in 1902, there could not have been a more unlikely marriage than that between the man and woman who became the parents of Anaïs Nin: Rosa Culmell y Vaurigaud and Joaquín Nin y Castellanos.[1] Rosa was thirty-one, the eldest and favorite of five daughters of a wealthy Danish merchant and his French-Cuban wife. Her twenty-three-year-old bridegroom was a penniless musician of minor Spanish nobility who had fled from Barcelona after he seduced a student and her father threatened to horsewhip him if he showed his face there ever again.[2]

Family legend has it that Rosa first saw Joaquín in a music store, where he was "dazzling the locals"[3] by playing the piano. She took one look at "the handsome young man in the shabby trousers"[4] and for her, it was love at first sight. For him, it took longer, perhaps until he learned how well situated her family was, both socially and financially.

Rosa's father, Thorvald Culmell Christensen, was the youngest of three adventurous brothers born in Denmark who set out to make their fortunes in business in the new world.[5] According to his descendants, Thorvald wanted to distance himself from his elder brother, who became rich supplying African slaves to Cuban sugar plantations, which he did by reversing his surnames and calling himself Thorvald C. Culmell. He prospered in his own import-export business,[6] and his wealth made him a paragon of society, but he remained conscious of the social distinctions between Cubans by birth, Cubans of Spanish descent who settled on the island, and non-Hispanic others who simply chose to make the island their home. Thorvald C always referred to himself as "an honorable man of good faith, closely tied to Cuba by family and interests even though I am a foreigner,"[7] probably a successful business ploy as well. He became so wealthy that by the 1890s he was able to build a splendid three-story house on the Malecón, the beachfront avenue where the finest families lived.

Thorvald C's wife, mother of his nine children, Anaïs[8] Vaurigaud y Bourdin, was of French descent. She preferred to tell her children and grandchildren that she was born in New Orleans, where her parents lived for a time after leaving France, but she was actually born in Havana, where they settled shortly after. The only certainty is that, like her granddaughter Anaïs Nin, she was exposed to a variety of languages and cultures in the early years of her life.[9]

The version of the family legend that her granddaughter Anaïs Nin preferred has it that Thorvald C threw the first Anaïs out of their house when he found her with a lover. The majority of her descendants, however, chose to believe that she "apparently saw too much of one gentleman in a platonic sense."[10] Whichever was true, when Thorvald C rebuked her, Anaïs Culmell abandoned him and their nine children and moved into her own house in Havana, where she lived out her life exactly as she pleased.[11] In a sense, their unorthodox married life was an eerie prefiguration of their granddaughter's.

The first Anaïs's willfulness created a serious problem for Thorvald C because none of their five daughters was then married. Had his position not been buttressed by great wealth and high political and social standing, his daughters might well have been declared unmarriageable in such a rigid and restricted society. However, his reputation had been above reproach since 1897, when he began several years of quiet diplomatic activity as an unofficial envoy in the negotiations that eventually led to Cuban independence.[12]

Rosa, the eldest, became a surrogate mother to her four sisters: Juana, Anaïs, Edelmira, and Antolina, and two unmarried brothers: Thorvald and Téodoro, who soon followed their brothers, Pedro and Enrique, into marriage and disappeared from the daily family drama.[13] Rosa and her sisters thus became the glue that held the Culmell family together, and they all figured largely in Anaïs Nin's life.

Juana, Anaïs Nin's godmother, never married; she was "engaged to a gymnast who died in midair and supposedly, she never recovered."[14] She became opinionated and domineering, especially toward Rosa, whose children mistrusted her because of her rigid disposition and because she frequently tattled on them.

Like Rosa (a mezzo-soprano), the third sister, Anaïs, also had a beautiful soprano singing voice. The two often performed for Thorvald C's guests, but there was little closeness between them. Of all the sisters, Anaïs was the coldest and most reserved and, after her marriage, the most oppressed. She married Bernabé Sánchez, who made his fortune raising cattle in Camagüey province. Anaïs Culmell de Sánchez lived alone most of the time in Havana, her spirit so crushed by her husband's machismo that she preferred to retreat into inaction rather than put his considerable fortune to any use at all.[15] He usually remained on his plantation in Camagüey with another "wife" and a second family; this, too, eerily prescient of Anaïs Nin's later life.[16] They had seven children, three of whom, Graciella, Eduardo, and Ana María, were important as confidants and sources of income at various times in Anaïs Nin's life.

Edelmira met her American husband, Commander Gilbert Chase, USN, a Virginian from a respected family and a graduate of the U.S. Naval Academy, in Havana.[17] Chase was subsequently stationed for many years at the Brooklyn Navy Yard, and he, Edelmira, and their two children, Gilbert Jr. and María Teresa, lived in a Victorian mansion in Kew Gardens, then countryside in the New York City borough of Queens. Edelmira became subsumed in an unhappy marriage and took to her bed frequently with various *crises de nerfs*. To keep her household running smoothly, she relied on her sisters and a succession of nannies. In the early years of their life in New York, the Nin children became devoted to both their aunt and uncle and were frequent visitors to the seemingly happy house that Anaïs, then writing only in French, called "Quieu."[18]

Antolina, the youngest of the Culmell sisters, was the most powerful and played the largest role in both Rosa's and Anaïs Nin's lives. She was closest to Rosa in personality, but nevertheless the two were always competitive and jockeying for primacy within the family hierarchy. Antolina, a beautiful fiery woman, was intelligent enough to spot what others needed and independent enough to step in and take care of it without fearing the consequences.

She married General Rafael de Cárdenas, had three children, and became one of Havana's most formidable women. After her marriage,

Antolina lived as independently as her mother, traveling often without a chaperone to Europe and New York. She cared nothing for organized society and lived quite outside it, but was always a force with which to be reckoned. "It's true, money can do everything," the eleven-year-old Anaïs Nin, already aware of Tía Antolina's power, confided to her diary.[19]

All five sisters became remarkable women. All became fluent in English, but only Rosa and Juana were educated at the exclusive Brentwood Convent School on Long Island, run by the Sisters of the Sacred Heart.[20] During their summer vacations and after they graduated, they were sent to live for several years in an uncle's château in France, where they learned flawless French. Juana, much more than Rosa, lorded her cultured sophistication over her younger sisters, even though all five had been given the finest "finishing school" education in Havana, preparation to make excellent marriages. Throughout the travel and education of their formative years, the Culmell sisters picked up other, more valuable qualities of unwavering dedication to each other, independence, self-sufficiency, and willingness to ignore social constraints to do what was best for themselves and their children. These qualities were most pronounced in Rosa and to a lesser degree in Antolina, but of all their seven daughters, only Rosa's Anaïs Nin inherited them.

Rosa, like all her sisters, was attractive, fairly tall by the standards of the time, with a full buxom figure, brown hair and eyes, fair skin, and a direct and forceful personality. Her father delighted in her lovely voice and allowed her to take private lessons; everyone who heard her sing thought she had professional talent, but Rosa was content to perform only for family and friends.

Despite a distinguished parade of suitors and proposals, the eminently marriageable Rosa was still single at thirty, at a time and in a country where the prevailing attitude was "If a woman is not married, she has no joy in living. To remain single is truly a calamity."[21]

Rosa's formidable personality may have been off-putting to the typical Cuban man of her social class and station. More important was that, in the motherless Culmell household, her role was that of "the Sacrifice," the daughter who either could not or did not want to marry, the one who cared for her parents if both were alive or, if the mother was missing from the household, acted as domestic manager, hostess for her father, and surrogate mother to her younger sisters and brothers.[22] Rosa chose not to marry because she had the inde-

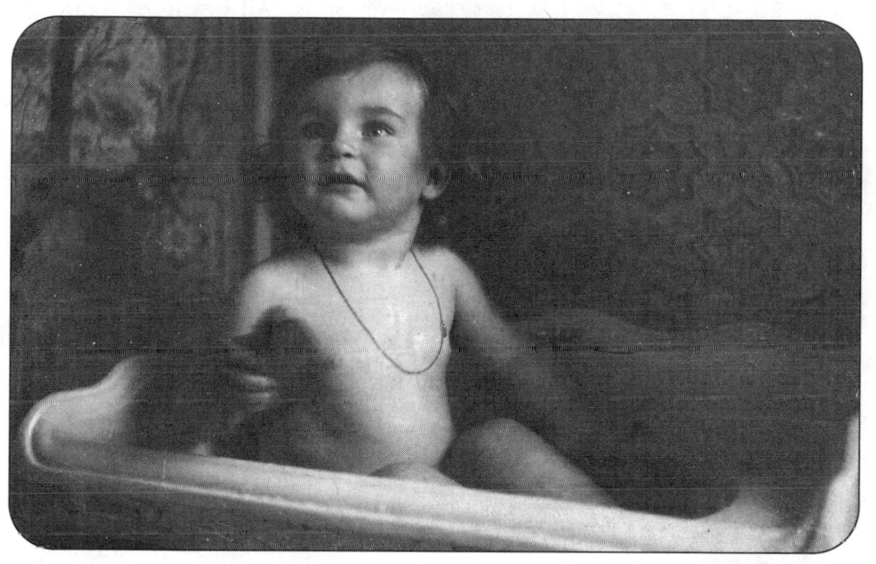

Baby Anaïs in her bath, taken by her father.

Baby Anaïs Nin in Havana with *(l. to r.)* her father, mother, and grandfather Thorvald C. Culmell, and *(top row)* Edelmira Culmell Chase, Thorvald Culmell and Juana Culmell.

pendence and status of a married woman without having to go through the formality of taking a mate unless she truly wanted one.

So, after the marriages of Anaïs and Antolina, Rosa was seemingly content to live in splendor on the Malecón. Guests were lured by Thorvald C's standing in the community and the novelty of his house,[23] but they came also to sing and dance, and sometimes to hear Rosa and Anaïs sing duets, especially from *Aida.*

Rosa was grudgingly assisted in her duties as hostess by Juana, whose prospective suitors were numerous although she had no intention of marrying.[24] Instead, Juana, too, lived contentedly in her father's house, painting flowers in watercolors and indulging herself with beautiful objects and fine clothes.

When the man Rosa really wanted to marry came her way, she was momentarily distressed when he stopped pursuing her and turned his attentions toward Juana, but pursuing beautiful women was more than his avocation, it was almost his second career.[25]

José Joaquín Nin y Castellanos, professionally known as Joaquín Nin,[26] was born in Havana on September 29, 1879, the first child of Joaquín Nin y Tudo, a Spanish Cavalry officer, and his Cuban wife, Angela Castellanos y Perdomo. A stigma was attached to colonial birth then, making it difficult, if not prohibitive, for Cuban men to attend the best Spanish schools or have free access to the professions. His children believed it was the root of Joaquín Nin's lifelong obsession with "the best," be it clothing, cars, or women.[27] Being baptized in Spain was thought to offset Cuban birth, so Joaquín Nin's was delayed until December 11, 1880, when he was christened in Barcelona. During the Baptismal trip to Spain, Joaquín Nin y Tudo decided to stay, becoming a mathematics teacher and writer of "really dreadful books."[28] Joaquín Nin lived there until he was twenty-one,[29] thinking himself Spanish and becoming a snob, for the Nins shared a distinguished family's name, Guell.[30]

As a very young child Joaquín Nin showed talent as a pianist and studied at the Barcelona Atheneum.[31] At thirteen, he gave his first public performance at the prestigious Círculo de Bellas Artes on a program dedicated to his father. His first solo concert, at age seventeen, was followed by one two years later that became his farewell before he departed abruptly for Havana.

One of the ways he managed to keep his reputation intact when he fled Barcelona to avoid disgrace was by dropping his family names and becoming simply Joaquín Nin. Arriving in Havana in

January 1901, he went to the home of his wealthy Castellanos cousins, a convenient place to lie low and live until he departed for Paris as a married man one year later. He gave his first concert in Havana on February 20, 1901. A few weeks later, Rosa Culmell saw her future husband in a music store, barely earning a living by playing sheet music and heavily dependent on the Castellanos family, which rankled. Joaquín Nin was a dandy with expensive habits, such as an overwhelming desire for photographic equipment. The Castellanos family paid for most of what he wanted, especially his Aunt Maita, who adored her sister's brilliant and charming son. The other members of the family tolerated her generosity reluctantly, and when Tía Maita died, their largesse ended as well.[32]

Joaquín Nin was thin, intense, filled with nervous energy and a disconcerting gaze. His dark blue eyes were nearsighted, which caused him to peer sharply through tiny wire-rimmed glasses and gave his face an expression that veered between thunderous disdain and scornful dismissal. At other times, his face often appeared childlike and authentically innocent. As he tossed his head, sweeping the long brown hair off his brow, he was the perfect image of a brooding Romantic hero. It was neither an act nor a ploy, for his ego was such that he believed he deserved unstinting homage and acclaim from women, but more so from the world at large.

Joaquín Nin truly believed he was a genius with a brilliant career ahead as a concert pianist, but not unless he got out of the backwater of Havana and into the mainstream of Europe. One of his teachers, Felipe Pedrell, told him not to return to Barcelona, a slightly more superior backwater than Havana, but to set his sights on Paris, difficult because the Castellanos family felt no responsibility if he left Havana.

Rosa Culmell could help him get to Paris, he knew, for he had been introduced to her by the owner of the music store as "a young pianist to whom the influence of a young woman of society would be very helpful."[33] He had to proceed carefully. Rosa's social standing was of the highest, and Joaquín was wise enough to realize that he could not trifle with her emotions if he wanted—actually, needed—to remain in Havana. He decided she was worth pursuing, not only for the status the courtship would convey but also for her sprightly intelligence, quick wit, and sound musical knowledge. These were qualities he admired in the independent, older, and far more mature Rosa, but what mattered most was that she adored him, for she was too honest and direct to pretend otherwise. Rosa seemed to be offering Joaquín all that he could possibly want at that stage of his life: the willingness to cater to his every whim, the wish to satisfy his every desire, and the money with which to do it. Years later he told his daughter that "Rosa's sister was prettier, but Rosa had a strength, a courage, a decisiveness I needed."[34]

Thorvald C, deciding that Joaquín was an unsuitable partner, sent Rosa to cousins in Matanzas, but she returned as determined as ever. Joaquín began a courtship campaign and Thorvald C relented, but only to let the penniless musician with the exquisite manners into the house long enough to give Rosa well-chaperoned singing lessons. Joaquín soon discovered that her voice was of such high caliber that she could easily perform professionally, which was exactly the wedge between father and daughter he needed. For the remainder of 1901, Joaquín prepared Rosa to participate with him in a concert that took place on April 2, 1902.[35]

The year of waiting intensified Rosa's determination to marry Joaquín, with or without her father's blessing. Despite misgivings, he gave permission. On April 8, 1902, six days after their concert, Rosa and Joaquín were married in the Monserrat church. Thorvald C's wedding gift to the couple was passage to Paris, enough money to buy a grand piano once they arrived, and a monthly income until Joaquín established himself, which they assumed would be soon.[36] They planned to study and give recitals and concerts together, but the emphasis was to be on furthering his career; she was to develop hers only as his collaborator and until he no longer needed her. Rosa wanted it this way as much as Joaquín, for although she loved singing, her primary ambition was to be his wife and helpmate.

A month after their wedding, they sailed for France. The first of their many major battles happened on the ship, when the captain asked Joaquín to give a concert. "I don't play for peasants," he responded, and Rosa erupted in anger at his arrogance.[37] From then on, their marriage, like the voyage, was a battleground on which the two jousted with bitter arguments and passionate reconciliations.

2

The Ugly Little Girl

BEFORE THEY LEFT HAVANA, Joaquín Nin decreed they would live in Paris's most fashionable suburb, Neuilly-sur-Seine, but the thrifty Rosa rented a modest apartment in St.-Germain-des-Prés instead. Rosa was thrilled to be in the center of Paris, which she perceived as the artistic hub of the universe. An avid reader, she spent her days exploring the quarter and buying vast quantities of secondhand books. Joaquín resented her for thwarting his will to live grandly, but as she provided the money, he chastised her for other things.

Rosa learned to defer everything to Joaquín to ensure household peace, especially during her pregnancy. Shortly before she gave birth, they moved to Neuilly. A daughter was born there at 8 P.M. on February 21, 1903. When baptized on June 21, she was officially named Angela Anaïs Juana Antolina Rosa Edelmira Nin y Culmell, but she was always known simply as Anaïs Nin.[1]

Joaquín Nin did not want a child, let alone a thin, "crying, bad-tempered baby girl"[2] with sad brown eyes. Rosa tended to equate Anaïs's delicacy with a weak constitution and hovered over her, to Joaquín's steadily increasing flashes of anger when she did not pamper him first. No matter what Rosa did, Joaquín found fault. When she spoke of giving up singing lessons, he accused her of finding another way to neglect him for the child. So she continued, and after participating in several of his small, local recitals, discovered that she enjoyed performing. Just as it became an important part of her life, Joaquín accused her of neglecting him *and* the baby and began to find reasons why she should not perform anymore.

Joaquín Nin became a Cuban citizen on July 7, 1904, because he thought it added a certain cachet to his professional biography, and gave his first major solo concert in Paris as a Cuban on December 19, 1904.[3] Rosa, pregnant with her second child, applauded from the audience.

In January 1905, Joaquín, Rosa, and Anaïs, now a plump, chubby-cheeked toddler, left for what was to be his triumphal return to Havana. His career seemed to be developing exactly as he had envisioned, as the Havana appearances led to extensive concertizing during the next several years.[4] But during the 1905 trip to Havana, although his talent was recognized, neither his reputation nor his income was improved. He was dependent on Thorvald C's stipend to live as elegantly as he wished, so the trip served a dual purpose: to bring in needed income and to show his father-in-law how successful he was becoming.

On March 12 Rosa gave birth to a blond, blue-eyed son, Thorvald Nin y Culmell,[5] and a few weeks later, Anaïs contracted typhoid fever. Her appearance changed startlingly: she became so thin that her bone structure seemed brittle, and the fever made her hair fall out in clumps. Overnight, she turned into "the ugly duckling," or "Anaïs stick-around," a bewildered little girl who clung crying in French baby-talk to her mother's skirt.[6] From then on, she always seemed older than her age.

Many years later, Anaïs Nin described this period in her parents' marriage: her father "was always on tour, pampered by women"; her mother "made scenes of jealousy."[7] Anger and resentment complicated their initial jealousy. Rosa accused Joaquín of cultivating his appearance before the outside world, where he was "a prince, wonderfully courteous," his "manners as noble as possible," while at home, he was "crude, very different." Giving herself all the credit (most of it deserved), Rosa concluded that Joaquín did not learn manners until he "took his place in society," implying that his social success was dependent in large part on his marriage to her.[8]

Naturally the children were aware of the situation. "My father is gay and charming for visitors," Anaïs recalled. "In the house, alone, there is always war . . . I am continually aware of the battles. But I do not understand them."[9] The fiercest battleground was sexual, when Joaquín deliberately provoked Rosa to angry outbursts by withholding his emotions and hiding behind his camera as a detached observer.

When the Nin family returned to France, Joaquín agreed they should rent a smaller, cheaper house in St.-Cloud. Thorvald C was dying and they needed to economize to further Joaquín's career. Juana, in her thirties, traveled with them, ostensibly because she was unmarried and had to be chaperoned, but really to help with the Nin family's finances. She moved into the house, but the atmosphere was tense when Joaquín made sexual overtures. The sisters had bitter arguments over circumstances neither created nor wanted. Shortly after, they were reconciled when they returned to Havana for Thorvald C's funeral.[10]

Joaquín's treatment grew more hostile when Rosa returned alone. His main complaint was her sexuality, which he supposedly characterized as "voracious, sexually aroused to exasperation" by his lack of ardor. Joaquín continued to be excessively finicky, with "a passion for perfumes and refinements." He demanded a pristine wardrobe of starched shirts and impeccably pressed outergarments he could change several times each day, all of which Rosa and the maid had to provide before attending to the laundry, which they did first to maintain peace in the household before tackling the mountain of diapers soiled by two babies. Small wonder, then, that Rosa, trying to meet his needs, keep up with two small children, and nurture her own singing career, sometimes did fit his description of "unkempt, dirty, without coquetry or taste."

Between 1905 and 1907, Joaquín Nin was performing in solo concerts in Europe and Cuba. Rosa and the two children usually remained behind in St.-Cloud because Joaquín objected to their "cheering and clapping, applauding like peasants,"[11] but actually because he wanted to be free to pursue other women. In his absences, Rosa taught singing as a way to bring much-needed money into the household, for her inheritance was dwindling. In early 1907, they gave three fairly lucrative concerts in Havana, where Rosa sang and Joaquín accompanied her and the violinist Juan Manén.[12] There, Rosa learned she was pregnant again. Joaquín was furious and they returned to Paris in hostile silence.

Joaquín had remained close to Felipe Pedrell, his mentor in Barcelona and the master who had directed most of the important Spanish composers of the day. Pedrell advised Joaquín to go to Berlin to improve his reputation and his income. In order to impress the German music world, in which credentials were so important, Joaquín asked Vincent D'Indy, founder and director of the famed Schola Cantorum in Paris, to make him an honorary professor. Joaquín secured the right to the same title at the New University of Brussels as well. Thus, doubly armed with credentials, he took the two children and Rosa to Berlin, where their last child, Joaquín María Nin y Culmell, was born on September 5, 1908.[13] Shortly thereafter, Joaquín Nin left on a frenetic round of low-paying appearances in France, Germany, and Spain that did more for his ego than his purse.

On her own in Berlin, having had three children in five years, Rosa was left to cope during a bleak winter. She did not know the language, household help was minimal, she could not pursue her own singing career, nor could she teach others.[14] Joaquín did not send for her until late spring 1909, leaving Rosa to deal with moving herself and the children to Brussels, where he was appointed *professeur adjoint* at the New University. "Here," Anaïs wrote of their years in Brussels, "Father's personality becomes more distinct."[15]

They lived, albeit unhappily, as a family in the Brussels suburb of Uccle, where things began to disintegrate in 1912, when Anaïs was nine. Her large, sad eyes dwarfed her tiny heart-shaped face and she was still thin, with elegantly long fingers that her mother called (not always kindly) "the Nin hands."[16] When Joaquín Nin noticed Anaïs at all, it was usually to call her the "ugly little girl."[17] Such comments made Rosa coddle her all the more.

The three children were close because their frequent moves had made them dependent on each other as playmates. Although she and Thorvald were inseparable at games, Anaïs perceived that she and Joaquinito were more alike in terms of how they responded to life: "He has the same way of finding pleasure in the least little thing and in imaginary things, and I think that together, using only our imagination, we have a better time than any children in the whole world could with the most beautiful toys imaginable."[18]

Thorvald was sturdy, blond, and blue-eyed, a quiet little boy, studious and self-contained, who learned very early how to efface himself whenever his parents quarreled. His self-sufficiency had unfortunate consequences, for Rosa concentrated on the other, needier children, allowing Thorvald to become introspective and isolated. He showed a talent for the violin at an early age, and was a pupil of the eminent Mathiew Crickboom, but he had an even greater gift for mathematics. Joaquín was as disdainful of his elder son as he was of his daughter. Thorvald was "so Danish" in his physical form, which in Joaquín's vernacular translated as "so lacking in imagination."[19]

Joaquinito remained the family's "holy terror," who played so many pranks that he exhausted his mother, who often surrendered his care to Anaïs. One day when he was barely three, Joaquinito climbed up on the piano bench and began to play a surprisingly good succession of chords. From then on, only the piano calmed him. Rosa was delighted with what she presumed (correctly) to be nascent talent, and arranged for him to have lessons in solfège, the system by which European children learn to play, with her friend and former pupil, Conchita Badia. He cheerfully ignored Badia's instruction and created his own music.

Anaïs learned solfège for several years in Brussels, but she lacked interest as well as talent: practicing was "too difficult" or she was "too weak" or "too tired." She had a pleasant voice, but not one of professional caliber. In a house filled with music and dominated both professionally and financially by it, she was the odd person out. The only thing she seemed to do well was to make up stories, which Joaquinito listened to avidly and, more important, quietly. This led her to create games, such as dressing up in costumes they concocted from old clothes and bits of fabrics, to drawing and coloring illustrations designed to complement her increasingly fanciful tales.

Thorvald, dour to the point of truculence, was different from his brother and sister in another way. His play usually took the form of fixing a household object or building something mechanical, which caused Anaïs to say regretfully, "He thinks that imagination is more or less another word for 'lies.' " Thorvald was the first of the children to repeat the term that they all heard Rosa hurl angrily at Joaquín as they fought, and to make it a hurtful weapon of his own: "the Nin lies."[20] Even though she did not understand its meaning fully, Anaïs feared that she might inherit it. As she grew older, she not only did, she made the Nin lies uniquely her own.

In spite of their differences, the three children depended upon one another because of the beatings their father, in his unfocused rage, began to inflict on them and their mother. Joaquín was "fond of spanking."[21] Usually he withdrew in silence from the ordinary daily life of his family, closeting himself in his study or hiding behind a book at mealtime. The children behaved normally, if a bit more quietly, during such moods. It was only when they heard the start of venomous criticism of their mother and themselves that they tried to creep out of his sight. Unfortunately, his snide comments and vitriolic outbursts usually caused the strong-willed Rosa to retaliate with equal intensity. This provoked him to exert his control over the household by locking the children in their bedrooms and beating her. When he realized how indomitable her spirit was, he devised a more extreme form of cruelty: locking up Rosa first, then walloping the three children, so that her frantic screams intermingled with and punctuated their cries. Joaquín made the children march up to the dark and frightening attic, paddling them as they mounted the stairs with a hairbrush, a cane, or the flat of his hand.

"Each detail of its construction I can remember distinctly and with much regret," Anaïs wrote of the house in Uccle, fearful that the neighbors could hear the violence within it.[22] The children's shame intensified when, before them and some others, Joaquín beat a neighbor's cat with his cane for no apparent reason, flaying the animal with relish until it died.[23] Afterward, he seemed pleased with a job well done, while the children had nightmares.

Joaquín usually remembered to lock the attic so that if Rosa managed to unlock the bedroom door, she could only sob and pound helplessly on the one to the attic. He beat the boys first and usually sent them away before turning to Anaïs. No matter what weapon he used upon his sons, Joaquín used the flat of his hand on his daughter.

Anaïs Nin wrote about these incidents many times throughout her life, but one of the first is the most chilling. "I would do anything to keep him from lifting my dress and beating me," she wrote at the age of seventeen, after his desertion.[24] Thirty years later, during a period of complicated sexual relationships, she tried repeatedly to recall what had happened during these scenes of violence and wrote the following:

> My Father has taken me up to the little attic room to spank me. He takes my pants off. He begins to hit me with the palm of his hand. I feel his hand on me. But he stops hitting me and he caresses me. Then he sticks his penis into me, pretending to be beating me. Oh, I enjoy it, I enjoy it. In and out, in and out,

> with my ass exposed, my pants down, he takes me from behind. But my mother is coming up the stairs. We have no time. I clutch at him, suck him in, palpitating. Oh, oh, my Mother is coming up the stairs. My Father['s] hands are on my ass—hot—I'm wet—I'm eager, eager. Open, close, open close. I must feel him all before she comes. I must shoot quickly—stab, once, twice—and I have a violent orgasm—. I believe this really happened. I do not believe my father penetrated me sexually but I believe he caressed me while or instead of beating me. I remember the attic room when he took us to beat us. I only remember with sureness a time I wept so much he didn't have the courage to beat me.[25]

Anaïs Nin wrote that she blushed as she composed this account, trying to pierce the haze of childhood memory, to ascertain what was fact and what was fantasy, and to arrive at the truth. As a nine-year-old, the adult woman asked herself, could she really *not* have wanted her mother to come to her rescue? Did she, as a child, resent her mother, who was only, after all, coming to save her? What had happened on the day her father had already beaten her two brothers and, with them still in the attic, was about to start on her? What made him stop when he saw the look on her face, "the hysterical, unbearable, humiliated grief"? Why was she alone of the three children unpunished from that moment on?

The adult Anaïs Nin believed she was ten or eleven when her father stopped beating and fondling her, but he found a way to turn his "coldness, sadism, unspeakable cruelties, [and] cynicism" into another form of humiliation and punishment equally horrifying to all three children. The camera, formerly his shield, now became his weapon as he photographed them naked, bursting in unexpectedly when they were in their baths, making the embarrassed children stand and face the camera fully exposed while he focused and fussed with lenses and angles.[26] Besides photographing Anaïs naked in her bath, he followed her with the camera as she dressed in the morning and undressed at night. All the while, she remembered how he repeated the refrain "What an ugly little girl."

None of her children remembered if Rosa objected to the photographs, which is perhaps why Anaïs blamed herself for her father's disappointment in "Miss Asparagus,"[27] and thought herself unworthy to be his daughter. She was ashamed, she knew not why, of the bathtime photo sessions, but at the same time she was thrilled. How

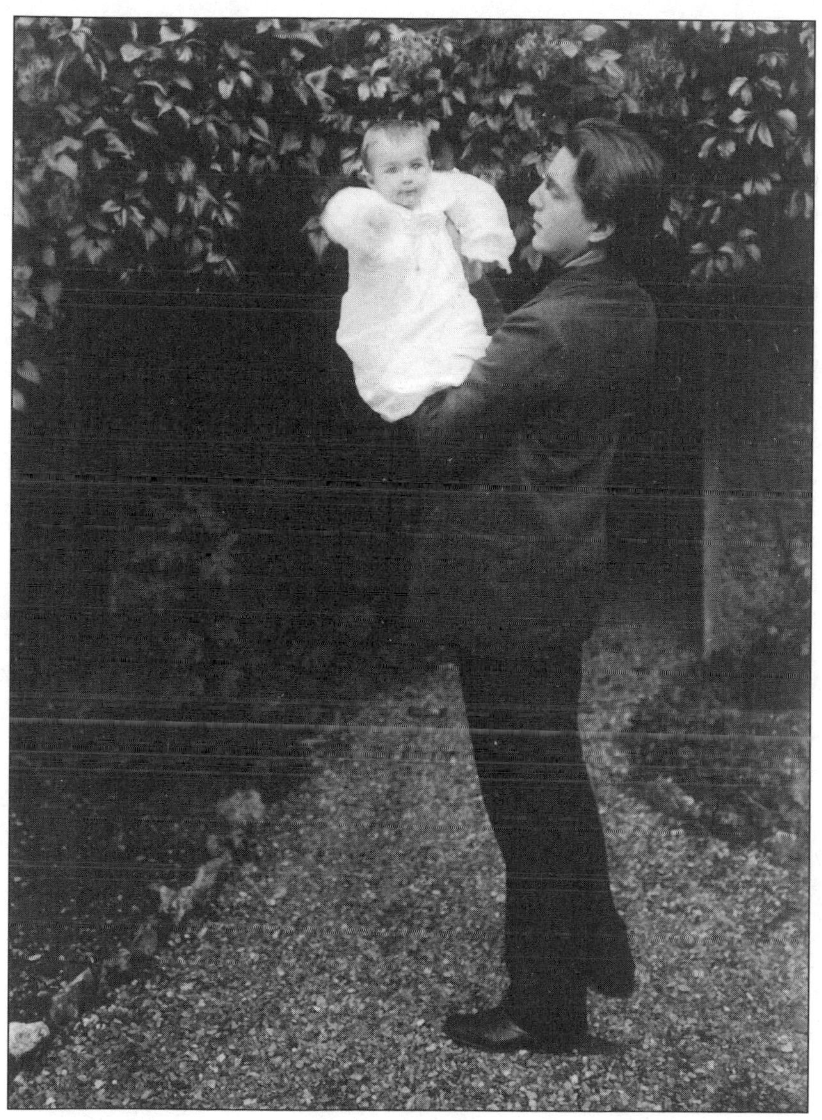

Joaquín Nin and his daughter, Anaïs.

Anaïs at her First Holy Communion in Barcelona.

homely could she be if he still gave her this wonderful, marvelous, personal attention? It was all very confusing. Something told her such attention was bad, but it all made her feel so good. And besides, her mother never complained or tried to stop it, so it must not be improper.

Anaïs's emotions were even more confused by Joaquín's genuine concern when she developed appendicitis on October 13, 1912. As he carried Anaïs to the cab that took them to the hospital, a helpful neighbor passed on what the doctor said as he left the house: "the little Nin girl will not survive this night."[28] Anaïs heard it clearly and never forgot it.

By the time surgery was performed, the appendix had ruptured, a condition that usually resulted then in death.[29] Anaïs was hospitalized for three months, growing thinner and weaker as an abscess formed on the incision, drained constantly, and refused to heal. Somehow, she survived.

Just before Christmas, a second and larger abscess formed inside the incision, an even greater danger to her life than the original ruptured appendix. Joaquín was resigned to her death, but Rosa never left Anaïs's bedside, veering between prayer, fasting, and vows ranging from devotions to various saints to threats to abandon her faith if her prayers were not answered. When Anaïs was at her weakest, Rosa resignedly surrendered her daughter's life to Sainte Thérèse de Lisieux, "The Little Flower of Jesus." As a paean to the saint, she brought gifts to the hospital for other patients, and on New Year's Day, 1913, in a wheelchair, Anaïs dispensed them. The abscess ruptured, and a second operation was performed to open the incision and clean out the infection. Surprisingly, Anaïs recovered swiftly. From then on, Rosa's dedication to Sainte Thérèse was unwavering; she believed a miracle had saved her daughter's life.[30] Anaïs became skeptical of her Catholic religion as a teenager and rejected it as a young married woman. Nevertheless, throughout her life she believed that something miraculous had anointed her and nothing could ever fell her.

When the hospitalization ended in late winter, the doctors advised recuperation in a warmer climate. Joaquín was scheduled to give a second concert in April 1913 in Arcachon, and he decided to move the family there so that Anaïs could recover and he could rehearse. They arrived on her tenth birthday, February 21, 1913.

Arcachon, a small town on the Atlantic seacoast of France, was a haven for intellectuals and artists, among them the Italian writer Gabriele D'Annunzio.[31] The Nins rented a large furnished house called "Les Ruines," built around the remains of a much older one.[32] Prophetically, the house's name described the marriage, for there, after eleven tormented and chaotic years, Joaquín demolished it.

Jealousy, which had always been a factor, assumed epidemic proportion as their battles escalated from Rosa's complaints that he paid her and the children too little attention to her overt accusations of infidelity. Most of the charges centered around the Rodríguez family, enormously wealthy Cubans who owned the famous Romeo & Juliet cigar factory. Joaquín not only befriended them but also persuaded them to become his patrons. Their younger daughter, "Maruca," was almost sixteen, beautiful and voluptuous, mature for her years, but whom Joaquín nevertheless persuaded to be an occasional playmate of the ten-year-old Anaïs.

Joaquín decided to give Maruca piano lessons, ostensibly to thank her parents for their patronage, which included renting "Les Ruines" for him and his family. Rosa sensed immediately that Joaquín's interest in the girl was more than musical. Joaquín denied it, but Rosa accused him, in full hearing of the children, of yet another of the "Nin lies." She tried as delicately as possible, so as not to jeopardize Mr. Rodríguez's much-needed contribution to the family's income, to keep the girl from coming to the house.

As Rosa's harangues mounted, Joaquín beat her and the children even more frequently and violently. He did indeed want Maruca to become infatuated with him, perhaps as a way to keep her father's patronage. The Rodríguez family was a godsend for Joaquín. Their nubile daughter was easily flattered by the handsome pianist's attentions and sympathetic to his sad tales of how his old, fat, and unfashionable wife did not understand him. Soon Maruca had a schoolgirl crush of major proportion. Joaquín wooed her carefully, observing all the proprieties of behavior while using every courtly technique at his disposal. Maruca was besotted and lost no time in telling her parents. They, of course, were horrified and immediately confronted him. For whatever reason—whether fear of losing their patronage or a desperate ploy to keep Maruca's affection—shortly after Señor Rodríguez confronted him, Joaquín Nin abandoned his wife and three children.

After his concert, Joaquín told Rosa he was going to Paris to rehearse for an upcoming tour. She asked why, if the studio in Arcachon no longer satisfied him, the entire family could not return to Uccle, where he had prepared for many previous tours. There were arguments, which all three children overheard.

"Was it a premonition? An instinct," Anaïs later wrote.[33] More likely, her instinctive fear had something to do with the "unusual" attention and the "care"[34] her father lavished during her illness and recovery. In his way, he had demonstrated parental concern, telling her to concentrate all her energies on recovering. Obediently, she exerted—probably for the first time—her tremendous willpower, for it was unthinkable to do anything other than what her dashingly handsome artist-father commanded. Hitherto the recipient only of his physical and emotional abuse, Anaïs now believed her father loved her deeply and was desperate to keep him within the confines of the family, for she was old enough to glamorize him and wanted his love to continue.[35] When Joaquín made his farewells, Anaïs became hysterical, screaming and clinging. He pried her loose and left anyway.

For several weeks, Anaïs believed that her father would write to her alone, and that his letter would set everything to rights. She had no reason to expect such a letter, as he had never written to her before, yet she was sure that he would single her out for this special attention, and by so doing, enable her to keep him as part of the family. She became convinced that only she could make him stay, and only through the dialogue of correspondence.

No one heard from Joaquín until a month after he left, and then it was Rosa to whom he sent a cold, perfunctory letter saying he had removed everything of value from the Uccle house and that his abandonment was permanent. He avoided any mention of divorce and advised her to go to Barcelona and live with his parents. Although he would not provide financial support, he would, he said, write from time to time instructing her on how to bring up the children.

Rosa kept her emotions to herself and began at once to cope. Leaving the children in the housemaid's care, she returned to Uccle to sell what Joaquín had not taken and used the money to move them all by third-class rail to Barcelona.[36]

She also wrote to her four sisters, but only Juana (who detested Joaquín Nin) and Antolina (who had both money and freedom to travel) were able to aid her while she was still in Arcachon. They both wanted her to return with them to Havana instead of placing herself under the jurisdiction of her father-in-law. But Rosa was equally determined to establish herself in the bosom of her husband's family, because she did not believe the separation was final and thought it best to obey him.

Several weeks later, after stubbornly refusing her sisters' money, Rosa said goodbye to them and ensconced herself and the children in Joaquín Nin's parents' apartment.

Even though the honest Rosa had not minced words and told the children that their father had abandoned them, Anaïs refused to accept it, inventing the myth that Joaquín was an artist and his career kept him away from the "family of clapping peasants" who "held him back." She excused his absence as calmly and rationally (irrationally, perhaps) as a precocious eleven-year-old could.

For several months, things went smoothly, even though Rosa worried about Anaïs. The girl no longer held her hands over her ears and screamed in terror at a raised voice, as she had done for a time after leaving Arcachon, but she was still skittish and frightened of many things, most of them concerning the possibility that she would be abandoned. She could not bear to say goodbye, and if her grandmother was going somewhere, Anaïs often had to be pried from her skirt and dragged away, sobbing as if she might never see her again. Anaïs was terrified each time Rosa left and did not calm down until she returned. She grew hysterical at the thought of losing anything, especially the faded stuffed doll called "Bouby" her father had given her. She believed that as long as she had Bouby, she still had her father, and carried it everywhere until she was married.[37]

All three children were afraid of their scowling and silent grandfather, but they adored their grandmother, who sang and played with them, told stories, and gave them treats. Anaïs was bewildered by the solicitous babble of Spanish that surrounded her, but she was relaxing under her grandmother's love and attention. This was, after all, her father's mother, and being loved by her somehow made him seem still a part of the family.

Anaïs's grandparents' marriage was serene because he was a tyrant and she was "sweet, submissive, and crushed."[38] Nevertheless, a quiet household was immensely soothing after the violence and noise of the past several years, and attributes of the children's personalities developed more distinctly within it. Anaïs grew even more needy, desperate to soak up love, attention, and approval from anyone who would give it. Thorvald kept himself to himself, and as he was quiet and obedient, no one asked if anything troubled him. Joaquinito could be counted on for obstreperous behavior.

Then the letters began. Joaquín wrote, but never directly to Rosa. Instead, he sent loving little notes to Anaïs, the letters she had dreamed of receiving back in Arcachon. If he wished to infuriate his wife, he succeeded brilliantly; clearly, he wished to manipulate his daughter, which he did, and with disastrous consequences for her adult life. Joaquín's letters did much to confuse Anaïs's perception of herself. He reminded her each time he wrote that she was a French girl by birth and should behave accordingly, despite the fact that her language was now Spanish and she was being brought up in Spain. She insisted that everyone speak to her only in French, which of course not all could do, and when they did not, she had tears and tantrums, accusing them of disobeying her father. He hinted that someday she would understand why he had no choice but to absent himself from the daily life of the family and then bragged of his conquests, both on stage and off. Everyone loved him, he said, and therefore so should she.

Of course she did, adoring, admiring, and even imitating her father for much of her life. Even in his absence, Joaquín Nin's innocence was one of adolescent self-absorption, for he believed himself to be the center of the world in which he lived and saw no reason why his children should not think the same. It was, however, a view that only his daughter inherited. Young as she was, Anaïs constructed her life around letters to and from her father. She made a ritual out of writing them, copying most of what she wrote into the little journal that eventually became her diary, reading and rereading what she wrote and then agonizing over the length of time it took him to answer.

Joaquín's replies were infrequent and brief, and he ignored Rosa's existence entirely. He wrote numerous precisely detailed letters to his parents describing how he wanted the children to be educated, especially their religious education and manners and deportment. Adamant that they consider themselves French, he insisted they read, think, and write in French and attend mass at a French chapel. His parents dutifully passed along his instructions to Rosa, expecting her to obey, but they never questioned why their son did not support the family whose daily lives he tried to control, nor did they ask when he would return. Instead, they turned against Rosa, who had tried to be self-supporting by giving lessons and trying to concertize. It wounded their pride because their son's reputation was besmirched, so they ordered her to stop. Rosa was in a quandary, for their income was not sufficient to support her and three children.

One of Rosa's staunchest allies in Barcelona was the Catalan feminist writer Carmen Karr,[39] who encouraged her singing ambitions but could not provide money. Once again Rosa's sisters came to the rescue: Juana paid for an apartment, and Rosa and the children moved out. There was still no talk of divorce, however, for Joaquín Nin liked things as they were, and he was better off financially than he had ever been. The Rodríguez family took the precaution of betrothing Maruca to someone else, and, with the wedding imminent, increased Joaquín's stipend, perhaps as a sop, more likely as a bribe. Now that he was free of all family responsibilities, the stipend was handsome indeed.

In October 1915, when she was twelve, Anaïs wrote a long passage in her diary wondering "Could the parting [of her parents] be my fault?" —a question so many other abused children and children of divorced parents have also asked. A surprisingly adult train of thought from such a young writer followed: "What has become of the sacred union of man and woman? Modern marriage has become like everything else these days. The result is old, young, and middle-aged are all children, thoughtless people, guided only by their natural impulses." It was a disgrace, she concluded, and "the name of this disgrace is divorce." It frightened her: "What happens to the children? . . . What a terrible uncertainty."

In the spring of 1914, Rosa could no longer support her children in Barcelona. Too proud to return to her in-laws and knowing her husband would not help, she turned again to her sisters. There was a hasty round of letters and telegrams. Antolina provided the solution: she would pay the passage if Rosa agreed to go to New York, where there was a much larger musical community than in Barcelona. There was every reason to believe that she would be able to make a living, and Juana agreed to help Antolina support Rosa until she could establish herself as a singer and vocal coach.

On July 25, 1914, Rosa, who spent her formative years in New York and spoke perfect American English, took her children on board the *Montserrat* for the voyage to a new life in yet another country, culture, and language. Rosa was determined to do two things: keep her little family together and ensure that her children grew up respecting their absent father. Neither would be easy: the two sons now conversed only in Spanish while Anaïs stubbornly spoke and wrote only in French.

Some years later, when Anaïs Nin was in her thirties and reconstructing in fiction the moment she left for New York, "anguish" became her prevailing metaphor: "The darkness before me was darker than the darkness behind me."[40] But at the moment of departure, when she had just begun to keep a diary, the frightened little girl, eleven-year-old Anaïs, could only ask, "What does the future hold for me? I am traveling in a country that has no landmarks."[41]

3

The Indispensable Lifeline

Anaïs Nin was, by her own account, "eleven years old when I walked into the labyrinth of my diary which I carried in a little basket."[1] She wrote steadily all through the *Montserrat*'s lumbering seventeen-day journey to New York. The ship docked in New York harbor on August 11, 1914, just as heat and high humidity erupted in a torrential summer thunderstorm. Lightning darted around the decks, and although Anaïs, who was sheltered below with her family, did not see it, she nevertheless embellished the story by writing at the time that "all the Spaniards fell on their knees and prayed."[2]

Commander Gilbert Chase was there to meet them with his son, Gilbert (Coquito), and Antolina's sons, Carlos (Charlie) and Rafael (Felo) de Cárdenas. In a babble of Spanish and English, they swept up the boys while Anaïs hid behind Rosa's skirt, clutching Thorvald's violin case and the tiny straw basket that held her first diary.[3]

Frightened by the commotion, bewildered by the clamor, Anaïs's terror intensified when Rosa and Joaquín went to the Chase house in Kew Gardens and she and Thorvald were taken to sleep in Antolina's Manhattan apartment.

The following morning, Anaïs and Thorvald were taken to "the country," as the borough of Queens then was. She found her brothers and all the Chase and de Cárdenas cousins playing games and sports, but she settled in her aunt's study to write in her diary. No one disturbed Anaïs, for Rosa cautioned everyone to let her adapt in her own way. The next morning, Anaïs rose early because she was afraid there would be no other time to write in her diary, and she could not bear to have a day pass without writing.

Anaïs Nin discovered the fascination of herself as a subject on the sea voyage to New York. Rosa had given her a little notebook in Barcelona to encourage her to write the magical stories she invented so easily for Joaquín (as Joaquinito was now called since his father's departure). She refused, saying she planned to become an artist, not a writer, and would use the book for her drawings. Soon, however, Anaïs began to write, choosing the facts of her life as her subject.

From the beginning, her diary was a subject of much speculation among the grown-ups. Some observed it kindly, as did the pianist Emilia Quintero, who said upon being introduced to Anaïs, "This must be the little girl who writes so well." Others, including her aunts, worried that it made her even more solitary and withdrawn and called her "the little girl who writes too much."[4] Rosa seemed as unfazed by her sisters' concerns as she was by their criticisms and continued to allow Anaïs to do as she pleased, which meant that the girl grew even more introspective and content to be her own best company.

Rosa originally bought the first notebook in the hope that it would distract Anaïs from her fear of abandonment and her excessive attachments. She believed that Anaïs should have an interest, something that was all her own but was also an outlet for a different form of creativity than music. Rosa wisely realized that in a house filled with artists Anaïs needed to feel she excelled at something within the family if she were to have not only a sense of belonging but also, and more important, a pride of place, which she desperately needed since her father's abandonment.

During Anaïs's illness, her father had told her repeatedly not only that she should get better but also that she should be bigger, braver, stronger in every way. She took his admonitions to heart and became a curious mix of qualities that characterized her later life. Even though she was delicate and frequently in ill health, she became competitive, with a compulsion for perfection, always expecting much more of herself than anyone asked of her. Part of this drive consisted of her fixation on wooing and winning her father back into the family, and the story was often told, mostly by the adult Anaïs Nin, of how she came to begin the diary as a letter to her absent father.[5]

When she was eighteen, she explained how this idea of the diary as letter came to her. She wrote about it in a letter to her father, asking if he understood why she needed to create such a myth, adding: "If you knew me, you would see that only I could imagine such a thing. One has to be quite separated from reality . . . [and] from the world in general to attribute to something ideal a misfortune that occurs every day and is caused by things so sadly human."[6]

She had held this idea for five years, but coming to New York was a bewildering event even for the best-adjusted of children. For one as introspective as Anaïs, it was a difficult transition that took years before she could cope. In her early diaries, which she wrote in French until she was seventeen, she drew pictures of huge buildings bending toward each other and towering over tiny stick figures. She wrote of the wonders of escalators and subways, of throngs of people on the streets and the cold impersonality of Manhattan as contrasted with the warmth and beauty of the countryside in Queens.

"I am going to tell my diary a secret," she confided one month after her arrival. "I have made a resolution not to have any friends and not to be attached to anyone outside my family. One can't be sure of staying anywhere and if one leaves, there is too much sadness."[7]

Still, the question of just how, why, and when she decided to write the continuing story of her life remains clouded in supposition, much of it self-created later. In the beginning, she drew pictures of herself and her family to accompany descriptions of her activities and the sights she saw. Very shortly, she became the heroine of her own life as she interpreted the events of her day, examining each activity and encounter in minute detail, telling and retelling all that happened, exploring each nuance in microscopic detail.

The notebooks were too successful as a distraction: Rosa had to chide Anaïs to stop writing and concentrate on school lessons and household chores, to go to bed at night. "Stop dreaming" soon became her most-repeated admonition.

From the first moment Anaïs began to write about her daily life, it was as if events had not really happened until she committed them to paper. When someone came to call, if she and her brothers were taken on an outing or given a treat, or there was a family celebration, everything had to be written down. But not just written; rather, analyzed from every possible perspective, from everyone else's point of view, and finally gathered up and filtered through *her* perspective, *her* point of view, and through the way in which everyone and everything revolved around and related to *her.* She was the center of her own universe, which is not really uncommon in a sensitive teenager. What is unusual is that she did not grow tired of minute self-appraisal but continued to write such a self-absorbed diary for the rest of her life.

She tried many different times and in many different ways to explain what the diary meant to her, and one of the most interesting was through a story she wrote in 1938 called "The Paper Womb:[8]" "There was always an anguish . . . about seeing things but once. There was a definite feeling that their meaning, their color, and their fleshliness of touch could only happen the second time. If there were no second time, if I were forced to go on, unknowing, blind, everything would be lost."

"She was a deep-sea diver from the start," her brother Joaquín observed, "and the diary was her indispensable lifeline." At the end of her writing life in 1973, Anaïs Nin said a lifetime of diary writing had been, from the first moment she wrote about herself, a concession "that life would be more bearable if I looked at it as an adventure and a tale. I was telling myself the story of a life, and this transmutes into an adventure the things which can shatter you."[9] And one of those first shattering incidents, which needed years of exploration, happened when the family moved to New York.

Rosa supported her family mostly on the generosity of her sisters Juana and Antolina and by giving singing lessons. Always in the hope of finding better and cheaper housing, she moved her children several times in the first few years to different apartments on Manhattan's Upper West Side.[10] She had aged considerably since Joaquín deserted her; concert bookings for a stout, middle-aged woman with a sad, lined face were nearly impossible to come by and did not provide enough money to support a family of four.[11] Within a year of her arrival, Rosa realized that her sisters' resources were finite and she would have to find other sources of income.

Deciding to end her dependence, the competent and capable Rosa decided to become an entrepreneur. With what she hoped would be the last loan ever needed from her sisters, she bought a five-story brownstone, mostly with Juana's money, at 158 W. 75th Street, and took in as boarders musicians who were also her friends.[12] Emilia

Quintero moved into a small room on the top floor, and the mother and sister of the young violinist Enrique Madriguera also were among the earliest tenants (later, he lived there as well).

Rosa installed herself and Anaïs in one bed and the two boys in another. "We lived four of us in the dining room and pantry of a once lovely house in New York," Anaïs recalled many years later. "We did not have a [private] bathroom."[13] These two rooms and the kitchen became their private quarters.[14]

But Rosa still could not make enough money to cover her expenses. She became a businesswoman accidentally when shopping for her sisters and brothers while they were in Cuba. Anaïs Sánchez asked her to go to New York's best stores—Lord & Taylor, Bonwit Teller, Wanamaker's—and buy expensive fashions for herself and her daughters. Rosa's brothers Enrique[15] and Thorvald soon asked for shoes, tobacco, and books as well as clothing.

Rosa arranged to open accounts in various stores, and when her relatives paid her, she paid the stores, keeping ten percent as her commission. Soon her personal shopping became her major source of income, especially when World War I restricted travel by wealthy Cubans to New York, and many of them, including the wife of Cuba's president, Mario García Menocal, became her clients. Her business grew so quickly that she took a small office at 1929 Broadway and hired an assistant.

Rosa, a self-taught businesswoman, made shrewd initial decisions. She invested in real estate, buying the contents of a ten-room house even before she owned a place to put it. Then, again with Juana's help, she bought a second house on W. 86th Street, installed the furnishings, and sold both house and contents for a modest profit.

Rosa's meager income seemed assured and everything boded fairly well. Two of her children had adjusted well to life in their third new country and language. Thorvald and Joaquín were robust boys who took to the English language with alacrity, thrived in school, made friends, and added baseball and other games to their musical interests.

It was different for Anaïs. She was first enrolled in a Catholic school but chafed at the strict discipline and complained that she was too advanced for her class.[16] In a pattern that repeated itself throughout Anaïs's brief education, Rosa capitulated and enrolled her in public schools, P.S. 9 and later Wadleigh High School. Anaïs was unhappy in each, finding them noisy and too casual.

Anaïs and Thorvald Nin in Évian-les-Bains.

Her main problem, however, was with the language. She picked up spoken English quickly but refused to master the discipline of grammar, spelling, and punctuation. Her relationship to English language and culture was further hindered by her father's belittling sarcasm in his occasional letters. He never learned the language and spent the rest of his life avoiding engagements in English-speaking countries because he was too proud to reveal his disadvantage. If he disdained the language, then so, too, must she, and she continued to struggle to write in a French that remained babyish as she matured into an American adolescent.

Joaquín must have realized that he had all but lost control of his sons, so he concentrated his long-distance intrusions into the family upon Anaïs, sending her French newspapers, books, and magazines. As the years passed and her French remained that of the small child she had been when she left France, he took to correcting her letters with his usual sharpness and sarcasm. In an uncharacteristic response, she chided her father: "You should learn English. I would like to tell you how much pleasure your letter gave me and my French stumbles, whereas in English (also in Spanish) I can find hundreds of words."[17] In another letter she told him that she now had "a deep love [for French] mingled with an exile's regret," but for English, which she had begun to use in her diary, she felt "tenderness" because her "whole life" was now "expressed" in that language.[18]

World War I added to her confusion about her identity. Her pride in France was coupled with fear for her father, who was in Arcachon. He was too old to be conscripted, but his letters must have hinted at more danger than he was ever in, for hers in reply were desperately fearful for his safety. Her mother took her to hear an unnamed Cuban poet who made a remark she never forgot and which, in many different forms, she confided to the diary for the rest of her life: "If one knows two languages, one is two people. If one knows three, one is three people. So, then," she asked. "What am I?"[19] It was a very good question.

Even though the school year should have dictated her daily routines, there was little structure in Anaïs's life. She was sick a lot, mostly with genuine illnesses, but many just happened to strike when she had spent much of the night writing in the diary and was too sleepy to get up. Her schoolday illnesses marked the beginning of lifelong hypochondria, but mostly served as an excuse to avoid whatever she did not want to do. Rosa, otherwise an exemplar of forthright diligence, coddled and indulged Anaïs, and if she doubted or disbelieved her excuses, she never said so.

Anaïs's teachers were aware of her shenanigans, especially one who failed her in algebra because she deliberately lacked even a modicum of common sense. Anaïs consoled herself by telling the diary that poets and philosophers always lacked common sense, "So I am content."[20] Such rationalization became an exaggerated trait that often had disastrous consequences.

Anaïs refused to think of herself as an American. Her attitude was more that of someone passing through than of a permanent resident, and her father did no good by accusing her of betraying her European heritage. Time and again, she rushed to reassure him that she was "the least American of the three of us."[21]

Rosa held social evenings centered around music and dancing to which all three children were urged to bring their friends. Anaïs seldom invited anyone, saying she was not like other girls, whom she compared to butterflies, but "like green moss, quiet and inexplicable."[22] If she could not think of herself as American, she had even greater difficulty coming to terms with her Cuban heritage, despite the fact that her father's citizenship made them Cuban citizens.[23] She was overwhelmed and embarrassed by the laughter and chatter when her Cuban relatives gathered, their music and dancing, quantities of food, and loving squabbling. Perhaps because her father had called them "peasants," Anaïs was "disgusted" by the "Cuban fashion" of "exaggerating everything and making a scene."[24] "Cubans are the most cynical, callous people in the world," she said, referring specifically to her Sánchez cousins.[25]

Although Anaïs disliked school, she made one friend at Wadleigh to whom she remained close throughout her life, Frances Schiff (later Bolton), who shared the same interest in literature and music.[26] Although both Frances Schiff's mother and Rosa Culmell held "dance evenings" for their daughters to meet suitable young men, the desire to become a writer and the fact that both kept diaries cemented the friendship between the two girls. Frances liked Wadleigh, but Anaïs spoke disparagingly of the school, saying too much independent thought and activity were allowed, and the other students were simply "an entire class of ignorant girls."[27]

Anaïs confided all this to the diary, but the remarks that follow were really why she disliked school: "I learn things that I don't want to learn, and sometimes I am afraid of losing entirely the delicate and exquisite mental picture that I have of the beauty of things around me." In short, she increasingly viewed anything outside the diary and the dreamworld it provided as ugly, intrusive, or disruptive. Except for Frances Schiff, she trusted only her mother and brothers and rebuffed or resisted friendships proffered by others. She preferred to view herself as lonely, solitary, and virtually friendless. The question remains: Was it a pose, arising from teenage *angst,* making good copy for the diary, or did she truly feel this way?

As she moved into her teenage years, boys began to tell her she was pretty. It was confusing, for she had difficulty accepting that she was no longer "an ugly little girl."[28] When the Catalan painter Francisco Pausas admired Anaïs's "Catalan" look, she could only accept the compliment after she connected it to her father, saying he would be proud of her because he was proud of his Catalan origin.[29]

She tried to relate everything about herself to her father, which angered Rosa so much that she used the family name as a code for everything negative. Anaïs was frequently accused of being in a "Nin" (bad) mood, or having "Nin" stubbornness, laziness, or temper. She, however, was proud that her disposition was "a faithful copy" of her father's, for "his is noble in its weakness and wonderful even with all its faults."[30] He was apparently to be admired, while everything her mother stood for was to be interpreted in a less positive light.

But all their disagreements centered around how much Anaïs disliked school. Anaïs persuaded Rosa to let her quit at age sixteen, the end of her junior year, and to educate herself at home. She produced a litany of specious arguments, indignant because her French teacher insisted she learn grammar and translation; algebra was "a nightmare" for which she had no patience, and English was a waste of time, for she already knew the books "by heart."

She was indeed widely read, having devoured Emerson, Stevenson, Scott, Coleridge, Dickens, and an English translation of Plato among many others.[31] In this alone she was correct to insist that she knew how to read and study. "I shall be able to manage it very well," she concluded.[32]

What finally clinched her leaving school, however, is astonishing; she persuaded Rosa that, having published several short poems in the school newspaper, she was now well on her way to making a living as a professional writer.

Letting Anaïs leave school was probably the greatest mistake Rosa made in her daughter's upbringing, but Anaïs was already a powerful manipulator and perhaps Rosa simply resigned herself to the inevitability of giving her what she wanted. It was tantamount to giving the already otherworldly girl permission to live in a totally unstructured manner, with few rules or boundaries for her daily life and nothing to turn her toward any socializing encounter. She could do exactly as she pleased, and what pleased her was to be alone with her diary. Within a month of leaving school, she described her life as "an eternal vacation."[33]

To justify how she passed her days, she invented all sorts of duties for herself and filled the diary with accounts of cooking meals and mending her brothers' stockings. In reality, they had two daily maids, and if Anaïs really did any of these household chores, it was because she wanted to do them, or, more accurately, to write that she had done them and not because they were required. She was as pampered and cosseted as Rosa could make her, given her limited means.

Rosa seemed unconcerned by Anaïs's isolation, but feared that she was too thin, despondent, and, despite all efforts to hide it, too worried about financial problems. Rosa persuaded Anaïs Sánchez to take Anaïs Nin with her children to Lake Placid for the summer in 1919 and spared no expense in buying her a new wardrobe.[34] Unfortunately, the trip coincided with the collapse of Cuba's sugar economy, and with it, Rosa's business as well.

Cuba had prospered during World War I, mostly because of the high price of sugar, but by 1919, the country was in severe crisis. Rosa's modest purchasing business paralleled the country's financial misfortune. Many of her wealthy Cuban customers ignored her repeated pleas for payment, and she was left with staggering store debts.

To keep afloat, she turned again to real estate. With the proceeds from selling the furnished house, she bought a cottage in Edgemere, Long Island, hoping to sell it at a profit, but there were no buyers. She could not meet the mortgage payments on the 75th Street house, for she rented only to musicians and many did not pay the rent. Creditors hounded, so she sold the house, kept the cottage on the market, and bought an inexpensive house in Queens. She also changed her name to avoid bill collectors, calling herself from then on Rosa Culmell.[35]

By November 1919, they were living at 620 Audley Street in Richmond Hill, Queens. The move seemed beneficial for everyone. Thorvald took the train to DeWitt Clinton High School in Manhattan,

Joaquín was enrolled in a Queens parochial school, and Rosa hoped that country living would force Anaïs outside and she would lose the unhealthy pallor that came from sitting alone in the house reading and writing all day long.

Anaïs had her own bedroom and was able to sleep separately from her mother for the first time since moving to New York. Rosa had spared neither effort nor expense to furnish the "dream" bedroom Anaïs had always wanted, all white wood and blue draperies, bedspread, and carpet.

Within a week after they moved, Rosa had a nervous breakdown. The stress of juggling real-estate transactions, stores that hounded her for money, and the added burden of coping with her well-meaning but nevertheless interfering sisters all caught up with her. She took to her bed and Antolina took charge, terrifying the children and making them wail by telling them their mother would die if things did not change.

At fifty, still indomitable and "not yet weary of the struggle,"[36] Rosa had one more plan in reserve. Anaïs was old enough to be presented to Havana society: a rich marriage would surely result, for she had become a lovely young woman. Everything rested, however, with the moody Anaïs Sánchez, who was willing to sponsor Anaïs Nin, but not until her eldest daughter, Cuca, was betrothed.

The Havana debut became something Rosa planned on, so it was only a question of hanging on until the former "Miss Asparagus" could solve her financial problems once and for all.

4

Miss Nin and Linotte

When Rosa recovered, she went to her Manhattan office every weekday even though there was nothing to do. Anaïs stayed alone in the quiet house, worrying that her mother, "having no substantial proof of my progress, no longer considers me a poet or an author who will be famous one day, but rather a daughter to be married off."[1]

Because of their straitened circumstances, Rosa dismissed the daily maid and made Anaïs responsible for running errands, shopping, preparing the evening meal, making beds, and doing dishes. Her diary tells a story of how she willingly sacrificed writing time to devote herself diligently to household duties, but her brother Joaquín remembers that she did everything haphazardly and absentmindedly.

She still had a great deal of freedom each day to "chat" to her "best friend," as she called the diary. Even she observed that her self-enforced solitude made her spend entire days without talking until the family returned at night. When she was with other people, she noted that she conversed only "with so much difficulty" and wondered if the pleasure she got from writing rather than from conversation might be due to "unbounded egotism, since I am continually talking about myself."

Even though she repeatedly claimed that everything she wrote in the diary was true, by the time she was seventeen, she was already consciously employing the technique of revision to refine the truth. In doing so, she was developing her style as a writer, which led to charges when the diaries were finally published that she rewrote the truth and therefore was a liar. In actuality, the matter was far more complicated, but it is safe to say that her obsession with refining the raw material of her life was so inhibiting that it interfered time and again with the creativity necessary for writing fiction.

In her formative years as a writer, she likened the technique of revision to a kind of "mental strainer" that "improved, purified, [and] filtered" her thoughts. She elaborated further upon her technique, saying she could remember a number of times in her past when she had deliberately not done certain things so she would not have to face "the shame of writing them down." Yet she insisted that if she had gone ahead and done things she was not particularly proud of, she had written them "straight out, spread out here with all the love of the truth which is *not* in my character but which *you* [the diary] have forced me to cultivate."[2]

She was already having problems telling the truth in her daily life. Rosa knew this and, on many occasions, either teased or admonished her to "go tell those lies to your diary." Anaïs, who dreaded being accused of "the Nin lies," was reduced to tears and furious protests: "No, no, I never tell lies."[3]

Actually, she lied frequently. Some of them were merely tales told to keep from being scolded; others were truly bizarre, such as the one that haunted her for the rest of her life. Anaïs Sánchez, at the Waldorf-Astoria with her children Cuca and Eduardo, invited Anaïs Nin to join them at the theater. Anaïs was detained on her way to the Queens station and arrived in Manhattan later than expected but still early enough for the performance. When the cousins asked what delayed her, Anaïs could not tell the truth, mundane as it was: "My imagination was there, my poor father's greatest fault and my heritage. What made me [lie]?" She could only answer: "I don't know."

The lie was truly a whopper. She invented a railroad strike, with angry workers stopping the train, breaking windows, and beating the conductor. Her imagined adventure was replete with blood, noise, and violence, and everyone believed her.[4] Astonished at her own creativity, she felt a double surge of power: not only could she invent so fantastic a story, she could make people believe it. Forty years later she still marveled that "the power of the spirit is frightening—for miracles, for creation, and for destruction."[5]

The next day, Anaïs Sánchez phoned Rosa, saying her children were afraid to come to lunch because of Anaïs's Nin's terrifying train ride. Rosa, furious, forced the truth and insisted Anaïs apologize for lying. Anaïs wept, threatened to run away from home, or do herself bodily harm. Then, begging, pleading, hugging and kissing her mother, she promised sweetly never to tell an untruth again if Rosa relented. As she had always done in the past and would continue to do in the future, Rosa "promised to help make [Anaïs's] falsehood as small as possible. She said she knew how I checked myself continually and tried [to tell the truth]."[6]

If Rosa's sons had even hinted at an untruth, she would have punished them severely, but she was complicitous in all things concerning Anaïs, excusing and forgiving her time after time. She knew others disapproved, but she ignored them, seemingly impervious to their concerns and criticisms. She allowed her eighteen-year-old daughter to spend her days aimlessly drifting, supposedly caring for the house, but really doing exactly as she pleased.

Rosa may have been unconsciously trying to compensate for Joaquín Nin's abusive treatment of the children, but Joaquín Nin-Culmell cautions, "As far as my sister was concerned, my father had not abandoned a wife and three children: he had abandoned *her!*" Joaquín Nin's abandonment of *her* resonated with more overtones, undertones, and nuances than Anaïs could enumerate in her rapidly accumulating volumes of diary writing. Even though society's view of families without fathers was changing, her own absent one became a defense to use when she was questioned or criticized, an excuse to avoid what she did not want to do, and a weapon to gain sympathy from those reluctant to give it. She was probably unaware of how much she used the persona of "the poor little Nin girl,"[7] but it became a formidable weapon for most of her adult life when she wanted something.

Love and warmth were qualities that filled the Nin household in Richmond Hill. Anaïs's cousin Eduardo Sánchez spoke of "the inexplicable charm" to be found there, where no one was ever bored and the atmosphere so imbued with the generous free exchange of ideas that everyone was encouraged to speak "of all the things one loves."[8] Many young men and women of Anaïs's age lived in the neighborhood and, in the custom of the time, there were social "evenings," music and dancing followed by games and refreshments. Rosa's entertainments featured some of the finest musicians who either lived in or were passing through New York. Cuban poets, among them the famous Gustavo Galarraga, came to call. Culture filled the house, and the music and conversation were fascinating and stimulating. The younger generation was expected to take its place among the elders and to discuss music and poetry with knowledge and appreciation.

Anaïs was "always very disturbed when someone says something nice, as though I didn't deserve to have people think I am good."[9] She had begun to divide herself into what she called "the double person in me: Miss Nin and Linotte."[10] "Miss Nin" was her public persona, the pretty young girl who shopped in the village, greeted the priest after Sunday mass, sometimes took the train alone into Manhattan to buy books, and went to parties in Richmond Hill. Linotte, however, "is impossible and must be hidden, hidden." She perceived the duality in her nature with rigorous honesty and was only momentarily unsettled by it. The secret, private self was the part she most preferred, and the preference did not worry her at all. Eventually, this latter became her true reality and certainly the dominating part of her adult personality.

All this had repercussions upon Anaïs's behavior as Rosa prepared to deal with her marriageable daughter. According to Cuban custom, Rosa commissioned a formal studio birthday portrait of Anaïs. It was to be sent to Joaquín and to the Havana newspapers in preparation for what Rosa hoped would be Anaïs's debut there in 1921. The photo shows a beautiful young woman, delicately graceful and appealingly innocent. "All those pictures are not me," Anaïs said, expressing a view she would hold for the rest of her life. "I only see someone who looks pretty, charming, and strangely like everyone else . . . suddenly I think: that's the way I look to everyone. Everyone sees me as I am in my photographs, not my ideas, my fantasies, my dreams, my observations." In her terminology, they saw Miss Nin; Linotte remained hidden.

Much of her thinking was shaped by her reading. As she was alone so much, she depended on books to provide her with ideas to write about. She was especially fond of journals, and Emerson's were among the earliest to spark her imagination. She copied his pithiest aphorisms into the diary, frequently commenting on what they meant personally to her. She also tried to write essays in the Emersonian manner, particularly imitating "Self-Reliance," "Love," and "Friendship." Too frequently, however, she found herself confronted with the problem that plagued her all her life: being unable to move from the journal into fiction; in this case, her essays disintegrated into diary writing and personal examination, usually after a paragraph or two at best.[11]

She found sustenance in Robert Louis Stevenson, solace in Frank Swinnerton, and exhilaration in George Meredith's *The Egoist,* with its various versions of love.[12] But since everything she read had to be related somehow to her own life, with herself as the heroine of every literary interpretation, she found the most profound analogies in such books as Eleanor Hodgman Porter's novels for young girls (especially her best-known creation, "Pollyanna"). She found in Porter's *Mary Marie,* "this little girl of crosscurrents and contradictions, the child of two unlikes," exactly how she wanted the story of her own life to proceed: "her parents are divorced, my parents separated . . . her father and mother fall in love again."[13] Mary Marie's thoughts so mirrored hers that it "hurt to see them printed there by someone else." She also liked Porter's "plain, ordinary [English]," which Anaïs spoke but never wrote because she loved "the other English, Scott's, Washington Irving's."

Her reading matured, but her diary writing did not always reflect it. As long as she wrote in French, it was the language of a very young schoolgirl and not capable of conveying the sophistication of her thoughts and ideas. When she began to use English exclusively in July 1920,[14] her writing became couched in rhetorical formality, imitating the classic literary French found mostly in the nineteenth-century novels and journals she so loved.

Any attempt to interpret her writing must begin with how the language she read influenced what she wrote and conveyed what she thought. If her prose seems sometimes garbled or her views excessively naive, it is usually because her knowledge of how to use language does not reflect the degree of sophistication in her thought. Her maturity becomes obvious to readers of her diaries the moment she abandoned French to write in English, but, as she continued to think in Spanish and French, awkwardness and infelicities appeared in her English grammar and syntax throughout her writing life. In any analysis of either her fiction or the diary, the dimension of language must be factored into every other aspect that constituted her own "mental strainer."

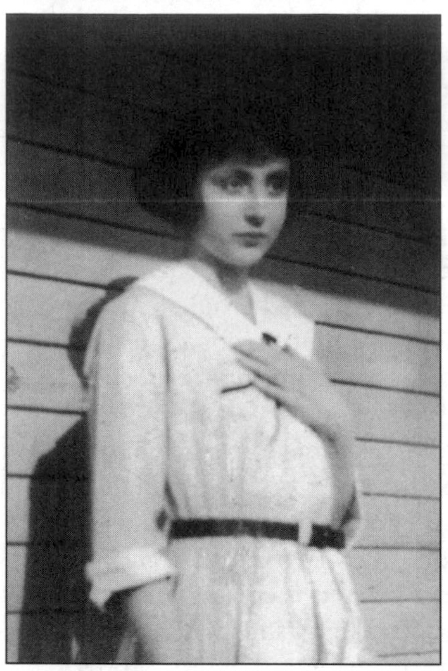

Anaïs in Richmond Hill,
age sixteen.

Anaïs in her "sweet
sixteen" photo.

Anaïs modeling, posing as Cleopatra, age eighteen.

Journals influenced her most, especially those written by women: "I am fascinated by journals and biographies. Nothing holds so great an interest for me now than the study of a human heart seeking to express itself in life."[15] The first to make a strong impression was by Eugénie de Guérin (1805–1848), who lived in an isolated château near Albi in southwest France. In 1834, Eugénie began a "Journal intime" (a title Anaïs liked and used for her own writing) for her younger brother, Maurice, for whom she had an intense, possessive love.[16] Although he died in 1838, Eugénie continued to write as if to him until 1842. Like Anaïs, Eugénie filled her days with household responsibilities and writing and disapproved of the "modern" lives of others. Anaïs loved Eugénie's journal for its "simplicity, purity, [and] goodness," saying it was "delicately written by an angelical woman."[17]

She loved the journal of Marie Bashkirtseff (1860–1884) for very different reasons: "[she] is not good, not simple, and writes with a frankness that borders on coarseness." Marie's journal so shocked Anaïs that when she wrote about it in the diary, she used French rather than English to distance herself from its harsh reality. Anaïs was fascinated from Marie's first stunning sentence, in which she said she would neither lie nor pose, but would tell the truth about everything.[18] Their lives also had certain parallels: when she was twelve, Marie's mother left her father and took her to France. Marie claimed she began the journal to reveal herself entirely to herself, but soon she, too, wrote with the intention of leaving her mark upon posterity by publishing it. As Marie Bashkirtseff's "Journal intime" supplanted Eugénie de Guérin's in Anaïs Nin's imagination, and as it had lasting influence upon the form of her diary writing for many years to come,[19] it is likely that Marie's journal first gave her the idea that she, too, should write for posterity and, therefore, eventual publication. Anaïs was amazed by Marie's "boldness, sincerity, vanity, conceit, arrogance, cleverness, exaggerations, flashes of wisdom, skepticism, folly." In short, a reflection of almost everything she had put into her own diary. Marie's diary strengthened her conviction that it was important to keep on writing despite teasing from her cousins and criticism from her mother.

When Anaïs was almost eighteen, her diary reflections moved beyond accounts of daily life and ideas gleaned from reading to thoughts about marriage and careers, what the future might hold, and what she wanted her life to become. Unmarried women with intellectual aspirations were known as "bluestockings," a pejorative meaning they were unfeminine and pretentious,[20] but Anaïs admired learned women, especially those with literary ambitions. Her fear was that she would not make a "good bluestocking," for then she would "have to get married" because she did not "know how to do anything else."[21]

The idea of having to work for a living frightened her. She wanted to be insulated from life's harsh realities and was already determined that hers would be "a dream made real."[22] This idea of living life as a dream became her driving ambition and caused her much trouble in later years when she struggled to position herself as a woman in a changing world. Yet, all the while she was thinking of how hers would be a protected life, she knew that she would have to go out into the world and support herself unless she married.

She formed a very clear idea of what marriage meant to her: "marriage is . . . like putting all the best that I have under the protection, the nobility, the grandeur of a man." But, "Just the same, I always compare my career as a bluestocking to a victory and marriage to a defeat."

Anaïs had quite a few conquests in her teen years, but the first real passion in her life was her Aunt Anaïs's son: her first cousin Eduardo Sánchez, and it caused a furor within the family. Eduardo, a Harvard student, had impeccable manners and was elegant in dress and deportment.[23] He was tall, blond, and green-eyed, reflecting his Danish more than his Spanish heritage. Although they had known each other all their lives, when they met as young adults in the summer of 1919, Anaïs was quick to note that Eduardo, a soulmate who loved poetry and kept a diary, was "a Linotte in masculine form."[24] His role within the Sánchez family was exactly the same as Anaïs's in hers: Eduardo was a dreamer in a family of doers.

Of all the Culmell sisters, Anaïs Sánchez married the wealthiest man. Eduardo, like his two elder brothers, was expected to help manage the family's enormous holdings in banking, industry, and land, but he preferred instead to pursue studies in astrology and William Blake's poetry. He confided this to his "cuisine," as he called Anaïs in his bad French, and the pet name did not escape his sharp-eyed mother's notice.

When Eduardo, his brothers, and other male cousins visited the

Nins on their way to and from their various schools, Eduardo and Anaïs were inseparable. The two were usually found quietly discussing literature, writing in each other's diaries, or reading passages aloud that they had written. Rosa was concerned about their deepening involvement, but more concerned that Eduardo's mother would renege on her promise to sponsor Anaïs's debut in Havana. The cousins exchanged frequent letters for more than a year, until June 1921, when, without consulting Rosa, Bernabé and Anaïs Sánchez forbade them to communicate in any way. Like his brothers before him, Eduardo was supposed to take his pick from among young Cuban women whose fortune and social standing equaled or surpassed his family's. He was not to waste himself on a first cousin, especially "the penniless daughter of a musician."[25]

A measure of Anaïs's naïveté was how bewildered she was by Eduardo's abrupt absence until Rosa, typically blunt and honest, explained. Anaïs was deeply hurt; thinking of herself as not Cuban, she deemed all Cubans "the most cynical, callous people in the world."[26] Rosa honored her sister's harsh edict and forbade any further contact between their children; the correspondence ceased.

Anaïs missed Eduardo because she was "so accustomed to knowing all that took place in his heart . . . through his diary." It was difficult to have to rely again on her own diary for companionship and to be without her alter ego (and equally important, his alter ego, his diary). His parting gift (disobeying his mother one last time) perfectly defined their relationship: a brown leather diary with gilt-edged pages and a tiny brass lock. He inscribed the inside cover to "my Lost Princess: When my wings shall cease to be clipped—then shall I stretch my pinions and fly to thee with all my joy, all the fervor, all the ardor of youth. Time can never crumble a true Devotion!! E.S." Anaïs consoled herself that the only thing to part them forever was that "during the period of waiting, we may find Love."[27]

"Love me, someone!" she had commanded at sixteen, seeking a "Shadow" to fill an "immense empty space."[28] As time passed, the "Shadow" assumed different guises, changing from "a strong, stern, severe figure . . . with nobly graying hair and steely eyes" (exactly how Joaquín Nin looked in the photos he sent her), to "very young, quite mad, with very little wisdom, of course, but a lot of talent."[29] Although the "Shadow" changed over time, the one aspect that remained constant was "he who will write in my diary with me."[30]

Perhaps, she thought as she recalled her friendship with Eduardo, she would marry after all. Her happiest dream was that she and her husband would spend every evening "read[ing] our diaries to each other, for of course [he] will have to begin his Diary as soon as he marries me."

Rhetorically she asked: "Do you pity him?"[31]

5

"What to do with Anaïs"

"THE QUESTION OF MONEY is always hanging over our heads," Anaïs noted with resignation.[1] By 1920, with Cuba reeling from the serious collapse of the sugar economy, Rosa's wealthy clients not only stopped paying for past purchases, they no longer placed new orders. She took boarders into the house and once again Anaïs shared her mother's bedroom.

Rosa was an excellent seamstress, and sewing was the one marketable talent she had left. Various Seventh Avenue merchants sent clothing that required delicate handwork, and she and her assistant sat in the little office on Broadway each day finishing as much as they could. Anaïs was pressed into service but soon became "ill" from the "strain." Rosa gave in and left her at home in Richmond Hill.

Anaïs wanted to help, but in her own way. Her favorite publication was *The Delineator,* a curious mixture of articles ranging from those espousing feminist views to others extolling the virtues of marriage and housekeeping. While championing woman suffrage, Butterick patterns were enclosed in each issue. It was Anaïs's favorite reading.

She entered a contest in which "younger readers" were asked to submit "your happiest poems, the most beautiful thoughts that you can put on paper" for a special summer issue.[2] She dashed off several and received "a kindly, encouraging [form] letter from the Verse Editor" who accepted an "Elegy" and said payment would soon follow—of one dollar.[3] Anaïs "flew" to her typewriter and dispatched several more, confident that she would soon be contributing handsomely to the household because of a second, personal letter from the "Verse Editor," who planned to consider her submissions for the "adult" rather than the "youthful column," saying "the check will be bigger"—by several dollars. Anaïs was overjoyed to think she was going to help the family's coffers through her writing.

Her next submission was a loose collection of adolescent romantic ramblings in blank verse called "Love Letters." When they were rejected, she responded as she would from then on to every real or imagined slight to her writing, with an offhanded casualness that disguised her true feelings. "Oh, the editor has answered," she told the diary, adding that she liked "the idea" of the poems but felt they needed "more polishing." Even a gentle rejection was too much; once rebuffed, she turned her attentions elsewhere and never sent another poem to *The Delineator,* nor was she ever paid—not even the promised one dollar.

She had been thinking of enrolling at Columbia for noncredit courses, and spent the summer of 1920 reading Bede, Caedmon, Cynewulf, Chaucer, and Spenser, (all from an anthology of English Literature), and just about anything else that came her way.

In September she was interviewed by a Dr. Glass, a member of the admissions staff, who told her she was a "mere child," a "mother's-baby-sort-of-a-girl, petted and spoiled and inexperienced and innocent." Anaïs was "tremendously indignant," as well she should have been: "Why didn't [she] ask me to tell her about Pascal, Socrates? . . . [about] Bossuet's beautiful and marvelous reasonings."[4] She decided "not to struggle" with Columbia until later that winter, after a proposed trip to Cuba upon which Rosa had staked her hopes for the family's future.

Rosa had always known that her estranged husband would not help to establish the children, either in marriage (Anaïs) or career (Thorvald and Joaquín). Thorvald was a brilliant student in his last year of high school and expected to go to college to study engineering. Joaquín continued to show precocious ability as a pianist, so his future education was directed toward a concert career.

Joaquín Nin chose this moment to strike with what Rosa had long feared. In December 1920, he sent a conciliatory letter, saying he wanted her and the children to return to France to live with him or else he would institute divorce proceedings on the grounds of abandonment. The letter was merely a legal ploy—announcement of his planned marriage to Maruca Rodríguez, now divorced and old enough to marry without parental permission. Rosa knew there were dangers if she did not comply: Joaquín was too selfish to be interested in raising his children but was still capable of taking the two minor boys just to spite her.

Rosa shared the letter with the children. Anaïs felt "estranged" from her father for the first time. She told him through the diary, "You are not loved any more by anyone under this roof except me, and I love you only because you are my father."[5]

By February 1921, Joaquín Nin realized that his ploy had failed. Rosa's lawyer advised her to write a detailed letter spelling out her conditions for moving to France so that she and the children would be protected. Joaquín's next and most devastating subterfuge was to enlist his mother against Rosa, persuading Angela Castellanos de Nin that he had repented and Rosa was "unforgiving and cruel."[6] The old woman accused Rosa of "calumniating [her son], staining his honor, depriving [his children] of his presence through her resentment and prejudices."[7] When that failed, he tried again to control Rosa through letters to Anaïs, instructing her to reply in Spanish because it was the language of her ancestors. Her succinct reply is notable because it was the first time she disobeyed him: "French is the language of my heart and English of my intellect. Spanish does not appeal to me one whit."[8]

Anaïs took Rosa's side without hesitation: "No one but his own daughter . . . could understand [Joaquín Nin] so well," she wrote in the diary. "I know the empty eloquence of his letters, his lack of sincerity, his actor's attitude in life." She also realized something upsetting: "It is you who have given me the traits I continually struggle to conquer, to uproot or at least control. You play with people's hearts, you move them and blind them." Her conclusion depressed her: "And the worst of it is that I love him . . . in spite of all the things I find out about him."

Rosa somehow found the money for Columbia, where Anaïs was finally accepted in the winter of 1921. The same Dr. Glass who delayed her admission by a year continued to stand in her way. She refused to let Anaïs take courses in philosophy and psychology but enrolled her in English composition and intermediate French, in which she had no interest at all.

"I can truthfully say I have studied four subjects at Columbia University," Anaïs wrote when the term ended: "Composition, Grammar, French and Boys." One semester was quite enough of "grammar and boys," and from then on she picked and chose only what she wanted of the other two.[9] She duly noted her composition professor's criticism in the diary that her "style" was "very beautiful, but . . ." She ignored his comment that 1920s writing was "terse, plain, direct." Even as she exhorted herself to drop her "elegant, elaborate speech, formality and pomp," she was proud to remain "old-fashioned" with a style that "specialized in fantasy."[10]

She believed she possessed the only two qualities that mattered for a writer: a love of the act of writing and facility of expression, which she attributed to her Grandfather Nin, a "rather poor" scholar, and her father, "a critic and champion of musical opinions . . . accustomed to using his pen when . . . not at the piano."[11]

"I have ink in my blood," she concluded. "But must I take it for granted that I possess their talent?" She gave Columbia credit for one realization only: "I know that my style is tedious, stilted, voluminous. I know that I have a tendency toward moralizing, which, at my age, is a thing that sorely tries older people's patience." These same faults, identified at the age of eighteen, were often cited as her major faults by critics of her adult writing, and ultimately led to her disparaging classification as a "major" minor writer.[12]

Once she dropped out of Columbia, "what to do with Anaïs"[13] became critical until Anaïs Sánchez reluctantly agreed to sponsor her for the Havana debutante season. In the meantime, she had to contribute some income.

Anaïs was pencil-thin, the look to which fashionable American women aspired in the 1920s. She had a crown of thick brown hair, a creamy complexion, and her hazel eyes could change disarmingly from blue-green to yellow-brown. She had never lost the trilled Spanish-French "r," which gave her English pronunciation a hint of a slightly exotic lisp.[14] Among Rosa's European friends were musicians who serenaded Anaïs, poets who said her beauty inspired them, and painters who wanted her to pose.

One of Rosa's boarders suggested that Anaïs register with various agencies as an artist's model, but Rosa forbade her, fearing it would damage Anaïs's chances for a Cuban marriage. Then, in June 1921, Rosa collapsed, again felled by overwork and strain.[15] She was deeply ashamed that her sisters had to rescue her still another time. By October, with financial disaster unavoidable, Anaïs became a model at the New York Art Workers' Club for Women, but bookings were few.

"I have been looking for work," she told Eduardo, confiding to the diary that he looked as if her remark "hurt him."[16] It led her to reflect at length on the nature of work, which she decided did not, in itself, insult, hurt, or humiliate, even though the process of looking for it did.

Soon she was steadily employed as an artist's model, and the work suited her. "I sit there hour after hour, so quietly, so still, I can dream, dream, dream, and dream to my heart's content."[17] She posed as everything from a French milkmaid to a Spanish gypsy, and was so popular with the famed illustrator Charles Dana Gibson that he painted her as one of his "Gibson Girls," her face adorning the cover of the *Saturday Evening Post.*[18]

"Dreaming," however, soon gave way to a harsh reality. A "Mr. Brown" tried to kiss her, insisted she dance, and held her too close. A "Mrs. Becker" tried to pay less than she owed. Other artists asked her to pose naked, still others (women as well as men) tried to fondle and seduce her, all of which she confided in highly indignant prose to the diary.[19]

Anaïs told Rosa everything that happened, and Rosa "was unhappy . . . to think of her 'little girl' "[20] having to work. "She had dreamed of my passing from her hands and her care to the hands and watchfulness and protection of a husband. . . . I answered her that there was only one man I would want to be 'protected' by and that he did not want to do so."

Anaïs was referring to Hugh Parker Guiler, with whom she had flirted discreetly for almost a year. They met on March 12, 1921, when his younger sister invited Anaïs to a dance at the Guiler home in Forest Hills, Queens. Anaïs attended in her "beautiful rose dress . . . transformed into an imp . . . perhaps with a dash of the devil."[21] She and Hugo danced the first and last dances together, but by the time the evening ended, they "almost forgot to dance in the excitement of the conversation." They discovered a shared "secret," writing poetry.

Despite their immediate attraction, there was no contact between them until June, when Hugo's parents went to Europe and he spent weekends with his aunt and uncle, the Parkers, who lived down the street from the Nins. Even then, Anaïs and Hugo did little more than nod to each other, for he was shy and awkward and she was too "old-fashioned" to make overtures. Rosa thought Hugo charming and indulged the flirtation by inviting him to sit on the porch one Sunday afternoon. Soon they were talking of Stevenson; of Emerson, whose essays Hugo carried in his pocket; of his beloved Columbia professor, the novelist John Erskine; and—to Anaïs, a miracle—of the diary that Hugo also wrote.

On July 1, 1921, Hugo invited Anaïs to an open-air concert at Columbia and then took her dancing. At the Forest Hills July Fourth celebration they talked of Erskine, Thoreau, Carlyle, Dryden, and Shelley, but especially of their diaries. Soon, Anaïs's became filled with notations of Hugo's looks, dreams, goals, ambitions, and whatever else she could learn about him. She decided that "outwardly he is all manliness, splendid, resolute. Inwardly he has the poet's wondrous wisdom. I can compare him with no one."[22]

Hugh Parker Guiler (called Hugo to distinguish him from his father) was the eldest son of Ena and Hugh Cheyne Guiler. He was born in Boston on February 15, 1898. The family moved to Puerto Rico in 1900, where Guiler Sr. supervised the industrialization of the sugar industry. Until Hugo was six and his brother Johnny three, they lived the life of "two little savages running around with a minimum of clothes in the garden of Eden."[23] They ate, played, and sometimes slept with the plantation's black servants, who were their only friends and playmates and who taught them fluent Spanish.[24] Both boys thrived, finding far more affection in the servants' quarters than they were ever granted by their dour, repressive Scottish parents, who decided that life among the natives was harmful and sent them to Scotland to live for the next ten years with their maternal grandfather and two stern maiden aunts.

The first four years the boys attended Ayr Academy in Alloway, a curious school where harsh discipline was coupled with a relaxed attitude toward individualism and creativity in a rigorous classical education combined with studio art. Hugo likened it to "a black cloud [of] terrible religious and moral oppression."[25] They saw their parents once every two years when they had "home leave."

Hugo bore lifelong psychic scars of his Scottish years: "I can vividly remember the excitement of preparing for my parents' visit. Johnny and I used to wish and hope and pray that they would take us away from that awful place . . . but . . . they would leave, and another grim year would begin anew in that dark, cold house with those two women who really did not know what to do with us."[26]

Hugo and Johnny remained in Scotland until 1914, when their father moved the entire family (it now included two sisters, Edith and Ethel) to Forest Hills.[27] The boys were enrolled as day students in St. Paul's boarding school in Garden City, "a miserable place, very snobbish,"[28] where Hugo was deeply unhappy. He excelled, however, carrying off the German prize, earning trophies as captain of its tennis team and writing poetry and fiction for the student literary magazine.

He graduated from Columbia in 1920 with a Bachelor of Arts in Economics and English Literature, and was chosen for the prestigious training program of the National City Bank of New York, which prepared graduates of the best universities to become senior officers in foreign branches and unofficial ambassadors of American goodwill. Hugo said he chose a career in banking initially for "a very Scottish" reason, financial security, but added astutely that "I had decided if I really wanted to go on with literature or the arts . . . I had to have some firm ground under me."[29] Everyone who knew Hugo had expected him to make poetry and literature his career, and no one was more surprised when he chose banking than Guiler Sr., a self-made man who frequently ridiculed his poetry-loving son by calling him "Professor."[30]

Anaïs also made an astute observation in August 1921: "I believe Hugo controls and forces back much that is impulsive in him."[31] To her distress, he did not contact her for more than a month because, as Joaquín Nin-Culmell observed, "Hugo's parents sent him away from Puerto Rico because they were afraid of the unsuitable influences of all things Spanish, and now here he was, totally enthralled by a little Spanish girl with no money, no real education, no social standing to speak of, and a Catholic to boot!"[32]

In late September, Hugo returned, bent on sorting out their differing views of life. He was concerned about Anaïs's lack of formal education. Anaïs, embarrassed, said she could not afford to return to Columbia. True, but also a convenient excuse: she was no longer interested in formal study. Hugo worried that she would be unhappy and frustrated as a housewife. As a potential executive in an international bank, he knew he needed a helpful and contented mate "to work with a holy joy, for the perfect ordering of practical things."[33]

She understood his many reservations about her suitability, but she was deep in the throes of a crisis of her own about how a woman should live her life—as an independent intellectual, a "bluestocking," or a *femme inspiratrice,* helpmate to a man. Hugo told her that he needed a business career in order to become a poet and writer because only through "the normal life of others" would he find the necessary "ideas and experiences and emotions" to write about. Anaïs agreed that his view was eminently sensible, for in comparison, her own life was "not as well balanced."[34] "Am I clever enough to be a woman and a writer? Is such a thing possible?"[35] she asked herself after reading Sydney Smith's treatise on "Female Education." She believed his thesis, "Choose between your home and domestic happiness [or] your pen and your books," could be combined into an integrated whole.[36]

She was ready to make a commitment to Hugo, but he continued to wax hot and cold. Just as she convinced herself they would not have a future together, she discovered in November 1921 that they were "beginning to say more with our eyes than with words. Sometimes the light in his makes me tremble."[37] By January 1922, he grew brave enough to kiss her hand. The "key to his character," she decided, was "patience . . . the most incredible, boundless, inimitable and exasperating patience in the world."[38] In April 1922, Hugo told Anaïs what she already knew: his parents disapproved of her because she was poor, Latin, and most of all, Catholic. In May he told her he loved her despite their objections. On June 8 they agreed to become engaged but told no one, not even Rosa.

Anaïs began a new volume of the diary. She had the habit of entitling each volume before writing in it, and now noted how uncannily accurate her titles had been. This one she called "Journal d'une Fiancée,"[39] for as far as she was concerned, marriage was only a question of time.

In a mood of blissful optimism she went alone to Woodstock, New York, a summer colony for artists and illustrators, whose models usually followed. Living on her own, Anaïs felt "a sense of power" such as she had never known: "thrown upon my own resources, here my real self must appear and assert itself . . . this new individual now

Mr. and Mrs. Hugh Parker Guiler, after their marriage.

Anaïs in hat she made.

Hugo as a young banker.

ruling me [is] firm, resolute, grave, almost sensible, exulting in her solitude and in the belief that she can handle life and not be handled by it."[40]

Then Rosa, fifty-one, embittered and exhausted, came for the weekend. Without considering Hugo, she asked Anaïs to promise that after her marriage they would all live together. Anaïs insisted upon "wanting to shape my own life, with Hugo . . . to be near, but not with, those we love."[41] Rosa responded angrily but prophetically: "You do nothing but dream, dream, dream, Fifille, and it is just that which frightens me for you. And with such a temperament as yours you are going to make yourself very unhappy."

Now that Hugo had in his own way proposed, Anaïs's diary writings were all about her future.[42] She turned again to literature for guidance but, of all she read, only Stevenson discussed marriage and he was "too sarcastic." Rosa told her marriage was not the stuff of dreams and to come down to earth. Frances Schiff was amused by her naïveté: "Our mothers, grandmothers, great-grandmothers all thought they would be happier. . . . Yet in the end, [their marriages] are all alike." Anaïs insisted that hers would be different: "all my life shall be spent in giving him happiness . . . I promise he shall never be hurt through my fault . . . I shall think first of him and then of my desires, and teach them to become his."[43]

In early September 1922, it seemed likely that they might never marry when Hugo's parents forbade him to marry a Catholic. Their threats to disown and disinherit him were coupled with his own hesitations: he was still not sure he could support a wife, for he understood tacitly that marriage to Anaïs meant supporting her mother and brothers as well. The tension brought him close to a nervous breakdown. His parents insisted on the time-honored upper-class solution: a cruise and three-month tour of Europe. He told Anaïs only that they wanted him to go away and sailed at the end of September 1922, the nadir of Rosa's business debacle.

Thorvald had graduated from high school in the spring, winning a prestigious four-year Regents' scholarship to Cornell. Rosa told him he could not go; she needed him to help support the family. Thorvald obeyed, giving up forever his dream of becoming an engineer. Of the three children, he was the only one Rosa forced to sacrifice his dreams, and it marked the start of his lifelong bitterness and resentment of his mother and siblings. The family crisis was so severe that even Anaïs became practical, working in a Seventh Avenue clothing factory during the day as a pattern model and posing for artists at night.

Joaquín Nin chose this moment to demand that his children join him in Europe—yet another ploy in his determination to divorce Rosa. Anaïs replied with a brutally frank letter about how his children were paying for the obligations he had so cavalierly rejected: "Our whole childhood was darkened by you. Our whole youth is difficult, hard, sad, because of you."[44]

Thinking it likely that Hugo was gone for good, Rosa's thoughts turned again to Cuba. The dauntless Antolina came to her rescue and agreed to pay for Anaïs's debut because she, Juana, and Rosa all believed that the Nin family's only salvation was for Anaïs to marry a wealthy Cuban. Anaïs told the diary (in self-pitying, heroically overblown prose) that *she* made the decision to "sacrifice" herself to a rich Cuban husband to end her mother's troubles, but she had no intention of doing so because she was determined to marry Hugo.[45] In sarcasm seldom found in her diary, she noted that the volume entitled with such pride and hope, "Journal d'une Fiancée," had become the account of her abandonment: "He, in the very midst of the first year of our love, can leave me. Only a miracle can make our marriage possible."[46]

With the protection of distance, Hugo sensitively and accurately recorded their behavior toward each other before their marriage. He wrote in his diary of how difficult it was to be his true self with Anaïs: each time he tried to be honest, she seemed so shocked that he became silent "for fear of losing your regard. It has almost seemed sometimes that I would have to be someone other than what I thought my best self in order to come up to your ideal of what I should be." His other concern was that she wanted only "the high peaks of life and not . . . soiling your hands with the common, practical things."[47] She was convinced that love could conquer everything and swore to change, which was exactly what he wanted to hear.

Determined to marry him, Anaïs wrote from Antolina's ranch outside Havana that she had been "transported to Fairyland." Indeed, she was the Cuban equivalent of Cinderella at the Ball. Society gossip columnists reported her every move, and Cuban newspapers raved about her beauty, calling her the "incomparable beauty who has captured the attention of all Cuba."[48] Of course, she sent all these clippings to Hugo.

Three weeks passed, and he wrote only one letter. "Here's what he said," she wrote to Rosa: " 'With the restoration of my tired body I am now able to know how blessed I am in your love, my sweet, my own Anaïs.' " For the first time, she did not tell Rosa everything, for she added only " 'etc. etc. and a whole lot of other things as well!' "

On December 5, Anaïs wrote to Rosa that Hugo had decided to marry her and he wanted Rosa to consider him as another son. He would assume financial responsibility for the family and would convert to Catholicism.[49] Hugo wrote the same to his parents. They replied that if he married Anaïs, they would never see him again; if he became a Catholic, they would disown him. They accused him of losing his mind and said they would cut off his money, leaving him stranded in Europe. Resourcefully, Hugo cashed in his first-class boat ticket and European rail reservations, then booked passage on a freighter to Havana and third-class tickets for him and his bride from Havana to New York.

On the eve of Hugo's arrival, February 18, 1923, Anaïs wrote the last entry in her diary as a single woman: "God help me, for I am entrusting all to love and binding my very soul to the fulfillment of my human mission. And while the knowing ones whisper: Love passes, Marriage is a failure, Man is selfish, I stand unwaveringly, in expectation, my soul filled by visions which elevate me above myself."[50]

On March 3, 1923, in a quiet ceremony before Antolina, Juana, Anaïs Sánchez, and several cousins, Anaïs Nin married Hugh Guiler in the Catholic Church. Rosa had neither money nor time to get to Havana. The Cuban newspapers duly noted that the "enchanting" bride had married "a distinguished young American who holds a high position in the National City Bank of New York" and bestowed upon them "the very best wishes for their every happiness."[51]

6

"Where shall this lead us?"

THEY WENT THROUGH the wedding ceremony in a daze, and after a small, subdued reception, left for a short honeymoon in a modest resort hotel outside Havana.[1]

As soon as they were alone, Anaïs put on her white satin nightgown and sat on the edge of the bed. Hugo became "exalted and romantic," falling on his knees to read a poem he wrote and to "utter wonderful words of worship." Then he turned off the light and both slipped into bed. Anaïs lay there expectantly, but Hugo was inexperienced and only rubbed his body against hers. "I did not know what to do either," she wrote. "All I knew was that it would hurt and that there would be blood." However, Hugo's emission penetrated no farther than her nightgown. Anaïs was amazed by how stiff the fabric was when she awakened the next morning. "I felt sad—vague," she wrote. "Hugo was sad, too. I thought that he did not love me."

She waited impatiently for him to "take"[2] her the next night, but he was impotent. He wept and apologized, but she had "a vague feeling that something was wrong. He does not love me, does not desire me."

For the next several months, they wore themselves out "with excitement and frustration." Hugo asked her to lie on the bed fully clothed, with her legs raised "so that he could look . . . between my legs, to caress the sex." Occasionally he placed his penis between her legs and each "rubbed" until they "came."

Their married life began in Rosa's house and Anaïs's blue-and-white bedroom. Hugh Guiler Sr. had indeed disowned his son, and so there was no contact between Hugo and his family. No one, not even his aunt and uncle Parker, who lived two houses away from the Nins, sent gifts or good wishes.

Life settled into a routine. Each day Hugo went to the bank while Anaïs fluttered around the house briefly in the morning, making vague attempts to do housewifely things before retreating to the sanctity and solitude of "their" room to write in the diary.

Rosa was grim, her happiness at having her married daughter under the same roof darkened by the shame of having most of the household expenses paid for by her new young son-in-law. Thorvald, now a working man, was a specter whose voice was silent and spirit quelled. His nightly presence infused the house with guilty unease; no one forgot that he was forced to sacrifice his dream of an education because of his mother's financial failure. Only Joaquín continued to fill the house with the joyful sound of music.

There were still boarders, further complicating the issue of privacy. As soon as it was polite to do so, the couple retired each evening to their room to write in a common diary. Literally, to write—for they were too embarrassed to express even the incomplete physical aspect of their relationship in a house that held so many people. In this common diary, Hugo drew upon all the clichés of romantic fiction to describe what his version of "making love" to Anaïs meant to him: ". . . the softness of her skin such as it is on her rose-tipped breasts along her curved in waist, and (softest of all) between her lovely legs. Hers was a body radiant with unearthly light, which, touching me, left me no longer merely [a] human lover sinking into satisfaction, but a god rising to take a goddess in her bridal chamber above the clouds."[3]

He wrote this passage a few weeks after their marriage, obviously content with their putative sexual relations. Anaïs wrote nothing at all about sex, either in their common or her private diary. She would not write about it for several years, and then she had only negative impressions of her husband's prowess, all of which began the first time they achieved coitus.

They lived in Rosa's house until early summer 1923, when they moved into a furnished apartment. Tired of their games, Anaïs insisted one night that Hugo "possess [her] altogether." He was "afraid to hurt [her]," but she demanded that he persist until "it was done."

She claimed then, and throughout their long married life, that Hugo was "unusually large" and she "rather small," and that their sexual relations were always painful. She also accused Hugo of being "in everything else sensitive, in this completely blind," of inconsiderately achieving orgasm without being mindful of her needs. Anaïs could not understand "this great abysm between the man I liked to live with because he was so attuned to me, so sensitive, enveloping, protective, and this man who appeared at the moment of sex and who was then an autocrat."

Otherwise, marriage to Hugo provided "a refuge, a soft, dark, secure hiding place," and he became her willing "shadow." She was content with what she later described as an "incestual brother-sister" affection.

Anaïs's dream of what marriage should be came true with Hugo, as he acceded to her wishes that diary writing be given high priority, indeed that it dominate their private lives. Each wrote comments about the other, sometimes even acting as scribe as one frequently copied letters into the diary that the other wrote to a third party.[4]

Each partner subjected the other to intense scrutiny, and Anaïs discerned an "irony of fate." She had hoped to find "strength and self confidence" in Hugo, but "he does not possess these things. I, in my weakness, am the stronger of the two." It was profoundly shocking: "Where shall this lead us? I, who believed myself made to cling, thrown upon my own strength."[5]

Hugo nevertheless became the stable pillar and de facto head around which the Nin family revolved. He went to the bank each day, and always gave Rosa the better part of his salary. She deferred to him, Thorvald was respectful if silent, and Joaquín "loved him like a respected older brother."[6] When they were alone, however, Hugo confided everything to Anaïs, from the emotional deprivation of his early years to his anxieties about advancing in the bank and his dreams of how their relationship should evolve. At her prodding, he began to write histories of the events in his life,[7] and spoke of the persons who had had the greatest impact upon his intellectual development, among them his professor of literature at Columbia, John Erskine, a literary critic, novelist, and musicologist, whose "middlebrow" writings were highly popular in the twenties and thirties.[8] Erskine "liked interesting people, like Hugo, and tried to fill the house with them."[9] Hugo revered Erskine for giving him insight into the dualities of "poetry and reason."[10]

Hugo wrote in his journal that Erskine's "sharp-edged sword of reason" gave him the courage to disobey his family and marry Anaïs. He struggled in a garbled account to explain "the sword of cold, shining steel I plunged into [his parents'] hearts, and went my way, laughing as I thought John would laugh." "Poetry *or* reason" became his lifelong dilemma, and he wrote here of the bank as a "great machine, final in its wisdom and authority," a "tremendous god, all demanding, all powerful." The bank required a "life of reason," and the divided Hugo believed that his only salvation was "love," which he feared would "struggle sometimes faintly" because of his job's demands. He noted how desperately his young wife wanted him to be a poet, but supporting her and her family dictated that he place imagination and poetry second to his daily work.

Curiously, as Hugo wrote this account, he discovered that not only was he good at his work, he liked it better than "the slow attainments of a scholar's life." He realized that banking was going to give him money, travel, and the opportunity to live and work in foreign countries. The only thing he had not factored into this pleasant personal equation was Anaïs and her view that life, no matter how successful and satisfying, if devoted to anything but art was somehow shameful and embarrassing.

An eroding split in Hugo's personality began to form. He saw himself as "in love with love and desiring above all else a wife who would be beautiful, mystical and intelligent. . . . Half-consciously, through my Scotch blood, I suppose, I prepared the practical means for the attainment of these ends."[11] Anaïs called him "the humorous banker,"[12] but the competing demands of his profession and his wife were exhausting him.

Anaïs was "sharply critical" of Hugo's love of banking, even though he was "always constructive and encouraging" about her immersion in the diary. Because she was unable to write anything else, she threatened "never to write again, to destroy the book, my Journal, myself, anything." Hugo assured her (even though he did not believe it) that the hours she spent on her diary were worthwhile, which provided the excuse that it left him no time to write in his own, which led her to chastise him for neglecting his and thus unconsciously devalue hers, and so on and so on. Anaïs's diary loomed so large in their relationship that it took on the aspect of a "third party" in frequent "tiffs."

Rosa shared Hugo's concern about the alarming amount of time

Anaïs spent each day immersed in the diary. Frequently they quarreled and Hugo had to intercede. He always supported Anaïs but usually wrote repentant letters to Rosa.[13] Anaïs avoided writing about the real reason for so much of the friction with her mother: the impending move to Paris. Hugo requested the transfer, as much for Rosa as himself, for Joaquín was accepted by the Schola Cantorum.[14] Anaïs believed that Rosa's presence in Paris would compromise her independence, but she only wrote about it guardedly in the diary. It took several years for Anaïs's written descriptions of her mother to change from "Dearest Mummy" to a virago hitherto absent, an obsessively clinging woman fighting to keep her strong-minded daughter under her control.

Everyone but Thorvald, who took no part in family life, worried about distracting Anaïs from her diary. Hugo stopped reproaching and took a positive tack, saying it was sound preparation for other forms of writing, and it worked. Anaïs began to write a play, but abandoned it after one scene and beat a hasty retreat to the diary.[15] Soon after, however, her "dream [was] fulfilled," for she persuaded Hugo to spend the evenings listening patiently as she read aloud to him from her early diary volumes.

Tension, always present, mounted in Rosa's household. A brief respite from money troubles came when Richard Maynard, a portrait painter, asked Anaïs to sit for him. Feeling flush, she persuaded Hugo that they could afford a better apartment and furniture of their own, and in Forest Hills no less, the affluent suburb where his parents lived. By October 1923, they were ensconced in such comfort that Anaïs was "dazzled by the picture."[16] It was the first of several times throughout their marriage that she persuaded Hugo to live beyond his means, for shortly after, they were forced to give up the apartment because the rent was too high. They moved back to Richmond Hill and bought an inexpensive little bungalow several blocks from Rosa's house.

Anaïs became obsessed with her first home's decoration. She was captivated by Moorish architecture and design and created an environment that compelled the eye, lulled the senses, and induced the intellect to believe it had been transported to a someplace mythical. She did it with hard work and little money, for most of Hugo's salary went to Rosa.

Things had come to an even sorrier state than anyone could have imagined, as creditors instituted procedures to seize Rosa's house and the nonexistent assets they believed she possessed. In January 1924, Antolina once again provided an escape, inviting Rosa to Cuba. She listed the house for sale and left with Joaquín, putting Anaïs in charge of renting rooms until it sold and making her responsible for Thorvald's meals and laundry. Anaïs was shocked to be transported so abruptly from the diary's tranquillity to such a grueling schedule. It made her realize that an entire year had passed and she was still writing in the same volume. "At one time I could fill a larger book than this in one month," she commented wistfully.[17]

Anaïs Nin identified her ultimate goal as a writer shortly before she married, but it became instead a quest that frustrated and eluded her for most of her life: "Mine is the story of the soul, of the inner life and of its reactions to the outward life."[18] When she wrote fiction, this "grievous fault" kept her from giving it "a human shape, a reality." She had no examples to learn from because she did not read contemporary novels, so she looked within herself for answers that she was too inexperienced to provide and to journals such as Amiel's,[19] who was her model until the early 1930s, when she discovered Romain Rolland's massive novel, *Jean-Christophe.*[20]

"I am practicing on myself as one does upon an instrument," she noted, further reflecting that "there are people in whom the flare* for the dramatic, the sense of the artistic possibilities of human behavior, is so strongly developed as to become an actual power in their life. . . . They do all things, consciously or unconsciously, with the purpose of the storyteller who desires his audience to be struck by an effect."[21] She did not, however, consider that she was, and would continue to be, among them.

She was pleased to discover that a story begun the previous fall had grown into a novel. Called *Aline's Choice,*[22] the heroine was a young woman very much like Anaïs herself, and the plot, more transposed autobiography than fiction, consisted of emotional and philosophical sections of her diary and some of her conversations with Richard Maynard, who treated Anaïs as a woman whose ideas were worth attention.[23]

Hugo expressed his pride in the novel in their mutual journal: "I believe that Anaïs Nin Guiler is one of the truly great writers of our time. Some day the world will recognize Anaïs Nin Guiler as one of

*Misspellings and awkward grammar in quotes by AN have been retained throughout.

Hugo and Anaïs's first home, the bungalow in Richmond Hill.

its great women of all times."[24] When he showed it to her, Anaïs copied it into her diary, and repeated it to others for years.

Hugo did make hesitant editorial suggestions, questioning whether she might place her characters more specifically in time and place, give them last names as well as first, and tell the reader something about how they made their living or were educated. She ignored these suggestions, saying hers was a fiction of the interior, of mood and essence. From then on, Hugo offered only the unqualified praise Anaïs demanded.

She still read everything she wrote each day to him at night. His response encouraged her to invite Eduardo Sánchez (who was becoming important as a confidant to them both) to read it as well. Eduardo was unstinting in his praise, comparing Anaïs's writing with Apollinaire, Rimbaud, and Verlaine, whom she read immediately. He had also discovered Proust and Joyce, whom she read with less enthusiasm.

Hugo's college friend Eugene Graves, honest and unpretentious, responded to her novel with reservations. As his letter was not unmitigated praise and admiration, she did not paste it in the diary but paraphrased instead in generalities, concluding that his "review" was "a far better piece of writing than you could find in any of my chapters. . . . I no longer believe in my book."[25] She seized the excuse of managing two households to abandon the novel.

Rosa sold her house in June 1924 and immediately enrolled Joaquín in the Schola Cantorum. Hugo now had to persuade the bank to transfer him to Paris, and Thorvald had to go, too, for they could only educate Joaquín if they lived together and pooled their salaries.

In early July 1924, the bank granted Hugo's transfer, to begin in January 1925. Rosa and Joaquín left in August, Thorvald (for whom Hugo secured a low-level job in the bank) in October, and Hugo and Anaïs planned to sail in December.[26]

The thought of moving to Paris brought back her feelings of rootlessness and exile. She had lived in the United States for ten years and was married to an American, but did not think of herself as one, believing that "we belong in certain countries more by temperament than by birth."[27] Someone asked if she would be happy in Paris.

"Indeed, no," she replied. "Paris will not satisfy me completely, any more than New York has."[28]

Rosa had no reason to inform Joaquín Nin of her move, and the announcement of their impending divorce reached her in Paris. She was furious to learn that he used grounds of abandonment and never forgave him.

She told Anaïs and Hugo she intended to contest the divorce. Anaïs assumed the role of mediator and wrote to ask her father to delay final legal action until Hugo's transfer was granted, for she feared that any unpleasant notoriety connected with her or her family might harm his career. All this soothed Rosa, who agreed to abide by Anaïs's wishes. Joaquín Nin, as usual, went ahead and did exactly what he wanted.

The enraged Rosa was served with her final decree in Paris. Anaïs spent her last months in New York as the go-between, writing long soothing missives to both parents, unwisely telling each what he or she wanted to hear and making it seem as if she sided entirely with whomever she wrote to at the time. Joaquín took advantage of Rosa's diatribes to gain Anaïs's "respect by his reasonableness and his restraint and patience."

"Eventually, she decided, "I will compensate him."[29]

In mid-December, Hugo and Anaïs were feted at several farewell parties, where they developed a deepening friendship with Pauline and John Erskine. She regretted leaving New York just as she was beginning to feel relaxed and sociable in his company. She did not want to confide this to the diary, which Hugo read as freely as if it were a novel, and hinted that perhaps Richard Maynard was right: she needed to keep it in a locked box.[30] She never did permit Erskine to read *Aline's Choice.* Instead, she put it aside and began a second novel, *The Blunderer,* about a young woman more experienced and far less naive about life than Aline, but she abandoned it after several pages.

Hugo wanted to reconcile with his family, and wrote to ask his parents to see him. After much discussion and negotiation, Ena Guiler wrote that Hugh Sr. refused to see his son but would allow her and the three siblings to meet him for tea in a Manhattan hotel. Hugo was to be alone, as they were not allowed to acknowledge Anaïs as his wife. "Hugo meets his mother, somewhere uptown, a meeting I arranged myself for their sake," Anaïs told the diary, bending the truth to suit what she wanted to believe.[31]

On December 18 they boarded *La France* for the six-day crossing and were surprised to find that Mrs. Guiler and Hugo's brother and sisters had come to say goodbye. Mrs. Guiler kissed Anaïs, and everyone wept.

When the ship was under way, Hugo wanted to stand on deck and watch the New York skyline recede. "No," Anaïs said. "I couldn't stand it. I want to forget all about it."

7

Battles of Interest

THEY ARRIVED IN PARIS on Christmas Eve. Holidays meant little to Anaïs,[1] which was fortunate because she and Hugo were immediately drawn into the family's emotional maelstrom. Rosa had rented attic rooms in a house on the boulevard Raspail and Anaïs found them squalid and depressing. She, who reveled in Greenwich Village, disliked Montparnasse: there were too many bohemians in too many cafés, too much drinking and carousing, and too much public affection, both homo- and heterosexual.

Joaquín had a crippling pain in his leg, diagnosed as tuberculosis of the bone.[2] It required fresh air and southern sunshine, but Rosa worried about interrupting his studies, paying for his rehabilitation, and leaving Thorvald on his own in Paris. Hugo assured her that he could meet her expenses, and shortly after the New Year she and Joaquín settled in the seacoast village of Hendaye.

Anaïs and Hugo stayed in the house with Thorvald, who was so unhappy that he barely functioned. Adrift, if not lost, in French culture and society, Thorvald was an all-American boy who liked baseball and plain cooking and had nothing in common with his young French colleagues at the bank.

Joaquín Nin seized the opportunity to make a dramatic appearance in his elder son's life, full of tears, apologies, and pleas for forgiveness. Thorvald refused at first to see his father, then began to visit him secretly after being overwhelmed with his seductive eloquence, flattery, and attention (none of which he received from his mother).[3]

"Father talked circles around my plainspoken brother," Joaquín Nin-Culmell recalled. "Mother found out he was seeing Father and was furious. Poor Thor was too honest to lie and it raised hell in his personality."[4] Plans were made to ship the twenty-year-old American boy to Havana, where Antolina found him a good job in the Cuban branch of the Bank of Canada.

Thorvald was not close to anyone in his family, but before he departed, he had an uncharacteristically personal conversation with Anaïs about their father's efforts to regain their affection. Anaïs asked Thorvald "if he ever considered that Father might believe his own lies." She told Thorvald how she feared to find "the Nin lies" in herself, and how her father represented "things which I have spent my life destroying in myself . . . the embodiment of falsity, of selfishness."[5] After their first meeting, she told the diary, "This stranger, my father, whom I have to reckon with and handle, has made me old overnight." She decided it would be best not to see him again.

Joaquín Nin was only one among the many in Paris who assaulted Anaïs with new and confusing sensations that she was hard-pressed to sort out. Within a month of arriving in the city, the reality confronting her led to a severe depression that did not lift for more than a year. "I wish that we had never come," she wrote on her fourth day there. "Paris must be seen romantically [or] it is a dismal failure. And Hugh and I are not bohemians, although we thought we were."[6]

She had a spontaneous realization that even if she was not sure to which country she owed her allegiance, she was sure that she wanted to write in English and be read by English-speaking people. Now that she was reading so much French literature, she saw how her own sensibilities had been formed by nineteenth-century English and American literature, which she found morally superior to French. She now believed that only Americans were honest, open, and direct; the "esprit, wisdom, culture, refinement" offered by her French acquaintances shone "like precious pearls in a decaying oyster." She recoiled from France and all things French: "I had to be transplanted to know where I belong. Now I know it, irrevocably."[7]

Hugo tried to describe Anaïs to a colleague at the bank, Horace Guicciardi,[8] saying she was was "very old fashioned, separating instantly the sheep from the goats with a kind of biblical rigor. And that is why she has been so forcible in her condemnation of a complex type like the French and so enthusiastic for a simple type like the Americans."[9] Hugo was proud of her "childlike goodness" and pledged to do all he could to keep her in "perpetual innocence." He could not understand why she became more discontented and disconsolate as each day passed, and to cure her depression, suggested a change of scene. They spent Easter in Hendaye and returned to the apartment of one of his colleagues, sublet for several months.

Anaïs was shocked to find the walls decorated with photos of naked women torn from soft-porn magazines. Her shock was compounded when Hugo said he liked them. He agreed to take them down, but asked her not to throw them away as he wanted to study them. Anaïs was further disconcerted when he told her shyly that he entertained himself during fittings at his tailor's with a collection of lurid photos set out to entertain restless clients.

Having admitted his burgeoning interest in sexuality, Hugo began to scour the bookstalls on the quays for erotica, spending evenings at home engrossed in Indian sex manuals purporting to be about god-sanctioned techniques for humans. He wanted Anaïs to experiment with him and was puzzled when she demurred. "Sex without love I hate," she wrote. "He wants to play with my own body, a desire created probably by the sight of the others, so that I am confused with them in his mind, probably compared."[10] She wanted to write of her increasing confusion about sex in the diary, but was too embarrassed to do so directly. The only word she could bear to write was "sensuality," which repulsed her. She insisted, "I love purity, but I can understand the impure."[11]

Hugo continued to adore her, to cater to her every whim, but nothing he did was enough to assuage a terrible need that even she could not fathom. He was satisfied with their relationship and felt that living in Paris was helping their sexual enjoyment of each other to grow and deepen, so he was puzzled by her vague, unfocused, and frequently unvocalized complaints.[12]

They began to have "battles of interests."[13] Hugo was absorbed in his work and often brought it home. Then some of his American colleagues invited him to "stag" events, and Anaïs became jealous. Hoping to please her, he said she would have to develop as an artist for both of them because he was so busy being a banker. Poor Hugo had no idea why this remark upset her so much.

She could not understand that he preferred his profession over sitting with her night after night while she read aloud from her adolescent journals. That he might want to relax by reading a novel rather than keeping a diary was simply beyond her comprehension. She began a subtle campaign to create settings where he would have no option but to write in the journal they were supposed to keep together, but he found excuses to elude her. He decided then that if he wanted to keep her, he would have to find a way to develop the artistic side of his personality.

Hugo used his first substantial raise to hire a woman to look after Anaïs and the apartment so she would have nothing to do but concentrate on herself—ostensibly, to gain weight and get well. She used the enforced time in bed to retreat even further into the diaries of her past, scrutinizing all she had written and mulling endlessly over its ramifications. Sometimes she rewrote past accounts as she began a new practice—typing out sections of previous journals to create brand-new ones. As the year ended, she realized she had barely filled one slim current journal, partly because of exhaustion brought on by depression, partly because she was rewriting the past for a purpose: to turn it into fiction.

She read the old diaries, but only those written in English, to see not only *what* but also *how* she wrote, in order to have something to compare with the few brief entries she was currently making. In doing so, she came to "the most extraordinary" conclusion, that she must not "disappoint" her sixteen-year-old self. As a twenty-two-year-old woman, she was determined to behave in such a manner that she could "stand . . . unashamed"[14] before the girl she had been.

During this time, she began to prepare entire typescripts of the early journals, but without commenting whether or not for publication. She studied her early journals as if they were guidance manuals of rhetoric and composition, but was "saddened and piqued" by what she found there, especially 1920, the year of her courtship and marriage, which she thought particularly phony and affected. The many thousand "borrowed phrases, gathered from miscellaneous reading" annoyed her.[15] This was an important moment in the diary's evolution, for she began a lifelong pattern: as she wrote new ones, she constantly revised the old. She never dated and seldom numbered the pages so that, as typescripts multiplied, even she was sometimes puzzled about their order and origination, which resulted in another lasting habit, a "Journal of Facts" and/or an "Index" at the end of each diary volume.[16]

All this resulted in an interesting idea, to write a book about writing a diary. "This," she concluded, "was what I wanted to do, what I am fit to do!"[17] She wrote as if possessed: "No traffic regulations, no pattern to imitate, no restrictions of tradition or taste evolved by others, no strict standards. I could . . . follow my moods and thoughts in utter freedom." Thus, Anaïs Nin, obsessed with creating her own genre, groped toward finding her own unique form from the earliest moment of her writing career. Because "the pure novel does not seem free enough," she searched for a new way to organize her thoughts and tell her story but also to find a form that allowed her to express the "queerness" within herself.

Hugo accused her of sophistry in her approach to life, and the concept became her new favorite self-definition: "I am the greatest sophist alive. And I am worried." But after she had thought about it for a while: "perhaps I think I am worried because I know I should, from a respectable point of view, be worried."[18]

In August 1925, Anaïs found their first permanent home in a new building at 11 bis, rue Schoelcher, abutting the Cimetière Montparnasse. She rented two large studios with balcony sleeping lofts, facing each other on the ground floor. Giving Rosa the one facing the rue Denfert-Rochereau, she and Hugo kept the one facing rue Schoelcher. Thirty years later, her apartment would become known throughout the world as home to the French writer and feminist Simone de Beauvoir,[19] but Anaïs Nin, the first occupant, set out at once to make it uniquely her own.

She and Hugo were quickly accepted by both the international business community and French and Spanish artistic society, but Anaïs smugly did not follow the "whims and judgments" popular among them: "I have not cut my hair, I have never worn pearls, we don't drink cocktails, we don't like the radio, we have not ridden in an aeroplane, we have no ultramodern furniture in our house."[20] Instead, with a 5,000-franc loan from Hugo's bank,[21] she indulged her flair for the dramatic and created fantasy settings with Gothic shutters, Moroccan furniture, and copper tables. "Oh Mummy," she wrote to Rosa, "I was beginning to think Paris an awful *hole,* and feeling homesick, but now I have a new interest in life."[22]

Domesticity consumed her until the apartment was furnished. Then she realized how much time was left to fill each day and how little she was writing. She worked sporadically on a second novel and wrote most of another play (soon abandoned) about a blind man who recovered his sight after many years.[23]

She did all this writing alone in a tiny maid's room on the top floor of the building. It had large French doors that opened out onto a small terrace, and Anaïs was so captivated with it that Hugo rented it for her to use as a studio and for their own private hideaway. They quickly dubbed it "The High Place" and spent many summer evenings happily looking out over the treetops at the lights of Paris. Anaïs went there each day after Hugo left for the bank, not descending until lunchtime. She was ashamed to confess to the diary, doing so in cryptic confidences, that she spent most of her time staring at the sky or napping, for creative writing continued to elude her.

Hugo reconciled with his father when the family, curious to see his success, came to Paris. When the Guilers refused to socialize with the Nins' Cuban relatives "to protect the girls from Catholics" until they were safely married, Anaïs felt secretly superior knowing, as they did not, that Hugo's conversion was now final.[24]

Her differences with Hugo kept building. To satisfy his ever-increasing interest in "sensuality" (she was still too squeamish to use the word "sex"), she read deeply in French literature, everything from "Ségur, France, Prévost, Loti, Stendhal, [and] Flaubert" to "innumerable dime novels."[25] Convinced that she now knew about *"everything"* (her emphasis), she asked Hugo if he was satisfied. He was, he said, and he wanted her to stay just as she had been when they met—virginal, innocent, and pure.

The trouble was, she wanted out of their "nice" life and did not know how to go about it. They were on a collision course when John Erskine came to Paris with his family for the Christmas holidays. He invited Hugo and Anaïs on a visit to Chartres Cathedral, where he introduced them to a woman who had a brief but nonetheless strong influence on everyone in the Nin-Guiler families, Hélène Boussinescq. "Boussie" was French, middle-aged, a teacher of modern American literature in a lycée, and the translator and friend of many contemporary writers, among them Sherwood Anderson, Waldo Frank, John Gunther, and John Buchan. The breadth of her knowledge was mind-boggling to Anaïs, who had hitherto believed her own reading more extensive than anyone else's. Now Boussie offered tart, opinionated, and often acerbic running commentaries on literature. The three rushed out to hear Stravinski's music and listen

Hugo in his Citroën, Paris.

Joaquín Nin-Culmell and Rosa Culmell with family friend
Mme. Brouardel in Hendaye.

to jazz, and quickly bought tickets to performances written or directed by Jouvet, Pitoëff, and Dullin because Boussie said they would be hopelessly old-fashioned if they did not.

Boussie was probably the first person Anaïs encountered in France who insisted that she bring every aspect of herself into the twentieth century if she intended to become a serious writer. Suddenly Anaïs felt it was important to be au courant about every cultural event that was happening not only in Paris but also in New York, a feeling she communicated to Hugo.

Boussie kept a literary salon, and there Anaïs's head reeled with the names of writers and critics she and Hugo heard for the first time. One who made a profound impression was Waldo Frank, whose *Rediscovery of America* Hugo called "the greatest intellectual experience for me since the discovery of mysticism," a view Anaïs shared.[26]

For the first time, she began to reflect seriously on this thing called Modernism. Music and fiction in the modernist mode seemed "discordant, harsh and mad," but as she listened and read more carefully, she understood that the artist or writer meant "to return to absolute truth in expression, discarding words and tones to which we are accustomed, in order to seek again . . . the complexities and discords of our lives and ideas."[27] There were exceptions, however, to how much Modernism Anaïs was willing to embrace. She was reluctant to read Freud because of her aversion to contemporary sexuality, and she hoped "never to have to read again" Proust, who later became one of her favorite writers.[28]

The biographic form appealed to her, "the informed free style, the telling of character without story."[29] But she soon realized that writing biography required dedication to the truth as well as felicity of style. Neither interested her, so she decided to create an imaginary character called Chantal who would tell a story, "to be fitted in the framework of my life, for I am impatient of facts and do not like to seek new ones."[30]

She was impatient about more than just facts. The concept of the self—more particularly her "Self" (or sometimes SELF, as she always capitalized all or part of the word)—preoccupied her. Her moods swung erratically from such dedication to Hugo that she spent hours polishing his "big" shoes (they were never just shoes), or utter despair that "a million things" drew her away from him. "My very real Self is not wifely, not good. It is wayward, moody, desperately active and hungry. . . . How monstrously selfish I am with this big noisy, voracious, passionate SELF."[31]

Her father contributed to her general irritability. Anaïs could see that he was at the pinnacle of his success when she and Hugo were invited to rarefied social occasions only because she was his daughter. His concerts sold out and people read his writings and hung on his every word; she was jealous and wanted this attention herself.

The question was, how to get it. The "second novel" on which she had pinned her hopes was "unfinished and useless."[32] So, since her writing was going nowhere, she decided to become a performer. A famous dancer called La Argentina was entrancing Parisian audiences during these years, and she also enchanted Joaquín Nin, her good friend. Seeing how warmly they greeted each other and how respectful each was of the other's talent, Anaïs decided that she, too, would become a Spanish dancer.[33]

She found a teacher, Paco Miralles, a "small, seedy, no talent, ladies' man who thought he was quite the charmer,"[34] and threw herself into dancing with more energy than she had shown in months. Hoping to maintain her energy and enthusiasm, Hugo bought her several expensive costumes as well as mantillas, high tortoiseshell combs, jewelry, and anything else that struck her fancy. Spanish dancing became expensive, necessitating further loans against Hugo's salary, and the pressure began to affect his health. Even after his salary was increased a whopping seventy-five percent, Hugo could pay only the most demanding of his creditors.[35]

In the midst of this financial turmoil, Hugo had to decide whether he would stay on in Paris or return to New York. Unlike Anaïs, Hugo had been entranced from the moment they landed, and in the almost two years they had lived in Paris, felt more at home than at any other time or place in his life. Nevertheless, he knew that the best course for his career was to think of Paris as a holiday and return to New York.

When Anaïs told him she shared his affection for Paris and wanted to remain, Hugo made a decision he knew was wrong even as he made it. He told the bank that he would stay there indefinitely.

8

Mediocre Unfaithfulness

THEIR PERMANENT LIFE in Paris began in luxury such as Anaïs had never known.[1] Hugo even bought a car, a Citroën he fussed over as if it were a child. They spoke of children infrequently now, for both preferred to concentrate on acquiring all that their new wealth provided. Like almost everyone in 1928, Hugo played the stock market, and their capital leaped and bounded up the financial graphs. In this climate of unending success, of money falling into their laps, of being welcomed into every sector of Parisian social and cultural society, there were too many wonderful diversions even to consider children. They decided to wait several years before trying to conceive.

Anaïs's diary musings of a house and garden happily filled with children and pets ended. Instead, by unconscious but still mutual agreement, they lavished all their care on her. She became their child, the center of their attention. Not just of hers and Hugo's but her mother's and brother's as well, for she insisted that whatever interested her must interest them all, and her role and status within the family were such that everyone complied.

When Anaïs took up Spanish dancing, her family had no choice but to become involved as well. She soon grew bored with the expensive costumes Hugo had bought and pressed Rosa to sew new, more lavish ones. Joaquín prepared musical scores and accompanied her on the piano, and Hugo actually learned to dance to be her partner.

Standing at least six-foot-three and wearing size fourteen shoes, Hugo was larger than the average dancer, and at thirty, also older. Although clumsy and ponderous, he embraced his lessons so earnestly that he performed better than anyone thought him capable. It is difficult to assess Anaïs's talent because "she started much too late [twenty-five] and practiced much too little."[2]

Nevertheless, she was determined to dance professionally, and when engagements did not come her way, sent out invitations and invited people to performances she and Hugo staged at home.[3] She and Rosa opened the doors between their apartments. Anaïs and Hugo dressed in theirs, where refreshments were served afterward, and danced in Rosa's where the piano was. Hugo encouraged her dancing with one very important exception: he forbade her to use the name Anaïs Guiler, as she was then known, even on invitations to their home. She became Anita Aguilera for as long as she danced.[4]

Why Hugo participated probably had much to do with their teacher, Antonio Francisco (called Paco) Miralles, who very soon after they met became Anaïs's *chevalier servant*.[5] Miralles was fifty, small, dark, and shabby. His personal hygiene often made the finicky Anaïs turn up her nose into her scented handkerchief, but his passion was thrilling, and soon she was joining him after class in the basement where costumes were stored. As she stood against the piles of shawls and dresses, Miralles knelt before her, lifted her dress, and "kissed my sex until I grew dizzy." Despite his entreaties, Anaïs told the diary she could never "bring myself to go to his hotel room as he begged me to."[6]

Hugo was instinctively intuitive where Anaïs was concerned, and began to accompany her to evening lessons. To keep Miralles's interest at a fever pitch, she scheduled extra lessons during Hugo's workdays at the bank. The groping continued, as did her self-analysis when it was over. How could she like it, she wondered, when Miralles's only value to her was as a teacher and she did not like the man at all?

She wanted to write about it in the diary, but could not think of how to disguise what happened between them. Not yet ready to put it under lock and key,[7] she considered keeping two journals at the same time. One would be "for things which do happen, and one for imaginary incidents": if she continued to live "doubly," she might as well "write doubly."[8] Anaïs called the woman whose life was to be the subject of the second journal Imagy, after her imagination and the imaginary events she created. Although she did write about Imagy, she never completed a second separate volume because her life was so packed with activity that she scarcely had time to write in (for want of a better word) the "real" journal, the current volume in the long line she was steadily amassing.

Having decided that she liked living in Paris, her depression was over. Her schedule consisted of frenetic socializing coupled with three to five dancing lessons a week,[9] activity that certainly belied her frail appearance. Also, she had no need to imagine an erotic life, for her encounters with Miralles continued, and she could scarcely find the time to write about them, let alone everything else.

So by default, the "real diary," which contained every aspect of her daily life, became filled with the doings of Imagy as well. She wrote of herself as being split into two women: the one she believed herself to be, "kind, loyal, pure, thoughtful"; her alter ego "restless and impure, acting strangely, loosened, wandering, seeking life and tasting all of it without fear, without convictions, restraint, principle, a demon."

Hugo's intuitions about Anaïs's heightened sensuality were correct then, as they would be throughout the rest of their life together. His response to the threat Miralles posed to Anaïs's fidelity was also typical of how he would react to any intruder into their relationship from that point on: he tried to share all her activities, bought her everything she wanted, tried to divert her with socializing, and took her on as many trips and vacations as he could manage. "We are out every night," Anaïs noted, "we are invited everywhere. We miss nothing."[10]

But still, some undefined emotion irritated her and (so Hugo believed) made her sick. She had "la grippe" four times that winter. These illnesses were probably real—the usual winter colds or flu—but they were also convenient excuses for periods when she was tired of people and parties and wanted to be by herself to write and think.

In late April 1928, word came that Hugh Guiler Sr. had died suddenly. Hugo was filled with self-recrimination because several months before his father's death he had felt compelled to be truthful and blurted out his conversion. He gave up Catholicism shortly after, when Anaïs decided religion was spiritually unimportant, but his father died without knowing it.

On the ship bearing them to the funeral, Hugo wrote a maudlin commemorative poem, much of it based on books of Eastern mysticism that influenced him (but not Anaïs). Hugo not only wrote but also believed that his father's soul had returned to occupy his body: "I feel him in me and am proud / He chose my body for his soul's new home."[11]

To their chagrin, Hugo and Anaïs discovered that Mr. Guiler had willed large sums of money in trust to his three other children, with Mrs. Guiler as executor, but they were still disinherited. Ena Guiler assured Hugo that he would be guaranteed a fourth of the estate after her death, but made certain he understood he would get nothing if he or Anaïs incurred her displeasure.

Anaïs steered clear of the Guiler family. While Hugo was in Forest Hills, she stayed in Manhattan and visited friends, including her cousin Eduardo Sánchez, now graduated from Harvard and in New York trying to become an actor. Eduardo confessed his homosexuality, and Anaïs was deeply shaken. He told her that he drifted into acting because theater people made him comfortable about his sexual orientation for the first time. Riddled with guilt and fear, and ashamed of what he had been brought up to believe was deviant behavior, he had begun a classic Freudian analysis. Four times each week, he told Anaïs, he lay on a couch covered with an Oriental carpet and talked about his earliest memories to an unseen woman who sat silently behind him. The usually reticent Eduardo told Anaïs how much he thought analysis was helping him and urged her to try it as well in the hope that it might free her of whatever inhibition kept her from writing fiction.

"The science was utterly unknown to me until the day I met Eduardo in New York," she wrote in the diary. "I am proud of never having had to turn to another for any explanations of myself."[12] She did not want an analyst because the diary served the same purpose: "I owe to it what some people owe to psychology: knowledge of myself, extreme consciousness of what in others is vague and unconscious, a knowledge of my desires, of my weaknesses, of my dreams, of my talents."

When she told Hugo how upset she was, first by Eduardo's confession and then by his suggestion that she begin analysis, he responded as he always did: he would read Freud, then decide about analysis for both of them. As always, he followed wherever she led and made it possible for her to proceed.

Hours after leaving New York on the voyage to Paris, their ship collided in heavy fog with a cargo vessel and was towed back to port. Passengers were transferred to another ship, which sailed the next day, but in the hullabaloo, the suitcase containing the most recent volume of the diary was lost. "You may be interested to know," Hugo wrote to Richard Maynard, "that in a rapid mental calculation of what [Anaïs] would save the only thing she considered important enough after our own lives was her journal and the only thing that worried her was whether they would allow her to take it on the life boat. I suggested to her that she might wrap it up to look like a baby."[13]

For the first time since her father died and her inheritance ended, Rosa had enough money for her and Joaquín to live comfortably and graciously. She had been received into the highest echelon of Cuban and Spanish society in Paris, and often entertained her friends and Joaquín's at recitals in her apartment. They were welcomed in the same musical circles as her ex-husband, where her son's talent as composer and performer were noted approvingly. Life in the Nin-Culmell household was more secure than it had ever been, even though Anaïs was overspending her allowance each month and deducting from her mother's stipend to pay her most pressing bills. The thrifty Rosa intuited that Hugo's support would always be chancy because of Anaïs, so she put at least one third of her allowance in savings until she, too, became infected by Hugo's stock market craze and let him invest most of her savings.[14]

One of Joaquín's first pupils was John Erskine's daughter, Anna.[15] In the autumn of 1928, Pauline and her children came to Paris for a prolonged stay because John was involved with two other women and she thought a separation was best for everyone concerned. John came long enough to see them settled before returning to teach at Columbia. As Pauline did not speak French, Anaïs took charge. It was the kind of service she had always provided, grudgingly for the most part for Hugo's rich clients, but for Pauline with special fervor.[16]

When John became famous for his Helen of Troy novel, money poured in, and he spent it equally fast. Women chased him, and, flattered by the attention, he often allowed himself to be caught. Anaïs no longer denied her attraction to John, but he held Hugo in such high esteem that, instead of succumbing to Anaïs's increasingly blatant flirtations, he made her his confidante. He told her about his

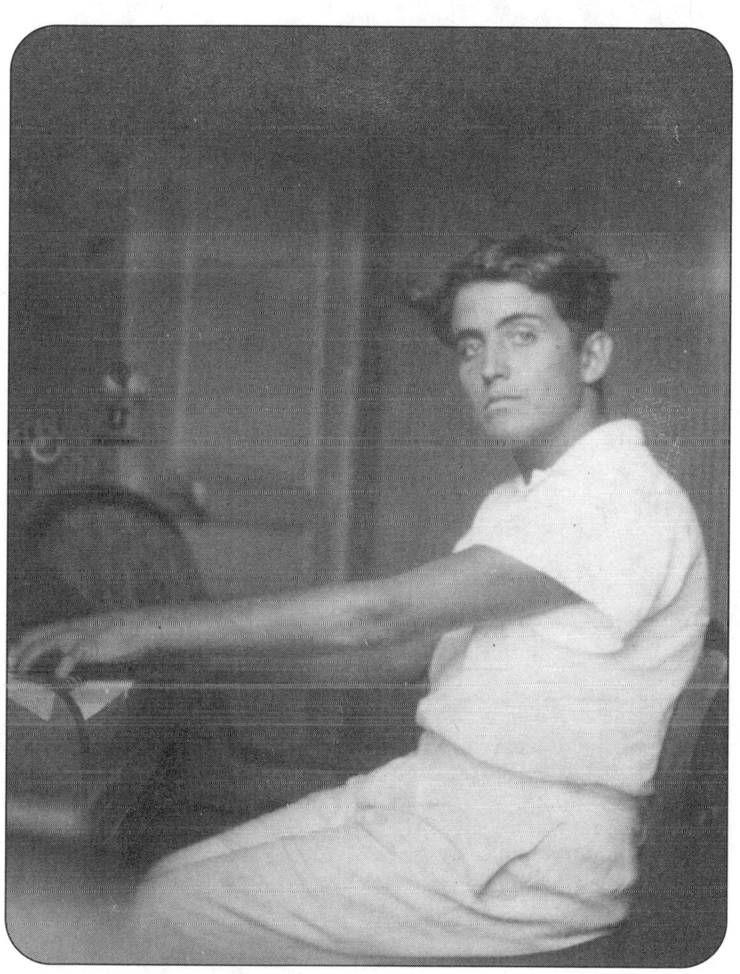

Joaquín Nin-Culmell at the piano,
rue Schoelcher.

Anaïs and Hugo, Spanish dancing,
rue Schoelcher.

affairs and how he had settled Pauline in Paris to have time alone to sort out his feelings for her and the two women he called Lillith I and Lillith II, after a character in one of his novels.

This was not exactly what Anaïs wanted to hear, for she had become accustomed to being the center of attention with the men she knew, and especially to receiving compliments about her looks, dress, decorating, and dancing. When these men did not volunteer the attention she craved, she frequently put herself in a position where they had no option but to pay the compliments she wanted or seem very rude. Some men resisted her ploys, but she still created long accounts for the diary about how they praised whatever it was that she needed to hear at the moment. She even copied into her journal passages that she said Hugo had written about her in his, but once again, these writings of his are in her hand.[17]

Now here was John, pouring out his heart in long afternoon tête-à-têtes in the apartment she had discreetly darkened and perfumed with scented candles, incense, and exotic potpourri, but about another woman and not her. Wisdom dictated that Anaïs steer clear of the Erskines' domestic dispute, but she nonetheless intruded, betraying the woman who considered her a great good friend by choosing John's side over Pauline's. Still, siding with John did not have the desired effect. Instead, when Lillith II came to Paris, he asked Anaïs if he could hold trysts in her tawdry furnished apartment on the square du Port-Royal, where she and Hugo were camping until the huge, elegant apartment that they had leased on boulevard Suchet in the fashionable sixteenth arrondissement was refurbished.[18] Amidst the detritus of other people's possessions, Anaïs and John sorted out the arrangements for his assignations.

She equated her role in Erskine's dalliance with "power," and she sought it with many other men in years to come.[19] No matter who they were or what the circumstances, "inspiring [and] pleasing men" made her feel powerful and in control. She compared herself to a "winged doormat," alternately behaving as a "sweet Spanish woman, malleable, attentive," and the next "independent and ready to fly off." It was a technique she cultivated, refined, and perfected. Hugo, uneasy the first time he noticed her trying it on anonymous men at a cocktail party, told her to concentrate on writing as her "art" and to forget about role playing with other men. She disagreed. Flirting with other men, not writing, "helped me to become a woman," she replied.

The flirtations were adding up, from Paco Miralles, John Erskine, Hugo's banker colleague Horace Guicciardi, and another mild one with Rosa's former boarder in New York, Enric Madriguera.[20] There were also countless unnamed others with whom she flirted in various drawing rooms in Paris. She confided to Eduardo that flirting with all these men allowed her to behave as if she were many different women, each possessing many different selves. "Women see themselves as in a mirror, in the eyes of the men who love them. I have seen in each man a different woman—and a different life."

There was also a young Cuban, a would-be writer and musician, Gustavo Morales, who seemed to Anaïs the most dangerous of all her conquests, even though he was openly homosexual. Morales was writing a pornographic manual of sadomasochistic practices, which may be why she wrote so pompously about him in the diary, announcing that she would take "a stronger stand" to win him: "I like to arouse feelings and I like to pretend. I like to create confidence between the man I am interested in and me, so that I may know him well, deeply, and so that he may know me, and enjoy me, without ever owning me."[21]

She tried to explain to Hugo how her "ideal goodness" clashed with her "desire for maturity." When she asked him "how far can one go in that direction" (i.e., other relationships), he told her he believed she would do no wrong because she would never willingly jeopardize their relationship. True, he agreed, there was nothing to keep either of them from doing exactly as they pleased because they did not believe in "the conventional ties of marriage," only their love, which was as close as they came to religion. When he spoke of the harm caused by "mediocre unfaithfulness," Anaïs listened carefully but was still worried because she wasn't sure what she sought or what she would do if she found it.

In one of the most telling passages in all her diaries, she carefully delineated how she perceived their relationship: "I never, never want to hurt [Hugo]. We are so beautifully mated, physically, mentally, temperamentally. But I cannot stay at home. I have a desperate desire to know life, and to live in order to reach maturity. Our marriage has given me but one kind of knowledge. Unless I am mistaken, Hugo, whose mind is always open to new ideas, whose mind tolerates mistakes when they are made in a sincere struggle for truths, Hugo will forgive me."[22]

And so her "sin[s] by the imagination"[23] continued. It took the dancing teacher Miralles's furtive efforts to seduce Anaïs to "enflame" her into wanting more passion in her life. But instead of turning to Hugo and suggesting that they try some of the experiments he read about, she was both ashamed that her desires were not the sort a wife should have and afraid he would discover that another man caused them. So she turned to the homosexual Morales for the satisfaction that eluded her. Obsessed with the idea of sex, he had no intention of providing the actuality of it to Anaïs or any other woman. He preferred to enjoy the discomfiture he created in the otherwise poised and attractive young matron, and she was naive enough not to know it.

By mid-1928, her feelings for Hugo as lover and confidant were eroding rapidly, and to evade them, she engaged in a frenzy of frivolous social activity for the better part of the year. To decorate their fairy-tale apartment on the boulevard Suchet, Hugo borrowed against his salary and persuaded his mother to loan him $5,000, which she did with the proviso that he repay her $100 a month at six percent interest.[24] Anaïs used $3,000 to turn the apartment into a Moorish-Oriental-Indian wonderland and hinted so broadly about wanting a fur coat that cost one quarter of Hugo's yearly salary that he used the remaining $2,000 as a down payment. The debts the loan was supposed to erase remained unpaid.

Hugo was appointed a trust officer and given a raise, which Anaïs calculated would allow him to retire at forty and let them live grandly, travel, and entertain. "A marvelous life," Anaïs concluded.[25] Hugo's new responsibilities required frequent trips to visit his wealthy clients. Anaïs usually remained at home, alone and brooding about the fact that she was still unknown and unsuccessful, be it as dancer, writer, or even actress.

Morales promised her a part in a play he had written, but this brief adventure came to naught. Miralles said he would not teach her anymore because she had changed his dances into something "vulgar and inadequate." She next took lessons in Oriental dancing with a woman who told her she was "too childlike, not sensual, animal, provocative enough." Once she saw that she was mediocre at best she sought a convenient excuse to drop performing and took to her bed: "Health very bad. Mood terrible."[26]

She was filled with a sense of urgency that life was passing swiftly and nothing was happening. She was still known only as "the daughter of Nin" or "Hugh's wife, Anaïs Guiler." She had anxiety attacks, palpitations, flutters, and flashes of fever that she feared were caused by her heart. Doctors told her politely that the symptoms were caused by her overactive imagination.

Coloring every action she took, every decision she made, was the thought that John Erskine was returning to Paris in spring 1929 to collect his family. She was determined to force him into a physical declaration of affection. When he arrived, it seemed things would happen just as she hoped.

In late May, John rang the bell on the boulevard de Port-Royal one afternoon shortly after Hugo had returned to work.[27] He and Anaïs fell upon each other, and soon he had unbuttoned her dress to caress her breasts. Lavishing compliments, he asked her "to disrobe" so that he might "see" her body. She went into the bedroom, returned with only a Spanish shawl wrapped about her, stood in front of him, and flung it open. He reached up, threw her onto the sofa, and lay on top of her. He did not undress, only unzipped his trousers to place his penis between her legs. She was fully aroused and began to caress him.

"I can't do this," he said abruptly, "for I am having a cerebral reaction. I cannot do this to Hugo." He jumped up to repair his clothing, then sat down at the far end of the sofa. She continued to lie there uncovered, hoping he would come back but too astonished by what had happened (not happened, actually), and too insecure either to move or speak to him. Eventually she sat up and gathered the shawl about her shoulders. He reached for her and began again to fondle her breasts, all the while telling her that, as a man of honor, he could not cuckold his good friend Hugo. They congratulated each other on their "technical faithfulness," and he left. The next day she and Hugo accompanied the Erskine family to the boat train. The goodbyes were strained, as no one wanted to meet anyone else's eyes.[28]

For the next year and a half, the memory of the almost-consummated relationship with John Erskine made Anaïs Nin miserably unhappy. As always, her family was eager to help her find what she seemed to be looking for with such frantic intensity, but of course it was nothing she could confide in them, or anyone else.

A few weeks after the Erskines departed, Thorvald arrived from Havana, suffering from an "unspecified illness" most likely caused by general unhappiness, loneliness, and frustration. He wanted to go back to New York but his aunts persuaded him to go to Paris and his mother made Hugo promise to find him a job in the bank. Thorvald's arrival set off a family crisis, provoked in large part by Joaquín Nin, who had introduced him to a life of culture and ease on his previous stay. Also, even though his father's attention was mostly insincere, it was still greater than what Rosa had left over to give from Anaïs and Joaquín.

Rosa, who had not seen Thorvald in several years, was in Hendaye with Joaquín when he decided abruptly to go to St.-Jean-de-Luz to spend the summer "recovering" in his father's and Maruca's care. Anaïs wrote a warning to Rosa not to try to see, scold, or write to Thorvald. Uncharacteristically, Rosa followed her advice.[29]

Anaïs and Hugo passed their summer in an atmosphere of increasing tension. Hers was due to unrequited sexuality, of yearning for John at the same time she was trying to "bury" him. His was due to mental strain over work and worry about their personal finances. He lost weight and feared he had ulcers and had to take several rest cures throughout 1929, usually in Caux, Switzerland.

The stock market crashed on Black Friday in October 1929, but the first time Anaïs could bring herself to write about it was November 12. Until then, she acted as if nothing untoward had happened, spending her "sick" time in bed reading old diaries and condensing them into new ones. She went to concerts and recitals, attended afternoon teas, and outlined plots for a succession of stories she intended to write.[30] On November 13 she addressed the crash a second time, writing, "Sad Days for everybody. Many ruined lives and suicides. All expenses to be cut short. Mother and Joaquín now entirely in our charge. No savings. Just the salary, which has never been quite enough."[31] A hasty telegram was dispatched to Mrs. Guiler, who agreed to guarantee payment of their largest outstanding loan.[32]

They looked for someone to assume the lease of the boulevard Suchet apartment so they could remain at the cheaper Port-Royal, but no one did so. Anaïs made elaborate plans to teach dancing, pose for artists, find a job. Hugo forbade the last: even after the crash, a man in his position could not permit his wife to be gainfully employed. His protest was moot, for Anaïs did nothing concrete and by Christmas Eve, nothing was resolved. There was no money but Hugo's salary, which the bank had cut as an austerity measure. Hugo was grateful that he still had a job.

Anaïs spent much of Christmas week in bed reading *Women in Love,* by D. H. Lawrence, convinced he was an important writer to emulate. She hung a photo of the sullen, brooding, bearded author above her desk and sat beneath it studying his fiction.

"I'm planning a study of Lawrence's writing," she decided impulsively. "Crudely entitled, for the moment, 'When D. H. Lawrence Found Himself.' "[33] Actually, writing about Lawrence would mark the real beginning of her quest to find herself as a writer.

9

An Unprofessional Study

PUSH HAD COME TO SHOVE. As all her diversions of the past two years cost money they no longer had, Anaïs decided it was the perfect time to settle down and write. She had begun many writings when she first came to Paris, from bits and pieces of stories to novels and critical commentaries, and had tried to resurrect some of them after the Wall Street crash, naively thinking they would pay handsomely if published, but her interest always lagged soon after the first flush of creativity. Her aim now was to see if anything was not only worth saving but also worth finishing.

So her perspective on her work was not helped when Hugo told her that her fiction was "good" but could not compare to her diaries. That she agreed with him made for a seemingly insurmountable problem: how could she risk publication of any part of the diaries and the publicity they would arouse as long as Hugo worked at the bank? Wives who aspired to be anything other than decorative ornaments were frowned upon. There was simply no question of her taking a job, even as a "woman's writer" in a Paris bureau of an English-language newspaper, which her new friend Wambly Bald told her was hers when she wanted it.[1]

Seeing no other alternative to earn money, she forced herself each day to write something, even if only notes for a possible story. Hugo told her it was all "punk," and for once she was not offended. "I know my style is degenerating," she admitted, because "the English language doesn't stand a chance." All too frequently "the genuine foreigner" in her melded French cognates and Spanish grammatical constructions into a curiously archaic but slightly charming written English.

Both Anaïs and Hugo were enthralled by a new publication called *transition*. From its first issue, Anaïs studied it avidly as a possible guide, even though she was bewildered by much of it. Many critics believed Eugene Jolas, the magazine's founder, stressed originality of form over content, but for Anaïs, this was its chief virtue because, of all the literary magazines that proliferated during this time, *transition* came closest to representing what she hoped to convey in her own writing. Jolas was also trilingual and was frequently accused of garbling all three of his languages, and she thought the charge that he published only submissions from writers who did the same would be in her favor.

Still, she realized how improperly she understood the language and, therefore, how she had probably misread many of the works that had influenced her. To compound this dilemma, she bragged about not reading original sources, preferring instead to glean her knowledge from "secondhand philosophies" and "indirect knowledge."[2]

Hugo frequently criticized her for using sloppy language, and even worse, slang. She asked why she could not use slang when Amy Lowell (whose biography of Keats she admired greatly) did it all the time. "Don't seek justification of your mistakes in other writers," he admonished.

He was, she concluded, an "inexorable" literary critic when he pronounced her "rich in ideas but weak on details." She was offended, but still took careful note of it. Rather than risk her ire further, he decided to correct only her grammar and spelling, which meant that he turned what she wrote into solid, readable prose, "mangling" (as she accused him) much of its vitality away. It did not help matters when, instead of incorporating his corrections, then rewriting, editing, and polishing her prose, she chose instead to compose something new every day. "How I loathe rewriting," she moaned. "The first thing I'll do when I have published and have enough nerve is not to rewrite."[3]

And so she remained undaunted, unknowingly stating her future credo in January 1930: "I feel that I must believe in myself because nobody else does, that only by stubbornness will I survive against other influences and pressure."[4] Not surprising, even before she had anything to publish, she spent weeks choosing a pen name, eventually settling on Melisendra because she liked the sound of it.[5]

For the next several months she wrote in a frenzy, pausing now and then to revise and reshape. In April 1930 she sent three short stories to Francis Arthur Jones, a New York literary agent,[6] but as "Miss Anaïs Guiler" rather than Melisendra. A week later, she sent a brief article called "Journal Writing Revalued": the culmination of a "book" about diary keeping and writing begun several years before.[7]

Jones returned everything, calling it "too slight" for American magazines.[8] This was probably true of the stories, but her article contained insightful commentaries about biography and autobiography, among them a distinction between "old" and "modern" content and interpretation that has since been debated by others who probably never read what Anaïs Nin had to say.

In September 1928, she began to lock up the diaries and carry the key on a gold chain around her neck. Her main reason was not her sexual adventuring but frustration at her growing inability to complete a publishable work of fiction, which she was too ashamed to confide to her "best friend." And she had an even stronger unwillingness to record a virtual onslaught of rejection, first from Jones, then Jolas, and then several other editors of small local literary reviews.[9]

To soften the blow, Jones wrote that her stories were "well written" and "unusual," but American magazines did not publish anything even slightly out of the ordinary. He did, however, ask her to send something about D. H. Lawrence. Between Christmas week 1929 and April 1930, Anaïs read almost everything Lawrence had published. In February she wrote a fan letter (unmailed) and a review of his fiction (even though she had no outlet to publish it).

By April the change in Anaïs's personality since the "John episode"[10] manifested itself in irritation with Hugo and further loss of weight. Now worried about her health along with their finances, Hugo was felled by stomach crises. They decided to return to Caux (where Hugo had taken previous cures) for the Easter holiday, to rest and read Lawrence and Huxley (her selections) and Keats and Waldo Frank (his).[11]

It was Lawrence, however, who preoccupied them both. Hugo read the novels along with Anaïs, and they had many discussions about Lawrence's theories of sexuality, trying to apply them to their own marriage and agreeing that Lawrence moved them both "to incalculable depths." Snowbound for most of their holiday, they studied Lawrence, made love, and grew closer than they had been since the "John episode."

To Anaïs's delight, Hugo began to share her view that a writer did not need to hide behind the evasions and allusions of poetry to write about sex. Now that he had read Lawrence's descriptions, he agreed that writing about sex with directness, clarity, and specificity was not only possible but necessary in the modern age. She found it amusing that Hugo, "who has the direct character, loves misty expression," while she, "indirect" in personality and inclination, was "direct and clear" in her writing. This last, of course, was then and continued to be a debatable point throughout her career, but in terms of their personal relationship, it was a breakthrough.

By early June, with a sheaf of notes on Lawrence's fiction, and unable to concentrate on any other form of writing long enough to finish it, she decided to go ahead with an essay.[12] She soon had a finished draft, but Hugo "corrected it to shreds."[13]

She had one critical study of Lawrence to consult as her own: Stephen Potter's *First Study,* a relentlessly formal academic treatise that generally ignored the topic of sexual relationships, which is what compelled her to write in the first place.[14] For Nin, Lawrence "opened a new world" within modern literature, and she wanted her contemporaries to understand it so they would pattern their lives accordingly. "Sometimes he failed," she admitted, but it was still "a daring thing to do."[15] The same observation could well be applied to her book.

Subtitled "An Unprofessional Study," it is a deeply personal text that tells as much about Nin's theories on everything from psychoanalysis to sex as about Lawrence's.[16] She wrote it during a time of personal crisis, when she was subjecting her sexuality to intense scrutiny that would have lasting repercussions. From Hugo and Eduardo, to flirtations with visiting bankers and society roués, to the pathetic dancing teacher Miralles and the teasing homosexual gigolo Morales, to the passionate strangers she yearned for in daydreams, every relationship in her life was metaphorically balanced on the brink of a bottomless chasm of irrevocable change. Whether the change would result, in Lawrentian terms, in a "strange conjunction," a "star equilibrium,"[17] remained to be seen, but Anaïs Nin Guiler believed that writing her book would provide answers to her questions.

According to "Anaïs Nin," the name by which she became known as a writer, from this book on, anyone attempting to understand Lawrence's "world" must do so with "a threefold desire." "Intellect" was necessary but could suffice only if coupled with "imagination" and "physical feeling."[18] Nin sought to explain the "texture"[19] of Lawrence's writing in much the same way that a young Samuel Beckett attempted to explain that of his literary icon, James Joyce: "His writing is not *about* something, *it is that something itself.* . . . When the sense is sleep, the words go to sleep. . . . When the sense is dancing, the words dance."[20] She noted Lawrence's propensity to convey meaning as if with "the nuances of paint" by using "words that had never been used for color," and to demonstrate "the rhythm of movement" through "wayward, formless, floating, word-shattering descriptions," sometimes using words "less for their sense than their sound." —All techniques she later made her own.

Controversy swirled around Lawrence during his lifetime and in the years immediately after his death. Many otherwise thoughtful and respected scholars and writers had castigated and reviled, mocked or derided his novels; few dared risk academic opprobrium by supporting his ideas. It was both a brave and foolhardy act for a twenty-seven-year-old outsider, a woman with little formal education, the pampered wife of "a bank sub-manager," to be prescient enough to recognize that human relationships, and by extension, social manners and mores, had undergone a significant upheaval since the end of World War I, and that Lawrence was among the first to express this change in fiction.

Perhaps it was naïveté that led Nin to write about Lawrence. She was innocent about the possibilities inherent in human relationships, and she wanted to learn what they were in order to better understand her own with her husband, and thus perhaps cure herself of longing for other men. She knew nothing about psychoanalysis, but was increasingly drawn to the new science because of Eduardo's urging. Also, she wanted to learn how to write fiction, and she needed a model to guide her. She wanted to take her subjects, language, and style from Lawrence and from other writers she admired, especially Sinclair Lewis, Waldo Frank, and Aldous Huxley. She liked the "tautness" of Lewis's prose but not his characters. She studied Frank's book about American culture and society, *Our America,* hoping to understand her adopted country and to learn how to write critical prose. Huxley's cool cerebral appraisal of human relationships in

Point Counter Point came closest to satisfying her need to understand her own, but "the human element was lacking."[21] Lawrence seemed to be the synthesis of everything she sought, and the writer who provided satisfactory answers to her different quests for self-knowledge.

She liked how he did not propose a "unified system" but offered instead "a constant shifting of values . . . a system of mobility": exactly her aspiration. She ascribed a belief to him that was one of her strongest: "any stability is merely an obstacle to creative livingness."[22]

The analogy between her way of creating characters and his bolstered her point of view in arguments with Hugo that concrete details were not always necessary. Neither she nor Lawrence created "a definitely outlined being who bears a resemblance to those we know." Both concentrated instead on "states of consciousness, subconscious acts, moods, and reactions." His way of "delving into chaos" excited her, for she correctly perceived that "chaos is a characteristic of our epoch."[23]

Closer to her own life was Lawrence's "search for balance in physical love." She was probably thinking about herself and Hugo when she wrote, "Lawrence realized the tragedy of inequality in love as no one else ever realized it . . . not alone of physical but of spiritual and mental love which is the cause of torment in human relationships." Her sad but nevertheless accurate conclusion was that "inequality of sexual power . . . causes disintegration in sexual relationships." She listed her traits and Hugo's in an effort to understand the balance of power in their relationship, but she "always [arrived at] the same sum: unequal values, positive qualities [his] against possible achievements [hers]. He is satisfied . . . I am not."[24]

She thought Lawrence also expressed her belief that most writers, indeed most people, refused to recognize the "entanglements" of "reality and unreality, fantasies and life," and that lies often provided a better way to deal with others than telling the truth. All these observations are in her chapter entitled "Experiences," the longest, most thoughtful, and most personal in the book.

"If you go very far," she wrote, "all values shift. . . . If you are terribly truthful the ground will always move from under you, and you will have to shift with the constantly shifting truth."[25] She also coined the term "mensonge vital," or necessary lie, which quickly became an important apologia for her behavior: lying was justified because the truth was "not always creative." Neither was it "worth

Hugo with Anaïs in window of rue Schoelcher apartment.

more" or "more right than untruth," nor was "loyalty [more right] than disloyalty, sincerity than insincerity." For her, "wisdom lies in knowing how and when to justly use them all."[26]

Nin also wrote a curiously feminist chapter on Lawrence's portrayal of women; curious because she considered woman's sole purpose to be helpmate to a man, ideally one who had a brilliant, creative mind and was successful and famous because of it. She admitted that women-artists were now succeeding in the world of men, but those she cited (Georges Sand, Madame de Staël, Jane Austen, George Eliot) only Amy Lowell was a near-contemporary, and Ruth Draper was truly modern.[27] Conspicuously absent was Virginia Woolf, whom she thought "over-intellectual" and indistinguishable from Rebecca West: "each write[s] like a man and I don't like it." She thought either woman could have written *A Room of One's Own.*

She agreed with Lawrence that, as society evolved, so would the number of "woman-artist[s]," or "artist-builder[s]," who would find in work "profound satisfaction" for its own sake. Lawrence believed contemporary women would tire of men whose only contribution to a relationship was "the dribblings of an idiot." The woman Anaïs had reservations about some of this, but the critic Nin gamely concluded that Lawrence was an "androgynous" writer who had "complete realization of the feelings of women."

Women in Love is the subject of the second-longest chapter in Nin's book, for this novel contains the most Lawrence wrote about combinations and permutations in human relationships. Nin was engrossed by how the four principal characters relate to each other in their male-female, male-male encounters, and how they carry "the burden of [his] earnestness"; how he turns them at times into his mouthpieces, spouting whatever rhetoric engrosses him at the moment as he puzzles out such questions as "What are you? What am I? What is love? What is the center of our life?"[28] Unlike so many of his early readers, she did not interpret this as "mindless sensuality and disintegration" but a consciously shaped "personal universe" arrived at only after intense "inward contemplation."[29]

With the Lawrence book finished, Anaïs hoped to concentrate on some of the stories that lay about in varying states of completion, but, as always, the summer brought with it an inundation of family visitors, both her Cuban relatives and Hugo's mother and sisters, who were on their way to England. The most notable, however, was Eduardo.[30]

As Eddie Sánchez, he had failed to become an actor in New York, so he returned to Havana and a sinecure job in one of his father's banks. Family legend has it that Eduardo told his father he suffered from "the sickness of homosexuality," but there was a new kind of doctor in Europe who could cure him.[31] When Bernabé Sánchez asked "Who is the best?" Eduardo was so surprised that he blurted out the first name that came to mind: "Jung." The proud Cuban father agreed to meet all expenses if his third son would go away until he was "cured," so that no one in Havana need know of his "sickness."

Once he escaped, Eduardo never again hid his sexual preference. He did not go to Zurich, nor did he become Jung's patient. Instead, he found an analyst in Paris and asked Anaïs to help him decorate an apartment. Then, in search of diversion, he went to Hendaye and spirited Joaquín off to tour several Spanish cities, thus earning Rosa's lasting opprobrium for "Eddie's bad influence" on her children.[32]

Too poor to travel, Anaïs and Hugo spent the summer of 1930 in Paris. They decided to cut costs by all living together in one large house, and in August she found one in the unfashionable tumble-down village of Louveciennes.[33] As usual, when she hoped to persuade Rosa to go along with her on something she wanted, her mathematical reasoning lay somewhere between overly optimistic and grossly incorrect: "Price 15,000 [francs] a year, which means a saving of <u>25,000</u> a year."[34] So, too, was her description: "the garden is beautiful. Steam heat, telephone, electricity . . . it has charm."

Actually, the house was dilapidated and impossible to heat. After the first freezing winter they were forced to close it from November to March and move into furnished apartments in Paris, thus paying more rent than if they had remained on boulevard Suchet (which they eventually sublet at a loss).

Anaïs was full of ideas for saving money, from keeping chickens in the falling-down coop to putting Rosa in charge of raising vegetables, canning fruit, and making jams and preserves. All came to naught, for the garden was and remained a thicket of nettles. Her aim was self-sufficiency, but as always, something interrupted her planned frugality and thrift. Eduardo, back from his holiday, had nothing else to do but live a "stumbling chaotic, life . . . the face turned adoringly to men, to whores, to insipid, marriageable girls. And to me, with the self-same power of attraction."[35]

He and Anaïs resumed their rapport as if no time had elapsed since they shared their diaries in Richmond Hill. Now, when Eduardo read the stories she wrote, he saw at once that they were all about her, that she had put herself into her fiction as much as she had done in the diaries. Like Lawrence, he added, she was creating her own world with herself as its center.[36] His remarks were barbed, for he also accused her of narcissism, which made her livid. True, she admitted, she "admired" herself "at moments," but she always kept her "love" for others and not for herself. When she wrote this exchange in the diary, she made it seem that he agreed with her; in truth, he made the accusation time and again, and it always made her furious.[37]

Hugo was often away, trying to persuade wealthy Americans vacationing in Europe to entrust their investments to his bank. Anaïs went occasionally, but although she liked the resorts, hated sitting with other wives while Hugo played tennis with their husbands and especially resented having to take visitors to Paris sightseeing and shopping. She liked the feeling of freedom that came with being drunk, and began to flirt with men in front of their wives. Several times, men's hands strayed along her body in clear view of everyone. Instead of being angry or ashamed, Hugo apologized for forcing her to subject her artistic soul to an evening with the Philistines of Mammon.[38]

Because she was alone so much, Eduardo became her constant companion. She had always thought of him as her alter ego; now she began to think of the two of them in terms of twinship, another variant of Lawrence's "star equilibrium." In language he might have used, she described herself and Eduardo as "two worlds of ideas" perpetually seeking unity even as their "two separate bodies fled from each other."[39] Actually, his was the body that fled from hers. Eduardo was involved with a young man of "dubious" (i.e., North African, Spanish, southern French) ancestry whom he picked up on the street. Much that Anaïs wrote in the diary about the soul-searching conversations she and Eduardo had about whether or not they should (or even could) consummate their passion was a transposition in which she inserted herself, for Eduardo was really talking about his lover, not her.[40]

The move to Louveciennes was their last, for 2 bis, rue Monbuisson became as permanent a home as they would have in France, and Anaïs hurried to settle her household. If she had an abiding compulsion, it was for order. Everything—from the linen closet to her writing desk—had to be neatly filed, collated, or arranged. Now she rushed the painters, stirring cans of turquoise and peach herself until they were the shades she wanted. The turquoise-and-white-tiled Moroccan fireplace that had graced the boulevard Suchet apartment was now the focal point of her salon, and upon its mantel was her treasured crystal fishbowl, in which the fish were made of brilliantly colored glass.[41]

Relations between Anaïs and Rosa had been strained but were worsened now that Eduardo was so often present. Rosa felt it her motherly duty to warn Anaïs about taking advantage of Hugo, who she feared would revolt and abandon them all. Anaïs construed even the most innocent comment as interference, so there were furious arguments followed by leaden silences. She never wrote the truth in the diary, only noted how "cross and domineering" Rosa was, and how she suffered from "contraditis."[42] Everything, she told Hugo, was always Rosa's fault.

Hugo resorted to poetry to keep his mind off their quarrels and his finances. Sitting on the toilet one morning, he wrote:

Five years since I wrote a line
And now it is here I start . . .
For one who dreamed in clouds . . .
I have not raised my head these years above the dirt
Nor even sung its honest earthy color,
So why should this not be
This poet's rightful golden throne.[43]

While he worried about paying next month's bills, she, who left school because she could not pass simple mathematics, amused herself by calculating how much money they would need for him to retire at the age of forty.[44] He did not tell her how absurd her figures were because she presented them as if they were a rare and precious gift. He continued to slog along.

Things seemed a bit better after she wrote the Lawrence book. There was a new seriousness to their sexuality and an eagerness to dispense with all forms of foreplay and go directly to coitus. Each discovered the satisfaction of multiple orgasm, and both were astonished by the pleasure. After ten years of marriage, they both spoke of this time as their true honeymoon.[45] Their eroticism was enhanced further when Eduardo began to compete with Anaïs for Joaquín's as well as Hugo's attention, a "frisson" that husband and wife exploited when in their cousin's company and that excited them when alone together.

In October, Anaïs received a copy of *The Canadian Forum* with her article on Lawrence in it, her first publication. She was thrilled to see her work in print but upset that no one recognized it as hers because she had used the pen name Melisendra. She concentrated on writing new stories, many of which she sent to magazines, but this time as Anaïs Nin. Mostly, they were vacuous tales of young heroines who modeled for male artists and, with their wisdom and beauty, helped these men secure fame and fortune.[46]

She sent them to the London literary agent Curtis Brown,[47] but no one there was interested. In Paris, she sent them to Janet Flanner, *The New Yorker*'s Genêt, who returned them without opening the envelope. The legendary bookseller Sylvia Beach had little patience when Anaïs sent four or five submissions and made as many personal visits. Beach finally suggested the name of a small, poverty-stricken French printer as a way to fob her off. Warren and Brewer, then publishing some of the most interesting international avant-garde poetry and fiction, returned her stories unread. *The Adelphi* magazine rejected her work, but at least was courteous enough to read it first, which is more than Mencken did when she sent it to *The American Mercury*. And so on and on. She made careful lists in the diary of all her rejections but kept on writing even as "my back is broken and I'm nearly blind."

What bothered her most was that nearly all to whom she submitted her work rejected it "without even wanting to take a look at my face." She was accustomed to persuading people to do her bidding by the magnetism of her personality, the seductive quality of her tiny voice with its unidentifiable accent, and especially by the mesmerizing way she locked her heavily kohl-blackened eyes with theirs. She was convinced that all these people would have published her work if they had only given her the chance "to work [her] magic" on them.[48]

She got her chance when Kay Bryant, Eduardo, and even Sylvia Beach all urged her to "go see Titus."[49] The American Edward Titus was editor and publisher of *This Quarter* and the estranged husband of the cosmetics magnate Helena Rubenstein.

In early August, Anaïs called on Titus (who was not there) with a sheaf of stories that his secretary insisted she leave. Anaïs waited a month, then returned and this time saw him in person. He had not yet read her stories, he said, but would do so at once, all the while appraising her openly from head to toe. He told her truthfully that the Lawrence essay in *Canadian Forum* was "original," but lied about his high regard for "Waste of Timelessness" and her other stories. Soon she was his "Honey girl," and became adept at fending off his more serious passes. Titus grew weary of pursuit, and turned her over to his young assistant, Lawrence Drake.[50]

Drake told her his office was too small to work in and took her to his apartment. She recognized the ruse but was fascinated by his "black eyes, black hair, olive skin, sensual nostrils and mouth," and especially "the new experience of his moustache." Soon they were kissing and petting, interspersed with great quantities of whiskey (for which she now had a prodigious appetite). Every now and again they glanced at her manuscripts.

Drake offered Anaïs the best chance for publication she had yet had, but although that was what she wanted, working toward it took second place to sexual experimentation. Whether truthful or not, Anaïs created in her diary almost a replica of her erotic encounter with Erskine. She wrote that after much kissing and fondling, Drake bared her breasts, laid her on the sofa, and asked her to disrobe. She apparently refused. Unwilling or unready to commit adultery, she grabbed his hand when he lifted her skirt and murmured something about "woman troubles." He then suggested "other ways." Her prose is sprightly as she notes how she complied with his directions and, with an innocence that seems incredible, knelt before him. When she saw his erect penis and realized that he expected fellatio, she jumped to her feet, horrified. She allowed him to place her on the sofa again and masturbate between her legs, "out of pity."

None of her stories was ever published in *This Quarter*. When Titus eventually accepted the revised and expanded Lawrence article as a book, he "suggested" that publication would be swifter if she paid for printing costs. Hugo paid, even though he moaned "I have lost my capital, capital that was to form the basis of our retirement to a life devoted to literature."[51] He willingly increased his indebtedness to help Anaïs, even after she told him about Lawrence Drake. Her version was highly edited, leaving out almost everything except that he made a halfhearted pass, which she fended off, and his request for fellatio, which she found lewd and revolting. When Drake accepted that there would be no sex, he stopped pretending he ever meant to edit the stories and asked her not to return.

She was fascinated by the "techniques" she had learned from Drake, however, and shared them avidly with Hugo, all the while feigning fastidious distaste for what Drake had proposed. She wrote a great deal about Hugo's passion during the next several months. In that, at least, if in nothing else, she seems to have been satisfied.

10

"A man who makes life drunk"

"IT IS NOW an accepted fact that I write unsalable stuff," Anaïs told the diary on New Year's Day, 1931.

The holidays had been quiet because money was scarce. Anaïs convinced herself that she wanted a job, but said that working for Sylvia Beach, Titus, or Jolas at *transition* would not pay enough to be worth her while. She claimed modeling was off-limits because of Hugo's position at the bank, conveniently forgetting that she had spent much of the past year posing free, and that Hugo's banking colleagues knew it, and dancing and teaching dance were "too strenuous." She talked a good game, but always found a reason not to play, and Hugo coached her by insisting that he would be a loser if he did not provide for all her needs. So Anaïs remained serenely unemployed while Hugo's hair receded and his digestion suffered.

During the first six months in Louveciennes (November 1930 to May 1931), Anaïs led a fairly quiet and productive life. Even though she was desperate to publish, she pored over the diaries, editing and annotating as carefully as if they were published books, indexing everything she did each day.[1] Since her childhood, she had ended each volume with a list of "Books Read"; now she added a list of visitors, social engagements, or activities.

If no visitors distracted, her daily activity consisted of "work in house, gardening, etc." Occasionally there was a notation of "chez Titus for editing," and even quite simply "writing."[2] Most of the time, she numbered the pages of the "journals" (as she always called the diary), frequently forgetting herself and repeating or misnumbering. When each volume was filled, she made a careful "Subject Index" of the contents, from "My darling [Hugo] is away for a week [page] 283" to "I don't like the silence of a room [page] 297." She never bothered to correct the numbering errors, but when she finished each subject index, counted the words in the volume: diary Journal no. 30, for example, had 46,800, each one in her impeccable handwriting without a single crossout, and all composed in less than six months. It is mind-boggling to note that she wrote all this in addition to hundreds of long personal letters, a Christmas-card list that took three full days to complete, and fiction as well.

These months were a period of relative calm before several different devastating storms. Still naming each diary before she wrote in it and unable to decide between two titles, she wrote both on the first page of Volume 31, June 1931. They were uncannily accurate: "The Woman Who Died" and "Disintegration."[3]

Perhaps because of Eduardo's influence and her own growing interest in psychoanalysis, Anaïs began to write descriptions of her dreams. She had also been reading "murky" Freud since the beginning of the year, fascinated by his "cases" and impressed by the scientific analysis he applied to the "deep subterranean world" of the mind.[4] She persevered, however, only because "at the end of Freud" reading Jung awaited her. Her list of "Books Read" included Colette, Gide, Huxley, and Dorothy Richardson (with whom she briefly compared herself),[5] but is mostly taken up with psychology and psychoanalysis.[6]

By reading psychoanalytic theory itself, she was departing from her preferred custom of reading secondary sources. This time she filtered her views, particularly of Freud, Jung, and Adler, through her own perceptions, reading (or, in some instances, misreading) their writings, doggedly insisting on applying their theories to her own life.

Adler, for instance, "bores one like a goody-goody idealist old maid."[7] She agreed with Freud that youthful accidents, incidents, or relationships may be the "cause of a lifelong deviation," but she worried that, as a medical doctor, Freud had not paid enough attention to the "transposition, sublimation [and] transfiguration of our physical and mental elements."[8] Jung, she reasoned, attended more to "how the artist uses them."

Her chief interest was how the artist ultimately makes use of real life. She interpreted Jung's theory of the collective unconscious (which she gleaned from his essay in *transition*)[9] to be "the intensification of our personal experience to the point of overflow into the universal—the impersonal experience. . . . A rich personal intensity breaks its own shell and its own obsessions—and touches the mystic whole." Arriving at "the mystic whole" became, in various guises, "living the dream," or "making the dream real."[10]

At times, Anaïs Nin was a prescient social critic. For example, she believed that, of the two theorists, Jung was more in tune with the tenor of the times because he defined "the nondirected thinking of our epoch." Couching her opinion in terms of "how the moderns" (i.e., Proust, Joyce, and Jolas) "have approached the dream realm," she intuited that "we no longer compel our thoughts along a definite track, but let them float, sink and mount according to their own gravity."[11] This, of course, was exactly what she tried to do in her writing, the very thing for which it was criticized and rejected for so many years.

She read Jung and Freud thoroughly and dutifully recorded her dreams.[12] When she dreamed of Erskine, she told the diary that he "really missed something good: an absolutely intelligent female, really subjugated."[13] —Her view, at the time, of woman's role played to perfection.

Hugo, who read psychoanalytic theory with her, also began what became his lasting habit of recording every dream.[14] Each had several that recurred, and one in common. Anaïs's was of a "monstrous" woman who took her to a tiny room and tried to seduce her. In his, Hugo decided to go to a hotel with a prostitute who had importuned him. They wandered disconsolately through many ghostly hotels, increasingly frustrated in their search for the perfect room until Hugo became "tired and bored" and gave up. Anaïs wrote: "H. interprets this that my attitude has liberated him, but that he is still calculating the practical inconveniences of that life and rejecting it again, as he did before."

A family crisis interrupted whatever action either might have taken to act out their dreams when Thorvald flew into a rage induced by "the Problem," or "Mr. Nin," as Anaïs now called her father.[15] Thorvald had made one final stab at banking in New York in a job Hugo arranged at the National City Bank. Disliking it, Thorvald quit and returned to Paris, intending to live with his father. Joaquín Nin was at the peak of his career during the early 1930s, and it was bolstered by his wife's fortune. He welcomed Thorvald effusively, making the taciturn young man, the most unlikely of the children, his deadliest weapon in the never-ending joust with Rosa for every possible supremacy.

As she had in the past, Anaïs placed herself squarely in the middle of their battlefield, writing letters that took the side of whoever was to receive them. She meant to placate, but when the recipients compared what she wrote, everyone became inflamed. Thorvald now believed the version of family history put forth by the ever-canny Joaquín Nin, with himself as a long-suffering martyr deprived of his children's company because of Rosa's hysterical need to punish him.

Anaïs still had a skeptical view of everything her father said or did, but she loved the secondhand glory that Cuban society in Paris showered upon her as "the daughter of Nin." So she wrote to Thorvald with the thought firmly in mind that her father might read her letters, which of course he did.

After several weeks of increasing vitriol, Thorvald wired that he would arrive in Louveciennes at midnight. Rosa and Joaquín were away,[16] and Anaïs and Hugo decided to sleep until he came. When he rang, Anaïs asked Hugo to stay in bed until she determined Thorvald's mood. Without greeting her, Thorvald opened his suitcase and took out her letters and telegrams, many several years old. He ensconced himself in an armchair and proceeded to read aloud in what she called "the Inquisition," pointing out her "contradictions." She insisted she had the right to hold different views at different times. And so it went—a round-robin of insults. He left abruptly in the middle of the night, even though Hugo joined Anaïs in urging him to stay.

Thorvald was a troubled young man who "thought he got a raw deal from his family."[17] Denied an education, he had drifted without purpose, alienated alternately from each parent, isolated for long periods of time from the warmth of the large extended Cuban family and from his American upbringing and the English language, which he considered his primary heritage.

Whatever goaded Thorvald into provoking the dispute with Anaïs was never really resolved. In years to come, it festered, causing him to lash out at her time after time. But on this occasion, he simply disappeared from her life for the next decade. He returned to Havana with money from Maruca (Joaquín Nin was notoriously tightfisted). On September 18, 1931 (pointedly, Anaïs was *not* included in the greeting), Hugo received a letter saying Thorvald had married a young Cuban woman, Teresa Castillo, and was living with her in Bogotá, where he was working for National City Bank.[18] He had thus effectively removed himself from the family, but Joaquín Nin did not give up trying to reenter it. As his son Joaquín would have nothing to do with him, he concentrated on Anaïs. She always told Rosa when "Mr. Nin" wrote, and Rosa always begged her not to reply. But Anaïs was intrigued, and liked the feeling of power it gave her to be the one to answer or not.

In late June, Hugo and Anaïs left for a week in Mallorca. Sorely in need of a holiday, Hugo became ill with flu, high fever, and chills. Anaïs nursed him for five bedridden days, the isolation and effort making her even more introspective. While sitting at Hugo's bedside, she entertained herself by practicing analysis on him, a willing subject. He told her his dreams in great detail, and from that launched into a long story of his personal history of sexuality, which she called his "confession."[19] She did all the analyzing and he did all the talking, for at this early date, well before she was even willing to consider becoming a patient, she was already thinking of becoming an analyst.

"My qualifications for Psychoanalysis" was how she entitled a very long list in the diary: "Preference for listening rather than talking myself; Gift for listening rather than talking myself; Natural habit of analyzing what is told me during and after talk; Exceptional good memory to retain confidences, tones, gestures; Habit of writing down confidences and clarifying them; Habit of brooding over people and spontaneous desire to heal them; Patience; Many proofs of understanding beyond my own experiences; Proofs that my mind works naturally in Freud's manner; Intuition."

When they returned to Louveciennes, she focused all these qualities onto herself and decided that she suffered from "anxiety neurosis. Cause? Sexual."[20] Hugo, still blissfully unaware of her encounter with Erskine, was looking forward to seeing him in New York and chattered happily about how eager he was for John to read her work. She was terrified by the thought not only of seeing him in Hugo's company but also of having him read her fiction.

She began her self-analysis "in my usual strange way: by putting all my clothes, papers, house and accounts in order. I always do that first." She listed everything she had done in the past year to overcome her obsession with Erskine, how she had turned to creative writing, decorating the house, uplifting conversations with Boussie, even using Eduardo as the substitute recipient of her erotic fantasies. It seems not to have occurred to her to take pleasure in the increasingly satisfying physical rapport she and her husband were developing in these years; only Erskine's rejection mattered. "Fortunately it will all be over soon," she wrote. "What an awful thing to think my physical mechanism is truly outside my control."

Their encounters in New York passed without incident, but Anaïs did not get over Erskine until she and Hugo were aboard the S.S. *Lafayette* returning to France. Hugo could no longer stand her moods and blurted out, "What is wrong with you?" So Anaïs told him.

"Today I died," Hugo wrote in the journal he and she sporadically kept together. "Thursday, October 8 [1931]. All the old infantile, weak romantic in me died."[21] Now Hugo knew why he had been "living with only half of her," her abstraction caused by John's "damnable 'unfinished business.' " He was not grateful for Erskine's respect and affection for him, "rather the reverse, for he left her spiritually and emotionally shattered . . . better if he had gone through with it." He also thought Anaïs would have recovered more quickly if the affair had been consummated "without wounding herself as she has done in body and spirit."

He quickly absolved Anaïs of blame and rationalized, even took perverse comfort, in all that had happened: "Ignorant and blind, I could not comfort her in her terrible suffering, a dual suffering," arising from the "strain of the uncompleted, unconsummated physical act" with John and her continuing love for her husband. Hugo seemed both proud and relieved that "[Anaïs] would never have left me of her own will, for him." With an amazingly casuistic line of reasoning, and in his usual dramatically overcharged prose, he convinced himself of the following:

> What is important to me, and what tonight I am trying to keep my eyes upon, beyond the knife-like pain that runs through me at the picture of that fair golden-white body offered ecstatically to J., rises to my mind and sears my flesh, is that what A. really did, in the most profound sense, was to reach up with a pure impulse and draw the true high-water mark of our love.

Anaïs and Hugo with John and Pauline Erskine
on an excursion to Beaune.

> For the sake of helping us both to reach that, she was willing to run the risk of sacrificing that love itself for which alone, in spite of the impulse for J., she lived.

Everything, Hugo insisted, was his fault. He berated himself because he concentrated on his work. He had been "too satisfied with living peacefully from day to day, always deferring doing anything creative and contenting myself with absorbing the written creations of others. Had I gone on, I would definitely have lost her sooner or later. . . . I have been lucky," he concluded, "for J. himself has been a mirage. Had he been the real thing my life would have ended."

"No one shall ever again take A. away from me, even for a moment," Hugo promised himself, as he plotted the course he must follow to keep her. It, too, led to a sad observation: "The plain fact is that as long as A. is spending 12 hours a day in meditation, reading, and creative writing, against the one hour or at most two that are available to me, she will *always* be getting ahead of me in thought and imagination."

The conclusion was perplexing: "Shall I remain in the Bank? If I decide that by doing so, I run the chance of again falling behind A. and obliging her to offer her body again to a 'symbol' then I shall get out of the Bank no matter what the consequences. For what does my income . . . or the possibility of acquiring capital . . . mean to me if I lose A. again to someone who is free to stimulate her mind while I dull the edge of mine. . . . The game is not worth the candle."

Hugo was in pain and in a bind. In anguish, he described himself as "a rat in a trap of my own making. Mother and Joaquín as well as A. are dependent on me. . . . A. herself is not well and I am terribly worried about her health."[22]

The only solution he could envisage was "to cultivate my off hours intensively." He had always wanted to write poetry, so "let me begin at once. For now there is no choice, it is death or life."

The next two days took their toll, and he lay ill in bed, tossing in half-sleep, trying to keep the image of John bent over Anaïs's naked body out of his mind. The day she told him what had happened, he confessed in the journal that "pity and reason" saw him through. Now, "a purely primitive man showed himself," and Hugo behaved as "nothing better than the savage whose woman has been possessed by another savage."

He made Anaïs tell and retell the scenario of her "almost-seduction" and how John asked her to put on the Spanish shawl and open it to reveal her naked body. "I cried out of my great pain, but also out of my pity for her," Hugo wrote. "For I know how wholeheartedly she offered herself at that moment and what it must have cost her to close herself up and not go through with it," a slightly different story from the one she had originally told in the diary.

Hugo needed to render Anaïs blameless in order to make his marriage survive: "And so my pity reasserted itself again over my pain, for I realize that she has suffered even more than I have." His account of what Anaïs told him covered thirteen tightly filled pages, all in his tiny, upright handwriting, with numerous cross-outs and corrections, in old fashioned, slightly melodramatic prose. Hers filled one succinct line in the "Journal of Facts": "October 9–15: rest."[23]

It was more like six days and nights of endlessly rehashing the tawdry details followed by intervals of violent sex. When the first session ended, they were both astonished to discover how much pleasure they derived from the violence and pain of the encounter. After that, they consciously goaded each other to try to reproduce the same sensations.

In Louveciennes, life resumed its pattern with the added fillip of sexuality as they enhanced the practices they had discovered on board the ship. Hugo left early for work and came home late, piqued that Anaïs seemed not to care.[24] "I do not criticize his work any more because such conflict kills him," she wrote, calling him her "little magnate" (his hard work had just won him another promotion). Hugo had no choice but to keep on trying to advance because he needed so much money to support the financial house of cards that life in Louveciennes now represented. The irony was not lost upon the "genius banker," who loved his work, but the comfort and security he earned through it brought scant respect and grudging gratitude from his wife, whose only desire was that he become something he did not want and probably never could be—not only a successful artist, but even more important, a rich one. So they continued to talk around each other, with no possibility that either one would understand or accept the other's point of view.

Hugo realized the magnitude of the problem; he was also resigned to how little he could do to change it: "Instinctively, all her life, she has been seeking a leader, a father, and she will never be satisfied with me, will wander forever, unless she finds that leader in me."[25]

Anaïs thought they should separate temporarily; she to go to Zurich to study with Jung, he to live in a Paris hotel and pretend to be away on business. Hugo refused. Determined they should "pursue new experiences," she suggested orgies, for she had become fascinated by the idea of sex with multiple partners.

Eduardo warned against both separation and experimentation because of Hugo's relative innocence as compared to hers. Anaïs felt sure the marriage could withstand anything because they were still in love with each other; even so, they agreed not to face "the issue," as they had come to call the idea of sexual experimentation. It lay between them, however, like an inert body, the personification of everything Hugo feared and Anaïs desired. Anaïs said the only tie that bound them now was "one of white-heat living . . . within the security and peace of marriage."

She was very fond of "widening circles,"[26] as she called them, and described herself and Hugo as "widening the circle of our sorrows and pleasures within the circle of our home and our two selves." It was all they could do under the circumstances, the only "defense" they could mount "against the intruder, the unknown."

The intruder came that winter, when it was time to settle the financial details regarding publication of her book on Lawrence. Titus wanted to make sure they would pay, and Hugo and Anaïs wanted to make sure he would publish it once he was paid, so Hugo consulted a lawyer who worked for the bank. Robert Osborn, Esq., had literary ambitions of his own and many literary friends, but most important, he would draw up the contractual agreements cheaply as a favor to Hugo.

Osborn told Anaïs that she must meet his friend Henry Miller, who was fascinated with Lawrence and thinking of writing a book himself. Anaïs was delighted and invited Osborn to bring his friend to lunch on December 5, 1931.

Joaquín Nin-Culmell never forgot his first sight of Henry Miller: "instant dislike."[27] Anaïs's response was quite the reverse: "He's a man who makes life drunk. . . . He is like me."[28] The next day she made another cryptic entry in the "Journal of Facts": "Hugo ill." Perhaps he was deluding himself when he told her she would fall in love with Henry's mind, but he still appraised the situation correctly when he said, "I'm going to lose you to Henry."[29]

"No, no, you won't lose me," she hastened to assure him.

And each—in his and her own way—was right.

11

Those Millers

On March 7, 1932, Hugo took up the journal he had begun more than five years earlier and in which he had filled less than a third of its hundred-or-so pages. Now he felt compelled to write, and his subject, as always, was his relationship with his wife. In this instance, his first sentence says it all: "This morning I asked Anaïs to tell me everything about her experiences."[1]

He must have paused, at least long enough to fill his pen, for the ink darkened when he wrote: "Another paradox. It hurts me to hear about them. I suffer." The ink lightens, then darkens again as if he hesitated, bore down hard, and came to a painful decision: "But I . . . would rather hear them even if I suffer, than not to hear."

Hugo was a quiet man who kept his emotions carefully hidden from everyone but Anaïs. Unfortunately, he was so sensitive to her every nuance that he understood all too well what was happening. From the day Henry Miller first came to lunch, Hugo feared he had lost whatever order and stability he had painstakingly built with Anaïs. He was sure of it when Miller brought his wife, June, to dinner on December 29, 1931. Three months later, life for Hugo had become a free-fall plunge into chaos.[2] Hugo, who loved Anaïs beyond passion or reason, could see no recourse but to let things play themselves out: "This seems a hell of a way to live but, like Anaïs herself, a very little goes a long way with me."

Hugo could not help but make comparisons: "I could never live a life like Henry's, spread[ing his] tentacles in many directions to grasp life"; Hugo preferred "to bore deep in one direction." All this was a euphemism for their attitude toward women, for Hugo wanted only Anaïs, who was so fascinated by Henry's tales of his adventures with two wives and many prostitutes that she insisted on telling Hugo all the gory details. In Anaïs's eyes, Henry became the paragon and Hugo the drone. Henry depended on strangers as well as friends to give him money, food, and lodging. Hugo worked hard and had willingly taken on the support of his wife and her family and made a success of it. Ten years later, his wife's chief response to his accomplishment was to tell him that he was not fulfilling himself as an artist. His response was to try harder to be and do everything she wanted, no matter the cost to his profession and his health.

Now her discussions of Hugo as an artist centered around sex, especially his (and by extension, *their*) lack of experience. When Hugo expressed his fears about what Henry's effect would be upon their marriage, Anaïs laughed them off, saying she was living her life "in advance" of him. "I am in love with Henry's *mind only,*" she wrote in her diary, which she uncharacteristically left lying about so Hugo would be sure to read it.

Anaïs was hoping to steer him off her intended course, which he knew, after Erskine, was sex with other men. Hoping to assuage his doubts, she wrote that by the time he was forty, Hugo would also be "seeking other experiences" and would need "contact with other men and women."[3] All Hugo could decide when he wrote about it was "I don't know."

When they first met Henry Miller, his "principal obsession, as always, [was] meals."[4] He swept into their lives because they offered one that was free and also very good. He owed money to everyone and had no fixed abode. Still, he was optimistic: "The food problem I've solved fairly well . . . rotating among my friends. Fred [Alfred Perlès] gives me breakfast about three in the afternoon. Cigarettes come as a matter of course. But a room! Shit, there's the rub!"[5] Michael Frankel and Walter Lowenfels, two expatriate Americans supported by their wealthy families, grew used to Henry's knocks just as their wives dished up dinner, and Richard Osborn had always found him a bed. But now Osborn was returning to New York and Henry was dependent upon Perlès, an Austrian journalist who worked for the *Chicago Tribune.* Henry's bed usually was the floor of Fred's office or half of his lumpy mattress at the miserable Hôtel Central. "I'm always living on the edge of disaster," was Henry's glum assessment of his life.

Henry came alone to Paris in March 1930, at June's insistence.[6] He never knew where June got the money to pay for his passage, but he had his suspicions, as he was suspicious of the money she sent sporadically to keep him there.

And so, for Henry, lunch at the Guilers' was as if the fabled stone cliffs of Sesame had parted, revealing a life of luxurious comfort he had not yet seen in Paris. Even though he thought the house overdone, its mistress puzzlingly dramatic, and her beloved crystal aquarium a bit strange ("the fish are made of glass here and the water is dirty"),[7] Henry still knew enough to send a bread-and-butter letter for the first lunch and the one that followed on December 12 (for him and Osborn, Hugo was away on business), as well as a dinner on December 23 (with Anaïs alone).[8]

"Dear Anaïs Nin,"[9] Henry wrote, offering to send a few pages of *Tropic of Cancer.*[10] He thanked her for "the hospitality, the sympathy and friendliness" she had shown him and looked forward to seeing again soon "the sparkling glasses and the shelves filled with books." But he had a problem: June had arrived in Paris out of the blue, as was her custom. "Everything has stopped since [June's arrival]," Henry wrote. "I have not been able to find myself. I have lost something."

Anaïs was wildly intrigued by a wife who would send a genius (as she believed Henry to be) to live alone in the world's greatest fleshpot. Unwilling to take such a risk herself, she fantasized about where the adventures of a life without boundaries or constraints might lead.

In their previous meetings, Anaïs had questioned Henry as much about June as she had about his writing. He told her everything, including the wildest details of June's escapades. Henry told her how he colluded with June's attempt early in their marriage at "efficient, somehow legitimized, prostitution"[11] when they rented a basement apartment in Greenwich Village and put in a supply of bootleg gin. It was what Anaïs had been dreaming of for the past several years: an acquiescent husband, a voyeur who would be there to observe her adventures with mysterious, phantom lovers, and when they were gone, who would replay them passionately with her.

In Louveciennes, the sexual tension became palpable. Eduardo, the most jealous, became the most vocal when he discovered how Henry not only filled Anaïs's thoughts and conversations but also how she showered gifts and money upon him.[12] Everyone else urged Anaïs to stop slumming and rid herself of the shabby, dirty derelict with literary pretensions and no talent for anything but panhandling and pornography. So naturally she sent a telegram as soon as she got Henry's letter telling her June had arrived, inviting them both to dinner at their earliest convenience. One wonders if he would have wanted the two women to meet—the steady patron he had every hope Anaïs would become and the flamboyant wife whose foul language and tart tongue could ruin his chances for regular meals, free gifts, and an allowance besides—had not June behaved so recklessly with money neither he nor she had.

Arriving broke, she went to the Princesse Hotel anyway, charming the proprietor into loaning money she promptly spent on clothes, makeup, and liquor. Henry was frantic, trying to figure how to sneak her and all her possessions out of the hotel, as he had no money either. Dinner with the Guilers offered a temporary respite, and Henry accepted for the very next night, fearing that Anaïs might have second thoughts and rescind the invitation.

Much of what happened in early 1932 between Mr. and Mrs. Miller and Mr. and Mrs. Guiler is shrouded in controversy, the conflicting accounts of two very dramatic people (Henry, forty-one, and Anaïs, twenty-nine) who turned their adventures into thinly disguised fiction and autobiography, a third (June, thirty)[13] who changed or recanted almost everything later in life, and the fourth (Hugo, thirty-four), an unwilling player and spectator to it all.

The catalyst was not Anaïs's attraction to Henry's physical form, for he was short, bald, myopic, and awkward, with a raucous Brooklyn accent and a vocabulary of equal parts slang and sexual expletives, all of which grated on her aristocratic sensibilities. Rather, it was his artistic vision, which was so like Lawrence's in the forcefulness and directness with which he wrote about contemporary sexuality. When Henry told her that Lawrence "missed the boat" in *Lady Chatterley's Lover* by including extraneous details of plot and setting rather than concentrating on his characters' "warm-hearted fucking all the way through,"[14] she felt as if she had been struck by a literary tornado. Henry, not Waldo Frank, Sherwood Anderson, or John Dos Passos, was the American writer whose work exemplified the sheer essentials of fiction. Henry Miller was the true modernist she had been

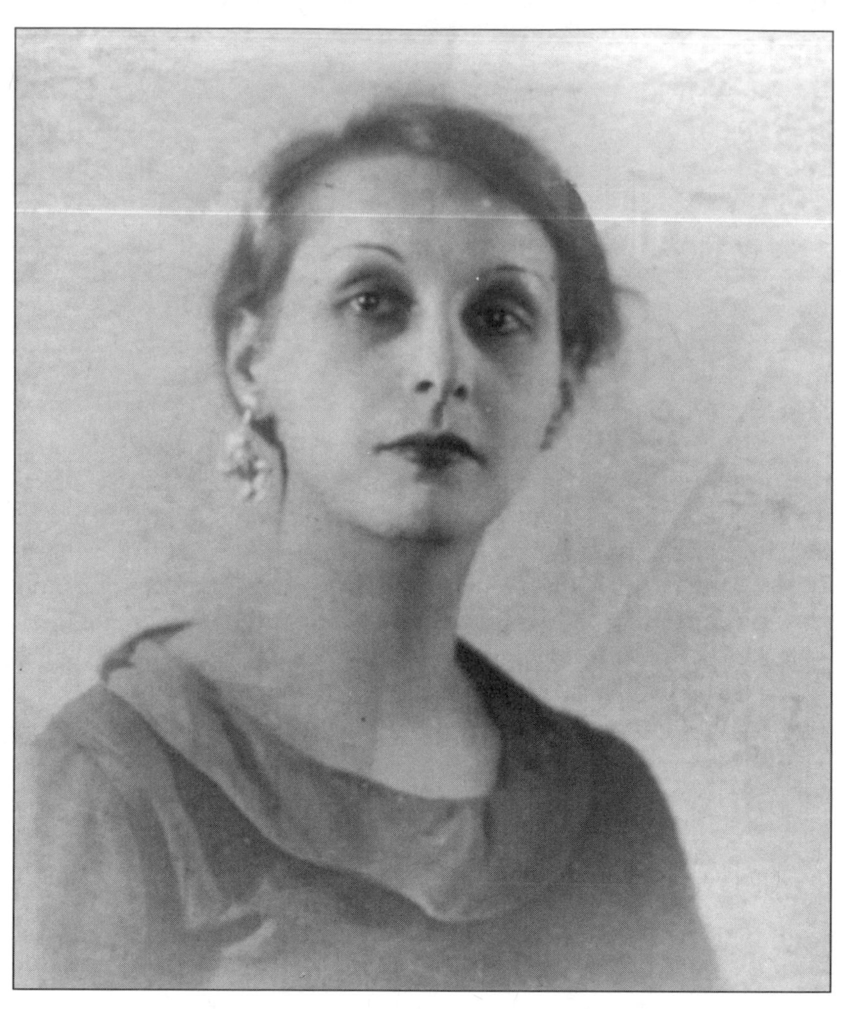

June Miller.

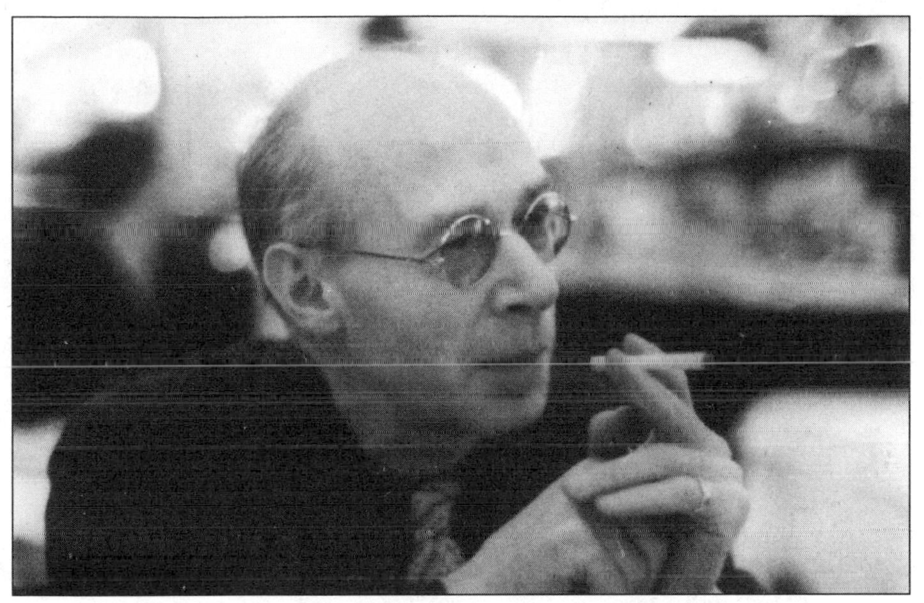

Henry Miller.

seeking, the one who, she was convinced, needed her to become his handmaiden.

She admired the poverty Henry was willing to endure to allow his artistic vision to flourish. Like most readers of English-language newspapers in Paris, she had read Wambly Bald's column about Henry several months before. Bald described a "legitimate child of Montparnasse, the salt of the Quarter," inventing a story that Henry was so down on his luck that he was reduced to sleeping on a park bench. "The only thing that bothered him," Bald wrote, "was that he didn't have a toothbrush."[15]

With Henry, Anaïs could play the role she first dreamed of at the age of sixteen, when she fantasized about putting herself "under the protection, nobility and grandeur" of a "Shadow,"[16] who would be a "great writer." She envisioned herself helping "a tiny little bit in the fantastic, poetic, imaginary chapters, when he is writing about illusions and poets and Autumn birds, flowers, the sea, against the government, to defend unfortunate prisoners and the poor. . . ." (Only briefly did she consider writing the book herself: "and he could correct it.")

Now here was Henry, admiring her book on Lawrence but intent on writing one of his own. His admiration of Joyce surpassed hers (she thought Joyce "a great stylist but sometimes vulgar"), but he shared her enthusiasm for Proust: "to Albertine" soon became a verb they shared. And when he told her he knew of no other *woman* writer of their generation or of any other period in history who possessed the courage to express herself as honestly and directly as she had in her Lawrence book, and that Lawrence himself would have been proud of her, she was enthralled.[17]

In the beginning, she told Henry in letters and herself in the diary that she would be the one woman he would never have.[18] "Excessive living weighs down the imagination," she decreed with dramatic pomposity. "We will not live, we will only write and talk." Henry disagreed, especially after she allowed him to read some of her diary. He told her she could write with such "imaginative intensity" only because she had not dared to live out what she wrote about. He accused her of finding it safer to adapt the facts of June's life to her fictional needs, or to "make notes" based on his stories about June's legendary exploits and how she dropped in or out of his life at will. All this made Anaïs fixated on meeting June.

Hugo walked the short distance to the Louveciennes train station to escort the Millers through the early darkness of the December night to his house. Anaïs waited until she saw them enter the tall iron gate, then flung the house's double doors open, flooding the garden with light. "I saw for the first time the most beautiful woman on earth," she wrote in the diary.[19]

Anaïs must have willed herself to see beauty, for although June was a striking sight, no one else had ever called her beautiful. Her outfit may have seemed slapdash, but June had dressed carefully because she had heard from Miller's "gang"[20] about the exotic stage-set of a house and its even more exotic mistress. She wore her favorite red velvet dress which had holes in both sleeves and several large spots and stains down its front, and a man's snap-brim fedora and cape, clothing she affected throughout her life.[21] Her face was covered with heavy white powder, and she rimmed her eyes with kohl as heavily as did Anaïs. June's *coup de grâce,* however, was lipstick that was either black or bilious green. While Anaïs wore large, striking pieces of costume jewelry, June wore only one earring—a cat's-eye—and a chrome bracelet set with a fake stone made of paste. Anaïs coveted the bracelet the moment she saw it, and June eventually gave it to her.

Although Anaïs was exceptionally slim, she was not the petite woman so many writers have described. She was five feet six inches tall, wore a size nine shoe, and had large, fine-boned fingers. Her hair was then died black, and she wore it in a fairly severe bun, which sharpened her face and gave her at times a birdlike appearance.[22] In her high-heeled sandals, she towered over the tiny June, who in her run-down heels stood five feet two inches at the most.[23]

Anaïs was determined to impress the Millers, and June, warned beforehand by the nervous Henry, was on good behavior, curbing her frequently foul tongue. Dinner, prepared by the maid Emilia, consisted of food tortured into shapes and tastes that disguised its straightforward origins. Candles were lit all over the dining room, and the fireplace threw a mysterious light and scent from the gnarled applewood Anaïs "preferred" to burn (actually, all she could afford). The table was an enchanted island of rose-pink because Emilia dyed a sheet to use as a tablecloth.[24]

Hugo, the perfect host, offered Henry cigars and brandy after dinner while Anaïs and June, like two proper suburban matrons, went up to her bedroom. The evening ended on a note of bourgeois comfort and propriety, but Anaïs was in such a frenzy of excitement that she could not sleep.[25] June left no record of what she thought of the dinner and neither did Henry. Only Anaïs recorded what June supposedly told Henry, but she does not say which of them told her: "Anaïs was just bored with her life, so she took us up." Anaïs thought it "crude . . . the only ugly thing I have heard her say."[26]

Anaïs found the reality of June better than any of Henry's stories about her. Having convinced herself that she and Henry would be lovers only of each other's writing, Anaïs now convinced herself that she was physically in love with June. This was partly because Henry had told her of June's several lesbian affairs in New York, and because she wanted so much to be important in June's life that she would have done anything to ensure it. The problem was, she did not know what lesbians did with each other.

Before Anaïs could act, June returned abruptly to New York after several weeks when the two women were poised on the brink of a sexual encounter that never progressed beyond kissing, hand-holding, and fondling. Anaïs initiated it by questioning June about her lesbian experiences, but June also coaxed things along, taking perverse pleasure in provoking Anaïs to constantly escalating displays of passion, which she promptly told in great (and sometimes exaggerated) detail to Henry. June enjoyed his torment over losing not his possible lover but his meal ticket.

In February, June returned to New York and Henry took a job, which Hugo found for him, teaching English in a lycée in Dijon.[27] Henry hated it from the moment he got there and wrote long love letters telling Anaïs. She replied daily, sending him her only money, cadged from her household allowance. She also sent gifts of ink, paper, warm socks and sweaters, and shipped her typewriter when he complained he could not write without one. To keep the household running, she borrowed from her mother.

The atmosphere of the Louveciennes house was so tense that quarrels, evasions, and accusations abounded, with everything centered around "Those Millers."[28] Hugo was jealous of the time Anaïs had spent in Paris with June, and now he was even more jealous of all she lavished on Henry. In Dijon, Henry was jealous because Anaïs still wrote daily letters to June (who did not answer). He worried that the women's friendship threatened to relegate him to a minor position in the triangle the three of them formed. Now more than ever, he needed to be first because he needed Anaïs's patronage. Eduardo was throwing attention-getting tantrums because Anaïs was not always available to listen to his interminable replays after each daily session with his new analyst, Dr. René Allendy. In a desperate move to divert her attention back to him, Eduardo repeated an earlier contention but now made it seem that it came from Dr. Allendy: the underlying cause of his homosexuality was unrequited sexual passion for her, and she must sleep with him because he would never be cured of it until she did.[29] Rosa, Joaquín, and Hugo, separately and together, confronted Anaïs, accusing her of bringing unhappiness and dissension into the household. "Get rid of those Millers," was Rosa's directive, but Hugo controlled the household's very existence and Anaïs controlled Hugo, so there was no possibility of that.

Hugo made an extraordinary decision in early March 1932, when the Princess Troubetskoia invited Anaïs to a party for the celebrated lesbian Marie Choissy, who wanted to meet her. It drove him to write a long, convoluted passage in his journal, beginning, "I love A. more than my life and suffer that she may have other experiences not only with men but now with women. The thought of anyone having a physical relationship with her just stabs me."

Anaïs had every intention of going to the party, but told Hugo she would abide by his wishes. He told her he would be unhappy whether she went or not, for by not going, she made him responsible for her sacrificing an important artistic experience. The confusion of what he wrote, about how art is suffused within the personality of anyone who becomes an artist, makes it seem as if he tried to convince himself it was true. He insisted, "with the profoundest conviction, that Anaïs carries that sacred fire in her. She is not merely an artist. She is the definition of art. Therefore, she cannot make mistakes. Whatever she does with that instinct burning in her, and it burns unceasingly, an immortal flame, is right, becomes right, for it is she who does it."

Anaïs did not attend the party because even though the idea of lesbian sex excited her, she was not sure about its actuality. She went instead on March 8 to a hotel room with Henry Miller, "the last man on earth" she would have considered for her first illicit lover.[30] Curiously, she did not write the fulsome details of the encounter in the diary (as she would do time after time in mind-numbing repetitiveness for the rest of their affair). After the first time she wrote only of "the tenderness of his hands, the unexpected penetration, to the core of me but without violence. What strange gentle power."

The next time she made love with Hugo, she wrapped her legs around his torso as Henry had taught her to do. "Darling, Darling, what are you doing?" she quotes him as shouting. "You're driving me wild. I've never felt such joy before."[31] Hugo put aside his fears of where she might have learned this new technique and wrote euphorically in his diary: "To really realize her one has to understand that here in the flesh is Cleopatra, Sappho, Helen of Troy, Christ, the fourth dimension, the woman's body that all men believe is just around the corner, the center of the magic circle in which we move."

But she felt guilty about the happy flush that covered her face, the jaunt in her step, the satisfied air of tranquillity that permeated her body and her newly blooming good health. She worried that people would notice, which they did. Her mother, furious that Miller spent so many nights "in the guest room" when Hugo was away on business, spoke to her only when necessary and then in tones of dour disapproval.

Anaïs did regret betraying Hugo, but her guilt was fleeting. She thought to assuage it by synchronizing the development of their extramarital sexual activity and decided to take him to an "exhibition" (something Eduardo had long been suggesting), a performance featuring any combination of prostitutes in any acts the clients wanted to watch.[32]

Eduardo first told her about exhibitions, but she telephoned Henry to find out which brothel put on the best ones. He said the best were at 32, rue Blondel, a high-quality house where they could join in if they were so inclined. On Saturday, March 12, she and Hugo went.

Each subsequently wrote about it, and each in a very different way. For Hugo, "the experience was filled with tremendous feelings." Anaïs wrote that she persuaded Hugo to go "just to see—do you want to? He is curious, elated, interested. Yes. Yes."[33] On their way, "Hugo hesitates but I am dancing and laughing at his side and I urge him on." Hugo gets directly to the point: they agreed that Anaïs should go in first to barter the price. Anaïs describes her feelings: "we have stood on a diving board and plunged. And now we are in a play, we are different."

Hugo writes that the *patronne* tells him they must take a table and buy a drink before choosing whatever combination of women they want. He explains that they want to see a man and a woman, but the *patronne* tells them this house has a "repertoire" only of women. When she asks him to choose, he defers to Anaïs, "feeling I was out of it and she might enjoy seeing an exhibition of lesbianism, of which I myself was curious."

Anaïs described how naked women milled about their table and shouted to be chosen. Hugo, "bewildered," deferred to her and praised her selection: "It did not take [Anaïs] more than three seconds to choose two girls. I was astonished by her quickness and sureness, especially as it was at once evident she had chosen the best in the room." Hugo did not describe the women but Anaïs did: "a very vivid, fat coarse Spanish looking woman and . . . a timid woman who had made no effort to attract my attention, small, slender, feminine."

The women sat at their table, naked except for small shawls that partially covered their breasts. Hugo had "the curious sensation of just sitting down for a solid chat with two young ladies who had, like all Frenchwomen, a gift for light conversation." Anaïs, "without drinking [was] drunk," able only to "sense things through a mist." She and the women discussed each other's nails, and they commented on her "nacreous" (a word she especially liked) nail polish.

At this point, the two accounts differ. Hugo thought the "real high point of the evening came during the conversation about finger nails when Anaïs smiles at them—her madonna face smiling with sympathy and understanding." This "high point" also ends Hugo's account. Anaïs's continued: the women led the way upstairs and she "enjoyed looking at [their] naked walk." Of the evening that was supposed to have been for Hugo, Anaïs wrote: "all the acrid savours of my blind desires, my frenzied yearnings for unknown experiences dissolved in that room." The women performed with dildos, demonstrating poses they called "Arabian, Spanish, Parisienne, love when one does not have the price of a hotel room, taxi . . . when one is sleepy." But Anaïs said she and Hugo learned nothing new because "in moments of white heat" their "instincts had taught all."

Anaïs interrupted to ask, as if the prostitutes were shopgirls showing different kinds of merchandise, for "lesbian poses." The large woman demonstrated oral clitoral stimulation and brought the small one to orgasm. After ten years of marriage and several sexual encounters with Henry Miller, Anaïs Nin discovered the clitoris, spellbound, as she learned for the first time of "a new secret place in the woman's body, the source of a new joy which I had sensed sometimes but never definitely."[34] She was so excited, she was "no longer woman," but "a man touching the core of June's being. Madness." And Hugo was "in turmoil." She asked if he wanted one of the women: "Take her. I swear to you I won't mind, darling."

"Utter madness" did not engulf them, and "the room seemed dirty" in their "half-sanity." They left and went dancing, then went home and made violent love. She thought the evening a great success because Hugo was "now liberated." But she also wrote that he raised the question of what they would have done "if there had been a man" instead of two women. "So we don't know yet," he concluded.

She thought the evening was "beautifully carried off, triumphantly, joyously." But the fact remains: he could not write a word about what they witnessed and her last line seems a telling indicator of the deflation they both felt: "We are killing phantoms."

The next day, Hugo was felled by symptoms that attacked when he was under stress: massive stomach cramps, severe headaches, and unfocused anxiety. When Anaïs went to the pharmacy he apologized for the inconvenience. "You are worth mending," she replied.

She had mended herself a month before, spending February at a Swiss spa where she had massages, drank the waters, and had the tip of her downward drooping nose surgically removed. Also, she wrote letters to Henry and composed two different diaries in leather-bound journals, one red and the other green because Hugo had discovered the red (or "real," as she called it) when she forgot to lock it away.[35]

He knew of her affair with Miller, but he wanted to read written proof of it. All he found was euphemism and evasion. She had written only of her "lack of resistance before an impulse, a craving," and her "mad act" (which could have meant anything). She described how Henry had driven her to "the humiliation of having one's beastly instincts free." Next came a topic that infuriated Hugo, as she wrote about how she urged Henry to "resign [from the lycée] and come home," and she would meet all his needs so that he could do nothing but write. Her next entry states that Hugo read this journal and "now he suffers."

He confronted her with the diary as evidence of her infidelity, and she did then what she would do for the rest of their more than fifty-year marriage: she persuaded him—because of course he wanted to be persuaded—that this was an "imaginary" journal "of a possessed woman" and not the "real one." The "real one," she insisted, was just like the red in size and shape but it had a green cover.

She had temporarily misplaced it, but would find it and show it to him when he returned from the bank that night. She then rushed to the little shop in Paris where she bought all her diaries in those years, and worked at double speed and in deep secrecy to write enough entries to bring the green journal up to date with the red. And so she convinced Hugo that the red (which was really "true") was "false," and the green "decoy diary" (which was really "false") was true.[36]

Thus Hugo willingly assumed the role he would play for the rest of their lives together: the big buffoon to whom she lied and cuckolded at will. Just as he had earlier written that "a little" of Anaïs went "a long way" with him; now he said he cared not "what" she did (carefully avoiding "with whom" she did it), just so she always returned to him.[37] He made his bargain and went on to live with it, head held high and seemingly impervious to the snickers and japes of incredulous outsiders.

After several weeks of writing in both diaries, she decided she could not keep up the pretense any longer and abandoned the red. The green thus became, by default, the "real" diary for the rest of the time she wrote in it.

The question of lying loomed large, however, throughout the short time she wrote in the red. Henry had caught her in several lies of no real import and could not understand why she resorted to such convoluted tales when a simple explanation would have sufficed. Her explanation was that she was "in full rebellion against [her own] mind." Unlike Hugo, Henry was not taken in by her tall tales and insisted she tell the truth. Angrily, she defended herself: "I lie by impulse, by emoting, by white heat."[38]

Her lies were not harmful, she wrote, because "even when I lie, I lie only mensonges vital, the lies which give life."[39] She defended them as "not superfluous, unnecessary or venimous or self-glorifying," and justified them as "different kinds of lies, the special lies which I tell for very specific reasons—to improve on living." That she lied to "improve the reality" became both excuse and justification, as she exhorted others to "live life as a dream, make the dream real."[40]

The expression "mensonges vital" occurs frequently in the diaries from this point on, mostly as a means of helping her remember the many lies she told.[41] She continued to personify the diary as the best friend and confidante she never found in another living person. It remained the one place where she believed she told the absolute truth, and *mensonges vital* helped her to believe that she was doing so without actually having to do it. That is, by admitting that she was writing a lie, she avoided having to write the truth, and the lie then became the written repository for the truth, which only her memory could release. She could stand to acknowledge the truth in her mind, but she simply could not bear to write it in the diary.

But the necessary lies took their toll in other ways. Joaquín told her that Eduardo accused her of having no sense of reality: "That's why she likes Henry. She gets reality through him, from him." Anaïs needed to find someone other than herself to blame, and Rosa, distressed by the havoc she feared Henry would wreak upon the family, was closest to hand. Anaïs lambasted her mother for having kept her weak and dependent rather than allowing her to grow "wilful and strong." —A remark that requires careful appraisal rather than quick acceptance.

Rosa finally delivered an ultimatum: she would not stand by and watch Anaïs ruin her life and destroy Hugo's in the process. If Henry was not out of their lives when she and Joaquín returned from Spain, she would move from Louveciennes.[42] If Rosa left, it would be the first time in Anaïs's almost thirty years of life that she was not living with her mother. Fear of being without Rosa gave way to glee: Anaïs envisioned having Henry move into Joaquín's bedroom and studio, but she quickly realized that he was "no Proust, lingering and dwelling on the meaning of life. He is always in movement and lives by gusts."[43] The only gusts at Louveciennes would be those kicked up by Hugo's anger, so she abandoned the thought.

Then there was the tremendous disappointment when the Lawrence book was published in 1932. Waverley Root, later a food critic, gave it a "patronizing and revoltingly sexist review,"[44] calling it heady stuff for a mere woman to have written. Mentioned in passing in a review of other books about Lawrence in *The Times Literary Supplement,* it was otherwise ignored. "Dismay, pain, among the prejudiced ones—always that small closed world which fires me to rebellion and debauch," she told the diary.[45]

"Fuck them all," Henry said, urging her to go off with him somewhere to live like peasants in eternal sunshine off the fat of the land and write whatever they wanted. This, too, terrified her, for what would she do if Henry forced her to choose between him and Hugo? Nothing gave her pleasure anymore: "I don't dare enjoy Henry's bohemian life without feeling it a harm done Hugo." So she returned, temporarily, to her life as a proper banker's very proper suburban wife.

She turned again to Eduardo, who by default had become the only living person in whom she could confide. "Eduardo says I need psychoanalysis," she wrote in April 1932, when he also said the one thing that persuaded her to reveal her deepest secrets to someone other than the diary: "He said Dr. Allendy would be like a father for me (Eduardo loves to tempt me with a father!)."

She lost no time in making her first appointment.

12

The Well-kept Mistress

HENRY LASTED THREE WEEKS in Dijon before he quit and returned to Paris. Anaïs was determined that he concentrate on his writing, so she guaranteed him a monthly stipend, swearing it would never be less than $200 (half the $400 Hugo gave her to run the house and pay her personal expenses). No matter how unsavory the details, Henry always told the truth to his pen pal Emil Schnellock, but this time he merely said he was "getting sound financial help of late" and would "someday . . . spill the beans."[1]

As the Depression deepened, Henry knew he would soon be "free again" when his proofreading job was eliminated. "Fred will look after me," he wrote, in the apartment Anaïs found for him and Perlès in the working-class suburb of Clichy. "I will stay home like a well-kept mistress and polish my nails."

The apartment had few furnishings, so Anaïs spent what little was left after doling out Henry's allowance and paying her household expenses to buy dishes, cutlery, sheets, and curtains. She installed a Victrola and recordings of Bach and Beethoven, his favorites; he needed reams of paper, vast quantities of ink, and a comfortable cushion for his chair; hoping he would take up diary writing, she also bought various kinds and sizes of notebooks.[2]

Her ministrations caused Henry to wax poetic about the virtues of French women as compared to American. "No better wives in the world," he decided, because "love and fondling" made them "obedient, very affectionate [and] animal-like." Henry thought it "beautiful."

He was, of course, describing his own "Mona Païva—over the i two dots," as he called Anaïs when he wrote to Emil, too embarrassed to give her real name. "Mona" was also the name Henry called June in his fiction; by conferring it on an idealized Anaïs, he enmeshed and entwined his love-goddess wife-muse with the "friend-confidante-colleague-helpmate-lover, all in the same person."[3] It made him feel omnipotent.

In Henry's words, once he was settled in Clichy, he and Anaïs spent most of their time drinking and "fucking." Anaïs's language was much more lofty: she preferred expressions such as "moist flowing honey" for the fluids of arousal, and it was always "my love" who "took" her with his "glowing, pulsating member."[4]

Because Hugo was often away, Anaïs spent most of her time in Clichy, leaving her house, two dogs, Hugo's several cats, the chickens, the grounds and the gardens, all to Rosa's supervision. An emotional triangle formed, as Fred made no secret of the fact that he, too, would not mind bedding down the likes of Mona Païva. The three spent their days writing, "every day, in the hope of being published,"[5] then ate the supper that Anaïs shopped and paid for, prepared, and cleaned up after, all the while talking about literature.

Late at night, after as much cheap wine as they could imbibe, sex sooner or later became the topic, usually starting with how best to express it in their writing. The two men frequently traded overtly hostile remarks, with Anaïs as the object of their preening and posturing. Often these bouts ended when Henry took Anaïs to his room where, in the midst of their violent and noisy lovemaking, she was aware of Fred stumbling around beyond the thin wall that separated the two bedrooms.[6]

Fred's descriptions of Anaïs, "Pieta" in his book *Sentiments Limitrophes,*[7] read as if he had an unrequited crush on her, which is perhaps why he was often harsh. But as Fred was genuinely fond of Henry, he was grateful to Anaïs for Henry's keep and for making his own life comfortable as well and was not about to offend her. He believed that Anaïs "tried to make people believe she had a soft personality, but in reality, there was a hard inner core to her."[8] Fred believed Anaïs thought Henry "a genius," and that she was "in awe of him because he was a better writer than herself." He was mistaken, however, when he added, "She loved Miller and I was his friend, so she liked me," for Anaïs not only disliked Fred, she distrusted him.

When Henry described life in Clichy, he tried to give the impression that eating and having sex mattered most to him and Fred, but it was really writing on which they concentrated.[9] They were as influenced by Jolas's views in *transition* as Anaïs was, especially his manifesto, "The Revolution of the Word," and slim book, *The Language of the Night.*[10] Two comments in particular from the "Revolution of the Word" struck Anaïs: "the imagination in search of a fabulous world is autonomous and unconfined," and "The writer expresses. He does not communicate." Jolas's decrees gladdened her undisciplined heart, for she had always resisted anyone who tried to impose order upon her free-floating prose. Narrative for Jolas was not "mere anecdote" but rather "the projection of a metamorphosis of reality." The literary creator had every right to discard the rules imposed by textbooks and dictionaries, to use words "of his own fashioning and to disregard existing grammatical and syntactical laws." "Time" in any sense at all, was simply a "tyranny to be abolished." Jolas, it seemed, spoke directly to the writer Anaïs Nin, and she was thrilled.[11]

Anaïs described what she and Henry could do for each other's writing: "I need a father, a guide. I need Henry's experience, his knowledge, his maturity . . . He needs my clarity and subtlety."[12] She showed him her diary entries about June to help him get over his block and write about her, but also (and more important) because she had written nothing beside her Lawrence book that she was not ashamed to show him. Everything else seemed old-fashioned, precious, naïve.

Henry's contribution to her writing was significant. He took it seriously and was always willing to discuss it, word by word, line for line. No idea was too silly, too outrageous; everything was open for discussion. But unlike Hugo, Henry did not give her total admiration and frequently made her angry with his critiques. She curbed her anger and listened carefully to what he said. When he offered to correct her English, she agreed because her mind raced so fast that "language will always drag and lag behind."[13]

He was fascinated with the diaries and found Anaïs's comments about June liberating. He praised her for being able to analyze June so dispassionately. Anaïs knew a weapon when she saw one and used the diaries to deepen the wedge between husband and wife.

Henry also saw enough ideas in the diaries for any number of novels, and he urged her to turn them into fiction. "The 'I' has become a terrible habit," she confessed.[14] In a long, anguished passage about a work of fiction she proposed to call "Novel of Henry and June,"[15] she attempted to explain her dilemma so that she might better understand it herself: "I tried to write as in a novel. It was hard. Then I wrote in the first person and it came easy. It is a slavish habit. I make use of all the talks I hear between Henry and Fred . . . [and] Fraenkel and other people. I note everything down. Why, why can't I write a novel, objective, with all my inventions? It is such a roundabout method [to] write a diary which I will have to transform later into a novel."

This inability to create fiction was one of the reasons she entered psychoanalysis.

On April 22, 1932, she wrote the first of many long passages in the diary about Dr. René Allendy, whom she visited initially because Eduardo wanted her to so badly that he paid for it. She was uneasy about the visit because Eduardo had insisted she must also undergo analysis to free herself of the compulsion to write in the diary. He meant it to comfort her, but it had just the opposite effect, for to give up writing in the diary meant relinquishing control of her life.

She was reluctant to trust Allendy: "I want him to say . . . something unsubtle and formulistic," she wrote later, "because if he does there will be another man I cannot lean on and therefore will have to go on conquering myself and my life alone, without help."[16]

René Allendy was one of the most prominent of the "first generation" of psychoanalysts in France, mainly because he was one of the twelve founders of the Société psychanalytique de Paris (SPP), although arguably its most "marginal."[17] A homeopathist who was fascinated by the occult, he was the author of more than twenty books about everything from *The Symbolism of Numbers* to *Capitalism and Sexuality,* writings best classified as falling somewhere between the quirky and the bizarre, "as vast as his personality was strange [and] best consigned to oblivion."[18]

Allendy's interest in astrology drew Eduardo to consult him, but Anaïs was more interested in his theories of how dreams reflected the Collective Unconscious. His most basic tenet was that neurosis was an illness of which the artist must be cured in order to function properly in the world and create. When Anaïs learned this, she was inclined to trust him, for she wanted nothing more than to rid herself of the block that kept her from converting the diary into fiction.

Anaïs Nin was the ideal analysand for Allendy, who was interested in writers and whose treatments (though classically Freudian in his early years of practice) were influenced by his "psychobiographical conceptions of art."[19] From the first "conversation," as she called their sessions, she recorded everything in the diary as soon as they finished. She also began to interpolate her digressive thoughts and observations. She was often frustrated: "There is a baffling problem in my writing down my talks with Allendy. I do not seem able to relate the fumblings, the shadowy portions. . . . We did not arrive suddenly at the clear cut phrases I put down. There were hesitations, innuendos, detours. I don't give the progressive development. There is a sifter inside my head. Is that good or bad?"

Any analyst will testify to the faultiness of memory when an analysand tries to recollect exactly what happened in a session. However, as the only surviving record of Anaïs Nin's analysis by Dr. René Allendy is in her diaries, we can relive it only through her written memory of the actual session. In this instance, her account of the first few sessions is probably one of the most trustworthy segments of her entire oeuvre, simply because she strove to re-create it as accurately as possible so she could return to study it time and again and thus gain a better understanding of herself.

In the first conversation, about Eduardo, Allendy asked if she realized that she was the most important woman in his life. She quotes him as saying, "Eduardo has been obsessed with you. You are his imago. He has seen you as the mother, the sister, and the most unattainable one. To conquer you meant conquering himself, his neuroses, the world."[20] She told Allendy that she did not want to hurt her cousin, but her feelings were familial, and to sleep with him would be like committing incest. She quotes his reply: "It would be good, it is almost necessary for Eduardo's cure, that you should have relations with him." She writes that she demurred; sexual relations for her had to be based on love. Allendy is quoted as saying, "You take these things very seriously, I see," a remark that emphasizes his view of women as little more than "the cup which receives the seed and preserves it."[21]

Anaïs insisted she would do anything to help Eduardo short of sleeping with him. She begged Allendy not to destroy Eduardo's newfound self-confidence but to call her instead "neurotic, afraid of sex." She felt "strong enough to take any neurosis" upon her own shoulders to spare Eduardo's macho Cuban feelings. Allendy supposedly thought this a good solution, as it would show Eduardo "there are other neurotics in the world." His next remark, however, was the hook that reeled her in: "and of course you may be. You seem to lack a bit of confidence."

She was stunned. "That word [neurotic] acted on me as if he touched an open wound." Emotion poured out as she told him how her father's rejection had affected her, how her father said he did not want a girl and that she was ugly, and how he never caressed or complimented her. She relived the time she almost died in Brussels, the beatings in Arcachon, and "the hard cold blue eyes upon me" as he photographed her naked in her bath. She blushed to remember the "unnatural joy" she felt when he sent a simple note when she returned to Paris as a married woman, addressing her as *"ma jolie."*

She told Allendy that, having gotten no love from her father, "I suffered within Mother's own body the injuries she suffered." Remembering how her father had told his children in Arcachon that he did not want them, she said, "What he meant for Mother, I also took for myself."

She told him about John Erskine and Henry Miller, ages fifty and forty-one respectively, adding as an aside that, like her father, both her extramarital lovers played the piano. Allendy pounced upon this: "You seek the conquest of older men in order to feel that you can win your father." It made her think about how "a child's confidence once shaken and destroyed [by an adult] should have such repercussions on her whole life."

Allendy had given Anaïs the first of the classical Freudian interpretations that characterized her analysis, mechanically noting down her declarations and appending a moral judgment stripped of all interpretations to everything she told him.[22] She was such a novice, however, that everything he said about her relationship to her real father and her search for substitutes rang so true that she could not stop thinking about it.

Allendy told her she had behaved beautifully to her cousin, for "in general a woman considers man as an enemy and she is glad when she can humiliate or destroy him." She asked how, as a woman, he thought she should behave. Women's responses were "still an enigma," Allendy replied, and thus far had not contributed anything to psychoanalysis because they were not worthy of serious study. In his view, woman's primary role was the one Anaïs had embraced so eagerly, helpmeet and handmaiden to men.

She thought there was nothing more to say about Eduardo, so she prepared to leave. When Allendy said, "I don't believe you need me. You seem very able to take care of yourself," she felt "immense distress" and said she wanted another session, this time to talk about herself.

But when she spoke to him next, and talked about the problems with her writing, he had no advice to offer. Anaïs had written two pages of a "new novel" under the influence of "modern writing" and in "a surrealistic way"[23] but could not write her way out of the impasse in which she was sure analysis had thrown her. She was exhausted by such intensive scrutiny of her past, but what really frightened her was that she was too tired and confused to write about it.

Analysis also made her long for Hugo, who was always traveling these days. Sometimes she lied to Henry so that she could spend the night alone in her own bed, clutching some object of Hugo's in order to feel him near. He was the only one, she decided, "who possesses me internally." It made her impatient with Henry. One night when he was talking about literature, she caught herself "listening like a child." At first she liked the feeling, but then she grew furious with herself.

When she described her anger to Allendy, he told her it was a natural reaction: "You *need* a father. We all do." And then he launched into an explanation that she accepted wholeheartedly, thinking it contained the very key to her behavior: "You loved your Father devotedly, abnormally, and you hated the sexual reason which caused him to abandon you.[24] This may have created in you a certain obscure feeling against sex. This feeling asserts itself unconsciously in your desire to win over older men without giving yourself. You are willing Henry to a kind of castration. Your feelings towards men are ambivalent. You need to dominate, and yet you want to be dominated."

For the first time they talked about Hugo. She told Allendy that because she was so sure of his love for her, she was able to give herself "entirely" to him. Hugo was the only person who really loved her, she said, "without egotism." Yet she was unable to accept the tranquillity and stability of Hugo's love, which led her to seek the pain of various forms of abuse, especially rejection, and was also the reason she willingly engaged in rivalry with June.

Allendy had the answer to this at once. It was all due to her "strong sense of inferiority . . . consistent desire to be punished, humiliated or abandoned," and "strong sense of guilt" for having loved her father too much. It was what led her to love her mother so intensely during her adolescence and why she sought "punishment" in all her adult relationships. "There is a desire to punish and castrate men," he warned her. "You are trying to identify yourself with me, to do my work. Have you not wished to surpass men in their work?" He seems to have wanted to punish her for the very strength he accused her of not having.

She denied trying to identify with him or trying to compete with men, offering examples such as how she had given Henry her typewriter, how she had sought to help him with his book on Lawrence rather than promoting her own, and how she had no intention of attending to her own writing until all Henry's needs were met. Allendy changed tactics and questioned her again, lacerating her sharply about her lack of self-confidence. She left the session repeating over and over, "I bleed. I bleed."

Several days later, she returned, but this time with "a growing resistance to analysis." She told Allendy that she did not like him (which often happens at this point in treatment). What she did like, however, was that he had "proved stronger than I." Yet as the hour progressed, she sensed that he was creating difficulties that were not real, that he was seeking to "re-awaken" her fears and doubts: "And for that I hate him." In reading the notes she made of her dreams, he decided there was a strong "masculine" element in her writing, which he deemed a negative quality. It made her question her "lack of confidence in her womanly power."

At this point she took control of her analysis—at least in her mind and her diary. Allendy began to question her about "dédoublement,"[25] the splitting or dividing of the self, in her case because of her dependence on the diary. She had not hidden her obsessive need to write down what they discussed the moment they finished talking. He noted how she seemed not to pay attention to their conversation in her eagerness to go away and write about it.

She gloated about her techniques for eluding him. Coyly, she asked about the books he had written, expressing great interest in wanting to read them. Diverted, he described them. She began to play a dangerous new game and knew exactly what she was doing: "I experienced a mischievous dédoublement. I mean that I was quite aware that he expected me to become interested in him and that I didn't like playing the game while knowing it was a game."

She left feeling less confident and more self-conscious than ever. Her victory over Allendy was so easy that it made her uneasy. So she practiced controlling Henry and decided it was not very exciting because by the time she finished manipulating his emotions, he was behaving toward her "like a serious husband."

Ever since she assumed full responsibility for making Henry's life tranquil and stable, he had been writing steadily and she was happy in the belief that she would eventually be known as the muse who made possible the most creative period of his life. She decided there would be no more sex with him because he needed a critic, companion, and guide more than a mistress. In the confusion induced by Allendy, she thought it likely that she would once again serve Hugo as a traditional, faithful wife.

Several days later, she returned to Allendy, filled with hatred and rage, feeling sorry for herself, trapped by the various kinds of economic dependence she had created. He asked why she had created these circumstances, why she did not confide in others as they did in her, why she insisted on being so reserved, on not having good friends with whom she could relax and be herself. Was she afraid that if she were honest she would be loved less? "Yes," she said, "quite definitely." Well then, when others confided in her, did she love them less? "No," she said, thinking of Hugo's and Eduardo's confessions. And then came the question she had been evading all along and simply could not answer truthfully: "Have you ever imagined what a relief it would be if you could be entirely natural with everybody?"

Allendy asked why she wore such exaggerated makeup and dressed and walked so seductively: "Only people who are not sure act seductively." His comment triggered memory of a dance recital, when she thought she saw her father's disapproving face in the audience and became clumsy and thrown out of kilter, even though she knew that he was nowhere near Paris. Allendy's diagnosis was swift: "You wanted him to be there. As you have since a child wanted to seduce your father and did not succeed you have also developed a strong sense of guilt. You want to dazzle him physically and at the same time when you succeed, something makes you stop with fear almost. You tell me you haven't danced since."

"No, no," she insisted, it was all due to her bad health that she stopped dancing, not to her father. "I have no doubt that if you

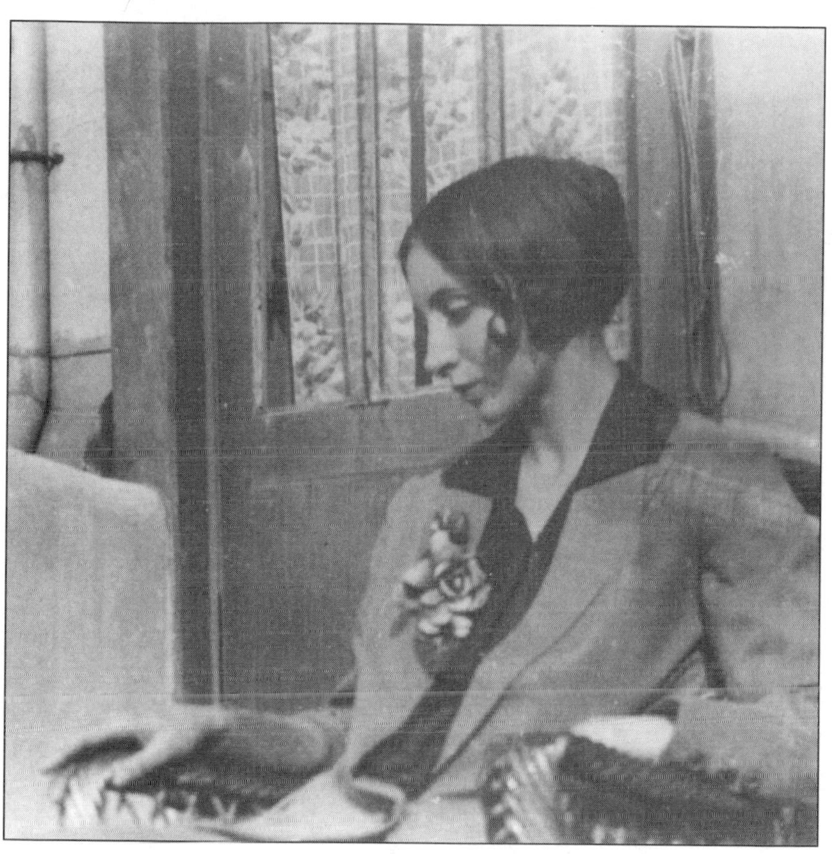

Anaïs Nin in "The High Place."

Dr. René Allendy.

should succeed in your writing you would also give it up," Allendy stated.[26]

She confessed at the next session that her finances were in such chaos that she would have to curtail analysis. Because everything she could scrape together went to meet Henry's needs, she had even stopped paying her household bills. Allendy told her she could pay partly by working for him, translating psychological writings he wished to read from English into French, doing research for his own writing, and cataloguing the work of others.

But she soon discovered what hard work it was, and how ill-equipped she was to translate technical psychological terms. Besides, she was working closely with Henry, who had embarked on the losing battle of trying to write his own book about Lawrence. Henry was not sure if he admired Lawrence or if he needed to denigrate him in order to assure his own primacy as a novelist. He was churning out reams of thought, all of it contradictory. Anaïs put her own writing aside to try to impose some sort of order upon Henry's, which left no time for the disciplined attention Allendy's required. Anxious as she was for the sessions to continue, she did not want to do the work to pay for them.

Perhaps that was why, in her next session, she turned the discussion to her body, pirouetting as she demonstrated how she was underweight and underdeveloped. Her breasts were too small, she said as she added calculatedly, "perhaps because I have masculine elements in me." He began to question why she felt this way, when she stood up and abruptly unbuttoned her blouse: "You are the doctor, I'll simply show them."

Allendy laughed away her fears. " 'Perfectly feminine,' he said, 'small but very well formed.' " A long passage follows in which she described his lyrical description of her beauty, charm, grace, wit, elegance, and many more qualities besides. It echoes suspiciously the many others she dutifully recorded in the diary, giving detailed descriptions of effusive compliments supposedly paid to her, in all their minute detail.

At their next meeting, Allendy told her he was observing the "unnaturalness" of her personality. She was "completely artificial" and "concealed" her true self with a manner "seductive, affable, and gay," while inside, she was "a hidden wreck." She was trying so hard to succeed in one of the arts in order "to assert [her] superiority," presumably over men.[27]

All the while, she was playing a game even though she did not admit it. Each time he questioned her too probingly, she turned the conversation to her body, particularly her breasts or her long legs. When she sat, she deliberately hitched her skirt above her knees. With her top button undone provocatively, she bent over and cupped his hand as he lit her cigarettes. She denied all flirtations to herself—that is, to the diary—but she knew what she was doing. If she knew that it was only a matter of time before she allowed him to seduce her, surely he must have known as well.

"Psychology will help me to be more truthful with myself," she wrote after her first session with Allendy. Unfortunately, it only provided another "artificial personality" behind which she could hide whatever her real self was at the time.

13

The Banker Woman

"Mr. Nin," also known as "the Problem," was back in Paris and causing trouble simply by being there. Joaquín was giving his annual recital at the Salle Chopin-Pleyel in late May, and Rosa was as excited as if she were the performer. Anaïs worried, too, but only about how to persuade Allendy to attend and how to keep Hugo and Henry apart.

She wanted to nudge her relationship with Allendy onto a different, more personal level than that of doctor and patient,[1] preferably in a setting such as her home, where she could control it. She hit on a less obvious (and perhaps less threatening) plan: to invite him to Joaquín's recital, and began by inventing a dream. She told Allendy she dreamed he attended the concert and provided the self-confidence she needed to get through it. Before he could ask why she would need support when it was Joaquín who was to perform, she turned the dream into a joke and asked offhandedly if he would attend. To her surprise, Allendy accepted.

The concert was successful despite a rocky beginning. "Mr. Nin" swept in as if he were the evening's host and positioned himself at the door to greet the guests. Rosa made such a howl of protest that Joaquín's manager, afraid blows would be exchanged, asked Joaquín what to do: "I told him literally to tell my father to sit down and behave himself or I would come out and tell him myself. Lovely prelude to a difficult recital."[2]

Anaïs wrote about the evening over the next several days, an account that had serious intimations of her future relationships with her parents: "I observed my Mother's red-faced vulgarity and my Father's cold, aristocratic reserve. I hate my Mother. Joaquín's success. *Her* Joaquín. *Her* children. 'The strong possessive instinct is a sign of retarded evolution; the really evolved human being has a sense of the universal,' Allendy says."

Rosa was preparing to leave for Hendaye, still threatening not to return to Louveciennes. Mother and daughter were barely speaking, and there had also been a steady exodus of maids since Henry all but moved in whenever Hugo was away. Anaïs was of two minds about Rosa's threatened move. On the one hand, it would mean total freedom; on the other, it would mean serious financial repercussions if Hugo had to support another, separate, household.

Anaïs performed a magnificent juggling act, giving a few francs to her most pressing creditors as she wheedled more of their still-needed services, cajoling others to wait a little longer for payment. She needed money each month for Henry's allowance, so she lied to Hugo about such things as cracked masonry on the house walls that had not been repaired. She inflated her dressmaking bills by ordering cheaper clothes or none at all. When Hugo demanded to see the new wardrobe and when she had nothing to show, he erupted.

Hugo usually gave Rosa's stipend to Anaïs, who then persuaded Rosa to lend her some of it to pacify her many creditors. Now Rosa refused, saying she needed to save money to move. She thought first of buying a modest house, but Anaïs squelched the plan, knowing it would tie up Hugo's income indefinitely, and threatened to have him cut the stipend drastically unless Rosa rented. Knowing that she would do it, Rosa left quietly for Hendaye with nothing settled.

Eduardo went on holiday, also angry and barely speaking to Anaïs because of how lovingly she behaved toward Henry and Allendy at Joaquín's concert. Eduardo was goaded into another flurry of insistence that she sleep with him, and when she refused, he threatened to tell Hugo about her affair with Henry. Anaïs laughed, and he went off in a huff. Hugo was away as well, practically commuting to Berlin. Henry was happily settled in contented domesticity that centered around writing prolifically each day. With her men occupied, Anaïs was left free to concentrate on Allendy.

She began their next session as she usually did, by asking him to talk about his political theory of analysis in his new book, *Capita-*

lisme et Sexualité, which was attracting attention in manuscript among French intellectuals well before publication. Allendy had barely started before she turned the conversation toward Joaquín's concert and herself.[3] She told him she had been deeply disturbed by his "sad eyes" and "troubled face" whenever she caught his glance. Her remark made him blush, so she quickly asked for his impressions of the other men in her life to remind him that there were indeed other men who desired her.

He said Henry looked "like a German painter—too soft, perhaps two-faced";[4] Hugo was "an unconscious homosexual" ("Now I'm surprised!" she wrote without further comment);[5] and he was struck by Joaquín Nin's youthful appearance. He seemed prepared to talk about her father in detail, then caught himself and asked why she did not want to be analyzed on that particular day. To Anaïs, it was a sign of success: she had succeeded in winning his confidence. Her aim henceforth was "to analyze him, to find a weakness in him, to conquer a little because I have been conquered."

When she wrote of that day in the diary, she elaborated upon conquest, now a major theme in her life. Carefully avoiding all mention of John Erskine, whose name she hardly invoked anymore, she listed her "conquests so far"—Hugo, Eduardo, and Henry. Now she wanted another: Allendy. Several days later she returned to her game. "He drives his questions relentlessly," she noted, "but he is confused. He does not see clearly." In a daring new move, she canceled her appointments for the following week without explanation.

She liked the anxiety he showed a week later when she arrived on time and as if nothing amiss had happened and launched directly into a detailed description of her sexual liaisons with Henry. She had told Allendy how they had intercourse in Clichy, various hotel rooms, and the house and garden at Louveciennes. Now she took perverse pleasure in watching his face as she recounted what they did to excite each other. She did not like "lying together like lesbians," she told him, and fellatio repulsed her. Allendy's response was not the prurient one she hoped for; instead, he said he worried about what Hugo would do if she became pregnant. He traveled so much she might be unable to convince him it was his child. At her next session, Allendy gave her a diaphragm, which she kept for a week before returning it clean but used, saying she had repented and had no further need of it.

Several weeks later, on her way to a summer holiday with Hugo, she told Allendy that she was ending the analysis forever. In that case, he said, they should spend their fifty minutes in conversation, which they did. As she prepared to leave, he asked her quietly to kiss him goodbye. She bent over and they touched both cheeks lightly in the French manner. Once on the street, she was angry that he had not been seized by passion.

She brooded about Allendy's seeming passivity, just as she had brooded for years about how John Erskine rejected her at the crucial moment before intercourse. Suddenly, the idea came to her that Hugo should begin analysis with Allendy in the fall. The thought gave her the same "frisson" as when she invited Henry and his friends Walter Lowenfels, Michael Fraenkel, and Fred Perlès to Louveciennes. She could hardly avoid inviting Fred, Henry's roommate, but invitations to Fraenkel had a more serious purpose. He and Lowenfels had founded Carrefour (Crossroads) Books and agreed informally to publish Henry's novel. Anaïs wanted to curry favor on his behalf.

But the "frisson" on such occasions was not enough, and she courted discovery by inviting Henry alone. After an informal dinner, Hugo told Anaïs he felt better about being in Henry's company because he was now very sure their relationship was only one of two writers working together. She rewarded Hugo by being unusually passionate that night in bed, while Henry lay sleeping just down the hall in their guest room. She wondered if he heard.[6]

On Sunday, September 18, 1932, Hugo had his first session of psychoanalysis.[7] There was only enough time for him to touch upon the major points he wanted to explore, all of which revolved around his relationship to Anaïs. Allendy had a ready diagnosis: Hugo's basic problem was probably rooted in his "preponderance of mysticism," which "perhaps weakened the sexual side" of his marriage to Anaïs.

Hugo thought a great deal about this because it rankled. Allendy, he wrote, "must not get the idea that I am not satisfied sexually." On the whole, Hugo thought he and Anaïs were "doing well" despite the increasing frequency and vehemence of their arguments since Henry came into their life. "It is true we fuck better in the collision of meeting after a trip. Perhaps Anaïs is right in saying we should have regular separations. There is such a thing as getting into a routine and letting sex degenerate into a habit. But today was perfect. I took her like a whore and that satisfied both of us."

Hugo's analysis was brief, as was his record of it. He had serious reservations about Allendy from the beginning, especially after he read *Capitalisme et Sexualité.* It was difficult for Hugo to accept Allendy's frequently facile and superficial criticisms of the capitalist economic system and weakened his confidence in the analyst himself. He found it difficult to accept Allendy's dictum that his every view was "part of my opposition to my father."

Allendy regarded Hugo's marriage to Anaïs as his only victory over his father, who won the ultimate and final victory because his death left Hugo riddled with remorse. Allendy insisted that Hugo had since unconsciously denied himself sexual pleasure and could take only small satisfaction in his business successes; furthermore, Hugo added to his self-punishment by "directly bringing upon myself the loss of all my money and the burden of debt in addition." Hugo agreed that he was prone to triumph in his business dealings through indirection and evasion: "What an admission I have just made! That I succeed by . . . a woman's methods!" He decided that, by using "indirect methods" to keep Anaïs bound to their marriage, he was defeating his purpose through less-than-masculine tactics, but "if I remember the danger I need not fear the comparison."

Allendy also told Hugo that his "individualism" was in grave danger because he was not rooted in a family, culture, or country. His lack of roots caused him to cling to Anaïs and make her the center of his world, a too-heavy burden that frightened her even as she strained to accept it. Hugo agreed that he often felt like a drifter, especially as a teenager when his parents and everything American had become foreign to him.

At this point, Hugo ended his analytic journal and recorded only his dreams.[8] In retrospect, he stopped at a perilous point of self-discovery, poised on the brink of having to confront the insights Allendy might have shown him.

Hugo and Anaïs probably should have found comfort in their mutual status as displaced exiles, but did not. It was a major topic throughout their intensive therapy, which began in 1930 and continued until they died. They sought the answers to many questions, but primary among them was the search for their proper identity and the place where they truly belonged. It was something they never really resolved. But in their first year of analysis, their major difference concerned their response to each other. Hugo wanted only Anaïs for comfort, solace, sexual pleasure, and satisfaction of every possible kind. As the year came to an end, she made the abrupt decision that she could find none of these qualities in Hugo and would have to seek them elsewhere.

Anaïs returned from her summer holiday determined to produce a work of fiction. Henry presented a stumbling block, however, which she did not discern until she read of a parallel relationship: "I've just been reading the life of Georgette Leblanc and Materlink. Very interesting. She reproaches him all the time for not having given her credit for all the inspiration she gave him. He used to write down all she said and say it was his!"[9]

She had written approximately forty typed pages about June—notes, snatches of dialogue, and texts—that ranged from descriptions of body, clothes, and mannerisms to analytic interpretations of her personality. There was also a sustained and thoughtful literary analysis of the role June played in Henry's life and work as his wife and fictional muse. Anaïs hoped her reflections would become a bridge to help her cross from the first-person introspection of the diary to the originality of pure fiction.

Henry read these pages avidly, finding in them the subtle kinds of character analysis that his emotional involvement with June kept him from being able to express. Anaïs's writing was measured and precise, exactly the opposite of his booming, pell-mell barrage. Hers slowed him down and made him think, especially about unity and organization. "Would you mind if I borrowed these?" he asked, and then went on to incorporate almost everything, just as she wrote it, into his own book, *Tropic of Capricorn.*

At first Anaïs was thrilled to think that she had produced something good enough that Henry would want to appropriate it. As he had had "enough romance to nourish his work"[10] from other women, she saw his blatant grab of her writing as the necessary means to dissolve his creative block in writing about June. Anaïs described their working relationship dispassionately in the diary: "We make notes and plans. We dissect June's lies. Henry asks me questions." So she continued to be his "critic, companion and guide," but was disturbed enough by the way he so casually took her work and made it his own that she discussed it with Allendy: "I gave away to Henry many of my ideas on June and he is using them. I feel impoverished and he knows it because he writes me that he feels like a crook. . . . I am sad, sad over all this. I feel empty handed, sucked dry!"[11]

Allendy told Anaïs that she had turned Henry into a trophy, deliberately instigating a rivalry with June to see who could win him/it; that she had the temporary advantage because she was on the scene and June was not; that by giving away her work as well as her sexual favors, she had armed herself with two other weapons to June's single one, herself. He cautioned her that no matter what Henry's relationship with other women, the moment June appeared, he would return to her. Allendy advised Anaïs to give Henry up rather than risk abandonment again. She rejected his advice, saying he did not realize that she was the stronger: "It is I who am making Henry."[12] Allendy insisted that her control was illusory, that Henry was weak, a parasite who would prey on her, "cruel, criminal and drunk."

Anaïs was unswayed: "I don't know why Allendy must stress [Henry's] weakness when that is just what interests me, to change and re-create it." She insisted that she learned much from "filling out Henry's portrait of June," that it allowed her to "write as a *woman* and as a woman only." She had come to terms with Henry's theft of her June material, but she was "still rich" and "happy."[13]

She believed she had guided him from unpublishable ramblings to the two successful *Tropics: Cancer* and *Capricorn*. She took credit for identifying what were to become his major themes, the lives and adventures of himself and his friends, and their extraordinary (i.e., for the historical time in which he wrote) sexuality. She insisted that in a number of crucial instances (June, for example), she provided the outline of what he should write, and he merely filled in the detailed observations.

With Miller's projected study of D. H. Lawrence, this is certainly true. When Henry found himself unable to decide how to construct the text, Nin dutifully made another forty-or-so pages of notes on Lawrence, which he studied rigorously and tried to incorporate into his own work. Henry, however, could never decide whether to praise Lawrence's genius or attack it in preparation for declaring himself the better writer and Lawrence only the precursor who paved his way.

Miller's influence on Nin is easier, at first glance, to categorize. He

Henry Miller in the doorway at Louveciennes.

read her manuscripts as carefully and thoughtfully as she read his, with the same rigorous analysis and criticism. However, his influence was mainly grammatical.

"Jesus! Get cured of this once and for all!!" he wrote in the margin opposite a particularly convoluted sentence in her "Rab" story. "It is one of your ever-recurring and abominable locutions. Study it! See what's wrong with it, in English, in French, in Spanish, in any goddamned tongue!"[14]

Although Henry read her diary avidly whenever she let him, he still had serious reservations about how much time she devoted to it. Another of his comments refers to the same story, a description of two people lying together after sex in which Anaïs piled adjectives upon superlatives, dangled participles, and unconsciously created comedic images that she certainly did not intend. Henry told her that there was an "emotional falsity" about this story, and that she should "take out all the inflation and leave the hard bare rock of concrete reality" if she wanted to evoke poignancy.

He was "laying [his criticisms] on thick," he warned, because he wanted her to "see how certain aspects of 'diary' writing lead to false accents."[15] All her attention to the diary was not helping her to write fiction, he warned, "because it is a writing behind walls, without hope of criticism or of suffering the strong light of day."

"Get me?" he asked, but of course she did not. She continued to use the word "ensorcelled," which drove him into fits of rabid hysteria: "You've got to think, to know what each word means before you can throw them about recklessly." And on this tack, he scribbled furiously: "Qualms not calms—look it up!"

The point, however, is that she had begun to write fiction with great seriousness. Each time she took the train back to Louveciennes, she pored over his corrections and made clean copies rather than writing in the diary. "Rab" (Henry) and "Mandra" (originally herself) had coalesced with her invention of "Alraune" (originally June, but now a combination of herself and June) into a new sheaf of pages she hoped would become a novel tentatively entitled "Alraune."[16] (It eventually became her first published novel, *House of Incest.*)[17] As Nin herself said almost every time she discussed her work, this novel is the primary source of everything fictional that followed.

Jung's maxim, to "proceed from the dream outward," became the controlling metaphor for how she wrote about her life as well as how she lived it. She applied Jung's exhortation to her first faltering attempts to create fiction out of a mélange of psychotherapy, surrealism, symbolism, sexuality, and sexual preference. All these were worked and reworked until the book was finally published in 1936. At that point it consisted of two tales, both basically about self-love, the first lesbian, the second incestual, two themes that had long fascinated her.

First, however, there was June.[18] Henry was happily settled into the most stable domesticity he had ever known, "almost a dream" in which he "worked without effort" and lived "a healthy normal life."[19] With Anaïs paying the bills, he "felt safe, secure." But Henry was nothing if not timid. He thought he had been so discreet about Anaïs that June would never find out about the affair. He had not counted on Fraenkel, who spent his summer holiday in New York and maliciously told June about Henry's great good fortune in acquiring Anaïs as his patron and mistress.

June booked passage to Paris and Henry waited nervously for her to descend upon Clichy. He took the precaution of returning to Anaïs all the love letters she had written to him, as well as the manuscripts of *Cancer, Capricorn,* a sheaf of notes, and the "Paris notebook." Then he breathed easier, hoping June would be so pleased to see his clean, well-ordered apartment that she would forget to ask how he afforded it.

Allendy was right: Henry had become the trophy and the two women engaged in a roundabout but deadly battle to win him. Still, it was a curious tournament in which both seemed to ignore the prize as they focused on each other, developing an intense friendship, the kind and degree of which has been an object of speculation ever since. Perhaps each vied to seduce the other as a way of diffusing attention from Henry. June, broke as always, had only words for weapons, but she used them to dangle the tantalizing possibility of sex before Anaïs because she knew how to manipulate her curiosity. Anaïs had access to Hugo's money and used it to shower June with gifts, elaborate meals, handfuls of francs for spending money, and the hint that she might just acquiesce and offer herself as a sexual object.

Henry was confused. June moved in with him but was away from Clichy most of the time. Anaïs seldom knew where June was, or when or if she would show up. One afternoon, Anaïs arrived in Clichy to find Henry writing, his manuscript carelessly tossed across the bed he slept in with June, intermingled with some of her belongings. Aroused by the sight of the bed, she "made Henry take [her]" on it several times, she "in frenzy," he "in fear" that June would return at any moment.

June, however, seemed to have no time for Henry, preferring to concentrate all her attention on Anaïs. She touched Anaïs's hair or brushed her cheek with gestures a lover might use, even rubbing her body against Anaïs's in full view of Henry and Fred. They all consumed gallons of wine and their sexual intensity grew in direct relation to the drinking.

In Clichy one night, June got falling-down drunk and collapsed on the bed in her own vomit. Anaïs spent the night lying next to her in the fetid gloom, fully clothed, staring watchfully into June's face as she snored with open mouth. Henry lay fitfully dozing in Fred's room, afraid to go in for fear of what he would find them doing.

The next morning June told Henry the lesbianism had all been an act put on for her own amusement and to trap Anaïs into telling the truth about her and him. Now she knew everything, she said, and wanted a divorce. Legend has grown around this incident, in which June is supposed to have said, "Now you have the last chapter for your fucking book."[20]

June reduced Henry to a quivering bundle of frazzled nerves by threatening him and "the banker woman" with bodily harm. Fred and Anaïs were concerned that he would collapse, and decided that Henry must leave Paris until June sailed. Anaïs raised the money to ship him off to London, ostensibly to see Rebecca West, who had written a favorable review of her Lawrence book and might like Henry's work as well as to help him find a publisher for it.

Henry was delighted with the idea of spending a Dickensian Christmas in London, but just as he was leaving, June arrived in Clichy and the frightened Henry let her take everything in his wallet. Fred found him cowering in bed the next morning and scraped together 200 francs for his fare. When Henry landed in Newhaven, British customs officials refused to let him enter because he had only the equivalent of one British pound. They feared that he might stay permanently and surface on the dole, so two policemen escorted him onto the next ferry back to Dieppe. A chagrined Henry showed up in Paris less than forty-eight hours after he left.

He went directly to Louveciennes. Hugo was in London on business, Rosa had moved with Joaquín to an apartment in Paris, and the maids were in Spain. Anaïs and Henry were alone for almost ten days.

Henry may have mourned his loss of June, but "He allowed her to go," Anaïs wrote. "He is passive. He does not act."[21] It was what she had counted on. She installed him in the guest room and devoted herself to his every need during the day. At night he slept with her.

Henry made his own observations on his luxurious new circumstances: "I . . . lie in a bed of state with red velvet covers. I have my own toothbrush. My own toilet. And I have Jung, Freud, Spengler, Rank et alia to keep me company. . . . I do nothing but take off my pants.

"Life is like that," he gloated. "Nothing more than taking off your pants. The rest is an alibi."[22]

14

Lover of the World and Men

Anaïs Nin's diary writing changed abruptly in 1933, from journals of introspection about life and art to ones replete with violence, brutality, arrogance, and grandiose proclamations of superiority. They are often angry, bitter, and cynical.[1] The main topic is sex, for she wrote about little else that year.[2] She portrays herself as a woman shorn of reason, careening through life like an out-of-control bulldozer, riding roughshod over the normal boundaries of social behavior. The titles of her diaries reflect her state of mind: "Schizoidie and Paranoia," "Flagellation," "Incest," and the ominously doubly underlined "Father."[3]

Now when she saw Allendy, there was no pretense of analysis. Mostly, they fondled and masturbated while discussing his two passions, astrology and alchemy. When they did talk about her analysis, it usually revolved around Henry, whom Allendy called "the dangerous destructive man."[4] It made her furious, for Henry was her "earthly paradise" and she waged "a desperate effort to preserve it." Anaïs declared "war now, between Allendy and me."

She won this battle when Allendy turned her into his analyst and confessed that he suffered from an intense inferiority complex, saying he had "to do one too many things to deserve love, while Henry, who did nothing to deserve love, got so much of it." They were somewhat alike, Anaïs concluded, because she resented June, who "did not ever deserve all the loves she got!"[5]

At this point in her analysis, she made two important observations. The first concerned the concept of "absolution," introduced when Allendy gave her "a deeply needed religious absolution for my past." She wrote defiantly that she chose to stand with Henry against the world, united by "great hatred of idealism and idealists" and the "great desire" to destroy and "wound the world which has wounded both of us."

This angry response was provoked by the scant, snotty notice—only a few mean-spirited reviews—garnered by her book about Lawrence. Hugo's belief in her talent had helped in the past, but as he was only a banker, his faith did not count for much. Now she had Henry, and he had become her "new religion." She elevated him to something between messiah and master because he was a writer himself, recognized her worth, and valued everything she wrote. The fact that he valued her body as well as her writing cemented her faith: she may have held the upper hand in most other aspects of their relationship, but Henry was her "lord and master in sex, as it should be." She knew she could "count on the ever restless, fiery penis!"[6]

She entitled her second observation "the analyst's triumph," which dealt with her exaggerated need for what she called "gestures."[7] Suddenly for Anaïs, an "illumination was unleashed," triggering a litany of "gestures" she felt she had deserved, had wanted desperately, and had not received: of how she wanted June to give her "things" even though she had no money to buy them, of Erskine's refusal to give her sex, of her own inability to decide what exactly she wanted Hugo to give and when she wanted it to be given. If, she decided, she had been able to realize and accept that all these persons "loved" her without gestures, then she would not have been so devastated when they were not forthcoming.

She insisted that Henry was the only man with whom she was ever involved to "bless" her with gestures.[8] Even so, because of his phobic fears—starvation, privation, and penury—she knew instinctively that his "love was less deep" than all the others put together. She knew that two fragile ties, sex and a monthly stipend, bound Henry to her.

She wrote her own self-analysis, one that was both prescient and accurate but at the same time a kind of frenzied shorthand for everything that had happened in her past relationships and would dictate how those in her future unfolded. And, of course, once having written it, she heeded none of it: "I had to possess the man body and soul.

I would not listen to any reason, compromise, deficiency, neuroses which made fusion impossible, that my possessivity was tremendous in proportion to my fear of abandon etc. It became clear to me how desperately I had sought to possess Allendy wholly, as a trophy, whereas what I want is a Father, a friend."[9]

This knowledge did not, for example, keep her from continuing to try to seduce Allendy. She invited him and his wife to Louveciennes for dinner, pleased that he was ill at ease and discomfited.[10]

Her behavior grew increasingly reckless. She got out of Henry's bed in the afternoon and went directly to Allendy's office. As she sat on his lap, she gloated over "the faint odor of Henry's semen" which she "so hated to wash completely away." Hugo went to Brussels on business and she and Henry were in bed when he came home unexpectedly. She dashed out in her negligee to kiss him passionately, giving Henry time to gather his clothing and sneak into the guest room. But he saw Henry's coat, hat, books, and papers scattered in the downstairs hallway, and a "look of absolute knowingness"[11] engulfed him. Anaïs quickly invented a story about phoning Henry because it was the maid's night off and she had heard strange sounds the past few nights. Hugo only said, "I imagined that I could hear Henry rushing from your room."

"What an imagination you have! Do you think if I were to deceive you I would do it as blatantly as that!" It was too easy: "Poor Hugo, he needed to believe. He wanted consolation, support, protection, security . . . he was tired and worried about money matters. I gave him enormous tenderness. . . . He went to work almost gay."

From then on, Hugo was always careful to tell Anaïs to the exact half-hour when he would come home; she never told Henry this, but delighted in watching him become increasingly terrified as she dallied in his bed until she heard Hugo's deliberately exaggerated noise announcing his arrival.

When Hugo returned from London with his sister Ethel,[12] Anaïs decided to toy with lesbian sexuality. Without other explanation, Anaïs told the diary she had "no choice" but to instigate the kissing and fondling she had learned from June, then repeated June's contention that she was "too awkward" to love women because of her "unknowingness," but also because she preferred men. As she analyzed her behavior in the diary, she was startled to realize that she enjoyed dallying with a woman in order to "watch her passion just as June watched mine. I was saying June's words and remaining conscious while I said them, just as June did." She liked the "power" it gave her, but she wanted to be the object of adoration, and therefore preferred to have men make love to her.

Still, the idea of power was so stimulating that she decided to test hers over Ethel by taking it a step further. Anaïs pretended to beg Ethel not to tell Allendy what she had done (Ethel was now the third member of the Guiler family in analysis with him). Ethel agreed, which was exactly what Anaïs did *not* want. She wanted Allendy to know, hoping it would arouse his desire for her. "Noooo—you must tell him," Anaïs said, as if changing her mind after careful thought. "I love to tell him the truth."

When she wrote about how she duped Ethel, she justified "all this trickiness and deception" as her "defense against a treacherous life too tragic and too destructive and too terrifying for me." It marked the start of her use of the word "neurosis," which figures large during her years of European analysis. She blamed her "distorted morbid neurotic fear" on her father's abandonment: *he* was responsible for all her reprehensible behavior, not she. It was his fault because he had not answered her letters with loving tomes of guidance but had instead criticized her written French as well as the content.

Her violent mood swings and reckless behavior frightened many people, especially Hugo and Henry. Hugo was working harder than ever, coming home many nights on the last train or the first in the pre-dawn morning, staying only long enough to shower and change before returning to the bank. He never knew how he would find her. She drank huge quantities of whiskey, which unleashed all sorts of bizarre behavior, from rambling, disjointed conversation to bouts of hysterical tears, to tearing at her clothing or picking compulsively at threads in rugs or upholstery. Each of these happened from time to time, but when they all occurred in the course of one evening at Louveciennes, Hugo was deeply concerned. He calmed her by making her spend a few quiet hours in the library, poring over astrological calculations and charting her horoscope.

Thanks to Eduardo,[13] astrology had become Hugo's new hobby, and he did the family charts and those of all their friends. He was shocked to discover that his Aquarius and Anaïs's Pisces were basically incompatible, whereas Henry's Capricorn showed that he had all the attributes of Anaïs's perfect mate and should have been her husband.[14]

Henry was also frightened by her fluctuating emotions. He begged her to end the deception and run away with him. She said it was impossible, as they were "two egoists, two narcissists, two independent and wilful and temperamental beings" who would starve without Hugo's support.[15] He still urged her to "tell Hugo the truth and let things bust up." She knew she could not, for her "greatest fear" was "abject cowardice, cowardice, cowardice." As long as she had Hugo and the security he gave, she could act out her every fantasy, and nothing or no one could harm her. Henry would doom her to a life of "fear," and she dreaded "his life itself."

Henry never did offer her the total, unselfish, and unflinching adoration that Hugo did. Rather, he thought he had the freedom to criticize her dress, deportment and behavior, just as he did her writing. He thought they were in a relationship of two equals—at least in the beginning. Once, when Henry was too ashamed to face Hugo, insistent that he could not cuckold him any longer, he threatened to stage a showdown and tell the truth about the money as well as the sex. Anaïs locked her eyes with his coldly and said: "One more word on this subject and I will walk out [of Clichy] and you will never see me again." It was a very long time before he even hinted at the subject. Henry was easily cowed because he, too, had one abnormal, exaggerated fear—of starvation.[16]

And so Anaïs gloated of "swallowing sperm with Allendy's head falling on [her] breast" and "Henry's erect and fiery penis" in her womb. It was not "playing tricks on men," rather, "on life, which does not answer what I have demanded of it." She took pride in lying "bravely, ironically, dually, triply," and in "this juggling and this treacherous handling." Her role, she bragged, was "the lover of the world and of men."

It was time to demonstrate her power over Allendy, to do more than grope furtively in his office. She persuaded him to invite her to a hotel. He chose one where afternoon assignations were commonplace and where she suspected he had often been before. She prepared herself by drinking quantities of whiskey and met him at the appointed hour.[17] He undressed her quickly while she observed his body: "white, flabby." He began to beat her buttocks—"slap, slap"—while she laughed to herself at his antics. She eventually had to arouse him manually and fake an orgasm. Suddenly, "inexplicably," she felt "sadness and sympathy" for him. "Laugh it off," she wrote that night. "Conquer it. Make the man happy. That is all. A gift. I make a gift in return for the tribute of his love. And I feel free of debts. I walk joyously away, debtless, independent, uncaptured."

Because she did not want to be with him again, she told Allendy that she felt remorse about having sex with her analyst and would not do it again. He insisted, so she met him again in the same hotel room. He reached into his pocket, snapped out a whip, and began to hit her. It made her laugh. "Don't make marks," she cautioned. "I don't want Henry or Hugo to see them." He was furious and hit harder. Only then was he aroused: "He fucked no better than before. I played a comedy. He said he had reached the height of joy."

Anaïs could not stop thinking about the whip. At first it was an "experience, a curiosity," but she did not "know yet how to treat that whip." While Allendy struck her, all she could think of was how she wanted to write about it in the diary, "the absolute truth," because "reality deserves to be described in the vilest terms." It is a curious statement, for as her lies increased in number and complexity, she resorted to lying in the diary "by omission." It perplexed her to be writing about the most sordid sexual experience of her life with grandiose zest and glee, which is perhaps why she turned Allendy into a fool who disgraced and demeaned himself, and herself into the observer who reports everything that transpired while remaining unscathed.

"What amused me most was to be able to deceive Allendy so deeply. Psychologist! intuition! Astrologer! Hah!" She laughed at how he pretended to be a savage: "He was not really deeply savage. <u>I'm</u> savage . . . woman the <u>whore</u>. After all, I <u>liked</u> that whip. That whip was virile, savage, hurtful, vital. It still stings!"

When Rosa removed herself from the daily life of Louveciennes, she also removed what was in effect the last bulwark of accepted social constraints in Anaïs's life. Before the advent of Henry's stipend, Anaïs had borrowed small sums from Rosa on a fairly routine basis, but somehow or other usually repaid them. Rather than face Rosa directly, Anaïs resorted to sending chatty little letters that usually ended with something like "Mummy dear, can you wait for the 2,000 francs [Rosa's entire stipend] until next month as I can't send it on just now."[18] Through caution, thrift, and much juggling of her own, Rosa kept her mouth shut and somehow managed.

❧

At a recital, Anaïs chatted with the Spanish composer Gustavo Durán, who had just seen his very close friend Joaquín Nin in St.-Jean-de-Luz. After praising her beauty and the clothing and makeup that enhanced it, Durán told her how much she resembled her father. "Your father is very sad about losing his children," he told her. "He talks about them all the time, but he asks especially about you."

"Tell him to come and see me the next time he is in Paris," she said offhandedly. But she was so flattered that she wrote about it at length in the diary. Several days later, to make sure Durán would convey her message, Anaïs invited him and the painter Nestor de la Torre (who was also a friend of her father's) to Louveciennes.[19] The ploy worked, for both men wrote glowing letters to Joaquín Nin about his beautiful daughter and her fairy-tale house.

Some days later she received a letter from her father. He had heard many stories about her marvelous house and wanted more than anything not to see *it,* but to see *her* in it. She was like a teenager with her first invitation to the prom: "Father's letter! Father's coming visit! They are like a flower in the pages of a book. In the center of *my* book, *my* journal, *my* life. My first idol."

Her writing veered directly onto another train of thought: She congratulated herself that she had always "been faithful to love," and had not yet "given" herself, except to men for whom, in some way or another, she always persuaded herself to "feel love." But now that her father wanted to be a part of her life, she thought about how she would relish "the coquetry, the immense coquetry . . . the game." Her writing suddenly changed, becoming darker and thicker as if reflecting the intensity of her declaration: "I refuse to live in the ordinary world as an ordinary woman. To enter ordinary relationships. I want ecstasy!"[20]

She had just celebrated her thirtieth birthday in her usual way, quietly reading her old diaries, and chanced upon a passage written three years earlier about what, ideally, she wanted to be:

> Eternally a woman of thirty, full-breasted, tall, black hair, oriental-Spanish eyes and aquiline nose. Very pale. Exotic look-

> ing. Extremely experienced. Author of five or six books of six different kinds. . . . Unmarried (lovers permitted). Rich enough to help out writers and publish a magazine. A great traveller. At thirty-one, I would meet Hugo and have two children (Hugo being the only man I would like to have children from) and sit in an old garden like this one [Louveciennes] and be really happy.[21]

The thirty-year-old woman who met her fifty-four-year-old father later that spring after a separation of almost twenty years was, in reality, the author of one generally ignored book, childless, already married for a decade, had traveled relatively little, and sat in her garden only when too sexually exhausted to go anywhere else. In most respects she was decidedly unhappy.

Henry had a burgeoning admiration for Walter Lowenfels, the experimental poet who became the prototype for his character "Jabberwhorl Cronstadt" in *Black Spring.*[22] Lowenfels believed in the importance of art in and of itself rather than as a vehicle for enhancing the artist's ego, which was perhaps why Anaïs feared his influence on Henry, which she called his "new idolatry."[23] Usually all she needed was to express grave reservations about Henry's enthusiasm for someone she did not like and he would give the person up quietly. This time, however, he insisted that Lowenfels was an important source of information about everything new and modern in literature, politics, and life in general. Lowenfels, for example, introduced Henry (and by extension, Anaïs) to Rimbaud's *Illuminations,* and more important, to Rimbaud's maxim, "We must be absolutely modern," not only the decree around which the Surrealists rallied but also one of the most influential statements of the 1930s, and certainly one of lasting importance to Anaïs Nin's fiction.

As the friendship between Lowenfels and Henry continued and deepened, Anaïs retaliated by initiating one with Antonin Artaud, of whom she wrote reams of extravagant factual notes in the hope of turning him into a character in her fiction. Anaïs professed to be unaware of Artaud's openly expressed homosexuality until she provoked Eduardo to a jealous rage at the thought that Artaud might possibly eclipse him.[24] Artaud soon became the catalyst who aroused anger and jealousy among all the men in her life. Anaïs noted the "advance into greater and greater complications . . . it is getting more and more difficult to make four men happy."

Suddenly, the usually pliant Hugo refused to bend. Jack Kahane refused to pay the printing costs for *Tropic of Cancer* and expected Henry to find the $600. Kahane had agreed to distribute the book, but for a hefty percentage of the profits. Anaïs told Henry to sign the contract: she would persuade Hugo to pay even though currency fluctuations made their scant savings "dwindle into nothing." Hugo told Anaïs he would always give her whatever he had, but he had no money for Henry.

She felt exceedingly sorry for herself: "Oh, the burden, the anxiety, the sacrifices . . . the gifts I must give! The problems, traps, pressures of reality, economy, anxiety." She moaned about holes in her shoes and not having stockings, and borrowing the maid's money to buy Hugo's dinner: "I'm still a neurotic . . . choked by anxieties. Will the furnace explode?"

But she still had weapons. When she threatened to sell her fur coat and pawn her jewelry, Hugo gave her the $600. She gave it to Henry with a letter stating that it was a gift, and any profit to be realized was his alone. Then she took up the diary and began to sing Hugo's praises for his selflessness and generosity. Hugo became "the most perfect of beings" who had given her ten years of "unmerited worship."

Several days later, Hugo left for London and Anaïs stepped into Artaud's "fantastic regions."[25] She claimed that she took him to the same hotel and the same room where Allendy had taken her. There, she "yielded" to Artaud's "devouringly fierce kisses," as he bit her "mouth, breasts, throat and legs." After all this foreplay, she noted quite matter-of-factly that he was impotent. She told him impotence had "no significance" for her: "it is a scene I know by heart."

She used this encounter to enrage Henry. "I invented a great deal. . . . I entertained and excited Henry. I was feverish and he was jealous." And so she played off each man against the others, going "from one's bites to the other's sperm." Her "recipe for happiness" was "mix well the sperm of four men in one day." It was no wonder that her health broke down. She was so tired that she could barely drag herself into the garden to sunbathe.

In mid-May, at the very moment Anaïs was forcing Henry to eat an early lunch so she could ship him back to Paris and keep an afternoon rendezvous with Artaud, her father telephoned to say he was on his way to Louveciennes. She telegrammed Artaud not to come, then rushed around putting the house and herself in order.

Joaquín Nin arrived by car, alone, glowing with good health, his face unlined but powdered and faintly rouged; his clothing rich and impeccable, exuding a faint whiff of expensive cologne. He stared at her openly from head to foot, taking in every aspect of her physical being. She stared right back, flushed with pleasure.

"But you are like me," he purred, and then went on to compliment her on the Nin hands, the fine bones of the Nins, the dark hair and fair skin. She was so flattered that she forgot to be wary. When Hugo came home that night, he warned her against becoming just another of her father's many seductions. "He is not called 'Don Juan' for nothing," Hugo cautioned. She laughed and said she planned to see her father as often as possible.

By mid-June, Hugo had two alarming concerns: her health, for she was so exhausted she could barely get herself out of bed to sit alone in the garden and drink restorative tonics; and her growing intimacy with Joaquín Nin. Joaquín invited her to go with him and Maruca to St.-Raphaël for a summer holiday, but Hugo refused permission: they did not have the money to buy the new summer wardrobe without which she could not stay in a luxury hotel. And even if they did, the tightfisted Nin did not offer to pay her expenses. Hugo did agree that she could go alone for a few days to a modest hotel in Valescure, a village near St.-Raphaël.

Anaïs left Paris on June 19. On June 21 she wired Hugo that she was with her father, who was ill and needed her assistance, as Maruca had not traveled with him. She found Joaquín Nin ensconced in luxury, lying on his own personal bed linens, satin sheets surrounded by pillows puffed and propped just so. Books and magazines were neatly piled on little tables, and medicines were arranged precisely on his dressing table. A dresser held expensive cookies he nibbled on and Quaker Oats and maple syrup he ate for breakfast. Everything was neatly presented, first to be perused, then prepared for his delectation.

Antonin Artaud.

The next day they drove around the Grande Corniche. He regaled her with stories of his love affairs, bragging about "playing with souls." She watched his face and "knew" he was truthful, "talking to me as I talk only to my journal." Also, she noted dryly, it was "at a certain moment inevitably untrue."

Joaquín Nin was much improved except for some residual effects of lumbago, so he invited his daughter to spend the evening in his room. As he lay in bed, he described her mother's gross sensuality as a bride. Anaïs was "profoundly shocked," first because "it is strange to discover the sexual life of one's parents," and then because her mother had always seemed so reserved and puritanical about "sex, religion, morality."

Joaquín Nin's version was of a poor, picked-upon aristocrat, badly mated to an older, vulgar shrew who yelled, screamed, made scenes, and was careless about her personal hygiene. What prevented this elegantly refined man from leaving his impossible union was the deep love and devotion he felt for his children, his "strong Spanish clannishness, sense of paternity, sacredness of family."

His tale touched Anaïs so profoundly that when she began to record it in the diary, she decided to write only about "the King, the solitary and obstinate visionary . . . visionary of balance, fairness, logic, transcendentalism." It is an astonishing reversal, an instantaneous rejection of everything Rosa Culmell stood for, and a total repudiation of her character and behavior. Anaïs was well aware that she was sitting with *her father* and listening to stories of his sex life with *her mother.* There was never any doubt that she was his daughter and he was her parent, at least not in her written account. How or why she lost sight of it is known only to her, but it may have happened when they shared tales of their mutual "diabolicalness." She told her father how she had taken Artaud to the same hotel and room where Allendy took her. He smiled, saying he had often done that very thing. It gave them a strong, shared bond, he said, and proved their superiority to everyone else.

They continued to chat desultorily, but she was infected with a "malaise," a "difficulty in finding our relationship." Boundaries had begun to blur as each vied to top the other with accounts of how they had betrayed mates, confounded lovers, and triumphed over inferior partners in their various assignations. As she bade him goodnight and bent for his fatherly kiss, she suddenly realized that she did not have "the feelings of a daughter." She offered her cheek, he bent his head and kissed her neck. He "disturbed" her; she was "afraid" of him.

The next morning she found him unable to move, almost paralyzed with a relapse of lumbago. She spent the day in his room, wearing only her "satin negligée." They continued along the lines of their conversation the night before, exchanging stories of their conquests. She told him of Allendy's whip, describing the part of herself that seemed another person, aloof and observing as the whip descended, offended by the "commonness" of what was happening to her. Joaquín Nin listened absorbedly but said nothing. After a long pause he said, "You are the synthesis of all the women I have loved." She watched him "watching [her] constantly." She stretched out at the foot of his bed and allowed him to caress her foot. He told her how "beautifully formed" she had been as a child and how much he loved to take her photograph. She remembered none of the fear and shame these moments induced in her as a child, recording only the pleasure of his compliments as an adult. The hours passed languidly.

Then he told her of his dream the previous night, of how she masturbated him "with jewelled fingers," and how he kissed her "like a lover." Silences, long silences, punctuated every statement that dotted the stillness of the peaceful summer afternoon.

Until he said: "I don't feel towards you as if you were my daughter."

"I don't feel as if you were my father," she replied.

Another long pause, and then he asked, as if it were a problem she, too, shared: "What a tragedy. What are we going to do about it? I have finally met *the* woman of my life and it is my daughter . . . I'm in love with my own daughter." Very quickly she responded: "Everything you feel is reciprocal."

More long pauses, more expressions of nonfamilial feelings. Suddenly he shouted: "Bring Freud here, and all the psychologists. What could they say about this?"

"Another suspense," she wrote, noting how she was afraid to say anything that would shatter the mood. He asked her to move nearer, and then to kiss him on the mouth. She was "tortured" by "a complexity of feelings," among them that she was about to "kiss a brother" rather than a father. As she lay across his erect penis in her slippery thin negligée, he in a loosened bathrobe, she felt "more terror than joy, the joy of something unnamable, obscure." They exchanged caresses upon their bare flesh while he cautioned that they "must avoid possession." In the meantime, he made her nipples harden and inserted his finger in her vagina until "With a strange violence," she lifted herself, threw off her negligée, and mounted him.

"You, Anaïs! I have lost God."

If Anaïs Nin the diarist is to be believed, for the next two weeks, father Joaquín and daughter Anaïs indulged in a nonstop orgiastic frenzy, all of it written in what one reviewer of the *Incest* volume described astutely as similar to the "portentous, heavy-breathing prose of a cheap romance novel."[26]

Anaïs Nin transposed the events of this affair to her current diary in a carefully regulated, slightly smaller-than-usual writing, even though it is her same, smooth-flowing hand. There are no hesitations, erasures, or corrected misphrasings; if this were the only volume that survived her life, one might be tempted to say that it was the product of many different and perhaps even differing accounts, all edited and neatly copied into the one final passage she chose to commit to posterity. But since all the writing in her original diaries is like this passage, flowing from beginning to end in one continuous stream of final, finished prose, it seems more likely that she recorded what happened between her and her father either exactly as it occurred or in the way she chose to commit it to memory after the two-week idyll ended. Either way, it is a disturbing account.

Nin the diarist regales herself with compliments paid to Anaïs the daughter. She writes of how her father wanted to replace all the other men in her life and become her sole lover, which, she said he boasted, he could have done if he were forty instead of fifty-four. She makes him regret that he might be incapable of "riquette" (their pet name for his erect penis), and says he is afraid she will "abandon" him (the word underlined heavily). She tells of how she protested the contrary verbally, but wrote of how thrilled she was by his insecurity. To know that "he the lionic, the jungle king, the most viril man" she had ever known feared that she would leave him threw her into a frenzy of "profound passion."

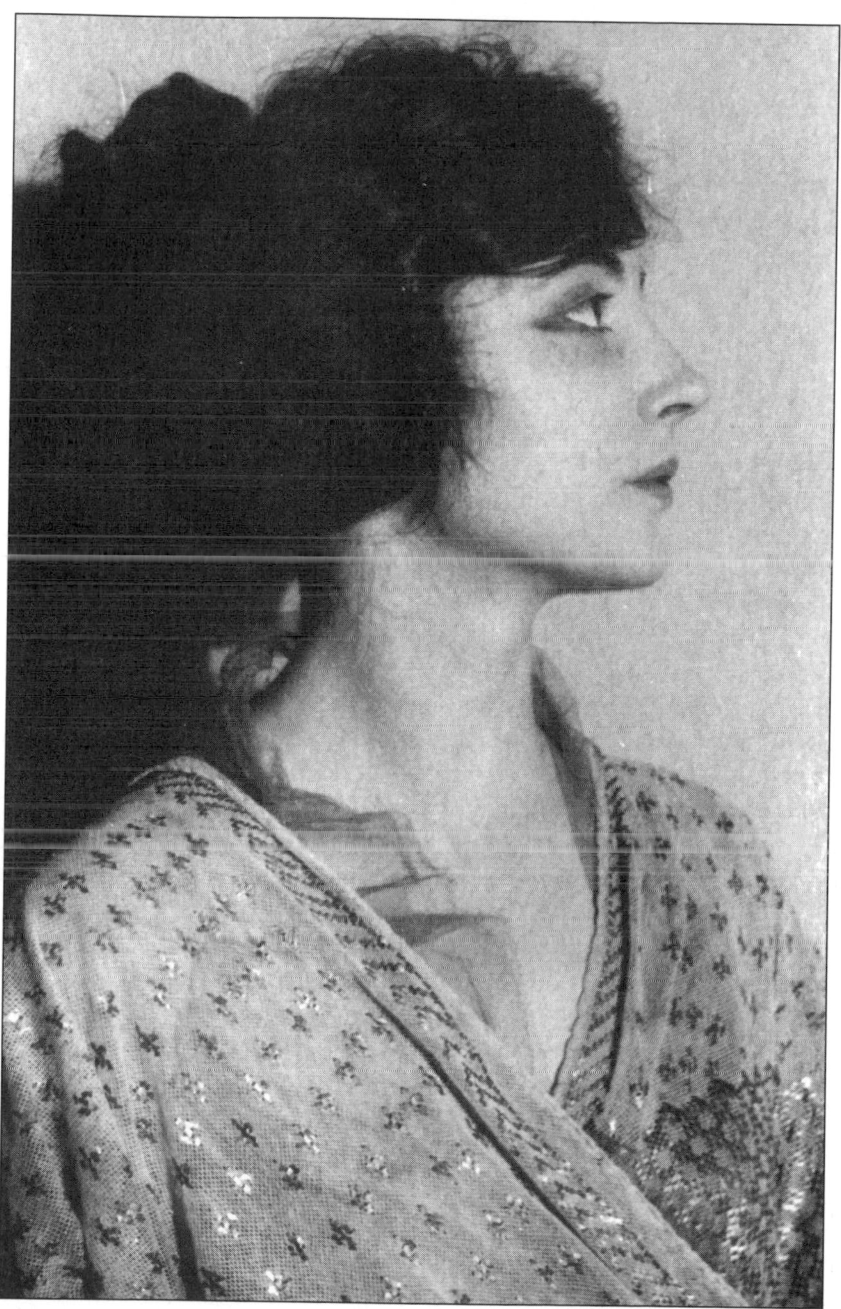

Anaïs, while writing the Red and Green diaries.

At the end of the holiday, Anaïs surrendered her father to Maruca's ministrations. Privately, she marveled at "the miracle of unison" that had filled her and her father's lives with "the same experiences and emotions." But she still needed a rationalization for what had happened between them. It was only an accident that their "passions broke the dam" and "forced" them to lie to others and to themselves. In a heavily underlined passage, she explained away what, as two consenting adults, they had done: "We have never reconciled ourselves to our own treacheries, to the flow of our nature, to our ascension and evolutions, which make us humanly unreliable." As far as she was concerned, she and her father were both liars, and liars cannot (and should not) be held responsible for the consequences of their lies.

Also, her only perfect "unison" was now with her father; Henry was lumped in with Hugo as another who did not satisfy her. She called it their "illusion," but her father had his own word for it: "Synchronism." She liked it because included in its meaning was the idea that "even the strongest cannot bear solitude. We crave unison."

And so she ended the two weeks in a state of euphoria and a belief in the rightness of all she had done and departed feeling free of any lasting repercussion. Two weeks later, after a continuation of her holiday, she returned to Paris glowing with radiant good health. Hugo, whose written French was much better than hers,[27] sent a letter to Joaquín Nin to thank him for his many kindnesses to his daughter: "Anaïs is back from Valescure, radiant because she has found her father again—a new, very young father who exists for her for the first time in her life . . . the father of her dreams. She has always dreamed of a father . . . like you. I feel as though I have also acquired a father and a brother at the same time, and I am happy."

Hugo was so elated with the change in his wife that he cast his new father-in-law/brother's horoscope. "Amazing discovery, astrology," Anaïs marveled. "It reveals that Father's moon is in my sun, the strongest attraction between man and woman. When Hugo showed me this, my last vestige of guilt disappeared."

HIM

AFTER NINE DAYS of unbridled sexuality with Joaquín Nin, now known as "HIM" in the diary,[1] Henry seemed like a stranger to Anaïs. Their secret holiday week in Avignon was not the joyous sexual reunion Henry envisioned, and when it was over, Anaïs disappointed him further by making him return to Paris alone on his bicycle. For several days before going on to meet Hugo in Annecy, she filled her diary with thoughts of her "Roi Soleil," another of the names she called her father. A curious sort of amnesia seems to have engulfed her as she wrote, for her father's was the only perspective she considered. His had been the tragic, stoic life, not Rosa's, and he had borne his solitude for fifty-four years with courage and dignity. The little girl whose father had abandoned her had no place in this account. Neither did she write about the adult woman who wanted so much to please her absent father that she deliberately created situations (her houses) or circumstances (her dance recitals) where others would be likely to carry tales of her talent and beauty back to him.

Instead, she turned this man, the lover whom she no longer regarded as her father, into her double, a disturbing other whose personality included aspects she had only just begun to fathom in her own self. As a means to self-understanding, she set herself the task of exploring "the life of my King, all the twists of his mind."

Somehow, she managed to push the repeated acts of incest to the furthest reaches of her mind and thus turned the liaison into something more than an affair. It was absolutely necessary that it become almost a marriage, preordained and forgiven, if not actually sanctified. She persuaded herself that loving her father was only an extension of loving herself, and then, in the very finest sense.

This state of mind gave her the stability to proceed peripatetically on to her next liaison, with her husband. But as her every thought concerned her father, she could not wait to compare husband and father/lover in the diary. When she did, suddenly everything was "so extremely simple: "[Hugo] lives for me, there is only me." But her constant need to write down endless comparisons colored their time together. In the privacy of their room, in the midst of Hugo's loving tenderness, she was an onlooker rather than a participant. "I watched our life in amazement and it is all care . . . tenderness, gifts, protection." As always, it was not enough to satisfy her.

No matter which of her men she was with, Henry or Hugo, she thought of her father. While Hugo slept, she filled the diary with images of how she and her father had courted discovery by fondling each other in public gardens, hotel lobbies, and elevators. Her excitement was tempered by fear, as guilt began to set in no matter how hard she tried to stop it. Once again she turned to Lawrence in search of an example to give herself permission for and absolution of the taboo she had already broken. She rationalized that Lawrence would have agreed that she had no choice but to make love to her father because all her other affairs had been with "timorous men, sexual weaklings" who forced her to seek the only man who was her equal, by which she meant their mutual disregard of accepted moral and social behavior in their unending quest for self-satisfaction.

She remembered how delighted she was when her father said he believed the sole purpose of other people's lives was to give pleasure and purpose to his. She shared but refined this view, because she thought woman's primary role was handmaiden and supplicant to a great man. Conflict arose because she considered herself an artist, too, and therefore entitled to the same treatment and behavior as a man. It boiled down to a confusing broth: how to blend female acquiescence with male independence.

Guilt still set in, and she could only mitigate it by heaping most of it onto Hugo. In her reasoning, if he had been able to satisfy her unfathomable needs, she would not have participated in mutual seduction with her father.

She could not sort it out: "All this incestuous love is still veiled and a dream. I want to realize it and it eludes me." Who was this adult stranger that she, an adult woman, met and with whom she fell in love? It was another person, entirely different and totally separated from the young father who beat the tiny child or worse. How could she reconcile the one with the other, or would that be truly terrible, more than her mind could bear?

As she resumed the daily juggling of her five men (Hugo, Henry, Allendy, Artaud, and now "HIM"), a remark of Richard Osborn's suddenly surfaced in her mind, that she and Henry were "equal matches in treachery." She always blamed Hugo for her inability to be faithful, and now she blamed Henry as well. Osborn's remark became an excuse to end the affair.

When she and Henry were together, she was acidly cold. He wrote her letters that were affectionate and placating; she sent acerbic replies questioning the way he edited her texts. She tried to keep him occupied somewhere other than Louveciennes, but he turned up uninvited, quaking in his usual galloping insecurities about money, needing a roof over his head, and fearful that he would surely starve one day. Anaïs assured him that she would provide enough for him to keep on writing no matter what the state of their personal relationship.

Henry was about to move to 18, Villa Seurat, to a studio apartment in a house owned by Michael Fraenkel. In his gratitude for Anaïs's guarantee to pay the rent, and hoping it might change her mood, Henry told her that he was like D. H. Lawrence and "needed a good woman behind him." She laughed to herself: "the irony of it all is that he has been miraculously faithful to me." Her intention was to get Henry happily settled in the Villa Seurat and then abandon him as a lover. She planned to do the same with Artaud and Allendy.

She saw Artaud first, in the same hotel and room where she now held all her assignations. Always prescient, he took one look and accused her of the "abomination" of incest. He had not heard gossip, he said, but he knew this just as he knew instinctively there were other men with whom she was having affairs. She denied nothing. He called her a "dangerous, malefic being" and stomped out. She reveled in the pleasure it gave her to "torture" Artaud and consoled herself that "one becomes more evil [as] one becomes stronger."

Next, she went to Allendy, and told him she no longer wanted his professional services. But as he was not as intuitive as Artaud and had no inkling of her behavior, she told him every prurient detail. She did not want any opinions, she said, she was telling him only because she needed a "confessor." If analysis is indeed the religion of the twentieth century, it certainly worked as such in this instance. By telling Allendy the analyst everything, Anaïs's confession purged and freed her of negative emotions and absolved any hint that she had sinned.

She would at last do only what she wanted with her life. From now on she would be like her father and put her needs before everyone else's. "If I am perverse, monstrous, etc, in certain eyes—tant pis! All I care about is *my own* judgement. I am what I am!"

The horrified Allendy regaled her with disastrous mythological tales of incest. In the face of her resolve, he sputtered to a defeated end by calling her an "unnatural being." She told him calmly that quite the contrary, what she felt for her father was a "natural" love and he had no authority to question it.

Henry was aware that her father had a great deal to do with her changed attitude toward him, but he had no idea then (and possibly never had) that Anaïs was involved in an incestuous relationship. He was still trying to placate her in order to keep her patronage. He told her he could not possibly be jealous of Joaquín Nin because "somehow that love seems to be so honest, so sincere, so plausible, so valid, so—" She interrupted him: "Don't say natural." "Yes!" he said, "I was going to say natural." It made her laugh so uproariously that she cried.

❧

That August Joaquín Nin sent a telegram asking her to come back to Valescure. Maruca was unable to be with him, and he needed a nurse. Even though Hugo was against it, Anaïs rushed off.[2] What her father really wanted was to resume the affair.

As soon as she arrived, they took a trip by car through St.-Cannat to Évaux-les-Bains.[3] The sex was more intense than ever, but this time it was punctuated by long periods of introspective self-examination. She wrote several pages in the diary complimenting him on his many "admirable" qualities, but also recorded everything he said about her, which was mostly critical. He addressed her as if she were a child, admonishing her to sit up straight and not to put her elbows on the table, to speak only in French (which he corrected) and to enunciate clearly. She explained his asperity away, saying he was a man of "two aspects . . . severity [and] sudden tenderness."

He asked time and again if she slept with Henry. "My first lie, no my third," she wrote of her reply. He criticized her for staying married to Hugo, for being nice to the entire Sánchez family, for not putting her own needs before those of others. All these people only weighed her down, he said, cheated her and sapped her vitality, and Henry was the worst of all, a "weakling who is living off your virility."

That night, after they had made passionate love, he begged her to remember "the date of San Juan, June 23—[the date of] our marriage." She went to her room, drank an enormous quantity of whiskey, and began to write in the diary.

She must have been very, very drunk, for this is the only time in her life that the copperplate engraving of her handwriting is almost unreadable. One can imagine her sitting up in bed, trying to print each letter with a minimum of ink blotches, squinting at the page and forcing the pen to make stick-figure letters that eventually became a confusion of run-on, unpunctuated words.

Every time they lay together after orgasm, Joaquín Nin begged his daughter not to write about what they had done in her diary. Begging gave way to threats, cajolery, and tearful pleas. He said if she committed it to paper, it would be "stoicism" (a misuse of the word), in which she would twist everything that had actually happened between them to what she wanted it to be on paper. She recorded his greatest fear, that Maruca would discover their "physical tie."[4] "No need to write it," he wheedled, "we are old enough to remember it all." Defying him became "a kind of supreme treachery," but she truly believed that she owed "faithfulness" to the diary more than to any human being.

❧

Back in Louveciennes at the end of August, she wrote pages of obsessive prose about her father, repeating "I love him . . . love him . . . I want nothing else, nobody else. He fills my life, my thoughts, my blood." Nestor de la Torre and Gustavo Durán told her she was her father's "only adventure." She "wanted to die with joy."

Joaquín Nin remained in Valescure until October, and even though his wife was with him, he and Anaïs exchanged love letters on a daily basis. He destroyed hers as soon as he read them; she honored his plea to do the same only after she dutifully copied every word into her diary.[5]

❧

What is amazing about the autumn of 1933 is how much Anaïs Nin wrote. Hugo was now the senior officer in the bank's trust department and working hard to persuade the French nobility and the upper classes of several countries to let him manage their money. Because of this, Anaïs's role as his dutiful young wife expanded, and she was constantly busy both entertaining and being entertained. She took wives of visiting magnates shopping and to lunch, and found them hairdressers and dressmakers. She gave exquisite dinner parties and dined in such elegant homes as those of Nellie, the Comtesse de Vogüé, and Louise de Vilmorin and her wealthy husband, Henri Hunt.

They and many others are mentioned only casually and in passing in the original diaries, but she gave them larger, more important roles in her life when she prepared the published diaries in the 1960s. Then, she reflected backward in tranquillity as she shaped the dust of history into the pattern she wanted to settle around her, modifying true roles, making outright changes, or melding people, places, and events into whatever she needed them to be. Sometimes she turned casual acquaintances into close friends and confidants, at other times they became exquisitely created small set pieces, cameos of characterization, all meant to enhance her standing in the world at large.

In the midst of the socializing, running the house with only one maid, and satisfying the needs of five men, she wrote. She employed a typist (called "Miss Green" in the diary) and kept her busy every day with masses of notes about June and Artaud. These would eventually become part of her first published novel, *House of Incest,* still entitled "Alraune" at this early stage. Mostly it was yet another attempt to capture June on paper, only this time she tried to play it off against Artaud's life, which she was trying to convert to fiction as well.[6]

Throughout 1932, Anaïs tried to determine why Henry preferred his wife to her. She felt "despair of not being June," so she "became June . . . absorbed June . . . went beyond June . . . and glorified [herself] for containing June." By spring 1933, when June had left Henry for good, Anaïs sent him a letter saying "<u>in me</u>" was the June he needed.[7]

By November 1933, all this had changed. Her material was now divided into "Alraune I" (title, rather than the character mentioned

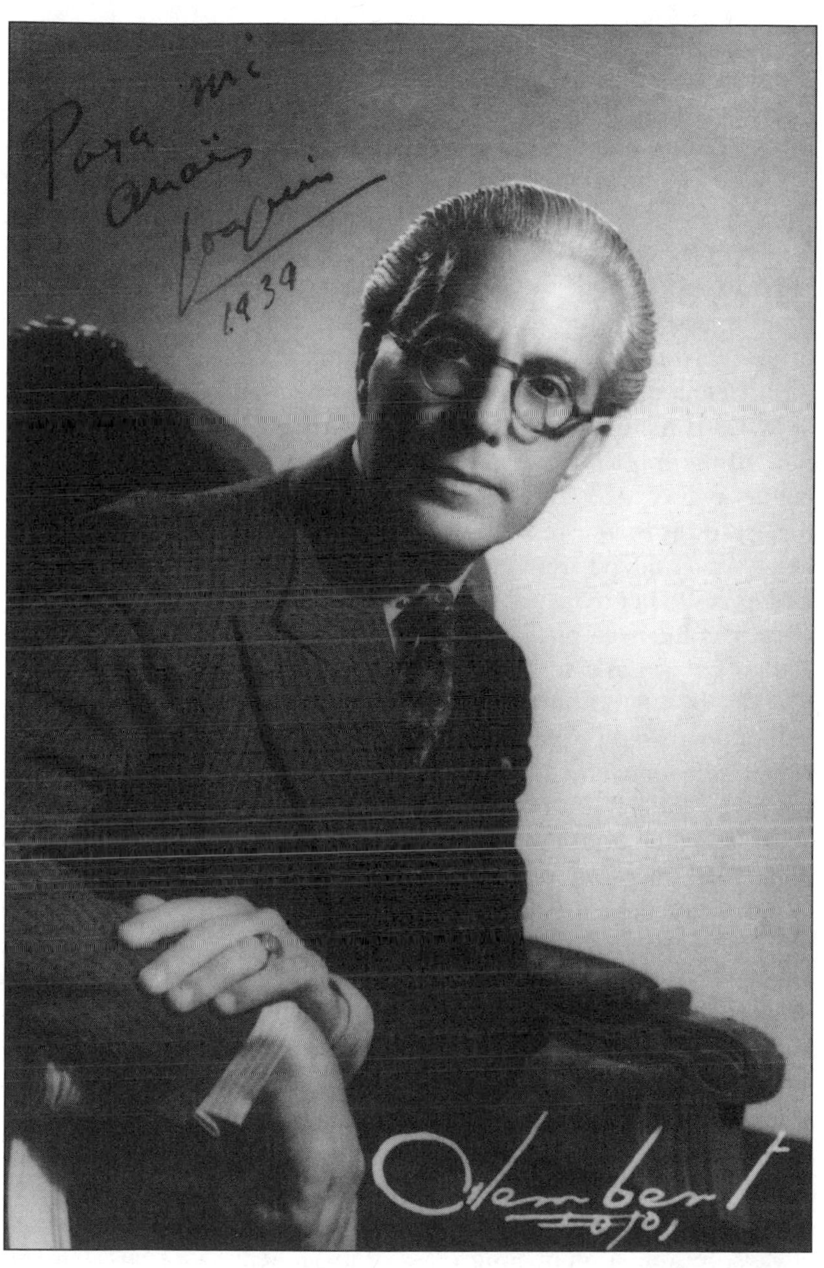

Joaquín Nin.

earlier), and "Alraune II." The first eventually became *House of Incest,* the latter her second published book, *Winter of Artifice.*[8] The novels evolved gradually over the next several years, however, for she had more pressing material to convert to fiction.

She wrote long, feverish passages about the eternal quest of woman-as-writer for a unified self. More than thirty years later, she wrote a passage that expressed what she was trying to understand: "You cannot relate to others if you have no self to begin with. In order to respond, to excite, to participate, to love or serve or create or invent, there has to be a self to generate such emotions."

She felt good about her most recent writing and decided to take it to William Aspenwall Bradley, who, with his Russian wife, Jenny, formed the most famous international literary agency in France for half a century. Anaïs first heard of him through John Erskine, who had been his friend since they were students at Columbia.[9] With his help, Anaïs edited, rewrote, changed chronology, deleted all the references to her religious piety, and changed many of the names. By starting at the beginning, she hoped that some sort of process would evolve by osmosis to free her of the first-person tyranny of her childhood self and push her forward into pure fiction.

Bradley read these rewritten diaries carefully, as he had promised Henry he would, and then pronounced them unpublishable.[10] Henry thought Bradley's "pungent criticisms" were accurate, as was his "irritation, fault finding, [and] exasperation. . . . You must let me help you. You must toughen up for criticism." He cautioned that "the hours that go to the [diary] are an evasion [of] the ever-impending problem—that of mastering your medium, of becoming the artist you are. . . . You need to write much much less and sweat more, go through agonies of torture in acquiring [your] craft."[11] It was excellent advice, which she did not heed. Instead she accused him of stealing her material.

One afternoon, as Henry was preparing himself for sex by shaking sandalwood powder on his penis, when "he was excited and I was in a fever,"[12] Anaïs reminded him of another of his many irrational fears: when someone knocked unexpectedly on his door, Henry always became a blubbering mass of apprehension. Anaïs, remembering that "he couldn't fuck me because someone had knocked," teased further by saying she had written the entire episode as fiction, and very successfully, complete with all his neuroses.

"You ought to let me have it," Henry insisted. "I want to write about it."

Another time, she made "a high handed use of the word 'gnashing' in a sexual description." Henry laughed and she turned on him angrily. "What I meant is the hard rubbing of flesh," she said prior to flouncing off. "I move we try it out," he said, knowing exactly how to calm her down.[13] In both instances, she surrendered the material to him.

⁂

Joaquín Nin sent another telegram asking Anaïs to return to Valescure. This time, debtors hounded and Hugo had no money to give her. He stopped her monthly allowance and doled out small sums each morning before going to work. In late October he dispensed 500 francs to last seven days. "And Henry needs at least 300!" she wailed.

She decided she was "deeply unfaithful" and in full "rebellion" against her father and the "don't[s]" and "nay[s]" that had dominated their last time together. Joaquín Nin tried to enlist her sympathies, but "my King is a weak man, too," Anaïs observed darkly.

She decreed portentously in the diary that as soon as Henry's book started to sell, and as soon as hers (the eventual *House of Incest*) was published (which she expected to be momentarily), she would leave Hugo and live with Henry. "With our two books out we should not be left to starve and I can always find work."

This intention lasted only until Joaquín Nin came back to Paris. With Hugo away in Geneva, they went to bed in Louveciennes. She felt only "mildly amorous" and yielded "only for his pleasure, gayly, indifferently." His status had fallen until he was only "a very expert and delightful lover," and it was "all very light and swift."

She told him he should seek other lovers, but he implored her to be faithful to him because their "love" was the "apotheosis" of his life. She thought otherwise: "I believe he wants to make our love the ideal finish to his Don Juan's career, but I don't believe he can do so . . . and if so, how can I be the first to destroy the ideal?"

Things had changed. Now she studied her father the same way as she looked at her husband and all her lovers, through the eyes of an observer. "I am hellishly lonely," she wrote. "What I need is someone who could give me what I give Henry: this constant attentiveness. I read every page he writes, I follow up his reading, I answer his letters, I listen to him, I remember all he says, I write about him, I make him gifts, I protect him. . . . He cannot do this. . . . None of these men can do it for me. I *have* to turn to my [diary], to give myself the kind of response I need. I have to nourish myself. I get love, but love is not enough. People do not know how to love."

On November 7, 1933, she went to the office of the psychoanalyst Otto Rank. She had her diary with her, as she always carried the current volume in her capacious handbag so she could write at a moment's notice. In a café, she recorded what had happened: "Rank told his butler he could not see anyone, but when he caught sight of me he was immediately intimidated and impressed, very affable and accessible. —I see him today at three."

16

"An emotional love tapeworm"

Anaïs had not gone to Otto Rank directly: first, she sent Henry, who was stymied by his inability to write "the Lawrence-Joyce-Proust book" (which had now become "the Lawrence book") and to revise *Tropic of Cancer.*[1] He agreed to go to Rank for an "interview" because of his respect for *Art and Artist,* but in "full panoply, with questions and with indictments."[2] Henry prepared for their meeting by reading, thinking about, and making notes on Rank's book. He also sent portions of the Lawrence manuscript and *Tropic of Cancer* so Rank could prepare as well.

His analytic hour passed, said Henry, with "the rapidity of a nightmare," and his "swift contact with the very core of the man" made him emerge "cured." He was in need of a "high challenge, the acid test," and Rank had not disappointed him. Anaïs was thus prepared for an instant cure as well.

She had been reading Rank's writings for well over a year, ever since Henry discovered *Art and Artist* and showered her with a deluge of his written thoughts and reams of quotations from the text.[3] In Rank's view (which she shared), the artist who departed from affiliation with and expression of the "collective" point of view was frequently shunned by society. This happened because the artist's thinking and expression were so far in advance of his cultural surroundings that he either frightened or amazed others who shared them. They were either unable or unwilling to confront the reality, the sur-reality, or even the dream that the artist portrayed. They could not grasp the meaning and intention of the work, and thus the artist was consigned to various forms of loneliness, ranging from separation to ostracism. For Anaïs, the fledgling writer in 1933 and the recipient of worldwide accolades in 1968, Rank's theory held true, for he demonstrated in both instances "how art is born of a fear of loss and change." These two concepts engulfed her at the time she sought his counsel.

Otto Rank had been in Paris since 1926: "Jew, foreigner and not a medical doctor, he was warmly welcomed in literary salons but not by the French psychiatric establishment."[4] Having fallen out of favor with Freud, he was a semi-outcast. Rank had been a former member of the "Secret Committee," a small group of intimates convened by Freud ostensibly to ensure the perpetuation of psychoanalysis, but in actuality to ensure that no dissenting theorist (primarily Jung) usurped his supreme position. Freud gave each of these men, his "angenommene Kinder" (adopted children), a carnelian ring meant to signify their special position.[5] Despite his banishment, Rank wore his proudly.

Rank remained one of Freud's closest disciples until he published *The Trauma of Birth* in 1924. The book was reviled by orthodox Freudians, and the master himself expelled Rank in 1926. He left Vienna for good and settled in Paris with his wife, Beata (called "Tola," herself a pioneering analyst), and their infant daughter, Hélène.[6]

When Otto Rank met Anaïs Nin, his marriage was foundering, he was in serious financial straits, and he was himself in the midst of an emotional crisis. At a time when the rules governing relationships between analysts and patients were not as clearly defined as they are today, it was not surprising that Nin's and Rank's became "a mixture of the bed and the [analyst's] couch," in which they were "sometime friends, other times lovers, and fellow professionals in still others."[7]

Rank's first dictum was that he did not object if Anaïs wrote an occasional passage in a "sketch book," but she must break herself of the "opium-diary habit."[8] She resorted to drastic measures to do so, checking into a hotel on January 14, 1934, without the diary and her favorite pen. She lasted several hours before cadging pencil and paper from the manager and writing a series of feverish notes. Her ravings seem to have calmed her, for she then wrote about how soothing it was to feel the flow of words leaving her hand. On February 6, unable to contain herself any longer, she began to write directly in the diary, unwilling to be without "the inexorable necessity" any longer.

Rank went off for a midwinter holiday and asked her to use the several weeks of his absence to create a body of new work as a way to wean herself from the diary. She wrote a great deal, but nothing was in any shape to show him. Even though she was the patient, she was determined to best her doctor: "Actually, I only stopped writing [the diary] for two weeks because I felt the need [to rethink and rewrite some earlier volumes]."

Too poor to move into Paris, Hugo and Anaïs spent the winter of 1933–1934 in Louveciennes. There was no money to buy coal, so they chopped up old doors and broken shutters and burned them in the little stove, which did not provide adequate heat. With Anaïs's guardian-restraints out of the way (Hugo was in Geneva and Rosa in Mallorca), Henry all but moved into the house. There, he spent his days in the marital bed, bundled into Hugo's warm kimono, trying to write his Lawrence book.

She was writing, too, "a few pages of the June-Henry novel [*House of Incest*], the final version, mad, neurotic, obsessed. I wrote in Alraune, adding diseased and monstrous pages. Whenever I returned from my Father, I added a few pages to the Double story [*Winter of Artifice*], a book which Rank nurtured and inspired by his insight into the drama."

In Anaïs's mind, the affair with her father was truly over when she said goodbye to him in the south of France six months previously. She was indifferent to him now, rushing home each time she went to dinner at his house to write more pages for "the Double story." They all dealt with her "incredulity"[9] at his "pretense of faithfulness." She judged him as she judged herself, and therefore, "my double cannot deceive me." Her strongest emotion now was "profound disillusion," which she had felt ever since writing the full account of their first two liaisons in the diary. Now when she wrote about the "Sun King," it was to dwell on his weaknesses, advancing age, and infirmities: "I either love him or hate him. Just now I hate him." Still, she continued to have sex whenever he initiated it, all the while claiming that she no longer wanted it.

She told Rank of the incestuous affair in March. Sparing no detail, she described her "malaise" one day as her father worked to bring her to orgasm and how he attributed her lethargy to her "terror of being caught." No, she replied, it was because she saw Maruca too often to enjoy his caresses anymore. No, Rank corrected, it was because she felt guilty. If that were true, she asked, how was she to separate herself from her father?

Anaïs Nin's diary is the only written record of Rank's alleged advice. She quotes him as saying: "You will deliver him of his sense of guilt towards you by hurting him. Then he will feel delivered because he will have been punished. Abandon him as he abandoned you. Revenge is necessary, to reestablish equilibrium in emotional life. [Revenge] rules us deep down. It is at the root of Greek tragedies."[10]

Her attempts to end the affair provoked Joaquín Nin to invite them often for dinner, which led to "scenes with Hugo, over nothing," and "an interesting encounter" when he invited Henry to lunch. Joaquín Nin was falsely cheerful and friendly, greeting Henry with "here is the monster who created Anaïs the phenomenon!" Anaïs was upset because Henry thought it a compliment. Her only joy came when she laughed as he ladled a huge serving of dessert into his finger bowl.

By the end of February, Anaïs and Henry both had enough work that they considered finished to call on Jean Charpentier, literary critic of the prestigious *Mercure de France.* One sentence in the diary described the meeting: "All strategic points in literature are held by little men."

Charpentier's scorn for their work made her want to isolate herself with Henry in "our world."[11] She was so keen to get away from Hugo, her family, and his, that she invented an enormous lie. She had never met Caresse Crosby, the widow of Harry, who shot himself and another man's wife in a scandalous murder-suicide several years earlier in New York. Caresse installed herself in a charming old millhouse in nearby Fontenay-aux-Roses and became a major player in the literary, artistic, and social settings of Paris. Anaïs compounded the lie, telling Hugo that she and Caresse had become the closest of

Otto Rank, wearing the ring given
to him by Sigmund Freud.

friends and that she would be spending much of her time at the isolated millhouse because Caresse had given her a studio where she could work uninterrupted. She lied further and said there was no telephone, although there was, and most of Caresse's friends knew it and could easily tell Hugo at any moment. Thus, she spent more time than ever before "at Caresse's," which was really at Henry's.

To avoid having to confront her increasingly blatant errant behavior, Hugo immersed himself in astrology with the noted astrologer Conrad Moricand.[12] His only arguments with Anaïs these days were about money, for he had all but given up caring about Henry. Mostly, Hugo managed to be away from Louveciennes. If they were not separated legally, they were separated physically for increasingly long stretches by his work, an arrangement that suited them both. When he came to Paris, there were no longer joyous reunions and showers of gifts. He refused to cater to her convenient bouts of "bad health" and insisted that she go with him to business dinners and do her part in helping him to secure clients. He expected her to behave like a good corporate wife; rattled by his uncustomary firmness, she did. That spring, 1934, she turned her wiles on her husband to woo him back, and tension between them was dissolved as they resumed conjugal relations.

Other family members nibbled away at her time with Henry and her attentiveness to Rank's analysis. Ethel Guiler treated her steady boyfriend badly and he spent almost every evening complaining to Hugo at Louveciennes while Ethel flirted upstairs with Anaïs. Anaïs flirted with Eduardo's younger sister, Ana María, who was in Paris shopping for her trousseau. She said she did it because she wanted the virginal Ana María to know what life was all about before she disappeared into the constraints of a Cuban marriage. It was probably true, but she was fascinated by the young girl's beauty and charm, which she insisted mirrored her own. If Anaïs Nin's father was one sort of double, she was convinced that Ana María Sánchez was another, younger version of herself.[13]

It was probably the only time in her life when she wrote more fiction than she did in the diary, but she recognized her limitations: "I will never write well. Not like Kay Boyle," whose stories Henry admired. "I am deeper and stronger, but not in craft." Then she listed her failures: "bad craft, spelling, foreign locutions, grammatical unevenness, extremes." —The very criticisms that would hound her published work for years.

Also, she wrote: "I break down under criticism. Coward. Can't bear it. No self-confidence . . . Hell." It didn't help when she showed what she hoped would be the final manuscript of *Alraune* (published as *House of Incest*) to Boussie, Joaquín, William and Jenny Bradley, and Bernard Steele, and every one of them had the same reaction: distaste for her "decadent style" and "confusing story." Only Henry came through for her, as he would time and again, arousing her "fighting spirit and strength," goading her into writing a "bigger book."[14]

She needed an excuse to quit and fell back upon the one that always worked: "Health, of course, the son of a bitch, fails me always." She had just surrendered 5,000 hard-gathered francs to Jack Kahane for Henry's book, and was exhausted from the strain of collecting the money against Hugo's wishes; the house was cold and her wardrobe shabby. How better to cheer oneself than by giving an elegant dinner party! On April 15 she invited Otto and Tola Rank to dinner. Afterward, she made one comment in the diary: "a disappointing evening, with cold, snippy, frost-bitten Mrs. R. cutting everybody's wings."[15]

Next day she analyzed herself: "I have an emotional love tapeworm. Never enough to eat!" In short, she was bored and looking for the next conquest. Rank was the obvious candidate, but something happened before she could turn her full attention to him.

She first wrote to the English critic and novelist Rebecca West in the autumn of 1932, after West had written brief praise for her book on Lawrence. Anaïs read West's most recent novel, *Harriet Hume*, and sent a letter of appreciation, thanking West in return for hers. West did not reply.[16] Nin waited a month, then wrote again, saying she rarely sought out strangers, but having read *Harriet Hume*, seeking to know its author was a "logical outcome." Once more, West did not reply.

In March 1934, Anaïs wrote yet again, asking West if she would read Henry's Lawrence book and recommend it to a British publisher. This time West replied with a two-word cable: "Why? How?" Incredibly, it was all the encouragement Anaïs needed to go to London. She persuaded Hugo to give her enough money for a week's stay and went at once.

The two women left conflicting accounts of this meeting. Anaïs wrote two versions: her unpublished diaries are a chronological narrative of each of their few meetings in the 1930s, whereas the published version is a mélange of distorted chronology, participants, and events.[17]

Before she published the diaries in the 1960s and 1970s, Nin's publishers required her to contact all living persons to secure their agreement that they would not take legal action. West was among the few who told Nin to delete all references or risk a lawsuit.[18] In the early 1970s, West received Evelyn J. Hinz, a Canadian scholar whom Nin had chosen as her biographer. When Hinz showed her the passages in the published diary, West was furious to find that Nin and her British publisher had disregarded her instructions. As far as she was concerned, everything Nin had written about her was either a lie or distortion.

West wrote immediately to Gordon N. Ray, then writing the biographical study entitled *H. G. Wells and Rebecca West,* to correct the record as she remembered it and to explain her version of the encounters with Anaïs Nin.[19] Both women's accounts provide an interesting comparison of "narrative truth and historical reality."[20]

West described herself in 1934 as newly married to Henry Maxwell Andrews and deeply involved with him in literary and political work, most of it connected to the Fascist persecution of Jews in Germany. When the uninvited and unwelcome Anaïs arrived, West's house was full of people who were also involved in writing, proposing conferences, and eliciting public support of British officials who supported their views. Despite West's best efforts not to receive it, Anaïs succeeded in presenting her with Henry's Lawrence manuscript. She read a few pages and decided it was "a farrago of nonsense,"[21] but she liked Anaïs, and feeling sorry for her, all alone in London, gave an impromptu dinner party, took her to the theater to see Charles Laughton's *Othello,* and invited her to a family lunch. "We gave her a full and happy four days," West recalled, "and as she was a total stranger I don't think I did badly for her."

Anaïs's account consumes many pages in her unpublished diary, starting with her reception by West's hall porter (whom she did not have), and her initial impression of West as "Pola Negri without beauty and English teeth. . . . She is deeply uneasy. She's intimidated by me."[22]

Anaïs said that at luncheon, she was "more and more disillusioned by [West's] sexlessness, her domesticity and by her last book on St. Augustine. . . . Naturally she admired Henry's book on Lawrence and passed over *Black Spring* in silence."[23] The next evening, she wrote of Rebecca (for they were now on a first-name basis) taking her to see Charles Laughton in *Macbeth.*[24]

Anaïs's next diary entry is of her last night in London and cementing their friendship in Rebecca's bedroom before dining at the Ivy, an elegant literary and society haunt. According to Anaïs, they shared confidences about their lack of formal education and having both been abandoned by their fathers in childhood.[25]

But something happened at the dinner to unsettle Anaïs. In her account, Rebecca supposedly said, "What puzzles me is that you should come to London with two [sic] manuscripts by Henry Miller when you're a so much better writer than he is, so much more mature.

"I was mute with surprise. . . . It stunned me. No, she must be prejudiced. NO, NO. She's wrong." Later, she added: "Henry will never forgive me for this—if he knew. I realized suddenly that Henry would not want me greater. That it would kill his love."

In mid-May, 1934, Anaïs copied a long letter from Rebecca into her diary,[26] telling her that Henry's Lawrence manuscript was "impossibly badly written."[27] Rebecca did send it to her agent, but he declined to help place the book.[28] Anaïs was surprised by Rebecca's eloquent praise of the "Rab/Mandra" portion of *Alraune,* which, inspired by their evening of shared confidences, Anaïs had given her before she left London. Rebecca thought it "simply superb," especially those parts "unaffected by Miller." Rebecca ended by hoping her astringent remarks would not cause a break between them, for she was planning a trip to France and hoped to see Anaïs again.

When she told Hugo and Eduardo what Rebecca had said about her writing, they were not surprised. "I don't believe them. They hate Henry," she thought. But during their next session, Rank asked her a disturbing question:

"Why has Henry written about Lawrence when you have already written about him?" She admitted that his question "skirted a mad doubt" that came to her at times: "The best pages of Black Spring are derived from Alraune, only more power always, a masculine expansion." She decided that everything was all right because each imitated the other. For her the only question that mattered was, "How great a writer is Henry?" If others had no faith in him, then the fault was hers: "I haven't done enough for him if he is still raw, immature, rough-hewn, uneven."

In anger, hoping to change his opinion of Henry, she made Rank read the newest revised version of the Lawrence book. "But where is Henry Miller?" Rank asked, pointing to long passages Miller had plagiarized not only from Nin but also from Spengler and himself. Depressed, she admitted: "I finally realized that I was blinded by Henry's gigantism, his long speeches, his accumulation of notes, his enormous quotations. It is a tragedy because he . . . has deceived himself as well as me." She admitted that she might be "blinded critically" but praised Henry for giving her an "awareness of reality."

Anaïs pondered Rank's comments about Henry but could not agree with him entirely. For her, Henry was still the "uncreated, unformulated being who is struggling to be born and whom I have not yet given birth to." But, she worried, if she had not succeeded after several years of trying, would it ever happen? Was she truly mistaken? Had she misjudged his "talent," his "genius"? Was Henry really the inferior writer everyone else took him to be?

She feared that her investment in him was "all the more tragic" because "I became pregnant five or six weeks ago. I carry in my womb the seed of Henry's child."

17

Birth

FROM THE MOMENT she realized that she was pregnant, Anaïs insisted that the child was Henry's and not Hugo's, even though she had been intimate with both men during the period of conception. That she had also been intimate with her father did not bear thinking, let alone writing about, and Joaquín Nin was never included in her list of possible fathers.

She was determined that Henry would be the father, and was just as equally determined that the child would never be born. But from the beginning, everything she did concerning her pregnancy was contradictory, including the account she recorded in the diary. "I must destroy it," she wrote, even as she launched into a glowing list of "the infinite possibilities of motherhood."[1] These she quickly shunted aside, for in her mind, she had to choose between the real child and the childlike and dependent Henry, who could not provide for her, let alone for it. She said she could not in good conscience ask Hugo to raise a child of Henry's, but her reasoning had a more personal dimension: what if the child were to look like Henry from the moment it was born? It could undermine, if not rupture completely, the security of her life as Hugo's wife. She simply could not risk it.

As soon as she was certain, she told Hugo that she was pregnant. Despite the fact that he knew (even though he never confronted her with the knowledge) that the child could just as easily be Henry's, he insisted that she carry it to term. She objected: "He is trying to assert his will over mine . . . angered I should not bow and obey." Hugo did everything, up to and including dire astrological predictions, to convince Anaïs not to abort, but she remained steadfast.

She did not tell Henry that she was pregnant, a curious omission if the child were indeed his. Instead, she told Rank, for whom she now convinced herself she had a "strange, ideal attraction . . . a subtle undercurrent." If Rank was surprised by her news, he did not show it, for they spent the rest of the hour teasing that she became "pregnant and fecundated" by his analysis. He asked what she planned to do. "I don't know. I'm all confusion," she replied.

But the next day she took herself to a "sage-femme," a midwife/abortionist, and here her account begins to defy interpretation. She said the woman did not have an instrument "small enough" to induce abortion—this at a time when legitimate physicians were well equipped with curettes and medications for the relatively painless procedures of dilatation and curettage, and back-alley quacks routinely resorted to hatpins or coat hangers.[2] In Anaïs's account, the woman told her to come back in a week, when she would have the proper tools.

A week later she visited the sage-femme again, but did not permit her to induce abortion because the "instrument" was frightening. She decided to take potions instead. Then she went to Henry, who was "depressed and desirous," but "after much teasing and unsatisfactory games (I cannot at the present indulge in real lovemaking), he forgot himself and I swallowed his sperm for the first time." She dressed quickly for her session with Rank.

She did not assume her traditional posture, but for the first time stretched languidly on his couch and invited him to lie beside her. They began to kiss until they "forgot" themselves: "I found myself drinking his sperm. And he threw himself over me and whispered wildly in my hair, 'You! You! You!' " When the analytical hour ended, she returned to Henry's. Omitting what had just happened with Rank, she told a happy Henry that "a woman should be nourished with nothing but sperm." They spent a pleasant evening "discussing the benefits of psychoanalysis."

"I am like a whore who gives herself but remains full of anger and contempt and bitterness," she wrote, admitting that the only way to feel better was to launch a new conquest. The Ranks' marriage had been one of convenience since they came to Paris,[3] so Anaïs suggested he spend a weekend with her. At the last moment he became ill with anxiety, which Anaïs thought was because Hugo had become his patient. Rank broke confidentiality and told Anaïs of Hugo's "incredibly naive portrait of [her] fundamental innocence."[4] The discomfiture of both men amused her greatly. When Hugo went to London on business, Anaïs persuaded Rank to stay overnight in Louveciennes. She found in him "all the elements of sensuality"; only "expertise was lacking."

For the next two months, she sallied back and forth between Henry and Rank, "absolutely fucked out," until August 1, 1934, when she joined Hugo for a brief vacation. She found him "absent, dim, joyless, slow, late, forgetful, nebulous." She did not have the energy to argue with him; she would "let him be."

She was now, she thought, three months pregnant. If she ever told Henry, she left no written record. Her attitude toward the child remained complex: she wrote in the diary of how her continuing pregnancy "baffled" the sage-femme as she "clung" to "the egg."

As August ended, she went to a doctor who discovered that all the sage-femme's potions were ineffectual and her pregnancy was more advanced than she thought: "I have to be operated and the child is six months old and alive and normal! It will be almost a childbirth. It will take over a week." She persuaded the doctor, a German-Jewish refugee,[5] to abort the child, and he gave her legitimate medicines to induce labor.

Now she began to think of it as a human being. For a brief moment she thought of giving it to her sixty-three-year-old mother to raise. Then she returned to her original thinking, that she could not ask another to shoulder her load, and furthermore, a child could not be permitted to complicate her life because "I am a mistress, I have already too many children. . . . Too much work to do, too many to serve."

On September 17, 1934, the doctor came to the now empty apartment on the boulevard Suchet.[6] While the dejected Hugo went to the pharmacy for medication to bring on labor contractions, a chipper Anaïs was already writing about this first stage of the abortion in the diary, noting that as the doctor "operated," she "charmed" him in a conversation about Jewish persecution in Berlin.

But the medication did not work and, to her surprise and displeasure, she began to have occasional spasms and labor pains. On the morning of the eighteenth, he injected her a second time, again with no results. On the nineteenth, when she had still not aborted, Hugo drove her to the Clinique Eugène Manuel, where she was shaved in preparation to deliver the child, an indignity she had not counted upon.

For two more days she labored intermittently but the child was not aborted. Hugo was with her, Henry was in the waiting room, Rank was in London, and Eduardo made himself scarce. Rosa was in Mallorca and Joaquín was studying in Spain; neither had been told that Anaïs was pregnant.[7]

On the twenty-first, when spasms of pain grew fierce, an hysterical Anaïs begged Hugo to telephone Rank in London and ask him to come. Hugo did and Rank agreed. Anaïs then combed, powdered, and perfumed herself, even painted her eyelashes. She made Hugo send for Henry, who came into her room looking "haggard and desperate," and Eduardo, who eventually turned up. Shortly after, Rank joined them. "All this love calling me back to life," she told the diary.

Several hours later she was taken to the delivery room, where she labored intensely but "kept my eyelash stuff on." In the early hours of September 22, she gave birth to a stillborn girl, whom she insisted upon seeing, saying she was "scientifically curious."

The next morning she perfumed and powdered herself and put on the rose silk jacket Hugo bought after her "carefully thought request for the appropriate hospital costume." All her men came to visit, bringing gifts. Henry's was the announcement of the imminent publication of his book.

"Here," Anaïs said, "is a birth which is of greater interest to me."

The account of the birth in the diary almost defies interpretation. It is a portrait of monstrous egotism and selfishness, horrifying in its callous indifference. Underlying all the pain Anaïs endured is her cheerfulness at having disposed so relatively easily of the problem. That four men and one physician assisted her without compunction is distressing, even as it provides insight into the power she wielded in each of her relationships. She disregarded any human element inherent in this birth, and from the beginning of the pregnancy seems

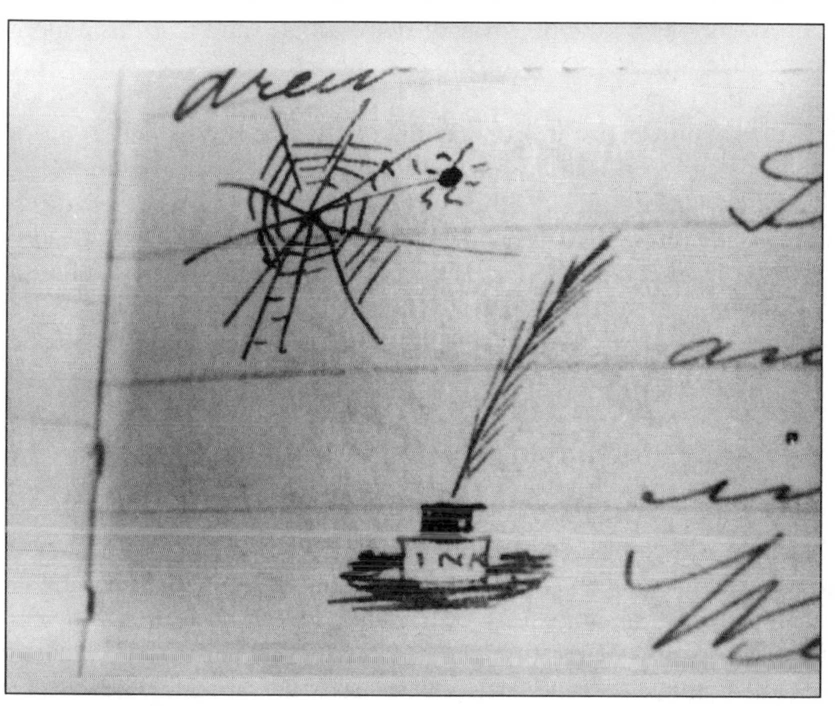

Anaïs Nin's drawing of herself and the diary.

to have considered it nothing more than an experience she could write about. If the reader can accept her point of view, the birth episode is probably her finest writing.

The prose is taut and precise, and not one excess word impedes or in any way detracts from her vividly graphic description of childbirth. It is shocking in its intensity, and riveting as she accretes both the details of the process and the detachment of her observations. What makes this writing ultimately so horrifying is the realization that Anaïs Nin is once again the observer of her own life, and that this experience, like any and every other, became real only when she wrote about it.

There is no regret in her account, only a confused collection of excuses and justifications for her action. As she looked at the dead child, she "hated it for all the pain it had caused me and because it was a little girl and I had imagined it a boy." Suddenly, this little girl, who had earlier been portrayed as "perfectly formed" with a beautiful head, hands, and feet, metamorphosed into a monster carrying "a tumor in the head" which was aborted in the nick of time, for if she had carried it one more day, "it would have infected me. I would have died."

Only for a moment did Anaïs consider, if the child had lived, "what this little girl might have been." Quickly she dismissed the thought. She justified waiting so long to abort it because it became "a hostage held against Rank's departure," which she carried only until she could get him to cut short his business in London and rush back to demonstrate "the immensity of his love." Another justification was that it was also "Henry's child" and therefore had to be "pushed away" so that she could keep him in his childishly dependent state. It also had to be dispensed with so that she could "live only for myself, for my love and my life as a woman individuated." If the child had lived, the ordinary requirements of raising it would have separated her "from man," and she could not have that: "For man, for love of man, for my life as woman, I killed the child."

The day after the birth, all the other men went elsewhere, but Hugo remained by her side and, together, they drank champagne. Mildly drunk, she fell asleep again: "Glory, glory of deliverance. The sleep of deliverance."

Within weeks she resumed her peregrinations from man to man. Rank took her to "visit" a first edition of *Huckleberry Finn* (he was a passionate collector of Twain memorabilia). She celebrated by taking him to the Suchet apartment for a tryst. When it was again rented, she found a nearby hotel, which meant that Rank neglected patients whose money he sorely needed. Anaïs rejoiced that he gave up money to be with her. At a nightclub, she deliberately aroused one of Hugo's clients so that his erection was visible to everyone. Hugo was mortified but said she was grieving for her lost child. Everyone said they quite understood. She had a brief fling with the publisher Louis Andard, whom she met on the train to Dinard.[8] Afterward, she made him pay 100 francs for a stunningly contradictory reason: "I desired to accept as June did, I wanted to use him as June did, but I needed it to pay for my trip to Rouen to meet HIM" (now Otto Rank).

"HIM" (Joaquín Nin having been consigned to oblivion months ago) was on his way to the United States because he could no longer sustain his lifestyle in Paris. He intended to take Anaïs with him. The first mention that she was considering a career as a psychoanalyst came in a postscript to Rebecca West written the previous June. She told West that Rank was instructing her so that she could live alone and be independent, and she expected to open her own analytic practice in the fall. Her only training—if it can be dignified by the term—came in early July, when she attended a few early sessions at Rank's annual institute at the Psychological Center he founded.[9] She was convinced she would be besieged with clients in New York and would make a fortune as an analyst. And besides, "Rank said he could get me a dancing job."

Meanwhile, her machinations continued. She prepared to close Louveciennes for the winter, with Hugo "anxious for me to go to New York, to get me away from Henry." Concurrently, she told Henry that she was finally leaving Hugo and moving in with him. In truth, she made most of her preparations "discreetly, quietly. The noise and flair of my departure would cause pain."

But both men could sense she was leaving and both retaliated: "Hugo deprives me of money, Henry takes refuge in his work." Then Hugo became hysterical and wept, begging her not to go. Her response was irritation when she learned he would be in New York on business in January 1935: as she was sailing in early December 1934, it gave her only a month alone with Rank.

Plans changed somewhat when a tenant assumed the lease on Louveciennes. Anaïs emptied the house and stored some furnishings, but sold most of them to pay pressing bills. Hugo rented a modest apartment near Rosa's, and Joaquín became an unwitting go-between when Anaïs asked him to receive Rank's "business" letters. He agreed, having no reason to suspect anything amiss.[10]

All through November, Rank sent a barrage of letters that read as if written by a dumbstruck lovesick kid. "You!" became their private expletive of love, so each time he wrote the pronoun, he capitalized, underlined, or otherwise embossed and embellished it. They gave each other nicknames: he became "Huck" because of his obsession with Twain's novel; she became "Puck" because it rhymed and was the name of a mischievous sprite in English folklore. Rank was so besotted that he took steps to help his nearly thirty-two-year-old mistress resume her dancing career. He sent clippings from New York newspapers about La Argentina: "Darling," he wrote, "yesterday I spoke to that girl who studies with Balanchine and she will ask him to see you and tell you what to do."[11] He met "a very prominent lawyer of the Paramount film company . . . he offered me letters of introduction to all the big fish. . . . Naturally I thought of you and whether I could get you in the pictures." Several days later he wrote again, advising her to "have that operation so not to be bothered with your monthly period."

He thanked her effusively for a signet ring she gave him their last night together, but made no reference to what he had given her: the carnelian intaglio ring that Sigmund Freud placed on his hand when Otto Rank became a member of Freud's Secret Committee.[12]

On November 10 she thought herself about "to go mad": Rank deluged her with "nerve-wracked" letters, Hugo indulged in "new cruelties with money," Henry was "childishly irresponsible and weak." And she tried to seduce her brother's spiritual counselor, the Abbé Altermann, supposedly "to deprive Joaquin of his faith and keep him from becoming a monk."[13] Disturbed by her callousness, the Abbé called her "une âme très disputée."[14]

The next day, she sailed for New York. Rank paid her passage because Hugo simply did not have the money.

> *"Listen to me, honey, I love you, you're marvelous, Isn't it grand honey to arrive in New York while I make love to you? I'm mad about you honey. You won't do me wrong. You won't forget me honey. I love your hair honey. Listen to me . . ."*[15]

—Thus Anaïs described her arrival in New York and her shipboard fling with an unnamed man. She cut a patch off the dress she wore as the ship docked, and when Rank asked why, said someone spilled liquor and ruined it.[16] It was the man's sperm, but she could not tell Rank, as he had given her the dress in Paris.

Rank took her to the Adams Hotel on E. 86th Street, where he rented "a darling little room with bath and everything right next to mine . . . not connected, so close and at the end of a hallway so we'll be absolutely by ourselves."[17] She stayed there for several weeks, during which time Rank worked very little and played tourist.[18]

She used all sorts of ruses to cadge money from Rank so she could keep Hugo's allowance for Henry's passage. Telling Rank that she needed another address because of Hugo's imminent arrival, she moved into the Barbizon Plaza to be with Henry. Rank kept her room at the Adams for her to consult patients and also paid for the one at the Barbizon. She persuaded him that they should sleep together only "on the holidays," an excuse to keep most of her nights free for Henry.

Rank prepared Anaïs to receive her own patients, but with her analyst doubling as lover, she made no progress in her own therapy. Even before she began her seduction of Rank, she told Eduardo why she intended to do it.[19] She believed that Rank wanted her "dangerous, rebellious perverse [June] side." She admitted that she had never really wanted to become an analyst and liked watching Rank "undermining the psychoanalysis from which he lives. I would not mind doing him harm. . . . He has met me and lost his head [and is] aware of the joy I feel in this triumph." Eduardo was horrified but shrugged it off, telling her since she could not have God she might as well have all the analysts. "I don't give myself to them. I keep myself," she replied.

And then she turned on Henry, asking, "Do I arrest myself on the brink of destruction and self-destruction in order to canalize[20] it all into art?" She postponed the answer by inventing a new question: "Should I go to Jung now and get another scalp?"

On December 26 Henry cabled: "Wire me immediately . . . that you are not betraying me." She replied by letter: "I am your woman always, Henry . . . have faith in me."[21] In the meantime, she slept with a half-dozen men who were business clients of Hugo's. Even John Erskine telephoned, but him she refused to see.

Henry sailed on January 7, his fare paid by Anaïs with the money garnered from Hugo and Rank. He was so rattled that by the time they cleared customs and got to the Barbizon, he was exhausted with nervous tension. She wanted to put him to bed to sleep, but he went only after he arranged "the Spanish shawl, the orange velvet cover, the orange coffee cups, all the symbols he brought of Louveciennes, the studio." She pitied him for his dependence on objects even as he told her that he no longer wanted her support because he wanted to marry and protect her "more than anybody, more than anything."

After he was settled, she left to spend the night with Rank, telling Henry she was on her way to Forest Hills because her mother-in-law forced her to stay several nights each week. When she returned the next morning, he confronted her with a sheaf of telephone messages from other men and said her lies put him "in despair."

Rank knew about Henry and he, too, was sad. It only made her behavior more outrageous. She had her own patients now, and actually lay down on her analytic couch with one man while Rank was in session in the next room. "I want to betray him there on the couch we lie on, pulling down everything sacred, desecrating, cheapening."

She scorned even those who could have helped her with her writing. John Erskine arranged for her to meet Theodore Dreiser, thinking he could help her publish *Alraune.* She rushed to see Dreiser in his apartment at the Hotel Astoria, but wrote in the diary only of his fascination with her beauty and his attempts to seduce her, which may or may not have been true. Her bizarre deceptions grew ever more grotesque and blatant, and both Henry and Rank went on accepting them humbly, as if she were bestowing special favors upon them.

Rank deluged her with presents, dumping on her bed one day a load of filmy underwear and nightgowns, creams, powders, expensive perfumes, chocolates, and a suitcase for her to put them in when she accompanied him on a lecture tour to New Orleans. "The minute he is gone I am taking all that stuff to Henry and I'm wearing it for him." And she did. "The real life of objects," she added. "He gave the chocolates to me and I gave them to Henry, who ate them."

Erskine came unexpectedly to see her; "full of mischief," she told him about her love affair with her father. "Really startled him," she noted with satisfaction. It must have, for she never saw him again.

In March she was overcome with panic that she was pregnant. Rank had been on a lecture tour of the United States and would know that he did not impregnate her. She had no money for an abortion, so she persuaded a doctor to give "medicine for delayed menstruation." His diagnosis was low thyroid and the medication did induce a period, but she was certain she had aborted again.

She did not join Rank in New Orleans, but used the traveling money to pay Henry's rent. Rank was so angry that he took back his gifts.[22] When he returned several days later, she crept into his bed, but he did not return the presents despite her wheedling.

A curious thing happened then: "The man who took away the diary as a neurosis gave it back to me as a unique work by his enthusiasm for it. He incites and inspires me to work." Rank now said he admired her diary so much that he joined her in a "twin diary," he writing on one page and she on another. It is, at the present, the only known writing in his hand that pertains to her treatment, all in the dense, obtuse, convoluted style of all his other, published, writings. In one entry, Rank wrote that Anaïs needed lies to help her "maintain the split."[23] She denied that she lied outright, saying that she did so only "to make the other happy by keeping up illusions, or rather building up illusion." In an exceedingly convoluted passage, Rank said that it had to be counteracted when it became too real in her mind by "stark reality (life service which is not real, not life either, but through the pain is *made* real); creating reality (just as much as unreality) by having it pain, but again as a balance having unreality which is happiness."

As he wrote his analysis, his mind seems to have worked so fast that his pen could not keep up with it, for grammar and punctuation both falter: "Lying for fear of loss (anger) loss of love! Loss of being loved interpreted for the other but maybe or is it for the other too, creating a uterine world for the man in which he can live, uterine world means ego world, where everything is as he wants it to be, or as he needs it, she knows that in his feelings when and what he needs, that's her adaptability, she is man's environment, changeable, possible environment."

At this point he practically stabbed holes in the paper as he wrote, "Where is your true self? Not in your writing, nor in your living, nor in your playing. WHERE?" Then he stopped writing for good.

Rank told her he now believed her many volumes of diary writing to be "an invaluable document, written from a woman's point of view, in which a woman's psychology is revealed."[24] He said the diary greatly enhanced his knowledge of women and their ways of thinking. He even admired *Alraune* and said that if no one would publish it, he would have it privately printed.

Rank gave her patients to see, mostly society matrons from Greenwich and New Canaan, Connecticut. A number of the wives of rich corporate executives he treated came into the city quietly to seek his services, and he turned them over to Anaïs.[25] When Hugo finally arrived in New York at the end of May 1935, she arranged for them to be invited to several of her patients' homes, and Hugo conducted some successful business transactions with their husbands.

Two of her best-known patients were the orchestra conductor Antonia Brico and Laura Archera, the violinist who later married Aldous Huxley. Others were men like the business friend of Hugo's who bought an occasional analytical hour hoping it would result in a tryst, and others were ordinary persons who genuinely sought help.

Despite the chaos of her life, Anaïs Nin seems to have given occasionally sound counsel to her patients.[26] Her advice fell into what is now called "self-help," and was generally upbeat and positive, as she told the patients how far they had come in their quest for self-understanding and how courageous they had to be to complete their treatment.

But she could not let her patients go when it was clear that their therapy was ended. One woman, a young wife of nineteen when she first consulted Anaïs Nin, remembers feeling (without knowing anything else about her except that she wrote diaries) "pulled back every time I felt well enough to get on [with life] by myself."[27]

Henry was also seeing patients,[28] thanks to Rank, whose willingness to send innocent people to Henry Miller can be attributed only to the depth of his infatuation with Anaïs Nin, especially as they fought daily about her continuing affair with Henry, which she now told him bluntly she would never end.

When Hugo finally scheduled his long-delayed business trip in May 1935, Henry gave up his patients and moved from the Barbizon to the less-expensive Roger Williams apartments on E. 31st Street. June had received a Mexican divorce the previous December, and Henry had been halfheartedly proposing marriage to Anaïs ever since. Now, with Hugo's arrival imminent, he decided to force her to decide between them. Finally and firmly, she put an end to all talk of marriage. She asked Henry: "why not take it humorously? We don't want to be free—economically—by living dully as ordinary people. You don't want an ordinary job. I don't want analysis or anything as a routine but as an adventure. Well then, we will have to conform to my job as Hugo's wife. Accept the separations. I'll continue to play tricks for us to live together as much as possible."[29]

After this, she noted that "Henry got frisky and playful again."

They had been apart for six months when Hugo cabled on May 2 that he would dock in Montreal on the fourth, where he asked her to meet him for a combined week of business and second honeymoon. As he was staying in New York until July, she also rented a furnished apartment at 7 Park Avenue. Rank was convinced at last that she would never leave Hugo and came to the apartment for a showdown. He accused her of using him: "All this was true. I could only say 'and didn't I give you anything in return.' " When she reached Montreal, letters from Rank awaited, signed "Miserable Huck" and begging her forgiveness.

Meeting Hugo again was "a great emotion." She greeted him in a white transparent nightgown and found it a pleasure "to submit again after Rank." Hugo had been living in London and the bank planned to make him senior trust officer there. He rented an apartment on the pleasant Charlotte Street, made new friends, and was flattered by attention from attractive women.[30] She noted his new clothing, a high-collared emerald-green sweater, gray-checked trousers, and several coats, "all as the artist wears it." But he talked only about "power," a word found in nearly every sentence she repeated for the diary. "He says he'll play the artist but he likes the power of his business successes. While he told me all this, I studied the stucco walls."

In May, Rebecca West visited New York and took Anaïs to a dinner party given in West's honor.[31] Anaïs was thrilled to be introduced as "the beautiful woman who wrote the best book on Lawrence," and proceeded to try to direct everyone's attention toward herself rather than toward Rebecca. This did not sit well with either the guest of honor or her hosts. Several days later, Rebecca discovered that Anaïs had initiated an affair with one of the guests, Norman Bel Geddes, "the P. T. Barnum of design."[32] Rebecca was furious, especially because she liked Hugo. "Your husband is so sweet," she said to Anaïs. "I was surprised he should be your husband."

On June 15, Hugo and Anaïs sailed for Paris on the luxury liner *Champlain*. Henry followed on the rust-bucket *Viendam*. Anaïs left the unhappy Rank to deal with her confused and angry patients. Her excuse for leaving was that "Hugo came to fetch me and Henry didn't want to stay in New York."

Back in Louveciennes, Anaïs was depressed by the decrepitude of her house and the lives of everyone she had left behind. Paris was now "like a second rate fair. Shoddy. Askew and small. And they say it has charm."[33]

"This is a new me," she wrote. "A me that does not belong here anymore. Living in a dead house . . . without home and resting place . . . because now I have accepted my solitude and so I have no home and no marriage."

Hugo went back to London, hinting that he might make their separation legal if she did not join him. She knew she would have to find a mollifying reason to remain in Paris.

Henry came to stay in Louveciennes, bringing Fraenkel and Fred. She was angry at Henry's lord-of-the-manor attitude. He and his friends consumed vast quantities of food, drank gallons of wine, and smoked endless cigarettes, leaving Anaïs to clean up the mess. But from their indolence and sloth came a decision with far-reaching consequences: as no one seemed eager to publish the work of any of them, they might as well buy a printing press and do it themselves.

18

Friendships with Women

ANAÏS RATIONALIZED that she made the decision to let Henry and Fraenkel control the printing press they were determined to buy not with her money but with Fraenkel's: "They can put it in Villa Seurat (what I now call 'Russia and the collective life,' in contrast to the haven of Louveciennes). I could not bear them all to be here."[1]

She resented Fraenkel, whom she referred to as "the Jew," even as she admitted that she was jealous of him. Although they exchanged letters about their writing for the next several years,[2] he thought of her only as Henry's mistress and patron. Fraenkel agreed to name the still-hypothetical printing press Siana (Anaïs spelled backward) but also decreed that the first book to be printed was Henry's "Scenario" (a section of *Tropic of Capricorn*). "Only then Alraune, which he seems to fear, always to envy. I don't know why."

He was especially dismissive of diary writing and snorted when he happened upon her treasured copy of Amiel's.[3] If she tried to engage him in a discussion of the diary as serious literature, he either made a disparaging remark or left the room, while Henry sat sheepishly silent. Anaïs was infuriated by them both.

Writing fiction was a painful process, worsened because her amorphous plots disturbed both men. *Alraune* was now separated into two parts: the first, still entitled "Alraune," became the "night" portion, later the section featuring Sabina in *House of Incest*. The "day" portion centered on Jeanne and was now called "Chaotica," a title eventually abandoned.[4]

"I don't want to see a hideous reality!" Anaïs complained after one too many of Fraenkel's criticisms that she had written a story dependent upon "two faces and night and day symbolism" and did not make any recognizable distinction between what she called "day-face or night-face." Instead, she gloated about her expressions: "I coined that! I think it's wonderful!"

As always, she needed a scapegoat, and Henry was closest to hand. Happily settled among other writers and artists in Michael Fraenkel's house, Henry organized his life around long stints of daily writing on *Tropic of Capricorn,* which meant he was not paying Anaïs the attention she craved: "As soon as his life settles into the mold he likes, gibberish, café, idleness, sleep, foolishness, childishness, I feel resentful, bored and unhappy." It took her several days to admit that her anger was actually because "he is writing about June and not about me."

After "another evening and morning of the blackest misery," she sat down alone in Louveciennes and began to "copy the New York diary," which meant "writing in between the lines . . . expanding and dramatizing." Some of it eventually became material for *House of Incest,* but with one major change: "I should probably be writing about my father but now I don't want to for I regard him more like Joaquín, as a brother." Later, she transposed accounts from the diary that were about her father into fictional events featuring her character, Jeanne's brother. But all the while, she was angry with herself for not being able to create and maintain a momentum similar to Henry's.

In Louveciennes, she longed for everything she left behind in New York. The diary version of life there became tales of success and adulation. She described "flirtations" (her euphemism for brief sexual encounters), "affairs" (Bel Geddes), and even "Cuban vice consul at the last moment, one hour before sailing!"

With time and distance, her analytic practice was recorded for posterity as a great success: "I came away loaded with triumphs as woman, as analyst . . . women of fifty clutching at me. I developed a great gentle firmness." Even the taciturn Walter Lowenfels, sparing with praise for those he admired, supposedly "capitulated" when she saw him briefly and let him read *Alraune:* "he said I was a human being and a creative artist and that he underestimated me."

By mid-July 1935, she had no more compliments to give herself and now told the diary she was "very sick, neurotic, repressed and finally physically ill."

Suddenly, the names of all the expatriate artistic community in Paris filled her diary, and always in connection with Henry. She introduced herself to the writer Richard Toma, whom she met as he rang Henry's doorbell one day. Fraenkel introduced her to James and Nora Joyce one afternoon in Sylvia Beach's bookstore. Fraenkel (not Joyce) told her that James Joyce admired Henry's writing. So, too, he said, did Ann and Julien Green and Moune and Stuart Gilbert, two couples to whom he introduced her and who became her friends (not Henry's) for many years afterward. "Marcel Duchamp is in the air," she wrote, "and Paul Eluard to come [to the Villa Seurat]."

She decided to introduce Henry to a celebrity of her own: "How would you like to meet Brancuzi," she asked. "I don't like prophets," he replied, declining the invitation. He preferred the Hungarian photographer Brassaï, the sculptor Chana Orloff, and the painter Foujita. She didn't like them or any of Henry's other friends from the Quarter, who all seemed "flabby, weak, or winey or without grandeur." And she especially resented that "[Henry] is becoming a celebrity, getting letters from Ezra Pound, T. S. Elliot [sic], a review by Blaise Cendrar. A hundred and thirty copies of Tropic of Cancer sold to date."

In such a mood, a confrontation was inevitable. She poured vast quantities of angry ink into the diary, writing vitriolic prose about Henry and all that he owed to her: when she became an analyst, he had to "rival and imitate"; she wrote about Lawrence and he pushed her work aside, seized authority, and wrote about Lawrence himself. Worse: "he takes all he has learned from me and analyzes Fraenkel, giving it to him as his [Henry's] own, identifying himself with Rank while hating Rank."

Time passed, and they talked less and less about the still-mythical Siana Press. Anaïs's mounting anger with Henry and his friends was interrupted when Rebecca West and her husband came to Louveciennes in August. Hugo was still working in London, but was home on vacation. Together the two couples journeyed to Rouen to see Rebecca's son, Anthony, who was studying there. The two women then spent several days in Louveciennes and shared confidences, but Anaïs did not tell Rebecca of "my love affair with my father and that I killed my child. I don't know how far she will follow me into strangeness."

Rebecca proceeded cheerfully to cement what she thought would become a solid friendship.[5] She read Anaïs's burgeoning manuscript and made thoughtful comments; Anaïs instructed her in the art of applying false eyelashes and mascara. The two women painted each other's nails and compared their analyses, their husbands, and their lovers.[6] "Rebecca's life, too, I feel I will influence. Toward freedom." Anaïs wrote confidently.

A cluster of confusion envelops Anaïs Nin's written record of her daily life after Rebecca's departure. There are many more references to love, a new lover, and to being in love again, but this time, she was not looking "for the father or the child," but awaiting "The MAN."[7]

Then, abruptly, she changed the subject: "—Oh god, I forgot. Kahane has accepted my novel of June-Henry. Is making me sign a contract for my next two books, and as my literary agent for all my work. Yes, I have a contract in my pocket." This passage appears almost as an afterthought because it was not entirely true: Kahane agreed to publish her work only as long as she provided the money to pay for it.

Again the topic veered abruptly, to "pregnancy again, which is bliss. But whose child?" Then: "How I regret each time its end." Without consulting a physician, she decided she would need a cesarean delivery, so there was "no use" in staying pregnant, which was "dangerous to my heart and general condition."

Her erratic thinking unleashed a frenzy of creativity. Both *Alraune* and *Chaotica* were subsumed into what would become her first published novel: *House of Incest.* She now believed her fiction would "never get stuck again" because she was "imitating the diary, approximating the tone of sincerity and the fullness."

She all but moved into the Villa Seurat, even though she resented having to shop for and cook elaborate meals for Fred, Fraenkel, and "Henry's timorous bourgeois weak winey friends" while they sat placidly writing all day long. "I can't lead such a wasted life," she observed, even as she did.

She explained her long absences to Hugo by saying that Fraenkel had given her one of the rooms in the house to use as a studio, and she could work better there than in Louveciennes. Hugo was not fooled, and after every ploy to keep her at home failed, resorted to violence. Each time he found her preparing to leave, he insisted on conjugal relations, sometimes so violently that she compared it to being raped. He tried another ploy, sending his card with flowers to the Villa Seurat, asking "May I see you tomorrow?"[8]

Anaïs was both disturbed and comforted by a "merciless" letter from Rebecca West,[9] to whom she had sent *Alraune,* a copy of Fraenkel's *Werther's Younger Brother* and several of his newer writings, and Henry's emerging *Tropic of Capricorn*—hoping Rebecca would persuade her publisher, the prestigious Jonathan Cape, to take them. West called them "repetitious, stale and borrowed" and found nothing of value in any of them. She allegedly thought Fraenkel and Miller "unworthy to for one minute be on your plane," as they had "no sense of reality." She also said, according to Anaïs:

> I cannot believe that such minds can ever profit from contact with yours. . . . I feel you are confusing what satisfies your maternal instincts. . . . I wish you'd forge ahead with the work of your genius, on its own level. . . . because these men are so empty . . . there is no end to what they can take from you and what you can give them, and that gives your nature its intensest pleasure. In reality it is a waste.

These were sentiments Anaïs Nin could have, and perhaps did, write about herself, as the passage West allegedly wrote is uncharacteristic.

That autumn Anaïs was sadly reflective: "no solid values . . . unreality . . . nowhere to stay." It was time to close Louveciennes for the winter, and this year they could only afford to rent several rooms in Louise de Vilmorin's vast apartment in the bourgeois Seventh Arrondisement.

Eduardo had been living with them, but he moved into his own apartment with a young Hungarian, Firi.[10] "He does the Coupole," Anaïs said disapprovingly, even though she went with him to avoid Henry, who was now begging for a larger monthly stipend in keeping with his growing literary reputation. Anaïs warned that his constant begging would drive her to abandon him. "You are not a man," she scolded. "You are the child who sucks one's breasts until they bleed."

As 1935 ended, she developed a plan. She would go back to New York, regroup her former patients, get new ones, and make her living as an independent analyst. She would, of course, take Henry, and thought it only a matter of time until she won Rank back and resumed her affair with him. She would also change the way she treated men, and would "take every lover who comes my way, to live my life as a woman, as sex, to make up for my stupid role as mother." But to do this, she would need a lot of money.

First she returned Hugo's affection and became a good corporate wife. In return for her temporary solicitousness, Hugo agreed to give her whatever money he could toward passage and expenses, but for one month only, January 1936. He expected her to return to Paris in early February.

It was a start. Next she went to Jack Kahane and persuaded him that Henry wanted her to have the 2,000 francs in royalties that were due him. Then she persuaded Fraenkel to give her 1,000 francs, in exchange for which she promised to try to place his manuscripts in New York. She sold some of her clothes and jewelry, but was so nervous about the trip that she went back to Allendy and was alone with him for the first time since she ended their affair. She persuaded him that she needed drugs, and he gave her "Chanvre indien," which he called "harmless" but which was really a derivative of *cannabis sativa* consisting mostly of hashish. She was to take it one week before her "moonstorm" (menstrual period).[11]

For the past several years, the week preceding her menstrual period had been painful, but now with Chanvre indien, everything changed. The drug made her "see everything enormous, ominous, tragic, etc. . . . humanly it is unbearable." It induced heightened creativity, which she credited with giving her "my book on my father," and the "Jeanne" section of *House of Incest,* which, in this drug-induced haze, she finally finished writing.

Chanvre indien had one side effect that she could not control: it made her hands twitch. So she took up rug hooking, an enterprise that soothed her for the better part of the next decade.

Drawing of Anaïs by her cousin.

Her father sent 500 francs "for pins" the day before she sailed on the S.S. *Bremen,* January 18, 1936. In her luggage she carried six bottles of "Dr. Jacobson's magic fattening powders." Eduardo found Dr. Max Jacobson, who would achieve notoriety in New York in the 1960s as "Dr. Feelgood," the physician who dispensed amphetamines to President John F. Kennedy, among other famous patients. Anaïs and Hugo became Dr. Jacobson's most devoted patients, and soon their family and friends were praising the vibrant and dynamic health given by his "magic cocktails."

Anaïs drank one as soon as the gangplank was raised, then went across the hall to Henry's stateroom, for she had scraped up the money for his passage as well. It was not a good crossing because "Henry becomes schizophrenic when travelling."

In New York, she booked rooms at the Barbizon Plaza and spent a fruitless afternoon trying to reach Rank. She wrote a letter to "Huck, my Huck," telling him that she had been thinking about his life and had many ideas on how to make it better and more peaceful.[12] He replied, not with a letter, but by underlining many of the passages in hers, addressing it to "Puck, my Puck." He agreed to meet her once, for an hour only, but never replied to the begging letters she wrote for the next several years.

In the early spring of 1936, Anaïs lived her life "as a woman" with reckless abandon. It was relatively easy to do, for Henry was never comfortable in the Barbizon and moved again into the Roger Williams Hotel. Her first encounter was with literary agent Barthold Fles, who she hoped would represent her. In her written account, Fles paused long enough to say he admired *House of Incest* before they pounced on each other and had sex. He did not help to publish it, however, nor did he agree to represent her.

Norman Bel Geddes was next. Maliciously, he arranged for Anaïs to be invited to a party he attended with his wife. There, Anaïs met the actors Raymond Massey and Adrienne Alan and the writer Glenway Westcott and MOMA Monroe Wheeler.[13] She wrote that John Huston paid her so much attention that "Bel Geddes who thinks I am a most exciting person gets jealous," but she refused to see him again.

She wrote an admiring letter to Waldo Frank, sure that once he met her he would find her a publisher. According to her diary, he came to her room and within minutes they, too, had sex and Frank's gratitude was immense: "God sent you, La Catalana, so that I might finish my book."

She contacted Donald Friede, hoping he would relent and publish her novel. He surprised her by saying that the moment they met he recognized how much they were alike. She quotes him as saying, "I'm a realist. Everybody around here fools himself about what he wants. I don't. I want sex. In fact, it is the orgy I like best and which I consider the most satisfying."

With Friede and a woman she calls "Mary, wife of a Time magazine high executive,"[14] Anaïs Nin participated in her first orgy and her first complete lesbian experience, "tasting a woman's vagina," which she did not like at all.[15] "Two things I always pictured and wanted," Anaïs wrote. "To slip my hand under a woman's skirt and to feel her backside. To feel and kiss beautiful breasts." Here, she wrote that she had not done these things with June, and regretted it. But all that she and Donald Friede did with Mary left her curiously unmoved: "we caressed and fulfilled our feminine obligations, but our real interest was in each other."

After the trio dressed, engaged in small talk, and sat around drinking cocktails, Mary and Anaïs left together in the elevator. "I would never have asked to see her again. I did not know whether my body had value in that fucking world."[16] But she had learned one thing that she never forgot: "And that is silence. Things are enjoyed in a kind of silence and awareness. That may be the law of enjoyment: not to think. I learned this in silence. I ask no questions."

Another woman, Thurema Sokol,[17] came into her life at this point, a woman with whom she might have developed a friendship but instead tried to engage in a sort of unfulfilled love affair. Anaïs Nin did not know how to forge friendships with women and had not had a close woman friend since her high school days with Frances Schiff Bolton. Even that was based on their mutual desire for a writing career rather than on the usual small talk. As a young wife, Anaïs depended on Hugo to fill her need for friendship, and since she met Henry Miller, she had had no time for anything other than "serving men."[18] With June Miller, everything in their relationship had been based on a contest, with Henry as the prize. Even Rebecca West, who was genuinely interested in being Anaïs Nin's friend in the mid-1930s, had to be controlled, bested, or placed somehow in an inferior, dependent position.

As Anaïs dictated the terms of the relationship with Thurema, it had no chance to develop in any terms but those she set for it. Having attained rapport only with men, she could relate to women with what she called, for want of a better term, "love." Thurema, married and the mother of a young son, lived quietly in a suburb of New York City, concertizing and attending to her family. When she realized Anaïs was fascinated with her, she returned the emotion in kind. They spent several nights together in Anaïs's room at the Barbizon Plaza, sleeping "head to foot in the bed," as Anaïs described it: "In the darkness, such loveliness, such a new experience to feel her softness and warmth. I did want to touch her breasts, but I didn't want her to misunderstand. There was no misunderstanding." Together they scorned lesbians, laughing at one of Anaïs's patients, the orchestra leader Antonia Brico, who was known for aggressively pursuing the young female musicians who played for her.

But Thurema came into Anaïs's life at a critical period, just after Bel Geddes, Friede, and all the other unnamed (and perhaps some still unknown) disappointing sexual partners. Thurema represented "love, purity, wholeness," which Anaïs had not found in her other relationships. Thurema told her that her quest for a father was futile; what Anaïs really sought was someone to mother her as she tried to mother everyone else. "Perhaps she's right, and I'm looking in men for something only a woman can give," Anaïs admitted. There was much passionate kissing and touching of each other's breasts, but Mary remained her only complete lesbian experience on that trip to New York.

All too soon, however, the familiar pattern in Anaïs Nin's relationships formed, and Thurema was relegated to the rank of those who disappointed her or in some way did not fulfill her expectations. "The passion died," and Anaïs was ready for someone else.

In late March she received a telegram from Hugo telling her that Thorvald would be docking in New York on his way from Europe to Havana. She had not seen her brother since he stormed angrily from

Louveciennes almost five years previously. He and his wife, Teresa, had moved from Bogotá to Puerto Rico and then to Havana, where they lived with their two children, Charles and Gayle.

There was a problem with Thorvald's passport and he was not permitted to leave the ship. Anaïs was invited on board, and in the ship's lounge, she saw "a face like a mask, so reticent, so closed, so estranged."[19]

Thorvald's relations with his mother had been strained since he left Paris and had been all but nonexistent with his brother and sister. However, he had remained on good terms with his father, and they corresponded frequently. And he knew that *House of Incest* was about to be published (by Fraenkel, who gave up trying to buy a printing press and instead forged an agreement with Kahane to publish the "Siana Series of the Obelisk Press": Henry's *Aller Retour New York* (based on his 1935 trip and funded by Anaïs) was to be first, Richard Thoma paid for his *Tragedy in Blue* to be second, and Hugo promised to raise the money for *House of Incest* to be third).[20]

Anaïs spread the news that her novel was to appear in spring 1936, and when Joaquín Nin heard its title, he was frantic. None of her letters soothed his fears, and taking his elder son into his confidence, he blurted out only that a terrible thing had happened, a great mistake had been made, and an isolated incident of incest had taken place. He placed all the blame squarely on his daughter, who he said had been "made queer by psychoanalysis."

Thorvald knew this when he met his sister, and he told her bluntly that their father had prepared him "to meet a madwoman," which perhaps explains his "reticence" and "brusque gestures" and why he "hid behind dark glasses." She countered by saying Joaquín Nin was "a pathological liar" who could not be trusted. Thorvald agreed with her and the conversation relaxed a little.

Here, the accounts of what happened between them differ considerably. In Thorvald's version there was some difficulty with his passport, and he was taken to Ellis Island and held overnight.[21]

Anaïs's story, told in the diary, is quite different: As Thorvald could not leave the ship, members of the staff invited her to stay on board and dine with him. Afterward, they kissed goodnight in "a storm of powerful intensity," and he held her "like a lover." She then went "to my own cabin,"[22] connected to Thorvald's by an interior door. They chatted from their separate rooms; then she describes three separate incidents of incest: he allegedly came to her cabin at night and the following morning, and the next night, to her room at the Barbizon Plaza.

All her accounts are written in effusive, maudlin prose, and all are couched in a very Rankian prose centering on images of maternity. The dominating theme, and her primary emotion throughout, is maternal joy at being able to give nourishment. The real-life brother has become the mythical son to whom the sister/mother has given birth. In the act of incest, his body metamorphoses into their father's, with whom she had previous incestuous relations. It is a neat and tidy account, and she seems pleased with the prettiness of it. Even so, large amounts of self-absolution and self-justification are necessary before she can close the account satisfactorily.

After Thorvald's ship sailed to Havana, she wrote of crying in unbearable pain for "so many loves." In self-dramatization, she asked, "What am I? The lover of the world. Crazed with love. Crazed with love. My whole body in pain. The pain of separation, loss, change."

There is no other mention in her diaries of this encounter with her brother, and that itself is enough to raise speculation about whether it happened as she wrote it. Another reason is based upon her method of confiding the events of her life to the diary. From beginning to end, Anaïs Nin had one clearly discernible habit: whenever she did something personally embarrassing, she usually mentioned it the first time casually, offhandedly. Days, months, sometimes years later, she wrote a second, fuller account, as if the passage of time gave her the necessary distance to write objectively about *most* of what originally happened. Finally, in a third or even fourth account written long after the second, she told all the details, no matter how unflattering they were. Sometimes she repeated the information in fuller and fuller detail until it became a referential code, a kind of shorthand for what happened in her by-then far-distant past.

The fact that she never mentioned this incident with her brother again makes one ask: Did it happen at all? Did it happen as she wrote it? Was it a "screen memory" for something else so deeply hidden that she was never able to pull it into her consciousness long enough to write about it? Only one thing is certain: her relationship with her brother Thorvald was strained to the point of rupture for the rest of her life.

19

Nanankepichu

To Anaïs's surprise, Henry said he did not want to return to Paris: "He feels now the power of earning money. He wants to stay here and work." She was astonished by how much money he made from his analytical patients, for his practice was thriving. His reluctance stemmed from the worsening political circumstances in Europe, and Anaïs was scornful: "He shows a strange and terrible cowardice, always a self-preservation instinct. He is driven by fear, not love."[1] In the end, however, Henry's fear of losing Anaïs's steady stipend proved stronger than his confidence about supporting himself; when she sailed on the *Bremen* (on April 2, 1936, two months after Hugo's deadline), Henry sailed, too.

They argued all the way to France, with Henry being uncustomarily insistent that the diary "harms [the] artist, and kills [the] imagination." She countered by saying "it is a friend, it makes me feel less alone."[2]

When the ship docked, Henry stayed out of sight until Hugo collected Anaïs and her belongings. To celebrate their reunion, Hugo arranged a holiday in Morocco and they left almost immediately.[3]

On their return, they found bundles of *House of Incest.*[4] "People fawn over me," Anaïs wrote, describing in minute detail every compliment she received. Best of all, however, was that "Fraenkel went to Spain in a pique," ostensibly because he could not deal with her success.[5] Henry was strangely absent from all her celebratory remarks.

Either she was totally ignorant of the realities of publishing or else she chose to ignore them, for she believed that she had great quantities of immediate royalties to spend. Hugo was so happy to have her back that he did not attempt to control her profligacy, and she indulged several times each week in massages, manicures, and pedicures at Elizabeth Arden's. She also bought everything from "turquoise colored paste for the eyelashes" to furnishings for the apartment she had just persuaded Hugo to rent.

On June 22, Hugo leased a grand seventh-floor apartment at 30, quai de Passy.[6] From every beautifully proportioned room Anaïs could look down across the cliffs of Passy to the Eiffel Tower across the Seine and most of the Left Bank. "I will pay your rent tomorrow," she wrote to her mother in Mallorca, but that month Rosa's stipend was never sent.[7] Instead, Anaïs gave an extravagant housewarming party.

She was grateful that night to George Turner, Hugo's colleague at the bank, for "his power to distract me from my sadness." It was how she excused their brief "fucking in the elevator" while Hugo waited in the apartment. "Who is George Turner," she asked rhetorically. "It doesn't matter, nothing matters but this drunkeness."

A "page of dates" is inserted into the diary at this point, and two entries in particular dominated her life for the next decade: "June 5, 1936: met Gonzalo; July 14: first sexual fusion."

Anaïs was not entirely accurate in this account, for she had, in fact, known Gonzalo Moré and his wife, the dancer Helba Huara, since 1931.[8] Gonzalo was half Scottish, half Peruvian Indian, a large, swarthy, and strikingly handsome man, and a dedicated Communist who, in his lazy way, engaged in political activism by working as a journalist and printer. Helba, whose career was dominated more by hypochondria than by dancing, was professionally renowned, welcomed into the finest salons, and had performed in the best revues at the best theaters.

By 1936, Helba was no longer dancing because an illness left her almost entirely deaf.[9] She, Gonzalo, and her teenage daughter by a previous marriage lived in a squalid basement apartment near the

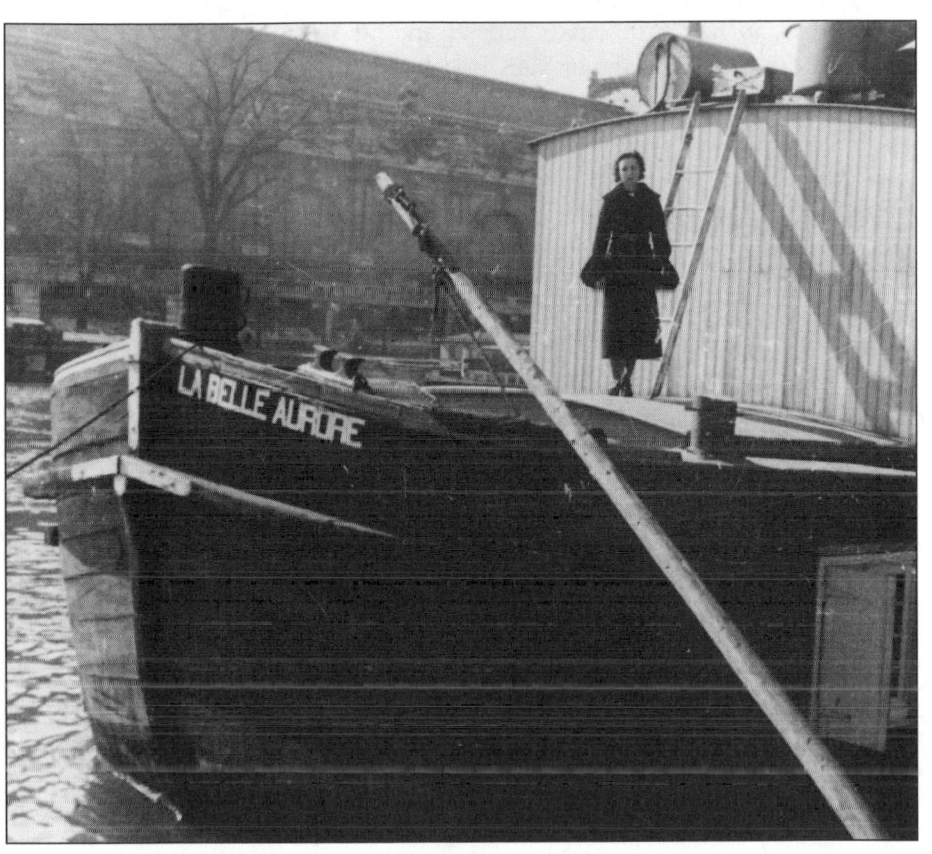

Anaïs on *La Belle Aurore*.

Métro Denfert-Rochereau, a hangout for Communists coming from or going to Spain. The most prominent objects in the apartment were Helba's vast collection of medicine bottles and pillboxes, and piles of filthy clothes.

Gonzalo had problems about arranging a clandestine love affair with Anaïs. Helba watched his every move, and he could not even spend an evening in a café without one of her cronies or his stepdaughter checking to see if he was there. The excuse was always that Helba was taken ill and needed Gonzalo or his money to pay for the doctor or the medication.

Anaïs described another problem in the diary: "He has pudeur [modesty], won't take off his underpants except in the dark . . . never once pissed with me, never walks naked, won't let me touch his penis, reticent in sex."[10] He was childlike and primitive, naive and trusting; when they saw a Tarzan movie, Anaïs compared herself and Gonzalo to Jane and Tarzan.[11]

From the beginning, Gonzalo and Henry knew of and resented the other, and in some instances, vied for Anaïs. Henry insisted that she spend every Saturday night with him, even though it forced her to invent increasingly bizarre tales to leave Hugo. Gonzalo discovered this (and despite Helba's surveillance), threatened to leave forever if she did not spend the following Saturday with him. Saturday came, and she tried to dissolve a sleeping drug in Henry's after-dinner tea. He noticed the muddy color but drank it anyway, and by ten o'clock was sound asleep. As soon as she heard him snore, she dressed and crept out, leaving the front door ajar. When she got to the nearby hotel where Gonzalo, despite his prudery, had booked a room, she gleefully told him of her escapade. Gonzalo was so frightened by what Henry might do if he awakened that he was unable to perform. She assured him of Henry's cowardice, but by 5:30 A.M. was on her way to the Villa Seurat. Henry woke at 6: "The luck of the bandits. No guilt. Pity and fear, yes, concern at Henry's possible anguish . . . but no guilt. Just love." She "gave Henry all he wanted," then went home and "gave a gift to Hugo."[12]

Gonzalo refused to go on meeting her under such circumstances and their assignations were stymied until October, when Anaïs conveniently forgot to pay Rosa her stipend and rented a houseboat on the Seine. Part of it sheltered a one-legged personage whom she called "the Captain," and whatever care was taken of the leaky, barnacle-encrusted vessel came from a young man of limited mental

Gonzalo Moré.

Helba Huara.

capacity she called René, who may or may not have been one of the homeless men who slept along the quays during the Depression. Gonzalo named it *Nanankepichu,* a Peruvian Indian word which he said meant "not really at home."[13]

She told both Hugo and Henry that the boat was her refuge, where she went in total solitude to write fiction, away from every possible corrupting influence that might cause her to revert back to diary writing. Both knew she was lying, but as always, accepted it. She was trying to break herself of pouring every emotion into the diary each day and then having nothing left over for fiction. Now her technique was to begin as if she were sitting down to write an entry in the hope that her fictional thoughts would flow as smoothly as her diary writing. She even went so far as to insert the blank pages on which she planned to write fiction into the diary, in the hope that some sort of "magic" would infuse her imagination.[14]

She also tried to write a play about analysis with Rank as the hero, but like so much that she began during this time, it came to naught. "Why should I strain and struggle to write," she asked rhetorically. "If you lived in a fairy tale, if you were swimming in caresses, if you lived among stars and clouds and felt the warm sperm pouring into you, would you write?"[15]

There was a great deal of tension between Anaïs and Henry as 1937 rang in, mostly because "he is at the moment inflated with people's praise."[16] Henry was as interested in painting as he was in writing, so he took her to Hans Reichel's studio, where powerful paintings of eyes disturbed her because they seemed to look straight into her soul. As they walked back to the Villa Seurat, Henry said bitterly, "now you are going to write quietly in your diary the whole thing. Then you must read it to me so I can get inspiration. Give me some of those finite phrases." It made her angry that he would so casually appropriate her material, but it inspired her to sit down and finish the childbirth story that had been preying on her mind. It was one of the few successful instances in which she used the diary as the means to write a complete story.

Another technique she found useful was one she called "dedoublement," or "the moment when I watch myself live."[17] She induced herself into this double-state through fantasy by imagining" someone else watching me. I play at the someone else who, like god, can see me everywhere and must therefore be the face of my guilt, not in relation to myself but only in relation to the one I am betraying at the moment." She did not know it at the time, but it was the genesis of her novel *A Spy in the House of Love.*[18]

But no matter how hard she tried, she could not write fiction. Having vowed to keep the houseboat "only for love" and never to take the diary on board, she repeatedly broke the promise. The first time was to "work on Volume 44, expanding my child story, the events following it, the taking of Villa Seurat with Henry, my enjoyment of Rank's passion, and etc. etc." The second time was to confide "I am in a desperate mood and no one can help me: I owe people 4,000 francs. I have only one pair of shoes to wear and no good stockings."

The bills were enormous, and even though someone finally rented Louveciennes, three hefty rents had to be paid: on the Passy apartment, Rosa's, and the houseboat. And now Henry was not the only one to whom she gave a stipend; Helba and Gonzalo had joined the ranks of her "children," a word she used from this point on for those whose financial security she guaranteed all or in part. Hugo knew how she dispersed the greater part of his salary, but as always, did not stop her.

The marriage was unorthodox, to say the least, but Anaïs was in fact a partner in not one but three marriages. For, with the advent of Gonzalo Moré, her sexual relationships settled into a pattern and routine that lasted from January 1937 until the outbreak of war in 1939. She was true in her fashion, for she was unfaithful to them all, but only with the others. In terms of sexuality, it was a period of relative stability, even though her not taking other lovers had a great deal to do with the simple matter of time, for she insisted on trying to provide every possible wifely support to each of her three "husbands." At the end of any given day she was so exhausted that she looked forward to a day alone as if she were going on a very special holiday.

It took all three men to satisfy her, for she thought each lacked something vital and could satisfy all her needs only in tandem with the other two. Hugo was the "young father"[19] who cherished and protected her, gave her independence, and tried to provide financial security. Gonzalo eventually overcame his quirks and peculiarities about sex and gave her the unbridled passion she wanted, even though it was never enough to satiate her; with him she also fulfilled her limitless maternal instincts because, as she and Helba agreed, he was too lazy and listless to take care of himself and "mañana" was his favorite word. Henry gave her respect for her talent, faith in her literary endeavors, and enough sustained criticism to nudge her—forcefully at times, gently at others—into the writer she eventually became.

Hugo continued to travel throughout Europe until mid-1937. That summer, he announced that he would be transferred to London and made director of the European trust department. He naturally assumed that his wife would accompany him. Anaïs waited until the last minute to tell him that she planned to stay in Paris and expected him to commute between the two cities. Hugo protested, but she played upon his sympathy, eventually convincing him that she could not leave her "children" for the selfish pleasure of going with him.

By this time she was deeply enmeshed in every aspect within the morass of Helba and Gonzalo's squalid existence. A list of Anaïs's errands for one day in the life of Helba and Gonzalo included "Get coal for Nanankepichu, wine for Gonzalo, and latest medicine for Helba."[20] Not only did she pay for Helba's medicines, she fetched and delivered them to the slovenly woman who had grown so fat she had difficulty walking. Anaïs was also expected to be on call to escort Helba in a taxi to whichever doctor—or doctors—she decreed in her daily hypochondria that she needed to see immediately.

All three—Anaïs, Helba, and Gonzalo—kept up the charade that Helba was entirely unaware of the affair. But Helba was no fool: in exchange for Gonzalo's sexual favors, she made Anaïs pay an escalating bill, first for doctors and prescriptions, then rent, food, clothing, and finally, even vacations and holidays. By 1938, when Joaquín Nin-Culmell assumed full financial responsibility for himself and Rosa, the Huara-Moré entourage was in line to replace them on Hugo's payroll. Henry was now making enough money from writing to meet his simple needs, but he still took his monthly stipend anyway.

When the bank summoned Hugo to New York that summer, Anaïs stayed alone in Louveciennes, resting from her ministrations to three men. At first she enjoyed several solitary days wandering alone through the house and garden until a strange anxiety beset her and sheer panic kept her from eating or sleeping. Her way of dealing with it was to write in the diary, which helped her to realize something important about herself:

> I cannot live alone because then I become diseased. My life gets unreal. I must confess I need Hugo's presence humanly. I need my lovers but lovers are less there. I like the day having order and pattern I must adhere to, but every night faced with solitude I cannot bear it. And now I know my diary was created not to be alone. What a weakness. I need this that I rebel against. I need this home which I say suffocates me, this husband I chafe against. I need all this web, ties, responsibilities, care, all that I curse as an artist.[21]

There was, however, one aspect of herself that she had not been able to come to terms with during her solitary prowling of the huge empty house: her fixation on June. Anaïs had had no contact with June since she divorced Henry five years previously, but she thought of June all the time. No matter who the man or how brief the affair, Anaïs compared herself to June as the ideal, and in every instance found herself wanting. June became both chameleon and paragon, the ever-changing ideal who was always just out of her reach; in her mind, she could never be as fearless, remorseless, indifferent, or even as insane as June.

June would have told Hugo straight out that she was not going to London, she would have told Gonzalo she wanted his body but not the impedimenta that came with it, and she would have laughed off Henry's well-intentioned but nevertheless relentless criticism of her writings. Anaïs was forced to admit that no matter how much she insisted she was living for herself alone, she could never attain June's degree of personal selfishness. For almost twenty years, June remained firmly fixed in Anaïs Nin's imagination as well as in her own personal judgment of herself, a towering figure whose influence equaled her father's. Joaquín Nin had told the small child she was ugly; June told the adult woman she was afraid to live. Anaïs could not forget what each had said, and as her voluminous diary shows, she could never record enough compliments or details of her outrageous behavior in compensation.

Although her two lovers never met face-to-face if Anaïs could help it, their interests nevertheless converged: each wanted a printing press, and each wanted her to buy it. Gonzalo wanted it for his Communist literature (which she thought enlightened), and Henry because "he thinks everything he writes should be published" (which she thought selfish). To purchase even one so old as to be in disrepair required more money than she could amass in several months' time.

Anaïs thought she would have a better chance of amassing money if she adopted one of Henry's techniques, the "begging letter." He was never too embarrassed to send out mimeographed letters to vast numbers of people describing his poverty and hapless plight in maudlin detail. Anaïs did the same, but with a little more discretion and only to a few intimate friends. No one offered to help.

She was "split in two directions."[22] When she lay in bed with Gonzalo reading newspaper advertisements and saw a small, manually operated printing press for 3,000 francs (about $150), she was all set to buy and install it in his studio, aflame to print her fiction and his propaganda. But the next night, after "a long peaceful talk with Henry in bed," she wanted to buy it for him.

Anaïs bought that same press in late August 1937, with some of the expense money Hugo was advanced by the bank to pay for his trip to New York. She "thought a little wistfully" how she would have enjoyed keeping it for herself, but the needs of her "children" drowned out her own.[23]

The press was installed in Gonzalo's studio, "a low-ceilinged room with two windows on an old French garden on the Rue de Lille." The bourgeois banker's wife who went to Elizabeth Arden for manicures discovered how much she loved the feel of setting type, and soon she was nearly as competent as her Communist lover. The process mattered more than the content, for she ended the session feeling "elation at producing printed matter."

Anaïs gave the press to Gonzalo rather than Henry because Gonzalo had just been appointed secretary of the (North and South) American Communist Party, which entailed printing many documents in large quantities and covering the costs himself. With the excuse that he was raising funds, he sat in cafés drinking and kibbitzing with fellow Communists, leaving Anaïs alone most of the time to do the work.

She was grateful eventually, for she refined her craft through trial and error and discovered how much she enjoyed printing. It was as soothing as rug hooking, but the final outcome was certainly more pleasing to her artistic sensibilities. It added another dimension to the tranquillity she gained by writing in the diary, for after a day of setting type, she was always physically at peace and mentally brimming with ideas for fiction. To turn to the diary after working at the press helped to start the fiction flowing, and she worked more and better each time she tried it.

The printing press brought another kind of comfort and security: if nobody else wanted to publish her writings, it no longer mattered. She could always print them herself, and almost from the beginning, she had every intention of doing so.

20

The Three Musqueteers

As the public's regard for Henry's writing grew, so too did Anaïs's resentment of his success. Accolades poured in from writers, critics, and scholars in Europe and the United States, and Henry "sat in the Villa Seurat like the ruler of a magic kingdom."[1] She wrote a letter accusing him of monstrous selfishness and irresponsibility, and blamed him for her search for "reality and warmth"[2] (Gonzalo).

Her literary reputation was not faring well. Reviews of *House of Incest* were few, and while readers of the birth story praised the harsh reality of her real-life suffering, critics ignored her genuine ability to re-create the event in fiction. Throughout 1937 she worked long, lonely hours preparing typed, edited copies of the diary for the French literary agent Denise Clairouin, whose initial comments were enthusiastic, but who ultimately offered a dispiriting overview: "the diaries will never be published [because] people can't stand such nakedness." Clairouin compounded Anaïs's despair by telling her she would always be a writer reviled by intellectuals and never understood or embraced.

Nevertheless, Clairouin believed in her talent and worked until the outbreak of war to place various incarnations of the rewritten diaries. She sent copies to Stuart Gilbert, who had written the most favorable account of *House of Incest.*[3] He liked the childhood diaries and those about her early years in Paris, but could not persuade a publisher to take them. He did, however, allow Clairouin to use his name as a reference when she sent copies dealing with the early years in Paris to the eminent British publisher Faber & Faber.

Just as *Tropic of Capricorn* was garnering raves, Faber & Faber rejected her diaries with a letter that would become the prototype for every rejection until they were finally published: "We have been having an exceptionally difficult time deciding about the diary. As you already know from my request for further material, we were very much interested. Yet after very great regret, we cannot see how to shape the material into book form which could be published in England. . . . In the end, the difficulties of the problem have defeated us, and I am sending the volumes back with a great deal of reluctance."[4]

Anaïs's usual response to rejection was to attack Henry over something unrelated. This time, her principal objection to his fiction was a prefiguration of much post-1970s feminist scholarship: "Instead of investing each woman with a different face, you take pleasure in reducing all women to an aperture, to a biological sameness." She accused him of hideously misrepresenting June in *Capricorn* by portraying "twisted, ingrown, negative love" and creating a "great anonymous, depersonalized fucking world."

If the charges were true, Henry replied, "I would want to run away and never see or hear from you again. I'd loathe myself." He implored her to meet him and discuss the letter because "the cause of the explosion has nothing to do with the real situation."

Her summation of their differences is astute: "What I write is less communicable than what he writes because he has a human love of writing, of words, and takes a sensuous pleasure in writing. It is flesh and life and food. Whereas, I, I have a sort of contempt for the sensuous joy of expression. I am like the woman and the mirrors, intent on my pursuits, my ideas, on satisfying myself. A lonely selfish quest, which isolates me."[5] She did nothing, however, to use this observation to effect any change in her work, so her frustration increased.

Much of what Anaïs had touted as praiseworthy in the preface she wrote for Henry's book she now held against him in her letter. Having commended him for his portrayal of "a world grown paralyzed with introspection," and its "unadulterated violence and obscenity," she now found these same qualities offensive. No wonder he was confused.

Henry might have understood better had he realized how jealous

Anaïs was, especially of his friendship with the young English writer Lawrence Durrell, twenty-three years old in 1935 when he sent a fan letter about *Tropic of Cancer.*[6] He was then married to his first wife, Nancy Myers, and was living on Corfu with her, his mother, and three siblings. Durrell had just published his first novel, *Pied Piper of Lovers,* such a resounding failure that his publisher suggested he use a pseudonym for anything he wrote in the future.[7] For Durrell, "the damn book [*Tropic of Cancer*] has rocked the scales like a quake and muddled up all my normal weights and measures. I love its guts."

Miller replied in kind: "your letter rocks me a bit too. You're the first Britisher who's written me an intelligent letter about the book. For that matter, you're the first anybody who's hit the nail on the head."[8]

As the epistolary friendship blossomed into mutual admiration, Henry shared the letters with Anaïs and let her read Durrell's "Christmas Carol," written especially as a gift for him.[9] Shortly after the new year, 1937, she sent Durrell a copy of *House of Incest* with a note saying that, after reading his story, she "wanted to throw my H. of I. into the Seine. Too heavy, too heavy." Durrell "travelled faster and lighter," she told the diary. "He danced on an echo."[10] He read her novel and wrote to Henry: "What a silly title, but I like it in spite of the technique." He thought it "really alive . . . with a queer kind of poignance. . . . Like sudden dazzling tears."[11]

Encouraged by his regard, Anaïs began her own correspondence with Durrell, so that when he and Nancy showed up unexpectedly at the Villa Seurat in late summer 1937, she felt she had "known [him] for a thousand years." She thought him "soft and feminine, healthy and humorous, fawn and swimmer." Nancy struck her as "a Greek boy . . . long waisted boy with beautiful long refined leopard eyes."[12]

Lawrence Durrell was one of very few men for whom Anaïs Nin never expressed a single sexual interest, nor did she consider him one of her "children." With him, the rapport was always based on a mutual quest for an understanding of the creative process in literature. But even though she was enraptured by his youth, energy and what she thought was brilliance, she was wary of his sycophantic qualities. He was Henry's liege man and "Henry treated him with the sort of reverence one might have for a beloved child, a wonder child."[13] She thought (correctly, as it turned out) Durrell would someday want to kill the king and usurp his position.[14]

Anaïs Nin had then had no other friendship with either a man or a woman such as the one she shared briefly with Durrell. Each confided the most intimate biographical details to the other and described how they would transpose them into their writing. Such confessions did not disrupt the friendship but rather enhanced it, as each managed somehow to preserve a respectful distance and decorum.

As soon as the Durrells arrived, she, Henry, and Larry were engaged in night-long talkathons, with Nancy (whose money paid for her husband's peripatetic life) sitting shyly outside their triangle or else playing the role that Anaïs had always filled, of handmaiden to literary men and provider of their food and drink.

The "three musqueteers" (as they dubbed themselves) began at once to psychoanalyze each other. Anaïs confided these conversations to the diary, reproducing them as accurately as she could so that later she could ponder the ramifications of what each person said and whether or not it was applicable to her. Her transcriptions of these exchanges are remarkable in the degree to which they recapture the spontaneous observations and insights of three writers who were still formulating their own personal literary systems.[15]

In them, Larry served as the catalyst to rejuvenate the by-now jaded observations and criticisms Anaïs and Henry offered each other about their work. As Larry carried no emotional baggage into the trio, he was able to say things that they no longer dared to say.

One of the most interesting of their conversations concerned "unmasking" oneself on the printed page and the danger it entailed. Specifically, the subject was Anaïs's diaries and Henry's two "Tropics," *Cancer* and *Capricorn,* but they tried to argue objectively: if a writer paused to consider what the reader's reaction might be to the rawness and intimacy of her (the writer's) experience, there was the possibility that she might hesitate, feeling the terror of revelation so sharply that she might decide it was not worth taking the risk of exposing her innermost self. If, however, the writer chose not to take the risk, the reader would be the poorer, having only a watered-down approximation of something organic and vital.

Larry's presence diffused their competition, so Anaïs offered Henry a backhanded compliment. After admitting that fear of revealing herself often kept her from writing fiction, she told Larry that Henry had proven himself the strongest of the three, for he had unmasked himself in both "Tropics." Henry was not afraid of being alone, she said; if she could not be with him it mattered not at all, for he just used the time to concentrate happily on his writing.

Her confession did not elicit the tenderness and concern she wanted. Instead, the two men seemed embarrassed by the introduction of personal emotion into an objective, critical discussion and joined to attack "my relating all things to myself, my personification of ideas. I defended myself brilliantly saying the relating was an act of life. To make history or psychology alive, I personify."

Inevitably, her self-defense led them to attack the diary, which they agreed was a "problem" she had to overcome in order to flourish as a novelist. Anaïs countered, saying she could feel the importance of an event while it was happening and thus knew it should be recorded. If she wrote it immediately, she captured the original emotion and experienced it anew each time she reread it. Their rejoinder was that she did not fully appreciate an event as it happened because her mind was busy transposing the actual experience to how it should be written even before it played itself out. Her rebuttal was that she did not interpret but, rather, recorded the original account. Subsequent rereadings kept it fresh, often prompting her to add to or enhance the original account with additional detail, further filtering and screening the original experience and giving it ramifications she may not have been aware of at the time it happened.

Henry brusquely dismissed her argument, saying it could not possibly work that way, for it would "upset all the art theories." Still determined to make her point, Anaïs countered with the Birth experience, "which varies so little, the version written as soon as it happened and the version three years later."

Larry joined sides with Henry: why then, he demanded, had she felt the need to rewrite it? —"For a greater technical perfection but not to create it anew." Larry remained allied with Henry, for having been drawn into the "Hamlet Correspondence" by Miller, Fraenkel and Perlès,[16] he used an analogy that Anaïs disagreed with to state his view of literary creativity: "I must rewrite Hamlet. I must make the leap outside of the womb, destroy my connection."

Anaïs noted that the discussion rambled aimlessly on, but she closed her diary account with a statement that reads suspiciously like one of her self-paid compliments, claiming that both men said: "we have a real woman artist before us, the first one and we ought to bow down instead of trying to make a monster out of her."

Later, in a long monologue, she pondered her role as writer, woman, and woman writer: "As soon as I won out I was doubtful deep down. I know Henry is the artist *because* he does exactly what I do not do. He waits. He gets outside himself. This last month I have been rewriting the whole diary in my head. What a prodigious thing I might do, *both* the document and the art product, both the human and the created, side by side, monster and woman, inside and outside. What a feat that would be! All I do is right for me. If today I can talk both man and woman's language, if I can translate woman to man, poor woman—"

She then made an uncharacteristic line of dashes, as if she were thinking through what she believed. What followed became a statement based largely on D. H. Lawrence's conception of male-female relationships, but written from her perception of what creativity meant to a woman:[17] "And woman, I repeat, never communicated directly with god but through man, never created directly but through man, was never able to create as woman. But what Larry and Henry don't understand is that woman's creation, far from being the man's, must be exactly *like* the child, that is, made out of her own blood, englobed by her own womb, nourished with her own milk. It must be a human creation of flesh, it must be different."

The evening's excitement wound down when she made an impassioned plea that effectively silenced them: "I have to be the resurrection! My creation must be that which can save man from the deserts he stumbled on, from the skeletonization of Fraenkel, the dissections of analysis, the cancer of egotism, the disintegration of knowledge, the black pest of brain cells." The two men disappointed her: Durrell woke his sleeping wife to take her to her bed, and Henry busied himself elsewhere in the studio.

The next day Anaïs resumed her traditional role by cooking a good dinner for Henry before he went to a literary soirée to which she was not invited. While she peeled the vegetables, she thought about "writing as a woman," of which she was becoming increasingly aware, of "all that happens in the real womb, not in the womb fabricated by man as substitute. Strange that I should explore this womb of real flesh when of all women I seem the most idealized, moon-like, a dream, a myth." She chafed at how to make men understand.

The next time she saw Larry, he wrote what he called "a poem" directly into the diary: "Anaïs is unanswerable. completely unanswerable. I fold up and give in. What she says is biologically true—from the very navel string."[18]

More and more, she found herself turning to "Peter Pan Larry" for the intellectual solace she no longer found in Henry. She wanted to pursue her theory that women wrote differently from men, which she had trouble formulating, let alone expressing coherently, and Larry was always willing to let her talk about it. In fits and starts, hesitations and inconsistences, she came to the conclusion that she expressed herself simplistically through a process of "expansion," which led to "deduction" (woman's way of thinking) and "core" (the deepest innermost place from whence women gain experience and vision). This she contrasted with "periphery" (where men, afraid of relationships, dispassionately find the material about which they create fiction). Even more simplistically, she said that because women were biologically different from men, it figured that they must not only write differently but must also write about different subjects.

In her quest to understand herself as a woman writer, Anaïs read M. Esther Harding's *The Way of All Women.*[19] She felt such kinship with Harding's Jungian views that she wrote two effusive letters but received no reply. Anaïs felt rejected and was bitter, but soon found another woman on whom to lavish praise.

Djuna Barnes's *Nightwood* was everything Anaïs was struggling to write in the three separate novels she now worked on concurrently (all of which were later incorporated into one, *Winter of Artifice*).[20] When Anaïs learned that Barnes lived in Paris, she wrote several letters offering to send copies of *House of Incest* and some of her work in progress, and asked for a meeting to discuss their work. Barnes never replied, and Anaïs neither forgot it nor forgave her.[21]

Other women, however, were kinder. A former patient, a wealthy woman from Greenwich with high-level contacts in the publishing industry, had been trying for the better part of a year to place some of the revised diaries in New York. There had been a string of swift outright rejections before one by Little, Brown, where the diary had been under consideration for a very long time. Like Faber & Faber, that house decided it could not risk having to settle possible lawsuits, nor could it decide how to cut potentially libelous material and still have a viable document.

Resiliently, Anaïs decided she would and could "change it, make novels of it, and it will be less dangerous for those whom it might hurt." Her intention now was to do what Otto Rank and Henry Miller had long been urging her to do: give up the diary as the repository of her deepest feelings and turn it into a notebook for novels. The prospect raised many questions: "What shall I do? How much can I reveal? Hugo might never read it, he never reads but what I put in his hands, but Henry? Is cutting what the censors want me to cut enough to preserve Henry's happiness? Oh, god, the duality!"[22]

❧

Larry and Nancy were overwhelmed by the noise and confusion of those who lived in the Villa Seurat. Anaïs let them stay first in her Passy apartment, then stashed them secretly in Rosa's while they looked for one to rent.[23] When Nancy told her she was planning to look at a "darling" little house on the next street to Villa Seurat, Anaïs thought quickly and told her not to bother, the house was already rented, then rushed to take it herself as she and Gonzalo had been without a trysting place since *Nanankepichu*'s owner evicted her for nonpayment of rent.[24]

Nancy and Larry were exhausted by the tug-of-war between Henry and Anaïs for Larry's primary allegiance. Larry wanted to steer clear of the continuing quarrel about the diary, but Anaïs demanded a commitment: "All I would like to hear you say is 'go on with the diary.' " As tactfully as possible, Larry told her he could not say it "wholeheartedly, without hesitation." He also told her he thought her novels were not very good and they "did not compare with the diary." His comments stunned her. She begged Larry to help her find the necessary faith to keep the diary going, but he kept silent. It marked the beginning of Anaïs's changed attitude toward him and Nancy (who had earlier accused her of straining for sensation in the diary).[25] Her friendship cooled, even though she treated Larry cordially and continued to help type the manuscript of what became *The Black Book.*

She was also critical of Henry's "vulgar and infantile side" when Fred Perlès became editor of the golfing newsletter of the American Country Club of France. In exchange for writing several pages of club notes, Fred could print whatever he chose. Henry appointed himself associate editor and decided they would boost themselves; thus the title, "The Booster."

Anaïs especially resented Henry's just-published *Scenario,*[26] a text based on her *House of Incest.* "Humorous ironic things are happening," she noted.[27] Henry was proud of his friendship with the American artist and art patron Kay Sage Tanguy, then the Princesse de San Faustino, but was embarrassed when he introduced her to Anaïs and Kay said that her novel was "perfection in itself" and the adaptation gratuitous. Larry told Henry, in Anaïs's presence, that the best part of his scenario was "about the man oiling the mechanism in his chest, the astrologer scene." Anaïs glared, for it was copied word for word from pages Henry insisted she eliminate: "HE wrote the film, but the ideas were mine, all of them. He only added Henry-like touches of asses, doves coming out of it, skeletons, noise and things I didn't like. And so I will see my ideas made popular by Henry and signed by Henry, the greatest piece of spiritual robbery I have ever seen."

Anaïs hated the article about the diary that Henry published in T. S. Eliot's *The Criterion,* and which he printed separately as a pamplet, "Un être étoilique."[28] She accused him of stealing her metaphor of ideas as mirrors and their infinite reflections, which he always objected to as phony and irrelevant.

"Henry is pushing me into prominence like a fanatic and has set himself the task of getting the diary published," she wrote. His essay had made so great a stir that "Monsieur [Jean] Paulhan of the Nouvelle Revue Française [leaned] over the diary, marvelling, exclaiming and looking at the Anaïs of today with admiration!" She could not help but think of "little Anaïs of eleven sighing to be made a member of the French Academy!" There were caveats in Paulhan's admiration, however: "We must study what this diary really is, for of course, in Mr. Miller's essay there is a lot of Mr. Miller."[29] And so, when Paulhan confronted the reality of the woman's writing rather than the man's refracted view of it, he decided it was not appropriate for his august publication.

Nor did anything happen at Scribner's, even though the famous editor Maxwell Perkins took the diaries home for the weekend to study. He told Denise Clairouin that Anaïs must certainly be "an extraordinary woman," but it was too massive and needed abridgment.

And so she set to work, refining the early diaries even as she wrote about her technique ("I proustianize, only dynamically") in the current one. First, she had to invent pseudonyms for everyone. Then, using as an example a passage about Rank and their first analytical session she had just written that day, she found the journal in which she thought it should appear and inserted it in place of the original account. In another passage dealing with one of her New York patients, she invented what she thought should have gone on in their session, "in a very natural spontaneous way similar to the mood in which I write the diary."[30]

"Watch me," she warned, "I am going to become a great artist. I have great satisfaction at what I [fictionalize] and no pain. I am removed."

But Scribner's did not want the revised diary, for the same reason as all the other publishers who rejected it—fear of lawsuits. So she sent it and the birth story to an unlikely venue, a Russian Communist journal in Moscow called *International Literature*. She was astonished when they refused it because of "themes . . . that we have found by experience Soviet audiences are not interested in." "So," she noted dryly, "the theme of birth does not interest the Soviet new country."[31]

Henry stepped in and grandiosely announced that he would publish the diary himself and would pay Kahane "by March 1st, 1938, failing a world war or a collapse of the monetary systems of the world."[32] It led to conflict within her family. Joaquín Nin-Culmell called Henry's essay and the "begging letters" (which Henry now dubbed "requests for subscriptions") demeaning and crass. Gonzalo thought only a Communist audience would understand her and was furious because to him, Kahane represented the Fascist world. Hugo was afraid of adverse publicity and begged her to keep Henry from sending announcements to bank officials or clients.

But Henry's efforts to publicize her work were succeeding. As the year ended, Anaïs received a letter from Dorothy Norman, the American founder and editor of the avant-garde magazine *Twice a Year*, who was struck by the "purity" of the "birth" story and wanted to publish it.[33]

It was Dorothy who finally gave the childbirth incident its official title, "Birth," after rejecting as "too tricky" Anaïs's preferred "Dead Birth," and also her idea of leaving it untitled and prefaced only by a quotation from D. H. Lawrence: "If women can bring forth hope, they are mothers indeed."[34] Dorothy Norman was also the first editor to guarantee publication of the diaries, despite the ever-constant threat of legal action, and excerpts did appear in *Twice a Year* several years later.[35] Dorothy also assumed the stature of mentor, guru, guide, and role model, a woman whose example loomed large in Anaïs's efforts to stand alone as a literary figure. That she remained so for so long was most likely due to the fact that she and Anaïs were separated by the Atlantic Ocean.

By early January 1938, failure, change, and closure were dominant motifs in the "moquette" Anaïs used as a diary, a printer's book of bound blank pages given to her by Henry. On the inside cover, beneath his flourishing signature, she wrote, "This was the dummy Henry intended to publish. I only collected 2,000 francs. The plan failed."[36]

Anaïs and Hugo argued as they divided up the household goods at the Passy apartment before he moved to London. She didn't tell him she refused to go because she could not give up Gonzalo ("who has no semen but insists on trying anyway") and Henry ("who takes me once a week which is right for his age and rhythm"). So she sent her "guardian angel, young father, fixed stability, protector, brother and child" to begin an independent life in a city where he already had a large circle of friends, some of them attractive women who made no secret of their interest.

She moved into the Hôtel Acropolis in St.-Germain-des-Prés, "dazed, dazzled" by her freedom, "face-to-face" with revising the diary into fiction: "There was no more evading it." Work soon came to a stop when Henry's essay appeared in *The Criterion*. "It gave me away," she wrote, "the conflict was so violent I got sick. I lost my elan."

The essay was a puff-piece, a public relations stunt designed to bring attention to Anaïs and the diary in equal parts. But it is also an essay that has stood the test of time, prescient in its description of how the historical moment was responsible for the changes in personal and biographical writing in the twentieth century. It was an article bound to cause extremes of commentary, from the scathing to the derisive, for Henry compared Anaïs's "monumental confession" to "the revelations of St. Augustine, Petronius, Abelard, Rousseau, Proust, and others," august company for a woman who had published one largely unnoticed novel. At a time when all autobiographical writing was considered akin to gospel truth, Henry was declaring a heresy as he proudly proclaimed that Anaïs mythologized, and her diary was "a mythological voyage towards the source and fountain head of life . . . an *astrologic* voyage of metamorphosis." He added the specter of astrology, and the critics had plenty of ammunition. The embarrassment and turmoil that suffused Anaïs was obvious to everyone but Henry, who was quite proud of himself. Once again she listed her many resentments, starting with his marriage to June.

She decided to demonstrate her superiority to June by seducing Hugo's and Henry's astrologer, Jean Carteret, who was homosexual. Pretending to be more interested in astrology than she really was, she lured Carteret to her hotel, greeted him in a red velvet kimono, and tried to entice him. He departed angrily, muttering "you bitch, you bitch, you bitch."[37] She liked his characterization and recorded it cheerfully in the diary.

Sitting idly in the Café Flore one afternoon, she saw a newspaper advertisement for another houseboat, the *Belle Aurore,* owned by the actor Michel Simon. He wanted 2,000 francs rent, she offered 1,000, and on February 28 it was hers. A week later, Jean Carteret returned from London, where he had gone to visit Hugo, and she finally seduced him. "I have no desire for Jean, but a magical connection," she wrote, giving him the credit for seeing her through the panic of March 1938, when Hitler marched into Austria.

She recognized Hitler's action with one line in the diary, an aside designed to precede a discussion of her central role in the impending world catastrophe: Gonzalo said he could not make love to her while the whole world suffered, then threatened to kill himself, her, and Helba, rather than live in a Fascist world; Henry begged her to keep his manuscripts safe and find the money for him to leave Paris; Hugo implored her to come to London, but she refused; and once again she thought she was pregnant and took injections to abort.[38]

Through it all, Jean Carteret was "phosphorescent with creation," as he allegedly told her she must not forget: "Your role is to keep your head above the water, to save others from drowning. You must always remain pure, alone, and represent that which can guide them. You cannot get confused or identified with the collective action. Your influence is different. Your communism is human, cosmic, not direct."

She took it upon herself to organize and supervise the lives of everyone she knew, from close friends to distant acquaintances, and juggled her creditors as she struggled to make her houseboat habitable.[39] Windows leaked, rain poured in, there was only a tiny stove, and Gonzalo usually forgot to bring the coal. The bums who lived along the quays frequently broke the locks, searching for something to steal. It was not the dramatic, romantic fantasy she wrote about later in the published diary, for she spent most of her time in Left Bank hotels recovering from the colds and bronchitis she got on the boat.

But still, she was moderately happy. While others worried about the political situation and made careful contingency plans in case war ensued, Anaïs paid no attention to outside circumstances and carried on as if there were no other world but the little one of honeycombs and circles that she drew from time to time in her diaries, with herself at the radiant center and everyone else at varying distances, depending on how she perceived the role each played in her life.[40] She thought it an unthreatened continuum that would last forever.

A number of recent events had set Hugo, now in London, to thinking intently and critically about his marriage.[41] His brother Johnny had divorced and seemed much younger and happier. Joaquín Nin-Culmell was supporting himself and Rosa, so Hugo's financial load was lightened.[42] Also, Anaïs insisted that it was only a matter of time until her writings made her self-supporting.

In London, Hugo discovered that people found him interesting in his own right, and not just because of his dramatic and flamboyant wife. He had taken art classes to fill time and learned of his talent in drawing and sketching. He was so skilled at casting horoscopes that friends and business associates sought his advice, and he had become a very good cook, comfortably hosting cocktail parties and small dinners. But despite all his successes, Hugo pined for Anaïs, who still found him lacking qualities she thought she needed. "I know I am cruel to him . . . it is all I can do to control my sexual hatred. It is suicide, I know. I am pushing him away [and] may lose him."[43] Still, she did nothing to change her ways.

Any number of books published throughout the 1930s dealt with modern marriage, and Hugo read most of them in search of advice and understanding. A few triggered something in Hugo, for he clipped articles and reviews that he kept for the rest of his life.[44] All dealt with the fact that the 1930s had produced the highest divorce rate (to that date) in history, placing much of the blame on the concept of married life as an endless honeymoon rather than an arranged, necessary alliance. Hugo read and thought about divorce, but all he wanted was Anaïs. He was learning to make his life without her, and although this period marked the beginning of what appeared to many as separation tantamount to all-but-legal divorce, they still remained married.

ANAÏS NIN

❧

There were problems with "La Belle Aurore," or the "péniche," as Anaïs called the houseboat in her letters and diaries. At the same time, she was plagued by impacted wisdom teeth; persistent anemia (Hugo donated two pints of blood with which she was transfused); bilious vomiting, severe eyestrain, and crushing headaches. In August she gave up the houseboat, defeated by colds, rheumatism, and expenses. The last straw was the King of England's visit, when all boats on the Seine were ordered to leave the city limits as a "security measure." As the tenant, she had to pay to have it hauled to a dock in Neuilly, one block from the building in which she was born. It was also one street away from where her father now lived alone in reduced circumstances.

Maruca had finally tossed the old roué out, citing his multiple infidelities as grounds for divorce. "I have strange news for you," Anaïs wrote to Rosa. "Mr. Joaquín Nin is being divorced by his second wife and left alone in the world at 58, bringing on his head his own punishment for his monstrous egoism."[45] Then she added a sentence with a curious turn of phrase, telling Rosa that she had "definitely divorced"[46] him as well. It was not true, for Anaïs did everything she could to exacerbate the marriage's disintegration.[47] Maruca's lawyer persuaded her to pay Joaquín Nin a modest sum and settle him in a grim linoleum-floored apartment in a building with a communal kitchen that served unappetizing meals. Bewildered by the abrupt change in his fortunes, Joaquín Nin aged overnight and turned to his daughter, who enjoyed his distress but was brusque and businesslike in their dealings.

"All the problems are falling on my shoulders," she wrote at the end of August 1938, as the specter of war hung over everyone. Henry got sick and stopped correcting the first volume of *Capricorn,* which he had just finished writing. Gonzalo was strutting and pontificating about a new Communist world order, and her father and Helba both clamored for a specific brand of digestive biscuits that only Anaïs could bring them!

By the end of September, Anaïs was convinced invasion was imminent. Foreign telephone service was suspended, so she was cut off from Hugo in London, and the rest of her family was dispersed throughout the Western Hemisphere. Her father was selling his few possessions and his extensive collection of books on music for money to go to Cuba.[48] Rosa and Joaquín were leaving for a concert in Havana, after which they would live at Middlebury College, where he would teach.[49]

Anaïs put as many of the diary volumes in a bank safety deposit box as would fit, but that left forty-five others. She put them in trunks in the cellar at 12, rue Cassini, where she took an apartment because it was next to no. 6, where Balzac wrote *Seraphita,* the only book that held her attention during the last frantic days of 1938. She also dumped Henry's things there, including his manuscripts of the two "Tropic" novels.

Henry came back to Paris from the Dordogne (where Anaïs had paid for him to hide temporarily), "terror stricken, trembling and howling." She sneered at his "egotistic instincts . . . cabling right and left drunkenly for money to sail to America."[50] She ignored him for Gonzalo, even though Gonzalo's political rhetoric bored her.

Henry was determined to press on with the Villa Seurat series, which was to appear under Kahane's imprint and be paid for by Nancy Durrell. His and Durrell's writings were scheduled to be the first two publications and one of the three separate novels Anaïs was working on concurrently was to be the third. At the time she was not sure whether it would be "Henry/June, Father, or confessions/dream book," but she was certain that whatever she published would be called "Chaotica." Finally, she amalgamated all three into one, but Henry refused to accept her title. "Henry found it," she wrote noncommittally in early 1939. "Winter of Artifice. Durrell is bringing it out in February."

Almost immediately there was trouble. Durrell was a rigorous editor, determined to save her from appearing foolish in print. She sent a harsh letter, demanding that he publish it as she wrote it, for she resented "having you revise and examine and disintegrate me."[51] Larry apologized, saying every criticism or correction was based on deep affection. Anaïs confessed "my great weakness . . . criticism breaks me down because . . . I feel handicapped. I feel I am making superhuman efforts to dominate not only a language that is not mine but to say things I should have said with music and dancing. Worst of all, I suffer because when I look at the bad phrase I can't see it's bad. Imagine a painter being color blind!"[52] Their rift was repaired, but when Hugo made one minor criticism about "several weak phrases," she erupted and turned all the anger she could not direct toward Larry against him.

Early in 1939, at Hugo's insistence, she traveled to London. They went to the theater almost every night, and two plays filled each with separate strong emotion. For Anaïs it was *You Can't Take It with You:* "A big family all doing exactly as they please and God takes care of them, but finally, God must take the form of a rich man." In the taxi going home to Hugo's apartment, she began to sob uncontrollably. When he begged to know why, she told him: "You are the one who makes it all possible for all of us to do as we please. Because of you, Joaquín can play, Helba can cuddle her diseases, Gonzalo can serve Communism and not work for a living, and I can write and live in a dream." Hugo consoled her, saying that she and all her "children" brought him pleasure and a sense of play he might otherwise never have found within himself.

The next night it was his turn to weep after seeing *Frou-Frou,* a fluffy comedy about a "toy" wife: "He wept because he wants me as a Chinese wife, dressed, perfumed, etc., an ornament, a charm," she told the diary. "All the same, I have my rebellions."

She left him in bed with the flu and returned to Paris to hear her father play a farewell concert before he departed for Havana. He billed it as his one-thousandth performance in the City of Light, and the hall was packed with fans and friends. Maruca was noticeably absent; Anaïs sat with an uncomfortable Henry in the balcony. In the midst of his first selection, Joaquín Nin suddenly stopped playing and clutched at the keyboard. "He does not faint, he simply stops playing. He died on the stage and his ghost is going to Cuba." For a brief moment she noted that "pity convulsed me but no guilt or regrets."

Joaquín Nin, ill, bewildered, and defeated, sailed for Havana on the day that Hugo arrived from London. Anaïs surprised her husband at the boat train but did not bid her father farewell. She never saw him again before his death, alone and penniless, in Havana in 1949. Throughout the last decade of his life, when Joaquín Nin wrote, pleading for financial assistance, Anaïs did not reply.

There was a brief respite that summer, 1939, when all the players in Anaïs's life ended up on the Riviera in a predicament that resembled

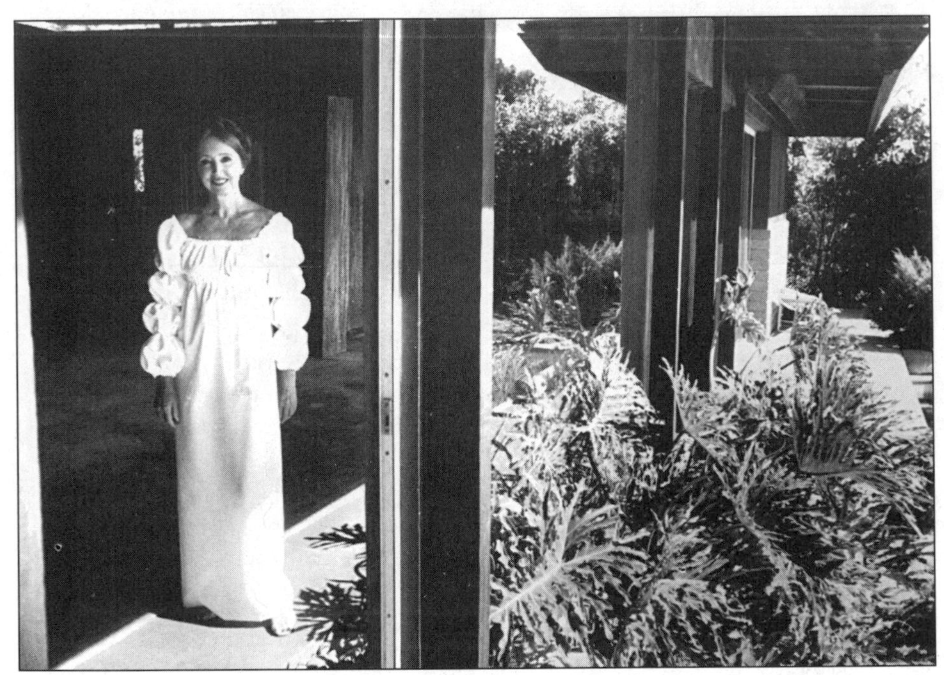

Anaïs at Rupert's house.

a Jacques Tati comedy.[53] She and Hugo went to Nice for ten days in June. Before they left, Henry clung to Anaïs, fearing that war would begin and he would not be able to reach her. So she found enough money for him to get to Marseille, promising to visit secretly until money he begged from Larry arrived and he could book passage to Athens. When Larry's money came, Henry blabbered that he was afraid to leave France, meaning Anaïs. When she presented him with a wad of cash, Henry booked passage before collapsing in panic. He was persuaded to go only after Nancy sent a second bundle of money.

Helba was jealous when she found out that Hugo was taking Anaïs to be pampered on the Riviera and complained that she needed a holiday as well. So Anaïs found the money for her and Gonzalo, too, but only to St.-Raphäel, which was cheaper than Nice. Anaïs had to keep them secret from Hugo, for when he returned to London, she intended to move to St.-Raphäel and keep her presence secret from Helba. Somehow she managed, and stayed until mid-August, telling Hugo she was improving her health when she was really exhausting herself sexually with Gonzalo.

And yet, impossible as it seems, she labored over her writing. Proud of how hard she had worked in the year just past, Anaïs wrote an enthusiastic letter to Rosa in the United States, listing everything she had published: "an essay on Rank in *Purpose,* a study of Conrad Aiken in *Seven,* a fantasy called 'Paper Womb' in *Delta,* a 'silent keyboard' in *the Phoenix,* 'Birth' in *Twice a Year,* 'The Rag Pickers' in *Seven,* fragment from the diary in *Seven,* Fragment from *House of Incest* in *transition.* Not so bad, eh?" she asked proudly.[54]

When she returned to Paris in late August, it was to find a steady stream of telegrams and letters from Henry informing her where to "send dough" and in which currency he wished to receive it. On September 1, war was declared, and on September 2, Hugo arranged for her to fly to London. Once there, she rushed around sending money orders to her "children" in Paris and to Henry in Athens. She called on Rebecca West in the hope she would help find an English publisher for the diaries, but Anaïs's earlier view still held true: "like all rich people she loves me when she sees me and then forgets me, specially when it's a question of helping. She's too busy."[55]

Two of Henry's letters, "monuments of egotism," were forwarded from Paris, ordering her to get "dough" and flee to Ireland, where they would sit out the war together. "Well, I think it is done," she wrote. "The war has hastened the separation."[56]

As September dragged on, she was desperate to return to Paris because Gonzalo, lazy even in war, had not bothered to write. She persuaded Hugo to cut through the red tape and he got their visas in a single day. In pre-dawn darkness they crossed the English Channel into France. "I am out of the English prison," she noted, "but what for? To see Gonzalo again I risk Hugo's life and mine in a crazy voyage." After several days of trying, Hugo secured another visa and went back to London, leaving Anaïs (so she told him) to deal with packing and preparations for departure.

Seemingly oblivious to the political drama playing out around her, she lived as if external events would not touch her daily life until several things made her realize how drastically Europe was changed. Everyone who had the means had by now left France, and suddenly Anaïs was truly isolated. All visas were canceled, phone lines were down, mail delivery impaired, and she could not receive money from Hugo in London.

Hugo expected the bank to keep him in London, and set up a bank account for Anaïs to live indefinitely without him in New York.[57] She saw no reason to comply. The war was her excuse to stay in France with Gonzalo and without Hugo. She thought she would be untouched because she was a citizen of a neutral country, and was all set to declare herself a French resident alien when Gonzalo was summoned by the American Communist Party to get to New York as quickly as possible. And so she had to choose whether to stay with her husband in England or flee with her lover to the United States. She persuaded herself that she was racked with conflict, when in truth it was a choice she made easily.

In one of her most casuistic passages of diary writing, she decided that she would have to "sacrifice" herself: "The most alive thing in me today is the passion I have for Gonzalo so I must follow it. I can't kill it without killing myself and making a widower of Hugo. It is not what I want, it is after all, what I must do, make a choice which tears me apart. But why must [Hugo] be fated to suffer, only because he doesn't inspire me with passion." And so, infusing herself with nobility of purpose, she made plans to sail on an Italian ship from Marseille, but only after she scraped together as much money as she could to pay for Helba and Gonzalo to follow shortly after.

Henry was in Corfu, "hanging on at Larry's place" and "rolling in all sorts of dough," because Dorothy Norman and James Laughlin (among others) had responded to his begging letters. He thought "the war won't last long—it will probably end in compromise,"[58] and sent a formal letter authorizing Anaïs to remove any or all of his books and manuscripts from the Obelisk Press offices and put them into storage.[59] Anaïs removed everything she could to the cellar at 12, rue Cassini with her own archives, but only as a matter of courtesy and without feeling.

When the Durrells went to Athens at the end of October in search of work, Henry used money sent by Dorothy Norman (after a second begging letter) to join them. A month later, he questioned Anaïs's evasions about his demands for ever-larger sums of money. "Use your wits!" he commanded.

Hugo recognized Anaïs's delaying tactics, so he arranged a transfer to New York without telling her until it was done. Then he sent a telegram instructing her to get herself to Lisbon by December 7, where they would fly together to New York on the Pan American Clipper. In lieu of clothing, she packed five diary volumes in the one suitcase she was allowed, all it would hold without being overweight; the other forty-five she put into the vault at Hugo's bank. She left Henry's archives on the rue Cassini, to survive or not.

Hugo and Anaïs landed in New York on December 10, met by Rosa alone as Joaquín was in Boston giving a concert. Soon after, they were ensconced in the Savoy Plaza Hotel, all expenses met by the bank. "I landed with my diaries but without my soul. I feel like a ghost . . . I enter a palace of Byzantine luxury. I have the grippe."[60]

Henry wrote on December 23, saying he would arrive in mid-January. "Try to have $20 on you when you meet me at the dock as I may need some for tips . . . I may be broke."

"This is a dying love," Anaïs noted in the diary. "I know it now. I am desperate for news of Gonzalo."

21

The Literary Madam

GONZALO STIRRED LONG ENOUGH to get himself, Helba, and her daughter to Marseille, where they boarded a Greek ship on January 5, 1940. Anaïs was terrified Henry might be on it, as his ship was to stop in Marseille. That both her lovers would arrive in New York at the same time was the stuff of farce, but not to Anaïs. She was relieved when they sailed separately.[1]

Two days after she arrived in New York, her calendar was filled. "I see Frances Steloff, the gentle Jewess who bought all my Lawrence and H of I copies; Dorothy Norman . . . Stieglitz the photographer who admires the 'Birth' story."[2] Anaïs was pleased with the new life: "I look beautiful. Luxury enhances me . . . I am immensely popular, wanted everywhere, invited, sought out, pursued, loved."

She and Hugo were invited to country weekends by his banking clients and the wealthy women who had been her patients and were still devoted to her. She met other expatriates through Kay de San Faustino (divorced and soon to marry the painter Yves Tanguy), among them Valeska and Bravig Imbs, he an artist-designer and memoirist of his expatriate years, she a genial hostess of White Russian descent; Hazel King Farlow, sister of Peggy Guggenheim; Laura Archera, the violinist who had been her analysand and was soon to marry Aldous Huxley; Brigitte and Hugh Chisholm, who introduced her to New York society; and a woman she had pretended to know for years but was now meeting for the first time and whose love affairs required the same complicated logistics: Caresse Crosby.

With all these people, especially the expatriates, Miss (as she was always respectfully addressed)[3] Steloff's Gotham Book Mart became a meeting place where they shared "poignant regret for dying France." Anaïs admitted what they all tried to keep from each other as they jockeyed for new positions and reputations: "all of us had run away from America and now we want to conquer it."

Anaïs was eager to get her career started, so she and Hugo spent a weekend at Woodstock, New York,[4] with Blanche and James Cooney, publishers of *The Phoenix,* a literary magazine with strong political underpinnings, named after D. H. Lawrence's personal totem.

Jimmy and Blanche sent invitations to writers throughout the world to join them in creating a literary magazine. Henry, "scanning the heavens for signs useful to him," saw the announcement and wrote at once, inviting the Cooneys to publish whatever they liked of his work—especially his more than 300 pages on Lawrence since no one else wanted it.[5] Jimmy realized the publicity potential if he printed something by the banned Miller, so the "engaging, irreverent, sophisticated and disarming hustler" (as Blanche described Henry) was elected European editor. Henry had worked hard for the better part of a year, but by the end of 1938 his enthusiasm waned and he resigned.[6]

Anaïs was among the first of the "staunch and stalwarts" the Cooneys agreed to publish, and she remained dedicated to *The Phoenix,* even though only one short story, "Orchestra" (later incorporated into *Winter of Artifice*), had appeared in 1938 and nothing else since. But when the Cooneys read Henry's "Être Étoilique," they were eager to publish at least part of her diary, and this hope was enough to keep Anaïs interested and involved. She had sent a large packet of possible selections from France, as well as photos showing her in Spanish dancer's garb, in the garden at Louveciennes, on the deck of her houseboat, and various portraits ranging from her teenage years to exotic young adulthood. "I smell the incense," Jimmy said as he and Blanche pored over writings they deemed "elaborately erotic, vaguely mystical, [with] professions of clairvoyance, intuition, all aspects of the extraordinary."

The Cooneys shaped a sizable portion of the diary into a coherent narrative that was scheduled to appear in the spring of 1940; in January 1940, Anaïs and Hugo made a trip up the Hudson to Woodstock in the dead of winter to meet them—Anaïs's way of ensuring that it did.[7]

The Cooneys were struck by the way Hugo deferred to Anaïs, "But every now and then what started as a chuckle in the civilized Hugo would become a giggle and rise out of control."[8] In late January, Hugo returned to his work in London, leaving detailed instructions about Anaïs's financial future if anything should happen to him. He told her to rent an apartment, but she moved to a cheap hotel near the one where Henry planned to live. She had the flu when he arrived, but roused herself to meet him on the dock with money in hand. Still sick several days later, she dragged herself to another pier to meet Gonzalo and stood in freezing sleet for several hours until someone told her his name was not on the ship's passenger list. Two days later a cable arrived, saying he was departing "next Monday." She was furious.

When the Huara-Moré entourage finally arrived, confused and disheveled as ever, Anaïs was on the dock to meet them. Both had flu, so she was subsumed in the bathos of their lives, involved in the ongoing comedy of trying to hide with Gonzalo in out-of-the-way hotel rooms from the ever-vigilant, always suspicious Helba. When Anaïs did succeed in spiriting him away, he either refused to disrobe unless the room was pitch-dark (Helba teased him that he was so fat no woman would want to see his body), or else was so worried Helba would find then that he was impotent. On the rare occasion when Anaïs persuaded him to stay the night, he would silently sneak away as soon as he thought she was asleep. One night she caught him and demanded to know why: it was because of his false teeth, he said. He was embarrassed to take them out in her presence and could not sleep while wearing them.

In late February Anaïs received a letter from a young poet calling himself Robert Symmes, who had heard of her from Jimmy Cooney. He and several friends wanted to meet her. She was in bed with flu, but still created a stage setting by displaying all her favorite Paris objects in her hotel room.[9] A Chinese lacquer chest was invitingly open at the foot of her bed, on which she lay in a frilly peignoir under an ornate bedspread from Madagascar. Symmes came, with a young painter named Virginia Admiral. To Anaïs they appeared as if "out of

Wonderland, les Enfants Terribles of Cocteau, of the Grand Meaulnes. He is beautiful. They are dazzled by my beauty."

The adopted son of well-to-do, eccentric Californians, Robert Symmes later reassumed his birth name and became known as the poet Robert Duncan;[10] Virginia Admiral was a young painter from Chicago. They met when students at Berkeley in the late 1930s and were good friends who came to New York together.

Robert had spent time with the Cooneys learning to operate Jimmy's large old hand press and setting the type for his own poems. When the Cooneys left Woodstock to establish an agrarian commune on the coast of Georgia, Robert bought their press to publish his own magazine, *Ritual* (after his poem of the same name). It was the second incarnation of *Epitaph*, a magazine he and Virginia founded and co-edited during their Berkeley days.

Virginia objected to Robert's initial call for contributions through an advertisement in *The Phoenix*. He wanted *Ritual* to be "a magazine devoted to the dream," one of Anaïs's favorite phrases, and to his other interests, later to be bones of contention between them but which intrigued her at the time: "ritual, incantation . . . omens and fetishs . . . of idiocy and of madness, both simulated and pathological . . . the double-vision of the paranoic and the mumblings of the schizophrene."[11]

Robert wanted to lure "the gentle Anaïs," who was all too willing to contribute her writings and invest money in *Ritual,* so he stressed its emphasis on "metaphysical experience at its highest intensity."[12] Anaïs, realizing that the path to commercial publication was uncertain, intended to build up a solid list of publications in various little magazines as a way to bolster her planned assault on commercial American publishers. She was pleased that her work seemed destined to appear in a wide variety, from Dorothy Norman's *Twice a Year,* aimed at "an upper crust liberal audience"; to *The Phoenix,* advocating utopian agrarian pacifism; and, she hoped in *Furioso,* "a publication of some significance in modern American literature."[13]

Anaïs had been writing a "houseboat" story for some time, seeing it through various incarnations as "the barge story" or "water birth." But she could not conclude the work: "it gets dehumanized and becomes a fairy tale . . . a process of evaporation."[14] She finally resigned herself to reprinting a portion of *House of Incest*[15] because Duncan sent a long letter several weeks before their first meeting in which he described "the link" between it and the "Birth" story.

This was his first letter to her, but Anaïs replied on a level of closeness she often assumed with strangers.[16] Soon, "reaching from the dream outwards," the phrase she adapted from Jung as her credo toward life, became a private shorthand between her and Robert. Under Anaïs's influence, he even started a diary,[17] and for the better part of a year they wrote together, side-by-side in her various domiciles until September 1940, when she moved into her first permanent New York apartment, a fifth-floor walk-up in a tenement at 215 W. 13th Street.[18]

Despite the fact that she was ill for the first nine months of 1940, she led a peripatetic life. She was once again visiting Dr. Max Jacobson, whom she and Hugo had been indirectly responsible for bringing to New York.[19] For more than forty-four visits during several months, Dr. Jacobson prescribed "magic cocktails," but she was still persistently anemic.

Early in 1940, Caresse Crosby had hosted Henry at her Virginia plantation, Bowling Green, and, using her health as an excuse to evade Hugo and Gonzalo, Anaïs joined Henry in the first of several visits there. She and Caresse became good friends, especially since Caresse planned to start her own publishing venture and was interested in the diary. Anaïs was working on "1,000 pages of unabridged diary" and planned to have it ready by the end of her stay.

She had another reason to accept Caresse's hospitality: "I am in debt again. America is monstrous." In Virginia, she had no rent to pay nor food to buy, and could evade the new supplicants for her money, among them Duncan and his friend, the poet Kenneth Patchen. Patchen seems to be the only person she ever refused, saying his "big strong wife" Miriam should be willing to work to support him.[20]

Her finances were in their usual disarray. Hugo gave her $400 on the first day of each month for household and personal expenses. She divided it immediately between Gonzalo (whom Hugo knew about) and Henry (whom he supposedly did not). For the rest of the month, she lied to bill collectors, wrote checks for things she was supposed to buy with cash, and tried to borrow from friends. "I have to expect

Hugo's revolts, take his scoldings," she wrote. "When he relents, forgives, gives more, I feel even worse."[21]

Hugo returned in late May, so her financial problems were momentarily eased as he swept her away for a week of luxurious pampering on his expense account. Afterward, she spent several nights with Gonzalo and then went again with Henry to Bowling Green. Caresse had other houseguests: a young poet named John Dudley and his wife, Flo, and another poet, their friend and traveling companion whom Anaïs called only "Leaf."[22]

She and John Dudley became lovers. He was twenty-six and she thirty-seven, but she wrote that he was "amazed" by her body, that "of a girl and yet more than a girl, ageless." She was grateful for his "worship and youth," so much more pleasing than Gonzalo's "heaviness, inertia."

In July she and Hugo rented an apartment in Mamaroneck. He planned to commute to work and spend his free time sailing a small boat he had bought. Helba was petulant at being left in sweltering Manhattan, so Anaïs found an apartment for them, noting "they are so slow they won't move in by the time I am ready to leave." Within the week, she persuaded Hugo that she had to work with Caresse on the diaries and returned to Virginia. "I had Henry at siesta, John on the pine forest floor and Gonzalo at night [on her return to New York] in the Hotel Pennsylvania. I am happy."

On August 22 Anaïs discovered that she was three months pregnant and Dr. Jacobson arranged an abortion. As she lay there waiting, the woman next to her whimpered through the examining room curtain that her husband did not know what she was doing. Anaïs thought how surprised this unknown woman would be to know that Hugo knew about the abortion and had accompanied her to the doctor's office,[23] but that her problem was to keep it secret from her lover Gonzalo, because he believed she had not had relations with her husband in years.

"How much is to be said against the ban on abortion," Anaïs wrote afterward. "Motherhood is a vocation. It should be freely chosen, not imposed on a woman." Rereading old diaries did not give the comfort and validation she sought: "I know now there is something very wrong with me. I need proof of love constantly and that is wrong and cruel for others." Still, she believed that her creativity sprang directly from a connection to a specific man and she could not write without one.[24]

Despite yearning for a new lover, she took time out for a "ménage à trois" with Dr. Jacobson and "his girl, the German-Jewish Nina." She did not want to, but felt she owed it because he arranged the abortion. When it was over, she told him she would "see" him whenever he wanted, but only alone, as she no longer had any interest in orgies. She told the same to Donald Friede, in New York again after six years in Hollywood. She ordered Friede never to contact her again.

With writing uppermost in her mind, she gave the diary pages originally intended for Caresse to Duell, Sloan and Pearce. Some weeks later, Pearce told her it was "marvelous" but should only be published in a limited edition because too much that was censurable would be lost otherwise. She took it next to Henry's agent, John Slocum, who agreed to represent her and shepherded the diary through the offices of every publisher in New York for the better part of a year.

Also at this time, she began to see much of Duncan and his friends. Anaïs engaged Virginia Admiral as her typist at ten cents a page but instructed her to stop when she reached ten dollars, all she could afford each week. It galled her when she learned that Virginia and Robert were typing Patchen's *Journal of Albion Moonlight* for free because he said he had no money to pay them.

It was especially galling because Duncan had broken with his adoptive parents and was homeless and dependent on others for meals and money. Duncan "would never borrow from his friends what he needed to survive," Virginia Admiral remembered, "but he had no compunction about borrowing from Anaïs and her cousin, Eduardo."[25]

As Anaïs had no money to give to Robert, her way of providing his security was "to give him as a present to her rich Cuban cousin."[26] Knowing that Duncan needed a secure abode, Anaïs told Eduardo she thought they were astrological soulmates, and after doing his horoscope, Eduardo agreed, but their affair was fraught with tension from the beginning. Robert believed Eduardo was far too demanding because he had the money and therefore the power to control it, and he resented the role Eduardo made him play, a putative wife in every sense.[27]

At the same time, Henry infuriated Anaïs by establishing a close friendship with Patchen, whom she called his "creation." Henry seemed astonished when Patchen tried to borrow money from him, and wanted Anaïs to increase his allowance so he could pretend to make a tidy income from his writing—for after all, he had no other visible means of support—and could then give it to those who turned to him in increasing numbers for financial help.[28]

She knew that some of her money was going through Henry to the one man she despised, Patchen, but could do nothing to stop it. She resented that Robert and Virginia worked for him without pay, all the while begging handouts from her. In what Virginia claimed was "utter innocence," she and Robert invited Anaïs to join a "Committee to Help Patchen" when Henry gave them the idea to write a begging letter. Anaïs wanted to hide her dislike, so she agreed to join but did not allow her name to be used, nor did she give money.

She was upset when Wallace Stevens sent $15 with apologies that it could not be more. No one had ever offered to help her financially, probably because everyone knew her husband held an important banking position, but she resented the fact that people routinely assumed she had large sums of money to give and were often rude and demanding when they asked for it.

Anaïs found it ironic, "like some Dante punishment," that Henry was "condemned to write about sex when today he is a mystic." He was weighted down by his father's prostate cancer and his mother's assumption that he would pay the bills, and the pleas for money from all those who envied the seeming ease of his life. He was unable to write the one thing that guaranteed a steady income, pornography for "the collector." He and Anaïs were sure "the collector" was Barnett Ruder, a New York rare-book dealer who denied it throughout their long affiliation, insisting that he only represented a mysterious "old millionaire down south" for whom he sought writers to create original pornography, payment one dollar per page and a minimum of one hundred pages per month.

At first it seemed easy, but gradually it changed from "forced and unnatural" to "hard labor." Henry was writing about June (in what became *The Rosy Crucifixion*) and did not want to use any of that material, so he invented bizarre tales for several months until the collector—according to Ruder—said that he was disappointed and would have to find another writer if the stories did not improve. Henry was frantic with worry until he learned that Doubleday Doran had accepted his proposal to write a book about the United States (which became *The Air-Conditioned Nightmare*), but they offered only a $500 advance, not enough to cover even basic travel expenses.

He blithely told Anaïs he would reject the advance, fully expecting her to pay for the trip. She "begged" him not to reject it, and to ensure that he would not, agreed to meet all his expenses above and beyond the $500.

Thus her "one true friend," the diary, helped her to begin a new career as a pornographer. She became "the literary madam of West 13th Street" when she suggested "we feed [Ruder] the diary as I have no money for travelling expenses." Ruder said he would not agree outright to letting a mere woman take over—for what did women know about pornography?—but would give her the job only after he read something. She gave him "Vol. 32, the beginning of my love for Henry and June," but because she had no faith in herself as a writer, she pasted an exotic photograph of herself as a Spanish dancer inside the front cover. "Now," she said, "I wait."

When Ruder, supposedly acting for the mysterious "old man," accepted volume 32, it came at just the right time: "We were borrowing from Millicent the maid and four days to go for Hugo's pay."[29] Anaïs used her first earnings to pay for Helba's doctor and Henry's latest travel expenses, deferring her own household expenses until Hugo's next payday. By the start of 1941, she was deep into pornography and into her past diaries as well. She was "astounded" by her rereadings: "Is it creation to make something live forever? For the first time I believe this: [the diary] will live forever. It has not died."[30]

Ruder told her, however, that she must eliminate all her irritating artistic elaborations, which filled space but did not provide what he wanted, one lurid account of sex after another, as fast as she could write them. She "let . . . go and wrote fous descriptions of sexual scenes for 34, the erotic madness days," and was so "powerfully excited" by her own writing that "I had an orgasm while I wrote, then I went to Henry and he was passionate, then to Gonzalo who was passionate. Responded to both."

Throughout the first six months of 1941, she was obsessed with rewriting the "true" diaries for publication, inventing sexual scenes for the "porno diaries," and her health. She summed up her problem with the diaries in two sentences: "I've written 60 books no one wants and now I have to write new ones to order. What irony!" Ruder was a hard taskmaster who often refused her stories as "not erotic

Anaïs in the 1940s.

enough" and "definitely lacking in the sexual elements."[31] Anaïs was indignant: "there were ten scenes in 100 pages!" In the meantime, the real diary "finally ended its tour of the publishers." Slocum had submitted it to every publishing company in New York and none wanted it. The reason was always the same: no one dared risk censorship or lawsuits. Even Dorothy Norman refused to publish further extracts after the one that appeared in *Twice a Year.*

"All my strength goes now into Erotica," Anaïs wrote. "The diary is abandoned. I look at it tonight to feel it is there, but I have nothing to say." Now she was asking Ruder for advances to pay her own debts rather than to take care of others. Hugo was furious when their telephone service was canceled even though he had given her money twice in one month to pay the bill. She stopped going to Dr. Jacobson because she could not pay for Henry's and Gonzalo's weekly visits at $38 each, let alone her own. She lost ten pounds she could ill afford and had constant pains in her stomach. Everything was exacerbated by her "moonstorm," the menstrual periods that brought manic and depressive mood swings and became more painful with every passing month.

Just at this time, Robert Duncan came into her life with devious, devilish intensity. Robert had broken with Eduardo, who sought solace with the Cooneys on their Massachusetts farm;[32] he wanted to get onto Anaïs's payroll and bring his friend, poet Sanders Russell. Robert ignored social boundaries with everyone, but ran roughshod over Anaïs and Hugo, helping himself to anything he wanted in their apartment.[33] Still, in the original diaries (as opposed to the published versions, where she is sharply critical of him from the beginning), Anaïs adored Robert Duncan. "He is the only one besides Henry who can do to me what I do to others. He can see right into the ocean of the diary, its meaning and direction. He is never lost. I can trust his vision of my work." All this would soon change, but until his Army induction in May 1941, he was her "twin," a figure of speech she liked to use to describe the literary alter ego she constantly sought. For days on end they wrote together, pausing only for meals (which Anaïs shopped for, cooked, and served). "I only go out to see Gonzalo," she wrote, "otherwise we get drunk on writing."

Each was critical of the other's style. Picking out a phrase from *Winter of Artifice,* Robert accused Anaïs of writing like a "ventriloquist's trick: Henry Miller speaking." She retaliated by saying that was how she wrote five years ago, and would not do so now, nor should he do the same by imitating Patchen. She accused Henry of "ugly, untransformed" language, right for him but wrong for her and Robert. Their task, she said, was to be "magic, primitive and not prosaic."[34] This made her think of Jean Carteret, whom she wanted Robert to replace in every aspect of her life, including the sexual. Although she had managed to seduce Carteret, Robert eluded her. She decided to settle for the "twin" whose diary "could flow into [hers] and become part of it."

Anaïs wanted to change various aspects of her life, starting with the company she kept. She was never entirely comfortable in New York social settings, from the most august Park Avenue drawing room to the most decrepit Greenwich Village artist's studio. She persuaded herself that it was because she mourned her lost Parisian life, but more likely she was uncomfortable among people who were at ease (or at least appeared to be) while she was so insecure about everything from her dress and makeup to her lack of education.

Everything came to a head after one of Dorothy Norman's elegant dinners. Quite casually, Dorothy asked Anaïs what she thought about Patchen's poetry being published in *Twice a Year*.[35] Anaïs could not hear his name without the blood of anger coloring her response. When she read his *Journal of Albion Moonlight*, she described the experience as one that caused her to "turn inward and cease to expand." Suddenly it struck her that turning inward was exactly what she wanted to do, and in her own convoluted reasoning, Dorothy's high regard for Patchen became a convenient excuse for Anaïs to abdicate from society, be it high, café, or artistic. Most of their social invitations came through Hugo's banking connections, every one of which Anaïs found a way to sunder. She stopped the one activity she liked, going to Harlem nightclubs with the many visitors in Caresse Crosby's circle who sought her when they came to New York.

Hugo was taking lessons in engraving from Stanley William Hayter, who had moved his Atelier 17 from Paris to the New School. He wanted to give a party in Hayter's honor, to which he invited (among others) Pierre Matisse, Harvey Breit, Matta, and Isamu Noguchi. "I didn't enjoy it, but the others did," Anaïs wrote in the diary. "I shrink. I can't talk." Only Noguchi captured her attention, the "diluted Japanese, enigmatic with a cliché surface, an American outer shell." She had sex with him several times but he must not have inspired her, for her descriptions of the encounters are among the most perfunctory in all her diaries.

Anaïs was ill-at-ease because she did not like conversations that did not center around her and was uncomfortable in settings where she could not convince herself that every man in the room desired her. She dismissed the likes of Mike Gold, Edward Dahlberg, Lewis Mumford, Charles Henri Ford, and Dwight Macdonald—to name a few of the men she met at Dorothy's—as self-centered bores because they tried to engage her in conversation about such things as the war or the latest brouhaha in *View* or *Partisan Review.* She dismissed Alfred Stieglitz, Dorothy's great love, as old and feeble, slowly dying; she avoided the many intelligent women who frequented Dorothy's home, nor did she mention any by name in the diary.

"I have no interest in anyone [in Dorothy's world]," she wrote. "Everywhere I find little Millers." Most of these were young homosexual men who sought her patronage and who later ridiculed her as a "fag hag" who tried to seduce them in exchange for a few bucks.[36] She was wise enough to realize that such alliances were "destructive," and thus she arrived at a decision that was to influence how she lived for the next several years. It was, she felt, "time to retire [from] human life. Not so drunk and not so open."

She turned to the diary, mostly because it was the only writing that did not make her so blocked that her arm grew rigid and she literally could not move her pen, which happened now when she attempted to write fiction. Robert tried to help by getting her an assignment to write an article on astrology for *Vogue.* She thought she wrote it "lightly," but Robert thought it not "flippant" enough. "You must flip!" he insisted. "I can't flip," she replied sadly, and abandoned it.[37]

And so, more than ever, she depended on the money Ruder provided, all the while beset by insecurities of every sort. When she gave Norman the first diary excerpt for *Twice a Year,* culled from the "true" diary, Anaïs told her how grateful she was for her "faith," which she needed at that particular moment. Then she did something she had never done before with another woman: she told Dorothy Norman her deepest insecurities: "As you know I have come to an absolute impasse with my work . . . I felt as if I were being forced back into solitude. For me, not being printed means solitude, no contact with the world. Always I'm aware that I cannot talk. I talk in writing. I am truly mute without writing. In writing I can touch people, so when I am not printed I feel as if my very being were entombed, my existence denied. This is not merely an egotistic pain. It is for me an act of love that is rejected.[38]

Having taken Norman into her confidence, she fully expected to be rewarded in a number of ways, starting with publication of further diary extracts. She also expected Norman to heed her advice and ban Patchen from the pages of *Twice a Year,* but Dorothy printed Patchen's poems and Anaïs never forgave her. Their pallid friendship continued for another year, and it brought a new woman into Anaïs's life whom she immediately compared with June: the actress Luise Rainer (then married to playwright Clifford Odets).[39]

People said they looked like twins, and Anaïs delighted in the comparison. Both were boyishly slender, with heart-shaped faces and the same slight lisp and indefinable accent. Anaïs was nine years older than Luise, and soon found herself being treated as elder sister, confidante, mentor, and protector.

Luise shared many of her emotional traits, especially the need to be the center of attention, so she insisted that Anaïs write a play about June in which she could star, because Anaïs's tales of June's destructive antics fascinated her. Anaïs agreed, for if Luise gained attention on the stage, the resultant publicity would be hers as well. But after several frenzied weeks of trying, Anaïs realized she could not write about June and had no idea how to construct a play, so the project languished.[40]

Because Luise insisted, Anaïs became her analyst. Luise's many neuroses so frightened her that Anaïs went in person to beg Dr. M. Esther Harding, the Jungian analyst whose writings had been so important to her several years previously, to accept Luise Rainer as her patient. It marked the end of their friendship, for under Dr. Harding's care, Luise decided that she hated and distrusted Anaïs. Anaïs was relieved.

As she could not afford regular dental care, Anaïs lost another molar to disease. She did not heal easily, so suffered from bleeding gums and infection after the surgery. Anemic and discouraged by "the struggle for health and the time it swallows," she still forced herself to continue on her self-appointed rounds. Once when Robert did not leave the studio until 1:30 A.M., she was too exhausted to rouse herself from bed the next day. "I am so ashamed of this," she wrote. "I want to deceive everybody by seeming youthful." Staying young began to preoccupy her. She commiserated with Caresse Crosby, then involved with the young African-American actor Canada Lee (with whom Anaïs also had a fleeting affair later that year). Both women feared aging and "worried about [our] lives growing shabby. Love has brought poverty, restrictions."[41]

"Look where I am!" she wrote of an evening spent watching the play of Richard Wright's *Native Son,* on a date with "Mr. Ruder, who is ugly and vulgar and familiar." She wailed at "the prostitution" into which the needs of Henry and Gonzalo forced her: "Look!" she commanded. "Look at Anaïs Nin in her dark wine colored velvet suit (seven dollars at Lerner shop) in her frilled grey blouse from New Orleans given to her by Caresse, in the six year old wine colored velvet hat with a feather that I wore [in Paris], with a cape cut out of the dilapidated fur coat, with mended stockings, walking down with a twaddling deformed long nosed monster who has the Jewish racial trait of invading the privacy of others without being invited! . . . However, people do say I look dashing and elegant."[42]

In June, Anaïs persuaded Hugo to rent a studio in Provincetown. At the end of Commercial Street, it was so close to the beach that at high tide water ran underneath it. It was restful, in fact too restful for Anaïs: "there are shoals and shoals of homosexuals here and no one for me," she wrote to Robert, who had been drafted, inducted, and soon after imprisoned in a Kentucky military facility for proclaiming his homosexuality.[43]

She had time to reflect about "an undercurrent" she had not previously touched upon in other diaries: "the story of our aging, all of us, of age."[44] She had "no sense of [her own] age" until she looked at Henry one day at Caresse's and saw an old, skinny, bald man sitting beside her. It was the same day that he "experienced a sexual *défaillance* and diminishing interest in women." Hugo had gray hair now, jowls and a potbelly. Gonzalo was fat, "a man who cannot drink, is often ill, gets pains and is depressed."

She turned a sharp eye on herself and found little wanting: "Physically there are no signs. My body is that of a girl. I weigh 113 lbs. My waist is still pronouncedly indented. My breasts are dainty, the tops roseate." Only her hands looked aged, "but they were always old," and there were "fine wrinkles" around her eyes and "a few gray hairs." On tired days, her chin drooped, "but the experienced girl at Elizabeth Arden said apart from the lines around the eyes, all is well. The muscles are firm." Anaïs was satisfied: "I can deceive anyone. . . . I pass for thirty easily." She was then thirty-eight, but already lopping years off her life. She told her mother she had begun to admit only to "thirty-two, thirty-three," and begged Rosa never to reveal her true age.[45]

Her introspection dissipated several days later when she saw a large blond man, a "Siegfried," "parading" on the beach, "such wonderful don Juan plumage . . . flexing his muscles." The next day she passed him and smiled, and the day after saw him going into a house near hers. The day after that they talked and dined together at a famous Provincetown hangout, the Flagship. Several days later they were lovers.[46]

Edward Graeffe sang tenor roles in Wagnerian operas and was spending the summer in Provincetown preparing for his debut that autumn at the Metropolitan. He was taller than either Gonzalo or Hugo, of robust build, and thirty-two, six years younger than Anaïs. When they walked into the Flagship, "people are stunned by us. All the homosexuals tried to interest him," she gloated, "but he is with me."

The new lover, Graeffe, caused the recurring comic logistical problem with the old lover, Gonzalo,[47] and with Hugo as well. It also brought a momentary realization of Hugo's "divine goodness." When his holiday ended and he returned to New York, she sat in a café one afternoon telling the diary how all her sexual dalliances were nothing more than a recurring self-inflicted "wound." She wondered why it and Hugo were not enough for her. There followed a startling admission: "I am in truth a very very sick person, who needs a love like Hugo's to keep her from insanity and death."

She returned to her studio determined "to set order in my life." Robert Duncan had been given a "Section 8" undesirable discharge from the Army and he wanted to sell his printing press and return to Berkeley. Anaïs "took the decisive step of buying the press from Robert to do Volume I [of the diary]."

The "Literary Madam" was about to add another title to her *curriculum vitae:* Anaïs Nin, publisher of Gemor Press. She was also about to begin a new period in "my autumnal life with Gonzalo, the autumn of my face and not of my body, the autumn which has marked only my eyes and a few strands of my hair, and not my soul yet because my soul was always aged."

She added one more comment that would become the most accurate description of how she lived the rest of her life: "I am ready to return to New York with the full conviction of my unhappiness and the desire to escape into pleasure. Or merely to escape."

22

Changes

THE YEARS 1941–1943 were characterized by severed relationships, as Anaïs Nin sought to effect elusive "changes" too difficult to define. There was a complicated rupture with Robert Duncan, dishonorably discharged, broke, and homeless in New York. Anaïs could not take him into her W. 13th Street studio because his tauntings had enraged Gonzalo, who went on a rampage, destroyed the furnishings, and smeared the skylight windows on which Anaïs and Robert had lovingly painted fanciful crayon designs.[1]

Robert could not stay with his best friend, Virginia, because he seduced both her and her new husband, the painter Robert De Niro Sr., then bragged to each about his conquest of the other. With malicious glee, he told Anaïs, who was haunted by the aftermath of the seduction and wanted to convert it to fiction.[2] Robert told her that Virginia and Bob got into a violent domestic fracas over each other's infidelity. Virginia accused Bob of being "a real shit," and suddenly, through the thin walls came a voice from the next apartment saying "Yes, Bob, you really were a shit." For days afterward, Bob De Niro, who had never seen the person in the next apartment, stalked the hallway and walked the streets of Greenwich Village, peering into faces, trying to imagine if anyone possessed the voice of his faceless accuser.

How Anaïs longed to turn this into fiction! But something always seemed to be lacking, some element that would permit a faceless voice to dominate the story. She was stymied until she recalled a morning the previous summer when she sat idly flipping the pages of Hugo's *Forbes* magazine as he ate breakfast. She remembered a headline that provided exactly the element she needed: THE LIE DETECTOR GOES INTO BUSINESS, followed by a mundane article about how department stores in Chicago were using polygraphs to help convict shoplifters.[3] Anaïs Nin personified the Lie Detector into a spectral figure that was the genesis of what many critics believe is her finest novel, *A Spy in the House of Love*. Writing it consumed her fictional energies for the better part of the next decade.[4]

Anaïs returned penniless from Provincetown and Hugo had $7 to last until payday a week later. Henry wired from California asking her to send dough fast. Anaïs "quietly telegraphed [him] to try other sources" and was surprised that she felt "no anguish."[5] Next, she refused Robert, who left angrily for the Cooneys' after taking whatever he wanted from her apartment.

Throughout the following year, she repeatedly posed a rhetorical question: "Is devotion to others a cover for the hungers and the needs of the self, of which one is ashamed? I was always ashamed to take. So I gave. It was not a virtue. It was a disguise."[6]

Robert returned briefly to New York in the winter of 1942, supposedly on his way to Berkeley but still seeking Anaïs's support despite her insistence that she could not afford it. In retaliation, he invited Hugo to lunch and methodically recited a detailed list of her infidelities, then taunted him as a cuckold. Hugo calmly paid the bill and left without responding.[7]

Dorothy Norman was next. Anaïs asked for a $200 loan to buy a better press than the one she originally intended to buy from Robert (it was too antiquated to be trusted). Dorothy refused, even though Anaïs offered to do $400 worth of work to pay for it. Anaïs was furious at Dorothy, "who lives in the utmost luxury, and meanwhile makes the writers wait for their checks, and pays the minimum price of a penny a word!" She was no longer grateful to "the only person who printed me in America."[8]

Anaïs's long affair with Henry took more than a year to fizzle out for good. Henry could not adapt to the New York literary life and stayed away from it as much as possible. His trip across the country to research *The Air-Conditioned Nightmare* piqued his interest in Los Angeles. At the end of 1941 and for most of 1942, he freeloaded off friends in Hollywood, trying to decide whether or not to live there permanently and urging Anaïs to leave Hugo and join him.[9] They played out their break in letters in which his self-justification rivaled hers. Henry claimed that he had partially paid for Anaïs's ten years of financial support by his efforts to convince her that she had enough talent to establish an independent life, then grudgingly admitted that, "on the other hand, I prevented you, by making myself dependent on you." He resented her "balk[ing] and bring[ing] up the past," and urged her to "honor the moment."[10]

Hoping to coax her to join him, Henry bragged that he was actually earning money from his writing, "one thousand dollars last year," but he did not mention "at least $500 in debts" that Anaïs knew about.[11] It made her so angry that she wrote the letter that ended their affair, saying she wished now she had attended to her own needs rather than helping Henry's. No longer dependent on her money, Henry had no qualms about telling the truth. He lashed out on January 15, 1943: "The one obvious thing which you refuse to admit to yourself is first, your lack of faith in yourself, second your lack of faith in others. . . . Finally, I come out here to stand on my own legs. And though I drew on you less . . . it is at this point you crack up, at this point you cry out: 'Too much! Too Much! I've given up everything.' "[12] He stopped abruptly and did not sign the letter.

For a brief period, Anaïs was, in her own way, monogamous. She was loyal to Gonzalo and Hugo, refusing the attentions of such men as the British poet George Barker and the brash American novelist Edward Dahlberg. Only "Chinchilito,"[13] as she nicknamed Edward Graeffe, was able to tempt her from her relative faithfulness when he passed through New York to sing at the Met.

One of the things that irritated her most about Henry was her own inability to express clearly what she meant by all the "changes" she believed had occurred since she returned to New York. She knew that she was unhappy but did not know why. Much had to do with the lack of American interest in her writing and the end of what might well be called her first "other" marriage—i.e., to Henry. But there were other indefinable changes that confused her even as she effected them.

She refused to support John Dudley and Robert Duncan, burdens she would have been incapable of rejecting only a short time ago.

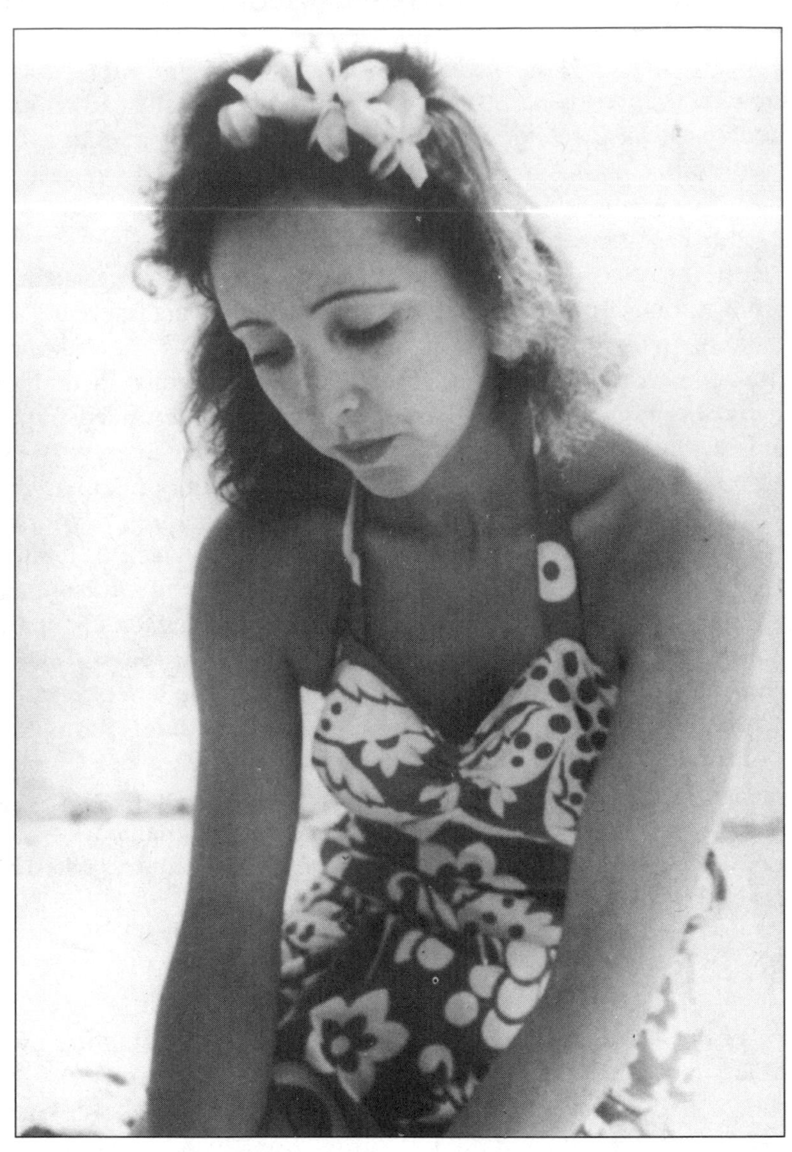

Anaïs in Provincetown.

And she, who feared abandonment above all else, now ended many so-called friendships, Luise Rainer and Dorothy Norman paramount among them. Much of her self-examination and introspection centered around her erotic relationships, and this brought on a detailed account of her long history with Hugo, for in just a few months, March 1942, they would celebrate their twentieth wedding anniversary.

Anaïs's introspection crested just after Hugo celebrated his first artistic success, an exhibition of his engravings at the New School. Stanley William Hayter, whom he and Anaïs knew in Paris, had reestablished his famous Atelier 17 at the New School, and Hugo enrolled in his classes. His interest in engraving stemmed from William Blake's technique, "where etching and engraving are combined on one plate, and then printed in relief, as in a woodcut, to produce a spectacular range of color and texture.[14]

Hayter[15] deemed Hugo's vision as original as his technique,[16] and arranged for him to have a solo exhibit, in November 1941, which was a huge success. Hugo sold four engravings on opening night.[17] He made $200 and gave half to Anaïs for her printing press. "The first money he earns outside the bank he gives to me," she noted sadly.

Hugo's success instilled tension into the marriage, especially when the rest of the engravings were quickly sold and he found himself with an admiring following of other artists who sought his counsel and expertise. Anaïs was not quite sure how she felt about the success of Hugo's first attempt as an artist after so many years of her own failure and rejection. On the one hand, she was delighted, for Hugo's glory reflected to a degree back onto her; on the other, if the banker were to become eminent as an artist, she would no longer be the creative center around whom their marriage revolved.

She could not explain why, but she reread *Lady Chatterley's Lover*, and it brought back memories of her bridal timidity. Then she thought back to her childhood, and how shy she was when her parents were still together. She compared it to living in an actor's house where there was sparkling banter and witty dialogue, a marvelous party to which she, as the daughter of the house, was invited, but how instead she always found a quiet corner in which to hide: "I felt born on the rim of an eternally elusive world . . . abandoned by those who are talking and laughing, as if they had left me out, whereas it is I who get cut off by my own nature and separateness."[18]

The writer James Leo Herlihy, who met Anaïs Nin several years later, in 1947, and remained devoted to her throughout her life, described this as one of her most striking qualities. "It was as if there was a wonderful party going on, and Anaïs was invited, but she went to sit outside on the fire escape because she couldn't enjoy it. She wanted the party to be *for her;* she wanted really to *be* the party. Nothing else would do. No praise was ever enough. It was sad, because she was so wonderful to be around."

Her marriage was in part a way to indulge her feeling of being an outsider, for Hugo encouraged "the hiding away," and provided "the refuge."[19] But her husband, to whom she looked for every security, was a "shadow" of herself, a man who wanted no identity aside from hers, who echoed everything from her joys to her sorrows and praised her "courage and weakness equally." It satisfied them for their first ten years, until she read *Lady Chatterley's Lover* and made two startling discoveries: that she had never experienced the sexual sensations Lawrence described, and that searching for them would become her unending quest.

In the second decade of marriage, she divided daily life neatly into what she called "the great abysm" of day and night. During the day, Hugo remained attuned to her every desire, while at night, he became an autocrat of the bedroom and "exerted the will of the husband. No attempt at charming, seducing the woman, playing on her moods, awakening her desire. Merely the immediate consent to the sexual urge which came up in him with such firmness. Like an order." It was not a conscious cruelty, for Hugo was no more satisfied than she with their sexual rapport, and the dichotomy caused him to enter analysis within the year and to remain in treatment for the next forty-odd years.

Anaïs believed they were unable to satisfy each other physically because their love was so fraternal as to be incestuous (a word she still refused to use for what had happened with her father). She asked: "how is it that Hugo's sexual nature adapts itself so well to the incest, and not mine?" Then she answered: "Because I have known authentic passion, perhaps." Not until later did she realize that she was "afraid of intruding erotic life" into her marriage for fear of upsetting the many delicate balances between them.[20]

She thought of all her extramarital relations, from brief encounters to the two long-lasting affairs with Henry and Gonzalo, as a perpetual traversing of mysterious states that Hugo had never dreamed of and therefore could not even try to understand. While she voyaged in search of adventure, he stayed at home, always ready with a safety net to catch her when she fell, and by tacit agreement "secretly aware of her ordeals, never aware of what caused them." She thought about Hugo's puzzling need to absolve her of any complicity or guilt. With John Erskine, for example, he turned what happened into "the grief" Erskine had inflicted upon her: "Hugo asked no questions. For him it was a sufficient miracle that I should come home. His entire concern was that I should come home."

No family member or friend of Mr. and Mrs. Hugh Guiler, and no scholar or critic of the writer Anaïs Nin, has yet accused Hugo of either consciously or unconsciously manipulating his wife. No one has suggested that he indulged her in so many different ways, from supporting her "children" to paying for her self-publication because it was his one sure way to keep her "coming home." Neither was theirs a simple marriage of a devious, promiscuous wife and her densely stupid and easily cuckolded husband. It was an infinitely complex relationship between two intelligent people, held together on a very primitive level by that too easily tossed off word, love, but also knotted into an unravelable skein by every emotion that gained either momentary credence or disrepute throughout the excessively self-absorbed times in which their lives unfolded.

On January 8, 1942, with Hugo's $200, Anaïs bought an old treadle press, a "Clamshell" (a standing platen model), and every tray of Bernhard Gothic Light type that she could find.

She wanted *Winter of Artifice* to be published in the United States, especially as Miss Steloff had sold all the European copies Anaïs managed to ship from France. But she had just been through another disappointing year with various would-be publishers. Caresse Crosby had planned to resurrect her late husband Harry's Black Sun Press and kept the novel for a year before returning it with little more than perfunctory apology. A young couple Anaïs met at the Gotham Book Mart, Seon Givens[21] and Wayne Harris, then a "Mr. Beamish," joined the growing list of those who planned to become publishers but whose ideas came to naught.

"There is no protection," Anaïs wrote, expressing every writer's complaint. "Anyone can come and say: I'll publish your manuscript and then keep it in a drawer. No advances, no security of any kind.

At the end of a year it is returned. Meanwhile the writer is bound and cannot show it to anyone else. The book is advertised as coming out, and people send in orders, interest is aroused, then nothing happens. It grows stale. When it is mentioned again it almost sounds like a hoax."[22]

On January 14 the Clamshell press was delivered to a studio Anaïs rented at 144 MacDougal Street as a trysting place for herself and Gonzalo but which now became their workroom. Gonzalo showed up that day, having decided to accept Anaïs's offer of employment. He came and went as he pleased, but Helba swiftly told Anaïs that she expected their allowance to be increased now that Gonzalo was "officially" in her employ.

Owning the press became the catalyst for change that Anaïs had long sought. She admitted what she had known all along, that Helba was "a great criminal cripple," and as "the apparent victim," she must "beware." Anaïs was truly at "the end of that road of compassion": the Huara-Moré contingent remained on Hugo's payroll, but their allowance did not increase.

"The truth is now that I want nobody around me who doesn't accept me as I accept them. I want to work. I have no time for new struggles." The resolution made her feel so good that by January 20, she was working steadily for six or eight hours each day. She had two assistants because Eduardo, deserted by Robert and seeking some sort of stability, now worked with her and Gonzalo. The three were happily united in a common cause, to print her novel, but first they needed a name for the press. Anaïs chose Gemor (pronounced "Geemore"), an amalgam of Gonzalo's first initial and last name, because he was a printer by profession and they were his apprentices.[23] It was also her way of trying to ensure his dedication to the project, for without Gonzalo, she and Eduardo did not yet know enough to print a book by themselves.

"The relation to hand craft is nourishing, beautiful," she wrote as she learned to place the lead letters into the composing stick and to adjust to "the adroitness of spacings, the tempo and temper of the machine." These were "victories, concrete, definitive, proved," giving her so much more satisfaction than the abstract theories that swirled around her in the New York literary milieu. On February 21 she noted "3 days to do 2 pages," which was all she could manage in the twelve-to-fourteen-hour workdays until March 10. Then she wrote "began to do 4 pages a day," but only because Jimmy Cooney was helping.[24] "I have not spared my hands. Some of my nails are broken." She had also not spared her book. "I have slashed into its imperfections. It is shorter, purer." She reprinted only two of the three original sections: "father and the voice, *not* the Henry June novel," so the book was substantially shortened as well as rewritten.[25]

As luck would have it, while she worked slowly and carefully to set the type for the "father" section, the classical radio station she listened to played her father's compositions for most of the afternoon while she "slowly, word by word, erect[ed] the lasting monument of his failure as a human being."

As she relived her experiences with her father, with Rank, Gonzalo, Henry, and even her youthful flirtation with Eduardo, she felt a sense of power and satisfaction that for the very first time was based not on the sexuality of seduction, but, rather, on bringing this project to a satisfactory conclusion. She called herself "the woman of tomorrow," secure in the knowledge that she could "expand to the new consciousness." It inspired her to look critically at her work and to see what was worth changing when next she wrote fiction. She criticized her excessive subtlety, saying it kept readers from understanding her meaning. The stories she was then writing, about Artaud, Moricand, and Carteret, were too "mysterious" and had led her into "strange regions." She felt confident that all this would change with her next novel.

Her confidence was further enhanced when Virginia Admiral presented her with the last of the typed copies of her sixty diary volumes. Anaïs commissioned this Herculean task because, with the United States now at war, she was afraid of losing them again, as she had temporarily lost them in France until one of Hugo's banking friends arranged to ship them to New York. When reunited with them, her first act was to buy a large safe that now sat squatly consuming space in her small studio apartment.

This period marked the first concentrated rewriting of all the diaries and was the first consistent and complete reinvention of her past. First, with the original diaries beside her, Anaïs rewrote by hand all those parts that she thought were publishable. This included almost everything but the incest with her father and most of the entries about her brother Thorvald. Then she gave the rewritten volumes to Virginia Admiral, who typed them onto "easily transportable" rice paper. Each separate diary volume was then inserted into its own cardboard folder, secured by brass tacks. The diaries she rewrote by hand were locked away with the originals, and the typed copies were made available to selected readers.[26] And so, when Anaïs offered to let someone read the "original" diaries, she was really showing those she had hand-copied from the true originals. Mostly, however, she showed the typed copies, all the while insisting each was transcribed word for word from the originals.[27]

With the originals securely locked into the darkest recesses of the safe, and after having been rejected by every New York publisher, Anaïs permitted another unnamed agent to send some of the typed copies to publishers outside New York. Her hopes were dashed by Houghton Mifflin of Boston in a prescient though negative letter:

> There is no doubt it is a remarkable performance that should someday be published and may well achieve permanence as the ultimate in neurotic self-absorption, a kind of decadent St. Theresa. Certainly the writing is extraordinary, the cadences, the ability to communicate an intensity of emotion. But I don't think this is the time to bring it out. Today such morbid preoccupation with one's inner life will seem trivial. My guess is that it is a book to see the light about five to ten years after the war is over. When the author does prepare it for publication, my advice would be to cut out the redundancy rather than the sex. In fact, I'd trim lightly there, and with an ear merely on the law. The erotic element is part of its uniqueness. It underlines the candor and leads even the unwilling reader on.[28]

The rejected typed copies joined all the others in the safe and she concentrated on printing her novel. By Tuesday, May 5, at 11:35 P.M., she and Gonzalo finished printing, and by May 15, the bound copies were back from the bindery and neatly stacked in the studio.[29] Miss Steloff kept her word and took twenty-five copies, which she sold in several days. She reordered, sold twenty-five more, and reordered again. Anaïs sold sixty, and soon more than half the edition of 500 was sold. And thus "began a series of successes, compliments, letters and continuous sales."

Otto Fuhrman, a respected graphic artist and professor at New York University, praised the book's appearance, which pleased Anaïs as much as the compliments of those who liked its content. James Laughlin of *New Directions,* who was always skeptical (and sometimes highly critical) of her writing, commissioned William Carlos Williams to write a 4,000-word review. Edouard Roditi offered to review it in the *New York Psychoanalytic Review,* and Harvey Breit praised its "terrific sensibility" and planned to review it for the *New Republic.*[30] Her friends Lucia Cristofanetti and Frances Brown[31] said they were "deeply moved," as did many anonymous women who wrote or telephoned to say how much they identified with the two characters, Djuna and Lillian. Even Luise Rainer wrote from Hollywood, saying Anaïs was "the smartest woman alive" and her biggest mistake had been in trying to help Luise solve her problems!

Her pleasure soon dissipated into what she insisted was "bad luck with the critics." Paul Rosenfeld of *The Nation,* a good friend as well as one of her few supporters, wrote a favorable review, but Anaïs Nin resented his complimenting her "veiled autobiography."[32] To her, Rosenfeld betrayed, "with the best will in the world . . . the secret I threw a veil over and proclaims the father [in the novel] is Joaquín Nin." William Carlos Williams, who wrote the first extended critical appraisal of the novel, earned the same ire.[33] He, too, was accused of (again "with the best will in the world") presenting her as "a female ogre, the enemy of man by my honesty." Williams's transgression was to state that Nin's writing clearly demonstrated how women's writing differed from men's, something she had long espoused herself. He also argued cogently that her writing deserved serious critical attention and that she was more than a coterie writer, but no matter: anything that was not gushingly effusive praise was negative, period.

By October, when interest in *Winter of Artifice* was ended, Anaïs worried about expenses, itemizing them time and again in the diary, as if by being written down they might magically coalesce into something manageable. As usual, she lashed out at Hugo, accusing him of bringing "undertaker gloom" home from the bank. Her conclusion was callous: "our inadequacy and spontaneous nonchalance (Henry, Gonzalo's and mine) make [Hugo's] existence necessary and indispensible." She resented needing him.

Just when it seemed things could not get worse, they always did. She admitted that her dream of the press making Gonzalo independent was "a mirage. Zero! Now What?" Hugo had no money to pay their taxes because he had invested every spare cent into the press, and publicizing her book and his engravings with an elaborate party at the Gotham Book Mart and several "teas" and "cocktails." There were also mailings, flyers to promote the book, and shipments to subscribers. And Anaïs needed several visits to Elizabeth Arden and a new wardrobe as she soared into society, this time not only to promote the novel but also in the hope that she would get commissions for Gonzalo to print.

She "sparkled" at the elegant soirées of Valeska and Bravig Imbs, hoping that the Irish writer James Stern, then a correspondent for *Time,* would write about her (he did not). Hugh Chisholm asked her to print his poems, but gave only a small deposit until the job was finished and then reneged on the rest. Caresse Crosby offered a commission, but Anaïs knew she was "poor and crazy. Has plans but no money." Kay Boyle threw a bone by offering to let Gonzalo set her daughter's poems in type. He refused the "worthless echoes of adolescent reading," so a desperate Anaïs executed the commission herself.[34]

Then came her biggest financial blow: Ruder was drafted and disappeared into the Army, thus ending the erotica and her only income. The war was causing everyone who had been important to her since she arrived in New York to change, go on to new things, or drift away. Some were resorting to ploys not to be drafted, Others (like Eduardo) were thinking of joining the Army despite the ban against homosexuals. Even Hugo and Gonzalo, both aged forty-four, had to register for the draft.

In some desperation, she confided to Henry that she planned to return to analysis to make enough money to settle her debts. His response was not what she expected: "Don't fool yourself by thinking that you are doing good . . . you will be treating yourself . . . maybe you can complete your own analysis—and then see beyond it."[35] She noted the date when she replied, November 19, 1942, telling him she had her own plans from then on, "and it won't be Hollywood." She considered it the end, but he kept on writing his self-justifying begging letters.

Rid of Henry, she analyzed all the couples around her, especially "myself and Hugo, myself and Gonzalo." What struck her most was "the drama of woman's development." At mid-twentieth century, when women had more opportunities than had been available in earlier decades, she believed they had consciously chosen a perverse kind of freedom by allying themselves with "the weak child man" and becoming the "sublimated mother of the artist, the poet, the primitive . . . the weakest [men] in the new world." But women also created "again and again, and thus gave birth to art and the artist."

In the meantime, she "yielded to a moment of desire" for George Barker, whom she compared to the hapless Waldo Frank, her least satisfying lover to date. Barker "made love like a cataleptic . . . propelled by acrobatic excesses, jerks and spasms without orgasm." Worst, he talked throughout, and what he said stunned her: "You, Anaïs, will always be erotica. No matter how you present yourself, as printer, writer, analyst, it's useless. You are an erotic symbol and people will always treat you as such. They will always seek to enjoy you, never to help you. You a psychoanalyst? I don't believe you know a word about it. You're going to practice witchcraft."[36]

The next day, Barker had the temerity to show up at the printing studio and ask her to set fifty pages of his poems in type as payment for their sex. Anaïs refused, but not with the indignation most women would have felt. "I had to say no, and every no I say is a laceration."

At the end of September 1942, she had a breakdown. All she could say was "no puedo más, no puedo más" (I can't do any more), as she sat crying in the hallway of her apartment building, too weak to climb the five flights of stairs. Gonzalo found her and helped her up to bed. For two days she lay weeping uncontrollably, so confused that she could not answer Hugo's most simple questions.

On the third morning, she remembered the name of the analyst recommended by her high school friend Frances Bolton, the respected Jungian Martha Jaeger.[37] Still sobbing, Anaïs telephoned for an appointment and stopped crying only when Jaeger insisted she repeat the time and place of their meeting to ensure that she was coherent. Before she hung up, Anaïs whispered to the doctor that she had one other serious problem she had to address: she was quite sure that she was pregnant again.

23

The Hurt Self

AT THEIR FIRST APPOINTMENT, Dr. Martha Jaeger said Anaïs needed therapy every day and they would discuss payment only after she was stabilized. After three days, Anaïs stopped crying and Dr. Jaeger named a reduced fee and offered hope that the sessions could soon be reduced to twice weekly. Within a fortnight they were, as soon as Anaïs's gynecologist diagnosed a "psychological" pregnancy. Dr. Jaeger said she was "trying to give birth to something, what we don't know yet."[1] Martha Jaeger told Anaïs she had "no sense of reality about the limitations of the body," and they set out to explore why Anaïs had spent so many years obsessively taking care of everyone but herself.

Anaïs admitted that she sought a woman therapist because she could not help wanting to impress and seduce male analysts. It led her to invent untrue tales and then believe them because her male analysts treated everything as serious subjects of discussion, all of which left her ultimately so confused that she gained nothing from therapy.

Anaïs tried (as she had with Allendy and Rank) to write verbatim in the diary what transpired in her sessions with Jaeger. It is representative of the confusion that engulfed her, for she wrote what Jaeger told her about women awkwardly and without her usual elegance and style. She had recently become aware of what she called woman's "particular tragedy" and was startled to find herself in the midst of a "brand new drama. The father is absent. This is one of the mother, or woman."

> Woman is only now becoming aware of her individuality, of her different than man's cosmic relation. It is a difficult, deep thing for woman to commune with. She can only do it by a unversal motherhood or whore-priestess way. "The High Priestess," said Jaeger, when I spoke of my yielding to my father. It is strange how I turned to the woman and the mother for understanding. I have had all my relationships with men, of all kinds. Now my drama is that of woman in relation to herself, her conflict between selflessness and individuality and how to manifest the cosmic consciousness she feels. I used to identify myself to my father, but I acted like my mother, the sacrificed one. My father was the ego, my mother the sacrifice.

Dr. Jaeger appears to have concentrated on Anaïs's repressed anger, her rage toward those who took advantage of her personally as well as those who scorned or rejected her writing. Anaïs presented a placid face to the world but gave vent to violent emotion in the diary, where she was "the hurt self, the deeply hurt, maimed, suppressed, repressed, anger, vengeance, vindications, revolts, subjected for the sake of the other, the spectacle of illness conquered for the sake of the other, selflessless."

This reflection led to an important observation: "I marshall innumerable betrayals and disillusions which have undermined my faith, but all this is subjective and inwardly self-created." Unfortunately, the next sentence bore the ominous truth about her future behavior: "I can see it so well when [others] do it, yet I can't see myself doing it."

In spring 1943, blaming her dissatisfaction and disappointment on individuals no longer soothed her, so "New York" became a euphemism for everything wrong in her life. Her memory of Paris had hardened into a myth of perfect happiness, and by comparison, New York was not even a close second. New York had no sidewalk cafés where one could sit for hours, she complained, conveniently forgetting the coffeehouses she frequented in Greenwich Village and Little Italy. She had initially chosen to live in the Village because she thought it the most charming and European section of the city. Now it was a pallid disappointment, despite the fact that whenever she walked its streets she almost always stopped to chat with the likes of

Edgard and Louise Varèse, Alfred Kazin, Yves Tanguy, or Kay Boyle—to name a sample of the people whose names appear in her diary during this time.

One observation stands out: "the experience of New York was an experience with the Jew. I must go into that." Following it is a list of names of everyone she knew, from Dorothy Norman and Frances Steloff (both Jewish) to Caresse Crosby (who was a proper Bostonian and not Jewish at all). Her list is long and includes other non-Jews such as her friend Thurema Sokol, the Chilean Surrealist painter Roberto Matta, and the Surrealist writer she disliked most of all, André Breton. It also included her new friends, the art dealer Bernard Reis and his wife, Rebecca, whose hospitality she accepted several times each week.[2]

Her puzzling fixation on the Jew, in everything from intellect to identity, was somehow tied up with her views on creativity and the sacrifices she believed she had made to become an artist. Just as she needed to turn against Hugo when anything in life did not fulfill her expectation, she now selected the Jews and everything Jewish to be the targets of her dismay that the New York intellectual community had not taken her writing seriously, nor had it made her rich and famous. It is difficult to call her an anti-Semite, because so many of the people she genuinely cared for throughout her life were Jewish, and she was both interested in and respectful of their beliefs and behavior. All the Jews she knew in 1943, however, seemed to be so much more successful than she. All had comfortable incomes and pleasant homes, held good jobs or used inherited money well, and were generally respected. It is more likely that she was envious rather than anti-Semitic.

Dr. Jaeger wanted Anaïs to explore the question of her "creative self," and "fear of failure" complex; could it be that she feared public recognition, and therefore courted the failure accorded to one who spent time perfecting someone else's work rather than her own?

The question unleashed an outpouring of every literary and publishing insult Anaïs Nin had ever suffered: ". . . the lamentable story of DHL book published by Titus a few months before his business went bankrupt, the book only partially distributed, half lost, not sent to reviewers and no royalties. Fraenkel advancing money for H. of I.

but losing interest when it was out and not distributing as promised. No reviews. No response. I finally sold 50 copies to GBM at 50 cents apiece which [Miss Steloff] resold at $5 and I was grateful that she took them or they would still be in France. Durrell supplied money for W. of A., Obelisk issues it a week before the war, no distribution, no reviews. I print it myself and James Johnson Sweeney accepts a deluxe copy from Hugo and never writes even a note of thanks, acknowledgement, courtesy even. Times refused to review it. . . . Harpers did not even trouble to read it. No one would mention story of the printing even though they write up lesser feats by women (Vogue, T & C) . . . NY World Telegram asked for copy then did not review because of 'limited space. . . .' Art Digest did not even acknowledge book. . . . Vogue read it and did nothing. Time magazine—Robert Fitzgerald and [James] Agee did nothing. Rosenfeld and Carlos Williams wrote only at my request. Marc Slonim, no word. No word from Charles Henri Ford . . . Viking Press . . . Kay Boyle, etc. No one ever mentioned the Artaud story in Experimental Review, or 'Woman on the Myth' in Twice a year. 'Birth' had repercussions but only told to me. On honor roll of . . . Best Short Stories of the Year is the only exception in the way of public notice."

She responded angrily when Jaeger asked if these disappointments were of her own making. "Other women with lesser works have gained notoriety. Kay Boyle and Djuna Barnes are covered with medals!" Jaeger stuck to her original point and insisted that everything Anaïs told her was merely a distraction for the very real guilt she felt at trying to compete with men through her writing, a guilt that dominated her behavior. Anaïs was determined that Jaeger should be wrong and repeated her assertions to the diary: "I did not want to rival man. I did not want to be a man. I did not want to steal man's creation, his thunder. Creation and femininity seem incompatible. The aggressive act of creation."

Jaeger asked why she was afraid to admit that she wanted the same recognition for her writing that was accorded men for theirs. Anaïs said she could not, for her lovers would no longer believe they were "the strongest, and they would love me less." Jaeger asked her to explain: "an act of independence seems to me will be punished by abandon[ment]. Men fear women's strength. I have been tremendously aware of men's weakness, the need to guard them from my strength. I have made myself less powerful, I have concealed my powers."

Except for analysis, Anaïs did not confide in the diary very much during the first ten months of 1943 because she was rewriting many of the previously published stories for what would become her second self-printed book, *Under a Glass Bell.*[3] Anaïs acknowledged Martha Jaeger's role in giving her "integration,"[4] but to read between the lines of her diary is to see something very different. Whether she could admit it to herself or not, she was tired of Gonzalo, and her way of justifying it was to concentrate her emotional life on Hugo. Now he became her "fundamental love," and she devoted herself to him and her home. What she did, however, was "cleaning, painting, reanimating, renewing," of a highly obsessive nature. She made lists; praised herself for "order and cohesion"; wrote lists of what she must do to change the behavior of her friends, then "cornered and harangued" them until they agreed with whatever she wanted, just to make her stop.[5] She called this frantic activity "Épurement [purifying]," concluding that it was "meaningful and important."

Then she decided she must use the printing press for public good, especially "the plight of the Negro, Communism, etc." Gonzalo scoffed at her new idealism, saying she had no aptitude either "for politics or the nitty-gritty daily reality of it." She could learn, she insisted, just as she learned how to write by printing what she wrote. Gonzalo begged to differ. "You are a sloppy printer, you can't figure anything out, you can't measure type."[6] She had to admit it was true, but when Gonzalo told her to enroll in a printing class at the Workman's School, she said "All this bores me, has always bored me," and did nothing.

In early November 1943, Anaïs crumpled into a shapeless, formless depression, part of it caused by her mother's visit.[7] Anaïs's appointment book is filled with notations of lunches and dinners with Rosa, but after each she usually wrote: "Hell on earth."[8] On November 17, the day after Rosa left, Anaïs wrote the phrase again, this time adding "suicidal, depression, rebellion, bitterness, physical hysteria." Two days later she was "sick in bed," and on November 22, went first to Dr. Jacobson for shots of his amphetamine cocktail, then to Dr. Jaeger for an emergency session. Afterward she went to Elizabeth Arden for a massage and then went home to bed.

The depression was exacerbated by severe ovarian pain, which had begun several years earlier but which now intensified each month during her "moonstorm." This time it was so severe that Gonzalo insisted on taking her to a "Dr. Lopez." She was sure she was pregnant, but Dr. Lopez was brusque and dismissive, telling her she suffered from "painful ovulation."

As soon as Anaïs was sure she was not pregnant, her mood swung upward. The press kept her busy as she printed Christmas cards for herself and some of her friends, set type for a book by "Berthier," and rewrote some of the stories for the forthcoming *Under a Glass Bell.*[9] She also launched a round of social activity that included a brief affair, and described herself as "Incurable Anaïs, who feels reassured by others' praise!"[10]

Martha Jaeger's husband commented on the change in Anaïs's appearance, and she agreed: "the siren has disappeared, and with it torments and anxieties and loneliness." Approaching her forty-first birthday, she noted that there was now an "audible cult" for her physical presence, and that she created a stir wherever she went, even though she "dressed very simply." Because she still had very little money, she perfected the trick of using unlikely objects as accessories to complement an inexpensive and unusual (for the time) dress. She scattered little Japanese umbrellas, for example, the kind that usually decorated cocktail glasses, throughout her elaborately knotted hair and wore a cheap kimono to a formal dinner party.

She was growing tired of printing, but her perilous finances left her no alternative but to print another book to try to recoup the losses incurred with *Winter of Artifice,* which still had 150 unsold copies. But she had written nothing new. Even though there was no market for her fiction, she decided she had nothing to lose by collecting the stories she had published in the little magazines. Everyone told her it was unlikely that readers would accept a collection of esoteric stories created in the prewar European literary climate, but she had nothing else. So she gathered the stories about Moricand and Carteret, of Artaud, the houseboat, and the abortion/birth, and put them together in a book she called *Under a Glass Bell,* named for the gardening apparatus French farmers use to keep delicate plants safe from predators or frost.

Once again she worked long, hard days, setting the type while Gonzalo pulled the pages. Hugo provided engravings to go with the text, but to print them, he had first to mount the copper plates onto wooden blocks and she had to buy a second press that was better able to print clean copies than the original Clamshell. She found one for $75, and for another $100 got all the Bernhard Gothic Light type that she needed to be fully operational.[11]

She was still looking for excuses not to have to print anymore, and Gonzalo inadvertently gave her what she wanted. His anarchist and Communist friends in Greenwich Village were snickering at the press's name, which they associated in a salacious manner with Anaïs. He complained that as a proud Spaniard he could not invite his friends to visit his workplace because they would see him taking orders from a woman. "This consequence of our romantic venture I had not foreseen!" Anaïs wrote as she justified what she wanted to do. "Besides, the lack of adequate response to my writing and printing is forcing me to withdraw. It's the end of the press as far as I am concerned. Another failure." But she still had to try to recoup some of her losses. Her only concession was to limit the edition to 300 copies instead of the overly optimistic 500 she had printed for *Winter of Artifice*.

In search of diversion, she began to go to parties in Harlem and to form friendships with Lucas Premice and his daughters, Adele and Josephine. She also embarked on several casual affairs with young Haitian men posted to the diplomatic mission and went frequently to the home of Rebecca and Bernard Reis, whom she both liked and resented: "patrons of the arts and surealist reviews, who call themselves communists but whose house is full of surealist Trotskyites." Everyone who congregated at the Reises' was included in her venom, and the list was long: "Matta as surrealist, neurotic, politically pernicious anarchist; 57th St. galleries for their snobbism and acommerciality; Max Ernst and Breton as dead, also Jolas, Léger, Kay Boyle; Buñuel for using naked truth of his film politically; Peggy Guggenheim for completing corruption of the surrealist group; Charles Henri Ford for publishing disintegrated and clownish *View;* Sidney Janis and James Johnson Sweeney as art critics of this group; Kurt Seligman a false mimetic decadent; Tanguy as stagnant self repetition."

—and on, and on. But—and it was suddenly a very big "but"—she recognized that "they are a force by their coalition, certainly the *only* art group."

Anaïs duly noted that Hugo was invited by Betty Parsons to have a one-man show at the Wakefield Gallery, but she could not permit Ian Hugo (as he called himself in art to keep that career separate from

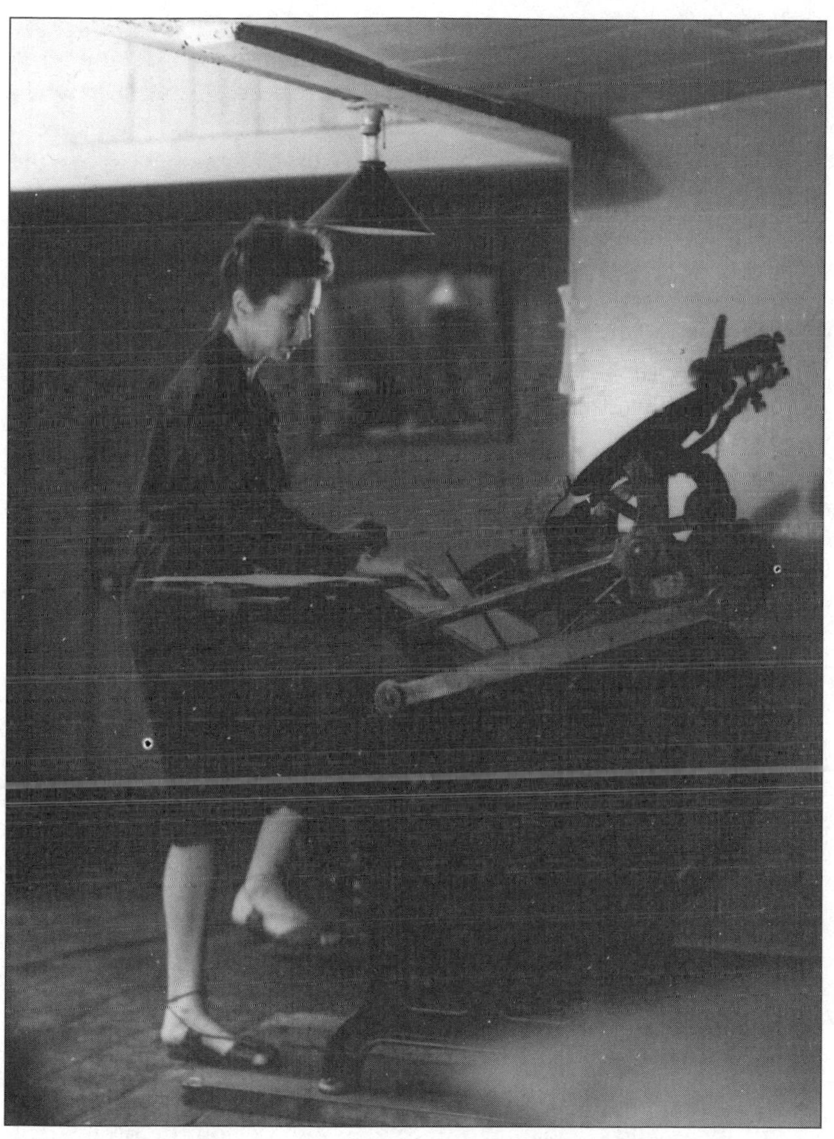

Anaïs at the Gemor Press.

banking) to succeed unless his achievement was somehow tied in with hers. He was given the show, she told the diary, only "because first of all, Betty Parsons loved the *Winter.*" Hugo worried about the effect this attention to his art might have on her, especially when *Vogue* asked to do a photo-article about him and posed him in front of some engravings. "He is concerned because *Vogue* never gave me any attention," Anaïs noted. She praised his generosity of spirit, but her innermost self resented it.[12]

The show was a success and Hugo sold a few engravings, but it was very expensive. Early in February, he collapsed, done in by their $1,000 debt (more than $10,000 by 1990s comparison), which mounted alarmingly every week.

"I can no longer cope with our economic problems. It is for you to solve this now," Hugo told Anaïs as he metaphorically turned his face to their bedroom wall. Eventually, in embarrassment and hoping for secrecy, Hugo secured a loan from another bank. He told Anaïs she would have to assume responsibility for repaying it, but both knew he would not hold her to it.

Anaïs and Gonzalo finished printing *Under a Glass Bell* at 5 P.M. on Wednesday, February 16, 1944. She had bronchitis, but went to work because she knew it was the only way to ensure that Gonzalo would do the same. Bill collectors hounded them, and when the pages were printed, Gonzalo told her offhandedly that the owner of the print-shop whose machine they needed to print the cover refused to do any more work for them unless Anaïs gave him $50, which of course she did not have. She went to plead her case in person, but the printer told her the only other option was to find her own proof press and do it herself. First she went home and sobbed, then she got out of bed and scoured the streets of Greenwich Village until she found just such a press belonging to a printer only slightly more down-and-out than Gemor Press. She persuaded him to give it to her on the promise of payment when the book was published. Happy to be rid of it, he obliged.

And so, when all the pages were printed, there was no celebration. Anaïs was ill and could only sit at the table bearing all the neatly stacked pages and look at them, too tired to do anything else. The bound books were in hand on February 24, in time for Hugo's engraving exhibition at the Wakefield Gallery. Anaïs joined him, Betty Parsons, her brother Thorvald, and her friends Lucia Cristofanetti, Thurema Sokol, Jimmy Ernst, and several others for a happy, diverting Sunday afternoon hanging the prints. Several days later, she described the opening as "a big brilliant noisy crowded gay party," and Hugo was suddenly a success. Incredibly, so, too, was she, for everyone loved her stories.

Everyone wanted to entertain them. Frances Brown Field gave a party for Hugo. Becky Reis opened her house to the New York art community to celebrate Hugo's show, and critics who had hitherto ignored Anaïs attended, giving her grudging attention. The Graphic Arts Society would be pleased to receive copies of every book she had printed and would print in the future. Anaïs was jubilant: "I am receiving my due! Affection, response, feelings to answer my feelings. Sincere success, no falseness. . . . A wonderful harmony with Hugo's work."[13]

Success brought with it frenetic activity, and a look at Anaïs Nin's diary and appointment book for this time shows the spectrum that comprises a woman artist's daily life. Pages of calculations list her debts ("accounts of loan"), followed by optimistic lists of money ("Incoming") she hoped to earn. Every day, she packed heavy boxes of books and carried them to the post office, hoping the return mail would include checks to cover expensive postage. So far, the Gotham Book Mart wanted fifty copies, Chaucer Bookshop took seventy-five, and Wakefield Gallery (to complement Hugo's exhibit) took another fifty. Subscriptions came, among them Wallace Stevens, who wrote a generous letter of praise and remained her admirer for the rest of his life.[14]

She reminded herself to "finish last things" at the press, then dash to her landlord's office to demand that someone fix her stove, on the blink for three weeks. She was entertaining constantly to promote herself and Hugo, and one note in particular captures her frazzled state of mind: opposite a reminder to buy "6 fonts of Bernhard Gothic light Italic 12 point, $2.85" was a heavily underlined memo to pick up "Ritz crackers and 6 bottles of beer" before rushing home to "CALL THE PLUMBER!!"[15]

She took care of Hugo's work as well as her own. "Buy Hugo plain envelopes," she noted next to a list of specific tools he asked her to buy for his engraving needs and the names of the widely dispersed shops that carried them. She matted, packed, and mailed his engravings, and kept lists of who bought what and how much they paid. In short, she was embarked on another round of manic activity with "no rest, no repose, no relaxation." Her primary sensation was one of "bursting from the shell of [her] own persona-mask—becoming visible and audible."

She could scarcely believe what had happened with the book she had printed only because she had nothing else at hand. "I thought people would find the stories esoteric, remote." Instead, they responded to the "pure poetry" of them as they had not done with the "psychoanalytical attitude" that permeated *Winter of Artifice.* Her friend Dollie Chareau commented that all the stories "end in B minor."[16] "Almost monotonously so," Anaïs agreed. Looking at them all together, she realized they were her written expression of a "secret revolt, despair." They were the written approximation of "a downward and negative curve" in her personality that was evident only when the stories were read one after the other as a consistent whole. She equated her literary negativity to what she considered the most appropriate analogy: "the sudden failure to attain the orgasm as it were, the unsatisfied act."

"So. So," she mused. "It is to be thought over." She gave this expression in the three separate introductions she wrote to the stories.[17] In one she quickly abandoned, she was "in a difficult position of presenting to the American public stories I wrote in the period when I was dreaming"; in another, she explained that the stories were written before "the Spanish war," and were now so irrelevant that she thought they should probably be destroyed. Then she decided that it might be good to offer them during the much greater catastrophe of World War II, so that others, too, might decide that there was only one answer to the horrors of the contemporary world and its suffering: "to dream, to tell fairy tales, to embroider, to elaborate, to follow the labyrinth of beautiful edifices." She insisted that her readers understand that "the fact that I describe the adult fairy tales, the fantasy, the decadent poet's world, does not mean I remained one with it and permanently identified with it." By 1944, she wanted her readers to know that even if it was not apparent in this collection, she had changed enormously and "a writer must be taken as a whole, as representative of history."

Unfortunately, most critics did not grant this wish, for throughout the rest of her writing career, she was seldom "taken as a whole." Her place in history, so inextricably entwined with the stuff of her life, has always been the subject of literary and critical dispute. But this was still to come, for the writer Anaïs Nin was suddenly "brought into daylight."[18] There was a grand party going on; it was for her, and at last she was the party.

24

"Begin anywhere and flow along"

ANAÏS WAS FEELING STRONG and self-confident as both publicity for and sales of *Under a Glass Bell* mounted. Caresse Crosby invited her to sign books at her G Place Gallery in Washington in conjunction with an exhibition of Hugo's engravings. His work did not sell, but 150 people attended and most bought at least one copy of her book.[1] Anaïs returned to New York to find the entire first edition of 300 copies sold out less than three weeks after publication. Miss Steloff was so confident she could sell more that she urged Anaïs to print another edition of 1,000.

Her friends in the literary world boosted her success wherever they could, and one of the most far-reaching in terms of recognition came when Paul Rosenfeld told Edmund Wilson, the respected *New Yorker* critic, that he must read her stories. On April 1, his review appeared, the same day a photographer from *Town & Country* arrived in the print studio to photograph Anaïs at work. "I did not seek them out," she noted carefully in the diary. "I had arrived, they telephoned me." She received in her "best plumage, a lace blouse borrowed from Barbara Reis, my tuxedo suit, and the coat of the woman Captain of Action. And *The New Yorker* was lying there, the pinnacle of authority, a review by Edmund Wilson."[2] The photographer obliged by shooting her in the finery, but then made her remove her makeup, change into a simple white blouse, and don the heavy canvas apron she wore when printing so that he could capture her working at the press.

She did not seek Wilson out and did not know him personally when he wrote his review; Wilson wrote favorably because of his reaction to the book itself and not its author. His review did more than all others to establish Anaïs Nin as a serious writer of some importance.

Wilson endeared himself to her by acknowledging the unpublished diary, "long a legend of the literary world," saying it was regrettable that no one wanted to publish it. He then drew her ire when he deemed her earlier publications "rather fragmentary examples of a kind of autobiographical fantasy . . . a little disappointing." Not so, he believed, were the stories in *Under a Glass Bell,* which "belong to a peculiar genre sometimes cultivated by the late Virginia Woolf."[3] His conclusion, however, was as startling to Anaïs as it was to many of her readers: "the main thing to say is that Miss Nin is a very good artist, as perhaps none of the literary surrealists is." Mentioning that she herself had printed the book, he urged readers to order it through its distributor, for "it is well worth the trouble of sending for." It was every writer's dream review, and the orders poured in to the Gotham Book Mart. The only dark spot on the author's radiant happiness came when friends and admirers inquired what her next literary triumph would be.

"If only I could begin to write, I would be happy," she noted, for she disliked the short story form and had none further to tell. She preferred the "weaving" of a novel, where she could "begin anywhere and flow along." With the success of the stories, this became difficult because "the faculty for re-living in the diary has gone." She thought she had lost the "inner eye mirroring all," as well as "the withdrawal to commune, to relive, to ruminate, to serve." It was unsettling to feel an emotion "like being constantly out of doors, in the daylight." She had waited all her life for public recognition, but it was still a little frightening after so many years of rejection.

There was also the worrisome business about the press and what to do with it. She did not want to set type for another book, and despite Wilson's review, no commercial publisher had asked to see her next manuscript. She had to create something new and begin the arduous process of printing it.

Gonzalo's Spanish refugee friends teased him unmercifully about the "Anaïs Press." What exactly was his job, they snickered, working for a woman in a room dominated by a large double bed? He boasted that he was responsible for the entire project, from design and layout to finished book. If he took the credit, she decided, he could do the work, so she gave him the press.

Anaïs found a storefront studio at 17 E. 13th Street, and with money borrowed from Thurema, had the printing equipment moved there. Gonzalo hung out a little sign, and the Gemor Press was now entirely his. He agreed to pay for the equipment at the rate of $25 per month, and did manage for a month or two. Then the payments stopped and Anaïs did all the work alone while Gonzalo drank with his friends in a local bar.

Even though it was supposed to be his business, Anaïs went to the shop every day, arriving between 9 and 10 A.M., and usually stayed into the early evening. If Gonzalo showed up at all, it was around 2 P.M., and he always left before she did.

Henry continued to write, even though Anaïs seldom answered. His latest "Open Letter"[4] brought results, and in April 1944, Henry told Anaïs he would send her one hundred dollars every month.[5] He wrote an adulatory letter about *Under a Glass Bell,* so effusive that, given his always stringent criticisms about her work, he must have designed it specifically to get back into her good graces. "One is stunned, prostrated" before her great art, he concluded.

Anaïs sent him the first of what became her ritualistic annual applications for a Guggenheim Fellowship (which she never received).[6] She proposed "to convert and transpose the diary of 65 volumes into a full, long novel: The Diary supplies an endless and deeply revelatory source of documentation. Because it was originally not written for publication, the emphasis on total truth and emotional spontaneity forms a solid foundation for a new contribution to woman's psychology. What a woman will only reveal to herself can form the basis of a new drama in emotional, feminine terms."

The rest of the proposal listed the fairly ordinary topics she intended to cover, among them the drama of the uprooted child brought to the United States and the adult's subsequent return to Europe. Several, however, were not ordinary topics of discussion in 1944, among them "the masculine, objective woman," and "the maternal, courageous woman spending herself on active loves." The longest section concerned "the drama of psychoanalysis." Here she intended to use her personal experience and how it had influenced and affected her before relating it to present-day attitudes toward psychoanalysis in general. Anaïs planned to dramatize a series of differing therapeutic treatments by having the main female character undergo and come into conflict with them, thus discovering her own individual significance in the process. The character would "become aware of the evolution of woman in her own terms, not as an imitator of man." The novel would show a woman clarifying her instincts and intuitions, and in the process discovering her role in "social history and the reconstruction of the world." Putting to good use an article she had previously reviled, she cited William Carlos Williams's article on *Winter of Artifice,* especially his discussion of "feminine writing."

What Anaïs Nin proposed to investigate was a subject that has inspired feminist scholarship for the last quarter of the twentieth century, but unfortunately she was too far ahead of her time. When her application was denied, she sent a note to Henry saying she had abandoned the project and planned to condense all sixty-five diary volumes into one. He was appalled at the magnitude of the task. "Where will my poor hundred a month take you on that job?"[7]

Anaïs gave Henry's first $100 to Hugo, and it started an argument that continued for months. Hugo took the money because he desperately needed it, but hated himself for doing so. Anaïs owed money to Thurema Sokol, Martha Jaeger, Sam Goldberg, Max Jacobson, and various other doctors as well as drugstores. She begged her mother to "please help me because I have to sell 365 books before I cover my expenses. . . . I have to pay back $100 for the paper and $100 for the linotype and $240 for the bookbinders, so you see I still need your cooperation."[8]

She had not paid the rent on the MacDougal Street trysting place for six months, and the landlord tossed the bed onto the street, changed the lock, and rented the studio to someone else. In a way it was a relief, for it left her with only Gonzalo and Helba's apartment, the printshop, and her own apartment's rent to worry about.

To distract herself from Hugo's distress over her financial problems, she began an "erotic relationship" with Harry Hershkowitz, an ex–merchant seaman who was sent to her by Henry. Hershkowitz wanted to write, but his primary aspiration was to become the second Henry Miller.[9] She discovered something about herself that gave her great joy: when Hershkowitz told her he planned to appropriate her imagery, phrasing, and some of her actual writings as his own, she reacted violently, as she had not years ago when Henry did the same thing. Instead of placidly submitting, she attacked: "Why should you? Write your own story. Find your own style." Afterward she noted that it had taken her a lifetime to stand up for herself enough "to be able to enjoy a man without love." Now she did it easily, without qualms.

Henry came to New York in December 1944, summoned by his ill mother. He asked Anaïs for a quiet tête-à-tête, but she deliberately selected Childs restaurant, with its ladies' tearoom atmosphere, knowing how uncomfortable Henry would be. She no longer wanted Henry because he had become an old man, which was also why she was tired of Gonzalo. Actively seeking a very young lover, she soon found a great many.

Rank, Henry, her father, and all her other lovers in the 1930s represented what she called "years of erotic madness" with adult men, but the period 1945–1947 represented erotic madness of a different kind, usually with mere boys half her age. These affairs were interspersed with sustained creativity, for in that time she published at least one book each year.

She began the book that became *This Hunger* at the end of 1944. Everything was a "fragment," on which she worked "unconsciously." The book eventually became three separate stories about three women, Lillian, Stella, and Hedja, each originally intended to portray herself in one of her several incarnations as well as her friends. This all changed as she wrote, but initially Stella was patterned after Luise Rainer, Lillian after Thurema Sokol, and Hedja after Lucia Cristofanetti.[10]

To "the Luise character" she intended to give "my father, lovers and friendship with Thurema." It was to be an "interiorized, Debussy" portrait, but the "pages and pages" that suddenly poured out were no good because she was so "lost in the maze of the diary" that she was unable to "disguise" herself as Luise. She wrote "feverishly, intensely," what she called "important pages on woman's history, on anxiety," but in the cold light of the next day's rereading, she always concluded that they could "never surpass the diary."

Previously she had defined herself as handmaiden to a male writer; now it would seem that she decided to rid herself of the actual male, assume his attributes and identity, and become the writer herself. Yet everything Anaïs Nin had already written was totally or in part based on a woman bent on discovering her own identity, no matter how complex, garbled, and meandering the process. Also, everything she proposed to write in the future (such as the novelized version of the diary) was based on a woman's acknowledgment of her profound difference from man in every aspect of her being. So her muddled attitude remained a puzzle that she never really solved, for all the while she groped toward artistic independence, she also grasped every man who came along in the hope that "he" would be the one with whom she could play whatever she envisioned woman's role to be at that particular moment.

A married suburban businessman who dreamed of becoming an actor-writer did not "yield," but eventually grew tired of her attempts to seduce him and drifted off. Rather than replacing him with another to whom she could "yield," she yielded instead to the new novel with a series of unconscious images and associations based upon mirrors in gardens.[11] It gave her the "thread of connection" that became the "essential symbolism" of *This Hunger:* art and reality.

More and more, she realized, *This Hunger* would be about sexuality, specifically hers, as portrayed by both Lillian and Djuna (a newly created character), and Henry's, transposed to Jay (Lillian's husband). She knew she had to respect "the frenzied taboos created by people's fear of the truth," so she wrote veiled descriptions of sexual scenes in an amorphous prose meant to exemplify the hazy, mirrored reflection of various combinations of lovers in "the naked garden in Paris." Having decided this, it was now time for another new man.

A fan letter brought her William "Bill" Pinckard, a Yale freshman who wrote at the suggestion of his professor, Wallace Fowlie, an admirer of her writing.[12] She replied in detail, as she did to every letter she received.[13] Several weeks later, Pinckard came down from New Haven to meet her. She knew at once she wanted to have sex with him, but on this occasion they had only tea.

Seventeen-year-old Bill Pinckard came to New York every weekend. Anaïs was struck by his "incredibly slender white hands, more feminine than mine. The extraordinary beauty of his eyes." She served tea to him and "Pablo," the nickname of an Irish boy whom she met in a Village coffeehouse. She called them her "sons" and wanted to be Léa to their Chéri in imitation of Colette's novel, but they were uncooperative. Frustrated, she declared herself "the celestial madame," in danger of being castrated by the world unless she found "a man lover soon." She and the boy Bill became lovers on Easter Sunday 1945, while Hugo was on Long Island visiting his mother.

Anaïs, forty-two, urged Bill, now eighteen, to leave Yale and break with his parents so that he too could live in the dream. He did. Frances and Tom Brown gave him a room in their nearby house and Anaïs gave him meals and pocket money. She and Pablo did not become lovers, but she did allow him to move into her apartment. The sexual tension was unbearable as her husband and the two boys competed for her attention.

Suddenly Bill Pinckard's father descended from Park Avenue in search of his renegade son. He stormed into the Browns' house, seized some of Anaïs's writings as evidence of depravity, then had his lawyer threaten to bring suit against her for corrupting the morals of a minor unless Bill returned to Yale. He would also inform Hugo's superiors of his wife's licentious behavior, and, as there was still uncertainty about Anaïs's nationality even though she traveled on an American passport as Hugo's wife, Pinckard Sr. threatened to have her deported to Cuba.[14]

Within the week, Bill returned to Yale and Hugo took Anaïs back "tenderly" when she asked for "forgiveness." She also resumed her sexual relationship with Gonzalo, but reluctantly: he and Hugo were "both aging, as I am not aging."

To Anaïs's utter astonishment, "the tension grew so great that Hugo packed his bag and left" during a weekend when Bill escaped his family's surveillance and Anaïs flirted with him in Hugo's presence. Hugo checked into a cheap hotel near their apartment, then telephoned Anaïs and asked her to come to his room at midnight, and pretend to be his mistress. Instead, she took Bill to a dance recital. Unnerved by her household histrionics, he refused to spend the night with her.

Unable to "face the empty night," Anaïs roused Gonzalo from bed at 1:30 and made him go to Hugo's hotel (he had inadvertently chosen one for men only: "what masochism!" Anaïs wrote). When Hugo came to the lobby, Anaïs shrieked "Hugo, come home!" The next day she wrote in the diary: "with Hugo back I could sleep. Battered. Defeated. I asked his forgiveness. He asked mine for stifling me."

She returned to *This Hunger,* unfortunately through the diary, becoming "swallowed in its hundreds of pages" (actually, thousands

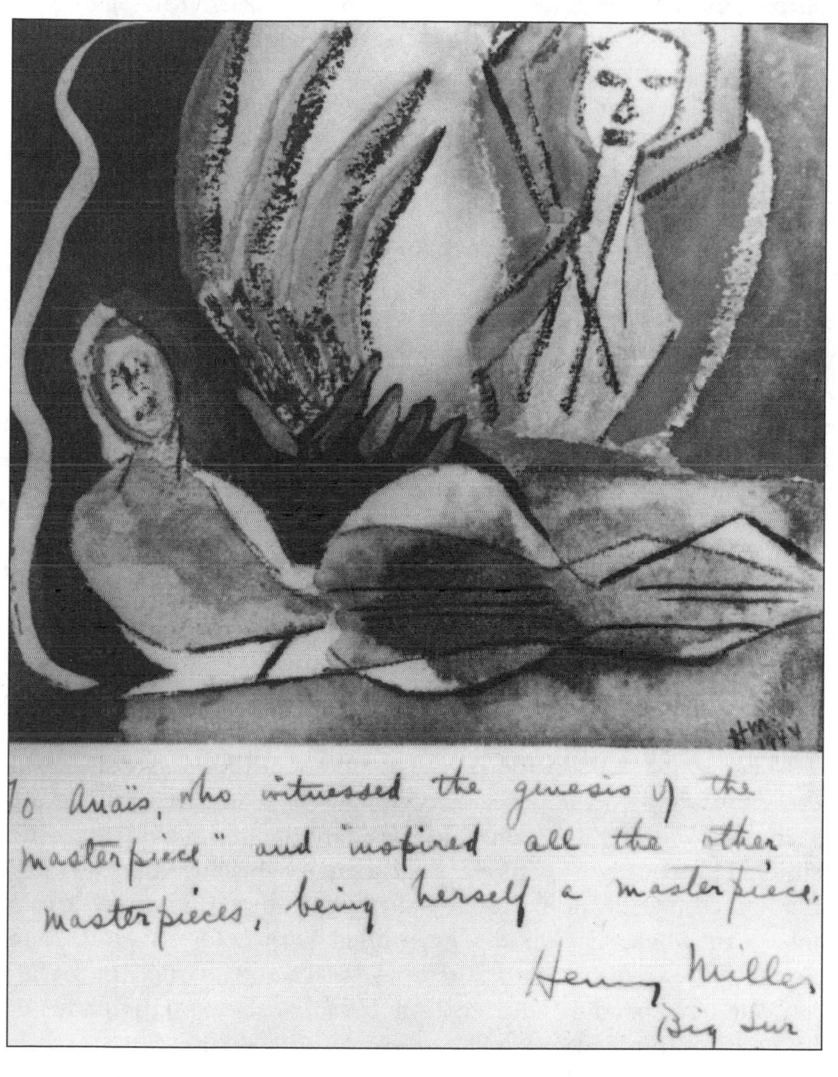

Painting by Henry Miller, inscription to Anaïs.

by this point), and "amazed" by its content: "No writing can ever surpass this hot lava out of the volcano of experience flowing freely." She was blocked, and not for the first time, with what would be her continuing problem for the rest of her life: to write of her experiences freely, and of what she called "the major themes," her relationships with Henry, Allendy, Rank, June, and her father, she would have to "crucify Hugo." In a spirit of reconciliation, she let Hugo read what she wrote about Lillian and Jay. Hugo accused her of writing about herself and Henry, so she invented the character Djuna: splitting herself "for Hugo's sake." Thus, Jay became married to Lillian and Djuna became his anima, "the mystic who guides Jay but is not in love with him." Anaïs fervently hoped that protecting Hugo would "force [her] to become an artist, to create (not falsify)."

Still, she could not integrate her women, and it was becoming confusing to intermingle herself with them. She was revolted at "the falsifications" and wanted to stop writing fiction to devote herself entirely to the diary. She herself provided the best description of her technique: "Truth and reality are at the basis of all I write (I can always prove the incident which caused the writing, produce the character, the place), but because I insist on extracting the essence, on giving only a distilled product, it becomes a dream, where all reality appears only in its symbolical form. Everything I write will have to be translated, just as when you read dreams."

Needing "to reassert the dream," she spent money wildly, even though Hugo made her swear she would reform if he returned to the marriage.[15] After a massage and pedicure at Elizabeth Arden, she stole a large bottle of perfume from a display because they "owed" her something for all the money she spent there. She threw it in a trash can when she found it was filled with colored water, then bought "an expensive Maria Stuart hat," black and heart-shaped, with intricate pearl beading, and a cotton dress that she thought made her look "all of fourteen."

❧

She was looking for another boy lover, but instead she found Edmund Wilson.[16] The previous spring, she had invited him to lunch to thank him for the review of *Under a Glass Bell.* He was on his way to England as a war correspondent, and while he was gone, they exchanged friendly letters. Now he was back and in the midst of a divorce from Mary McCarthy. At loose ends, he telephoned and asked her to meet for drinks. Wilson described how Mary had stripped their house of furnishings he specifically wanted and now mourned. Afterward, he launched into criticism of Anaïs's fiction. She was surprised at how well he knew the stories, but even more when he told her he had marked many passages that described Mary perfectly. "That would be the last thing *she* would want to hear!" Anaïs muttered under her breath.

By the end of the evening, she described Wilson as "under [her] spell," and returned with him to the eerily half-empty house and the nuptial bed that Mary did not want. She planned to sleep with Wilson only once, but several days later, when Bill Pinckard sent a letter telling her he did not want to see or hear from her again, she "succumbed to his [Wilson's] worship, desire, ardor, madness," and a full-fledged affair was under way.

Even though she told her mother she was "very happy and enjoying my success,"[17] she was seething with dissatisfaction. Bill Pinckard was now a "tough cruel little brat," and she was furious that he rejected her. Soon she was ill with bronchitis and anemia.[18] Hardly able to function, she sought another analyst, this time a man, Dr. Clement Staff. For the first time, she could not commit what happened in the analyst's office verbatim to the diary but could only make notes. She made garbled and muttered comments about herself, writing that behind her "masochism" lay "sadism."

Dr. Staff told her that masochism produced nymphomania and was "a devious way of seeking love," and so, too, was her compulsion to write a diary. She did not brood about it long, for two more boys came along to join Pablo in "a cajoling caressing relationship. All but possession."

At the end of October 1945, having temporarily given up on finding a lover, she began the rounds, "peddling my new book without joy." It was "not wholly accepted by anyone, not wholly loved and much opposed." She singled out Wilson's "stupidity," Diana Trilling's "implacable anger," Leo Lerman's "betrayal," and lumped all the rest of the reviewers into a group that "only accentuated the lack of understanding" of all her readers.[19]

Wilson judged the book repetitious, without interconnections, and "a little uneven," but he praised her—accurately—as "one of those women writers who have lately been trying to put into words a new feminine point of view, who deal with the conflicts created for women by living half in a man-controlled world against which they cannot help rebelling, half in a world which they have made for themselves but which they cannot find completely satisfactory." Isaac Rosenfeld's review said her four heroines emerged "without personality, as mere personifications of neurotic anxiety." Diana Trilling was the most cutting of all. For her, Nin's characters were "only the sum of their clinically significant emotional responses." Trilling found the book "inferior to a good analytical case record" because "its psychoanalysis is not science but pretension."

None of these reviews, despite the scathing comments quoted above, was entirely negative. Each critic praised Anaïs Nin as an original writer whose themes were a necessary antidote to the socially relevant fiction that dominated American publishing in those years. Many spoke of her insights into the changing status of modern women, and others praised her willingness to bring the questionable science of psychoanalysis out of the darkness to which it was then relegated.

Nevertheless, in deep depression, she took to her bed, emerging only to visit her several doctors. Jacobson gave her his new "compound" that he developed for the army.[20] Staff told her she had a "great hostility to reality and the adult world" and urged her to begin regular sessions because she was "in grave danger of breaking [down]." A third unnamed doctor diagnosed a tumor in her left ovary, but said it was fibroid and would dissolve in time. No surgery was recommended.[21]

She was a mess of indecision, uncertainty, and confusion when Kimon Friar, chairman of the Poetry Center's reading committee, invited her to read from her work on November 3, 1945.[22] Dressed in her new black suit and fuchsia blouse, with Hugo and Eduardo to cheer her on, she performed. As she spoke, she realized that her audience was "wowed," and a frenzy of energy was unleashed in her. Her new friend, or more accurately, her new rival, the filmmaker Maya Deren,[23] gave a party afterward to celebrate Anaïs's success. There, she "danced wildly, sexually." The next day she pronounced herself cured and told Staff she would no longer need him.

Staff was so concerned that he telephoned Hugo, urging him to see that Anaïs remained in therapy.[24] But she ignored them, confident that it was only a matter of time until commercial publishers sought her next book, for Wilson had taken it himself to several of them.[25]

On November 19 she accepted Kimon Friar's invitation to listen to him lecture at the Poetry Center. She was in a sad mood, so she dressed as "Marie Stuart who had her head cut off by the jealous Queen Elizabeth" in a tight black dress, the expensive heart-shaped hat, and a white veil. There was only one seat left at the end of the long table where Friar lectured, so she took it, and Hugo sat behind her in a row of folding chairs. Next to her sat a handsome young man who asked if, because of her unusual dress, she might be French. Her first impression was "he is like Bill. He is luminous and manly . . . the same tall, slender body, the same clear skin, full mouth. . . . He is twenty years old."

His name was Gore Vidal.

25

Colette and Chéri

THE WAR WAS OVER, although to read Anaïs Nin's diary, one would hardly know there had been one. Occasionally, she apologized to her mother for forgetting to send ration coupons or thanked her for sending maple candy and syrup to replace sugar, which Hugo could not do without. Other than Eduardo and Duncan, both of whom were discharged shortly after being drafted, she knew no one in the military.

Anaïs seldom encountered a uniform, so perhaps it is not surprising that in her first of many diary entries about the young man who sat next to her at the 92nd Street YMHA, she mistakenly identified him as "Lieutenant" Gore Vidal. Actually, he was a warrant officer, the highest rank an enlisted man could attain and a singular feat for a twenty-year-old.[1] He was then stationed at Mitchell Field on Long Island, awaiting discharge and working part time as an editor at E. P. Dutton & Company publishers. His first novel, *Williwaw,* based on his military experience in the Aleutian Islands, had just been published.

That Sunday afternoon in November 1945, when the young man in uniform asked the woman in the dramatically veiled hat if she were French, he knew full well that she was the writer Anaïs Nin, whose hand-printed books were becoming increasingly popular with certain literary coteries, particularly gay men.[2] He told her a great deal about himself, starting with his graduation from Phillips Exeter Academy in 1943, his enlistment in the army, and how he spent the rest of the war as master of a small ferryboat plying the Aleutian Islands, transporting cargo, passengers, and supplies.

He also told her that his father was Eugene L. Vidal,[3] who had been Director of Air Commerce under Roosevelt and was now the president of Eastern Air Lines.[4] His mother, Nina Gore Vidal Auchincloss Olds,[5] was the daughter of Oklahoma's famed blind senator (and its first), Thomas P. Gore, to whom Gore Vidal was devoted. His ambition at that time was to follow his grandfather in politics. "Gore Vidal: Future President of the United States," Anaïs noted that night in her diary. "I believe him."[6]

Anaïs learned all this in the brief intermission, including the fact that Gore Vidal's mother instigated divorce proceedings when he was ten and was largely absent from his life afterward. Their mutual loss of an adored parent at roughly the same age cemented the bond that each felt from the first exchange of pleasantries.

He asked when she received callers; she suggested he come that evening. Hugo tactfully absented himself, just as he had done that afternoon and every other time he saw Anaïs focus on whoever captured her attention at the moment.[7] According to Anaïs, she and Gore spent the evening exchanging personal information with the same breathless intensity that had characterized their earlier meeting. What happened after that is clouded in the controversy engendered by two very strong personalities, each of whom insisted on a very different account of their relationship when it ended.

Anaïs Nin left voluminous diary entries of its day-by-day, year-by-year progression, as well as a complete separate volume called "The Gore Diary."[8] In the beginning, when he signed a copy of his first novel, *Williwaw,* Gore compared "Anaïs chérie" to Joan of Arc, writing that, like the Maid of Orleans, she was responsible for a king being crowned. As time passed she became caricatures in his novels, starting with Marietta Donegal, who aspired to be "a love goddess [and] a legend in her own time . . . as, in fact, she herself has so often noted in the five volumes of memoirs she has to date given us"; and most recently, Priscilla, who kept an untruthful diary in which she "distilled" her meaning and wrote "something unpleasant" each day about everyone she met.[9]

As Anaïs and Gore kept their relationship sequestered and separate from their other friendships, few people can actually attest to first-hand observations of what went on between them.[10] Their letters do provide insights, and in important instances, document and verify the greater part of what she confided to the unpublished diary.

According to Anaïs, Gore wanted her to leave Hugo and marry him, but he made it clear from the very beginning that he would never consummate the marriage. What Gore wanted was impossible for her: "to live with me, close to me, possessively, emotionally, but to sleep with boys. . . . He wants me to share this."[11] According to Gore in 1992, "How could she even have dreamed that I would marry her, a 42 year old woman . . . a henna haired French adventuress, an adultress with black gums."[12]

Anaïs was convinced she could change Gore's sexual orientation if only she could seduce him, and she spent the first six months that they knew each other trying to persuade him to have intercourse. Each time she confided to the diary that she was about to succeed, her subsequent entry would describe his newest male companion. And so she resumed her affair with Bill Pinckard.[13] Gore was furious at what he insisted was betrayal, expecting her to remain celibate and available as muse and inspiration whenever he needed or wanted one, while he was to be free to pursue men at will.[14]

Anaïs believed they shared a "quest for the cheated childhood," and was convinced that all Gore's problems would be resolved once he came to terms with his troubled history with his mother.[15] She urged him to consult Dr. Staff, but he went once and refused to go again. Gore told her Staff said it would do her good to have a "relationship without sexuality" because she "oversexualized."

Staff tried to prepare Anaïs for the break he was sure would come when Gore discovered that she was forty-three and not thirty-two, as she had told him. She laughed, saying she always called him "chéri" and instructed him to call her "Colette."[16] She insisted she had prepared herself to be his muse and mother. Then Gore demanded that she tell everyone they were lovers because he was not ready to admit his homosexuality publicly. She complied, thus giving credence to the rumor that has persisted ever since.[17]

In severe frustration and to satisfy her physical needs, she turned to "Chinchilito" (Edward Graeffe); Gonzalo and Hugo (on the same day); a young man from the Village, Marshall Barer (always stopping short at consummation); and when he was in New York, Bill Pinckard.[18] Afterward, she had such hostility toward Hugo that she asked

Staff to explain it. He told her she did not hate Hugo; it was a form of self-hatred.

Her loathing of Edmund Wilson was so extreme that it gave rise to every negative thing she ever thought about herself. "I have never described even in the diary the act of self-murder which takes place after my being with someone. A sense of shame for the most trivial defect, lack, slip, error, for every statement made or for my silence, for not being earthy enough, or for being too passionate, for not being free or being too impulsive, for not being myself, or being too much so."

Happily for her, Bill Pinckard was on leave and she was able to forget Wilson's age and ugliness in Bill's beautiful youth. She told the diary she was *in flagrante delicto* with Bill when Hugo returned unexpectedly from a business trip, and she hid him quickly in the stairwell until Hugo was safely in the apartment. Whether or not Hugo was aware of what he interrupted is not known, but within the week he, too, began analysis with the doctor who would treat him until he died thirty-nine years later, Dr. Inge Bogner.[19]

Whatever the reason, there was an immediate change in Hugo, a forthrightness and firmness that was always present in his business dealings but hitherto lacking in his private life. He took his first stand by telling Anaïs that he would no longer support Gonzalo and Helba, but through his intercession, the Community Service Society paid the Huara-Moré rent and $30 a week for a year, a decent stipend in the 1940s. Gonzalo, the ostensible owner of a printing shop, was expected to earn the rest of their expenses through his labor.[20]

Anaïs did not contest Hugo's decision, but made excuses for herself and him, saying the press "collapsed under a mountain of debts, corroded by Gonzalo's irresponsibilities." Long before Hugo forced the rupture, she had wondered "what kind of fire" she ever saw "in this sick primitive."[21]

Anaïs Nin was suddenly invited to speak at several New England colleges and universities, and Staff wanted to prepare her for hostile criticism. He was concerned because she had earlier told him about a serious attack of panic when Gore suggested taking her to a party to meet friends of his mother's who moved in the highest social and political circles in New York and Washington. Anaïs was incapacitated by anxiety akin to the distress she felt as a child when her father entertained and she feared to be found lacking in some way.

To prepare her for her tour, Staff thought she should be ready to respond to views such as Diana Trilling's in her review of *This Hunger.* Like Trilling, he too had been puzzled by Lillian's "unreal and not substantially treated" home, husband, and children. But that was exactly the point, Anaïs insisted. How could she spend pages making them so when they were not real to Lillian? "I didn't get that," Dr. Staff supposedly replied. "You see," Anaïs explained patiently, "if I spend too much time to make a world real I can't spend time on the drama of its unreality."

Anaïs believed that, despite what some critics were calling her "incompleteness, preciosity," her fiction was increasingly appealing to readers who agreed that she captured experience as it was lived in real life, with all its neuroses, anxieties, and abstractions: "I am giving the vision of the neurotic directly. I am writing as most people today are feeling. I can bring them to a clarity about these feelings. All the world cannot [afford] analysis. I can bring the neurotic [world] into [their] reality."

She claimed that Staff conceded she had proven her point, and thus bolstered, prepared for her first reading at Harvard. She recorded later that she wore her black dress and "vivid fuchsia scarf" and "won many people, even some prejudiced ones"; and that the distinguished literary critic F. O. Matthiessen attended and praised her writing.[22] She estimated that 200 people came to Widener Library and 100 were admitted to the room, which was supposed to hold only 50. The next morning the Harvard Film Service recorded her story "Rag Time."[23]

The following day, she took the bus to Dartmouth, and then went on to Goddard College, again recording in the diary a lavish and adulatory reception of herself and her work. Each visit was "one long constant interview," but she was thrilled because she "learned to talk freely, to parry, attack, resist intellectualization, to answer irrelevant questions."

She was glad to reach Amherst after a five-hour drive over snow-covered roads.[24] Kimon Friar was a member of the Amherst English Department, and his original intention (which Anaïs never knew) was to have her merely appear on a program that was supposed to star Djuna Barnes. When Barnes learned that Anaïs was to share the platform, she was affronted and invented a terrible cold.[25]

Few members of the college's literary community attended her reading, and only a handful of students. Afterward, there was a reception at a mathematics professor's home, and he tried to engage her in a discussion of various themes he perceived in her fiction. Determined to have an admiring audience, she quickly created a distance between herself and the faculty by gathering a group of students. She gave them her undivided attention, and they were entranced. From this time on, she counted on students to become another version of her "children," to give her the adulation she feared adults would not.

Friar introduced her to the poet James Merrill, then a twenty-year-old undergraduate.[26] Merrill, whose father was a founding partner in the brokerage firm of Merrill Lynch, lived not in a dormitory, but in a house, where he invited Anaïs to be his guest for dinner. He also invited his classmate and friend, William Burford, who provided the "real high point" of her trip. The nineteen-year-old heir to the Skelly oil fortune, Bill Burford was studying history and political science in preparation for a career in the Foreign Service.[27] When she left that night, Anaïs invited both students to send her some of their writings. Merrill, more worldly than Burford, eluded Anaïs's orbit and politely declined, but Burford was drawn into a correspondence.[28]

Unlike Gore, who wrote infrequently, Burford promptly answered every one of Anaïs's barrage of letters.[29] Hers are soulful epistles usually running to ten or more pages; his are prickly missives, full of intelligent undergraduate theorizing about art and literature. Each was often angry with the other for real or imagined slights, and much of their correspondence was taken up in accusation and rebuttal.

Burford was astonished to discover that her knowledge of fiction ended with the French Surrealists and the Americans Sherwood Anderson and Waldo Frank. What she knew of contemporary literature seemed to be based on book reviews or shreds of commentary gleaned at parties. His impression is both perceptive and correct. The long lists of "Books Read" that she appended to every diary shrank to a desultory few when she met Henry Miller, as did the long, thoughtful reflections on how they pertained directly to her life and her personal theory of literature. Pressed by Henry to read his sheaves of notes from Nietzsche, Kafka, and Doestoevski, Anaïs's sustained development as an autodidact all but ended. The frenetic activity of her daily life certainly contributed to the decline of her reading, so perhaps it is not surprising that it became intermittent and haphazard.

In what she called her "second period of erotic madness," she no longer sought a father but rather a "child" who would become at times her "brother" and at other times her "twin-lover." Anaïs became fixated on William Burford by default.[30] William Pinckard, in Japan, sent a steady stream of intensely personal letters filled with erotic longing. Gore was in Guatemala, sustained by his young lover and the easy flow of writing that became his controversial (for the time) novel of homosexual love, *The City and the Pillar.* Anaïs had only a continuing procession of young boys who came and went from Greenwich Village with interchangeable ease, and she cast herself in the role of Colette's Léa instructing whichever youth was her Chéri of the moment.

She also compared these boys to the legendary nineteenth-century foundling Kaspar Hauser and cast herself in the role of his savior.[31] In Anaïs Nin's many diary references to the German foundling, Hauser is always idealized as a beautiful blond boy, tall and fair. Most important, she makes him possess an innocent intelligence that only she would be capable of educating, and a sensuality that only she could develop fully. When this idealized boy came to maturity, he would be her true "twin" and, together, they would go off to some natural paradise, to lead a life in full harmony with each other and at one with nature.

Hugo was spending long periods of time in Cuba on business and was not available to assuage the anxiety that caused Anaïs to invite a succession of unnamed Greenwich Village boys to share her bed every night.[32] Part of her anxiety stemmed from her "best friend," the diary, for she no longer found the sustenance she required from writing in it. She may not have recognized how dramatically the content of the diary had changed since she left Paris, or that the current volume, number 69, would become the last. After that, when she wrote what passed for diary writing, it would be on whatever paper of whatever quality and size came easiest to hand, all of which she stuffed into manila folders along with correspondence, news clippings, photos, theater playbills, and whatever else struck her fancy. Since arriving in New York, she wrote few of the long portraits of friends (or enemies), there was no discussion of books, and little of theater. Her entries were no longer daily, and when she did write, it was mostly about machinations on behalf of her writing, her peripatetic daily life, and especially her version of what she and Clement Staff said to each other.

The problem was the "thundering solipsism" of which Gore Vidal accused her many years later. To him, she was "shrewd, but not an intellectual."[33] Burford's impression supports this view. Anaïs often spoke of creating a "circle,"[34] her word for a salon where like-minded people would gather to share their ideas. The nineteen-year-old thought this was splendid and looked forward to participating in the re-creation of "a contemporary Mme. de Staël and Benjamin Constant."[35] Throughout the winter of 1946, he drove down to New York several weekends each month in the hope that the circle would be realized, but was eventually disillusioned: "She was interested in a literary gathering in what seemed to me to be the wrong sense. She did not want a mix of politics, history, and literature, but wanted everything to become more psychological, more personal." He was also frustrated because she refused to perceive the reality of others: "She had to turn everybody into some kind of player in her world, [into] projections of herself. She missed their real character."[36]

Having decided that Burford was an astute critic, she intended to use his talent to foster her reputation. Through Henry, she met Florenz and Oscar Baron (then known by his family name, Baradinsky), the owner of the Alicat Book Shop, press, and art gallery in Yonkers, New York.[37] The Alicat Series of one-dollar chapbooks was started several years earlier when Florenz asked her husband for one of Henry Miller's books as a Christmas present. Instead of buying one, Oscar printed something new: Miller's essay "Obscenity and the Law of Reflection." Within the year, Miller's influence on the chapbooks was apparent, as works appeared by Michael Fraenkel, Anaïs Nin, and Ian Hugo.[38]

Anaïs Nin contributed an essay entitled "Realism and Reality," one of her first attempts to explain herself as a writer.[39] Not content to elucidate her credo, she wanted someone else to comment favorably on her work as an introduction within the pamphlet itself. Burford was her first choice because she thought he was malleable and would write a paean to her brilliance and talent. He accepted the assignment and wrote a thoughtful essay that examined her work for what it was, rather than, as her harshest critics were then doing, for what it was not. Although his essay was generally positive, he was temperate in his judgments and less than effusive in his compliments. Almost fifty years later, he remains the soul of discretion and will say only that he was "surprised" when he read the published essay, for "many parts" were not what he originally wrote.[40] Anaïs Nin's revisions to his text hastened the end of their friendship, for Burford no longer trusted her: "If she had been honest enough to explain why she was dissatisfied, I would have re-written pretty extensively to satisfy her, but she never did, she just changed it."

As 1946 ended, the loss of Burford was not long mourned, for Gore was back and her first commercially published novel was about to appear. She wrote joyously to her mother: "I signed a contract with Dutton, will get $1000 royalties for my new book, which they will print next fall, then they will reprint all my other books with Hugo's illustrations. I'm very happy."[41] She used a tiny portion of her royalties to augment Hugo's major contribution, and together they paid the rental deposit on a two-bedroom penthouse apartment at 35 W. 9th Street.

She owed her commercial publication to Gore Vidal, who was delighted to help her in 1946 and characteristically intemperate in a 1992 memory of the event: "You have no idea what I had to do to get her published at Dutton's. I had to sign a two-book contract with that house when I was dying to get away from them. It was the only way they would publish her." He described himself in those days as "the most famous young writer in America" and Anaïs Nin as "the most famous unpublished novelist on West Tenth [sic] Street."[42]

She signed the contract in mid-January and had a firm deadline to deliver a new novel by the end of February. The problem was the usual one: she did not have a new novel. The solution was also the usual one: to recycle an existing work and add something new to it. The negative criticisms in reviews of *This Hunger* had sunk in, despite how blithely she tried to toss them off.

As Diana Trilling had singled out the "Hedja" section for harsh criticism in her review, it was among the first Anaïs jettisoned when shaping the new work, which she called *Ladders to Fire.*[43] Much of the new novel was based upon a dance recital by Martha Graham's troupe. Anaïs believed the dancers expressed "a new way to execute the concept of the neurotic world vision" and it led directly to what she called "The Party" section. The writing flowed easily, and she compared it to one of Graham's ballets, "full of rhythm, rich, full of color and strangeness, like a mobile modern painting." Contentedly, she submitted the manuscript and waited for publication.

Anaïs Nin and Gore Vidal.

Ladders to Fire was reviewed on October 20, 1946, in *The New York Times Book Review,* which called it "Surrealist Soap Opera." It was the first of what turned out to be few, but all unrelievedly negative, reviews. Undaunted, Anaïs organized a letter-writing campaign to rebut the review. She probably typed them all herself because the typewriter is the same even though they were signed by Gore Vidal, James Merrill, poet Charles Duit, and several others.[44] In the face of unmitigated critical hostility, Anaïs Nin took up her pen and began to write again. She had a two-book contract with E. P. Dutton and was determined to hold the company to it.

Things were not all bad, however: she was invited to Black Mountain College to speak in the distinguished creative artists series, and John Crowe Ransom said he would be pleased to have her contribute to the *Kenyon Review.*[45] She was also invited to speak at Sarah Lawrence College, where she met the critic Maxwell Geismar, who with his wife, Anne, became good friends to her and Hugo. All this activity marked the beginning of the formation of her strongest following, students and the very young, who found something in her writing that mature critics either could not see or did not value.

Re-energized, and publicly confessing to "thirty-four or five," she sent another cautionary missive to Rosa: "We are not in France and maturity is not considered an asset here. Please, please tell Joaquín to keep it [her age] quiet, as it means a great deal to me."[46]

On February 21, 1947, she was forty-four years old. Her first act at the start of this new year was to take her typewriter to be fixed because it "skipped frenziedly,"[47] It was, she said dryly, "the right illness for my typewriter." It was also an apt description of her life in the past several months, a confused jumble of too many young men, all "jeune fille with phallus," who "are ashamed to be wives."[48]

She frequented parties where the only men were homosexuals who had come to meet each other, and the women were what would be known in a later decade as campy harridans. She went to one party in a sari, flaunting bare shoulders covered with bite marks she claimed were made by one of her dalliances. The men at the party were "aroused by her beauty" and by "stroking" her, and soon they were biting her, "hard, like an orgy without final climax." Hugo was there, watching from the sidelines. Later, as they walked home together through the frigid streets he said quietly, "I looked at you and you did not belong there. You were so much more. You must find your level."

To the world at large, she appeared happy, convinced that at every party "there is always someone who knows me, whom the others envy and asked to be introduced to me . . . they come, they are worshipful, they are grateful." Still, it was "not enough. Terrible depression."

Each visit to Dr. Staff revolved around her "first humiliation at the hands of man," her father's "violent spankings." Staff asked her to consider the possibility that because of her father's abuse, she had somehow linked humiliation with pleasure. She said it was true, that from the first spanking, she had accepted a kind of "slavery" even as she went on to abandon, punish, and hurt all those who had hurt her. In this category she included her father, Henry Miller, Otto Rank, and Edmund Wilson.

She also included Gore, for she was shocked by how he portrayed her in his novel, *A Search for the King*. She perceived it as "a caricature, a cheapened superficial, distorted image in his own terms," and little more than "a pulp novel." Gore now became "a nice little monster I have taken to my breast," another in the long line of those who did not live up to her initial expectations. Their personal relationship remained intact, but the literary jousting and jockeying for power had begun.

Despite this reckless and debilitating behavior, she still wrote "every day, all day." She was finishing her second novel for Dutton, *Children of the Albatross* and something—she knew not what—was "seeking to break through." Kimon Friar asked her to read again on another program at the 92nd Street Y, this time with the poet Jean Garrigue and Marya Zaturenska, who had just won the Pulitzer Prize in poetry. Friar said his invitation was in recognition of the poetic element in her fiction, which she had long wanted readers to be aware of and critics to note.

As she sought to immerse herself in her new novel to forget the embarrassing memory of a particularly debauched party, she wondered how to include a new perception of aging into the closing pages. She decided that it was not a physical phenomenon; rather, it began when a person grew weary of "repetitious motifs," when "the next move, the next word, the next lover" became all too boringly familiar.

Perhaps, she mused, she was ready "for a new experience, a new world, a new lover, a new passion—perhaps for the biggest one of all!!"

26

"Life again, life!"

IN YEARS TO COME, Rupert Pole's favorite story about Anaïs Nin was how they met, in an elevator, on their way to a party given by Hazel Guggenheim McKinley. Rupert's romanticized version is that each noticed ink on the hands of the other and exclaimed in mutual delight that both were printers. As Anaïs had not worked at the press for a year or more, and as she was so fond of manicures at Elizabeth Arden, the story is unlikely but charming.[1]

The day before Hazel McKinley's party, February 18, 1947 (which just happened to be Rupert's birthday), Anaïs made an impassioned plea to her only confidant: "Oh my diary, may I be granted the wish to live alone—may it happen Hugo may feel free without me, for I would not have the courage to desert him—may it happen simultaneously and painlessly. For then my life would match my writing and my writing my life and all would be integrated."[2]

Even though she wrote about wanting to live alone, Anaïs was always looking, wherever she went, for *the* new lover, the ideal man she still believed would come her way. Nevertheless, her initial reaction to Rupert was tempered by caution. He told her he was Welsh, an unemployed actor working in a printshop.[3] When she remarked on his full-length white leather coat, he told her it belonged originally to his step-grandfather, Frank Lloyd Wright.[4] Rupert thought its sheer drama might enhance his acting prospects, but so far it had not brought much luck. A third-generation Angeleno (as those born in

Los Angeles call themselves), he was twenty-eight in 1947, unemployed, and newly divorced from the aspiring actress (and also his cousin) Jane Lloyd-Jones, with whom he had performed as an entertainment duo on cruise ships.[5]

He was stunningly handsome, with the finely chiseled facial features and slim, muscular body found more frequently on Greek statuary than human beings. He was also painfully shy and socially insecure. Awkward and ill-at-ease at the party, he spent most of it sitting on a small sofa, talking to Anaïs.

When he learned she had never been west of northern New Jersey, he described the landscape and sky of Colorado, New Mexico, and California. She discovered that he was "full of aphorisms, Lao Tze's sayings, mysticism, pacifism, [and] Krishnamurti." Rupert believed daily life in New York was "inbalance" and as he was "earthy," he wanted to return to the West and "a better balance between body and spirit."

"Danger!" she told the diary that night, "he is probably homosexual." Anaïs could hardly believe her good fortune. Here was a beautiful young man who looked like Bill Pinckard but was not afraid to express feelings and emotions and who spoke of his inner self as easily as she did. She could hardly contain herself but managed to act "passive and careful not to be moved." She thought, "some deep part of his being is unknown to him, protected by this manly heartiness."

Two days later, he telephoned. Hugo was in Cuba, so she invited Rupert to come to dinner after work. He arrived around 8 P.M., still in work clothes. She noticed then what immediately struck most others who came to know both men in the years that followed: Rupert looked like a younger version of Hugo and had many of the same mannerisms.[6] He stayed all night.[7] The next morning she refused invitations from the five men (casual liaisons all) she had slept with during the past week, feeling the need to recapture her "purity" for Rupert.

To kill time until he phoned again, she worked on *Children of the Albatross* and met her March 1 deadline, finishing "a slender volume, but so rich." Ten days later she was depressed, as she always was upon finishing a book, but also this time because Rupert had not contacted her since their one "magnificent night." He seemed surprised when she phoned and said he would be busy until March 12. Hugo was returning from Cuba on the 10th and leaving again a few days later. She asked Rupert to call then, thinking he would surely take her somewhere special, but he was frugal and insisted on cooking together instead. After dinner, he entertained her by speaking Spanish, playing his guitar, and singing. He was "healthy and beautiful and alive," so it was enough for her.

But there was much to worry about in the handsome young man who came and went as if she were a diversion but not much more. Rupert told Anaïs of a "puritanical girl friend" who "thwarted his lustiness." She worried that he could discuss this so casually, fearing he regarded her as an older sister, if not a mother. She worried privately about the sixteen-year age difference between them.[8]

Anaïs sought Rupert out one cold winter night in 1947 at the printshop where he worked. She took him to a Spanish restaurant and because Hugo was at home, asked if they could go to his apartment. She noticed his viola in the corner of the tiny, messy studio, and he told her how important music was to him. He read to her from Kahlil Gibran's *The Prophet,* which he called "my bible," then told her he had to return to California because his parents insisted that he live at home and establish a career. "Go with me," he said; "yes," Anaïs replied without hesitation. Later, she wondered what she had done, agreeing so blithely to go off on a cross-country jaunt with a mere boy in a 1941 Model-A Ford roadster that he called "Cleopatra."[9] But she knew that she could always change her mind.

Rupert's invitation was a godsend. She had been looking for something or someone to get her out of New York since the disappointing publication of *Ladders to Fire.* She had since developed an understandable paranoia and was convinced that she and her writing were the targets of either vicious digs or snickering asides. Although this was true in the main, she was also, as usual, overreacting: even as the critics who deigned to review the novel were united in their general negativity, there was a growing appreciation among those who ignored reviews and read the novel anyway. Nine months after publication, more than 4,000 copies of *Ladders* had been sold, a very good number in those days for such an offbeat work of fiction.

Many new people came into Anaïs Nin's life at this time. Among them were Larry Maxwell, who owned a Greenwich Village bookshop on Christopher Street called At the Sign of the Dancing Bear, and the young NYU student who worked there part-time, Lila Rosenblum.[10] Larry thought Anaïs was simply "incomprehensible,"[11] but they became professional friends, adversaries, and combatants for the better part of the next decade; Lila then became a devoted friend throughout the last third of Anaïs Nin's life.

With the end of the war, many expatriates whose names had filled her diary went back to France or, like Henry, to someplace new within the United States. Greenwich Village was now populated by a new and younger crowd. Many of the men were returning veterans who were unwilling to settle down; many of the women were not sure if they really were artists and writers or only rebelling against bourgeois backgrounds until they found someone to marry. What both knew, however, was that they were capable of influencing the direction of contemporary culture, and the war years were a great void which they were determined to fill with something new.

Without being aware of it, Anaïs Nin was in a special position during this pivotal moment. To her contemporaries, those who controlled the dissemination of culture in the United States, she was a fringe literary figure, a coterie writer meant only for rarefied audiences. But to the new crowd who filled the coffeehouses—Anaïs Nin was not only the last remnant of an exotic prewar life to which the passing of time had given a romantically rosy glow, she was also someone who wrote about feelings, sensations, and inner selfhood when most other published writers did not.

Gore returned from Guatemala, causing the usual emotional upheaval. Anaïs had managed to control her erotic longing for him, but he still found ways to upset her. Now she told the diary that he definitely wanted her to marry him and bear his child by artificial insemination.

Even Hugo had become a genuine worry. His frequent business trips to Havana were only partially for the bank that had employed him for twenty-eight years. He had been offered a job in The Trust Company of Cuba, a bank controlled by the Sánchez family, now under the direction of Graciella Sánchez's second husband, Roy Archibald. Anaïs deplored the idea that the Sánchez family might determine her financial security, but compared to Hugo's present salary, the one they offered was astronomical.

There was also the continuing war with her publisher, at least according to Gore, who reported his ongoing battles to protect her interests at Dutton's in (for her) insulting and humiliating detail. Most of the people who knew her best in the years following adopted the expression coined by her brother Joaquín of Anaïs as "a steel hummingbird . . . determined to be famous."[12] Her efforts to promote her novels attest to this fact. She wrote to every college and university that had previously hosted her, asking for invitations to speak again, and also to universities where she knew no one, frequently sending her photographs and books.

Disappointed with Bill Burford's article, she was determined to find someone who would write glowingly about her, as Henry had so many years earlier in his "Être Étoilique" article, and thought Leo Lehrman might be the one to do it. Then an editor at *Harper's Bazaar,* Lehrman had been responsible for the photos of Anaïs at the printing press and also for a composite photo of her dressed as each of the four women in *Ladders to Fire.*

She wrote to Lerman, asking if he would commission a profile to appear when *Children of the Albatross* was published in fall 1947. Lerman said he was agreeable in principle but would have to wait before making a firm commitment. In the meantime, he asked, why didn't she begin by writing her own self-portrait, which might help him to decide whether or not to assign a writer to the project.

"That was the one question I hoped you would not ask me, but answer for me," she replied.[13] She then wrote a three-page letter, typed, which went through countless handwritten revisions first and which reveals the fragmented state she was in throughout 1947. She wrote of playing a thousand roles in life while her real self remained unknown, and she spoke of often thinking about ending her life in suicide, as Virginia Woolf had done. She admitted that everything she wrote, no matter what the genre, originated in the diary, which was all true and merely "transposed" from her life. Everything that mattered, she insisted, was in the diary, which to her sorrow was unprintable.

But she still aimed to publish it, and began another round of rewriting that bested her all-out effort five years previously with Virginia Admiral and Robert Duncan. She engaged Lila Rosenblum to help, mostly to correct her grammar, spelling, and punctuation. Anaïs wrote new versions of old events on lined pads, which Lila corrected. Then Anaïs recopied the corrected pages into booklets, some of which she had Lila type. This generally led to further rewriting and correcting, and when she was finally satisfied with the typed copies, she destroyed the originals. It was a process that went on and on, sometimes "hundreds of times." She inserted all these carefully typed pages into loose-leaf folders, and when she gave them to someone to read, always insisted they were reading her original diaries.[14] Anaïs Nin carried on this process of self-expurgation all her life.

But in the spring of 1947, all the self-inflicted pressures of the "thousand roles" she played were suffocating. Her anxieties crystallized around the thought of making the trip with Rupert, whose name she could not even use when talking to Dr. Staff. When Staff asked her to describe Rupert, she said, "He has these airy spaces he leaps into," and feared he was too young to remain in her life for long.[15]

Staff asked if he was a good lover. This was what frightened her most, she admitted, for she thought him the most potent lover she had ever had. It was the very quality in a man she had learned to fear and mistrust because of her father and Henry, both of whom evinced faithlessness she felt was due to extremes of potency. It was what had caused her over the years to turn to "less and less potent men" and finally to homosexuals. Dr. Staff asked if perhaps Rupert's healthy sexuality represented a return to a kind of normality she had always lacked; in essence, a return to life. Yes, she agreed, "life again, life!"

Dr. Staff raised the question of what she would do about Hugo. She told Staff she would never leave Hugo, and besides, Rupert would probably tire of her when he saw how old she really was and how she would collapse under the rigors of the trip. Staff asked why it could not last forever and she had a ready answer: Rupert's profession. He planned to study forestry and become a ranger who fought fires. Also, he was decidedly not an intellectual and wanted to do outdoor work and live in Western isolation, preferably in Colorado. Ultimately for Rupert, "home is important, a HOME."[16] She, proud that her roots were portable and could be set down wherever she happened to be, could not understand this. And there was the question of children, which he wanted very much. She had no wish to have a child, and as she was now forty-four and experiencing gynecological problems, she thought it a moot point.

She and Hugo were quarreling a great deal now, something they had not done since the early years of her affair with Henry. The question of living separately came up from time to time, but only obliquely. Anaïs had been careful to keep Hugo and Rupert from meeting, but she was sure he suspected someone, probably Gore, especially when she casually mentioned that Thurema Sokol was thinking of taking an extended drive across the United States, and what would Hugo think if she went with her. It was a daring lie, for she had no way to keep Hugo and Thurema from meeting accidentally while she was away. Hugo did not give permission but said instead, truthfully, that he was deeply in debt and had no money to pay for such a trip.

It led to the most ferocious battle in years.[17] She accused him of being "10% artist, 90% banker." He retaliated by telling her she was "100%" living in a dream world he could no longer support. She rebutted, saying she might be "90% artist," but was also "10% realist," which was more than enough to deal with being his wife.

Typically, she sought other men. When Hugo brought the African-American novelist Richard Wright to dinner, Anaïs decided to embarrass Hugo and dazzle Wright with her wiles. "One visit and he falls in love with me," she wrote, insisting in the diary that Wright wanted to take her to France with him.

Throughout all this, Rupert, her "fiery one," was nowhere to be found. He took it for granted that she would go with him when he left New York at the end of April, for Rupert had the same quality as Anaïs of seeing only what he wanted to believe. Meanwhile, she busied herself with prepublication publicity for *Children of the Albatross* because, if she did manage to go with Rupert, she would not return until just before the book was published in mid-October. Some of her self-promoting letters brought results, and before she left, she had invitations to speak at the University of Chicago and Berkeley in November and December. These engagements especially pleased her, for she reasoned that if things went well on the first trip, they would provide an excuse to make a second one to see Rupert.

Logistics were daunting as she tried to plan her escape. Anaïs believed that Hugo accepted her story of driving with Thurema, who agreed to steer clear of him as well as she could. There was the question of mail, and how to receive it, and how and when to speak by telephone to Hugo without inflaming Rupert's jealousy.[18] Gore was furious that she planned to leave New York. He was scathingly sarcastic about Rupert, and she was uncertain whether or not he would act on his threat to tell Hugo who her traveling companion really was. Even Gonzalo surfaced again, this time pleading for money to keep from starving. She gave him a pittance as an advance for printing another thousand copies of *Under a Glass Bell,* which Larry Maxwell promised to distribute to other bookstores and sell in his own. She swore Maxwell to secrecy and told him the truth about the trip, and he agreed to act as her mail drop and telephone connection to her life in New York.

On April 23, 1947, she wrote in very large letters on a separate page in the diary, "Part Two of my life. I feel loved. I feel invited to the world. I feel free." The next day the diary went "into the vault" in preparation for their Monday-morning departure. Anaïs called Clement Staff one last time, overcome by such severe anxiety that she could barely dial his number. He told her it was simply a projection of the guilt, really a myth of her own creation, that engulfed her every time she took a step, no matter how feeble, toward leaving Hugo. He told her to make up her mind one way or the other, but not to vacillate in-between. She went, but did not stay, and was in-between for the rest of her life.

They were both silent during the first mile as Cleopatra penetrated the Holland Tunnel and roared toward New Jersey and mainland America.[19] She was swathed in lavender and purple, her outfit topped by a wide-brimmed hat to shield her fair skin from sun and wind, as Rupert insisted on driving with the top down.[20] He wore a tightly belted dark blue wool coat, scarf, and Tyrolian hat, and smoked a pipe. "I am running away with a most beautiful man," she thought, unable to believe her good fortune. When they stopped for breakfast in New Jersey, she had a slightly different thought as Rupert pulled out a tiny notebook and carefully wrote down how much it cost. "Expense book," she wrote in the few pages of scattered notes that constituted her cross-country diary, "Hugo's son."

The trip was a rambling one that took them south through Washington and the Great Smoky Mountains to Virginia, and on to New Orleans, where they visited Gore Vidal. It was a tense visit, as Gore lost no opportunity to flirt with Rupert and taunt Anaïs.[21] From there, they went to Arkansas, Oklahoma, and the Texas panhandle into Albuquerque, Santa Fe, and Taos, where they called upon Frieda Lawrence. They went north to Denver, where Anaïs had arranged to have mail sent to general delivery. Rupert was angry and jealous when she received letters from Gore and some of her other lovers.

They had their first real quarrel when she delayed their departure to write an angry letter to Gore after brooding over his latest insult—

the character of Maria Verlaine in *The City and the Pillar*—a woman who had seen two wars, had lines around her eyes, and could not find a satisfying sexual relationship.[22]

Cleo chugged over the top of the Continental Divide down to Fraser, where Rupert had a job interview. Then they visited Rupert's father, Reginald Pole, in Tucson, and Lila Rosenblum, who was now a student at the University of Arizona.[23] They went through Navajo reservations in Arizona; the Grand Canyon; thence to Las Vegas; St. George, Utah; San Bernardino; and Los Angeles. Anaïs's memories were intense: of making love on sun-warmed desert rocks, of sleeping outdoors in the cold desert nights, of the wind howling through the Grand Canyon, and especially of the smell of mile after mile of orange groves as they entered Los Angeles.

They spent their first day on the beach in Santa Monica, after which Rupert took her to a modest hotel in Hollywood and went home alone to his mother and stepfather. He could not spend the night with her, he said, as his mother expected him to stay in his boyhood room. Anaïs was astonished to discover just how frightened Rupert was of presenting her to them, or even of the possibility that they might discover she was in the same city.

The day after they arrived in Los Angeles, Rupert hastily trundled Anaïs off to the airport. She could not believe how easily he surrendered her, and sat alone weeping until her plane was called.

Back in New York in late September, she resumed her frenetic life. She was no longer keeping a diary, only a jotting of engagements and random notes. On October 11 she noted, "hysteria, depression, death wish." On the 12th, "a crisis with Hugo." In between, there were trips to the dentist, working on proofs at Dutton's, evenings with the retinue of men, and preparation for a tour of the surprisingly large number of colleges and universities that invited her to speak. She also visited Clement Staff, daily at times, then every other day.[24]

There was also the pressing need to have an abortion, for she was pregnant with Rupert's child. She had told Gore about Hugo's inability to give her money for the cross-country trip and he generously sent her $1,000 in traveler's checks, most of which she still had. A young admirer, Sherry Donati,[25] found a doctor, and after a relatively painless procedure and ten days of rest she was fine. "I didn't tell the Welshman or he would have married me," she joked to Gore.[26]

Anaïs in Rupert's "Cleo" on her way west.

Rupert Pole in his actor's publicity photo.

On October 20 she left for a four-day visit to Black Mountain College in North Carolina, where she was to speak to students about the craft of writing. There, she met a young man from a working-class Irish family in Detroit who would become one of her closest confidants, the writer James Leo Herlihy. Many years later he could still remember his first impression of Anaïs Nin, "an utterly magical being."[27] What struck Herlihy was her reply to a student who asked why she wrote and what was her ultimate aim in writing. "I want to give to the world one perfect life," she replied, then went on to explain that by "living the dream" and "perfecting [her] reality," she would be able to offer a model to generations to come.[28] "Picture, if you will," Herlihy said many years later, "youngsters who were just developing after the drab grayness of wartime, and who saw this sparkling, tinkling creature as perfection itself. When she told us that we, too, could live out our dreams, well—we were converted, to say the least."

Back in New York, she found a letter from Gore: "Are you trying to tell me (perhaps you have told me) that the Pole affair is everything you want and need?"[29] If so, he advised her to leave Hugo, for she had "no real ties" in New York. "Why don't you make a life for yourself," Gore asked vehemently. "You have no idea how important it is to have a way of life."

The letter added to her confusion, for publication was near and anxiety mounted. All she could think of was to get away from New York and the spite, backbiting, and especially from the men who, having heard she was "easy," assaulted her in bedrooms, baths, and kitchens at the parties she attended night after night in search of she knew not what.

She decided to move to a sleepy little Mexican fishing village she first heard of when Thorvald sent a postcard: Acapulco. At first she planned to live alone, but almost immediately plotted to lure Rupert there during his Christmas vacation from UCLA. She called him "Chiciquito" (little boy) in her pleading and imploring letters. "Write to me," she begged, for he hated to write letters. And because he was "so beautiful," she implored him not to let anyone steal him away from her.[30] Unable to keep from falling into her old pattern with other lovers, she sent him fifty dollars.

Children of the Albatross was published on November 3, and she read from it at Harvard, Dartmouth, Amherst, Chicago, and Berkeley. Dutton paid for her travel expenses and arranged a schedule of readings, including several in the Los Angeles area. When she told Rupert she would be there, he commanded her not to come. He did not dare to see her as he lived in his mother's house and felt watched and restricted. By early December, she was back in New York preparing to spend Christmas in Acapulco with Rupert and telling an astonished Hugo that she planned to buy a house and live there indefinitely.[31]

She was convinced that *Children of the Albatross* was going to make money and that it would lead to future contracts giving her a minimum of a thousand dollars in yearly advances, a very good sum for the late 1940s but not nearly enough to support two separate households, even if one were Mexican and inexpensive. But the novel received the same sort of criticism as its predecessor, that it was abstract and obscure, impossible to discern her meaning and intention.

In this novel, the character of Djuna is a mature woman (and Nin is careful to stress that mature does not mean old) who has many male "children," all bisexual or homosexual. She brings them to her "house of innocence and faith,"[32] where she encourages them to develop their artistic tendencies, whether in dance, painting, or music. She celebrates freedom with some and provides sexual initiation to others. Looming throughout this novel is a tyrannical father-figure, a patriarch who denies individuality and autonomy to his daughters as well as his sons: a mélange of her father, husband, and lovers. Lillian, Sabina, and Jay are in this novel, continuations of themselves in the earlier book, their characters not much developed here, and appearing again in the next installment of Nin's Proustian *roman fleuve*.

She knew now that each novel needed to be part of a whole, and she already had its overall title: *Cities of the Interior*. She thought the next installment would probably be centered around an Ur-mother figure, whose determination to spread "goodness" to everyone costs her dearly in the long run. Beyond that, she was not certain what would happen within its pages.

When she broached the idea of a new contract to her editors at Dutton, they hesitated, probably waiting to see how well *Children* would sell before committing themselves. They did, however, agree to print *Under a Glass Bell,* for surprisingly (at least to Anaïs), there was a steady stream of requests for the one among her books she thought least worthy of readers' attention.[33] Because it remained popular, she believed the same sort of interest would eventually spill over to her novels. It made her confident that she could support herself in Acapulco, so she set off to buy a house and wait for Rupert, hoping to convince him to join her in a life of beachcombing.

Hugo sensed that she was about to take her most definite step to date away from him. It caused him to make an abrupt decision that changed his life: Hugo resigned from the City Bank Farmers Trust Company, a year and a half short of being vested in the pension fund. On December 11, 1947, Hugo sent Anaïs, who was in Acapulco, a twelve-page handwritten letter with minute details of their financial situation. He said he decided to resign on the eve of his fiftieth birthday rather than waiting until he was fifty-five because it would allow him to take the money already invested in the pension fund, and pay his (actually, Anaïs's) enormous debts and still have $150,000. He did not say, but the implication is clear, that if he did not pay these debts, many of which were long overdue, there could be some sort of scandal that might cost him his job.[34]

Hugo took his $150,000 and invested it through Anaïs's cousin Charles de Cárdenas (Antolina's son). He also named Charlie and one of his banking colleagues executors of an entity called Cartera Investment Inc., which was to be Anaïs's to invest, free and clear of him. He calculated that the annual income would be $5,000 after taxes, and he expected her to split it equally with him. When combined with her projected $1,000 from publishers, she would have approximately $300 a month. He also told her that, as they had no heirs and no one to whom they felt obliged to leave the bulk of their money, they should feel free to spend at least half the capital during the next twenty-five years. This, Hugo calculated, would give each of them an additional $3,000 per year. He hinted at greater sums to come, as he had agreed to work as an investment counselor for Roy Archibald, in the Sánchez family's banking interests.

Hugo's machinations were dependent in large part on her Cuban relatives, which tempered Anaïs's wholehearted enthusiasm. His financial arrangements probably had something slightly shady about them, for he warned Anaïs not to draw money directly from her accounts, but to arrange well in advance to receive her income in the form of "gifts" from her cousins Charlie or Graziella, which would be paid to her in funds taken from her Swiss bank accounts. He told Anaïs that he had just asked Charlie de Cárdenas to cable $4,000 to her in Acapulco, but she must not count on any other funds from their New York bank, as he had to pay their (her) debts.

Hugo ended his letter apologetically, saying he had not been opposed to her plan to purchase a house but was pressing for details so that he might contribute his business acumen. And, as usual, after she made an unwise, impractical decision, he found a way not only to bail her out but also to say she was right and proper to have done it in the first place and he was "confident everything would work out as planned."[35]

On Christmas Day, Hugo wrote again from the Hotel Nacional, Havana, saying he would fly to New York the next day to tender his resignation: "I find I have some emotion about the event, which I suppose is natural after 28½ years of submission to authority. The symbol of the father and the rebellion against him repeats itself, though I am conscious of it, which should make it less hard."

This followed his letter of Christmas Eve, in which he wrote, "I never felt happier in all my life and I sing to myself all the time. It is only sad not to have you with me to share it. The more I see of other people the more I realize how much you mean to me."

27

An Edifice of Lies

Beginning in the winter of 1947, Hugo traveled a great deal in his new job with the Archibald financial foundation and boasted that within a year he would be a millionaire. He made frequent trips to Brazil, where he wrote guarded letters telling Anaïs that she must not mention "the mines" to anyone.[1] He practically commuted between Paris, London, and Brussels, and always stopped in Geneva, where the Archibald brothers, Roy and Henry, had their headquarters. And he shuttled between New York and Havana, where Charles de Cárdenas consolidated all their business dealings.

Having given up the idea of buying a house in Acapulco, Anaïs spent most of her time on the West Coast, first in Los Angeles, then in San Francisco when Rupert (to escape parental supervision) transferred to Berkeley.

To keep Hugo from suspecting a lover, she invented a complicated web of lies about her health, made delicate by the ridicule of New York critics and the hostility of the reading public. Hugo went along with it, albeit unwillingly.

She joined Rupert briefly in Fraser, Colorado, where he had a summer job in 1948, and when she wrote to friends, pretended that she hauled water, chopped wood, and was a real pioneer.[2] Only Hugo's letters, sent on by an obliging landlord, interfered with her peace of mind, until she noticed how ill-at-ease her presence made

Rupert before his rough, earthy companions. She was distressed to see his relief when she pretended the altitude gave her heart palpitations and returned to Los Angeles. There, Hugo's barrage of letters continued. He needed and wanted a wife, "not a mistress who can never be counted on . . . but a wife who is there, contentedly.[3] Anaïs promised to return soon, but was nearly trapped by one of her many lies, the invention of a Los Angeles therapist (she was still seeing only Clement Staff in New York). Hugo told her not to disrupt her treatment, but Anaïs insisted on interrupting the mythical analysis and joined him in Acapulco for Christmas, 1948.

But then she needed an excuse to leave Rupert, so she invented a family reunion in Acapulco arranged by Thorvald for her and Hugo to meet his new wife, Kay, and their baby, and to entertain his two older children, Charles and Gayle. The only true part of the story was that Thorvald had indeed remarried and fathered his third child; he and his family were nowhere near Acapulco.[4]

The holiday was pleasant because one of Hugo's New York friends gave him an old movie camera and he spent the month filming, mostly Anaïs. He became an accidental filmmaker when his random shots later coalesced into *Ai-Ye,* his first complete film. After Acapulco, they flew to Los Angeles, where Hugo showed it to the avant-garde filmmaker Kenneth Anger, who told him he had a definite talent and ought not to risk it by studying with anyone.[5] Hugo followed Anger's advice.

Meeting Anger brought Anaïs into the fringes of an entire community of writers, producers, and directors whom she came to know, but not well, among them Gavin Lambert, Curtis Harrington, and their colorful friend Samson deBrier. These casual friendships also began years of frustration on her part, as she sought to convince someone—anyone—to turn her novels into films.

The winter of 1948–1949 marked the start of "a period of financial recklessness." Anaïs allowed Hugo to return with her to to Los Angeles because Rupert was in Berkeley. Money flowed, as they lived on Hugo's capital and enjoyed the beach at Malibu, shot film on Catalina Island, and went sight-seeing up and down the Pacific Coast Highway as an excuse for Anaïs to practice her wildly erratic driving.[6]

And when Rupert went to the mountains of northern California for fire training, she allowed Hugo to drive her to San Francisco in her Christmas present, a new Chrysler convertible.

She had rented a "tea house," her euphemism for a tumbledown shack in the midst of an eerie garden on an estate in the Fog Belt.[7] Like the houseboat before it, Anaïs refused to see the teahouse for the uninhabitable shack it was. Built mostly underground, it had hard-packed dirt walls and the warped plywood door did not lock. There was a primitive chemical toilet and sink but no bath or shower. Undaunted, she rigged up a "sailor shower" like her new best friend's, the artist Jean Varda.[8] Hugo insisted she move the moment he saw it. They settled on an apartment at 258 Roosevelt Way, with a fireplace and view of the distant Bay. Anaïs lived with a mattress and a card table, waiting for the furniture that had been in storage in France since they left in 1939. It cost Hugo dearly to have it shipped, but he didn't care.

Hugo left for New York, and Anaïs spent a quiet period in her new apartment rewriting some of the diaries of her years with Henry in Paris. When Rupert returned to classes in late spring, he spent Saturdays with Anaïs and returned to his room at International House on Sunday to prepare for the week's classes. He stuck to his rigorous schedule until he came down with bronchitis, then moved into Anaïs's apartment so she could nurse him. Liking it, he stayed permanently.

She gave Rupert the second bedroom, which had been her study, and she made do with a small corner of the living room. It marked her first logistical problem: where to keep the original diaries someplace so Rupert would not find them. She had to hide Hugo's daily letters as well, in a locked suitcase tucked into a hall closet.

Anaïs was not lonely when Rupert was away on subsequent firefighting training sessions, for she befriended Ruth Witt Diamant, a literature professor at San Francisco State University who admired her fiction and whom she took into her confidence about Rupert and Hugo. In years to come, Ruth provided excuses, served as a mail drop, and remained a devoted friend. She also chastised Anaïs, insisting that as an internationally published author she had an obligation to make herself known in the Bay Area. It was one of the few times Anaïs refused to appear before an admiring public. Her life was one of quiet domesticity punctuated by lovemaking, and she did not want anything to disturb it. As Rupert was both shy and anti-intellectual, she also did not want to risk exposing him to a group of sarcastic writers.

She did meet George Leite, a poet and editor of the little magazine *Circle,* with whom she had occasionally corresponded since he published "Hedja," and Bern Porter, working then as Leite's assistant.[9] In the group that surrounded the editors of *Circle,* only Robert Duncan remained hostile. Still smarting from their breakup, he now called her "Anus Ninny" to anyone who dared mention her name in his presence.

When the furniture from France arrived in April, Anaïs quickly realized she had no place to put the huge Spanish-Moorish bedstead and Arabian mirror, and everything else seemed out of place. She sold everything to the poet James Broughton, who sometimes dealt in antiques, saying "they furnished and decorated my days with Henry [and] Gonzalo" but now were little more than "wreckage from great emotional journeys."[10]

Hugo found someone willing to take over the lease on the 13th Street walkup and used the extra money to redecorate the apartment they had leased in early 1947, a two-bedroom penthouse with a large terrace in an elevator building at 35 W. 9th Street. It was the first major decision affecting the way they lived that Hugo made without Anaïs's consent. He hoped the opportunity to redecorate without worrying about money would lure her to New York, but she stayed on in San Francisco, still "playing for time" to be with Rupert until the summer, when once again he would work in Colorado.

Surprisingly, Anaïs was living frugally, despite Hugo's lavish gift of an annual income. Hugo, on the other hand, was thinking grandly. While in Havana, he arranged for Tía Antolina to send Anaïs a "gift of some $50,000," his cryptic description of commissions on various stock transactions with Charlie de Cárdenas. He instructed Anaïs to use it as needed, for he was confident of replenishing it frequently. He was pleased that he could give her what she wanted, "namely capital" that she would not have to share with him. The only disadvantage, he noted cautiously, was that she would now have to be nice to her aunt and pay attention to her, for technically, the money was Antolina's gift to Anaïs.[11] Shortly after, she noted in her diary, "short trip to New York. Strong sense of duty."

She spent the summer sitting listlessly in the new apartment, depressed because Rupert did not write, and because he forbade her to write more than one short letter each week. He was embarrassed that his fellow rangers still teased him about his "writer girl friend" and made sly digs about her age. Rupert had one flaw, Anaïs decided, his temper: "I can only use a word applied to women for what he becomes: nagging, pernickity, finicky, and fussy."[12]

At loose ends, she wrote one word in the diary, separate from other text on the page, centered and very carefully lettered: "Drugs." Most likely it referred to the sleeping pills and mood elevators her regular physician gave her, the variety of pills she now got from Jacobson, and the shots she took regularly when in New York.[13] At times, she wrote, she thought of death. She did not mind the disintegration of the body; what bothered her was to think that everything she "learned, accumulated, and experienced" would be wasted. "Surely it cannot disappear," she wailed, and began another round of diary revision, determined that it must be immortal.

In July, Hugo said he wanted to spend the next two months in Mexico, but August was Rupert's one month free from school and he wanted her with him in California.[14] Rupert intensified his pressure on her to divorce Hugo, and to prevent him from staging a possible confrontation, she said she would do it as soon as Hugo's analysis ended: surely within the year. Hugo was not to be deterred, so Anaïs invented another family emergency to explain her absence that August, telling Rupert that she had to go to Mexico City to take care of Thorvald's two older children because he was incapacitated following back surgery.[15]

When autumn came, she was detained in New York despite Rupert's anger and her own desire to be with him. Her editor was not enthusiastic about *The Four-Chambered Heart* and hinted that Dutton was seeking reasons not to publish it. To placate Rupert, Anaïs used all her powers of imagination, inventing writing assignments for *Harper's Bazaar* and Fleur Cowles's *Flair,* interviews with all the major newspapers and magazines that supposedly had discovered her fiction, and a job reading manuscripts for her publisher, whom she could not afford to offend. When Rupert remained angry, she pulled out her trump card: Dutton wanted to publish the diaries, which they now declared would be "the next best seller," and she could not leave until contracts were signed.

There had been a terrible struggle when she left California the last time, as Rupert insisted, job or no job, he would not let her return to Hugo. She convinced him that the money from her putative job was too good to turn down until she could find something to take its place in Los Angeles. She also promised that she would not live with Hugo but would stay in Thurema Sokol's apartment, whose address she then used as her mail drop. To keep Rupert from checking, Anaïs told him that Thurema had had the phone disconnected for the summer but she would call him at specified times from pay phones.

On October 20, 1949, she was granted a temporary semi-truthful respite from her lies when her father died in Havana and she told Rupert she was too distraught to travel. She wrote a poignant passage in some of the diaries she was revising, about how she wept because she had not been able to see him one last time in order to forgive him for abandoning her, but her brother Joaquín remembers her coldness when she heard the news and how she refused to help arrange their father's funeral or the disposition of his few possessions.[16]

Because Hugo was in Cuba again, she left for San Francisco in November, reversing the various lies for his benefit. Her story now was that she could not return to New York or join him in Acapulco until she found someone to rent the apartment, as she could not afford the drain on her finances. She invented speaking engagements in the Bay Area and said she could not risk offending the sponsors by canceling. Hugo's response was always that she did not need to worry about money—there was plenty of it—and she must come at once. She dared not risk inventing a third therapist, so she pretended she had enrolled in film classes to surprise him and could not leave until they ended. It provided her next excuse, that she was in the midst of making a film and could not leave her actors in the lurch as she had guaranteed their salaries. By December 4, Hugo told her not to bother coming back to New York until he resolved his anger at her prolonged absence. He said he needed to stop deluding himself about the cause of so much of his past unhappiness and face "a whole accumulation of things in our relationship."[17]

Dr. Bogner must have been working to persuade him to accept himself for what he really was rather than what Anaïs wanted him to be, as this passage attests: "Bogner tells me I am primarily a businessman and not an artist. And I just love to make money. I love to have plenty of money to have the things that I desire—boats, airplanes. I want money because I want to be free, but I intend to avoid any enslavement to acquire it."

Hugo said he now felt less angry with her, but: "The question you must ask yourself is whether you want to continue to be married to the person I have painted to you as my real self. Whether you can continue in such a marriage without the unhappiness that has resulted from each of us keeping before us a false and unreal picture of the other."

Frightened by Hugo's assertion of an independent self, Anaïs packed Rupert off to his family in Los Angeles and packed her own bags for Acapulco, afterward returning meekly to New York. In February 1950 she wrote apologetically to Rupert that she could not celebrate their birthdays, his on February 18, hers on the 21st, but did not say it was because Hugo wanted her there for his on the 15th. Desperate not to arouse Rupert's suspicions, she made Thorvald's mythical back condition deteriorate so dangerously that he had to be flown to New York on a stretcher and in a cast. In case that was not enough, she gave Thorvald, whom she had not seen in several years and from whom she was estranged, a bad case of bronchial pneumonia.

Seeking resolution to her divided life, which she called the "trapeze,"[18] represented by the planes that flew her from one end of the continent to the other, she decided the best tack was to persuade Rupert to run away with her to Acapulco or Europe. He was obsessed with the idea of security and refused to give up the Forestry Service, but his salary was so small that he could not support her on it. Rupert insisted that she would have to find work paying an equal salary if they were to have even a minimal standard of living. He expected to be posted to a ranger station in the Sierra Madre mountains once his on-the-job training was complete, and even with government housing, things would be very tight.

Rupert was exceedingly parsimonious and he expected Anaïs to give him a minimum of several hundred dollars each month, most of which he planned to lock away in savings until he had enough money to fulfill his dream of buying a house. He knew nothing of how much money she had and she was careful to keep him from finding out, but her biggest mistake happened when she gave him the entire four hundred dollars that comprised her monthly allowance from Hugo. Now Rupert wanted that much or more every month. If he ever found out that she had $50,000 quickly dissipating dollars—all her own—in a bank account, she knew he would demand a showdown with Hugo and insist that she divorce him at once. He insisted he was going to tell his parents that he planned to work as a forest ranger in the Los Angeles area and was planning to marry Anaïs, so they would just have to accept it.

Alarmed, she fired off another of the letters that always made her seem like an older and wiser sister, if not a mother, to Rupert. "If I were you, I would not say too much. Don't praise me. Don't reveal the depth. I wish I were there to help."[19]

There was also her distress about *The Four-Chambered Heart,* which Dutton did not want to publish.[20] The publisher did not want to honor the contract, and the first ploy was to tell her that publication would be delayed for at least a year. Angry with the "hypocrite moron"[21] editor, Anaïs went to Charles Duell, a partner in the firm of Duell, Sloan and Pearce, whom she met occasionally at various book-launching parties, and explained her situation. He agreed to publish it if Dutton released her, which they were only too happy to do.

The Four-Chambered Heart received better reviews than the previous novels, but as they were not sheer unmitigated praise, they were still less than heartening to Anaïs. Two of the more important reviewers, Hayden Carruth and Charles Rollo, both granted nuggets of praise: Carruth called it "some of the finest writing of our time," and Rollo noted Nin's ability to "celebrate the fusion of two human beings."[22] However, she wrote to all her reviewers, influential or insignificant, thanking them for whatever positive comments she could cull.

Rupert gave her the title for this novel, really the story of herself and Gonzalo. He often instructed her at mealtimes about botany and zoology, and she always pretended to be fascinated with what he said.[23] On one such occasion, when he was cooking his favorite food, steak, he launched into a description of how a cow's heart is divided into four chambers. She decided that it was the perfect title for the novel of a good woman, Djuna, whose kindness is tested by her father, but more especially by her lover Rango's wife, a thinly veiled Helba.

Anaïs had a new and different reason for reacting so strangely to reviews that, granted, were generally negative but not nearly as adverse as those for *Ladders to Fire.* In *The Four-Chambered Heart,* she transposed great chunks of the novel word for word from diary accounts of the affair with Gonzalo and her indignation, disgust, and rage with Helba. Reviews that criticized the novel were, by extension, criticizing the diary, and she could not bear it.

As Rupert knew nothing of Gonzalo, it is unlikely that he connected the novel with Anaïs's life. Hugo, who knew all the sordid details whether or not he ever faced them, probably did connect the life and the work, but Anaïs did not think much about him. She chose to believe that her husband, involved in the lives of Gonzalo and Helba on the same daily basis almost as closely as hers had been, was totally unaware of the degree to which the novel paralleled her life.

No matter how hard she tried, she could not find convincing-enough reasons to return to Hollywood. Hollywood offered "relief" from New York, but she could not write there. She knew she was in trouble with Charles Duell because *The Four-Chambered Heart* had not sold as well as he expected. She needed to produce another novel as quickly as possible, but one question continued to haunt her: "Shall I go to the end this time? One handles the truth like dynamite." She could not decide how to further the fictional adventures of Djuna, and she was tired of Rango. She hit upon Sabina as the focal point of the next work, but could not determine how to wrap a plot around her. The only thing she thought settled was the title, "Sabina and the Spy Catcher," as she then called the Lie Detector.[24]

She hit upon another way to further her career and divide her time between New York and Los Angeles. Hugo was working on his second film, and if she acted as his agent and distributor, the Hollywood movie industry provided an excellent excuse to travel to the West Coast. Throughout the next twenty years, she did work hard to see that Hugo's films were shown, often taking them to various colleges and universities, where they were shown on programs in which she also read from her work.[25] Hugo sometimes accompanied her, but she insisted they act as if they were not related. As he was known professionally as Ian Hugo and Anaïs used her maiden name, it was easy to do.

She really believed, however, that her novels would make splendid films and set out to make it happen. Two of Anaïs's dearest friends, James Leo Herlihy and Lila Rosenblum, were living in Hollywood in the early 1950s, and both tried unsuccessfully to introduce a touch of reality into her thinking.[26]

Irene M. Selznick was among the first producers Anaïs contacted, and her response was typical of most of the rest. Selznick said politely that her "overall reaction" to *The Four-Chambered Heart,* which she found "extremely interesting and very well done," was that it did not lend itself to dramatizing. Anaïs was infuriated.[27]

As she was "absolutely determined to be famous," Anaïs did not hesitate to approach any celebrity she thought might further her aim.[28] The next time she was in California, she invited Christopher Isherwood (whom she had never met) to visit her at Sierra Madre, the tiny mountain village one hour's drive east of Los Angeles where the Forestry Service had stationed Rupert. Isherwood said that having read the books she pressed upon him, he did not see any as a movie, "If only for the simple reason that [they are] about people whom movie goers would not understand."[29] She was disappointed in his "obtuseness."

She sent off her annual application to the Guggenheim Foundation, then wrote to the Ford Foundation to ask if they supported writers and filmmakers. Nothing came of either request. The only positive response she got was one she did not pursue at the time: a young literary agent named Gunther Stuhlmann asked if she had any work in progress. As she was hurrying off to Sierra Madre, she did not reply.

Rupert told his superiors that his wife had a very important writing job that took her to New York several times each year, so he was allotted married quarters, a one-bedroom beige stucco cabin with green trim in a cluster of others that differed from it only in the number of bedrooms. Each cabin was functionally furnished, the only graceful element the fireplace, much used during the cold, clear, mountain nights.

Each wife was as much a member of the Service as her husband. "Mrs. Anaïs Pole," as she was known in Sierra Madre, described her life during the only tranquil time she had to write, on an airplane crisscrossing the country, on flimsy Japanese paper she now used as a diary because it was light and took so little space: "1 hour in the kitchen—dishes, cleaning, burning garbage. 1 hour of 1 room a day, thorough cleaning, sweeping rug, mopping, cleaning pipes. 1 hour of errands, shopping, shoes repaired, cleaning suits, tailor, post office. 1 hour sewing or mending socks and underwear. 1 hour for myself, bathing, care of face, hair, etc. A little while for letter writing, reading if I'm tired, and then another hour in the kitchen to cook dinner."

Tourists thought nothing of barging in, searching for everything from directions to a nature trail or a drink of water and a bathroom. There was a small swimming pool behind the quarters, and Anaïs swam for exercise every day, one of her few pleasures. Even there, she was interrupted by tourists.

Her life with Rupert was rigidly scheduled: every Monday night they drove to Pasadena or Hollywood to see whatever B-feature was playing, for Rupert liked the act of "going" to the movies but was not really interested in what he saw. On Tuesday, he played his viola ("not too exactly, but with fervor . . . he does not practice") in chamber music with friends in their homes. When the Pasadena Orchestra gave a concert, he and Anaïs attended. On Wednesday, they saw another movie. Thursday was reserved for dinner with his family and more music, for the Wrights played quartets after eating. On Friday they saw another movie. On weekends, Rupert was frequently on duty, answering tourists' questions, guiding nature walks, and giving lectures about local flora and fauna while Anaïs stayed gratefully alone in their quarters. After just one week in Sierra Madre, she felt "stupified and diminished, colorless and empty," and more than ready to return to New York.

Rupert was as demanding a taskmaster as his superiors. Each time she returned with her "earnings" from the magazine articles, lectures, and whatever else she was inspired to invent to explain Hugo's monthly allowance, Rupert took it all and socked it into a savings account for the house he intended to build. "I have to ask him for money," she complained.[30]

There were other tensions, centered around his family, when Reginald Pole moved from Arizona to Los Angeles. At first Anaïs liked the old man's quirky personality, but soon tired of how he dropped in unannounced to stay for meals and then long after, nattering nonstop about his various ailments. Anaïs dreaded hearing the telephone ring in the middle of the night, summoning her and Rupert to the transient hotel where Reginald lived because he had imagined another of his never-ending stream of medical emergencies.

When Rupert finally summoned the courage to introduce Anaïs to Helen and Lloyd Wright, both detested her on sight. Anaïs recorded their reasons: "I was a married woman, older than Rupert (they did

Reginald Pole, Anaïs, and Rupert *(carrying Tavi)*, evacuating during a forest fire in Sierra Madre.

not know how much older), an artist, and all artists are egocentric and foreign, and there is far too much sex in my books."

At first she accompanied Rupert to their Thursday dinners, but their hostility mounted rather than lessened as time passed. Anaïs gave up and sent Rupert alone because she did not want to become the cause of a rupture between him and his parents, but she also sent a long letter to Helen Wright explaining why she would no longer be there.

In her letter, Anaïs could not resist using the words with which Helen Wright greeted her the first time they met: "You are not the woman we had dreamed for Rupert." However, she added, she was the one he chose. The letter also contained the most exaggerated lie Anaïs ever told, and one which would lead her into a legal morass from which she never extricated herself. Anaïs told the Wrights that she had divorced Hugo in Mexico. For Rupert, she invented a complicated story that a divorce was in progress, but complications concerning her citizenship had arisen and the process was stalled. She persuaded Rupert that, after almost thirty-two years of marriage, she was still a resident alien who could be deported at the whim of the United States government, and that the divorce could not be approved until she satisfied the residency requirements of the United States, Cuba, and Mexico.[31] She said this meant that she had to exit and return from the United States several times each year in order to keep her status legal, which gave her an excuse to go to Mexico with Hugo whenever she wanted.

Each time Rupert met her at the airport, she braced for his barrage of questions about her divorce. As one flight landed, Anaïs wearily listed the major lies she had used in the past five years: "Americanization, divorce, jobs, lectures, magazine work, publication of my books, Christmas holidays with my family, illness of Thorvald in New York hospital, problems with *Spy,* disguises, metamorphosis to cover my trips, my other life." She clutched her huge, heavy, "much travelled grey suede and black leather handbag" as they walked through the terminal, refusing to let Rupert touch it: "if spilled accidentally [it] would throw on the ground proofs of my deceptions—travellers checks I can't explain, money, Cuban passport, etc. etc. It is the bag I carry and watch over."

"No," Anaïs protested, "I cannot live this way." But for the rest of her life, she did.

28

The Trapeze

No matter in which direction she flew, Anaïs was exhausted when she boarded the plane, but several martinis gave her energy to write throughout the pre-jet twelve-hour flight. Almost always, she described her precarious double life with two men and wrote a litany of complaint about each.[1]

The affair was in its fifth year, and she was as amazed by its longevity as were the few trusted friends who knew of its duration.[2] With Rupert, she lived from one visit to the next, thinking he was only interested in "a few years of fun" before he threw her over for "the American girl and *Time*," his two major interests. She was never so aware of her forty-eight years as when they were at parties and he flirted with every nubile beauty in sight. And she despaired each day when he arrived for lunch or dinner, kissed her briefly, then turned on the radio full blast to listen to what she called "the commentators" and bury his nose in *Time*.[3]

But as nothing had separated them in five years, and even though she despised their daily life, she began to think they might never part. The relationship satisfied her as no other had ever done, even though she resented having to construct a "web of lies, lies, lies" to join a man whose "life is small," who was "only equal to manage the small kingdom," and whose "main desire is for a house built out of his own hands." She could not explain what led her to return to him time after time.

The young, beautiful Rupert with whom she agreed to cross the country in an open car, the shining boy with the "nomadic impulses, the quest of the marvelous and the strange," was now a weak and insecure man thickening around the middle, his mind "poisoned by the commentators," sick of forestry and afraid of the larger world because he did not know how to do anything else. It was hardly the romantic passion she envisioned when they first set off in Cleo.

Each time she left Sierra Madre, she told herself it would be for the last time, that she had broken her last Arden-manicured fingernail polishing a floor on her hands and knees. But leaving Rupert was sad and painful, compounded because she always flew to New York via San Francisco, resuming her life with Hugo by first visiting her mother and brother. In 1950 Joaquín joined the faculty of the Music Department at Berkeley (he would eventually become chairman), and Rosa lived with him. Anaïs was there for Rosa's eightieth birthday, and the flight to New York was all the more reflective as she relived her past life.

As the plane droned steadily onward, she thought about the life she had just left and wondered why she had such a "compulsion" to return to it. Despite several decades of evidence to the contrary, she believed that she would leave Hugo; but then, she wondered, why was she so afraid of what life with Rupert entailed? She listed the reasons.

First of all, he nagged about money.[4] His salary was $250 per month, and he expected her to live on $200. The extra $50 went into the bank, along with the $400 she received from Hugo. If Hugo was short of cash and she brought back less, Rupert scolded her for not "working" hard enough at her various "jobs." Then the Forest Service instituted a new decree: married rangers would have to pay for hitherto free housing. Rupert's cabin was assessed a rent of $100 per month, and he was upset to think of his savings being depleted by that amount. His solution was to tell Anaïs that she simply had to "earn more" each time she went to New York.

Hugo had taken back Tía Antolina's "gift" when some of his investments failed, so Anaïs no longer had access to what had been her own money. Once again he doled out her allowance each month. The irony of having to wait sweetly for one man to give her money that a second took away without a qualm did not escape her. "No wonder neither of them wanted an American wife," she noted bitterly on one of the few occasions she claimed her Cuban heritage, but then only long enough to blame it for her submissive docility.

Within a scant two years after Hugo's initial largesse, his financial situation plummeted alarmingly. He was forced to unload his stock in the Brazilian mines, not for money but for other stocks that soon became worthless. He had indulged himself by buying an airplane in Brazil and it was repossessed. He made other disastrous investments in New York so that, by the beginning of 1954, his initial $150,000 capital had dwindled to $64,000, and he and Anaïs were in their fifties with every possibility of a long life before them.

To preserve his capital, Hugo was now dipping into Anaïs's $50,000, much of which she had dissipated on expensive flights, trips to Acapulco, and all the self-pampering on which she gorged when in New York. As a way to curb her expenditures, Hugo made a sudden, startling decision that added enormous complications to Anaïs's life: he decided to let her manage their household. Each time the plane landed, as soon as Hugo collected the luggage and tucked her into the luxurious convertible he had bought for himself, he demanded an accounting of their finances. She always knew that the minute she gave her report he would shriek and tear his hair at how alarmingly the money had diminished.

Their discussions followed a ritualistic pattern that always ended with Hugo's declaration that they could no longer afford expensive "cures" such as her "California ranch," for somehow she persuaded him that she lived in an isolated mountain cabin on a vast ranch run by an eccentric woman who had no telephone and required her paying guests to live in quiet isolation.

Anaïs's way of dealing with the lies she had to invent was to tell as much of the truth as possible without telling all of it. When Rupert, obsessed with accumulating money, said they could manage with the quirky Cleo and sold the Chrysler convertible Hugo gave to Anaïs, Anaïs told Hugo that she sold it because the eccentric ranch owner did not allow cars on the property. She said friends in the village of Sierra Madre drove her to the post office each day to get her mail and took her to Hollywood or Pasadena when she wanted to shop or see a movie.

After Helen and Lloyd Wright grudgingly mellowed, she told Hugo that her friends the Wrights invited her to spend holidays with them. When the actress Anne Baxter, Frank Lloyd Wright's granddaughter and Lloyd's niece, insisted on hosting her extended family, Anaïs told Hugo that Anne also befriended her. And when Hugo feared that she was too isolated, she invented a nonspecified "friend" who invited her to chamber music concerts several times each week. Thus, she told Hugo a great deal about her daily life just by steering clear of conversational shoals that included a male companion.

It was more difficult to create plausible lies from New York, as Anaïs needed all sorts of checks and balances to calm the ever-jealous Rupert, vigilant for evasions and contradictions. She told him she never saw Hugo because he was bitterly estranged since she instituted divorce proceedings. Sometimes she told him she stayed in the apartment Larry Maxwell kept over his shop, which Rupert could not telephone because Maxwell's phone was permanently disconnected. Rupert's letters, however, could be (and were) sent to the bookstore. She used the same story about lodgings by sometimes substituting Eduardo (he had no apartment in New York during these years).

Some years later, when Daisy Aldan and Marguerite Young became members of Anaïs's "underground" who provided cover stories and alibis, she did give Rupert their numbers.[5] No matter what hour he called, Anaïs had either "just stepped out," or was "working." Quickly, they dialed West 9th Street, and Anaïs scrambled to the pay phone on the corner. It was expensive to call Sierra Madre, but she made a fortuitous discovery: a lead washer was the same size and weight as a quarter, and best of all, a package of 100 cost only $1.98. After a certain time, however, she had to roam farther afield in search of pay phones, for inspectors staked out her favorite spots, hoping to catch the perpetrator of the blank duds.[6]

Despite Anaïs's attempt to cover every possible untoward event, things still went awry, such as the night Rupert attended a party in Hollywood and some of the drunken guests teased him about what Anaïs did on her trips to New York.[7] One pressed a slip of paper into Rupert's hand with a New York number and urged him to call it. He did, but only after returning to Sierra Madre.

Three people were startled when the telephone rang in Hugo's apartment between 3 and 4 A.M.: Hugo in his bed, Anaïs in the second bedroom, and Jim Herlihy on the living room sofa. Hugo had started modern-dance lessons with Lavinia Williams and her company and damaged his back muscles in his enthusiasm. He was immobilized by traction, and Jim, who had neither job nor apartment, volunteered to nurse him. Rupert's call shrilled from the bedside phones of all three, and they all picked up the receivers, so Rupert heard three hellos. "I'll take it," Anaïs said coolly, "it's for me." She calmed Rupert by telling him part of the truth: Hugo's dancing mishap became a serious fall with the threat of lifelong paralysis. Carefully omitting Jim, she said the other male voice belonged to the worried doctor, who was spending the night in vigil.

Rupert accepted her story. The next morning Hugo did the same when she invented a former mental patient who also lived on her mythical Sierra Madre ranch and was infatuated with her. Jim watched her performance in open-mouthed amazement. Privately he told her that the wrong "twin" (as they called each other) was planning a career on the stage.[8]

He began to use her expression for the double life, a "trapeze," and urged her to extricate herself: "Whatever happens, remember that your work is far more important than the trapeze. . . . If something happens that you should tumble from [it], remember you have already spread a large net underneath yourself, of friends, and again, the work."

As time passed, and she did nothing to ease the burden of keeping two men happy no matter how great the expense to her health and sanity, Jim tried again: "I hope you can do something on that end of the tightrope that will keep Hugo from expecting you so often. New York is good for you, but the frequent trips are not. Make up something about a motion picture scenario. You can always say the deal fell through at the end. The going to and fro must be a terrible strain."

She was troubled again by the "fibroid," or "fibrone," as she called it, an ovarian cyst that had been diagnosed several years previously and was supposed to "dissolve itself." Either it had not, or she was having psychosomatic symptoms, for the area where the right ovary was located was as painful as when her appendix was removed and the incision failed to heal. Dr. Jacobson inserted a "crystal graft" just above the painful area, which only made it worse.[9] There was always the unthinkable, that it was not a benign growth, but if this occurred to her, she did not write of it nor did she seek other treatment.

She continued to see Clement Staff each time she was in New York, but their sessions had fallen into such a routine that any resolution seemed impossible: she always raised the same old questions and he proffered the same old answers. She told Staff she could not continue the highwire balancing act and he told her there was an easy solution: to dismount from the trapeze. She said she could not leave Hugo ever, nor could she leave Rupert until she found another woman to take her place. Staff said it was not her responsibility to sacrifice her health, spirit, and possibly her life, just to keep two grown men happy when both were perfectly capable of managing on their own. Had each not proven it by existing quite well when she was away with the other? Whatever it was she wanted from Clement Staff, most likely his undivided sympathy for her selflessness and sacrifice, she did not get it. So she looked somewhere else.

When Hugo's back healed and he began to travel again, Anaïs suggested that since he paid his analyst whether he attended sessions or not, she might as well take the hours he did not use. Hugo mounted what was for him a major protest. He had been in therapy with Inge Bogner for more than six years and believed he was making excellent progress; he certainly did not want his wife to interrupt or complicate it. He was frankly relieved that Anaïs could not sway Clement Staff and he wanted her to remain with him. Several weeks later, however, Anaïs went to "the woman analyst who has done so much [for Hugo] and has so much influence over him."

Aside from her dissatisfaction with Staff, part of the reason Anaïs wanted to see Inge Bogner was simple curiosity, because the woman analyst had effected so much change in Hugo. He was quite different from the gloomy, lumbering old man who wanted to nap after dinner and go to bed early. Now, besides his modern dance, he was playing the guitar again. When Anaïs was away he gave dinner parties after which he showed either his finished film (*Ai-Ye*) or footage from the one he was currently shooting (*Bells of Atlantis*). He made friends in the New York film community, and several were involved in his new work. The gifted cinematographer Len Lye was demonstrating new techniques for superimposing several different images onto one film, and the young electronic sound makers Louis and Bebe Barron were composing new music specifically for his project. Hugo was frequently backstage when Judith Malina and Julian Beck's Living Theatre performed. He befriended the Cuban artist Wilfredo Lam, and gave a huge party for him to which he invited a variety of new friends, including composer John Cage, anthropologist Carl Withers, and literary agent Frank Dobo. The dancer Pearl Primus insisted Hugo was so talented that he must join her on a European tour. And Hugo even had a brief affair with a young dancer in Lavinia Williams's company.

The affair shocked Anaïs, even though she pretended to be glad that Hugo was capable of being intimate with another woman.[10] In order to accept it, she needed to devalue Hugo, so she wrote of how unspecified persons told her he frightened the young woman with his violent lovemaking. The underlying current in her remarks was the fear that if Hugo could find emotional and physical satisfaction with other women, he might no longer need or want her. It marked the beginning of one of the recurring periods throughout the next decade in which she lavished attention upon Hugo and insinuated herself back into the center of his life.

Her shock at his affair was coupled in equal parts with surprise when she saw how so many people genuinely welcomed Hugo and enjoyed his company. If Inge Bogner had done so much for him, she reasoned, then perhaps the same could be done for her.

Dr. Bogner was a medical doctor with a specialty in psychiatry, a Catholic refugee from Nazi Germany whose family had long been active in socialist politics and humanitarian causes.[11] She received patients in her brownstone apartment on E. 94th Street, where she lived with a husband some years younger than she, the budding actor and opera singer Martin Sameth. Bogner (as Anaïs and Hugo called her) received patients in a large room that opened onto a small backyard garden. An alcove held a desk at which she never sat and several bookcases filled not with psychiatric texts but with fiction and poetry. The main room had a Yin/Yang quality about it, for everything was black or white and very soothing. As her patients talked, Inge sat quietly knitting. When necessary, she stared into their eyes, sometimes disconcertingly, as one was glass and she seldom blinked. Her patients were frequently puzzled at the way she remembered the most minute details of their testimony, for she never took notes and kept no written records.[12]

Inge Bogner intuited something about Anaïs Nin that Clement Staff did not: that she needed both men in separate parts in order to have one who satisfied her wholly. Indeed, when Anaïs first described Rupert to Bogner, she used the same words she wrote in the diary in 1947: he was a "young Hugo," probably the idealized Hugo she wanted but did not get when they were young. She confessed to wanting to adore Hugo in the beginning of their courtship and the years just after their marriage, to idolize and idealize him, but his lack of sexual knowledge and general physical clumsiness frustrated her at every turn. It did not help that he so idolized her that he was incapable of giving her the passion she wanted but treated her instead as a pristine madonna whom he simply could not violate. All this she told to Bogner.

Anaïs with Eric, Helen, and Lloyd Wright.

When she met Rupert, she knew from all her affairs that men differed only in the degree of kindness and understanding they offered. She knew exactly what kind of lover she wanted, and Rupert was experienced enough to fill the role. He also gave her the same unstinting adoration as Hugo, and no matter what the truth of her other relationships, she convinced herself that he was the first, and the only, to give her sexual fulfillment.

So with each man she now had exactly one half of everything she wanted. Hugo was rich, and he lavished money and gifts on her. She had all the beautiful clothes she wanted—and yet, because she lived in perpetual fear of discovery, she bought little because she was determined to fit everything that mattered to her into the two suitcases she was permitted on each flight. Hugo took her to Acapulco, where she stayed in the most luxurious hotels. He made her the star of his films and told everyone that he owed his every artistic achievement to her. In New York, Millicent the maid came every day to serve Anaïs's breakfast in bed and tend to the household responsibilities. Hugo also created a brilliant social life, arranging parties, dinners, and outings to fill as many days and evenings as she liked whenever she was with him. In short, Hugo gave her everything but the kind of sex she wanted, and that she got only from Rupert, who gave her a life she despised.

Inge Bogner understood Anaïs's dilemma. She commiserated and comforted, even as she tried to help her choose one man or the other. Bogner tried to bring Anaïs to some kind of peaceful resolution before any of the tragedies inherent in her dual life might erupt if discovered. All the same, Anaïs hedged her bets: she took the hours with Bogner that Hugo could not use, but she continued to see Clement Staff as well.

And the lies accreted.[13] "All divorce matters going smoothly by dint of much [Mexican] graft," she wrote to Rupert from Acapulco, where she was spending two months with Hugo. The real reason for such a long stay was that Hugo intended to complete the film that became *Bells of Atlantis.* Her lie for Rupert was that the divorce would not be legal in Mexico or the United States unless she had a twelve-week Mexican residency. Rupert accepted the story, but as time dragged on and there was no divorce, she needed a new stalling tactic. She pretended that Hugo suddenly rediscovered his deep and abiding Catholicism and refused to divorce her for religious reasons. She told

Rupert she had to begin anew with Catholic annulment proceedings. She counted on being able to use that one for at least a year.

From New York, she was forced into concocting a new tale about her "job" to replace the old one when *Flair* magazine folded. She had Rupert believing that for the past five years, she wrote unsigned articles directly into French and Spanish for foreign editions that never appeared in the United States, about everything that was new and interesting in American art, music, and literature. For these articles, she claimed the job required her to be in New York every six weeks for a period of never less than that time. To Hugo, she said she could not live in New York longer than six weeks, and only if she had the same amount of time in solitary isolation on the "ranch." But within this large framework of one general lie, many others were constantly needed to deal with unforeseen circumstances.

She persuaded trusted friends to write letters that were specifically meant for one man or the other to read. She wrote to Gore Vidal, who was in and out of Hollywood in the next decade, directing him to say that various important Hollywood producers were supposedly panting to turn one of her novels into a screenplay, and she must return at once.[14] To explain where she got the money for her airfare, she told Rupert that Gore gave her a free courtesy pass to use on any airline, a gift from his father, then president of Eastern Airlines. Jim and Lila,[15] both in New York, provided excuses for her to go in the other direction by writing that various publishers wanted to see her. Sometimes she made them telephone in the evenings when she knew Rupert would be at home, and pretended to be talking to a "boss," who urgently needed her to manage an office or cover a story.

She and Hugo wrote to each other every day, but as she was the one who collected the mail at the post office box, there was no fear of Rupert's finding the letters. The problem was how to store them, for Anaïs kept every scrap of paper she either wrote or received. In Sierra Madre, they went into the bottom of her makeup case or into a locked suitcase. In New York, she had a locksmith install a security lock on the closet in her bedroom that she called "Pandora's Box."[16] There, she kept whatever diary she was writing at the time or those she was rewriting; the rest were in a Brooklyn storage vault and only she had the key.

Anaïs wrote to Rupert several times each week, even though he hated writing and seldom replied. She created incredible tales of her difficult life in New York, of waking each day after a night on someone's sofa, rushing to a drugstore for coffee and a doughnut, and then running to her "assignments," which she invented by reading a variety of magazines, always making sure that Rupert's favorite, *Time,* was among them. Lunch was usually a "drugstore sandwich," and in the evening, she was usually "so tired" that she collapsed in someone's apartment and fell asleep early, listening to the radio and yearning for her "Darling Chiquito." Usually she enclosed a token gift with her letters, something that always came from Woolworth's and cost less than a dollar. Rupert scolded her extravagance when he wrote, so she always concluded with something about how she, too, longed for the home where they would settle forever in blissful domesticity as soon as she contributed enough to make further traveling unnecessary.

Anaïs usually wrote these letters from the sun-filled bedroom where she lay propped on pillows after Millicent removed the breakfast tray and Hugo went off to the office he rented (another huge expense) to give credibility to the independent investment counseling he hoped would replenish his lost capital. She sometimes shuddered to think what Rupert would do if he ever learned the truth about the luxury of her New York life.

It almost happened in August 1952, during Rupert's annual vacation. Anaïs tarried too long in Acapulco with Hugo because she was having a good time; then she delayed her return to Sierra Madre by stopping in Miami to help him entertain clients. They were no sooner back in New York when Hugo, accident prone all his life, fell and broke several bones in his foot, re-injuring his back in the process. He was not only in a cast but also in traction.

She thought she would not have to worry about Rupert because he was finally trying to leave the forestry service and had a job interview in Puerto Rico. He intended to fly there during his vacation, but when Anaïs did not return and he feared he had lost her, Rupert decided impulsively to drive to New York. The night before he was to arrive, he sent a telegram to W. 9th Street: "You can't say no. I will arrive Friday!"[17]

It was Anaïs's turn to panic. "I almost fell off the trapeze," she wrote during her next transcontinental flight. "I had to mobilize my underground. Lila, Lawrence Maxwell, Jim Herlihy and Millicent."

Fortunately, Rupert phoned Maxwell's bookstore before he checked into a hotel. When Larry phoned her, she left Hugo to the capable ministrations of Millicent and Jim and rushed to Rupert. As she did with Hugo, she now did with Rupert, telling him most of the truth but not all of it. She admitted that she was staying in Hugo's apartment because he was injured, stressing his helplessness. She also told Rupert an important truth: that she slept alone in Hugo's workroom. It marked the beginning of separate bedrooms for Anaïs and Hugo but not the end of their conjugal relations, which of course she never did tell Rupert.

Rupert was disappointed that she would not be with him all the time, but "took it well, was generous and compassionate." She took him to the movie "Blythe Spirit: the ex-wife haunting the second wife's house." She told Rupert that Hugo was like the ghost and Rupert surprised her by replying "but a needy ghost." For the next three days, they saw several other movies, went to museums and nightclubs, and she arranged for Millicent or Jim to spend the night with Hugo so that she might spend hers with Rupert. Each morning she arose early and tiptoed into the apartment. Although Hugo was awake and querulous, he never questioned where she had been.

In retrospect, and certainly to one who did not live it, the episode seems comic; to Anaïs it was a tragedy. She admitted that her love for Hugo was based on compassion and that she simply could not love him as she "should." Rupert's behavior was surprisingly mature throughout, and now, in an important reversal, she "placed him in Hugo's role" within her affections. The only ominous sign was that Rupert kept insisting she must forget about an annulment and get a divorce at once.

"I am immensely tired," was Anaïs's response. "I see Bogner every day. I got rid of the pain of defeat as a writer, but I can't make my life whole—or my love single."[18]

Jim Herlihy, who knew her best and loved her dearly, saw that she was at the breaking point and urged her to meet Rupert in Miami. Together, she and Jim concocted a story that Rosa was suddenly taken ill and Anaïs had to fly to her bedside. Hugo was ordered not to telephone Berkeley or even to write, because Joaquín did not want his mother to know he was so worried that he had summoned Anaïs. Hugo agreed, and Anaïs flew to Miami, met Rupert, and drove with him to Sierra Madre. She promised Hugo she would stay with her mother for one week only, but Rupert wanted to see more sights as they crossed the country and they proceeded slowly. On the day she was supposed to return to New York, she slipped away from Rupert somewhere in Arizona and phoned Hugo, saying she needed a few more days with her mother. He gave permission.

When they arrived in Sierra Madre, a letter was waiting from Jim telling her that he was exhausted by all Hugo's demands and could not live his own life until after 11 P.M., when he finally persuaded Hugo to go to sleep. Unable to face what awaited her in New York, Anaïs invented an earache and bleeding sinuses and told Hugo she could not fly for at least another week. After eighteen days away, she returned to New York and took up both her daily nursing duties and daily sessions with Dr. Bogner. Unable to sustain the strain of talking to two separate analysts, she left Clement Staff forever, and Inge Bogner became Anaïs Nin's analyst for the rest of her life.

Inge Bogner told Anaïs Nin that she resembled an accountant whose "strict Ledgers of Guilt" were kept with such mathematical precision that she, the doctor, could scarcely follow them.[19] When had Anaïs last enjoyed herself with either of her men? the doctor asked gently. Anaïs could not remember. Bogner illustrated how Anaïs slunk like a criminal loaded with guilt instead of freeing herself to live a healthy, integrated life. What was she afraid of? the doctor asked, and Anaïs could not at first reply. Sometime later she said "I must separate from Hugo and marry Rupert and stop feeling I am stealing my life from Hugo."[20] She told Bogner she had come to a decision: she wanted to live with Rupert. But the moment the session ended, she rushed to Hugo's apartment and "took up [her] duties again."

No one, it seemed, would publish her work, and she was seriously depressed about it. Nothing seemed to help her and Hugo was powerless to lift her daily gloom, which was why he relented and allowed her to consult his analyst. She did not tell him she needed Dr. Bogner because of the double life; she said it was because of the trauma involved in the constant round of refusals she encountered with her writing.

"Yes," he wrote to her in alarm after she sent several gloomy letters in succession from Sierra Madre, "there is no doubt that you have a big job to do with Bogner about your publishing and writing because it gnaws at you even when you are on the ranch."[21] Several days later, he wrote again: "If you ever want me to, I will, in my usual thorough way, put my mind and energies to the task of studying the whole selling end in the world of books and trying to find out who are the agents who could do a good job in their field or what, if anything, it would cost to promote the sales of your book. . . . I want to do everything I can to help you." Hugo wrote this even as he lay helpless in traction. Anaïs insisted time and again on the "enormous changes" she needed to make in her life, but with Hugo so willing to place himself and his considerable means at the disposal of her writing, this was not yet the time to make them.

Instead, she set to work with grimly thorough precision to put her lies in order. The various scraps of paper and the tiny pocket notebook that hitherto held her written lists of lies were too disorderly and confusing, so she bought a packet of file cards and a small folder, which she called "the Lie Box"[22] and tucked securely into the capacious handbag that held all the necessities of life for a bi-coastal commuter. She divided the cards into two sections: New York and Los Angeles. Each had several subheadings, of persons she could count on to lie for her and persons she must at all costs prevent from finding out about her double life.

Besides keeping all the lies straight that she told the two men, the Lie Box had another, equally important purpose: it helped her to maintain the diary's integrity. By the time she was settled onto the airplane and trying to re-create the details of her strained life in each city for what now passed as the diary, she frequently could not remember what was true and what she had invented. She feared she was in danger of jeopardizing the diary as "the only truly honest record" of her life.[23]

Within a month or two, the basic divisions within the Lie Box evolved into a careful network of semi-encoded names, dates, and cryptic descriptions of who knew which fiction, what lies each person had been told, or what lies each was willing to tell, and the frequent updates and revisions that were necessary to keep each story viable and believable. When the file grew too big to carry, she made two copies for the "Pandora's Box" she kept in each domicile: the locked closet in New York and, now, a locked metal box in Sierra Madre.[24] Thus, she carried only what she thought she would need at any particular time. As she went from place to place, she made double copies of new lies and invented new stories. After revising, upgrading, or discarding various persons or tales, she deposited the cards accordingly in whichever place she thought they best belonged.

The Lie Box was both a relief and a burden. It was a relief to know that she could pretend to be checking notes for one of her fictions and pull out a handful of the cards in front of either man, for neither ever thought of asking to read something until she was ready to show it. But taking care of it was a burden that curtailed what little time she had for her writing.

As for her writing, the next few years brought "continuous rejections by publishers" and "complete exclusion from poetry readings, critical estimates, debates."[25] There were numerous times throughout her life when one of her lies became the truth, and this was one: she lied to Hugo about why she wanted to consult Dr. Bogner, her double life, telling him it was because no one would publish her fiction. Now she seldom talked about the trapeze, as her sessions were devoted to her "total invisibility and failure" as a writer and to unearthing the "rebellions and terrible angers" caused by rejection.

Sitting in a restaurant with Hugo on his first night out of the cast and free of traction, she broke into tears, "weeping with a deep sense of loss . . . of myself giving up a writing nobody wants." She compared it to "a vast fracture of diamonds sinking into the sea."

Recalling the scene on the plane later that week, "toward a provincial stupid California" where "nothing tremendous awaits," she stabbed her pen savagely into the thin rice paper as she wrote about the humiliation of rejection: "A great loss [to literature], I honestly believe."

29

Literature's Invisible Woman

As 1951 ENDED, Anaïs Nin began a list of the publishers who rejected *A Spy in the House of Love,* the fourth novel in the series called by the overall title *Cities of the Interior.* There were eight swift rejection letters, but during the next two years, they doubled, then tripled. Most were sent in care of Max Pfeffer,[1] engaged by Hugo to be Anaïs's literary agent, and they reached her in Sierra Madre, where the isolation intensified her brooding and bitterness.

The rejections festered because there was no one with whom to share her anger and outrage. She had to keep up a strong positive front for Rupert because she used publishing possibilities as her most frequent excuse for trips to New York. And her mood was not elevated whenever she thought of the glamorous life Hugo led without her.

When not in Europe on business, Hugo was promoting his films to other professionals who welcomed him into their ranks. It was especially galling when *Bells of Atlantis,* starring Anaïs, was highly praised at the Venice Film Festival, which Hugo attended without her. While he was being complimented by Abel Gance for his extraordinary cinematographic eye,[2] she was in Sierra Madre cleaning up after Rupert's ancient cocker spaniel, Tavi, and being scolded by the authorities for watering the lawn by hand even though she was too frail to operate the clumsy sprinkler system.[3] "The full irony of escaping from Hugo's will to Rupert's tyranny" did not elude her.[4]

She could not, however, allow Hugo to be successful on his own: "I deserve half the credit for those films. I found the shipwreck and told him how to film it."[5]

Sulking, Anaïs composed a long litany of her failures:

> "Sabina" [*A Spy in the House of Love*] was turned down by eleven publishers. I was left out of Signet Anthology. Kimon Friar returns from Greece, arranges a series of readings at Circle Theatre (at my suggestion) and does not ask me to read. He includes Djuna Barnes in his Anthology of Modern English and American Poets but not me. I am not accepted by Bottegha Oscura. My ms. are returned by New Mexico Review, Kenyon Review, Harpers Bazaar, Partisan Review. All the doors are closing against my work. It hurts.[6]

She could have added other slights, such as Dutton's refusing to reprint her novels and returning the copyrights to her, which no other publisher wanted to buy. The only action she could take was to kill the messenger who brought the bad news, so she fired her agent. Hugo quickly found another, a young Frenchman named René de Chochor, then at the respected James Brown Agency. Still, the rejections continued with relentless regularity.

Several were brief, curt, and rude, but in one of life's little ironies, the first thoughtful and perceptive one came from Hiram Haydn, who later became the first editor of her published diaries. Haydn, then at Bobbs Merrill, was a gentleman of the old school whose letters of rejection were so kind that some authors frequently had to read them several times to make sure their work was indeed being refused.[7] "It is with great regret—and I mean that—," Haydn began his letter rejecting *A Spy in the House of Love*:[8] "First of all, there is no question but what it is an impressively written book. You are a real stylist, and the writing itself is a real joy. There are, moreover, many impressive insights into the nature of anxiety, guilt and other emotional states, insights which strike me as fresh, vivid and right. What then is the matter? I don't know how better to say it than that I am never persuaded of the authenticity of your people as people, and that the various values, symbolic or metaphorical, that they have do not, for me, compensate for this lack as I see it and feel it."

The other rejections fell into distinct groups. John Farrar, of Farrar, Straus and Young, represented the first: "The trouble is we already have several writers . . . who require the same belief, investment and intention for the long-time pull. The decision had to be: were we prepared to add another? . . . The answer is that, in fairness to you, we don't think we can offer the kind of publisher-author relationship your work both deserves and requires."[9]

A second group simply did not like her writing. James Laughlin did not find the novel "up to the standards of her earlier work."[10] Stanley Kauffmann, then at Ballantine Books, "watched her characters with interest, but not often with emotion . . . somehow I felt [the writing] was never addressed to me."[11]

A third group, represented by Coley Taylor of Pellegrini & Cudahy, was puzzled by "the tenuous continuity of erotic confusion." Like several other publishers, Taylor turned from "sympathy with the heroine in the beginning" to "indifference" to her and her fate. He thought her private adventures boring, even though beautifully written.[12]

Taylor's letter hinted at the one alarming theme lurking in all the rejections. Pascal Covici of Viking raised it directly: Nin's "romantic fantasy" was unpublishable because of its "erotic subject matter," which the censors were sure to ban. Covici thought it would be best published by "some small private press . . . in a limited edition." Theodore Purdy of Putnam's echoed Covici, writing that some of the passages were "almost pornographic."[13]

In Sierra Madre, Anaïs Nin "began to rage," specifically at writers whose work she felt covered many of the same themes as hers, and who were being published while she was not, such as Carson McCullers, Paul and Jane Bowles, and Jean Stafford, and was especially upset that "Tennessee Williams and Truman Capote are reigning." She also made an ominous comment hinting at trouble to come, that James Leo Herlihy had just sold his first story to *Discovery* magazine while she remained "The Invisible Woman of Literature."[14]

She paid attention to the criticisms in the more reasonable rejections, for she spent the early part of the summer of 1952 in Sierra Madre revising the novel. She was able to work because she made Rupert hire a cleaning woman two half-days each week. He objected to spending the money, but she threw a tantrum, as she now did whenever she really wanted something; confronted with her violence, he gave her what she wanted.[15]

"I am no longer angry," she wrote as she not only revised the text but, at the end of each day, wrote a critical analysis of how she arrived at her revisions. She concentrated on the Lie Detector and simplified the design of the entire novel, incorporating more fully the passages about guilt that pervade this work into the character of Sabina, what Nin called "reabsorbing the Lie Detector."

As she worked, she began to meditate about what she wanted the corpus of her writing not only to be in her own time, but also to represent in posterity. She pondered why she so stubbornly insisted on staking out a position for herself on the periphery, so to speak; why she could not bring herself to write the kind of literature the American public wanted to read; and most of all, why she could not make the changes in style and content that would lead to publication.

Nin's technique for creating fiction consisted of lifting passages about herself and others from the diary and then melding them into characters whose real-life antecedents she hoped would not be recognizable. She did not always succeed, as when Hugo erupted in fury over Rango (Henry) in *Ladders to Fire,* or when several critics speculated about her real-life father in *House of Incest.* In retrospect, it was probably her greatest misfortune as a creative artist that the diary loomed so large in her imagination, that she was so strongly the center of her own world. These two factors, prominent in everything she wrote, together ensured that she would never really ascend into the realm of pure creativity that is the hallmark of great fiction. She was never able to free herself from what one might well call the plodding literality of mining her own life which, in her fiction, resulted in only occasional treasures.

The writer Anaïs Nin was well aware of how much about herself and her relationships she refused to transpose into fiction, but she felt that her reason was sound. She believed that fiction was successful only when the author retained "a feeling of protection which is derived from mystery."[16] How could she write more about Sabina's marriage, she asked rhetorically, when it would only lead to revelations about hers with Hugo? No, she concluded, there was simply no way within her fiction that she could ever "tell all." Her readers would have to be content with whatever heavily transposed parts she chose to give of herself.

The Sabina of *A Spy in the House of Love* is another of Nin's unfulfilled women who enter into erotic involvements with a succession of men. Sabina's swirling cape (which Anaïs Nin herself wore with great panache) was supposed to represent both physical cover and emotional containment for a woman who concealed myriad aspects and many different facets of her personality beneath it. Like

Hugo with Anaïs, Sabina's husband, Alan, adores her but turns a blind eye toward her peccadillos. Also like Hugo, Alan is more father than husband, thus both frustrating and complicating Sabina's feelings for him. Each of Sabina's men is more disappointing than the last, and she gives nothing of herself to any of them. In the end, she is a collection of shattered, fragmented selves, racked by guilt over the havoc caused by her total irresponsibility.

Sabina is the "spy" of the title, a woman who telephones a man known only as the Lie Detector to invite him to follow her, teasing and taunting as she urges him to discover her illicit relationships and reveal her for the fraud she knows herself to be. This was, in the 1950s and remains so today, the most controversial aspect of the novel and the one that caused most publishers to reject it. Originally, the Lie Detector was a "fantasy personage," a projection of one of the many different emotions that engulf Sabina. But because so many publishers were perplexed by the shadowy entity, Nin "sacrificed the fantasy personage" as she "simplified the design, made the sequences more obvious [and] clarified Sabina's motivation."[17] She wanted the Lie Detector to represent "the subjective identification with what one feels [and] what Dandieu calls 'the primitive and childlike emotional participation.' " In Nin's mind, "When Sabina telephones at random to the Lie Detector to invite him to track her down, inviting pursuit (as a criminal does), the Lie Detector becomes a reality."[18] As she revised, the Lie Detector finally became a real (as opposed to imaginary) person whose only purpose is to enhance Sabina's increasing frustration, her frantic search for resolution and contentment, and her inability to achieve stasis either alone or within a relationship. The Lie Detector provides much of what is puzzling in the novel, as he allows Sabina to exhibit a self that is both sad and all-too-human in her failings. Although Nin's primary intention in this novel was to depict the inner reality of a woman's life, she has unintentionally presented a woman who struggles, albeit unsuccessfully, to forge in the larger world an integrated intellectual identity within a satisfying human relationship. *A Spy in the House of Love* is one of the first novels to deal with this theme that has preoccupied so many novelists in the last half of the twentieth century. Anaïs Nin is never given credit for being one of the originators of it, nor is her work included among its best examples.

Nin the writer struggled to understand and interpret how fiction had evolved in the mid–twentieth century, and perhaps because of her isolation in Sierra Madre, it was a topic to which she devoted long passages of diary writing. She was convinced that two separate themes had become alarmingly united, to the detriment of American literature: homosexuality and the cult of youth. She condemned them both. She judged homosexual fiction—and here she used as her primary examples writings by James Leo Herlihy and Gore Vidal, simply because she knew their work best—to be as guilty of deception as critics accused her of being: "because of fear of incrimination [they] do not tell the truth."

"Meanwhile," she continued, "the homosexuals are ruling the arts and mechanics of writing." In a precursor of some of the current arguments about political correctness, Nin condoned what she called "the preoccupation with affection for and acceptance of homosexuals on moral grounds." What she condemned was "the essential basic problem of homosexuality as a symptom of adolescence, of retarded maturity: The true degenerates are not the homosexuals for being homosexual but those who by a process of stunted growth continue to exhibit at fifty all the symptoms of awkward, aggressive, dissonant, unstable, adolescence."

For this she blamed the larger American culture with its "fixation on adolescence," rather than homosexuals themselves.

> Why should they make an effort to mature when all around them maturity is confused with aging and the American literature, Press, Psychology, is a glorification of seventeen years old period, and a ridicule, a burlesque, a primitive caricature of middle age as a physical decadence without a moment's recognition of the contribution of maturity to civilization. The cult of the child produced the type which pervades American letters—arrogant, narcissistic, intent on destroying the parent, as all adolescents are. . . .

She also observed that "only recently America has discovered that mothers and grandmothers could still enjoy a love life, be beautiful and desirable," but unfortunately this discovery was more often than not the subject of parody and ribald humor. As she approached her fiftieth birthday, it was something she thought about a great deal.

Much of her resentment was a natural outcome of her own work's rejection, but a large part of it was directly caused by her nomadic existence and her continuing inability to feel at home in any given culture. The little girl who knew three languages and therefore had three selves had become a woman who rejected them all and was at home in none. In her mind, Cubans had always been second rate, California was alien territory, and New York sneered at her. That left France, and she began to lay the groundwork for an eventual return—alone, without either man.

She thought of the critic and translator Stuart Gilbert as someone to help her, remembering his brief kindness in their several meetings before the war and his review of *House of Incest,* the first as well as the most positive the novel received. So she sent him a letter with some of her books: "The symbolic meaning of this is that I am hoping to leave U.S.A. some day for good, and that the books are slowly going out of print. The last one . . . I cannot get a publisher here for at all, and hope that I may be able to find [a publisher] in English and in France. I don't belong here, I came as a temporary visitor, and there is no great reciprocate love between U.S.A. and myself. It will be easy to emigrate."[19]

Without telling either Hugo or Rupert, Anaïs completed all the requirements, and in July 1952, took the oath of allegiance to the United States.[20] Jim, Lila, and Gore, whom she now called "The Magic Coordinating Circle" of her "underground,"[21] were the only persons she told; Rupert did not know until they began to travel together more openly in the early 1970s.[22]

Gore knew the most about her dissatisfaction with publishing and the United States, for he was the one to whom she poured it out in letters. The American publishing industry was "a world for plumbers and salesmen," and "even salesmen die of it," she wrote, in a confused reference to *Death of a Salesman.*[23] She complained that, had it not been for her "benefic husband," she would have "starved, literally as well as artistically" since arriving in New York in 1940. All she wanted now, she told Gore, was "to get out of this brutal, insensitive, unperceptive, superficial, and empty desert." It was all "such irony—this conviction coming together with my citizenship!"

Gore ignored her rantings and was among the few good friends who urged her to consider self-publication again. He suggested that she approach one of the better "vanity" presses about producing a beautiful book, then take care of its distribution and pay for it herself. He even volunteered to write a preface saying the American literary community should be ashamed to let "one of its best writers go unpublished," and to arrange for reviews by the best-known critics and her other "mighty admirers," so that they might "hurl" the novel in a "cause célèbre" at all those who scorned it.[24] He promised to "attend to all the details" of publication—short of paying for it, of course, which everyone took for granted would be Hugo's responsibility.

When Anaïs told Hugo, he did some of his thorough and careful research and learned that a publication called *New Story,* with editorial offices in Paris, would publish a section of the novel as a separate short story, but only for $1,500. He sent a check at once, and Anaïs eagerly awaited publication, which did not come. After repeated angry queries, the magazine's American editor, Robert F. Burford (no relation to Bill), sent an apologetic letter saying the manuscript had not arrived in time for the deadline. He would, however, be very happy to work out, for a second payment (unspecified, but the implication was that it should be larger), an agreement whereby the magazine "might" publish the entire book.[25] Hugo told Anaïs he could do nothing further for the time being. "It would be a marvelous life if Hugo would stop speculating and losing his capital," she noted grimly.

Anaïs thought long and hard about Gore's suggestion while she was in Sierra Madre, and wondered how she could wrest away a significant chunk of Hugo's capital, not only to get her book published, but also to keep him from frittering away the remainder of their livelihood.

So she kept on going to Rupert and the life she despised, only to discover something she had always feared: that Rupert was in the midst of a long affair with her friend Betty Berzon, and that there had been other women besides.[26] Hugo, too, had several relationships during these years, which catty persons were only too eager to report to Anaïs each time she returned to New York. It was certainly an ironic reversal, for she had been faithful to both men since meeting Rupert, and she continued this fidelity for the rest of her life, despite the many cruel stories that emerged after her death to cast her as an overpainted old harridan preying on young, beautiful, homosexual men.[27]

Drinking now helped her escape from "the terrible awareness which increases the sense of pain."[28] She wondered how much longer she could keep up the façade of being young, of how many more times she could "tint the hair so the gray won't show," and how many massages would be needed "to keep me slim and firm my body." Drinking helped her to forget that she was "forty-nine and tired." It also eased physical pain, and she was having a lot of it.

The most alarming symptom was the dull ache on her lower right side, just below the appendectomy incision. She had complained of it since 1946, but no doctor ever found anything concrete. When the pain grew steadily worse, Dr. Bogner, whose original training was in general medicine, insisted that Anaïs have a complete physical examination, including X rays of her entire torso. Anaïs suspected a tumor, but several doctors and radiologists assured her there was none, nor was there any visible cause of the back pain she suffered in the general area of her kidneys. "So," she concluded, thinking it was probably psychosomatic, "we have to accept I am presenting the symptoms of my father's illnesses. The twinship continues."

But the pain did not abate. She spent all of December 1952 and most of January 1953 with Rupert, bleeding heavily throughout. She did not put herself under the care of the local physician because she did not trust him. Also, and more important, she did not want Rupert to learn that she was in pain, for despite his five years of devotion, she still feared he might abandon her if she became visibly old and ill.

The moment she landed in New York, she consulted her own physician, who felt "a tumor as big as an orange in *right ovary,* pressing on appendicitis adhesions."[29] She consulted a second doctor who concurred in the diagnosis. On January 28, 1953, she checked into New York Hospital and "a benign cyst" on her right ovary was removed through a new incision, just below the appendectomy scar that took so long to heal when she was a child.[30] By February 9, she was at home and well enough to write a four-page letter to her mother, joking that the surgery was nothing compared to the bad food which, after a week in the hospital, "almost killed me!"

From that time on, her health was frail. She described her symptoms as "stiff aching limbs, cramps at night in my legs (rheumatic fever as a child), enlarged heart and heart murmur, chronic nasal passages irritation with bleeding . . . intermittent anemia . . . no [internal] heating apparatus, defenseless against cold and subject to several bronchitis a year."[31]

❧

James Leo Herlihy.

With Rupert so easily diverted by flirtations that their relationship seemed in jeopardy, with Hugo seemingly determined to divest himself of his capital through the most foolish means he could think of, and with her physical condition threatening to bring down the trapeze on which she shuttled between "the pillar [Hugo] and the tree [Rupert],"[32] Anaïs Nin determined that the only way to get her novel published was to pay for it as quickly as possible while Hugo still had money.

Hugo contacted Bob Burford again in March 1953, demanding his $1,500 or a firm agreement to publish the novel for that amount. Burford admitted that he had spent the money to sponsor a short story contest in the hope of building subscriptions, but that *New Story* failed anyway and he was penniless. He said he had relocated to Holland, carefully omitting that it was to elude French creditors. There, he and his partner, Eric Protter, founded Gargoyle Press. Citing higher costs for paper, printing and binding, Burford insinuated that if Hugo were to send a hefty additional payment, publication could be swift. Hugo turned the matter over to René de Chochor,[33] who contacted French lawyers and instituted proceedings against Burford and Potter. The publishers decided it was best to publish *A Spy in the House of Love* but under the imprint of their new name: New Story Books of Paris and New York, and The British Book Centre. The process of bringing out the book was neither easy nor direct, and Hugo ended up paying nearly triple his original investment.

Meanwhile, Anaïs reconstituted her mailing lists and—with Jim and Lila amending, adding, typing, and filing—prepared for publication. She kept Rupert in the dark about everything except that a publisher had miraculously volunteered to publish the novel. His first question was to ask how much of an advance she received and when could he deposit it in the savings account for his house. It meant that Anaïs had to find extra money beyond her $400 "salary," and she cadged an extra $250 from Hugo. She apologized to Rupert for the pittance.

The news from New York was no better: "Hugo says now we have to make $5000 a year to maintain our standard of living. I suggest instead we lower our standard and then we could both continue to be artists without trying to commercialize." As he had already relieved her of all that was left of the $50,000 gift (less than half remained when he took it back), she complained angrily when he engaged a publicity agent to promote his films. She made no mention of her own expenses in publishing the novel; the frequent plane trips; her massages, manicures, glamorous clothes, and Mexican vacations.

She told the diary she was "tired of the enormous price one pays for protection": "I should have started to build up my independence long ago. The status of wife is worth nothing. If I had worked I would be free today and not afraid to stand alone, as I am today."

At the same time as she romanticized life in Paris on the houseboat, she developed an irrational fear of suddenly dying. Deciding she had ten years to live, she estimated that she needed $200 a month or $23,600 to live alone. For the first time, she envisioned the course of action that would dominate the rest of her life: selling the original diaries and manuscripts. She had already had several overtures, among them one from Katherine Winslow, a Chicago book dealer specializing in Miller's work, who offered to place Nin's manuscripts at Northwestern University and to buy all remaining copies of her hand-printed novels.[34] Jim teased Anaïs: "not bad for a writer nobody wanted."[35]

In a curiously ambivalent gesture, after years of complaint about Rupert and the life in California, after laying careful (if impractical) plans to leave both men and return to Paris, after plotting how she could become financially independent, Anaïs Nin did something to chain herself firmly to her transcontinental trapeze for the rest of her life: she married Rupert Pole without divorcing Hugh Guiler.[36]

In March 1955, she and Rupert were driving through the Arizona desert, returning from a holiday in Mexico. As they drove through the dust and heat, Rupert began another harangue. Anaïs explained in the diary what she did and why on her next flight to New York:

> I exhausted all the defenses I could invent: that I was neurotic, that I did not want marriage, that I wanted to stay as we were, that I wanted to protect him from a feeling of responsibility, etc. To no avail. I know the persistence of his obsessions. I also feel tired of resisting, feared the effect of my frustrating him, felt also an ironic mockery of the laws, a feeling that if this had to be a source of irritation and insecurity, oh well, to hell with laws, I would gamble once more, one more gamble . . . and gamble on the consequences.

It did not occur to her that he would bring the car to a screeching halt in the next little one-street town they drove through, directly in front of a sign saying ARIZONA JUSTICE OF THE PEACE. Once more, she tried to stall, saying she did not have her divorce papers, she was not a citizen, whatever—but Rupert left her sputtering in protest and went up the walk and into the house. She described how he came back: "radiant, his eyes blazing, laughing, his lips humid, his smile incandescent: 'Let's get married!' "

She thought he was "so irresistibly beautiful . . . so happy" that she felt "like a murderer to kill his joy." But she did, persuading him that she was too tired, dirty, and dusty from the trip to enjoy a wedding day. A week later, Rupert insisted on driving back to the same tiny isolated town of Quartzsite, which she described as "so extremely ugly it was humorous."

She was the observer of her own life as the preparations for the ceremony began. She found great symbolism in "the minister's name, Mr. Hardley, a fat German man, joyous talkative [with] a beer barrel stomach,"[37] who excused himself to put on a freshly starched white shirt but no tie or jacket. She thought it ironic that the huge book on the ceremonial table between her and Rupert was *The Arizona Criminal Record* and laughed silently, thinking her name should be on the very first page. But as the ceremony began, she thought again, "oh what the hell"; she was about to make "one person happy in the present and that is a great and rare achievement."

Anaïs was "elated by the danger, the adventure, the challenge once more, the overcoming of difficulties, the chess games with the world's literalness." She could see clearly "all the absurdities" in what she had just done, but still insisted she had participated in the ceremony "with the utmost purity and wholeness," fully aware of its "deeper ritual." Throughout the past eight years, she had felt "so deeply married to Rupert so many times," and this ceremony was just "one more" of those times.

But as they drove back to Sierra Madre so that she could cook Rupert's dinner and he could get to bed early because of work on the morrow, she thought about something else: "New York Friday, and the difficulty of leaving."

30

Acting Out the Dream

After she married Rupert, Anaïs spent one of her first evenings with Hugo at the movies watching *The Captain's Paradise.* Alec Guinness played a bigamous ferryboat captain who thought he had created the perfect domestic setup: his little boat chugged back and forth several times each week between a proper British wife (Celia Johnson) in Gibraltar and a hot-blooded, sultry mistress (Yvonne De Carlo) in Algiers. Trouble was, the voluptuous mistress wanted to don an apron and stay at home cooking spicy dinners that upset the Captain's digestion, while the prim little wife wanted to throw hers away, along with the bland British food the Captain relished, to spend her nights on the town getting drunk and disorderly. "We laughed," Anaïs dutifully recorded, "but my situation is deeper and subtler and more intricate."[1]

Everything in her life now revolved around the two husbands and her determination to be "the perfect wife"[2] for each, but unlike the debonair captain in the movie, she was terrified that her two paradises might be exposed. Anaïs knew what she had done: "what human beings only dream, I acted out. I obeyed the dream. But I was unable to free myself of guilt. And Dr. Bogner was unable to give me absolution."[3] And just as she defined her problem, so, too, did she think she had the solution: "The idea of death . . . is the answer to the idea of guilt. Guilt is punishable by death." She was convinced that wrathful vengeance was imminent and her own death would soon follow.

She could not sleep without massive doses of sedatives, and even then her rest was interrupted by frequent nightmares. When she awakened, she felt her heart pounding erratically, "as if it were tired of pumping," and her body was drenched in sweat. At first she tried to attribute these manifestations of terror to pre-menopausal hot flashes, but the way her body shook during anxiety attacks made her realize that she could not blame her condition on natural changes. When she accepted that her mind was responsible for her body's havoc, the only escape she could envision was death. Although she wanted absolution in the sense of forgiveness for her sins, she did not ever think of looking for mental peace in the Catholic religion of her adolescence; she looked rather to the religion of her adulthood, psychoanalysis.

For the previous twenty years, whatever solace and comfort Anaïs Nin found had come from her belief in the healing powers of psychoanalysis. In all her past deceptions, she had been able to expunge herself of guilt and responsibility by applying psychoanalytic concepts garnered from a scattershot collection of readings (or more accurately, misreadings of secondary sources). And when none of these helped, there was always the diary into which she could pour her casuistic versions of reality.

Now, the one fear Anaïs could scarcely bear to think of was that psychoanalysis might ultimately fail to provide what she needed, for if the gentle, nonjudgmental Inge Bogner could not grant what she desired above all else, a very Catholic form of "absolution" in every religious and spiritual meaning of that word, where else could she ever hope to find it?

Bogner told Anaïs repeatedly that absolution would come only when she accepted responsibility for her actions and dismounted from the bi-coastal trapeze once and for all. Anaïs could not dismount, for doing so would mean the ultimate failure of her entire life, an admission that it was impossible to "live the dream," which she set out to do the very first time the reality of her existence paled. Everything she did or wrote was to make the dream possible, and now the dream of the perfect life was little more than several bundles of file cards flimsily held together by dried-out, crumbling rubber bands in something she called "the Lie Box." Only her willpower and determination kept the so-called dream together, but as usual, her body rebelled and sent her fleeing to the ministrations of the analyst.

Still, she had to find a way to justify her past actions: "And yet, I gave so much to others!"—A plaintive cry but one with a certain degree of truth. She insisted that no woman before her had ever been as kind and generous, which was certainly true, but she expected these qualities to absolve her sometimes heinous behavior. She believed that her very presence tempered all past transgressions, for no other woman "has given to as many people in one lifetime the feeling of "not being alone!"

After several anxious letters in which Hugo conveyed the details of their dwindling capital and heavy expenditures, he decided to seek other clients besides the Archibald brothers and rented an expensive office at 26 Broadway. When Anaïs was in New York, their breakfast conversations were once again of stocks, bonds, and "million figures, big talk, big schemes and perhaps this time he will make it. . . . He wants me to get elated . . . when the reality is that we are living on borrowed money."[4]

She assuaged her guilt at taking so much of Hugo's money to give to Rupert by volunteering to run Hugo's many errands in connection with his films, but resisted his pleas to take on a full-time job as his official producer. Instead, she did the gruntwork, dutifully riding the subway back and forth to a remote processing studio in Queens, sometimes making several trips a day when prints were not up to Hugo's exacting standards. She trudged from one shop to another searching for whatever equipment he wanted to buy until she found the lowest price. And when she solicited invitations to speak about her work at colleges and universities, it was always in conjunction with showing Hugo's films. But no matter how much she devoted herself to his most arcane request, she did not feel an iota of "absolution." And her guilt was now concentrated into one specific fear: if she were to die suddenly, what would happen to the diary?

Dr. Bogner's straightforward advice was that she should make a will. Anaïs refused, saying she felt obligated to leave her estate, which consisted only of the diaries, to Hugo, and she could not bear to think of his reading them. Bogner suggested naming a literary executor, but

Anaïs said the only person she trusted was Jim Herlihy, her "spiritual son." She rejected him because, although sure of his devotion to her, he was "too young and not objective and he does not love Hugo."[5] She asked Bogner to accept "guardianship" of the diaries because she was the only person whom they could not hurt, but Dr. Bogner declined.

In the increasing fragmentation of her daily life, Anaïs became fixated on the diary, the only thing that rivaled the importance of the two husbands. Now she turned her full attention to its many volumes, as if by putting them in order she could do the same with her life. As always, one of the major reasons she returned to the diary had to do with the failure of her latest novel to capture the public's imagination and make her famous. *A Spy in the House of Love* sold a disappointing 1,500 copies despite all her efforts to promote it and the alarming amount of Hugo's money spent to publicize it. Anaïs was embarrassed when the owners of The British Book Centre refused to distribute it any longer.

"No more novels," Anaïs decided. "I was given enough time to write, god knows, more than anyone else and I failed at it! I think what I should do is devote the rest of my time preparing the diaries for publication. And earn my living like everybody else around me."

The problem of selecting an executor was next to nothing compared to rounding up the diaries from the many safe places where she had stashed them throughout the years. Her last sojourn in Sierra Madre had been a "double exposure month," as she started to put the few copies she carried with her into formal order. She spent as much time as she could cadge from housekeeping duties trying to organize them but was thwarted by "re-numbering, re-checking dates and re-copying."

To straighten everything out meant several trips to a bank vault in Pasadena, where half the originals were stored, followed by a hurried one-day trip to San Francisco to bring back the other half, stored in Ruth Witt Diamant's basement. This was followed by countless trips to Bekins Storage in Arcadia, where she kept the first revised copies typed by Virginia Admiral, as well as the second series of revised copies typed mostly by Lila Rosenblum, with occasional assistance from Jim Herlihy.[6]

The task of editing was especially difficult in volume fifty, which contained her "sexual adventures" in New York and Paris, the disintegration of her affair with Henry, and the beginning of the one with Gonzalo. In a curious conjunction, Henry sent Anaïs a letter asking for help in remembering some of the events of their Paris years: could she recall the name of a restaurant on the way to the Porte d'Orléans, and who was the astrologer Moricand's friend ("not Cendrars—the other one"), and what was Moricand's hour of birth.

Anaïs talked about this to Bogner, and it led to a discussion of "displacement." What upset her in Hugo was the "bad habit" she detested in herself: "He manipulates 'the facts' to suit his fantasy . . . Hugo had to confuse finances to conceal his love of gambling (stock exchange), his love of adventure (association with [financial] adventurers). No wonder he confused me (wanted to!) as I confuse him to conceal my life with Rupert."

Bogner would not allow Anaïs to shift all the blame onto Hugo and accused her of applying a "subjective vision" to her life and work. Anaïs was furious: "I get very disturbed. I'm willing to admit errors in living, not in my work. I take her implication as a threat to the integrity of my work. She did not mean that. She meant that all truth lies in the relationship between subjectivity and objectivity, not in one *or* the other."[7]

The financial problems were worsening. Hugo's primary client besides the Archibalds was now "a Mr. de Saint Phalle and [Hugo] seems to be mucking that up as well."[8] When it came time to prepare taxes at the end of 1954, it was a shock to both that the entire income of the Guiler family came from the writings of Anaïs Nin: "Royalties on Spy: $178; Lecture and film showing at Brown: $100; Lecture and film showing at U. North Carolina: $100; Reimbursement by British Book Centre on unfair charge for books Hugo paid for: $144."[9] A grand total of $522 against expenses estimated conservatively in the range of $20–$25,000.[10]

Anaïs thought of selling the diaries to a collector, just as she had earlier sold pornography to Ruder's "collector."[11] She vowed to pursue the "fantasy" of selling the diaries until it became a "concrete fact." Each time she wrote to a college or university to request a lecture engagement, she also sent a list of the diary's contents and the names of some of the persons who figured in it, hoping to entice a library to buy it.[12]

Anaïs's fear about the alarming dissipation of Hugo's capital also led to a discussion with Bogner about how she reacted as an adolescent to Rosa's steadily worsening economic situation. In each instance, Hugo and Rosa shared an optimistic view of the large sums they planned to make, both basing their schemes on commissions that were never paid. For just as the rich Cubans stiffed Rosa, so, too, did the various investors for whom Hugo played the stock market with alarmingly regular bad judgment. As if by committing his losses to paper they would somehow disappear, Hugo was now obsessed with bookkeeping, giving it the same frantic attention as Rosa, when she juggled her balance sheets so many years ago.

Anaïs's reaction to her mother's plight had been "finally to go out and get a job," but she was then an attractive girl of seventeen. Now she was a still-attractive woman of fifty-two who had never worked and had always been supported by a man.[13] All she had to offer a prospective employer was her writing, and as no one wanted her novels, her last hope was to sell the diaries. It never occurred to her that they might also meet with the same sort of rejection as her fiction. Because they were the most valuable physical possession she owned, and because nothing else was as important to her, she never entertained the thought that others might hold them in less than the same regard.

She directed her literary agent, James Brown, to bring her a collector who would buy the original diaries and, at the same time, a publisher who would buy the latest revision for "future" publication, when "certain people have died [in] ten or fifteen years." Several weeks later she noted bitterly that Brown decided he could no longer represent her and she was once again without an agent.[14]

She turned to friends for help, primarily to Maxwell Geismar. She had known Max and Anne Geismar since he sponsored a reading of her work and a showing of Hugo's films at Sarah Lawrence, where he taught. The two couples became immediate friends, but Anaïs was always shy and insecure in their presence, especially if she saw them soon after she returned from Los Angeles.[15] Anne ran a gracious home in Westchester County, but was also a woman of wide-ranging and well-informed intellectual interests; Max was a respected critic and literary scholar.

Before she left for Los Angeles in the early spring of 1955, Anaïs gave Anne and Max a large pile of the second revision of the original diary (the ones Lila typed), each inserted into a three-ring folder secured with brass pushpins. She did not tell them that these were revisions, in many instances far removed from the original diary entries. Instead, she said they were typed copies of the original handwritten volumes and made them promise not to tell Hugo they had them, as if to reinforce the veracity of her claim. Both Geismars were enthusiastic about what they read.[16]

Soon Anaïs and Max were exchanging letters. Soon they were quarreling as well because Maxwell Geismar had too much intellectual integrity to give Anaïs Nin the complete and total admiration she required.[17] Max explained that he was "genuinely concerned" to help her find a publisher for the diary, and that his comments were offered in the most constructive manner possible.[18] Anaïs actually apologized: "I set you up as a symbol . . . the Voice of America, to say what no American critic said, [to give] total allegiance. But I see now that I was wrong. You couldn't do that because you have your own integrity."[19]

In a long second letter, Anaïs tried to explain the trauma induced by American rejection of her fiction, couching her statement in the ideological language she believed Geismar espoused in his own literary criticism. Although she did not phrase it clearly nor argue it cogently, it is nevertheless an interesting appraisal of contemporary American literature. In her mind, her fiction had been rejected by a "crabby, puritanical, restrictive and punitive sour parent,"[20] which was how she described American arbiters of literary taste. Now these critics no longer mattered to her, for she insisted she had "divorce[d] America" and overcome the hurt of rejection. To prove it, she cited her new story (which eventually became the novel *Solar Barque*)[21] and said she was writing "better than ever."

Despite her stated intention to live a quiet life devoted to writing, she spent long hours talking to Dr. Bogner about her hatred of America, which was where she concentrated her anger and rage toward the literary community.[22] Bogner pointed out that Anaïs told her how she was afraid to form friendships with French writers and how it was probably insecurity that led her to insist upon writing in English and establishing the persona of an American writer when she lived in Paris. Bogner also questioned why Anaïs settled so rigidly into relationships with Henry and Gonzalo, both unsuitable lovers for a woman of her class and station and every bit as foreign in France as she. Anaïs's reply was that André Breton once called her a bourgeois banker's wife, and the remark was so wounding that she withdrew entirely from French culture and society and chose the most nonbourgeois foreigners she could find.

Bogner told her she was really inventing excuses to cover not only her insecurities but also her many different kinds of rebellion during the years she lived in France. The comment struck Anaïs as an illuminating revelation, and suddenly she remembered how often she rebelled against all things French when she lived in France, not idealizing the culture until she left it. "So," she noted, "rebellion is an important part of my personality now, and the hatred has increased in violence as I get older because I feel I have so few years to live and I am still here!"

She remembered a conversation with Richard Wright some years before in which he said he had to leave the United States because the race problem festered in him and he could not expand as a writer if he stayed. Anaïs later repeated Wright's remarks to Max Geismar, saying she feared the same nonexpansion and festering was happening to her. He urged her not to give up on herself but to try to find a middle ground between the diary and fiction. And because several French publishers had made recent halfhearted inquiries about the status of the diary, Max also urged Anaïs to consider publishing it herself rather than risk the first appearance of such an important cultural document in a possible bad translation and improper publication.[23] Anaïs disregarded his concern as excessively isolationist and jingoistic and eagerly answered every inquiry that came her way. She exchanged letters with Éditions Plon in France, but nothing came of it. As her novels attracted a small but discerning audience in Holland, she attributed comments to Geismar that she invented herself and wrote to the publisher, Methorst, flogging the diary.[24] If Methorst would buy it, she offered to "sell a novel size abridged version of the diary for two hundred dollars outright, that is no royalties." All she wanted, she wrote, was "time to revise and abridge the diary. And two hundred dollars gives me freedom from work for a month." Methorst declined her offer.

Next she tried Northwestern University, where one of the librarians, Felix Pollack, had recently invited her to lecture.[25] Anaïs refused the chief librarian's "foxy" offer to photocopy the entire diary free of charge. Wisely, she declined to let any part of it leave her hands until or unless it was sold.

She also took *Spy* and a few pages of *Solar Barque* to the producers Sam and Bella Spewack, who told her the writing was "beautiful" but there was not enough of it to warrant a screenplay. They held up as the model of what she could do, should she put her mind to it, *Bonjour Tristesse,* the new novel by the young French sensation Françoise Sagan. Anaïs was enraged by the comparison and went off to Sierra Madre to repair her wounded ego, and because she was so close to Hollywood, to pursue the possibility of reading scripts or writing screenplays.

She wrote to Georges Simenon, who had become a new favorite, asking to translate his novels and then try to sell her translations to producers. Madame Simenon replied huffily, as if instructing an illiterate child, that all translation rights were firmly held by Doubleday.[26] Always attracted to Colette, Anaïs planned next to propose an adaptation of *Chéri* to anyone she thought might buy it, but at this point her life kept her from constructive endeavor.

As soon as she arrived in Los Angeles, she fell prey to recurring nightmares, many of which featured her mother, who had died peacefully almost a year before, on August 3, 1954.[27] In the year since Rosa Culmell's death, Anaïs wished repeatedly that her mother had not died until she was able to rekindle a feeling of closeness between them, but had to admit that their last visit was an ordinary one. She and Joaquín joked over martinis, then they and their mother played canasta. The next day they talked and reminisced, and the two women sat side-by-side on a sunny afternoon while Rosa worked at her lace making and Anaïs quietly hooked a rug.[28] On Sunday, Rosa and Joaquín attended mass, as was their custom, and after lunch (which Rosa did not eat), all three took a leisurely drive into the Oakland Hills.

In retrospect, she wondered why she had not sensed that her mother was preparing to die, why she had not "given her the words of love she needed for dying." After dinner that night, Joaquín drove Anaïs to the airport for her flight to New York. Hugo met her at 6 A.M. when the plane landed and told her that Joaquín returned home to find that Rosa had suffered a heart attack. She was taken to a hospital in a coma, and died without regaining consciousness. As Joaquín was taking Rosa's remains to Cuba to be buried, Anaïs did not return to Oakland but waited for her brother in New York on his way back from the sad task.[29]

Anaïs made her personal farewell to her mother in a diary passage tinged with an underlying layer of remorse and a vague, unfocused

Anaïs and Hugo in New York, 1940s.

Anaïs, Rupert, and Tavi on the Malibu land.

anger toward both Rosa and herself: "What a burden . . . when a mother serves you, does all the menial tasks, feeds you, works for you, sews for you, but then condemns what you are!"

All her life Anaïs remained confused about where individuality ended and selfishness began. She could not sort out her conflicting emotions, and after her mother's death, directed her unfocused anger toward Hugo, even though he was a paragon of gentle kindness. For the better part of 1955, they had separate bedrooms, he having made no objection when she moved her things permanently into the second one after her mother died. She thanked Hugo for helping her through "quiet, gentle sorrowing" without demanding conjugal relations and for living "a quiet, subdued life," in which there were "no fervors, no enthusiams, no hatreds."[30]

All this paralleled the time when Anaïs Nin wrote the section of *Solar Barque* in which Lillian returned to her home and children. Just as Lillian was "struggling with the muted tones she had not previously been able to hear," so, too, was Anaïs struggling to find some muted voice within herself that would tell her what to do about her bi-coastal life.

First she had to do something about the nightmares. Rosa appeared in Anaïs's dreams as her executioner, relentlessly injecting her head with enormous needles so that she would die and Rosa could read the diaries. Anaïs awakened with palpitations and skipped heartbeats. In a cold sweat, she sat up beside the sleeping Rupert and analyzed her dream: "I am suffering from guilt. The exposure of the relationship to Miller frightens me. Discussions of selling it—no, I must burn it. Nothing is worth harming human beings. The truth cannot be told. The truth is destructive. I must burn the diary."[31]

Her terror at the possibility of the diary's contents being exposed took on a new urgency when she received a letter from Fred Perlès, then visiting Henry Miller in Big Sur. Fred told Anaïs that he had written a combination memoir and biography called *My Friend Henry Miller,* which was about to be published by the British firm of Neville Spearman Ltd. Although the publishers did not insist that he let all the living persons mentioned in the book read what he wrote about them, Fred sent it to Anaïs as a courtesy.

Anaïs was horrified. Even though Fred carefully avoided stating directly that she and Henry had been lovers, the implications were clearly there. James Brown was still representing her at the start of the ensuing brouhaha, and she took the extraordinary action of phoning him from Sierra Madre (Rupert did not permit long-distance phone calls because of the expense). Brown fired the first salvo in a letter to Neville Armstrong, one of the partners in the British firm that bore half his name, asking Armstrong to delete all references to Anaïs or risk legal action.[32] Armstrong took an equally strong position in his reply, defending Fred's kindness in showing the book to Anaïs, saying there was "not one derogatory statement against her," and that everyone was astonished that "she should now take exception to things being written that happened twenty years ago." More to the point, Armstrong wrote, the book was already set in type and changing the text would be expensive; also, the firm of Neville Spearman had just contracted for Anaïs Nin's first commercial publication in more than a decade, having judiciously purchased (with her knowledge) *A Spy in the House of Love.* Armstrong pointedly told Brown that the Perlès and Nin books were each intended to enhance sales of the other, and ended the letter with a thinly veiled threat of his own: "we hold Miss Nin's signed contract," implying that legal action would ensue if she tried to break it.

After investigating, Brown concluded that there was no legal basis to stop publication of either book. Brown, Armstrong, and their various agents all agreed that "everyone 'behaved a little peculiarly' on the Left Bank twenty years ago," and that Fred's book could not be rewritten without at least referring to Anaïs's important role in Henry's life.

Undaunted, Anaïs pressed on, imploring Armstrong, "as one human being to another," to delete her name or risk damaging "a life-long marriage."[33] As she was contractually bound for *Spy,* she tried another ploy, telling Armstrong she would not think of entrusting him with publication of the diary (which he did not want anyway).[34] And then she played her final card, offering to pay for all expenses connected with changing her name to a pseudonym and for any text that had to be rewritten.

The debate dragged on for months, and in late November, Fred pulled his agent, the writer Margaret Crosland, into the fray. She tried to soothe Anaïs, who had by then been dismissed by Brown and was firing off hysterical diatribes on a daily basis without anyone either to represent or to stop her. Crosland, who numbered biographies of Colette and later Simone de Beauvoir among her many publications, told Anaïs that she both appreciated and valued privacy and also resented the many criticisms leveled at her for writing biography "with too much regard for the subject's private life."[35] Then Margaret Crosland dangled a most attractive plum, asking Anaïs to send any of her books she thought suitable for publication in France and other European countries, for she would be happy to represent her.[36]

Finally, the matter was settled with a modicum of satisfaction to everyone involved: Fred divided the real Anaïs Nin into two separate characters, herself and an imaginary courtesan, Liane de Champsaur; Hugo paid for reprinting costs, which were considerable; and both *My Friend Henry Miller* and *A Spy in the House of Love* were published to modest success and mixed reviews in early 1956.

The episode had lasting consequences for Anaïs. She decided not to destroy the diary, but to protect its privacy to the best of her ability. Even though she thought she had arrived at her decision independently, she was really carrying out the advice given by Inge Bogner almost a year before. On her next trip to New York, she consulted lawyers from the firm of Montgomery and Marcus and arranged for James Leo Herlihy to become the diary's guardian if she died.[37] Hugo became her literary executor, with the power to arrange for future publication of all her work, diaries included, but no person other than Jim would have access to them and only he could decide what or how much of their content should be made known, and when.

Jim accepted the daunting responsibility and sent Anaïs a letter from Key West, where he was then living, saying that he had two copies of all documents and would place the one addressed to him in her handwriting "somewhere that will give double protection," and would place the one from the law firm into his customary safe-deposit box.

Rupert was more insistent than ever on building a house. With his stepfather and brother, Lloyd and Eric Wright, Rupert purchased a plot of land in Malibu where Lloyd intended to establish a family compound. Every spare moment, he dragged Anaïs to the mountainside, expecting her to help clear the thick underbrush, even when the fog rolled in wetly off the ocean. Rupert's dogged persistence made her angry, but also made her think about why she had been faithful to him for almost a decade, content with his lovemaking, all desire for other men "annihilated," no traces remaining of the years when she imitated her father's "Don Juanism."[38] These thoughts inspired comparisons with her parents, and for the first time in many years, she took her mother's side: "I wonder if my mother felt the humiliations, the enslavement, the submissive serving role of woman, and was constantly in rebellion against it, as I am. The femininity is accompanied by such a loss of prestige and power—such servitude, that assertion could only assume a negative form—ANGER."[39]

Analysis provided a breakthrough in her anger as she gave Bogner credit for helping her to see people for the first time as they really were, not as she wanted them to be. There was also a stunning revelation: "I no longer consider the ecstasy of the heightened moment to be the height of life, I can participate in day to day activities now and be happy." This thinking prevailed even in her relationship with Hugo, as they went to the theater, took walks, and talked about his films. He bought champagne to celebrate her arrival, but "he did not make love and we kissed like brother and sister."

The absence of physical contact with her husband of almost thirty-six years was "frightening: he must suffer from it, but he would not [be aware of] it." When, she wondered, could she tell him that she had made her decision, and it was to be with Rupert. "All [Hugo's] relationships fail," she noted sadly, from his partners in business to the Barrons in his filmmaking to Millicent the maid. Anaïs's judgment was that Hugo "has no close friends and no women are in love with him."

She was not entirely right in this assessment, as Bebe and Louis Barron were quick to inform her. "Hugo is better when you are not here," Bebe told her frankly. "You are too glamorous, too exciting. It makes him passive. When you are not there, then he is the handsome, the active one, radiating. He needs to be the glamorous one."[40] Anaïs's response was to continue to perform her duties as Hugo's wife in order to get the next increment of her allowance to take back to Rupert.

The California winter of 1955–1956 was extremely harsh, and Anaïs badly needed warmth. She made a happy discovery, one that took her mind off herself for hours on end: "If your soul feels the cold, you go to Sears Roebuck, Pasadena, to the tropical birds department. They keep the place very warm. It is full of bird chatter and tropical plants, flowers."[41]

There, in a flowing Indian printed cotton dress, her eyes heavily lined in black mascara, Anaïs Nin drifted dreamily up and down the aisles, as exotic a creature as the caged birds she stared at, freed for a time from thinking about her own self-imposed imprisonment, the dual cages of her doubly married life.

31

Wider Perspectives

ANOTHER DEATH—that of Hugo's mother—and money troubles marred Anaïs's pleasure when *A Spy in the House of Love* was published in England, where her work was always received with slightly less hostility than in the United States. Hugo's mother died at the end of 1955, naming him sole executor of her estate, valued at more than half a million dollars. Hugo, Johnny and Ethel each received a minimum of $60,000; Edith, who had been left only $7,000, immediately filed a claim, arguing that Mrs. Guiler's will deprived her of a fair share. Hugo filed a counterclaim, insisting that their mother had already settled more than $100,000 on Edith during her lifetime. He had finished repaying all the loans he took from his mother shortly before she died, payments that included the high interest rate Mrs. Guiler charged for every one, so Hugo felt the inheritance was his just due and had no intention of sharing it with his sister. Edith sued, winning an equal share of the estate and the right to administer the funds herself, effectively stripping Hugo of control. He fought the decree and lost, thus incurring significant legal fees. But he still had a goodly sum.[1]

Medical expenses were the main expenditure for Hugo and Anaïs. Both always had a tendency toward hypochondria, but as they aged it increased, especially in Hugo's case. He saw Inge Bogner daily and paid her a minimum guaranteed fee of $500 a month, and his other bills for dentist, druggist, and doctors were never less than $600, usually more. Anaïs's bills were equivalent, so that a minimum of $2,000 depleted their monthly capital even before rent, food, and other expenses. Everything connected with his filmmaking was expensive, and his monthly outlay usually started at $300 but was often $500 or more.

By early 1956, it was clear that they could not continue to live as they had done since he left the bank. Hugo asked for his old job back, and when told it was not available, suggested he would be willing to accept a lesser position. His former colleagues refused that request also, making it clear that he was considered unstable after his abrupt resignation.[2] Hugo decided to close the Broadway office he had just opened at great expense and go into partnership with the brokerage firm of Emanuel, Deetjen & Co., where he and his former partner, Claude de Charriere, would now be entitled Managers of the Foreign Department. The firm guaranteed to pay them a salary plus commission for a period of ten months, and to pay the rent on much smaller office space. Hugo told Anaïs he made the move in the hope of being salaried "indefinitely" because neither he nor she could bear the strain of not having a secure income.

But Hugo's new position and guaranteed income did little to lessen the strain between them, and by the summer of 1956, a serious rupture occurred. Hugo insisted that she give up California, live with him permanently in New York, and be prepared to travel to Europe at a moment's notice. It is not clear exactly what sort of business Hugo transacted in Europe, but basically it involved moving large sums of money between New York and Havana, and Geneva, Brussels, and Paris. He began to travel from one city to the next almost as frequently as Anaïs flew to Los Angeles, making his headquarters in the luxurious Hôtel Crillon in Paris, where there was always a suite filled with amenities, compliments of a manager who knew how to keep an important client happy. Hugo was a demanding guest who expected to be pampered with alacrity, and no errand, no task, was ever too difficult for the hotel staff. Every businessman at Hugo's level has an expense account, but few had one that provided such luxuries. By reading his letters carefully, one can see that Hugo paid for his time at the Crillon with much of his own money, and did so for the better part of the next decade, all the while literally worrying himself sick about how swiftly he was depleting his capital.

Anaïs was sick, too, but from the strain of trying to keep two men content. In January 1956, when she was preparing to return to New

York, she sent a list of symptoms to her doctor, requesting an appointment for a physical examination. In language more surrealistic than medical, she described how she was sometimes awakened at dawn with the "faint feeling of a tremblor," in which her heart felt as if a liquid were "trying to pass through a rough channel." At other times, she felt "a kind of suspense," followed by "a heavy drop falling in slow rhythm." Most important, however, was her statement that "on the emotional level, I have been disturbed, but I am under analysis, for six years." She also noted that menstruation ceased when she was forty-two and hot flashes troubled her ever since. In summation, she was "basically depressed, with temporary elations."[3] She did not tell Dr. Harold E. B. Pardee what she already knew: that a Los Angeles physician had earlier diagnosed a bleeding ulcer for which she now followed a special bland diet.[4]

Dr. Pardee sent the results of her examination to "Mrs. Guiler" in New York several weeks later.[5] He found her general health "good" but hinted that her problem might be other than physical. When she inserted Dr. Pardee's letter and a copy of her list of symptoms into the diary, she scrawled above it "Pseudo Heart Problems."

There were some changes in her life with both men. Anaïs suggested a "trial separation" of one year, urging Hugo to find another woman, whether wife, companion, or mistress. Hugo reacted angrily, and threatened to tear all his engravings off the walls and destroy the plates. He would not consider a separation and, weeping copious tears, demanded that she not leave him. Anaïs noted that "his pain . . . cornered me into [staying]."

For the first time since she began her affair with Rupert, there was hope that they would soon lead a life more to her liking. He had finally tendered his resignation and in September was to begin the career he held until retirement, teaching science to junior high school students in Silver Lake, the Los Angeles district that became Anaïs Nin's neighborhood for the rest of her life. She liked the fact that he would work from 9 A.M. to 3 P.M., and would not be permanently "on call" nights and weekends, as he was in the Forest Service. With three months free each summer, she hoped they would travel to Europe and Mexico.

"I am glad I had the patience to wait until he was sick of it," she wrote to Jim Herlihy, adding that since Rupert resigned, "life got a little more glamorous."[6]

In another instance of deliberately pursuing a celebrity she wished to know, Anaïs sent copies of her novels to Romain Gary,[7] the French novelist who was serving as his country's consul in Los Angeles, and his then-wife, the English journalist and travel writer, Lesley Blanch. Gary immediately put her on the list for consulate parties, but it was his wife who held the most fascination for Anaïs. Lesley Blanch was the author of *The Wilder Shores of Love,* a book that made a profound impression on Anaïs because she found so many similarities to herself in the lives of four nineteenth-century Englishwomen who traveled to exotic destinations, fell in love with foreign men, and lived life pursuing outrageous acts of freedom in love. These women were Anaïs's precursors in living out the dream, and their tales fascinated her.

So, too, did the coolly elegant Lesley Blanch, whose sophistication and savoir faire Anaïs had not seen before in Los Angeles and to whom she took at once, hoping for an intimate friendship. Lesley Blanch kept herself to herself, and what Anaïs got instead was an invitation to many large parties at the consulate and to several smaller luncheons and dinners, but never the degree of intimacy she had had with such women as Thurema Sokol or Luise Rainer.

Nevertheless, it was exciting, after so many years in Sierra Madre, to be invited to parties in Malibu and Santa Monica, where the other guests were often actors such as Mr. and Mrs. Joseph Cotten, or Gregory Peck and his glamorous French wife, Véronique. Cole Porter, old and weak, sat quietly watching as Mrs. Cotten told everyone within earshot that she was a devotee of *Ladders to Fire*. "All in all, quite cheered by wider perspectives," she wrote to Jim, who was in the process of moving from Key West to Hollywood, where he had several interesting offers to act in films and write screenplays.

Their friendship had been strained for the last several years because of Anaïs's response to his growing success. Much as she loved Jim, it was difficult for Anaïs to watch him succeed, while she, his original inspiration, suffered as her work was resoundingly ignored.

No matter how scathing her attack, nor how insulting her criticisms of his writing, Herlihy was willing to give her his unstinting love and devotion in return, telling her he would always be there to help in any way she might need him. It did not take her long to realize how lucky she was to have a friend like Jim, and by the summer of 1956, she forgave him the transgression of following his own muse instead of imitating hers, and was confiding in her "twin" just as she had in he old days.

Hugo insisted that Anaïs meet him in Havana in May for a few days of vacation after his business was finished, and then insisted she return to New York and spend the summer with him. She was afraid to provoke his anger by refusing. Things were complicated because Rupert planned to leave the Forestry Service in late June, taking a two-month holiday before he began his new teaching career, and he wanted Anaïs with him.

Now that Rupert's new job would keep him at home regularly, Anaïs needed to justify keeping a post office box to him and the move to Silver Lake to Hugo. She convinced Hugo that it was to further her increasing involvement with Hollywood film studios who were interested in making screenplays of her novels, and that she had rented Christopher Isherwood's small apartment on modest Effie Street (he actually lived in a villa overlooking the sea in Santa Monica). She also told Hugo that Isherwood stopped the mail delivery, which is why she needed a post office box.[8] Really, she needed it to keep Hugo's daily letters secret from Rupert, but she convinced Rupert that she did not want obsessive and possibly dangerous fans to know her street address.

She was never entirely secure, however. First there was the telephone, which was always listed in Rupert's name. Anaïs told Hugo she neither had nor wanted one because too many people would interrupt the isolation and tranquillity for which she came to California.

There were so many details for which she had to be constantly on guard. She had to remove the labels on her many prescription bottles so that she would not be "Mrs. Pole" in New York or "Mrs. Guiler" in California.[9] It was the same with mail, as she cautioned all her correspondents to address her as "Miss Nin," and never by either married name. Her doctors were the worst offenders, for they insisted on addressing her by the name of the person who paid her medical insurance, and that was always Hugo.

Then came the invention of "work" in Los Angeles to explain her increasingly longer absences from New York. She told Hugo that she was working with producer Jerry Wald (whom she merely met at one

Dr. Inge Bogner and her dog.

of the French consulate parties) on a translation of Romain Rolland's exceedingly long novel, *Jean-Christophe.* She also said that William Kozlenko, another producer, was interested in adapting *Spy* (she later tried unsuccessfully to persuade him to do so), and she invented an occasional job for herself as a translator of foreign texts that movie studios wished to consider (which was not how studios acquired foreign properties, but Hugo didn't know it).

Hugo, however, was adamant: he wanted her in Cuba and would not take no for an answer. So Rupert was fed stories of upheavals at *Cue,* for whom she now supposedly worked, and of how she had been ordered back to New York to oversee the offices for the summer.

And so she flew to Havana, where something was very different about Hugo, but she, who had spent her life attuned to his every nuance and watching his every move, was at a loss to explain what it was. When they returned to New York, she suddenly realized: Hugo was having an affair that really mattered to him.[10]

The tables were ironically turned, for now Hugo was imitating her behavior: he ended whispered phone conversations as soon as she entered the room; if they went out to spend a leisurely afternoon window-shopping and browsing, Hugo excused himself several times to make calls from various street corner phones just as Anaïs did when she sneaked off to call Rupert. Hugo even bought two bottles of the same perfume and gave only one to her, a trick she recognized, for she always bought two of the same thing, one for each husband. Always before, when Anaïs was in New York, Hugo canceled evening business engagements to be with her; now he invented sloppy excuses and went off so jauntily Anaïs was sure he was with his mistress.

Anaïs was baffled because Hugo, who had been both demanding and domineering in recent months, was suddenly mellow, loving, and more appreciative of everything about her, even though he seldom initiated sexual relations. After three weeks, Anaïs decided that the time might have come at last when she could talk to Hugo about their respective involvements. She had no intention, however, of dissolving their marriage: "Now that we are not lovers, he will understand. I can talk to him. We can have different relationships."[11]

Early one Sunday, when she heard him stirring, she crept into his bed and began to talk, "very quietly and tenderly, trying to say it was right that he should have a mistress since I had left him alone, and barely hinting at our freedom, my situation, pleading for his understanding and acceptance." In all their years together, Anaïs's main complaint against and her most frequent accusation toward Hugo was that he "never faced reality directly." In this instance he followed suit by going into his "usual shock." Hugo shouted, "What did you expect me to do, to live without your desire?" And then began to bellow in outrage: "I must see Bogner. I have to talk to Bogner. I can't bear it." He would not let Anaïs continue the discussion. Instead, he curled into a quivering mass and was so distraught that she spent the rest of the day trying to comfort and reassure him, to keep him calm until he could call Dr. Bogner on Monday morning.

"He failed me in the same way he had all his life," she noted bitterly. "He didn't behave like a man, but like a child." All weekend long he repeated the phrase that Anaïs first heard so many years before when she told him about John Erskine: "I died." And then he began the litany of all his "deaths" (which were her fault) when he broke with his family to marry her, when he chose to go to work in London and she would not leave Paris, and finally, a whole host of times he "died" when "they" (to his credit, not "she" alone) did not give each other what each wanted most from the relationship.

The next day, besides seeing Hugo, Dr. Bogner scheduled a second emergency session for Anaïs, who was astonished at how strongly the analyst disapproved of what she had done: "[Bogner] reminded me she had told me Hugo would never be able to face a separation, but I said there is no question of a separation. If he has a mistress surely he can face that I should have a lover."

Hugo could not face the fact that she had a lover. His moods alternated between fury (at the lover) and fear (that he would lose her), and Anaïs spent the next three weeks "helping Hugo, who did not help me." Anger (that he could not accept her lover) fueled her reaction to his response much more than fear (that he would cut off her money), and she insisted that she would not allow him to "withdraw, sulk, etc.," but that they must face the predicament together: "Why do I accept [a mistress] and not you [a lover]?" The name of this lover, however, remained her secret: Hugo did not ask and she certainly did not volunteer the information.

"So once more, lies," Anaïs noted on June 27, during the flight back to Los Angeles. Hugo had banished her, telling her to return to Los Angeles and her lover and not to come back to New York until or unless he summoned her. Because he was a gentleman, Hugo agreed to continue her allowance, but he made her promise that she would not allow the unnamed lover to move into her apartment, nor would she at any time share permanent quarters with him. Blandly uncaring by this time, it cost her no emotional pain to make such a promise.

"I have speculated on your trips for years," Hugo said.[12] "Why didn't you merely ask me, I would have told you," Anaïs replied, all the while thinking that if he had asked, she would have told him "only the smallest fraction of the truth," that she had taken a lover "only recently." And then she realized what made her angriest of all about Hugo: "That [he] should be *now* what he should have been when we first married: gay, assured, fond of going out, of pleasure—which may have changed our whole life and marriage."

Her first few days with Rupert made her think she might at last be freed of the guilt about Hugo that had made her angry and ill. "But of course I wasn't," she noted sadly. "I spent my time writing him comforting letters."

Desperate to resolve the dilemma and fearful that "the mediocrity of our life is sapping at the relationship," she tried to persuade Rupert to move to New York and look for a teaching job there. He refused with the usual excuses: his father was old and ailing; his ancient cocker spaniel was fourteen and dying; teaching in New York would not help him to become certified in California; and most of all, he was determined to build a house. There was nothing to be done. She had either to accept him as he was or to give him up, and she was still too dependent on him sexually to take such a drastic step. There was always the fear that Rupert might find out she was a bigamist, but she simply put that fact out of her mind.

Anaïs knew finally, once and for all, that neither man would change his life one whit. She had two choices: either to accept life with both or break with one.

"Today I had to look at my angers in the face so they will no longer poison me," she wrote. She had made her decision: she would keep up the high-wire trapeze act as long as she could.

32

The Meaning of Freedom

IN THE FALL OF 1956, Anaïs Nin suddenly realized that she had produced only eighty-four pages of new writing in two years, and fewer than half were good enough to see print. She had been trying to finish what eventually became the novel *Solar Barque*[1] for more than a year, but the distractions of the Perlès-Miller book fracas, the tension with Hugo, and helping Rupert adjust to his new career left little time to write.

She was blocked as well by her anger at Maxwell Geismar's slightly less than adulatory review of *A Spy in the House of Love* in *The Nation*.[2] Hoping to repair their friendship, Max persuaded the literary editor that Anaïs was the perfect writer for "a comparative estimate of Mary McCarthy and Simone de Beauvoir—the blue stocking vs. the *bas bleu* and two of the most formidable dames of our time."[3] Had she written the article, it would have put Anaïs Nin's name before the public in a stunning new way that would have confounded her critics and perhaps brought her new readers. Whether it was fear of personal publicity (something she worried about because of her bigamy) or simply fear that she would not be up to the task (unlikely, given her strong sense of the importance and value of her pronouncements on literature), she did not write the article.[4]

Even though she published little, there was a spontaneous arousal of interest in her work during the latter part of 1956 and the beginning of 1957. Much of it was curiosity about the woman of dogged courage who kept on flogging the work she printed herself before a disinterested public. Also, she was becoming known as a Greenwich Village character, part of the local color among the new Beatniks who flocked to the cafés, jazz clubs, and bars.[5] However, the change in literary fashion probably had most to do with the arousal of interest in Anaïs Nin's fiction. Another of the cyclical changes in literary taste was evolving, and many questing readers were turning away from social realism toward younger, angrier writers who depicted an inner self adrift in a hostile world. As this new generation pursued the psychological dimensions of the individual and confronted a future fraught with political danger and the threat of nuclear annihilation, Nin's pursuit of the dream piqued their interest.

Nin sensed these changes, just as she had earlier sensed the impact of Lawrence, Freud, Jung, and so many others on culture and society, so she read—actually, studied—the writers who seemed to have the most influence on the rising generation. She did this in a thorough, systematic manner, and transcribed her thoughts and emotions into the diary as she had not done since meeting Henry Miller so many years before, when she surrendered her autodidactic search for literary models and fictional heroes and meekly accepted those he placed before her.[6]

Waiting for Godot was the first work to move her deeply and to have a major impact on her writing and thinking. Hugo took her to see the first New York production in spring 1956, and it captured her imagination for the greater part of the year. In the beginning, the fascination of Beckett's elliptic text stemmed from Anaïs's "enjoying being mystified for a change from some of the plays where you know exactly what is going to be said next."[7]

As she left the theater after the performance, Anaïs stopped to listen to the informal discussion that sprung up nightly among an audience debating its merits and defects. She picked up a copy of the English translation simply because it was there and Hugo offered to buy it,[8] but spent much of that night and most of the next day reading it. Then she wrote a long appraisal in the diary, one of her first about literature in many years.[9] She called Beckett's play a work that explored the "antipodes of the mind." What puzzled her most was how and why it had come to be so "mysteriously accepted by the people." She answered the question herself: "Because the human aspect of it, and the comic spirit, are common—smelly feet, passivity, hoboe's fantasy of someone who will save them, waiting, boredom." Yet

Anaïs still believed the language of the play was "not authentic" because "in the antipodes people speak the language of dreams." In her mind, the play succeeded only because "people have the illusion they have seen a profound spectacle," and "the intellectuals are tickled."

Sitting in Café Rienzi, drinking cup after cup of espresso, she and Jim Herlihy tried to analyze why they had not "fall[en] in love" with the play and concluded that it was because the plot was "personally distasteful: waiting, empty days, seeking to pass the time, passivity waiting for a rescuer." All these themes struck fairly close to home, as Anaïs sought some way out of the morass of her life, which is perhaps why they were so unsettling. In the end she decided that Beckett had broken new literary ground and "we must be loyal to all the explorers of man's dreams and nightmares." And, a new expression helped her and Hugo to defuse potentially troublesome disagreements: they were "waiting for Bogner" to sort them out.

She had a more immediate and personal reaction to two of Simone de Beauvoir's novels, *The Mandarins* and *She Came to Stay,* saying even if she didn't write about them for *The Nation* she should at least read them. She identified with Beauvoir's characters, seeing parts of them in herself and others who figured in her life, and also sensed that Beauvoir gave parts of herself to each of her characters, just as she herself had done in the several incarnations of Lillian, Djuna, and Sabina.

Love triangles were much on her mind as she read *She Came to Stay.* She could not get over how "the husband and wife were so determined to be together that both of them had to share the woman he lusted after."[10] Anaïs saw her counterpart, however, in *The Mandarins,* identifying with Anne, who had so much time to reflect as she flew between her husband in Paris and her lover in the United States, "living out her last love affair and then wanting to die." Anaïs thought it was happening to her, for she believed her "sharp, keen, wild passion for Rupert" had been killed by the ordinariness of their life together.

Rupert felt trapped by his teaching job, which made him miserable and in turn made Anaïs feel so trapped that she viewed Hugo as her savior.[11] Both had been deeply frightened by the violent argument that left them teetering on the brink of separation. Both were so terrified of parting that each was convinced that the other had changed and was now exactly the person he or she wanted from the very beginning of their marriage." Anaïs now regarded Hugo as perfection itself, and decided that she wanted to break with Rupert but could not because of his "overwhelming needs . . . the new job, bronchitis, his loneliness."

When it was time to go to Los Angeles, she was reluctant to leave her posh life in New York, where Hugo showered her with gifts and ordered splits of champagne to help her sleep at night.[12] She asked Bogner why she was so averse to going that she invented new lies about her "job" in order to stay two weeks longer with Hugo. Bogner asked if Anaïs realized that she seemed to "reach peace, comfort or serenity only when the sensual life is excluded," for she and Hugo were still in separate bedrooms.[13]

A pleasant surprise awaited, however, which made her think there might possibly be an intellectual life in Los Angeles as well as New York. Ruth Witt Diamant, the professor of literature Anaïs took into her confidence in San Francisco, wrote that she was sending "a couple of youngsters," the poets Allen Ginsberg and Gregory Corso.[14] To Ruth, Ginsberg was "a messiah of a sort . . . [weak] outside the particular agonies of his own experience . . . not tied to anything but effect"; Corso "twenty-two, precocious . . . noisy and emphatic, shouting of catalogues to make a poem. Occasionally he hits it so good that it seems worthwhile to encourage him." She was interested in Anaïs's "always accurate impressions."

Anaïs went to hear them read and summed up the experience as "like hearing surrealism born in the Brooklyn gutters . . . Jewish of course."[15] It reminded her of "Artaud's mad conference at the Sorbonne," especially when someone in the audience challenged Ginsberg and he shouted at the heckler to stand naked before the world as he did metaphorically when he read his poems. Angered to a frenzy, Ginsberg stripped, which Anaïs found "not shocking but so violent and direct and [it] had so much meaning (in terms of all our fears to unveil ourselves) . . . it was really like the old surrealist dadaist fights." It gave her hope for change in American literature after all, even though she was disgusted by the earthiness and vulgarity of the Beat Generation writers.

Seeing Ginsberg and Corso gave Anaïs Nin a new obsession. She devoured everything the Beats had thus far published even as she decried their influence on and popularity within American culture. They also gave her a new vocabulary expression, one she was particularly fond of using to sign letters to both husbands: "your Beat Generation wife."[16]

But all the while she studied Beckett's novels and plays, puzzled over the triangular relationships in Simone de Beauvoir's novels, dressed like a Beatnik, and even tried to behave like characters in the fiction of William Burroughs and Jack Kerouac, she was turning inward toward the diary.[17]

Now she had all the originals in one place: Bekins Storage in Arcadia. She made frequent trips there, often spending a large part of the day just sitting among them, comforted by their presence. Often she removed one at a time to rewrite, or "recopy," as she put it.[18] She then returned the original and one copy to the vault and sent a second copy to Jim Herlihy in New York. It was his ardor, she noted, that "incited" her to begin again on the diaries, for he was her "one faithful reader. I owe him so much. He has never failed me." At the same time as she praised Jim for giving her the impetus to return to the diary, she noted far too casually, "I couldn't finish Solar Bark."

Jim consciously patterned his remarks about the diary in a way that he hoped would permit Anaïs to rid herself of the block that had stalled the novel. Well aware of how violently she responded to negative criticism, he cautiously suggested that the portraits in the diary she was then shaping, of her friends Frances Field and Thurema Sokol, and her description of Gonzalo and the Press, were all vivid, *but,* he stressed, she must also organize and complete them.[19] In one sense his advice was helpful; in another it was frustrating: "I see in both lights, the human light of the diary and the essence and abstractions of the novels. In the Diary I follow the life-line. In the novel the fantasy. Where to begin?"

"I reread my novel as if someone else wrote it," Anaïs observed, both in wonder and fear. "I forgot what I have written." When she talked about it with Jim, he told her his reaction upon reading the few pages she showed him had been one of puzzlement, for it seemed as if she had either changed her mind about what she was writing on every single page or else forgotten what had already happened to her characters. "Is it the strain?" she asked, and then answered her own question: "such a dual life is an enormous strain."

It was easier to turn to the diary, where she had to confront the fact that her portraits were indeed wrong, for she was doing what Bogner accused her of, seeing her friends through her own eyes and not as they really were.

She discussed *Solar Bark* in her sessions with Bogner because she was overcome with anxiety as she wrote the sections dealing with the costume party on the Mexican general's yacht.[20] For reasons she could not explain, writing these passages made her relive the weekend before her mother died and the long-ago tension just before her father's "going away (sexually and on a trip)."[21]

Under Bogner's questioning, Anaïs remembered that she felt "responsible" for her father's unhappiness, "unrelated to him except when I was bad and he spanked me." Then it came to her why she was so obsessed now with not losing Hugo. She realized that the separation she had long told herself she wanted was not what she wanted at all, for if she lost Hugo, then she lost her father a second time: "I realized that the sexual wall that had been erected between us early in the marriage was that he was my father and now he was even more my father when he deserted me for a mistress."

Was this the moment, the adult Anaïs wondered, when the child Anaïs "originated the concept that sensuality and love are not reconcilable"? Was this what made her have sex with so many men other than her husband, even though she knew deep within her that they would all eventually disappoint her? What a relief it was to receive Hugo's telegram from Cuba saying there would be "no question of separation" and that he loved her.[22]

Anaïs resumed the writing of *Solar Barque* (as she was now spelling it correctly) with a clear understanding of how the novel would evolve. She noted astutely that, of all her novels, this one was the most original, containing "the greater part invention, very little reality." It had been so difficult to write in the beginning because it touched "the periphery of the diary," and therefore required "circumvention."

Nin's most maternal character, Lillian Beye, reappears and is the central figure. She finally learns that "the meaning of freedom is not flight . . . but commitment," as she gradually realizes that Larry, the husband who never satisfied her and from whom she fled to Mexico in search of an inner self, was infinitely more complex and a man of many more parts than she originally thought. Once she arrives at this conclusion, Lillian "untangles the knot of her own past [and] rediscovers her love of her husband."[23] Having made this startling discovery in her own life, Anaïs Nin finished the novel within a few short weeks.

She thought the British firm of Neville Spearman would probably publish *Solar Barque* because they had just published *A Spy in the House of Love.* She was disgusted with everything Neville Armstrong had done to sell the novel, especially the front cover, which showed a buxom woman, naked to the waist, coyly looking down at her full rounded breasts and strongly resembling the photo of Anaïs Nin on the back cover.[24] She also complained angrily to Armstrong about the brief biography under her photograph, which said she "worked alongside Henry Miller" in Paris and that a "full account of that period" could be found in the Perlès biography, "published by us simultaneously."

"I am in a quandary about giving you the next novel," Anaïs wrote to Armstrong,[25] but it was really a ploy, for she would gladly have given *Solar Barque* to him or anyone else who would buy it. Alas, it seemed her publishing history was repeating itself, for no one wanted it.

The novel languished and Anaïs's bitterness grew. Hugo came to her rescue again with a plan for self-publishing through the book-manufacturing firm Edwards Brothers, in Ann Arbor. He suggested that Anaïs re-create the Gemor Press, this time calling it The Anaïs Nin Press. Hugo would simply pay Edwards Brothers to print as many copies as she wanted, and Anaïs could take over the selling through her old network at the Gotham Book Mart, the Eighth Street Bookshop in Greenwich Village (Larry Maxwell had since closed his shop), and the Satyr Bookshop in Los Angeles.

Anaïs announced the formation of The Anaïs Nin Press with uncharacteristic modesty. Although she received congratulatory letters from friends who praised the endeavor, she was ashamed of the ruse and embarrassed by her most recent rejections. She told the truth to no one except Felix Pollack, the gentle librarian at Northwestern who had confided intimate details of his life to her: "About the Press. . . . It is to save face, it is made out of pride, because America has treated me so shabbily and I don't want them to know I am defeated."[26]

She was so desperate for commercial publication that she wrote several groveling letters to Armstrong, suggesting all sorts of combinations and compromises. When he declined them all, Anaïs had friends such as Geismar submit it to others, who also declined. In the end, Hugo duly paid Edwards Brothers and the novel appeared in 1958.

A crucial change in her friendships occurred during the mid-1950s, when Anaïs was in the depths of confusion over what to do about her bi-coastal trapeze. Because of her unsettled relationships with two husbands, she turned to women for emotional sustenance and formed deep and abiding friendships, something that had been notably lacking in her life and something that seems to have surprised her when she tried to write about it.[27] Anaïs always had friends—Thurema Sokol, Luise Rainer, Dorothy Norman, to name just a few—but there was always a subtext, usually of jealousy, competition, and in some cases, a sexual undertone (starting with June Miller and continuing to the mid-fifties with other women, such as some of her younger admirers in Los Angeles and New York).[28]

Now she began to see women as they really were, as separate persons with their own sphere of existence and influence. Other women no longer had to radiate around her as sycophants or disciples for her to like them, and she did not ostracize or banish them when they chose to go their separate independent ways. She actually studied some of these women, admiring the different ways in which they coped with life's raw deals and tried to adapt their methods of coping for herself.

Peggy Glanville Hicks, the tiny Australian composer who was then music critic of the *New York Herald Tribune,* was one of the first women to be welcomed onto the newly level playing field of Anaïs Nin's female friendships. Peggy, forty-three, lived serenely alone in New York, content to concentrate on composing and reviewing. When Anaïs shared the details of her bigamous life, Peggy refused to join the growing list of friends who tried to help her keep the trapeze airborne by providing alibis, but instead became one of the very few (such as Jim Herlihy) who urged her to choose one man or the other and dismount before she killed herself with worry and stress.

Cornelia Runyon, then in her seventieth decade, was another good friend who did not judge, kept secrets, and urged Anaïs to end the

Anaïs and Rupert at the "Come as Your Madness" party.

juggling act. Like Peggy Glanville Hicks, Cornelia was content with her work and was happy living alone for long periods of time. Again like Peggy, Cornelia counted on a large circle of loving friends for companionship, but if they were not available was serene alone, something Anaïs never accomplished.

Cornelia Runyon proved her friendship when she visited New York in the mid-1950s and was taken by friends to see the films of the interesting avant-garde filmmaker, Ian Hugo (whom she heard of then for the first time). Commentary was to be provided by her Los Angeles friend Anaïs Nin Pole.[29] Cornelia had no inkling of Anaïs's double life, having accepted her reason for frequent travel to New York as her "job at Cue." When Anaïs saw Cornelia enter the lecture hall, her heart nearly stopped. Quickly she ran to embrace her, whispering as she did: "You will keep my secret, won't you." She introduced the puzzled but unfazed Cornelia to "my husband, Hugh Guiler," and each expressed great pleasure in meeting the other. Cornelia Runyon never told a living soul about what she witnessed that afternoon. She maintained an artistic friendship with Hugo for the rest of her life, all the while giving Anaïs nonjudgmental comfort in frequent gripe sessions about Rupert and her stultifying life in Los Angeles.[30]

Anaïs took advantage of Hugo's liking Cornelia, and soon her name appeared in daily letters as a convenient excuse for any number of things about which she did not want to tell the truth. If she went to the beach with Rupert, for example, Anaïs told Hugo she had gone with Cornelia. And to make sure she remembered which "friend" she named, she made carbon copies of her letters.[31]

Renate Druks was another woman who provided Anaïs with years of excuses. Born in Vienna, Renate was divorced and lived in Malibu with her adolescent son, Peter Loomer. A kinship was established between the two women when Renate married a second husband fifteen years her junior, the UCLA football star who wanted to be a poet, Ronnie Knox. To Anaïs, Renate was "an amusing woman but a bad painter,"[32] but she liked the way Renate lived life with bravado and zest and eventually made her the focal point of the stories in *Collages* (1964).

Anaïs's letters to Hugo are full of parties, dinners, concerts, and other happy occasions, most of which never happened. Her days in Los Angeles were taken up entirely by the rhythms of Rupert's life. He left each morning by 7:30 and returned at 3. Always an early riser,

Anaïs was up by 6 to make coffee and think about what she would write that day. He came home each afternoon to prepare martinis and help Anaïs cook their dinner, always the same: he broiled the meats and she prepared the vegetables. Rupert insisted they eat by six o'clock at the latest.[33] The radio blared throughout the preparations, as Rupert listened intently to various news reports, but Anaïs tried to make him shut it off while they ate. Afterward, they did the same things they had done in Sierra Madre.

Occasionally they were invited to parties, such as those Romain Gary gave at the consulate; sometimes they went to a book launch or art gallery opening, but very seldom, for Rupert was uncomfortable in such settings. When Renate decided to give a costume party at her house in Malibu, Rupert was adamant that he would not go, especially when he learned that each guest was to come in a costume representing his or her "madness."[34] Anaïs persuaded him that they must go or she risked losing Renate's friendship.

The party was one of those occasions that have since become mythologized, partly because Anaïs wrote of it in the published diary, mostly because Kenneth Anger later re-created it in a film called *Inauguration of the Pleasure Dome.*[35] The costumes Anaïs created for herself and Rupert were so stunningly original that they, too, have taken on an air of myth as most of those who attended remember them with differing degrees of accuracy.

When Rupert finally agreed to go, costuming proved difficult because Anaïs was hampered by his "obsession with expenses." And so she directed the originality that characterized all her decorating toward creating costumes that cost next to nothing but which drew raves from all the other guests.

What exactly was his madness? she asked Rupert in the weeks preceding the party, determined to portray it as accurately but yet as artistically as possible. Shyly, he told her that he used to hear voices at night that kept him from sleeping. She suggested painting eyes all over whatever clothing he would wear, to represent both his own, which could not close in sleep, and those of the voices he believed were watching him.

"That's very good!" Rupert exclaimed, "because I always feel [other people's] eyes watching me. I always think people are looking at me. It makes me self-conscious."[36]

And so his costume was invented: "Black balled tights on which we sewed eyes of all kinds, in rubber and plastic, one pair staring from his sex. Torso painted by Gil [Henderson], strikingly. Hair ornament by Rupert Himself, a wire crown of staring eyes painted on ping pong balls."

Anaïs's costume was equally dramatic, especially for a fifty-year-old woman:[37] "Skin colored net stockings up to my waist. Leopard fur earrings glued to tips of my naked breasts, leopard belt on waist, rest painted by Gil, and my head inside a birdcage. Hair dusted with gold and eyelashes two inches long. Around my wrist strips of paper on which I had copied lines from my writing—out of context. I unwound these and tore off a phrase for each person at the party. Curtis Harrington called it 'Tickertape of the Unconscious.' "[38]

But despite all the attention and even the flattering moment when a complete stranger read his piece of tickertape and recognized the passage as one written by the novelist Anaïs Nin, the party was "painful." Rupert "resented" her dancing, and "withdrew and spoke to no one."

Several years later, Anaïs realized that she could count on her fingers all the parties she had been to in California, which is perhaps why they have since assumed a status out of proportion to their actual role and place in her life there. Her summation of the "Come as Your Madness" party probably best describes her life in Los Angeles: "the difficulties were greater in proportion to the pleasure."[39]

33

The Black Children

Gore Vidal reappeared in 1957 after an absence of eight years.[1] "Nothing was born of our relationship but destruction,"[2] Anaïs wrote, vowing never to give him the opportunity to harm her again.

They had a backstage reconciliation on opening night of his play *Visit to a Small Planet,* then poised to become a Broadway success and hit film. In a "deliberate snub," Gore did not invite Anaïs and Hugo, so Louis and Bebe Barron, who wrote the music, took them.[3] Gore was outraged when he saw Anaïs, but then kissed her on both cheeks and said she "still" looked marvelous. He asked her to telephone the next time she was in Hollywood, and several months later, she did.

Anaïs thought Gore had not changed much: "success, friendships, love affairs, travel, money ($6,000 a week!) do not show their mark."[4] She asked herself what about Gore Vidal had so fascinated her the first time they met, deciding it was his "sadness . . . which had created a bond, one entirely based on distress."

Lately in her sessions with Bogner, Anaïs had been working on what she called her "failed relationships," a category into which she placed Gore. Bogner told her again the reason for all these failures, that she "invented" other persons rather than seeing them as they really were. Unwilling to accept it, Anaïs searched for reasons why her "invented" relationships failed, but she put only men into this category.

James Merrill and William Burford led the group that consisted entirely of those who "suddenly 'turned' against my work," and Gore followed closely. Anaïs noted that before they met her and fell under her influence, all three planned to write as modern realists and disciples of Hemingway; after meeting her and reading her fiction, she believed all three had been dazed and bewildered by the creative possibilities inherent in her work, with its Surrealist form and psychological underpinnings. Her conclusion was that these men were frightened by her power to influence them.

Of the three men whose defection (as she viewed it) still troubled her a decade later, Gore hurt the most. But seeing him again in Hollywood allowed her to explain it away in terms that permitted her to resume a friendship of sorts—or more accurately, a guarded truce that lasted for the rest of her life. The only way Anaïs could sustain the truce was by learning to accept his conscious cruelty, the ease with which he inflicted public humiliation on her through his devastating fictional portrayals of women, and his seeming lack of concern about breaching the trust she conferred upon him so many years ago.

She finally realized how fortunate she was to have someone like Rupert in her life when several illnesses reminded her that she was showing signs of age.[5] One day, embarrassed by her appearance, she blurted out "oh so painfully" her true age. The sixteen-year difference between them meant nothing to Rupert, who responded with the same loving kindness he showed no matter what news she told him. Rupert told her the difference in their ages mattered not at all, that he was simply happy to give his youth in exchange for all else she brought to his life. If anything, her confession made him more considerate than he had ever been. She was touchingly confused by this man's unending devotion but very glad to have it.

There were other meetings with Gore, who was then sharing a house with an aspiring actress, Joanne Woodward.[6] One evening, sitting in the bar of the Bel Air Hotel, Gore began to talk about writing, and for the first time admitted to Anaïs that she had profoundly influenced the direction of his work.[7] He told her that he had been well "on the way to becoming another Hemingway" when they met. Because of her "seriousness and the depths" of her writing, Gore said he abandoned his original intention for his second novel, *In a Yellow Wood,* to concentrate on dramatizing the conflict between "convention and art," but could not "get beyond the hard surface." She said he told her that she was responsible for his not becoming the novelist he wanted to be, and the course of his writing would have been "much easier, more successful and more ordinary" had they never met.

"Who could have predicted then," she wrote in the diary, "that Gore and I would ten years later be driving in an open sport car in Hollywood, both of us tanned, and both of us having as he said, obtained what we wanted—he success and I love."

Actually, love wasn't all she wanted. She wanted to be published and to have the success and acclaim that came to the few fortunate writers who tapped deep wells in the literary imagination. She had every hope she would be one of them, for Tom Payne, a young editor at Avon Books, had just bought *A Spy in the House of Love* for publication. They arranged to meet on her next trip to New York (thus giving her a genuine excuse for more frequent trips, all because of "complications in publishing"). He asked about her newest writing and she showed him *Solar Barque,* which she was now self-protectively describing as "a scream through the eye of a statue."[8] With great trepidation, she gave Tom Payne the new work, but he liked it enough to suggest submitting it to his superiors.

Anaïs hoped to persuade the distinguished agent Georges Borchardt to represent her, but while she waited for his decision, she was contacted a second time by Gunther Stuhlmann, "an intelligent German who loves literature, does translations, worked with films." He was now a partner in "a young and active [literary] agency," Hinshaw and Stuhlmann, and said he had begun to "create some interest for your work in Europe, including the diary."[9] She would have taken such a letter seriously no matter who wrote it, but Gunther's included the magic phrase, "interest in the diary," and so she paid it special attention. She was still revising "The Black Children," as she and Jim now called the diaries. While Rupert was at school, she alternated revisions with housework, a combination that somehow soothed her. As she thought of those whose portraits she was perfecting for this volume—Frances Field, Thurema Sokol, Josephine Premice, Albert Mangones,[10] and Edward Graeffe—she realized for one of the very first times just how "grateful" she was for having found Rupert and "for the fulfilment of my last passion, the last, the most beautiful of all, because it involved heart *and* body."

She still wrote of dissatisfaction with life in Los Angeles but now spoke seldom of dismounting the trapeze, for she was determined to keep both husbands in her life, no matter how difficult. She continued to gripe, usually in tones of long-suffering nobility but, from this point on, described her never-ending juggling act with stoic resignation.

Having resolved how she would live her life, only the question of how to make the diaries suitable for publication remained, and that seemed irresolvable. "I don't know why I cannot give to the Diary the unity and continuity of a Proustian work," she asked.

Proust became the ideal she tried to emulate, and for a time, thought his "unique insight into character" the quality she needed to incorporate into her own work. Proust knew "that a single face can wear a hundred masks, that personality is reducible to a discontinuous series of psychological states." The problem remained how to accomplish his elegant and difficult writing in her own portraits, and ultimately, how to unite the diaries with some of the portraits already created in the novels so they could "flow together."

There was also the question of the diary's "power to recreate the emotional intensity of [a] relationship." She thought of Gore here, and of how, when she copied (i.e., rewrote) passages from their earlier relationship, how much more alive they were than the friendship that was unfolding in present time. Another example was that of Bill Pinckard, whom she ran into one morning in a Greenwich Village hardware store. He introduced Anaïs to his wife, whom she deemed "a very ordinary girl," and as she walked back to her apartment, she suddenly felt "jittery . . . very nervous." Not, she realized, at meeting Bill and his wife, but rather because of the "incandescence" with which she "adorned the relationship" while it was happening ten years ago. When she tried to describe what was troubling her now, she could only think of "the terrible experience of death in life which I have experienced more often than most human beings because I preserved them at their most heightened moment."[11] All these thoughts coalesced as she pondered how she might create an inner, psychological reality. Several days later, she was stunned to discover that someone from her past life had already done so, and with enormous success.

Gore, who did not know that Anaïs and Larry Durrell had been friends before the war, was indirectly responsible for bringing him back into her life. During one of their Hollywood talks about writing,

Anaïs in Southern France with Claude and Larry Durrell and their children.

Gore casually suggested that she could learn something from a new novel, *Justine,* whose author also probed inner psychological states of being. Anaïs sought it frantically.

"What a feast!" she proclaimed as she read it. "A banquet! An orgy of words and colors, riot of the senses—a male counterpart to my novels, errative, elusive, penetrating, a sensuous jungle, a trapezist of images, a jungler, a master of all prestigitations." She could not believe that Little "Peter Pan" Larry could have written such a stunning novel. An immediate comparison sprang to mind, for she had just read Jack Kerouac's *On the Road:* next to *Justine,* it "seemed like gorillas."[12]

Anaïs wanted to write to Larry but was embarrassed about how to do so. He had asked her for money during the war when he was stranded in Cypress and cut off from funds in England, but Anaïs, supporting Gonzalo and Helba and "drowning in debts," did not reply to his letter. Meanwhile, Henry tirelessly begged money from everyone he met and helped the Durrells. "We could have been writing to each other," Anaïs wrote ashamedly. "He was the better writer of the three of us."

Despite her chagrin, she wrote, saying "the advent of *Justine* was a phenomenon, after the miserly, sterile, frigid, plain, homely, prosaic, stuttering world of American writing." Two typed pages of equally effusive praise followed, into which she carefully inserted several remarks about how his writing showed so many "paralellisms with hers."[13]

From the start of the resumption of friendship, she told him the truth about herself: "I live a divided life. One in New York with Hugo-the-father, graceful apartment, chic clothes, white heat living, many friends, café life in the Village, trips to Mexico, business. And another life here with Rupert-the-son, grandson of Frank Lloyd Wright, nature man, beach man, a professor by mistake, by temperament a guitar player hating work . . . have friends but colorless because California is colorless, like a cheap drug that has been mixed with bicarbonate and toothpaste, a pseudo tranquilizer." She also told Larry that she could help him become published in Sweden because she was a best seller there, which she knew was not true even as she wrote it. *Children of the Albatross* had indeed been published by an excellent firm, but despite "brilliant" reviews, was remaindered.

Larry expressed pleasure at hearing from her after so many years and told her in full detail his plans for "the four Justines," as he then called the novels eventually known as the Alexandria Quartet.[14] After having been "in the wilderness" for so long, he and his new wife, Claude, were working hard to cement his success so that Larry would not have to return to work in the British Foreign Office. They were living in the South of France and wanted very much to stay there.

Several possibilities of how she could hitch Larry's rising star to her flatly fallen one sprang to Anaïs's mind. None of her plans was clearly thought out, but the first one she suggested involved getting him to agree to let her publish some of his writings on her "Press" (i.e., Edwards Brothers Printing Company), in the United States and in countries such as Germany and Sweden, which she targeted as likely venues for her own diary, the planned second book to emerge from "her" press.

Suddenly she had it: she dreamed up a scheme whereby she would become the publisher of his long-banned *The Black Book* in the United States, reasoning that, if it were printed here, it would not have to clear customs, and, therefore, banning would be moot. All would be well, she assured him, until "a Catholic fanatic" bought a copy, but by that time they would have sold several thousand copies and made their profit. She invented a "silent partner" who, she told Larry, thought the plan "practical, feasable and interesting." She said she already had the money to pay him because *Under a Glass Bell* "has gone well as a reprint." In truth, it had not "gone" at all, and she was counting on Hugo to finance whatever harebrained scheme Larry might accept.

She also told Larry she was "doing" a book called "Anonymous Diaries," in which famous diarists would submit several pages of handwritten text that would be reproduced in facsimile, and readers would have to guess which text belonged to which writer. And just in case he declined that one as well, she concluded by asking if he had anything else that he wanted to have privately printed, for she would take care of it.

Larry rejected everything in an exceedingly polite reply, saying he did not want to risk disturbing the many commercial publishers who were suddenly courting him with lucrative contracts.[15]

Undaunted, Anaïs wrote again, this time telling the truth, that she was now working for a magazine called *Eve,* whose editors would be happy to publish any fragment he might have to give them.

The editor of *Eve,* Lawrence Lipton, a patron of West Coast arts, had invited Anaïs and Rupert to his home several times for poetry readings and dance recitals. When Lipton told her he was planning to start a magazine aimed at the "new" woman, and asked if she had anything he could publish, she responded with alacrity. "Now they will publish 8,000 words of Solar Barque."[16] Even better, in the euphoric beginning of her connection with *Eve* ("The Magazine for the Woman of 1958"),[17] she believed she would be hired as a columnist and paid to write a "Letter from New York."[18] It was heaven-sent: a real job instead of an invented one, a genuine salary to augment Hugo's allowance (some of which she hoped to keep for herself instead of giving it all to Rupert), and a legitimate reason for her frequent trips to New York.

In California, *Eve* provided a "Bridge to the World" that helped her to reestablish "connection." Larry Lipton was treating her as a valued source of ideas and information and relied on her to discern what was important in all things cultural. Lipton also paid her the supreme compliment she yearned to receive when he asked her to write "whatever you think would be of interest to our imagined Eve, whom I am sure you know very well for after all she is really you."[19]

Despite working entirely on speculation, Anaïs devoted her considerable energy to making the first issue of *Eve* a success. Her ideas for articles were first rate both in intellectual quality and in general public interest. Without consulting Larry Durrell, she nevertheless assured Larry Lipton that she could "get a piece from . . . the writer of the moment whom everyone wants to publish (writer of the finest quality, author of *Justine*)."[20] She also volunteered to persuade Margaret Mead to let them reprint the chapter "To Both Their Own" from her new book, *Male and Female;* to track down Erich Fromm in Mexico and persuade him to write something new; to convince Santha Rama Rau to write an article about the condition of women in India; to have Max Geismar write book reviews; and to have someone else interview Peggy Glanville Hicks, not only because she was an important "woman composer," but also because her opera from Thomas Mann's *Transposed Heads* was to open in February 1958 at the Phoenix Theatre. Anaïs also proposed articles to be written by the Barrons about "Musique Concrète," wherein technical developments in the new electronic music would be transposed into lay language. Jim Herlihy's *Blue Denim* had made him a playwright of note and she wanted him to write about contemporary theater. These were only the ones that sprang immediately to mind, mostly ideas centered on promoting her best friends, but they all deserved it for they were producing high-quality work. She sent list after list to Lipton of story ideas that, had the magazine survived, would have ensured its excellence for many years to come.[21]

The way in which Lipton helped Anaïs most to recover her "Bridge to the World" was by praising *Solar Barque* as "a beautiful piece of writing"[22] and by urging her to give him any other fiction she wanted for future issues. And so, the happy combination of having her own editorial work appreciated by someone who valued her writing even more highly gave Anaïs "an objective role for a comeback."[23]

"All my work with Bogner bore fruit at this moment," she observed, saying "when creativity is fulfilled there is less fatigue than in frustration."

Anaïs took special care to record Bogner's statements in the diary, a clear indication of how important she thought them. She quotes Bogner as calling Henry's method of concealing the truth "exaggerated realism: When you are so intent on describing externals, so emphatic about externals, it is one way of concealing whatever thoughts, memories or associations lie behind or beyond these facts, the other dimensions."

Anaïs spoke of lying by telling Bogner that it was impossible to know when and if indeed June lied. Bogner said, "When a person lies so desperately on all levels, it is because the compulsive mechanism functions *continuously*, a symptom of great defensiveness, great fear of the truth leaking out." Anaïs did not admit to lying, but said that when she began to write fiction, she "went into surrealism as a method of equivocal truth telling" because it gave her the necessary "ambiguity, obliqueness" without which she could not have confided her thoughts and emotions to paper. Bogner asked how she used "fantasy," and Anaïs said it permitted her to "overcome the guilt for seducing the father" that colored so many of her adult actions. She told Bogner that the only way she had been able to arouse herself to feel passion with all her many lovers was to fantasize of her father, "lifting my dress, pulling down my panties, spanking me—no, not spanking me, he is caressing me, he is making love to me. My mother will catch me."

Though disconcerted, Bogner had a ready answer: "fact or fantasy, the guilt is the same."

A passage then follows that is without attribution; whether Inge Bogner or Anaïs Nin expressed it, or if Anaïs only thought it as she sat digesting and writing about the session: "It is only the sick who drag their past along and who decide that life is like a novel once written and definite, like a photograph. This is the way it is."

"But it is not," Anaïs reproved whoever made the statement above. She described what may have caused her to become the woman she now was: "If today, as a mature woman, I have a propensity to exaggerate, to be hypersensitive to injury, to break with those who offend me, could it not be possible that at my parents' first 'error,' first careless gesture, first inadequacy, I reacted unduly, and deepened and sharpened my anger, my revenges, my wounds—yes, it is possible. Just as the criminal who remembers only the wrongs, never the kindnesses and who retaliates more violently than the act against him justifies, so the neurotic, so the child, wanting all, and obtaining but a human fraction, conceives an exaggerated grudge."[24] Still searching for concrete incidents, all she could recall from her childhood were "sensations: curtains, table covers, veils, capes."

"Capes!" she noted with a sudden shock of recognition. She had become so associated with them that photographers vied to pose her in some of the many she collected. Her beloved capes gave her one more dimension of what she sought: to be "veiled from the world."

The euphoria of this discovery was soon muted when the publishers jettisoned *Eve* in early spring, 1958.[25] All Anaïs's work had been for naught: not only had she never received a cent in payment, now she was faced with writing letters of explanation and returning manuscripts to all her friends. It was like a death in the family when they all wrote to commiserate. Even Caresse Crosby, who had just had surgery for her failing heart, wrote from the Minnesota clinic where she was recuperating to say how sorry she was. The indomitable Caresse ("staunch, that's what she is!") thought to console Anaïs by inviting her to "bring Hugo" to Europe, but "not the paramour," whom she refused "even [to] acknowledge."[26]

Caresse's letter could not have come at a worse time. Anaïs was convinced that she, too, had a bad heart, but also, that she "wanted to have a bad heart, and to die."[27] Bogner assured her there were many reasons why she had frequent heart-attack symptoms, anxiety foremost among them, and that her so-called well-being during the months of planning for *Eve* was only temporary and not due to genuine stability. The analyst tried to make the patient see that putting her faith in something as ephemeral as the possible job on *Eve* would not resolve the underlying problem of her dual life, but Anaïs insisted that her symptoms were genuine and not caused by "hysteria." Her mind reverted back to how she invented a brutal railroad strike at age seventeen to excuse herself for being late to meet her Aunt Anaïs and the Sánchez cousins. "The power of the spirit is frightening," she realized, not only for "miracles [and] creation," but also for "destruction."

"I am going to die," she wrote in the diary, "and before I die, please give me what I want (Rupert)." Her problem now was a new version of the old one: Rupert finally had enough money for the down payment on his dream house. This was more frightening to Anaïs than any other aspect of her dual life. She began to have dreams of being imprisoned, both in cages and underwater, and she knew they were all related to the knowledge that once he got his house, Rupert would insist that she stay inside it all the time.

She tried to talk about her "portable roots" with Jim, and how she never wanted to be tied to property by ownership. He had a ready explanation, which seems to have given her solace. She had no single country, Jim believed, and therefore no national identity. Her country was the the peculiar landscape inhabited by artists. "They are your people," he told her. When she thought about it, she marveled that there could be so much inherent understanding between them. Their affinity was based on life, not art, she decided, and an affinity based on life was exactly what she must use if she wished to relate to Rupert. And the way to do this, as the experience with *Eve* had demonstrated, was to find a way to be happy with her art. It would make all else possible, but finding the solution remained the problem.

34

"Why not me?"

ANAÏS'S FRIENDSHIP with Lesley Blanch deepened as the two women commiserated about their respective marital situations.[1] Romain (forty-five, ten years younger than Lesley) asked her to divorce him so that he could marry the eighteen-year-old Jean Seberg, just plucked from Marshalltown, Iowa, to play Saint Joan in Otto Preminger's film of the same name. Now he could not make up his mind which woman he preferred. Lesley was the only one in her particular marital trio who knew what she wanted: to maintain her limbo-like situation despite the emotional cost. "The masochism of woman disguised by maternal role," Anaïs wrote, without a trace of identification.

Through her deepening friendship with Lesley, Anaïs was thrown into contact with Hollywood's glitterati. Among the stars who appeared at consulate parties was Frank Sinatra, to Anaïs the epitome of a Hollywood roué. There were also hangers-on and hopefuls, and a number of entrepreneurs waiting for the big break. These included a succession of marginal figures whose names appear in her diaries but who never became known in the industry and were mostly hustlers on the lookout for novels that might be adapted to screenplays. Anaïs paid respectful attention to them all.

There were, however, several who did work within or on the fringes of the movie industry and who tried, in some cases for years,[2] to turn *A Spy in the House of Love* into a screenplay. Among these were William Kozlenko, a fixture on the Hollywood scene, a "stubby, tough, fast-talking writer-editor . . . [who] reminds you of a literate Mike Todd."[3] *Spy* had been excerpted, summarized, and included in a book called *Masterplots of 1954,* one of Kozlenko's prime sources, even though he seldom read more than the titles. He thought *Spy* had something to do with the Cold War and Sputnik, a hot topic then, and one that would make good television fare. Anaïs, who knew little of the vagaries of Hollywood filmmaking, wanted nothing less than a major Hollywood movie, and at once, but Kozlenko was an unlikely possibility to make that happen.[4]

He offered a vague and unspecific option with nary a mention of money. "Please," Anaïs begged a cautious Gunther Stuhlmann, who was investigating the situation and proceding warily, "remember I told you this is my year and you are my agent! . . . Entre nous, whatever they offer is okay with me because I like Kozlenko—I trust him."[5]

Things soon changed: "[Kozlenko] said I was a great writer . . . but he wanted to make a playwriter out of me . . . of TV shows!"[6] Anaïs was insulted because she lumped television into the same category as *Time* and Rupert's "commentators." It seems unlikely that she would have agreed to Kozlenko's plan, but then again, perhaps not, for this was a period in which she pursued every possibility to get her name and work into print, no matter what the venue.

As Kozlenko's "option" grew even more amorphous, Anaïs bearded others, demanding immediate action. She literally backed Walter Wanger, then at 20th Century–Fox, into a corner at one of Lesley's consulate parties and would not let him go until he agreed to listen to her pitch in person at his office. Several days later she made the long trek from Silver Lake to the San Fernando Valley to present her novels in person, but Wanger did not receive her. He returned them in an embarrassingly short time with a perplexed letter in which he thanked her politely for delivering them but carefully avoided all mention of her writing.[7]

Lesley Blanch was indirectly responsible for another aspect of Anaïs's brief fling at living what she thought was the "real" Hollywood life. Lesley took her to the home of Laura Archera and Aldous Huxley to hear Dr. Oscar Janiger read a paper by Alan Watts, who was to discuss LSD. Watts compared several of the "organized visions," as he called his religious and mystical experiences, to taking LSD, which he described as akin to "a complex dream that lacked cohesion and would need to be interpreted and organized later to be understood."[8]

Anaïs tried LSD but could not understand what all the fuss was about, for taking LSD had been "no different than my writing." No matter who took the drug, whether poets, painters, musicians or scientists: "The experiences . . . resemble each other and prove Jung's Collective Unconscious. It is ironic that in our scientific era people who would not believe in the artist's vision are willing to believe [in] a drug, or to entrust themselves to a chemical."[9]

There was, however, one aspect of the "trip" that had lasting effects on what the published diary finally became. She believed that the drug activated her subsequent night-time dreaming, and the next day, when she tried to add these images to a "character" she was creating in her rewriting, she realized that "it was the first time I had looked upon the personages of the diary as personages . . . as characters, and that it revealed I was achieving the work of art and transcending the personal diary. I also began to see it as 'peopled,' in fact, crowded as any so-called 'social' novel might be."[10] Several years later, this insight became the catalyst for changing the diary's form and making it suitable for publication.

Determined that it would indeed be her year, and armed with a sheaf of copies of the *Masterplots* summary, Anaïs prepared to accompany Hugo to Europe. The first thing she did was to write Claude and Larry Durrell to tell them she was coming to France and hoped to see them. Shortly after, Tom Payne told Anaïs he had received a query from the British publisher Peter Owen, asking if the rights to *Spy* were available in England. She wrote at once to Gunther, and this news was waiting for him when he returned from Europe, where he had interested German publishers in *Under a Glass Bell,* and Italian, Swedish, and Dutch publishers in *Spy.* But the most encouraging news was that she had a "young fan" in Tom Maschler, an editor at McGibbon & Kee in London.[11]

From the moment he became her literary agent, Gunther Stuhlmann gave Anaïs Nin sound, solid advice at every stage of her career, but as always she did exactly as she pleased and left Gunther to sort out the details and deal with the frequent messes. He thought it wiser to wait for Maschler's offer than to sign with the marginal Peter Owen, but Anaïs continued not only to court but also to pursue Peter Owen.[12]

Owen expressed interest but was vague about specifics and withstood all Anaïs's attempts to pin him down; Maschler was charming and gallant, and Anaïs was enthralled by his understanding of her work, but he, too, was vague about contracts. What neither she nor Gunther knew was that Maschler was about to move to Penguin Books and wanted to place Anaïs's work with its parent firm, Heineman.[13] She left London dispiritedly with no contract from either Owen or Maschler.

From London, she went to the Brussels World Fair with Hugo, having told Rupert that *Cue* sent her to cover it. Hugo was extremely tense. There was mutual distrust between him and his erstwhile partner, and there was wheeling and dealing on a level so high, fast, and frantic that Hugo was hard-pressed to explain it and Anaïs could not understand it. Hugo was in constant flight between Curaçao, Havana, London, Brussels, and Geneva, selling properties and moving large deposits of money. Everything was top secret, hush-hush, and he expected Anaïs to support all his cloak-and-dagger drama with patience and fortitude. As Castro forged his relentless way from the provinces to Havana that culminated in his seizure of power on New Year's Day, 1959, the Archibalds moved swiftly to secure their assets, using Hugo as their intermediary, but they made the decisions and treated him as little more than a high-level messenger and low-level adviser. The Sánchez family (controlled now by Bernabé, Eduardo's eldest brother) did little despite Hugo's warnings, convinced they were inviolable no matter who took over the country.[14] The indomitable old Socialist Tía Antolina, the last of Rosa Culmell's sisters still alive, embarrassed them all by embracing Castro as the country's savior and vowing to put all her assets at his disposal.[15]

Hugo still believed that his financial future would be one of constantly escalating wealth, and demonstrated his assurance by booking a suite at the Crillon for the entire summer, even though he knew he would be in transit on his usual business routes until August, when he had three weeks' vacation.[16] He urged Anaïs to take advantage of the suite to reacquaint herself with the city she now spoke of rapturously as the place where she had spent the happiest years of her life.

"The idea of returning to Europe is a little overwhelming for the moment," Anaïs wrote to Gore. "The trapeze will be complex, like the airplane problem, to avoid collisions."[17] Logistics were eased somewhat because Rupert taught until mid-June, then would be safely confined to Los Angeles for the rest of the month while he took examinations for teaching certification. After that, he either wanted her in Los Angeles, or wanted to be with her while she "worked in the Paris office of Cue."[18]

Everything about the trip was upsetting to Anaïs. She had nightmares about cemeteries and feared death and loss, especially that she might lose Rupert during such a long absence.[19]

She dreamed of Tom Payne, of whom she had an occasional, extremely fleeting, erotic fantasy. In her dream, he was seducing an extremely fat woman she knew in Los Angeles and Anaïs wondered "why not me?"[20] She interpreted the dream as another version of being "left out of the family circle, [and] desperation at being left out of [*Eve*], a free lancer and not in the inner circle, the same old story but with a different twist." Then there were dreams of darkness and jealousy, which she hated; they represented "lights turned out," of parents who "quarreled all day" and "achieved closeness at night." It explained, she thought, her "abnormal jealousy of couples embracing, anywhere, even when I am with Rupert, a lover of my own."

Ultimately, however, her bitterness, fear, and unease centered around the question "why not me?" Why had Durrell found such great success with *Justine*? Why had Jim become "so rich and famous now" with *Blue Denim*, and why were his novels such a hit with her former editor (to whom she introduced Jim) even as he declined to publish hers? She wondered "why not me" even with Lesley, whom she sincerely liked and admired, as *The Wilder Shores of Love* continued to garner high praise and critical respect while Anaïs could not even get her work published.

Outwardly she remained serene, never giving any indication that she was angry, never directing any visible sign of anger at others. Instead, she unleashed it into the diary in two ways: she wrote diatribes against Rupert and his life in long, exhaustive, repetitious detail; and her behavior grew reckless, as she courted danger and discovery of the trapeze.

As she flew to New York in mid-June, preparatory to joining Hugo in Europe, she had an idea. Rupert thought Hugo was long gone from her life, which was why, after all, he had married Anaïs in 1955. He believed that she never saw him on her trips to New York and always stayed in someone else's apartment. Now she decided to invent a story that Hugo was waiting for her at the airport when she landed after a bumpy, sleepless night's flight, supposedly to talk about "death and wills."[21] Incredibly, Rupert not only believed her, he put a compassionate gloss on her tale: "Love, I understand how you feel about Hugo and know how difficult this must have been . . . but I think it good for Hugo just to see you and talk and to feel he may still help you in some way . . . talk of wills and leaving me something . . . is so silly. You, with the highest contempt for facts, are becoming obsessed with the fact of our birth dates to the complete exclusion of the fact of your mirror . . . or of the bond of our relationship."

Now she made an even more reckless decision: to bring Rupert to Europe and somehow swing upon her trapeze throughout the summer. She envisioned herself staying with Hugo in the Crillon and running across Paris to some dingy Left Bank hotel where she planned to cache Rupert, and pondered the logistics of keeping each man from finding out about the other. She drew Caresse Crosby into her dangerous game, coyly asking "which husband" Caresse wanted her to bring to Greece. Never one to mince words, Caresse blasted Anaïs: "You lay yourself open to the answer! . . . I can't accept that two husband myth. . . . That Hugo does accept it, though people laugh, shows what a very exceptional being he is. Nuff said and forgive me. Perhaps you never should have told me."[22] Anaïs did not take Rupert to meet Caresse Crosby, then or ever.

"Anything you do is all right with me, love," Rupert told Anaïs, as she concocted a story about why she needed to be in Europe: *Cue* was now having trouble in the Paris office, and only she could straighten things out; also, the editors wanted her to travel to various European festivals and write about them. Of course her "job" was paying all her expenses, and handsomely to boot, so Rupert should join her as soon as his exams were finished. He believed her and did not care "where or how" they lived in Europe, "as long as it's together."[23]

The tale she concocted for Hugo was more simple. As he would be so busy with business, Anaïs said she was loath to stay in Paris without him, even in the Crillon. She invented a friend, "Rachel," who was flying first to England to visit "her" six old aunts, sisters of "her" father, Reginald (all of which Rupert planned to do before joining her). Then "Rachel" would come by boat train to Gare St. Lazare, where Anaïs would be waiting with her luggage, and off they would go directly south, to spend three weeks driving a little rented Renault to Provence, Italy, and possibly to Barcelona, where Joaquín was spending the summer. When it was time for Hugo's three-week vacation in August, Anaïs would ship Rupert home via England and Ireland and join Hugo in Venice. Amazingly, her plan worked and neither man discovered any trace of the other's presence, even though there were several close shaves.

"It was not a happy trip," she wrote on the flight home at the end of August, when she gave full details to the diary of "Hugo and I" and "Trip with Rupert."[24] It gave her an excuse to decry Rupert's penny-pinching, his stubbornness, and, especially, his truculence over "his inability to control the situation." It also allowed her to contrast the way her two husbands traveled. Rupert scrimped during their modest journey across France and Italy (which her "job" paid for) so that he would have some of the expense money left to save for his house. He sent an apologetic telegram after he returned to Los Angeles begging "forgiveness parsimony," followed by an unconsciously ironic letter telling Anaïs he was so glad she could go to Venice if she had "to be stuck with [*Cue*'s] Business Manager."[25]

Hugo pampered her for three weeks at the Grand Hotel. "I know you are not supposed to go to Venice with your husband," she wrote to her brother Joaquín, "but I did and it was wonderful. What do you think of that!"[26]

When she returned to New York, the memory of her contentment in Venice was so strong that she continued to invent problems at *Cue* so that she would not have to go to Los Angeles, as life there "seemed shabbier than ever." She drifted about trying to make a new network of friends and heard of a group of artists who had moved south of Greenwich Village to Coenties Slip, the "last stop for the non-conformist, Bohemia on the Waterfront," the first wave of "Village expatriates in search of larger lofts [and] lower rents."[27] Among them was

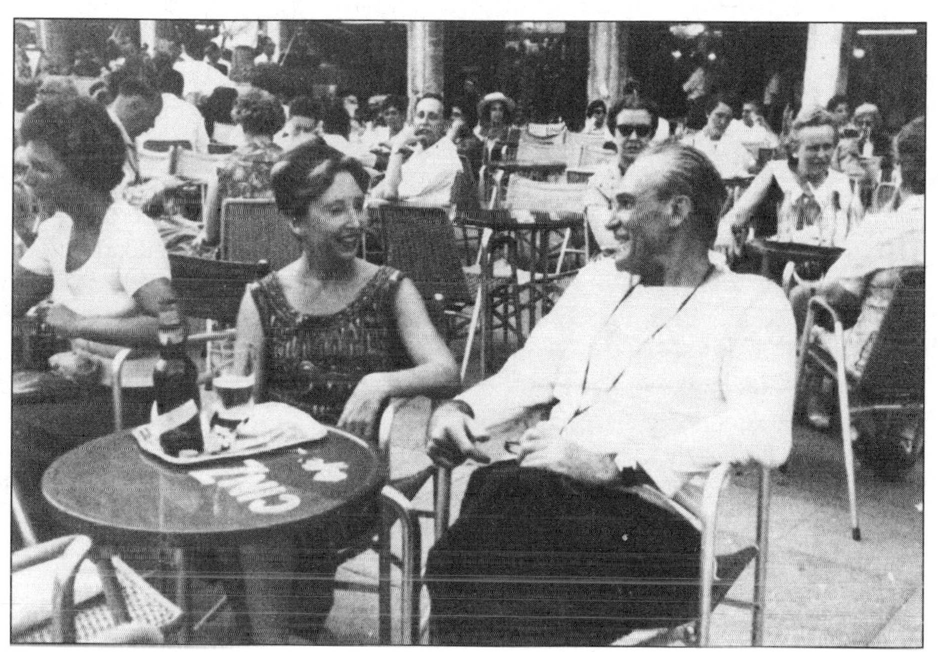

Anaïs and Hugo in Venice.

Lenore Tawney, the small, mystical being who created sculpture in fabric, weaving brilliant colors with feathers, found objects, or whatever else struck her imagination.

Tawney captivated Anaïs as the manifestation of the true spirit of pure art.[28] She lived alone, as she had since her husband was killed in World War II.[29] Her tranquillity and inner contentment were marvelous to contemplate, and Anaïs was dumbstruck by how serenely Lenore lived in what, for her, would have been isolation and loneliness. Anaïs was not seeking Lenore's friendship in the newly learned equality with which she embraced women such as Lesley Blanch; rather, she wanted Lenore to be as entranced with her as women such as Thurema Sokol had been throughout the 1930s and '40s. She did not seek to understand Lenore's "otherness." Instead, she wanted her to become "ensorcelled," which, given Lenore Tawney's artistic independence and integrity of vision, was impossible. Lenore Tawney joined June Miller, Rebecca West, Djuna Barnes, and even Lesley Blanch as another of the women who refused the "intense merging" Anaïs Nin sought all her life.[30]

Anaïs Nin needed to have Lenore Tawney adore her, which of course did not happen, and so she put compliments into her mouth. In the unpublished diary, she made Tawney say something that later she would make many others say in the published ones: "You are a great artist, Anaïs, for you I would give you my work in exchange for what your books meant to me."[31] Many years later, Lenore Tawney was puzzled to learn that Anaïs Nin had written this, for she had not even known that Anaïs Nin was a writer until, after several parties, she came alone one day to Tawney's vast loft, "a place where they once made sails, a studio as vast as a church." Tawney's account of the exchange is very different: "Anaïs paid me too many compliments. I didn't like them. She kept insisting that she had to have some of my work. In exchange, she wanted to give me her hand-printed books. It seemed very important to her so I finally agreed. Once I gave her the weaving, she stopped coming to the loft."[32]

In Los Angeles that fall, Anaïs brooded over Larry Durrell's success, especially when Gore told her *Justine* had been bought for the movies and he would probably write the screenplay.[33] She read and reread *Balthazar,* then wrote to Hugo: "Decided Durrell is a brilliant cheat, who does not have a deep knowledge of character. It shows in this Balthazar soi-disant psychiatrist. Promises relativity of truth but that lies in acceptance of subjectivity and that means introspection going in, and he has [none]."

She was angry about other books as well. How could American readers make *Lolita* a bestseller? "They ban stories of sex between men and women (Miller's) but not sex between a man of fifty and a girl of thirteen!"[34] And when Jim's new play, *Crazy October,* closed after several performances despite a glittering cast that included Tallulah Bankhead, she felt a grim satisfaction that she did not bother to hide from the author.[35]

She asked Tom Payne why Durrell's novels had been "treated with more fairness" than hers, and he had a swift reply, the only consolation she gained in a dispiriting time. "Three reasons," he said: "1. Your work is purer than his. He mixes the unconscious with long stretches of almost conventional novel writing. People can cling to that. 2. Time: you came too soon. 3. You are a woman. All the critics are men."[36]

Gunther was having no success in placing her work in Europe, and Neville Armstrong struck another wounding blow, saying he would not publish *Solar Barque* because he did not think he could sell even 500 copies in England: "The title seems all wrong and I don't want to say this but your readers . . . are waiting for a new novel with a strong, provocative title and theme, a title such as *House of Incest.* When you can write me the right book, it need not be too long because you don't write them that way, I can really sell 10,000 copies."[37]

It was the last straw. When Peter Owen offered to print *Children of the Albatross* and *The Four-Chambered Heart* in a niggardly contract that demanded a share of any future North American royalties and required Hugo to share printing costs, Anaïs accepted. Gunther was upset that she had not consulted him, but tried to make the best of it. His British associate, Mark Patterson, was furious because it placed him in an embarrassing position with publishers he had been courting on Anaïs's behalf.[38] He said she must decide who was representing her—Gunther (and therefore Patterson) or herself.

Fearing that Gunther would dismiss her as a client, Anaïs kept secret the real reason Peter Owen finally agreed to give her a contract. Owen had made one non-negotiable condition to publishing her novels: Anaïs told him Larry Durrell volunteered to write a preface for *Children,* and now she had to turn her lie into a truth.

She took Rupert to meet Larry and Claude on their drive to the south of France that summer. Fame engulfed the Durrells, as journalists, filmmakers and scholars passed through their village in a steady stream, and the superlatives abounded. The Durrells were also inundated with his children, Claude's, and other family members and visitors they hadn't seen for years. Larry and Claude coped with the barrage of people, broken plumbing, and chicken pox (the children and Claude), all the while trying to work. Both wanted to live permanently in France and write without having to take jobs to pay their various alimonies and living expenses. This was their main chance to capitalize on the success of his novels, and they knew they needed to keep focused on their work.

Anaïs came twice into this harried household, once with Hugo and once with Rupert, who the children thought a cowboy from the Old West, especially when he pulled out his guitar and entertained them.[39]

The Durrells were polite when Anaïs arrived both times with a shower of gifts, but Larry made it clear in his letters and during her visits that he was harassed and needed time to work.[40] She ignored his polite hints. What did he need or want to read? she asked. And when he provided long lists of books both expensive and difficult to find, she went out of her way to get them. She asked if he would like to come to Paris for several days as guests of her and Hugo, naturally to stay at the Crillon, and he accepted with alacrity. And when Larry complained that publishers were slow to pay, he was short of cash, and had overdue bills, Hugo sent several sizable money orders.

It was then that Anaïs made her request. If, she said, he were to write a preface, she was sure Peter Owen would stop vacillating and offer her a contract. She intimated that her publishing future was in his hands, and left Durrell no choice but to write it.

He dashed it off overnight, and Anaïs was horrified when she read it, calling it "obtuse and foolish, way off the mark."[41] She wrote Peter Owen to ask him not to use it. Owen naturally disagreed, knowing how many books Durrell's name would sell. Anaïs tried another tack, saying Durrell gave her permission to cut whatever she wished, and she wished to cut all references "of a personal nature." She also objected to specific images, such as Larry's awkward use of the word "embalming" to show how she "extracted poetic essence," of his description of her prose as "irridescent and rainbow-coloured and peacock's tail."[42]

When Anaïs realized that the preface was going to be included whether she liked it or not, she turned to Hugo to save her.[43] He offered Owen such diverse solutions as paying him for eliminating the preface and when that failed, threatened legal action. Owen ignored Hugo and published the book, preface mostly intact.

When the book appeared she was "enormously depressed."[44] Hugo suggested she write a "diplomatic" letter explaining what upset her; instead, Anaïs blasted Larry for the "great humiliation," and for making her feel like one of the many "nuisances" who plagued him. Larry said her letter filled him "with absolute amazement; really, amazement!"[45] He apologized for having wounded her "inadvertently," and said he wrote "with no thought except to show solidarity and admiration for an old friend and admired artist." He was genuinely puzzled: "Please when you next write tell me what I should ask you to forgive."

Anaïs calmed down. The next time she wrote to Larry, she admitted an "emotionalism which came out of a million accumulative distortions in twenty years of life in America, and which made me expect and count too deeply on your words." She asked him to "just forget about it." She wrote this second letter because she knew she might still need to make use of Larry Durrell and his connections and was hoping to hitch herself in any way possible to the filming of his novels in Hollywood. She still thought about reprinting his *Black Book* on the putative Anaïs Nin Press, and she also wanted to take advantage of a casual introduction he gave her when he told her to call on a young medical student in Paris, Jean Fanchette, who was beginning a bilingual magazine called *Two Cities*.

Larry hinted that Fanchette might be persuaded to publish a part of the diary that dealt with the Three Musqueteers during their Villa Seurat days, and it was all Anaïs needed to hear. When Fanchette told her that the first issue of *Two Cities* would indeed include a portion of her diary along with articles by Miller, Durrell, and philosopher Gaston Bachelard, she was hooked. Anaïs offered everything from editing assistance to selling the magazine via her American network of bookstores to Hugo's money if it were needed. "I rely on the help you kindly offered," Fanchette replied, and then proceeded to tell her what to do: "please insist [on] Miller's contribution."[46] Fanchette wanted an "original text," but if she could not wangle one, she was directed to secure permission to reprint Henry's preface to *Justine*. If Fanchette's peremptory orders were upsetting, the rest of his letter was soothing. As soon as he finished writing an article about Durrell for the first issue, he told her he planned to write another for a subsequent issue that he would call "L'art d'Anaïs Nin." She set to work on his behalf at once, but it was difficult from Los Angeles, where she spent most of the winter of 1959.

She had too much time to reflect on slights, real and imagined, and too much time to rehash the same old litany of her problems. A new word entered her vocabulary at this time: "Connection."[47] All her problems were related to it. She could not connect her "two loves," her "diary and novels," her "physical and spiritual life" and finally, she could not connect with "Rupert's life, the one he is at ease in."

Much of this musing was brought on because Rupert finally found the lot on which he wanted to build his house and Lloyd Wright grudgingly agreed to design it. Anaïs could no longer avoid the reality of what a house would mean: "a big burden, too tied down . . . no travelling."

As if she were preparing herself to break her bond to Rupert, she wrote pages, whether true or not, about all the other bonds she was responsible for breaking, from Henry and Gonzalo to the many men who flitted through her erotic life in the 1940s, and finally, to Gore Vidal.

Suddenly this writing changed, and in the center of a page, in very large letters, she commanded herself

ANAÏS BEGIN A BOOK—
WRITE
BEGIN ANYWHERE—

She tried to analyze why she could not fill out *Solar Barque* and amass enough pages to persuade an English publisher to give her a contract, so that Gunther could sell it in Germany and French and American publication might reasonably follow. She thought she knew why: "I am imprisoned in the Diary. . . . I am submerged by the enormity of my material. I . . . cannot construct."

"Where am I?" she asked, in large block letters in the center of a page. She left a great deal of space before she began to doodle a few random thoughts that she soon abandoned. Her final admonition to herself was once again centered, and in large block letters:

START A BOOK ANAÏS

35

"Too much to say"

THE TRAPEZE THAT HUNG SUSPENDED for almost thirteen years teetered on the brink of crashing as 1959 ended. Rumors of Anaïs's life with Hugo in New York drifted back to Hollywood, and a great many persons now knew about her double life. Unfortunately, whether with idle curiosity or true maliciousness, some guests at a party Rupert attended could not wait to tell him.

He brooded until it was 1:30 A.M. in New York, then telephoned Hugo's apartment. Anaïs, in her bedroom,[1] had just taken a sleeping pill and was dozing off when the phone rang. Half asleep, she heard Rupert's voice and became alert to the danger. "Wait a minute," she told him, then shut the door connecting her bedroom to Hugo's.

The next day she remembered that a long conversation ensued, but could recall only the gist and not the specifics. She remembered Rupert asking several times if she were alone in the apartment. She said "Yes" each time. When he hung up, she kept the receiver to her ear for a moment longer and "heard the click which means someone else was on the line."

Anaïs went into Hugo's room. "That's it," he said quietly. "No, it isn't," she replied. She begged Hugo to believe that a deranged man tracked her down in New York and was not worth such trauma, and he accepted her story.

When morning came, Anaïs and Hugo vied to see who could get

to Inge Bogner first (Hugo won). Anaïs then called Rupert and repeated that Hugo was never in the apartment when she stayed there, but was always traveling in Europe. He believed her as well, or, like Hugo, pretended that he did. Only Anaïs suffered from the double deception. She made herself so ill with worry that another round of visits to doctors followed.

For the past year, Anaïs had been telling Dr. Bogner that she wanted to live in New York with Hugo because their history was too complex to dissolve, their understanding of each other too strong to sever, and most of all, their life together had finally become everything she had always wanted—unparalleled luxury, European trips, a new wardrobe, and new friends who were either wealthy and cultured business clients or artists and intellectuals they met through Hugo's filmmaking. And it was actually a relief to Anaïs (and she thought to Hugo as well) that their physical relations now consisted mostly of cuddling, kissing, and gently touching each other.[2]

Rupert's telephone call gave Anaïs the perfect opportunity to dismount from the trapeze if she really wanted to, but she vacillated until she received the letter he wrote between his call and hers the next morning.[3] Whether Hugo was in the apartment was not the issue, Rupert wrote, for he was willing to accept that Hugo might be there some of the time: "The issue is that I can no longer believe all the things you tell me."

He saw only one solution: "no more separations. We can make it without the money. I only hope you love me enough to give up NY. Perhaps you'll have a better solution, but if it's devious I'll whack your little behind." He told her he loved and needed her, and wanted her to come back to him. Which is exactly what she did several days later.[4] She decided the passion was still there and she could not give Rupert up. Six weeks later, on schedule, she returned to Hugo, who was equally ecstatic to see her.

And so each man welcomed her, and each in his turn colluded with her double life by releasing her to go to the other. They helped her to remount the trapeze and to keep it firmly, securely in place. With their compliance, she remained on it for the rest of her life. Each man knew all too well how she deceived him in turn, but each allowed her to construct her web of lies and pretended to believe it.

She did not have to worry for long that Rupert might insist she give up her "job" and live permanently with him. He now had the lot on which to build his house, and he needed more money. He did not have enough to pay for the land outright, and the bank would not grant a construction mortgage until he owned the lot free and clear. Rupert borrowed what he needed from a loan company, taking on two mortgages. He needed Anaïs to contribute a minimum of $150 a week for the next twenty years or he would lose the house. It was a bondage she could have refused, but she assumed the burden as her just due.

At the same time, Hugo admitted how badly his income had plummeted when Castro assumed power in Cuba. He had often predicted gloom and doom in the past, but this time, Anaïs knew their situation was precarious when he ordered her to give up her "dual life."

She countered with her first serious attempt to sell the diaries, and approached the Institute for Sex Research at Indiana University (home of the Kinsey Report) when she learned it had a sizable collection of private diaries and journals. The Director of Field Research sent an alarming reply to her query, telling "Dear Mr. Nin" that the institute already owned "eight typed manuscripts" of hers, purchased from "a private collector." It consisted of the erotica she wrote for Barnet Ruder and single copies of *This Hunger* and *Under a Glass Bell.*[5] The institute would be happy to become the "guardian" of her diary but they had no money to purchase it. The director added that the unnamed seller had penciled a notation on the manuscripts that the material was "somewhat autobiographical."

This was even more frightening than Larry Durrell's few innocent personal comments in the despised preface and the equally innocuous biographical information Peter Owen wanted to include on the dust jacket of *Children of the Albatross.*[6] Swiftly on the heels of the institute's letter came one from Henry, telling her that he was about to publish *Letters to Emil* and a second book consisting of his and Durrell's letters. Anaïs was terrified. She continued to insist that Hugo knew nothing of her affair with Henry and would learn of it for the first time if Henry published the letters as they were originally written. She feared that Hugo would leave her, and the fear was heightened because, as Mrs. Anaïs Pole, she had just accepted the irrevocable legal burden of helping Rupert pay his dual mortgages.

And so, after years of being relegated to the oblivion of the unpublished, and therefore of no personal interest to the reading public,

Anaïs Nin was now confronted with pitfalls engendered by an audience curious to know about the personal life of the woman who had been Henry Miller's "friend." Also, the year was 1960, and women were beginning to seek the writings of other women. They passed well-worn, heavily thumbed copies of Anaïs Nin's novels from hand to hand, intrigued by the writer with such insight into their condition.

Men sought her as well; curiously, most were incarcerated in mental hospitals or prisons. She began an extensive correspondence with several in which she confided the innermost details of her life and thought. One in particular, Roger Bloom, a prisoner in the Illinois State Penal System, received weekly letters of ten or more pages that frequently served Anaïs in lieu of diary writing, for she kept carbons and inserted them directly into the folders that now constituted her diary.[7]

But all these people wanted biography, and while she soaked up their adulation like the California sunlight to which she was addicted, she rightly feared the risks that exposure of her personal life would bring. She began to annoy friends with repeated admonitions not to talk about her personal life. Eve and Henry Miller bore the brunt of her nattering with exceptional fortitude, but it took many conciliatory letters to calm her after Henry casually told the astronomer Sydney Omar when and where Anaïs Nin was born.[8]

She refused to heed Henry's advice that truth will out and she should stop trying to control it. Instead, she decided to create her own version of herself, to promote it whenever possible, and to stick to the details no matter how her questioners sleuthed or what they unearthed. In March 1960 she was invited by *The Harvard Advocate* to speak to students, and a staff member was assigned to interview her. Anaïs sent a two-page typed letter containing all the biographical information that she wanted to make known.[9] It included her Paris birth and French, Spanish, and Danish heritage, her parents' separation and moving with her mother to New York, and the beginning of the diary. She noted her return to Paris at age twenty (really twenty-two), but carefully omitted the reason (marriage to Hugo). She said she chose to write in English because her "most intimate friends" were Miller, Durrell, and West. Further rewriting her personal literary history, Surrealism became a minor and passing influence; from the beginning, Proust was major, as were Giraudoux, Pierre Jean Jouve, and Djuna Barnes. When she returned to New York, Edmund Wilson (not Gore Vidal, whom she did not mention) persuaded Dutton to publish *Ladders to Fire.* As a "special favor," she asked the reporter not to mention her marriage because she showed Hugo's films everywhere and "it is better for us to be known as separate artists."

She did not mention how distressed she was by the constant rejection of her fiction, but instead presented a glorified picture of her publishing history: she was "finishing" her career as a novelist to concentrate on her "major work," the diary, now consisting of more than "1,000 characters" and comprising ninety volumes. She now devoted all her time to "editing and copying [it] for future publication."

She was also preparing her public for how she wanted to be perceived: "I consider myself international. The world I have most devotedly pictured is the world of the artist. I have studied psychoanalysis and was a friend of Dr. Otto Rank and Dr. René Allendy." Content with this self-created portrait, she ended by asking, "Is this enough? Ask me anything you want to. There is too much to say!" —But no matter what anyone asked her in the years to come, Anaïs Nin seldom said more than this.

The fear of personal exposure intensified, because Anaïs Nin did write a book of sorts, an ending to *Solar Barque* that both encompassed and replaced the earlier work. Peter Owen agreed to publish it, but he had reservations. After telling her that "the writing is, of course, beautiful," he added that he was "rather worried about the form it takes and thought it would be a disservice to be anything but frank."

Owen was the first of the novel's many readers to feel that it was not a cohesive unity and that it did not provide a satisfactory summation and conclusion of all she had written in the previous novels. When he read it—before Anaïs Nin made fairly extensive revisions—it was two novels in one: Lillian's while she was in Mexico, and after that, as he noted, "Sabina and Djuna . . . and Pierre who really seems to have no importance or significance." Owen suggested that she either lessen Sabina and Djuna's roles or perhaps eliminate them altogether, jettison the unnecessary Pierre, and concentrate on showing all ramifications of the plot through the development of Lillian's character. If Anaïs would not agree to these changes, he had one other suggestion: perhaps she would write a short explanatory note of what had already happened in her previous novels as a way of preparing the reader to cope with the puzzling threads that she dangled in the new work without ever weaving them into whole cloth. Hoping to persuade her to follow this latter course, Owen noted that critics were liable "to pounce" on her inconsistencies, and added a phrase designed to strike terror in an author's heart: "Sales will be affected."[10]

Naturally Anaïs disagreed: "The real basic trouble lies in the fact that the book was designed to follow the other books and the denial of this continuity is bound to create a few inconsistancies."[11] Owen held the power, however, and he wielded it: no introduction, no publication.

Also, he wanted a tantalizing title, and for the first time ever, Anaïs was unable to think of one.[12] She finally settled halfheartedly on *Seduction of the Minotaur,* in deference to Neville Armstrong's earlier wish for one that would pique the same sort of reader interest as *House of Incest.* The idea eventually came to her that all the novels were interior explorations and were filled with threads of ideas and weavings of characterization, of labyrinthine plots and mazelike levels of understanding. Suddenly she had the title for the last book in the series: what had been *Solar Barque* would become incorporated into the new writing, henceforth to be known as *Seduction of the Minotaur.*

In the meantime, Owen continued to complain about the inconsistencies in the text as a stalling tactic, so Anaïs made a further compromise: to publish only the sections concerning Lillian and to omit those concerning Djuna and Sabina. It was a large concession, and to justify it while appeasing herself, she compared her novels to Durrell's Alexandria Quartet, insisting that, from the very first, she had envisioned everything she wrote as a series, and all were to be judged in their entirety rather than as separate entities.

Owen would certainly not agree to the major expense of publishing and promoting all the novels within one cover when he had such serious reservations about a text as vague and tenuous as *Seduction.* He was even reluctant to accept the title, and asked Anaïs to call it "Springtime," which in retrospect is both amusing and unsuitable.[13] Despite Gunther's frequent letters reminding Owen of his contractual responsibilities, he continued to hesitate over minutiae and to delay publication.[14]

Anaïs, embittered and hiding out in Los Angeles with Rupert

(where she would not have to face questions from her literary friends in New York, who were eager to know the new novel's publication date), described her feelings in a letter to Hugo: "I am finally facing the extent of my failure. Almost total, I might say."[15] She added that "in preparation for quitting," she was learning to cook "seriously" and had become "a very fine woodstacker."

In reality, she was helping Rupert to stack trees felled on the lot where he finally built his dream house, a steep hillside on Hidalgo Avenue, "the wrong side of Silver Lake," with a sweeping view of the reservoir that gave the area its name, and of the hills and mountains that ring Los Angeles to the north and east.[16] Lloyd Wright created the house's basic design, a shed consisting of a large central living area leading to a kitchen at one end and opening directly into a bedroom at the other. At the bedroom end of the house, a bookcase wall separates the living area from a bathroom and a narrow room with a large plate glass window that became Anaïs's study. Rupert did much of the construction himself, designing and supervising the building of the stone-walled fireplace that separated the kitchen from the main living area. To save money, he used inexpensive materials, and Anaïs's contribution was to stain the plywood walls and kitchen cabinets, dark but with a hint of purple showing through. She also selected the mosaic tiles for the countertops, a mélange of "soft grey mauve on the purple side."[17] These colors dominated the plaid fabric of the foam cushions on the plywood banquettes that served as seating in the living area, and the bedspread covering their mattress, which rested on the floor. The same fabric was used for the only curtains in the house, on the bedroom area's sliding glass doors, which like the living area opened onto a small terrace and pool, an extra expense not included in the price of the house. Rupert painted the pool black to make it look like a natural swimming hole. Anaïs swam every day, as it was her preferred form of exercise.

Jim Herlihy wanted to buy Anaïs a housewarming gift, and she was eager to accept because "economics on this side of the moon are strained." They were struggling to repay the $16,000 in house loans, the pool payments were an extra burden, and the car, she told Jim, was "on its very last lap, almost as impossible as Reginald."[18] Rupert's elderly father's mental functioning was impaired and he required supervision. Anaïs and Rupert strove to make the old man's declining years comfortable, but it cost them dearly in time, money, and emotional distress.

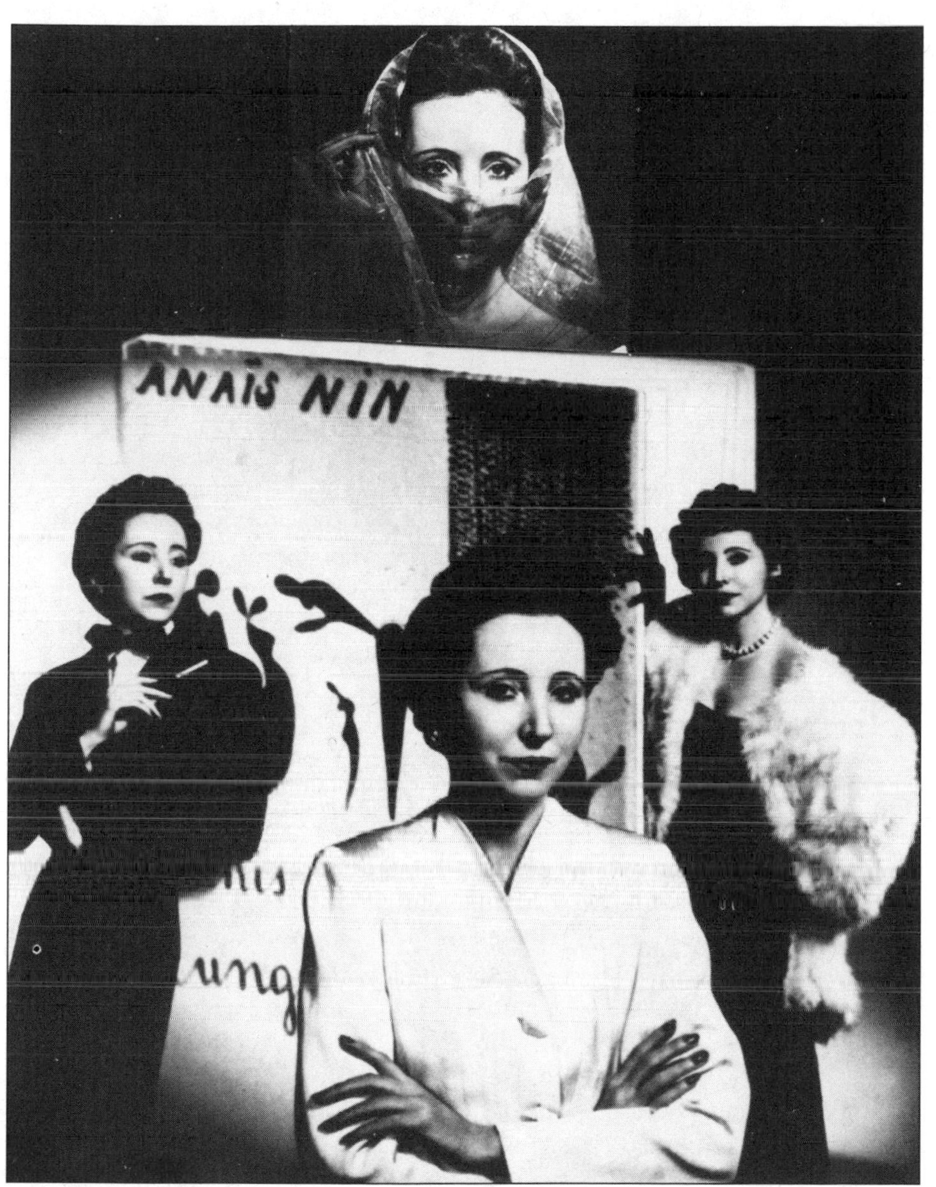

Publicity shot for *This Hunger*, disliked by Anaïs.

She had no emotional oasis throughout 1960, for Hugo moved as well. The building at 35 W. 9th Street was turned into a co-op, and tenants who chose not to buy had to move. Hugo did not have the $20,000 to buy it outright and knew that he could not qualify for a mortgage.

Anaïs was reluctant to leave Rupert alone when there was much work to be done in the house, so she invented reasons not to help Hugo find an apartment. First there was a "job" as assistant for program preparation on a radio show, which she told Hugo required her to remain in Hollywood.[19] More truthfully, she met Tracey Roberts, a young actress who wanted her to write a screenplay of *Spy,* wanting both to star in and produce the film. Tracey's machinations unfolded over a period of years with a succession of writers and became one of Anaïs's most dependable excuses when she did not want to leave Rupert.[20]

And so, Hugo looked for a new apartment without Anaïs's cooperation or approval and found one in a new development called Washington Square Village. He could afford the rent and it was large enough to accommodate his film equipment. The building was typical of the architecture of the 1960s: massive, brutal, and without charm. It did, however, have light, space, and a terrace. Anaïs was furious; that Hugo could expect her to live in such a functional, unadorned setting was so incredible she had difficulty comprehending it.[21]

She wrote angry letters, but Hugo held his ground. If she chose to stay in California, he would not put his life on hiatus until she deigned to show up and tell him he could start living again. Without actually saying it, Hugo was letting Anaïs know that he would no longer wait patiently for her to come back, but would live fully whether she was there or not. He also told her he was about to decorate the apartment; galvanized into action, she returned at once.

Hugo had just recovered from a serious bout of hepatitis, which Anaïs believed was responsible for a series of uncharacteristic demands, including a dog.[22] It was unusual, because Hugo had never had a dog, only a succession of cats who came to untimely and unfortunate ends. To appease him, Anaïs bought the first in a succession of white miniature poodles, naming him Bouboule.[23]

Confronted with the fluffball, Hugo told Anaïs he could not accept Bouboule until he discussed it with Bogner, as he did with any deviation from his normal routine.[24] Bogner told him to consider it "half a cat"[25] and enjoy it, but he objected to its care. Hugo abdicated responsibility and Bouboule became Anaïs's dog and fellow traveler on her bi-coastal and international trapeze.

Bouboule created an interesting wrinkle in Anaïs's double life. Rupert dubbed him Piccolo, and Anaïs was hard-pressed to explain to Hugo why the dog, who by this time was spending most of his time in California, did not come when called Bouboule. When the poor confused animal was a year old, Anaïs told Hugo that Bouboule/ Piccolo was so happy with "The Belgian Ladies" (another euphemism for Rupert) that she did not want him to travel anymore. Hugo was greatly relieved and went back to cats. Rupert kept Piccolo, who was succeeded by Piccolino and Pico in turn.

The direct route to money, via book publication, seemed blocked, so Anaïs seized upon the opportunity offered by Jean Fanchette when he named her American editor of *Two Cities.*[26]

Signs of trouble were there from the beginning.[27] In her typical fashion, Anaïs not only volunteered to have her friends submit their writings, she was also determined to dictate what those writings should be. Not surprisingly, she thought many should be about her, and enlisted friends, relatives, and even critics she scarcely knew, such as Edwin Fancher, a co-founder of the *Village Voice,* who had praised *Under a Glass Bell* there.[28]

Fanchette tolerated her peremptory ways, mostly because she willingly contributed money to pay the printer, the translator, the occasional secretary, and once even bought the paper on which *Two Cities* was printed. Anaïs persuaded herself to overlook Fanchette's "intransigence" at not deferring to her editorial demands because the first volume of the magazine, an "hommage à Durrell," contained Fanchette's essay on her work and she could not have asked for a more flattering essay had she written it herself. He called Anaïs Nin one of the twentieth century's most original and gifted writers and listed *House of Incest* among its masterpieces. Fanchette compared Nin to Virginia Woolf, whose writing was just at the beginning of the extraordinary renaissance that has characterized its reception and her reputation ever since. Whatever Woolf had done to enhance the reputation of "feminine literature," Fanchette thought Nin had already done it, and better.[29] For such a glowing tribute, Anaïs Nin forgave his many real or imagined slights and injustices.

Like the *Masterplots of 1954,* which listed *Spy* among them, Fanchette's essay became another tool in her ongoing campaign of self-promotion. Hugo paid to have an initial 500 copies off-printed, some of which Anaïs always carried with her, and which she frequently passed out to puzzled strangers who wondered what they had said or done to make this exotic-looking woman so intent on pressing an article about herself into their hands.[30]

When she heard of another periodical that was in the planning stages, Anaïs seized upon the opportunity to become its roving editor.[31] She pursued it more avidly than the others, but for the first time with a caveat: "I can't any more afford the luxury of working without pay, because I am deep deep deep in debts. Hugo takes care only of one side of my life. The other is a constant drain and struggle."[32]

Lila Rosenblum had been approached by a "reclusive young millionaire" to start a new magazine that was supposed to be an "Esquire for Women." It was to be called "The Fair Sex," and those who saw the dummy of the first issue later described it as "an impressive precursor to *MS.*" Several decades later, Lila recalled sadly that it was "too early, too premature."

Anaïs took Lila into her confidence and told her about the invented "jobs," the "pay" that was really Hugo's allowance, and the ensuing guilt and ongoing problem of how to pay her other debts. "I had pleasure in this 'fantasy magazine,' " Anaïs said, "but the real one is far better than my invention."[33]

Lila had difficulties getting "the investor" to turn over the money he promised, but she worked hard for the better part of 1961 on the dummy of the first issue, spending her own money in the process. Anaïs worked just as hard, and without pay. But as legal agreements between Lila and the investor were being drawn up by a reputable lawyer, and as a formal date was set for signing them, it seemed only a matter of time until Anaïs would receive her first real paycheck. Suddenly she was confronted with a problem of major proportion.

As long as she had no income of her own, she had no reason to fear the dreaded Internal Revenue Service, for she was officially known as

Mrs. Hugh Guiler and he filed their joint returns.[34] But once she was on a legitimate payroll, she would have to explain her annual W-2 form to Hugo, and why she did not contribute the salary to the family coffers.

A small matter such as bigamy had not stopped Mrs. Guiler from also becoming Mrs. Pole; neither would the small matter of a genuine salary stop her now. Anaïs Nin received her first social security card, number 058-36-0603, not as herself but in the name of Lillian Beye, the character in her novels with whom she most closely identified. Said Lillian Beye gave her address as 756 Greenwich Street, New York 14, NY, which just happened to be where Lila Rosenblum lived.[35]

Believing that she had once again managed to fit all the pieces of her several lives into a cohesive entity, Anaïs got to work convincing friends to contribute to *The Fair Sex*. She feared that she was already suspect because "I got so many writers working on Two Cities and my credit with them is bad now. They think I am always entangled with unpractical schemes." Nevertheless, she was sure she could persuade Gore Vidal to write something. Breezily, she planned when next in Paris "to get in touch with Beckett, Ionesco," and noted that "the author of the Zoo Story, Albee, is someone to look into. Very striking writer."

Not only did she intend to use the magazine's pages to promote her friends, she also planned to get even with her enemies, and Maxwell Geismar was now one. Still smarting about his suggestion that she write on Mary McCarthy and Simone de Beauvoir for *The Nation*, Anaïs suggested that Max write for *The Fair Sex* about "women's writing . . . which has been devaluated and ignored in great part."[36]

Geismar declined, which was just as well, for when the long-awaited day came for Lila and "the investor" to formalize their agreement in the lawyer's office, she waited and waited, but he did not appear. The investor turned out to be a con artist: a gardener from Phoenix, Arizona, he passed himself off as a man of cultivation in the intellectual rather than the botanical sense of the word, and Lila Rosenblum was not the first he duped. Lila became depressed, but Anaïs tossed it off as just another betrayal. She turned it into a short story and gave a wry, humorous account in the published diary.[37]

Out of the blue, Anaïs was offered a full-time position to teach writing at Los Angeles State College with a salary that would have almost doubled Hugo's allowance. Rupert was flabbergasted when she turned it down, arguing that she could not become a teacher until she learned "to spar, to deflect hostility."[38] He was furious and suspicious of her real reason when the college continued to woo her, hoping to change her mind. She held fast and stalled with weak and unconvincing excuses.

Hugo was in Europe during August 1961, which gave Anaïs temporary respite to stay in Los Angeles and placate Rupert. "How hard it is to recreate faith," she wrote to Lila.[39]

To join Hugo required creativity and imagination. She printed a telegram message signed by a mythical boss at *Cue,* mailed it to Lila in New York, and asked her to send it to Silver Lake: "Can you replace Anne in Paris for two weeks 500 dollars August 16. Need you in NY August 15 one day . . . John Keating."

Lila sent the telegram and it had the desired effect on Rupert: "Now that the need of money is pressing, his security is rebuilt," Anaïs noted drolly.[40]

36

"Nin Rediscovered in Denver"

THE STRESS OF SUCH LYING was not without its toll. Anaïs resorted to the usual "sleeping pills every night,"[1] which caused "great depression and irritability" and impaired her writing. She drew upon her formidable willpower to prescribe her own cure, the elimination of all pills and alcohol, and as 1960 ended, was contemplating her publishing situation with renewed clarity and focus.

Her personal distress coincided with the most important change in her publishing fortunes, one that marked the start of her fame and led to the eventual publication of the diary. It happened by chance and grew out of an accounting muddle over her self-printed books that Larry Wallrich created when his bookshop folded.

Gunther Stuhlmann could not find an American publisher for Anaïs Nin's novels. In February 1961 she wrote him a sweetly shy letter, thanking him for his continuing faith. Although she was enormously grateful for his persistence, she was too tired to keep searching: "You have tried so hard! It is true my business is to write, but Gunther, I really can't go on writing and locking it up in a drawer!" She decided that she would prefer to be linked to Edwards Brothers for the rest of her writing career because she could no longer face the insults and humiliation that came with repeated rejection. She planned to straighten out Wallrich's distribution mess and take charge of the business affairs herself. Her distress was certainly well founded and valid, but the main reason for her desperate decision was that she had grown weary of dangling the diary before publishers as an enticement to get the novels published. That they did not want the fiction hurt, but the recurring rejection of the diary was deeply wounding.

Then, at the suggestion of Glenn Clairmonte, a regional writer whom she knew in Los Angeles, she contacted the Denver publisher Alan Swallow. For more than twenty years, Swallow had published poetry, serious fiction, and nonfiction—all from his garage. At a time when independent publishers were beginning to be engulfed by large corporations, Swallow was an anomaly who remained independent and although not rich, was certainly profitable.[2]

Anaïs contacted Swallow because she admired his courage in publishing Maude Hutchins' novel, *Victorine.* She decided to swallow her pride and submit her work to a commercial publisher for what she intended to be the last time. As always when she wanted something badly, she was so overeager that she wrote one of her garbled letters.[3]

To entice Swallow to publish her fiction, she dangled "a new unpublished manuscript," even though she had none. So eager was she that she guaranteed to "sell" (i.e., that Hugo would buy) 1,000 copies of anything he printed. Then she dangled her ultimate plum, the "one added factor" of inestimable magnitude: "I will give an option on the Diaries (for the future)."

Swallow's reply was the one she had yearned for: "I think it makes just about perfect sense that I become your U.S. publisher."[4] He told her he published only books he admired, and he admired hers, "so it should be a fairly good 'wedding' of work and publisher." Anaïs Nin could hardly believe her good fortune.

He agreed that all the novels should be published in one volume with the overall title of *Cities of the Interior.* As *Under a Glass Bell* had always been her most popular book, he saw no problem with keeping it in print, as well as *House of Incest.* He also agreed to what she thought was a small miracle: "to buy from you your present stock and to pay, in addition, on sales, a royalty." Anaïs was astonished: Swallow was not asking her to pay. He willingly took all the risk and did not ask her to invest a single cent of Hugo's money.

Swallow began the difficult work of building an audience for Anaïs Nin's fiction as soon as she signed his contract. An announcement in *Publishers Weekly* heralded five forthcoming titles: *Seduction of the Minotaur, House of Incest, Winter of Artifice, Under a Glass Bell,* and

Cities of the Interior. "Nin Rediscovered in Denver," read the headline when they began to appear within the following year.[5] But a year later, despite 400 copies sent out for review, *Seduction of the Minotaur* received scant notice and then mostly in columns that lumped new novels together and summarized them briefly.[6] When Anaïs received her royalty statement in March 1962, all five books had earned a grand total of $32.56.[7] It was one of a series of blows that came barreling at her one after the other, each threatening to undo her precarious double life.

First there was the tax return she needed to file for 1961. Hugo asked Anaïs to send documentation of her earnings to his accountant Roger Boulogne, who had hitherto handled his business matters and whom he now engaged to take care of the personal as well because they fluctuated so greatly. He believed he needed Boulogne first to unravel them, then to keep both him and Anaïs under fiscal restraint. Boulogne's attitude toward the Guilers' joint income tax was professional where theirs had been casual at best. He demanded a full account of Anaïs's earnings, but she was as dismissive of money matters as she had always been. "I still think it would be a mistake to draw attention to me," she replied to Hugo rather than directly to Boulogne. "I really think it should be left alone." She summarized her earnings for 1961 as $300 paid to her by *Vogue*[8] and said that all her other activity had been done without receiving a cent in payment. Hugo accepted everything she told him, and thus Boulogne had to as well.

But the question of her earnings soon became a serious and continuing problem for Anaïs because both men were obsessed with finances. Each wanted to see all her statements of income to make sure that she was not being gypped, and probably each wanted to try to figure out why she was not making any money. Her reputation was growing, and the invitations to speak in colleges and universities that would overwhelm her a few years later were beginning to mount steadily. She was traveling from both domiciles to meet these obligations, so each husband was aware of the engagements and naturally wanted to know how much she brought home. She parried their questions by saying that all earnings were paid directly to Gunther, to be dispensed periodically by him. He became her most convenient excuse, and to ensure there would be no incriminating evidence to prove otherwise, she instructed Gunther to say he was ethically bound to divulge financial statements only to her, his client, and not to Hugo or Rupert. Fortunately, both men respected her professional agreement with her agent and neither attempted to contact Gunther.

Thinking she had weathered another crisis, Anaïs was then assaulted by the most serious to date:[9] Hugo's firm asked him to resign his partnership. He persuaded someone he knew at Hayden Stone to take him on, but it was at a reduced "draw against commission" of $1,300 a month, barely enough to meet his expenses in New York, let alone to pay for Anaïs's Los Angeles life. The grand days of the Hôtel Crillon and first-class air travel were over for Hugo, for there was no more expense account and only small investment funds to manage. He was shattered by the change in his fortunes.

Anaïs sprang into action to protect her California life. The first economy was to persuade Hugo to move to a cheaper apartment in the same building. Now she had to "think quickly" to justify the bi-coastal jaunts because Hugo naturally (and happily) assumed that she would continue to be dependent on him and would therefore have to share his reduced circumstances. "So now I have to earn this money I tell Hugo and Rupert I earn when I am away from home," she noted grimly.

Another crisis, this one involving Henry Miller, gave her a temporary respite. Henry had been taken up by Barney Rosset, the heroic publisher of Grove Press who championed banned writers and mounted court challenges of U.S. censorship laws. Rosset had just won a decision with *Lady Chatterley's Lover* and planned another test case with *Tropic of Cancer.* He had paid Miller an exceedingly high advance (for those days) of $50,000 and wanted to recoup it by publishing the book. Interest in Miller's work had been growing in the United States, and the success of Durrell's Alexandria Quartet brought with it a reflected and heightened curiosity about the two men and their friendship in Paris. To a much lesser degree, the reflection fell upon Anaïs Nin. Unfortunately, most of the growing interest was directed toward her "friendship" with Miller rather than toward her work, which of course rankled. As any curiosity about her personal life was a matter of concern, this new interest in connection with Miller was truly terrifying.

The public perception of Anaïs Nin at this time can be seen in an article about Miller's banned books written by Joseph Kaye, the New York correspondent of the *Kansas City Star.* Kaye thought her an "early Greenwich Village beatnik . . . who also writes in the unorthodox manner of Miller."[10] He was "staggered" by her appearance, "clad in a stunning Grecian robe and gold slippers." Like so many others, he was awed by the long flowing Mme. Récamier gowns and the gauzy Indian cottons she wore. She was fifty-eight but could have passed for a woman in her late thirties or early forties. Her hair was newly lightened to a becoming blond, her body was slim and taut from swimming, daily massage, and scrupulous attention to her diet.[11] Her face was exquisitely made up and she positioned herself carefully in the apartment's flattering soft pink lighting.[12] Kaye was so captivated that he swallowed her version of her life without question, that she had "helped Miller considerably when he was penniless in Paris."

This was good publicity but it was also dangerous. Some scholars were interested in biographical material about Miller and Durrell, which meant they were interested in her as well; others were interested in publishing collections of their letters and asked to include hers.[13] Miller, whose fear of loss was as strong as his fear of starvation, was so worried that calamity might befall his archives that he assigned everything in his possession to the UCLA library, including several hundred letters from Anaïs, many of them passionate love letters written during their long affair in Paris.[14]

When she found out that Henry had entrusted these letters to UCLA, Anaïs's primary emotion was not fright but fury. In retaliation, and because she was desperate for money now that Hugo's allowance was truly jeopardized, she sold some of Henry's letters to her.[15] Then she fired off a venomous diatribe, demanding that Henry return hers, which she declared were not his to give or sell.[16] Henry professed himself "just amazed" at "all this anguish."[17] He promised to see if the library would return them, but cautioned that they might now consider the letters to be their property. If such were the case, he said he would do everything in his power to ensure that no one could read them without his permission. And once again, he tried to tell his "dear Anaïs" that no matter how much she tried "to keep certain facts regarding your life a secret, certain things will leak out no matter what you do or say."

But to Henry, the most puzzling aspect of her diatribe was why, when she was so determined to impose secrecy on their relationship, she should now want to publish an edition of his letters to her. "What pleasure does that give you, feeling as you do about me?" If she insisted on proceeding, he insisted on assigning all rights to her so that she might receive the royalties and thus reap the profit. The situation was now reversed; he knew about her straitened circumstances and wanted to help. "How can I ever repay you, in money, for all you did for me? Or do you really take me for an utter ingrate. I would give anything to annihilate this fear, suspicion, doubt, or whatever it is that plagues you." Melodramatically, Henry poured it on: "My time draws near," he wrote, before adding truthfully, "The last thing I think of is to mar the few years left me by acting the fool or the scoundrel."

She accepted his offer of royalties and ownership of copyright, and a week later he sent his first check for $2,500, "the best I can do at this moment."[18] He also asked her to visit him in Pacific Palisades, where he was now living with his new wife, Lepska, and his two children by Eve, Valentine and Tony.

It was not a soothing visit. Typically, when Anaïs encountered persons happy and fully integrated into their lives, her reaction was to devalue them. She did this with Gore Vidal and James Leo Herlihy when their work made them comfortable and successful, and now she did it with Henry. She almost could not bear the sight of him in a pleasant home and the easy and emotionally honest way he joshed happily with his children.

Henry was almost seventy-one and looked his age, which gave Anaïs "a strange uneasiness" because it also indicated that she, too, was growing old. Henry told her nothing in life mattered but one's personal relationships. Anaïs snorted: "the Henry who wants to be thought a saint."

"What about you?" he asked. "Are you or are you not married to Rupert? Are you a bigamist?"

"No, I'm not," she responded firmly. "I just say we are because of his family, his students."

She told Henry about Hugo's losing his job, and how his gift of royalties temporarily relieved her of a possible crisis with one or both husbands. Henry repeated his conviction that she was not doing herself, Hugo, or Rupert any good by living a lie. Seeing her bristle, he changed the subject to their mutual pen pal, the convict Roger Bloom. Anaïs was furious. "On him he lavishes compassion, he can identify with Roger. . . . Not with Hugo, or my desire to protect Hugo from the truth."

The visit ended on a sour note when she began to nag again about her letters and Henry said if she wanted them that much, she should visit the UCLA library and steal them.

She did one better than that: she contacted library officials and suggested an exchange, saying she would give them Henry's letters if they would return hers to him. The head of the Special Collections Department sent a testy letter agreeing to her proposal, but only if the exchange were made simultaneously. Anaïs did not surrender all the letters, and Smith could not help wondering what all her fuss was about when he read those she gave him. He said it made no difference to the library which side of the correspondence was there, and "It really should make no difference to you, as these letters will not be made accessible to anyone until after your death, and I will furnish you with a written promise to that effect."[19]

The next in the series of crises concerned the original diaries, long housed at Bekins' Arcadia storage facility. At a party, Anaïs overheard a discussion of California marital-property law and was stunned to hear that Rupert, as her legal husband in that state, had the right to share all her assets. To her this meant the diaries, her only possession of monetary value. Without checking to see if this overheard conversation was valid, Anaïs began to plot how to move the diaries to another state. She could never rid herself of the fear that Rupert would abandon her for a younger woman and would demand his financial share of the diaries. This frightened her, not because of the money involved, but because it would give him the right to read them, and she could not bear to think he would learn how she wove a lifelong fabric of lies.

She became obsessed with moving the diaries away from California, and without investigating to see if New York had the same marital-property laws, decided to move them there. It was a complicated procedure, starting with Bekins refusing to release them until Jim Herlihy sent legal documents revoking the earlier agreement that named him co-trustee.[20] While Rupert was teaching, she packed a few heavy boxes whenever she could find an excuse to keep the car. Then she had to bide her time until she accumulated enough money to ship them. Her expenses included $600 for a lawyer, $150 shipping costs, and $30 each month for vault rental. Hugo's income was $1,500 or less each month, and because he had such high medical and telephone bills, he had cut her allowance in half to $200.[21] This was a firm figure from which she had to pay all her travel expenses and live. There was no other recourse, as Hugo depleted, then closed all their accounts. For the first time ever, Anaïs had no access to bailout money.

Several days after she shipped the diaries, she followed them to New York. When she arrived at the Railway Express office, she discovered that the shipment was "misplaced."[22] After several tense days during which she replayed the trauma of their temporary loss during the war, she systematically traced their cross-country transit. Her "persistent detective work" paid off, for they were eventually found. Greatly relieved, she locked them into a Brooklyn vault and kept the only key.

That, too, was a worry. Anaïs consulted a lawyer and made the first of several trusts to ensure their safety. She named Gunther Stuhlmann and Inge Bogner as joint trustees and gave them each a key. If she died before the diaries were published, and if they were subsequently sold, Gunther and Inge were to divide the money equally between Hugo and Rupert. If and when the two husbands died, her brother Joaquín and Hugo's brother, John, were to share the proceeds.[23] Neither Hugo nor Rupert knew about this trust, for she told only the two executors. Having taken such action, she was momentarily at peace for the first time in a very long time.

When Anaïs returned to Los Angeles, she had a sudden startling realization: she was happy in Rupert's house, took great pride in it, and was now calling it "our home." She could not believe her joy when she woke up and heard the birds singing. She loved to take her morning coffee onto the terrace and watch with pleasure as her "Japanese gardener, Rupert," made everything bloom and flourish. And she particularly loved it when the sun was setting behind the hills that bordered the opposite shore of the lake. Then, she and Rupert liked to swim nude in the pool.[24] These happy moments were, however, always tainted by guilt over Hugo. He was now her "cross," and Rupert was her "happiness in the physical world." It would have been so easy to plant the hitherto "portable" roots and to live in the house's shelter forever, but everything was tainted by money worries.

No one wanted to buy the diaries.[25] To earn extra income, she and Rupert hit upon the idea of becoming café performers in the coffeehouses that were proliferating in Malibu, Santa Monica, and Venice. Rupert suggested they adapt the "party" section of *Ladders to Fire* into a series of dialogues they could read together. Hoping to take their act to San Francisco, Anaïs described it in a letter to Ruth Witt

Anaïs with Rupert and Piccolo.

Diamant: "[Rupert] took the structure from theme of Chess Player. He sits on a stool and reads the Chess Players part. He indicates 'moves' on an imaginary chess board. He moves each time he becomes a different character (drunk, lover, zombie, etc.). I move each time I become a different woman (Sabina, Lillian and Djuna). There are stylized changes of voice, rhythm, gestures—not exactly acting, but certainly dramatic."[26] The coffeehouses were delighted to have them perform but did not pay them, so they never left Los Angeles.

The news from Gunther was equally dispiriting. Although he managed to sell *Seduction of the Minotaur* to an Italian publisher, the advance of 50,000 lire translated into less than $100.[27] Added to the grand sum of $270 from Alan Swallow, Anaïs's earnings for the year 1962 promised to be less than what Hugo used to give her for one month.

There were also serious problems standing between her and any publication of Henry's letters, which he now wanted to delay. His correspondence with Larry was to be published in the fall; he wanted the book to sell but was afraid to tell Anaïs directly, so he used the excuse that he did not want to "glut the market" with his letters to her.[28] Gunther tried to explain just how tangential was her claim to Henry's letters since he was the legal owner and especially since she insisted on publishing only his half of the correspondence. Gunther believed the only thing she had to gain would be publicity if she wrote an introduction, and to do so would again raise speculation that risked disclosure of her past.

Financial desperation led Anaïs once again to try to persuade someone to turn *A Spy in the House of Love* into a movie.[29] For a brief time, until Hugo lost his job, she hoped he would produce and direct it.[30] Wisely, he told her no one whose opinion mattered would take it seriously if done by her husband, but his financial setback soon made the question moot. He suggested Jean-Gabriel Albicocco, the French director of Italian descent whose most recent film, *The Girl with the Golden Eyes,* was one of his and Anaïs's favorites.

Anaïs wrote to him, enclosing a copy of *Spy* and suggesting possible treatments. In what seemed to Anaïs her second miracle in a year, Albicocco agreed to write a treatment, the first step toward a full screenplay.[31] The contract stipulated payment of 20,000 new francs, or $4,000, one half upon signing, the other upon delivery of the script.[32]

All this happened because of Albicocco's wife, Marie La Forêt, who

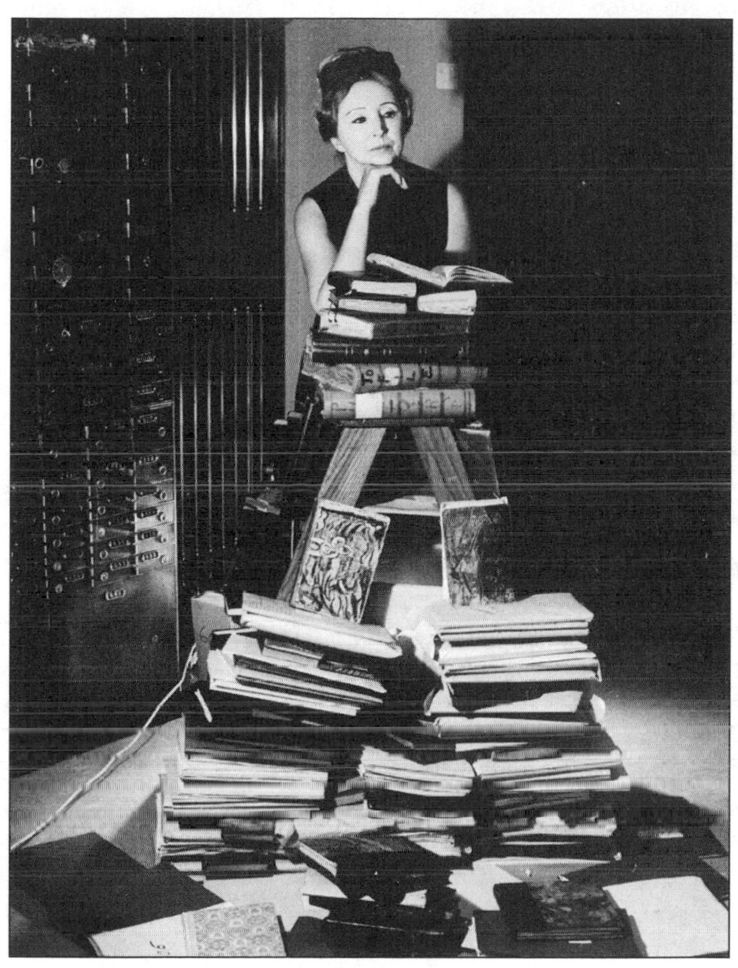

Anaïs Nin and her diaries in a bank vault.

read the book in English and felt an immediate sympathy with the women characters, and Tracey Roberts, the Hollywood actress who had long wanted to bring *Spy* to film.[33] Through Tracey Roberts, Anaïs met an ongoing series of screenwriters, all of whom she thought exhibited "a curious attitude toward Sabina." Tracey herself called the novel "The Lost Weekend of Sex," which irritated Anaïs, but she thought that the taint of nymphomania could easily be rectified in the film simply by showing that ten years elapsed between each of Sabina's affairs. With the screenwriters, however, she noted that all were "fundamentally unsympathetic" to Sabina's behavior, and most were "even hostile." To Anaïs's dismay, "they denigrated [Sabina] on the old morality rules! There was either an open contempt in the characterization or vulgarization or depoetization."[34]

One scriptwriter who actually moved the project further along than most was a young UCLA professor, Jascha Kessler, who agreed to write a full screenplay with all due speed.[35] He never learned what Anaïs disliked about what he thought was a "sensitive interpretation of her novel," for she cut him coldly as soon as she read it. She repeated Kessler's experience with any number of writers and producers for the next decade. Tom O'Horgan really wanted to stage the diaries and agreed halfheartedly "at least to consider" staging *Spy,* but it was not a serious proposal.[36] And there was a wealthy French-Canadian "heiress,"[37] a phantom wraith whom Anaïs pursued throughout 1963–64, but who eluded her time and again. Only Henry Jaglom remained in her good graces, probably because she could never pin him down to anything concrete.[38] Unfortunately, nothing concrete transpired with Albicocco either. He and his co-producers, Jacques Lanzmann and Maurice Conne, squabbled during preparation of several different contracts (all of which Anaïs was eager to sign); she was disappointed when they drifted off to other projects.

Anaïs, who said she could not accept a full-time, well-paying teaching job because she could not "spar" and "deflect hostility," now advertised for private writing students and charged them $10 an hour.[39] She had few takers, and they tied her down for a semester without real recompense.

She pretended the teaching was wildly successful and used it as an excuse to spend the summer in Silver Lake and avoid commiserating with Hugo, whose attitude was one of unrelieved gloom and doom. She needed to be especially conciliating when Hugo's letters began to rebuke her for behaving like "a child not helping [him] in reality," and insisted that she must "earn money, have a job."[40] "I thought you wanted me to depend on you," she responded. "On the one hand you wish me to make money as you mentioned three times in the past months, on the other your pride is always disturbed."

The diary and its fate loomed large in Anaïs's mind during these times when she needed enormous tact and discretion to deal with Hugo. Since no library wanted to buy it and no publisher wanted to print it, she had to think seriously about what ultimately to do with it. But there was an equally important consideration: namely, how to finish it, how to give it a sense of closure. She had not written each day since the mid-1950s, excusing herself by saying "everywhere I turned lay pain."[41]

She wanted to make the diary a final, finished document, but something was missing and she knew not what until she participated in a radio program honoring Antonin Artaud. She was asked to contribute personal reminiscences on a program that included the translator of one of Artaud's plays, a student who had written a thesis, and a scholar who translated some of his poems. As the program proceeded, Anaïs realized that the others were so busy arguing their theses that they did not listen to her anecdotes. "We never came to my portrait of Artaud," she wrote, "and in a way I was glad because I was struck by the awareness that the Artaud I knew was the human being, intimate and confessional. And I could not give them that! They did not want it!"

She returned to Silver Lake silent and depressed. She thought of everyone she had written about, how the "narrowness" of her vision did not permit her to see their alterity, their otherness. She realized the necessity to reach "outside" her "personal range" and expand the portraits beyond her personal reactions, and admitted that many of her portraits had been consciously created in retaliation for insults, humiliations, and slights, whether real or imagined. She wondered if she would ever succeed in "conquer[ing] my anger." Her task now was to strive for a "reciprocated love between artist and the world," for only then would "this anger disappear."

Instead, however, the anger hardened into a fixed and driving presence and caused her to focus on selling the diaries just as they were because she needed money. She could not manage on Hugo's $200 a month, especially if she had to fly to New York, which she no longer wanted to do. She asked Gunther to help her sell the diaries and he arranged for her to meet a dealer in manuscripts when she was next in New York.[42]

The dealer made a good first impression, so Anaïs took him to the Brooklyn vault and let him inspect all five metal files and more than ninety volumes of diaries. After intense scrutiny, he estimated that her archives should consist of: "All the diaries to date and those to come. All manuscripts to comc. First editions of *Under a Glass Bell, Winter of Artifice, House of Incest.* All correspondence. Photographs. 1,000 pages of erotica. Miller ms. [and] Miller letters." He thought $50,000 was a fair price. Anaïs was disappointed: "I said it was not enough. I said I would think it over."

No one she trusted was available to consult: Hugo and Gunther were away, and she did not dare tell Rupert because he would insist she take the money. She could not meet Dr. Bogner until the next day, so she confided in Sylvia and Ted Ruggles, former neighbors on 9th Street, and was upset when they urged her to accept the dealer's offer.

During her next day's session with Dr. Bogner, Anaïs admitted the root cause of her anger: "Think of the Diary being sold for the amount Grove Press gave to Tropic of Cancer!" Bogner told her to examine Henry Miller's alterity, to create a portrait that recognized him apart from her complex web of feelings about him as a useful way to rid herself of jealousy, competition, and anger. She also asked Anaïs to consider carefully whether she really wanted to part with the most valuable part of herself.

Anaïs Nin made her decision: she not only wanted $100,000 for the diaries, she wanted it only *after* they were published. When they were admired, respected, and feted by the world, then—and only then—would she accept the money she felt they were truly worth. She wanted these diaries to bring her what she believed she deserved—literary adulation and financial remuneration. In 1963 she thought she had only a few years left to live. Publishing the diaries became her single, abiding passion.

37

"Story of the Diary"

SHORTLY AFTER ANAÏS NIN decided she would not sell the diaries until they were published, she received a note from Professor Harry T. Moore of Southern Illinois University, the D. H. Lawrence scholar who had just agreed to write the introduction for Swallow's reissue of Nin's book.[1] Anaïs launched into a correspondence with Moore, hoping he would persuade the university library to buy her diaries. Moore told her it housed an impressive collection of contemporary archives, the most recent purchase being Caresse Crosby's, which included Anaïs's letters and Hugo's engravings. When Moore extended a speaking invitation to coincide with a special exhibit of Caresse's papers, Anaïs went because she wanted to see which letters Caresse sold and how incriminating they were.

The lecture attracted a large audience, as all her lectures did these days. Students still found her tales of the Surrealists fascinating, but what entranced them most were the merest tidbits about Miller and Durrell. She found it disconcerting to field the questions of young women who wanted to know (to "pry," as she put it worriedly) how she forged an identity as a woman writer in a male-dominated society. It made her realize that she had to walk a very fine line when she told highly dramatized tales of her life without even hinting about the person who made her glamorous existence possible—Hugo. Nin emphasized such biographical staples as being the daughter of the famous composer and pianist Joaquín Nin, with the underlying but always unstated assumption that her background was one of family wealth and privilege before her father's abandonment. After that, the persona of a woman writer rising triumphantly from poverty could not have a rich and doting husband as part of the picture. Her problem was how to mesh the various parts of her self-created history and still keep her secrets.

While she was at Southern Illinois University, the curator of the rare book collection invited her to view Caresse's papers privately. She did not like this man, and described him in one of the most unflattering of all her diary portraits as "Pinocchio in person."[2] That night, he inspired a long passage about biography and autobiography in which she crystallized her hesitation about selling the diaries.

Although she made him a figure of derision, the librarian was still "the holder of controls, secrets, the ruler of manuscripts, the one who slides open file drawers and shows you letters . . . diaries, first editions, treasures, indiscretions, betrayals, [all] sold for gold." It upset her to see letters, photos, and diaries preserved under glass as fixed and final artifacts that were no longer part of an ongoing life and was especially shocked to see her letters to Caresse given prominence of place, all because she was on the campus. She was upset that Caresse sold her archives "forgetting the intimate, sacred or secret trusts." Still, she admitted "to be just, I do the same in the diary. Her secrets are there. They will be exposed."

She had no misgivings about exposing Caresse's secrets, but was determined to hide her own at all cost. Her first meeting with Oliver Evans had been more than a decade ago, when she invited Tennessee Williams to tea in New York and he brought a friend who turned out to be Evans. Now, Moore, who was general editor of a series of academic publications, commissioned Evans to write a book-length study of her work.[3] Evans knew she was married to Hugo. He taught at San Fernando Valley State College, so he also knew she lived with Rupert but not that she was a bigamist. Realizing hers was a delicate situation, Evans prepared the groundwork carefully, hinting that he would need her guidance regarding personal information for his book.[4] She said she regarded him as "a friend" and agreed to tell "whatever you wish to know."

Evans was too polite to ask direct questions, so Anaïs was lulled into thinking there was no need for vigilance. Then he sent printed proofs of an article about her[5] in which he said she was married to Hugh Guiler, also known as the artist Ian Hugo. Alarmed, she tried to make Evans "omit Hugo's name . . . it is terribly important." She knew she had to tell him something, so she hinted that she was telling him everything while cautiously avoiding doing so. Hoping to engage his complicity, she wrote, "I know it's madness. Any day, at any moment, everything may collapse. . . . So please help me. Someday I will tell you all."

Evans accepted her explanations as a gentleman, but as a scholar and critic, he realized the obligation to explore in his book the fusion of autobiography with fiction. In his next letter, he asked her to elaborate upon personal references. On the one hand, she could tell him what he wanted to know and hope for the best when he wrote his book (and she dearly wanted him to write this first-ever book about her); on the other hand, she had two choices: she could withhold the information and risk his finding it elsewhere or she could tell him but forbid him to use it, and thus risk that he would abandon the book she was counting on to place her in the canon of contemporary literature alongside Miller and Durrell, where she wanted so desperately to be.

It was a continuing battle for control until his book was published in 1968, and unfortunately Nin won, for Evans acquiesced far too much in accepting the version of her life that she required anyone who wrote about her to espouse. Evans did strive for scholarly objectivity, however, and as his book was not unmitigated hagiography, Anaïs Nin disliked it intensely.

After her experience with Evans, controlling what critics wrote about her became as important to Anaïs Nin as seeing her own work published. She was temporarily thrown by the few scant reviews that *Ladders to Fire* received in France. All were written by men, and all objected to Nin's women characters and their search for an inner self. With a certain degree of intuitive accuracy, she insisted "there is something in my work which irritates men critics. Is it the idea of woman trying to find herself and not accepting objective patterns but seeking through the unconscious for the truth?"[6]

Despite her insistence that she would not let hostile criticism sink her, Anaïs drifted into another brooding depression as she hibernated in Silver Lake. Hugo rescued her yet again, when he told her about meeting the French novelist Marguerite Duras at a film festival.[7]

Duras casually told Hugo that she had read an advance copy of the French edition of *Spy* and thought it would make a good film, and she might even like to write the treatment.[8] She said she knew the director Michelangelo Antonioni, "who would of course be an ideal director."

Hugo was writing this to Anaïs when she telephoned unexpectedly. She was so elated, she was ready to jump on a plane and fly to New York that night. Even though Duras's remarks were exceedingly casual, Anaïs swung into action, telling her Hollywood contacts that Duras was committed to write the screenplay of *Spy.* Anaïs called Jerry Bick, the erstwhile agent for all her film machinations who had been involved sporadically in Tracey Roberts' haphazard attempts to turn *Spy* into film. When he heard Duras's name, Bick prepared a letter in which Anaïs Nin agreed that Jerry Bick would represent her in and be compensated for any or all contracts to adapt the novel to film. She signed it without showing it to her legitimate agent, Gunther Stuhlmann.

Anaïs further exaggerated the degree of Duras's interest by telling Bick that she had guaranteed Antonioni would direct. This convinced Bick, who telephoned the director Robert Wise, then preparing to film *The Sound of Music* in Austria. Having no reason to doubt Anaïs, Bick explained what she told him, that Duras was all set to write a script of *Spy* for Antonioni to direct.

This was exciting news to everyone in the film community, for Duras was one of the few "bankable" foreign writers in Hollywood. Wise was so eager to work with Duras that he agreed to put up his own money to finance a treatment. If Duras could transpose *Spy* to the screen as "art-house material,"[9] Wise was willing to raise the rest to make the film. He told Bick he would pay Duras between $3,500 and $4,000 for a full treatment, from twenty to sixty pages of writing that would convey an overview of the novel and its cinematographic aspects and would provide the starting point for a script. Bick conveyed this information to Duras's American literary agent, Georges Borchardt, who told him the troubling news that Duras left all decisions regarding her filmwriting to a "Monsieur Rossignol," who worked for her French publisher, Éditions Gallimard.

By this time the proverbial too many cooks were fanning fires that were spontaneously combusting everywhere. Hugo was repeatedly telephoning Borchardt on Anaïs's behalf, as were Gunther and Bick, each trying to bring any or all of the parties to an agreement.

Gunther begged, pleaded, and cajoled Anaïs, urging her not to communicate with anyone but him, but Anaïs was so determined to make this film that she evaded Gunther and continued to promise anything without thinking what might happen if she had to make good on a single one of her inflated promises.

Hugo, the one person who knew from the beginning the truth about Duras's putative participation, seemed equally devoid of reason throughout this bizarre drama. He scraped $1,000 together, telling Anaïs to use it to ensure her success. When Bick persuaded Duras to accept $4,000 for a treatment, he told Anaïs that she (i.e., Hugo, whose existence he did not then know of) would have to provide most, if not all, of the money. Anaïs tried to prepare Hugo by telling him that preparing a script was "a gamble," and even if it could not be used, "[the money] goes to the writer anyway." Hugo said he was prepared to find whatever money she needed.

By April 1964 it was a stalemate. Only Wise, far away in Salzburg, was removed from the fray. As for the others, all three agents feared being cut out of the deal and forbade their clients to speak directly to each other. "My God," Anaïs wrote to Hugo. "I have three agents to pay. . . . I hope it won't all fall apart."[10] Anaïs decided it was time to use Hugo's money to take herself and Jerry Bick to Paris to see if Duras and Wise could be nudged into a formal agreement.

Wise explained to Duras that he would be using his own money to finance a film of *Spy;* if she agreed to accept a lesser amount than her usual fee to write both treatment and script, he guaranteed to pay her a percentage of the film's earnings. She agreed.[11]

Everyone was confident that a deal had been struck. It was now May 1964, and filming was supposed to begin in February 1965. Bick returned to Hollywood, and Anaïs went to Paris, where Éditions Stock had just published the French edition of *Spy.*

For the first twenty days of May 1964, Anaïs Nin realized every dream she had ever wished for her writing. Her editor, André Bay, arranged for the novel to be featured in every important bookstore's window display. There were publicity appearances, and at night cocktail parties and dinners with glittering personalities. Radio Canada recorded a broadcast on Nin's life and work, and she was interviewed on French television. There was even pre-publicity, as Stock announced with fanfare that *House of Incest* was scheduled to appear in the fall,[12] and while Anaïs was in Paris, touted the news that Edgard Varèse was preparing a composition based on the novel for a premiere at the Berlin Festival.[13] Everyone wanted to meet or interview this direct descendant of the Surrealists, who, as her publicity put it, had been for so long and so wrongly denied the publication, recognition, and adulation she so well deserved. Basking in this admiration, Anaïs returned to Silver Lake and set to work to eliminate incriminating passages in Miller's letters to her, to revise the diaries, and to wait for news that Duras had finished the film script.

The question of who owned the rights to Miller's letters was finally resolved in her favor, and Anaïs (through Gunther) received $6,000, her share of a $7,500 option to publish them from Peter Israel, representing G. P. Putnam's Sons.[14] It was an astonishing windfall and could not have come at a better time, for Hugo was down to his last few thousand dollars of personal capital.[15]

The $6,000 was not a great deal of money even by 1964 standards, but it marked a turning point in the over-forty-year marriage of Anaïs Nin and Hugh Guiler: for the first time ever, she was making a financially significant contribution to the marriage; more important, it marked the beginning of her role as the principal wage-earner, the main support of them both.

At the end of June, gossip from Paris wended its way to Hollywood that Duras's script consisted of little more than random jottings. The "gamble" had not paid off: Duras kept the $4,000 (most of it Hugo's money) but never wrote the script. In Hollywood, Jerry Bick and Anaïs Nin warned everyone involved not to discuss the situation,[16] then set to work to write their own before Robert Wise lost interest.[17]

Anaïs began to plot her escape from Hollywood, for she could not bear the derision she knew would be directed at her once the news got out of Duras's defection. She had already abdicated from the New York literary life by hiding out in California, and if she ran away from Hollywood, that left only France. Hugo dissuaded her from taking that step.[18] Anaïs accepted Hugo's advice and concentrated on editing the rewritten diaries for Gunther to submit to a publisher.

The process of trying to get them published was complicated by the *Letters to Anaïs Nin,* as the forthcoming volume of Henry's letters was entitled, and by her own collection of stories, *Collages.*[19] Alan Swallow was Anaïs's official American publisher, and according to their contract had the right of first refusal for both books.

Swallow was recovering from a heart attack and his health was fragile. His physician suggested curtailing rather than enlarging his publishing activity, which, to be generous, is probably why Gunther began to explore the possibility of placing the Miller book in New York rather than waiting for him. Gunther rightly assumed that the Miller-Nin letters would require a large first printing because of the success of the Durrell-Miller letters. Still, business ethics as well as contractual obligations required Gunther to present the situation to Swallow and let him choose from various options, from publishing solely, to co-publishing with a larger firm, to refusing them outright.

Neither Gunther Stuhlmann nor Anaïs Nin gave Alan Swallow this courtesy, nor did they ever tell him that the unnamed, unspecified book that they offered along with *Collages* was Henry Miller's *Letters to Anaïs Nin.* Instead, stressing his desire to protect Swallow's health, Gunther said only that he would investigate the possibility of co-publishing *Collages* and "another book" with a commercial firm more suited to large-scale publishing. Swallow "later found out" through other contacts in the publishing community and only after the deal was done that the "other book" was Henry's letters.[20]

The "commercial co-publisher" turned out to be G. P. Putnam's Sons, where Peter Israel originally contracted to publish both books—Miller's letters and Nin's stories—in the fall of 1964 under a joint imprint with Swallow Press.[21] But Miller's letters appeared, time passed, and there were all sorts of irritating delays with *Collages.* Israel's first excuse was that Henry's letters must appear sufficiently in advance to prepare readers for the stories. Time was lost when Henry refused to let Anaïs edit the letters as arbitrarily as she wished. She wanted him to wait for galleys to make his corrections, but he insisted on seeing what she rewrote to make changes before it was printed. After several weeks of dickering, Henry held fast, saying there would be no publication unless Anaïs showed him each individual letter as she edited it.[22]

Henry was stalling, consciously or not, because he did not want the letters to be published as she censored them. He also thought her rewriting would make them compare unfavorably with his sparkling exchange with Durrell, causing readers and reviewers not only to question their quality but perhaps also to draw attention to the very relationship she was trying so hard to hide. Having no other option, she complied with his directives because she was convinced that hooking her work onto the tail of the comet Henry's writing was currently blazing was her surest route to success.

But when the Letters were finally ready for publication, Israel refused to publish *Collages,* saying it was slight, lacked form, and "reads like a fictionalized slice from her diary . . . with a rather artificial beginning and end tacked on." He also objected to the "thinly disguised real people" such as Lesley Blanch, Romain Gary, and Djuna Barnes, fearing that "conceivably other readers would recognize other characters."[23]

At that point Gunther had no choice but to offer *Collages* to Swallow, who agreed to publish it. Only then did Swallow learn, and not from Anaïs, that Putnam was publishing the lucrative Miller letters. Swallow digested the situation for several weeks before writing a long, thoughtful letter to Anaïs (copy to Gunther). With his usual integrity and generosity, he began by expressing dismay at having to write and apologized for what he felt he must say.

He reminded Anaïs that, well over a year ago, he predicted "1964 was the year you'd break through into a wider public," and that *Collages* would change her "devoted" but "narrow" readership into one of broad-based appeal. His prediction proved correct when *Time* chose it for the annual "Christmas List" of the best books published that year and sales rose steadily during the holiday season.[24]

Swallow published Nin when no one else would and his difficult, dedicated work laid the groundwork for Putnam to reap the success that she and her agent had not offered to him. What he resented most was hearing through the publishing grapevine in November 1964 that Gunther had been offering the diaries to other publishers without mentioning, let alone stipulating, that Swallow Press was to co-publish.

Alan Swallow announced that, with deep regret, he was withdrawing from his agreement to publish her work. "I see no pride in publishing what I believe those books to be—trading upon Miller's name in one case, and emasculating (and it would be that, even if only 5% were cut out) the diary in the other case. I wouldn't want to publish such books. . . . I published your work because I believed in it . . . I've demonstrated that it can be done when no other publisher in the nation would do it. . . ." And then he delivered his most devastating blow: "As for the diary, keep it there; I don't want to see any more of it—unless I can be reassured that my original assumptions were correct, that the work is being done properly to the genuine quality of the original . . . that the one volume is the opening for a series of getting at this correctly and honestly . . . I don't want it if it is capitalizing on a version even slightly bastardized in order to get publication in a big time way right now."

One year later, in September 1965, she constructed a "Story of the Diary, Editing and Publishing," which was meant to be the official version of its long, complicated history and to be deposited with the originals by whichever library agreed to buy them. In her version, she said she always intended Swallow to be the diary's sole publisher but his heart problems prevented it and forced her to seek first a co-publisher, then a separate one. She further absolved herself by insisting that she had always been loyal and generous to her first patron.

Why, then, she asked herself within the pages of her official history of the diary, was she having nightmares? Why was she so depressed? She was so anxious to see Bogner that she plotted and schemed to find ways to go to New York, where she spent more time in the next few months than she had in the last several years. And when she was in California, she wrote at length about her qualms to Hugo.[25]

Not knowing what lay behind her anxieties, Hugo mostly repeated what he had told her several months before the rupture with Swallow.[26] He urged Anaïs then, and repeated it through early 1965, that she should find comfort in psychoanalysis. Throughout his now more than twenty years of analysis, it had become "clearer and clearer," Hugo said, "that you and I, because we have . . . had the courage to go into depth analysis over such a long period, have been in possession of the true key to the questions about the 'inner reality' . . . how few have had the courage, the persistance (and the money) to make that exploration!"[27]

Hugo's boasting and Anaïs's recurring nightmares both came from a fear that neither dared express, that until or unless she found a publisher for the diaries, financial realities would intrude upon their lives as they had never done before. Hugo was sixty-five and his working life was ended. "I have to find something else," he wrote to Anaïs, but all he could think about "for the moment" was "surrealism," which, in the context he used the term, was really a euphemism for analysis and his fear that he would no longer be able to afford it.

For the past several years, both her husbands had colluded in balancing Anaïs on her trapeze, and Henry's gift of the royalties to his letters gave her the impression that she would be able to swing indefinitely. Now she realized that the income Henry's letters earned would not be enough to pay her share of the costs of life with Rupert, let alone support to Hugo.[28]

In the past, she would have taken to her bed. Others would have had to care for her, or she would have fled somewhere luxurious to recuperate. She would have depended upon Hugo to rescue her. This time was different: she had to rescue him, for Hugo succumbed to a month-long bout of bronchitis serious enough to send him to the hospital. She not only had to minister to his considerable needs, she had to pay the bills, take care of the taxes, and settle the household accounts. She did everything with diligence, patience, and, surprising even herself, with skill and authority. Nothing was too much for her to handle; she coped with every crisis.

And throughout it all, she worked. Each day she revised and reshaped her written life. It became for the first time an entity quite separate from her, a text she scrutinized with a detached and critical eye. She who hated so much to revise that she would abandon rather than rewrite and edit, now pored over revisions, searching for a way to turn the innermost, secret thoughts and events of her existence into a palatable public commodity. There had to be a way to keep the integrity of the original diary and still disguise it enough to publish it not only in her lifetime, but also Hugo's, Henry's, Eduardo's, Rupert's, and especially while the two men to whom she had once been so close were still alive, her brothers Thorvald and Joaquín.

It was disconcerting that, as she wrote ruefully to Gunther, "they only publish me to be able to publish Miller."[29] It was certainly true of Peter Israel, who seized Miller's letters avidly but rejected *Collages* and refused the diary.[30] André Bay of Éditions Stock, hitherto oblique and evasive, finally stated his position directly: if he did not publish the Miller letters in France, he was not interested in publishing any more of Nin's fiction, nor would he even consider her diary.[31]

Anaïs was now approaching the 1,000th page of edited text that she wanted the first published volume of the diary to encompass. After years of indecision about the form most suitable for the content, she decided to begin *in medias res,* with the launch of her writing career in the 1930s rather than at the real beginning, when Rosa brought her children to New York. Anaïs knew that the best way to engage a potential publisher's interest was to stress the "portraits" of the important and interesting personalities who appeared within the context of her life. In the hope of piquing interest, she had prepared lists of these portraits for years, of everyone from Allendy to the Cubist sculptor Zadkine, and featuring along the way Durrell, Miller, Rank, Vidal, and Rebecca West. The emphasis, however, was never on the personalities themselves, but always on the great persons who were fortunate enough to have known Anaïs Nin, for she always kept

Anaïs as a popular lecturer.

Thorvald Nin, age fifty.

herself spotlighted and positioned at the center of her own stage. She believed it was a simple case of deciding which part of her life should be the first act, and how she should present herself before launching into the portraits of others. But publishers disagreed, believing that the greatest interest lay not in Nin herself but in those whom she knew, which was another way of saying her self-absorption soon grew tiresome and off-putting.

James Silberman, of Random House, was the most interested among the many to whom Gunther offered the diaries. In the first 150 or so pages of the 800 available to Silberman, Nin presented herself through "the day by day development of character,"[32] focusing on every nuance of her thought and expression; in effect, tracing the evolution of the serious young girl who blossomed into (as she saw herself) the influential and respected writer. Although these pages were cohesive, Silberman worried that "this unfolding will [not] be interesting to enough readers to make it possible for us to do the diaries on the scale Anaïs proposes." But she was still a long way from being able to accept criticism or suggestions. As far as she was concerned, the shortsightedness lay with Silberman and not with her: "What they [Silberman and Random House] want would be destroying the integrity of the diary. A Diary is not an action film."

Gunther was eager for Anaïs to accept whatever Silberman wanted, for it would be a coup to place her at Random House. Gently, he tried to tell her that one of Silberman's "recurring themes" was that the diaries must "justify the expectations which have been built up for so long."[33]

Silberman then suggested that Anaïs pattern her diary along the lines of Simone de Beauvoir's memoirs. Anaïs was furious: "There is more in my diary than in the diary of Simone de Beauvoir. There is no action in hers, and no life at all. It is deadly dull. And all this talk about expectations. It shows lack of faith. No, I feel, they are wrong."[34] She insisted that Silberman wanted to "turn it into a novel and take the authenticity out of it." She implored Gunther to agree: "Don't you agree it is silly to want to take out the growth of the personality, to have it all external? Tell me your real feelings. Don't spare me." A few days later, Silberman regretfully declined to publish the diaries.[35]

The rejection was a severe blow, soon repeated by other major publishers. Anaïs still kept pressure on Gunther to submit the diary elsewhere. Early in 1965, Hiram Haydn, of Harcourt Brace, read the

900-page manuscript (revised by Anaïs from its previous 1,000 pages). With the proviso that she agree to make significant cuts and edit as he directed, Haydn offered a contract to publish what became the first volume of *The Diary of Anaïs Nin*. It was clearly understood by everyone concerned that if the first diary did not meet the publisher's expectations, i.e., sell enough copies to pay for itself, no other volumes would follow.

Anaïs was strangely subdued by the news that the diary had at last found a publisher, perhaps because it had been so long in coming, perhaps because the shock was too great to absorb all at once. Whatever the reason, she did not record her feelings and emotions until almost nine months later, when she wrote the curious text, "Story of the Diary, Editing and Publishing."[36]

There was the question of how those she wrote about would react once the diary was published. Anaïs had already shown Henry the passages about himself and June, and even he, who cheerfully turned the stuff of his life into biographical fiction, was shocked and demanded all sorts of excisions. Anaïs complied because she needed his permission to publish his letters, and therefore, to remain in his good graces.[37] Next to read it was Joaquín, who worked carefully through the entire manuscript, "tolerant and understanding, noting only the usual errors which arise in every family about the past."

Joaquín Nin-Culmell proved to be a scrupulous reader who very quickly learned an important lesson: "My sister would not stand for criticism, no matter how small or insignificant. So I learned to praise what I liked (and fortunately, there was much of it), and simply did not speak of anything with which I did not agree or did not like."[38] He continued to point out errors of fact with diplomacy and tact, but retreated to the safety of correcting dates and spelling, eliminating repetitions, and checking for historical accuracy. "You have proved to be the most understanding of all my readers," Anaïs wrote to Joaquín.[39]

But there was also Thorvald, and whether she should let him read the passages about him. They had not seen each other for fifteen years when Thorvald retired to Miami and Charles de Cárdenas, whose portfolio Hugo had managed for years, became his neighbor. Thorvald, who "was bluntly honest about his opinions,"[40] lost no time in creating a potentially troublesome situation when he boasted about the far greater profit he received on his own investments than Charlie received on those made by Hugo.[41] Hugo depended on

Charlie's account, which represented a major portion of his greatly diminished income, and he could not afford to lose it. He asked Anaïs to go with him to Miami, to persuade Thorvald to stop preying on Charlie's fears.

Joaquín tried to prepare Anaïs for Thorvald's "bad temper and cutting remarks."[42] It was still shocking when she saw her brother's "violent personality, absolutely cold eyes, expressionless, a stony face, hard as marble. A stiff, forced manner, a terrible tension."

Anaïs told him of the diary's forthcoming publication briefly and in the most general terms. Although Thorvald said nothing in response, it set off an unfortunate climax to the unhappy reunion on the last day of the visit. Apropos of nothing, Thorvald suddenly denounced Anaïs's "twisted mind," called her a "liar," and poured forth a stream of insults. She lost control and began to scream and was overcome by hysteria. Hugo quickly collected their luggage, called a taxi, and set off for the airport. Trying to calm herself, she spent the flight writing a long letter to Dr. Bogner.

Gradually, as the disastrous visit receded into memory, the process of editing led to "another force, far stronger," her belief in the diary's worth. Her most important realization became "there was plenty enough to give so that what I could not give would not be missed. I could avoid the blank spaces." She decided not to worry about Thorvald's threats; he would appear in the early years of her life where it was appropriate and the devil take the hindmost.

This attitude prevailed with everyone, even though Hiram Haydn informed her that every person she wrote about had to sign a legal release or she would have to eliminate his or her portrait. She assumed that everyone would be delighted to be found within the pages of her book, and was amazed by how many refused, and, in some cases, how violently and rudely they did so. Although Lesley Blanch would not appear in the early diary, which was to cover the years 1931–1934, she threatened legal action if Anaïs even hinted at her name. Anaïs had already published a sarcastic and easily recognizable portrait of the breakup of Lesley's and Romain's marriage in *Collages,* and Lesley was not about to let herself be ridiculed again.[43]

Rebecca West was cordial but insisted she did not want to be mentioned because the passage about her was "too far from what I was feeling at the time."[44]

Most surprising of all, however, was the violence with which Eduardo Sánchez insisted upon being removed from the diary. Dependent upon his eldest brother's largesse thanks to Castro's seizure of his family's assets, Eduardo was taking no chances that Anaïs would reveal his homosexuality. Her method of dealing with Eduardo was one she used for many others as well: "Sweet revenge, as I had to find someone who initiated me to psychoanalysis, to Surrealism, and to be there occasionally at discussions. I turned him into a girl, Marguerite. Ha!"[45]

Of the wealthy and social Louise de Vilmorin (whose story she used in *House of Incest*) and other recognizable members of the family, she "changed all the names, alas, as family is very alive and very prominent." Of Richard Osborn, whom she could not locate and therefore could not ask to sign the legal release, she "had to keep him . . . though a minor character, played an important role, introducing Miller." The same with Lawrence Drake: she excused herself for writing of him without his permission because "sometimes a minor character is necessary . . . I [already] eliminated so many." And "Woman's Vanity" was her excuse for attributing D'Annunzio's remark about her brother's beautiful eyes to herself.

"I solved the problem of editing according to my own standards, ethics."[46] —Thus did she give herself license to change or revise anything from the years 1931–1934 that did not meet her satisfaction in 1965. Her thinking about how to depict the lives of others was "ambivalent" because hers was so "entangled" with theirs that "I could not give their lives. They did not belong to me." As she eliminated the passages demanded by more and more persons, Anaïs Nin believed that one clear fact remained: "There was so much richness of experience that the excisions did not matter. People would read between the lines."

She also believed that "one main theme emerged: I had to act according to my own nature or else the diary itself would be destroyed." She believed it was in her nature "to bypass the destructive aspect of others and to relate to their creative or numinous aspects."[47]

And so she came to the conclusion that her anxieties were based on the emotional baggage she carried from her past life, fears of "the Eye over your shoulder, parent, teacher, therapist." It was time to face the world, "not with a work of art, separate from myself, but with myself, my body, my voice, my thoughts, my feelings. Expose them."

Still, she had reservations: "Already I had had to suffer from the concept that all diaries are narcissistic, that introspection is neurotic." She chose to believe that she instead "overflowed with love of others" and that her intense introspection was "the only way to accomplish the inner journey of self creation."

"Help me, Dr. Bogner," she begged rhetorically, noting that the analyst had accused her of "reverting to the Catholic Confession." Nevertheless, she wanted what Confession offered: "Give me absolution. That would give me peace."[48]

Anaïs Nin credited analysis with helping her to see that she had committed no crime and therefore should feel no Catholic guilt. Also, that the diary was "beyond such petty judgements, beyond the personal," and that it required significant courage on her part to write it. "Let the woman lose her small personal fears," she admonished herself. "Let her dare to offer her creation and if necessary, suffer the consequences. Every artist has taken that risk."

Her "small, timorous concerns" fell away as she admitted that her "main mature objective" was now clear: "I believed every word I wrote. They were written by another self." And now, she must permit this other self, "the creator, to face the world."

38

Being Famous

The Writer writes his Letter to the World. When the World answers it is like the Sorcerer's Apprentice. He cannot control what he has summoned.[1]

"MY MAIL IS BECOMING a staggering problem," Anaïs wrote to Hugo on June 3, 1966, shortly after the first volume of the diary was published. The most important review—by Jean Garrigue on the front page of *The New York Times Book Review*—was also one of the best, summarizing it as "a rich, various and fascinating work" in which "the volatile human essence has been caught."[2] The literary world, having ignored Anaïs Nin for the past quarter century, suddenly perked up, and the attention she craved all those years descended in a deluge. Everyone, it seemed, wanted to know something about the woman who, in Garrigue's words, "For years . . . has been known for a diary only a few have seen."

Her fan mail gave the first indication of the onslaught that changed her life in a flash. It increased exponentially,[3] and she answered it herself, in longhand, at great length, and with an intimacy that often surprised the recipient. Each believed that Anaïs Nin[4] had proffered a very special friendship to him or her alone, and so all these people wrote again and again, in the same confessional vein, confiding the intimate details of their lives.

She was bombarded with requests for interviews and lectures that entailed frenetic travel. "Personal friendships, home life, sacrificed to public life, but as this is not what I believe, I will learn to control it," she wrote to her French confidante, Marguerite Rebois. "I am not fond of public life, as you know, by nature. But I am so happy as I have received all a writer can dream of—all the love I gave has been returned."[5] She truly believed she was obligated to return "love," but she went to excessive ends. Despite warnings by her analyst, her two husbands, editors, and friends, who all agreed that she was exhausting herself with minutiae and neglecting important issues for peripheral concerns, Anaïs Nin was driven to offer intimacy and friendship to total strangers so that none might accuse her of rejection or abandonment. And because she was no longer using this tremendous energy to write a diary, she put it into writing letters, which led to many bizarre encounters.

In one instance, she engaged in correspondence with an obsessed person who threatened to commit suicide on her doorstep if she did not enter a lesbian relationship. Nin then wrote to the person's analyst, describing how she would treat the patient, confident that she was qualified to do so.[6] The analyst was horrified and reprimanded her for writing, let alone expecting him to admit that the person was his patient or to discuss treatment. The analyst stated in the strongest possible language that the reply was only to tell Anaïs Nin that she must never write again, and in the best interests "of the person in question," she should "end all forms of contact."[7]

Her letters were not limited to fans, for she wrote to "thank all the good reviewers," and also wrote long diatribes in which she hectored and lectured any critic whose innocent opinions or innocuous prose struck her as negative.[8] Even Oliver Evans, whose book on Nin was nearing publication, received one last scathing letter denouncing it, thus ending all contact between them.[9]

She was more successful in befriending other scholars and bending them to her will. Bettina Knapp willingly submitted a review to Anaïs Nin before sending it to the editor who commissioned it, asking her to "correct everything you think is not right or for any other reason."[10] Nin made corrections and rewrote portions of the review, and when it was published, sent Knapp a glowing note saying "people who do not know we are friends sent it to me with their compliments—critics, other reviewers. It is really lucid and illuminating."[11] Anna Balakian, the respected professor of literature who (along with her sister, Nona Balakian, an editor at *The New York Times Book Review*) became one of Anaïs Nin's staunchest boosters,[12] did not fare so well, incurring Nin's wrath when she innocently sent a draft copy of her review of Evans's book.[13] Anaïs Nin's reply shows that nothing was too minor to escape her scrutiny, her displeasure, and ultimately, her veiled threats of retaliation. "Because you are an honest critic and not negative or destructive, I hope one day you will reconsider some hasty and innappropriate comments. . . . I feel that when you have time to read Novel of the Future you will not want these statements to take permanent form inside one of the Diaries."[14]

If she can be said to have kept a diary from 1966 to the end of her life, it is in her ten-to-twenty-page letters to total strangers. On a good evening, she boasted of writing between six and ten. She bragged that on each cross-country flight she could write "fifteen," "sixteen," and once an astonishing "twenty-four," each consisting of a minimum of fifteen closely packed handwritten pages, and usually more.[15]

To Anaïs Nin, the fan letters were a form of adulation, of validation and verification of her importance, first as a writer, then as a woman, and finally as a woman artist. These were important distinctions in her mind, and as her fame increased, she struggled to express the differences in her many public appearances. She loved the "cyclone" of attention that came with "radio and television two or three times a day."[16] She appeared on the popular television program "Camera 3," and pretended to be surprised afterward when viewers recognized her and stopped her in the streets of Greenwich Village.

But there were not many sixty-three-year-old women who walked those streets in broad daylight with hair entwined with ribbons and flowers and piled high on their heads, who wore long flowing gowns of white cashmere or silver lamé covered with dramatic capes that once belonged to parish priests or French policemen, and who painted their faces and lips dead white in the fashion of the day and darkened their eyes so heavily they were startling when glimpsed unexpectedly on a sunny afternoon.[17] She was a striking presence as she stood on line at the post office or methodically churned out page after page at the local photocopy machine. Her lifelong attention to physical appearance was now paying dividends; as she progressed through her sixties, everyone assumed she was a woman in her early fifties, and she did not disabuse them of the notion.[18]

Anaïs Nin realized how much her personal appearance enhanced the sales of her books and she did everything she could to capitalize on it, including registering with the respected W. Colston Leigh Lecture Agency.[19] She was immediately booked on a grueling schedule that would have defeated a much younger woman.[20]

Everywhere she went there were large audiences, packed lecture halls, and best of all, so many books to autograph for adoring fans who bought ever larger quantities. Within weeks of the first printing of 3,000 copies, Haydn ordered a second 2,500, and it too, promptly sold out. "Hiram Haydn very pleased, but always cautious," she noted acerbically. "Too small as things are going now."[21]

Money seemed to be rolling in, more than enough to keep both households on an even keel, but she soon found out this was not true. Rupert's needs remained fixed, providing the only surety in her financial circumstances. Hugo continued to travel between New York and Europe, the Caribbean Islands, and South America, his letters full of schemes to recoup his vanished capital, none of which ever materialized. Anaïs, who had never concerned herself with business, now learned very quickly how to apportion her income. She also realized that she could not continue to be married to two men, each of whom thought he was legally entitled to claim her on his income tax returns. Even she understood that trying to deceive the IRS was far more serious than toying with a phony Social Security card.

And so she simply told Rupert, as gently as possible, that their marriage was invalid because she had been married to Hugo all along and always would be. She laid the onus on Hugo, saying it would have been inhumane to divorce him even though she had always wanted to do so. She convinced Rupert that Hugo would not have been, nor was he now able to survive without her occasional presence in his life; also, that they were no longer lovers and that she maintained a separate bedroom in his apartment.[22] She also said that Hugo would require lifelong analysis (which he did), and that more to the point, he now required her financial as well as her emotional support. She believed herself honor-bound to provide Hugo with everything he needed for the rest of his life, not just to equal, but also to surpass everything he had ever given her.

Learning the truth about how Hugo had made his life with Anaïs both possible and comfortable, Rupert agreed that it was right and just that Anaïs continue to share her time and her income. Together, Rupert and Anaïs consulted Phyllis Ziffren Deutsch, who became the principal of the several lawyers representing Anaïs Nin Guiler's legal affairs for the rest of her life.[23] Deutsch filed for a Judgment of Annulment, which was granted on June 16, 1966.[24] Anaïs Nin became "a married woman" but not to Rupert Pole, who became " 'a single man,' whose marriage has been annulled since the last date of recording."

There was one other situation concerning Hugo that plagued both him and Anaïs for the rest of their lives: why he was totally absent from the published diary. The decision that all mention of the person who made possible Anaïs Nin's romantic and exotic life should be eliminated from its written record was his, not, as rumor has had it, hers. Through their daily exchange of letters, Hugo was involved in every step leading to publication of the first diary, especially in vetting the manuscript, even though Anaïs used her need of isolated tranquillity to prepare it as the excuse to stay in Silver Lake for most of the year. She was both grateful and appreciative of Hugo's judicious scrutiny, and tried to assuage any hurt he might have felt.[25]

Critics, reviewers, and the most sympathetic of her readers all wondered as they read the diary, "who paid?" for Anaïs Nin's seemingly charmed life.[26] Hugo was able to deflect questions but was irritated by the negative reactions of various family members and his and Anaïs's most sympathetic friends. When an old Paris friend complained that Anaïs had unjustly eliminated Hugo, he fired off a strong letter to her defending his wife, which he repeated in virtually the same form to Anaïs's many other critical friends and relatives.[27]

Once Rupert knew the truth about her marital status, Anaïs stopped lying about her New York life. But she told Hugo nothing about Rupert and continued to lie about Los Angeles. In a collection of jottings entitled "Notes for Book to be Published After I Retire, Title: 'Dream and Nightmare,' "[28] Hugo wrote nothing to show that he knew how or where she lived in Los Angeles. Instead, in the summer of 1969, they played out another of their domestic dramas, this time with Rupert's knowledge and compliance.

Hugo wanted Anaïs to spend the summer in New York, but she and Rupert decided to vacation in Greece and Turkey after she toured England, where Peter Owen had arranged publicity to launch the diary. Just as she was departing, Hugo told her that he had a detached retina, and had chosen to schedule elective surgery August 14—in the middle of her vacation.[29] Anaïs told Rupert the truth but made Hugo's surgery life threatening, with cataracts that were about to separate from the retina and tear it in half in the process. She accompanied Rupert as far as Izmir, then flew to New York, where she stayed several weeks to nurse Hugo.

He recovered swiftly, but as they sat in the gardens at Washington Square Village enjoying the mild late-summer weather, she was besieged by "anxiety and restlessness during slowed down, becalmed life." Hugo was "growing deaf . . . his memory which was always bad is worse. Business and filmmaking take all he has. In life he is a zombie." These became her complaints and excuses to avoid him for the rest of her life.

That autumn, when Anaïs was invited by her German publisher to the Frankfurt Book Fair and Hugo was in Paris pursuing elusive business deals that never materialized, Anaïs had no choice but to travel to and from Frankfurt via Paris. She described it to Gunther: "[Hugo] is in Paris on business and staying at the Crillon. Stock has reserved a room for me at the Pont Royal . . . I had lunch with Hugo (on my expense accounts). We laugh at the situation, each in a different hotel."[30] The Paris arrangement was actually a metaphor for how Anaïs and Hugo lived from then on: he pleaded with her to return and she used two excuses not to: everything she needed to edit the diaries was in Los Angeles, and a screenplay and subsequent production of *Spy* was imminent.[31]

Anaïs could not understand why Hugo wanted her with him, for they made each other unhappy and argued all the time. She could not understand why, when Hugo's letters described his ease as host for showings of his films followed by buffet suppers at which he served his excellent curries or gourmet casseroles, he became taciturn, clumsy, and glum the moment she was there. He had befriended a generation of young people—playwright Tom O'Horgan; Ellen Stewart, the founder of LaMama theatre; and other artists, writers, and designers, among them Victor Lipari, Frank Alberti, and Alexandra Souteriou, all of whom remained devoted for the rest of his life. His close friends included Jerzy Kosinski and his wife, Mary Weir, whom he described with vivacity in his letters, but he refused to introduce them to Anaïs. All his friends thought it was because the force of her personality was so strong that when she was with him, Hugo became little more than a dull gray appendage who disappeared into the background of the glittering figure she cut.[32]

People either loved or hated Anaïs Nin when they met her. No one was able to respond to her with any degree of neutrality: they were either dazzled by the mesmerizing charm she lavished upon them, making them believe they were the only person in the world who mattered to her at that moment, or they were repulsed by what they considered her crass and blatant attempts to seduce and entrance them.[33]

Hugo gave up imploring her to return and learned to settle for what little time she gave him. He still adored her blindly, as he had all his life, and she always behaved as a loving and devoted wife who lavished care and attention on him. Always the hypochondriac, Hugo became impossible to placate. Their devoted housekeeper, Millicent, then approaching her eightieth birthday, wrote letter after letter complaining about "Mr. Hugo's" insatiable demands. Hugo grew deaf, which made telephone conversations nearly impossible; his handwriting grew spidery and wobbly, which made reading his letters difficult without a magnifying glass; and he became even more accident-prone than he had been when a clumsy young man. It is hard to say if he exaggerated these afflictions as a ploy for her attention, or if they were genuine, but Anaïs never succumbed to his pleas and imprecations; she offered sympathy and expressed concern in her daily letters, but remained firmly entrenched in the Silver Lake house.

She left Hugo to his own devices, which included affairs with several much younger women. In the liberated and sexually free late 1960s and early 1970s, they were awed by the much older man's courtliness, gentility, and chivalry, a demonstration of manners they found sadly lacking in the men of their own generation.[34]

Anaïs had no intention of leaving Rupert now that life in Los Angeles finally became what she had wanted it to be all along: a nonstop round of parties and the devoted attention of a growing band of young women who called themselves her "daughters." She was comfortable being a star in the Los Angeles literary community, for its "second city" inferiority complex in regard to New York made her feel at ease and secure. Because there was no time to write much else, she began now to keep a calendar in lieu of diary writing, simply listing activities, events, people she saw, and people to whom she wrote.[35] There were always several notations each week of "music" or "music at home" (Rupert's group, for he was still a creature of habit). She liked the way he insisted on keeping their evenings "sacred," with the ritual of martinis and a swim, followed by a dinner they prepared together, but why, she asked rhetorically, did it have to be on the table at precisely five o'clock!

She dined at Deena Metzger's home, participating in her first Passover Seder. She had several meetings with Henry Miller and his acolytes, including Gerald Robitaille, whom she did not like. She attended such shows as "Single Wing Turquoise Bird Light Show at Sam Francis's studio," Beatrice Manley Blau's "thrilling" Winnie in Beckett's "Happy Days," and "Brecht play—bore." There was an unending procession of cocktail parties with everyone from Laura Huxley to Luchita Mullican, the actress Yvette Mimieux, and "Nancy ex Durrell," who was passing through Los Angeles. Meetings filled her calendar, especially with anyone she thought likely to film *Spy,* such as Jeanne Moreau, then living in Hollywood and who she also hoped would star in it. She lectured at places ranging from the local Jewish Community Center to Stanford University, where Professor Robert Newman of the Physics Department invited her to speak about the connection between "Integrated circuits and Surrealism" (she said, "the only parallel is that both scientist and artist at one point have to plunge into the unknown").[36]

Her life in New York was taken up with new friends and old: poet Sandra Hochman made her the honored guest at parties and dinners; Frances Field's husband, Michael, cooked gourmet recipes from his cookbooks; she renewed her friendship with Frances Schiff Bolton; and Anna Balakian introduced her to a prize student, Sharon Spencer, who became one of Nin's most perceptive critics and a friend in the last decade of her life.[37] Pamela Fiori, then an editor at *Travel & Leisure,* urged Anaïs Nin to write about exotic destinations, which eventually led Anaïs and Rupert to Bali and Morocco, and to articles in the magazine.[38]

Through letters, she began friendships with many persons who wrote about her work, including Harriet Zinnes, Wayne McEvilly, Duane Schneider, Benjamin Franklin V, and Nancy Scholar Zee.[39] Lili Bita, a Greek actress, began to translate Nin's novels into her native language, and her husband, Robert Zaller, collected a series of essays which became *A Casebook on Anaïs Nin.*[40] Evelyn Hinz, a young Canadian who also wrote about D. H. Lawrence, cooperated with Anaïs Nin on a critical study that met with her total approval.[41] Other women, such as Rochelle Lynn Holt, Valerie Harms, and Adele Aldridge, were inspired by Nin's example to establish printing presses of their own, and they also became her friends.[42]

A young scholar innocently suggested to Anaïs Nin that he was considering the possibility of starting a newsletter about her work and found himself deluged for the next decade with an avalanche of her letters and copies of writings about her. Richard Centing was a librarian at Ohio State University who needed to demonstrate scholarly ability in order to be granted tenure, and as nothing had yet been compiled about Anaïs Nin, he thought her life and work would make an excellent project.[43] His initial letter was simply to explore the possibility of a newsletter, but Anaïs Nin was determined that "The Café in Space" (as she called it)[44] would become reality. She focused her energies on it with more concentration than she had given to any other project except publication of the diary and did not give Centing time to reflect upon what he had proposed before she launched a subscription campaign surpassing all those she had previously mounted for her novels. On top of all her other activity, she prepared carefully typed, minutely detailed lists of names, addresses, and descriptions of more than a thousand persons to whom she expected Centing to send subscription forms. She herself guaranteed to buy a minimum of fifty copies each time it was published, but she usually bought several hundred or more.

Under the Sign of Pisces began quarterly publication in 1970 under the aegis of the Ohio State University Library and did not cease until 1981, after which Centing took full financial and editorial responsibility, renaming it *Seahorse* and publishing it as a labor of love until 1983. The newsletter became a curious mélange of thoughtful scholarship and good prose mixed with embarrassingly amateur writing and adulation by the "Ninnies," as her groupies were calling themselves in the most positive use of the term (but always outside her hearing). There were also articles selected or approved by Anaïs Nin, about others who were important to her in some way, but who provided no competition to deflect the limelight she so happily occupied within its pages. There may have been articles about Durrell, Miller, Djuna Barnes, and Marguerite Young, but most of every issue was filled with blatant publicity supplied by Anaïs Nin herself: "lectures—one every other day—almost everyday I meet someone doing a thesis—from Yale, etc. It is now an avalanche! Ramparts will interview me. . . . I have a list of colleges where books are taught. Vogue photo and interview will be in June."[45] She prepared the detailed lists as promised, and the moment the plane landed typed and sent it.

Having no discernment about the relative importance of activities and events, she fully expected her doings to be printed in each issue exactly as she wrote it. One such list, dated 1969, ranges from an invitation to attend the Frankfurt Book Fair as the featured guest of her German publisher to "informal discussion with Freudian doctors in their home." She was proud that her writing was being taught, no matter where, from "all books taught at Ohio University by Duane Schneider and Ben Franklin" to "Books taught at YMYWHA of Greater Flushing [New York]."[46] Centing's struggle for scholarly integrity was a losing battle. She rewarded his twelve-plus years of devotion to her and her work with a passage composed especially for her last published diary, volume 7: "Shocked by Richard Centing, who carefully records gossip against me. . . . This has shaken my faith in him. Yet he wrote about symbols in the Diary so understandingly and seemed so devoted and loyal."[47]

Benjamin Franklin V, for a time Centing's co-editor, also felt the brunt of her retaliatory prose when she became "angry" that he "constantly disparaged [her friends]" within the newsletter's pages.[48] In the published diary, Franklin became a member of "the bitchy society I am struggling against," and later, the subject of a discussion with Bogner as primary among those who "turned against me."[49]

Rare was the person who appeared within the pages of *Pisces* and did not feel what Meryle Secrest called Anaïs Nin's "annihilating need for revenge, [as she] acted out that need over and over again."[50] Perhaps because Nin had so little formal education, she did not understand that a scholar's rigorous appraisal of a writer's work does not automatically equate with the intention to destroy it. Nin regarded Nancy Scholar Zee's perceptive study, for example, as written by a voyeur whose intention was to reveal her double life by "putting together Diary and the novels as complementing each other. . . . She thinks to destroy me by her great discovery."[51] Kate Millett, who wrote a paean to Nin, "would have done a better job writing about women writers nobody writes about."[52]

All her paranoia—for that is what it was, really—boiled down to fear of exposure. Curiously, having offered parts of her life to the public and hinting tantalizingly at parts withheld, she seems to have been, on some deeply basic level, profoundly ashamed of herself. The words "absolution" and "resolution," comparisons with the

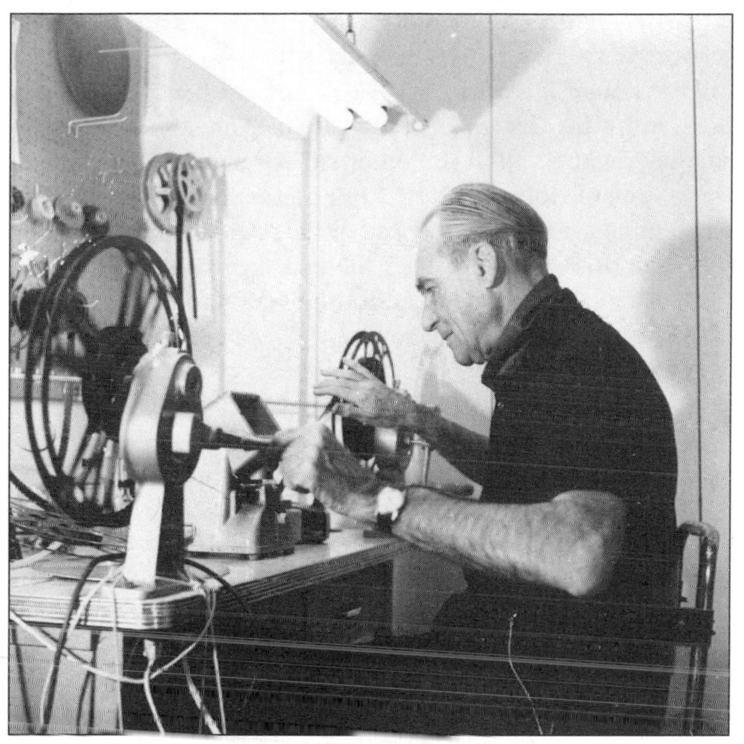

Ian Hugo *(Hugh Guiler)* in his film studio.

Catholic sacrament of Confession, and the quest for "peace"—all these begin to appear in her letters to Hugo and her brother Joaquín.[53]

"I know I give you a hard time," she apologized to Richard Centing, "but from the first I considered you a friend who understood the precarious balance of my life. I have to protect both lives."[54] As scholars became increasingly peripatetic, this became harder to do. She did not want Daniel Stern to visit Los Angeles because it would mean "entangling you in the other side of my life."[55] Professor William McBrien of Hofstra, a New York friend, innocently asked to visit during a professional meeting in Los Angeles. Unable to think of an excuse, she invited McBrien to Silver Lake without telling him of Rupert. When she opened the door, he was startled to see Rupert in the background and hear her whisper, "Dear Bill, you will keep my secret, won't you?"[56] He did, joining the ever-increasing list of persons who knew and liked both men too much to make jokes at their expense.

Anaïs had one other, very different, problem with *Pisces,* which she also had with everything written about her. "Send me twenty-five additional copies," she would blithely instruct Richard Centing, who also sent her the bill.[57] Harriet Zinnes was horrified when Anaïs rushed to buy more than fifty copies of *The Prairie Schooner* because she thought Zinnes had written an article about her, when in reality she was mentioned in Zinnes's review of Robert Duncan's poetry.[58] Because she wanted to influence the content of William Claire's literary magazine, *Voyages,* she bought multiple copies of every issue and tried to ensure that her friends contributed writings she personally vetted.[59]

To Hiram Haydn, she wrote a long letter of complaint "about the books charged to my account and adding up to more than my royalties."[60] She told her accountant that "Harcourt Brace is so stingy with its review and publicity copies . . . I have had to spend almost all my royalties giving copies to excellent reviewers. . . . Every lecture, every foreign contract, every translation, entails gifts, review copies, etc."[61] Gunther told her she gave away so many free copies that, to his great dismay, "there is no money due to you at this point, or to me."[62] She stuck to her convoluted view of the situation: "it is not fair that you should be deprived of your royalties because Harcourt is too stingy to give me copies of the diaries for all the public relations work I do."[63]

She never liked the first editor of the diaries, Hiram Haydn, even though she owed her success to his willingness to take a chance on the first volume. Her letters to Gunther are filled with such comments as "Can you talk to our dumb HH? . . . He called me yesterday in his usual oily, ponderous, false way."[64] Apparently, Haydn committed two additional unpardonable sins besides not giving her unlimited quantities of free books: he insisted that she provide him with signed releases from everyone she wrote about and he planned to use a photo on the covers of the paperback editions that she thought was unflattering and made her look "old" (she was then sixty-eight).

Anaïs's method of dealing with Haydn's stipulation was to tell everyone that they were free to change anything they did not like in their portraits, but if they changed "too much" (which she always left unspecified), she would eliminate their portrait. Most people wanted to be in the diaries, and so they gave her carte blanche. Usually, people signed without complaint, but all too often voiced objections once the book was in print. She carefully kept their letters of consent, many of them gushingly effusive in praise of their portraits, and when time and strength permitted, used them to silence what they called her "lies and innaccuracies."[65]

There were others who found their own methods of retaliation for what she wrote about them, such as Gore Vidal's splendidly wicked review of volume 4, in which he played a leading role.[66] Vidal's every sentence has a double edge, both sweet and sharp, as he knew exactly how to raise her hackles and disarm her at the same time. He led off with her age, the very thing he knew would enrage her, coupling it with the comment that always pleased her more than any other: she was "as beautiful as ever." He further rattled her composure by describing his own unflattering portrait of a thinly disguised Anaïs as Marietta Donegal in *Two Sisters,* all the while stressing that it was not *really* meant to be her. In the unkindest cut of all, Vidal insisted he had always been one of her "defenders," arguing that no matter what the shortcoming of her novels, the diary would one day "establish her as a great sensibility." But now that they had been published, he wrote slyly, "I am not so certain."

Neither was Hiram Haydn. The first volume of the diary sold a respectable number of copies in hardcover, around 10,000, before it was put into paperback, but volume 2 did not even sell the first printing of 2,500. Volume 3 did little better, and Haydn had been reluctant to publish volume 4, citing "mistiming" among other excuses for not offering a contract.[67]

In the meantime, the paperback editions were selling briskly, helped along, Anaïs was sure, by the flattering photo of herself that graced each cover. When neither Haydn nor publicist Hilda Lindley listened to her complaints about the cover photo they wanted to use, she went directly to John Ferrone, then chief editor of the paperback division.[68] She marched in bearing the objectionable photo and Ferrone became her friend forever when he looked at it, then at her, and said "but of course it's all wrong. We must have another."[69] She was delighted with the uniform covers of the paperback volumes, each with a different wash of color on a flattering closeup of her face.[70]

She continued to plead with Gunther to make Haydn offer a contract for volume 4, but there was little more he could do than hint to other publishers that all subsequent volumes of Anaïs Nin's diary might be for sale. Not surprisingly, none nibbled at his bait. She was worried because "this year [taxable 1969] I have had more expenses than income," and she urged him to "make our peace with Swallow." If Harcourt Brace Jovanovich (as Harcourt Brace was now known) did not want the rest of the diary, she wanted him to ask Swallow Press to publish it alone. Gunther was against it, but before he could do her bidding, Haydn grudgingly offered the contract for volume 4 with a pittance of an advance against royalties.

Anaïs was in desperate straits.[71] Besides the hundreds of free copies of both the diaries and the newsletter that she dispensed so freely, and the equally large sums she spent trying to buy up multiple copies of everything written about her, she was now in financial and legal trouble with her French publisher. The translation commissioned by Éditions Stock did not meet her approval, and her contract granted the right to reject it. But it also required her to commission another immediately and pay for it herself, and the cost was still mounting. She had been dropped by her lecture agency because she insisted on making her own arrangements, which interfered with theirs, and although she lectured constantly, more than two-thirds of her engagements were gratis. When she was paid, her fees seldom covered expenses, so she earned adulation but little money. Her expenses for stationery, postage, and photocopying were "frightening,"[72] and she continued to do all the work of self-promotion by herself. She called it "the hard grueling work of being famous."[73]

Money, and how to get it, was the refrain that played constantly in the background of her fame. She thought enviously of Henry and the comfortable life his writings bought for him. "After putting us through hell, he is now enjoying the diary," she noted bitterly.[74]

"Dear Henry," she wrote, saying it was easier to write than to talk to him about her situation.[75] Admitting that it was "quite clear I will never be a best seller," she asked him to "make me a gift of your letters (the personal ones I did not publish) as you did for the first batch which were published." She wanted only the royalties and agreed to submit any that she might eventually publish for his approval before doing so, but "this is only for the future, of course, as they cannot be published until after the death of Hugo."

Her intention was to sell the letters as quickly as possible, for despite the success of having four volumes of the diary in print in English and a steadily mounting number of translations, no one wanted to buy the originals, and she needed ever-increasing amounts of cash to support her new lifestyle. Except for an occasional commission, Hugo was now dependent on her, and Rupert still needed her contribution to the household. Duane Schneider told her that her fans were selling her individual letters for anything from $10 to $30, and she was outraged when Peter Owen sold her correspondence to the University of Texas for an "astonishing" sum of money.[76] Everyone, it seemed, was making money on something connected with her writing but her.

There were other irritations, and an inkling of trouble brewing among her audiences. Blanche Cooney, who worked in the Smith College Library, was responsible for an invitation to speak at the college on December 11, 1969. "Failure," Anaïs noted on her calendar. The women of Smith questioned Anaïs Nin about her commitment to feminism and pressed her to explain some of the choices she wrote of in the diary, most particularly her relationship to Henry as his helpmate. She tried to retreat behind her usual façade, citing privacy and individualism, but when she said that her aim as a woman writer was to give to the world "one perfect life"—herself—she was hooted and hissed.

The event still rankled two years later, when she wrote to Blanche Cooney to "correct" what had happened during "An Evening with Anaïs Nin" at the Old Cambridge Baptist Church on Harvard Square: "The Report you received on Harvard was not quite true. I received an ovation of five minutes before speaking from 1,200 persons and when the fanatical militant women spoke (only two of them) they were hissed away by the public. True the question period acknowledged clear disagreement from the subject but they were in the minority. . . . However, I am contributing to women's lib in my own way."[77]

Anaïs Nin had begun her talk by saying that this was the first time she would publicly address the criticisms leveled against her, namely that she was not a feminist because she was against political action and had never behaved in ways consistent with emerging feminist thinking.

"I am not speaking against political action," she insisted. "I am speaking of a better preparation for it. I was trying to make the bridge between examination of ourselves, which is not such a despairing and pessimistic thing, and group action. The tendency to group thinking weakens our will and our individual clarification of things. Without individual expansion and evolution, we get rigidity. This does not exclude action, social change."

The discussion continued at length, but there was neither agreement nor resolution between Nin and her interviewer, who tried to put a generous positive gloss on Anaïs's perception of the Feminist Movement.[78] But skepticism toward her "whifty"[79] approach to life was growing. At Bennington College, where she gave the commencement address to the class of 1971, there was a positive overall reception, but there was also a sizable contingent of women graduates who sat toward the rear of the class and whose attitudes veered between open sneering and politely hidden scorn. As the Vietnam war changed women's perceptions of their role in life, and as they became increasingly willing to take the risks entailed by political action, Nin's idea of "one perfect self" began to lack both charm and credence.

"Who Chose These Women, and Why?" was the headline in *The Village Voice*[80] a year after the Bennington commencement. "Anaïs Nin showed her nipples and the rest of her beautiful shape through a clinging silver dress, held a mask in front of her face, lowered it, and began to read from her diaries," wrote reporter Bertha Harris. "Maybe the sight . . . was worth it . . . but that was the beginning and the end to any aesthetic or feminist shape in the whole show." Harris described Nin as "a woman who . . . seeks to be feminist . . . speaking primarily on the thinkings and doings of men."

Even though there were growing clusters of women who questioned the validity of Anaïs Nin's feminist credentials because of her woman-centered (perhaps self-centered is a more appropriate term) writing, there were even more who embraced her as being emblematic of everything they sought to do and become. So for all those who rejected her because of what might be called her political incorrectness, there were many more who rallied round her credo of feminine fulfillment and adapted it to their own perception of proper feminist theory and behavior.[81]

As *Pisces* became securely launched, it was clear that Anaïs Nin had grown from her days as a coterie writer for the discerning few to a major cult figure. By the end of 1973, there were four volumes of the diary in a uniform paperback edition in the United States, and they sold a resounding 92,795 copies. That same year, 8,000 boxed sets of the first four were issued, which brought her total paperback sales to just under 125,000, a figure that has grown steadily in the years since.[82] And as sales figures for the translations of her work supplemented those in the United States, it was clear that her financial worries were over at last.

There was even interest in the sale of the diaries to university libraries, and several other private libraries approached her independently.[83] She was finally ready to let the diaries go, secure in the knowledge that they would be a separate, lasting monument to her achievement.

39

"The Book of Pain"

IN HER LAST TWO YEARS of life, 1974–1976 (she died on January 14, 1977), Anaïs Nin produced two extraordinary volumes of diary writing, chronicles of the unremitting, excruciating pain that accompanied the cancer that killed her. Each volume was also a testimony to the love she shared with Rupert Pole, deepened and strengthened by the devotion and care he provided unstintingly. Anaïs marveled at the outpouring of love from her friends and her brother Joaquín, truly what any human being would wish to have in times of such anguish. It sustained her throughout these terrible years, as did the arrival of the mail each day. It remained her "greatest treat and pleasure,"[1] filled as it was with letters, prayers, and gifts. There was also a steady stream of honors and awards, public recognition that validated her work and was finally enough to assuage her lifelong hunger for acceptance within the literary pantheon.

All these generous gestures accrued into an unending demonstration of how Anaïs Nin, through her life and her work, touched (and sometimes changed) the lives of so many people. She was fortunate, in her final years, to be able to have the peace of mind that came with such validation because what happened to her body was truly terrible.

The cancer began in the vagina.[2] In 1969 she experienced heavy bleeding, similar to a menstrual period. She had already had a hysterectomy, so the bleeding was reason for alarm. She consulted her gynecologist, who said the bleeding was "seepage from an incision which did not heal."[3] She chose to believe it was a residual symptom of the ruptured appendix she suffered at the age of nine.[4] When the pain in her lower back and the area where she believed her ovaries lay intensified,[5] she questioned him again, and he told her it was a side effect of the medication prescribed earlier by a doctor in Los Angeles to stem bleeding and prevent infection from discharge. He advised her to "wear a Kotex as if I were having a period. It was humiliating."

He also prescribed Darvon, a narcotic analgesic for mild to moderate pain, which Anaïs took every four hours even though it had little effect. Some weeks later, when she could not get out of bed until she first ingested Darvon and waited until it took effect, she returned to the gynecologist, who told her she had a small tumor, best treated by radiation rather than surgery. He sent her to New York's Presbyterian Hospital in late January 1970, for what she called a "radium tube" inserted directly into the vagina, where it was supposed to shrink any tumors or carcinomatous cells.[6]

Shortly after, the bleeding was stanched and the doctor told her she had made a "miraculous cure." Believing this because she wanted to and also because she had no reason not to, Anaïs Nin added to her frenziedly active schedule, traveling nonstop to give lectures, grant interviews, write articles for magazines, and contribute prefaces for the books of her friends. She flew to London, Paris, and Frankfurt to launch foreign editions of her diaries, visited Japan and Morocco, Singapore, Bangkok, and Bali, all of which she wrote about in travel articles. She posed for photographs, appeared on television, and was the subject of a feature film, *Anaïs Observed,* by Robert Snyder.[7] And as she was still commuting between Rupert and Hugo, there was an extra level of tension involved in appeasing each man's needs as well as hiding her frailty to keep them from worrying during her absences.

Obsessed with prolonging the enjoyment of her success, and considering how swiftly the cancer invaded her body, she counted on willpower and determination to carry her through each activity-filled day from 1970 until the end of 1973. She also used her illness in other ways, mainly to avoid unwanted questions. When she appeared at the 92nd Street Y in New York with the biographer Nancy Milford, who was to question her about women's autobiography in general and in particular her diaries, Nin waited until the very last moment before the program began, then whispered that she would not answer any questions about her personal life. As they were about to go on stage, she also whispered, "You do know, dear, that I am dying of cancer, so you will be gentle, won't you."[8] Milford was so stunned by Nin's revelation that her "hard, tough questions flew right out the window."

All this activity was played out against a backdrop of repeated visits to hospitals in New York and Los Angeles, and the continuing hard work connected with editing volumes 5 and 6 of the diaries. These two were the most difficult to write because once she finished the fourth volume, about her "New York period," there was "no one big theme [to] emerge," and thus, nothing to unify the subsequent volumes necessary for an account of her entire life.[9] Hugo pointed the way out of the morass in which she found herself by insisting that it was perfectly valid for the diary to become "more sketchy." He urged her to rely upon "memoir writing because . . . it follows the struggle, mood, and vision of that time." Anaïs was "superstitious afraid of breaking a good strong continuity," a valid worry because medications prescribed to dull her pain made her distrust her ability to concentrate. But once she agreed to an "impressionistic" as well as a "more sketchy" format, she was able to "fill out the portraits" and work toward finishing both volumes.

She was hospitalized again in March 1970 in New York for a second "radiation," after which she left for Los Angeles to spend several weeks with Rupert before flying to England and France for publicity purposes and also to meet Hugo in Paris. She told Richard Centing she was "under stress" and still lacked energy for anything other than a brief walk, but she told Hugo she could swim three laps in her pool before her breath gave out.[10] However, she could still write, and that was what mattered most.[11]

In late spring, 1971, she was hospitalized for the first time in Los Angeles, at Cedars of Lebanon Hospital. She described her physician, Dr. Weston, as "a top doctor though a bad psychologist,"[12] also as brusque and dismissive, dictatorial and tyrannical.[13] From the beginning, she questioned his treatment.

He did not tell her that she had cancer, probably because he assumed she knew. And so she returned to Silver Lake to spend the summer, thinking she had been cured. "I am perfectly well," she wrote to Hugo in July. "No troubles of any kind."[14] And then she told Hugo she had discovered that her gynecologist, a Dr. Parks, knew she had cancer all along, but neither he nor Dr. Weston had told her.

She learned the truth when Weston, leaving for vacation, introduced her to his replacement. The two doctors discussed Anaïs's case as if she were not there, "incidentally" mentioning cancer. Anaïs told Hugo what happened next: "I said 'not cancer.' He showed me Dr. Parks's file and it had a word I do not know, carcimonous or something like that, low grade, but it was cancer and not benign. He added I had made a miraculous cure, etc. but of course I was rather shocked as Dr. Parks had not told me." She was also upset at the possibility that Dr. Bogner might have known and not told her either.[15]

Between 1971 and 1973, she was hospitalized three times for radiation therapy and several other times for tests, all the while keeping up the frenetic activity that caring for her fame required. She also contributed to her constant exhaustion by rushing to New York to care for Hugo to the detriment of her own health.

The greatest reversal in their marriage happened in 1973, during the last period of Anaïs Nin's life when she was in relatively good health. She began to make money in goodly quantities while Hugo made none. By the third quarter of that year, Anaïs's income totaled $62,000 and seemed likely to go much higher.[16] She was commanding good fees for her articles, never less than the $1,700 for one on Bali in *Travel & Leisure;* she accepted lectures only with a minimum fee of $750, but they were usually always higher; and she received healthy sums in royalties from translations of her work.

Things were brought to a head with Hugo when International College asked Anaïs Nin to become a tutor in an independent study program for "men and women who wish to work as apprentice writers under her guidance."[17] Just as she had earlier refused to teach in Los Angeles because it would not allow her to make periodic trips to New York, she now wanted to accept this offer because she needed an excuse not to live with Hugo any longer.

Her roots were no longer "portable," for she loved the house, her very own "small paradise just five minutes from downtown."[18] She also accepted at last how ideally suited she and Rupert were for each other. Now that "love of beer" had thickened his body in middle age and gray speckled his hair, the difference in their ages no longer seemed so vast. He was about to retire from teaching, and wanted nothing more than to enjoy puttering with her in the house and garden and help her deal with the avalanche of work entailed by her fame. It seemed a miracle, as Anaïs told Bogner, that everything she had yearned for all her life had come to her, and how sad it was that she was in her seventies and too ill to enjoy it.

International College seemed to provide her with something she sought constantly: a reason both logical and truthful that Hugo would have to accept for her ever-longer absences from New York. In this instance, she was quite mistaken. At the end of 1971, when he was seventy-four, Hugo admitted that he was penniless and asked Anaïs not only for financial help but for her constant presence at his side.[19]

She certainly intended to give Hugo whatever he needed, but she discussed the situation first with Joaquín, who was shortly to retire from Berkeley, capping a distinguished teaching career as chairman of the Music Department. When he heard of Hugo's plight, Joaquín decided that the time had come for him to help the person who had financed his education. He loved Hugo and did not want to injure his pride. Writing as if his decision were sudden and spontaneous, Joaquín said that he had been "an old investment" of Hugo's and was now ready to "pay off." He promised to send Hugo $100 a month for the rest of his life.

Unlike Hugo, who required her to be present in New York before he doled out her "allowance," Anaïs simply contacted their accountant and arranged to have $1,000 a month placed directly in Hugo's bank. It was enough to support him fairly well, but it was not enough to support his films, his doctors, and his analysts, so Anaïs increased his stipend first by an additional thousand dollars each month, and when that was not enough, still more.

Hugo gratefully took the money Joaquín offered, but did not treat Anaïs's contribution nor himself with the same respect. She wrote repeatedly, urging him to consider the money as "our money," which he was unable to do.[20] Perhaps it was another ploy to force her to return to New York, but now he insisted he would economize by moving to a cheaper apartment and implied that he would have to dispose of many of her things if he did. No doubt he knew this would terrify her, for her room contained a locked closet in which she had had a false wall constructed.[21] Inside, the rear wall was locked by two more keys, and required knowledge of certain strategic shifts, lifts, and lowerings of the panel before it could be opened. Hugo may not have known this, but he did know she kept diary volumes there, moving them back and forth to the Brooklyn vault as she finished culling them for the published diaries.

Anaïs and Hugo fought throughout the fall of 1973, with each firing new salvos in the daily and sometimes twice- or thrice-daily letters that flew between them. Anaïs tried to resolve their verbal war by imploring Hugo to respect her need for a less stressful way of earning money than the individual lectures for which she had to travel in her impaired health.[22] Telling him she understood "the symbolic significance of money making," she praised him for having "supported and raised successfully a family" while managing to be an exceptional artist and "very remarkable man."[23]

Hugo needed several months of therapy before he could admit to Anaïs that his anxiety was mostly due to the feeling that "you had left me out of your life."[24] Anaïs tried again to tell him she was his "best investment" and "things are going very well":

> I already as I told you, saved, tax free, enough for any of your needs next year . . . I spend very little here except rental of the house I was glad to have when publicity started . . . as it is very appropriate a setting[25] . . . The important thing for the future is that 50 or over colleges are teaching me, which means selling many books and initiating new generations each six months. This assures continuity, which no best seller ever has. . . . My reputation is no fad. The Casebook . . . is an anthology of the best essays and will establish me. Evelyn [Hinz] has in the academic world by her dry analytical book (nobody likes). These are permanent things.[26]

Nothing she wrote calmed Hugo's mounting anxiety, so she asked Inge Bogner for help in October 1973.[27] Even as she wrote she knew nothing would come of it: "Only one person has known Hugo well, and that is Bogner. But she is so vigilant, so ethical in not sharing her knowledge, as if she knew neither of us."[28]

Anaïs spent the last days of 1973 and the beginning of 1974 with Hugo in New York. She was bleeding throughout this time "like a light menstruation." She could not avoid "the fear of recurrence of cancer is there."

Each day with Hugo was "uniformly dismal," and each day as she took the bus to see one or more of her several doctors, she jotted down what transpired between them.[29] Anaïs thought Hugo "a living symbol of the failure of psychoanalysis," just as she was "of its effectiveness." She resented Hugo's childish dependence on Bogner, and his grandiose schemes of setting himself up in Paris at the Hôtel

Crillon, to live as he had done in his glory days, dreaming that he would recoup his lost capital.

Anaïs railed against "the helplessness engendered in woman by the married state": "The man providing may be the ruin of her life. I had no courage to leave Hugo when I should have because I felt helpless and I don't mean only economically, but helpless and frightened of life. This debt of protectiveness is what I am paying back. He never refused me anything so I feel I cannot refuse him anything."

Fortunately for them both, Hugo received a small grant from the American Film Institute. His depression lifted at once, but hers deepened immeasurably, even as she sat for a series of photographs by Jill Krementz. "I was depressed all the while," she wrote of the photo shoot, but to see how the photographer captured her radiant face and the dramatic swirl of the black cape which enveloped her, no one would ever know it. Nor would they know she was about to be hospitalized for another bout of radiation.

"I asked [the doctors] if anything bad. They said no." Ten days later she wrote, "Test made. Yes, there is something brewing. I have to go to hospital for 4 days for painful insertion of radium bullet." She didn't mind "the pain (which is great)," but she did mind "the ruined love making for months because of a shrivelled vagina."[30]

On January 22, her luggage weighted down by books John Ferrone gave her to read during what she assumed would be four days of rest, and her briefcase filled with all the papers she needed to plan her "activities," she checked herself into the hospital. She was appalled to find that the time passed in a blur during which she was "an inanimate object . . . diffused and weakened by anesthesia." On January 27 she was dismissed. In early February, seven pounds lighter and still weak, she willed herself to pack her luggage and sent it by air freight, then called a taxi and got herself to the airport. This time she parted from Hugo peacefully, for he agreed that she should return to the healing sunshine of California. Rupert met her at the airport with a wheelchair, but she was too proud to use it.

Several days after that, she spent the morning tinting her hair ("Rupert does not want me to let it go grey"), packed a small suitcase, and left for Fresno, where she was to be paid $1,000 for a lecture. She went because she needed the money for Hugo and was afraid to turn down any fee that came her way.

By the end of March 1974, she was forced to admit that she had not recovered. She made the first of the occasional self-appraisals that soon became daily, detailed accounts written in the two journals that chronicled her last two years of life, "The Book of Pain" and "The Book of Music."[31] In this account, what saddened her most was that she had not recovered the energy she had before the January recurrence and hospitalization. Now she could "only swim six laps instead of ten." She could get out of her bath only by "holding the handles," and if she crouched over her files, she "had to make an effort to straighten up." She "dreaded crowds, standing up for hours, talking to admirers." Even worse, "the martini I love which breaks the tension between day and evening gives me pain."

Something happened that made her perceive the two men in her life very differently. She arrived home at 1.30 A.M. after having flown to Sonoma, in northern California, early that morning to give a lecture. Rupert refused to let her take a taxi and insisted on meeting her at the airport even though he had to teach the next day. "Hearing the complaints of women on men resenting their careers I see more and more how exceptional Rupert is," she noted appreciatively. Her mail that morning brought a letter from Hugo, "showing anxiety and doubts, asking Gunther over and over again if my royalties will be sufficient even if I should stop lecturing." Hugo she did not appreciate.

By May 1974, her activities were as intense as they had ever been, but several particularly stood out in her mind. In Los Angeles, Christy Logan staged *Collages,* and in New York, she participated in a program about diary writing with Dr. Ira Progoff, founder of the "Intensive Journal" method. Anaïs Nin was disappointed: "Ira is enclosed in his system and we could not combine the spontaneous diary writing with his planned therapeutic way of using the diary. I could see a stimulating combination of the two but Ira is convinced there is only one way. Our students shuttled between us because he can answer the question I never could answer: how do you write a diary and how do you begin!"

She was elated to learn that she was to be inducted into the American Academy and Institute of Arts and Letters in New York in May. It was not the French Academy, but to receive such acceptance and validation from the country that had snubbed her for so many decades was a thrill beyond measure. Despite her weakness and constant pain, she flew to New York to attend the ceremony, leaning heavily on John Ferrone.

For the rest of the year, Anaïs Nin ignored the toll on her body and traveled throughout the United States giving lectures, accepting awards, and promoting Robert Snyder's film. All the while she was bleeding, once again wearing a sanitary napkin, once again believing Dr. Parks when he told her she was not having a recurrence of cancer. Shortly before Christmas, she consulted Dr. Weston in Los Angeles because the pain was no longer bearable. He sent her to Cedars of Lebanon Hospital for two days of tests, and on New Year's Eve she learned that it was indeed a recurrence of cancer that was "threatening the uthera or the intestines."[32] She could not have any further radiation because she had been given the maximum (if not more) than the total dosage allowed without causing irreversible damage to healthy tissue and toxic side effects as well. There was no alternative but surgery: "If no invasion of bladder or intestines, all is well, but if there is, then I will be mutilated with a hole in my stomach and a bag for evacuation." She knew she had "the courage for the surgery, but none for the mutilation."

For the first time, she was entirely felled by her illness. The painkillers left her befuddled and she could not "surmount pain and work, not this time." As she waited to be admitted to the hospital, she asked herself, "Can the love given to me this year by so many keep me alive?" There was no doubt of Rupert's love, for he demonstrated it passionately and she responded despite the pain of sexual intercourse. On their last night together before her surgery, they drank champagne in their beautiful house and she felt "grateful, grateful, to have attained a great love, and gained love for my work."

On January 9, 1975, she was admitted for surgery. The next time she was well enough to describe what she had endured was on February 7, when she described the surgery as "a season in hell," with pain and complications so intense she never wanted to describe it. Instead, she wrote of losing the desire to live, of pain so severe that Rupert sat by her bedside begging her to stay alive. She remembered that he was "radiant, devoted" as he repeated over and over, "Hold on, Anaïs, hold on." To give her the will to live and whether she could hear him or not in her delirium, he recited a litany of "everything [she] cared about": of Henry Jaglom wanting to film *Cities of the Interior* and Tristine Rainer writing the script; of Judy Chicago including her in the *Birth* series; of being honored by the United Nations in "The Year of the Woman," and her invitation to appear on a panel with Germaine Greer and Françoise Gilot, which, sadly, she had to refuse; of her honorary doctorates at Philadelphia College of the Arts and Dartmouth; of her students at International College who had become her "daughters" and who gave her such joy through their writing.

After she rallied, her only writing for the next several months was a calendar listing the many friends who came to see her and the offers and honors that she had to refuse. Not until April 11, 1975, could she write "Worked on Vol. 6," but then it was only to try to remember where she had been before the surgery.

She tried to talk to Hugo on the telephone but he was either legitimately too deaf to hear her properly, or he pretended his condition was worse than it really was. She still insisted that "friends" were caring for her, and he never questioned her stories. Her feelings toward Hugo changed during her illness from compassion to irritation and finally to revulsion: she simply could not bear the thought of being with him or living with him ever again. She was well aware of everything he had done for her and was grateful enough to want to return it in kind, but that was all. For too many years they had been a mismatched couple who made each other miserable because of their long history together, which, for so many complex reasons, they could not sunder.

In the first letter she was able to write, just three weeks after the surgery, she described what had happened to her since the cancer was diagnosed in 1970.[33] It was accurate in lay terms, but the language is befuddled due to the heavy medication she now took:

> I had three radiations. Two in New York, one here. The flesh around the ruptured appendix of childhood was probably already weakened (I was three months draining the abscess). After surgery here the stomach wall burst in the same place. It is a hole about ½ inch wide, enough to let out a lot of liquid. As it is placed between stomach and small intestine and ilium, where [small] intestine meets the large one, so a great part of my food spills and through fisture [fistula], a bag has to collect the material. This bag leaks often because bile, stomach acids, etc., sneak out. . . . When they operate they make a bypass so the food will go the right route but this means an artifical drain, a planned hole, with a bag in another place. That is why I was not eager to have it nor were the doctors. We all hope it will heal as the first one finally did after two months. I have been back from hospital only three weeks. So there is hope of healing.

"No illness could have been a greater trial to my sense of aesthetics," she wrote many months later, when accidents with "the bag" became a relentless occurrence. Her description is harrowing:

> The continuous torment of the leaking bag, the over active fistula, hours spent lying flat in bed waiting for the nurse . . . the anxiety when a visitor comes that the leak should happen, awakening at night to find it has burst, wearing a dress I love and the fistula staining it, getting up two or three times a night to empty the bag, the feeling of an impure body . . . the saddest hours are those spent waiting for Jo, the nurse. When the bag leaks I have to take it off and lie flat in bed with wash rags to sponge off the horrible content of the fistula. The hole is deep, the discharge ugly, green, yellow. I often weep.[34]

Even the slightest movement was enough to dislodge the bag and send the acidic discharge spewing across her abdomen. Within a very short time, the skin around the opening was raw and abraded, prone to infection. When the discharge touched it, as it did all too frequently, the pain was searing.

Rupert could not bear to see her in such pain, so he learned to change the bag. When she could no longer ingest medication orally, he learned how to give injections. No task was too menial, difficult, or degrading for Rupert, as he took over all aspects of her daily care.

Joaquín volunteered to come to Silver Lake several days each week and take over "shopping, cooking, dish-washing and other chores I am well prepared to do,"[35] to give Rupert respite from his devotion to meeting Anaïs's needs.

"How could God do this to me?" Anaïs demanded of her devoutly Catholic brother. "How could he give me everything I ever wanted and punish me with cancer at the same time." "God does not operate that way, Anaïs," Joaquín told her sadly. "He is not a computer who keeps track of balance sheets and gives and takes away in equal measure."[36] Privately, she railed and cursed her illness; publicly, she tried to act as if she were entirely well.

Rupert sought alternative treatments and cures. Through Anaïs's Japanese translator, Kazuko Sugisaki, he learned of an experimental Japanese vaccine that was banned from the United States and tried (unsuccessfully) to acquire it.[37]

Dr. Brugh Joy became Anaïs's healer and friend, and she also experienced an attraction she had not felt in years. One day, when she realized that Brugh's "beauty . . . struck a chord it had not touched before," she cautioned herself not to become personally involved because "I have never loved Rupert more deeply and more passionately. He has energized me against other men."[38] Nevertheless, the attraction to Brugh Joy gave her something to grasp, as she believed for a very long time that he was helping her to become healed.

Brugh Joy became so important to Anaïs that for a short time Rupert even took her to his ranch, a drive of several hours and over bumpy, rutted roads for the last few miles. There, Brugh's other guests sat in a circle on huge pillows, holding hands. He placed Anaïs on a high table and passed his hands over her body, after which each member of the group individually laid hands upon her. "I felt such energy entering me that I felt compelled to leave the table and dance. But for the dizziness I would have danced, but as it was, I made just a few gestures. But the effect of the healing was startling." By the time they arrived home after the equally arduous return journey, the pain began again and did not respond to a double dose of medication.

Chemotherapy made her hair fall out. Rupert was determined that she would not feel shame at this so-obvious loss of her beauty, so he bought a selection of wigs, turning the "selection of the daily personality" into a game for both to play.[39] He did everything to lift her spirits from the depression that overwhelmed her. He cooked special meals and insisted she eat them, made her take short walks to keep up her strength, gently raised and lowered her into the swimming pool each day, and even made love to her there so that she would not dwell on the loss of her beauty.

"Rupert's faith is shining brightly," she noted in the diary, but then she added ominously, "I am not there. My body has slipped away."[40] She still looked forward to the daily arrival of the mail, but wondered why it no longer made her happy: "What is it? What has happened to me. A sorrow of enormous depth lies at the bottom. Oh, so heavy. I cannot resume my joy. It is not the concept of death, the parting from all love. It is a profound sorrow at the loss of my energy, my fire. There is a void, a void . . . before my illness I was physically and emotionally close to everyone. Now there is a distance."[41]

Complications piled one on top of the other. An abscess formed around the fistula; a second, then a third surgery was necessary. From "two bags," she now had "three bags," and when "they put the catheter in for bladder trouble" she was pinned down in her bed.[42]

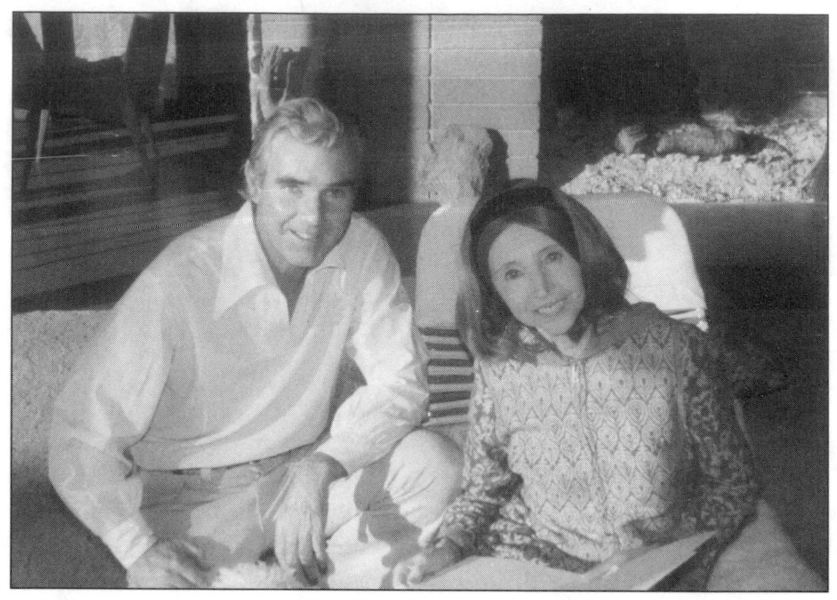

Anaïs in one of her wigs during chemotherapy, with Rupert.

Anaïs reading at WBAI.

Her depression lifted somewhat when Inge Bogner wrote that Hugo was finally ready to accept "separate lives."[43]

With predictions for her survival "so solemn," Anaïs finally faced "the possibility of death." "Small things," such as being too weak to open her mail, her eyesight too blurred to read it, and the nagging concern over the diaries, still in the Brooklyn bank vault, forced her to admit the time had come to be totally honest with Rupert. She told him every last detail about her double life in a "total confession." His attitude "was perfect . . . in millions of ways, Rupert was there." Now there was no need to conceal Hugo's monthly checks, and Rupert even dialed the telephone so she could speak to Hugo more frequently. When she became too ill to talk, Rupert took over the phoning and relayed reports of her condition.

Rupert "understood the motivation for the double life" at once, but Anaïs "never realized the weight of the burden until [she] shed it." She was "frightened" by the intensity of her "rebellion against Hugo," and by how peaceful she felt now that Rupert knew everything: "for the first time living one life, one love," she felt "a peace I never knew, an absence of strain I never knew."

They moved the diaries to a vault in downtown Los Angeles, just over the hill from the Silver Lake house. The volumes were placed in a small cell-like chamber, and from time to time, Rupert was able to carry Anaïs there to sit among them on the chair he created for her, an aluminum-frame webbed lawn chair covered with the softest white sheepskin. Volume 6 appeared, reviewed by Joyce Carol Oates in *The New York Times Book Review* with what Anaïs Nin expected: "petty and old fashioned, full of clichés." She had reached a new plane, however, for she "no longer suffered from those narrow judgments."[44]

Rupert took over the editing of volume 7 in August 1976 when "excessive radiation" made it impossible for her to continue.[45] She spent most of her time in bed because the warmth of the electric blanket helped her cope with the pain. She tried to write, but the medication impeded the clarity of her thinking. There was too much difficulty in establishing sequences, and her hand was now too uncoordinated to write clearly. In a natural reaction, Rupert began to watch television obsessively, while she begged him to let her get out of bed and help with the housework. She apologized for what she had done to his life, but he told her she had given him his life and taking care of her was his "most important achievement."

"It is amazing and beautiful how we work together," she observed. Rupert's "devotion" to the diary was "absolute" and she believed that his editorial decisions and his actually writing large parts of volume 7 "improves it." She decided that he had become "a writer in the process," and now "recognizes his identity as an artist."[46] To honor his commitment to her work, she revised her will and trust so that after Hugo's death, Rupert would become her sole beneficiary.[47]

Friends recognized the strain Rupert was under to care for Anaïs, and they came to help. Jim Herlihy answered the mail that poured in daily "in cartons and cartons." Once or twice she was well enough to visit him at his house on the other side of Silver Lake. She was delighted that his house seemed "fused with fantasy and beauty," and that he was happy. Barbara Kraft came several times each week, always bearing some small treat to cheer her. The former nun Corita Kent, famed for her silk-screen drawings, became a new friend when she wrote one day to say that she, too, was suffering from cancer.[48] Their friendship expanded through letters as Corita told Anaïs how fortunate she was to have Rupert, for she lived alone in Boston and was hard-pressed to deal with the depression that came with her illness. Hugo's young friend Frank Alberti visited from New York, taping one of the last interviews Anaïs ever gave, on their mutual passion, Marcel Proust. It was Frank who sent the news that she said meant more to her than membership in the American Academy and Institute of Arts and Letters, that an article on her Proustian affinities would soon appear in the Dutch "Society of the Friends of Proust" Bulletin.[49] Equally thrilling was when the *Los Angeles Times* named her Woman of the Year in 1976.

Anaïs's dream of finding a home for the diaries was finally realized in 1976 when Digby Diehl, of the *Los Angeles Times,* telephoned philanthropist Joan Palevsky and asked her to co-chair a fund-raising drive to buy Anaïs Nin's diaries for UCLA. "How much must we raise?" she asked. "$100,000," he replied. Joan Palevsky thought for a moment, then said, "Look, Digby, you and I are very busy people. Why don't I just write you a check for the full amount and then it will be over and done with."[50] Joan's generosity reduced Anaïs, in her weakened condition, to gratitude expressed in numbed disbelief. She invited Joan to visit, and discovered that they shared a love of France and French literature and were interested in many of the same writers.

There was so much to live for that she was determined not to die. "I will get well! I will get well!" she implored herself in October 1976. "Two years of this! Unrelenting pain and difficulties." The bag leaked constantly and the stomach acids burnt her skin. "Too much! Too much!" she cried, as they carried her to Cedars for a nerve block. All throughout the year, whenever she was hospitalized, Rupert filled her room with beautiful things. He hung Japanese paper birds and recorded the birds who sang in their garden so that she could play the cassettes while she lay in bed. Friends brought bits of macramé, drawings, and flowers. And when she needed blood transfusions, women turned out in droves to donate. Rupert brought his quartet one night to play for her.

In November 1976 she "dared to face my ultimate fear, despair, anxiety—I am not prepared to die." The last diary entry in her hand is dated "November 26," followed on the next line by "Dec. 6." It is followed by three blurred lines reproduced here exactly as she wrote them: "Nov 26 I went to the Hospital—and died. Died among clean sheets, medicines, finish like an insect"

Rupert's handwriting fills the rest of the diary. Whenever he arrived in her room, "everything seems all right. He takes charge."

Deena Metzger, whom she always called "Truthful Deena," came to see her. "Am I dying?" Anaïs asked. "No you're not, but you must prepare for death," Deena replied. Anaïs asked Corita Kent whether she should prepare for death and Corita told her "Death will be especially easy for you because you have already transposed." Anaïs was not so sure; she wept at "the mere idea of separation from Rupert."

When Joaquín came to visit during her last few months of life, he was unsure of her attitude toward the Catholic religion. To try to ascertain how she felt, he joked that Sainte Thérèse de Lisieux had saved her at the age of nine, and he would inquire as to why she was shirking her duties now. Anaïs smiled but said little. Joaquín asked if she would like to see a priest to make a final confession, and she said no. Earlier, she confided to the diary that she had lived her life without such rituals and preferred to die the same way.

In her last months of life, the cancer metastasized throughout her body, into her lungs and throat, impairing her speech so that she could speak only in a throaty whisper. Hugo was mostly deaf, but she still asked Rupert to get him on the telephone.

For the better part of 1976, her correspondence with Hugo frequently mentioned the word "absolution."[51] Anaïs pounced on his initial use of the word and asked him to explain it. As always, he hid behind Bogner, saying he should not have used it because "Inge will have nothing to do with that." From this far-removed beginning, the concept of absolution veered to become one in which the doctrine of the Catholic Church was paramount in its meaning whenever Hugo and Anaïs used the term.

In one of her last letters to Hugo, written large with a black felt marker, her once-firm hand only slightly shaky, as if she were willing it to be strong, Anaïs Nin Guiler asked her husband of almost fifty-four years to grant her "absolution." The purpose of the telephone call she asked Rupert to place was to hear Hugo say that he absolved her. Instead, what she heard was a confused old man who may or may not have heard what she asked, who was unable to do more than stutter and stammer about how much he loved her and how he so wished she would get well. He did not ask if she wanted him to visit, for he had long since given up asking, and accepted what became her official version of why she did not want to see him, that she wanted him to remember her as she was, when she was full of life and very beautiful.[52] It is probably a testimony to Hugh Parker Guiler's lifelong love and devotion that he respected her wishes rather than his own and did not try to see his wife before she died.

The question of "absolution" is also clouded by whether or not Anaïs ever asked Hugo to "release" her. There are several long letters within her archives in which she told Hugo the same truth about her double life as she told Rupert, but across each she has written "letter not sent," or words to that effect.[53] There is a very real possibility that at some point during Anaïs's final illness, Inge Bogner told Hugo that Anaïs wanted "a release from him because of guilt feelings."[54] Hugo claimed not to know exactly what Anaïs meant, let alone what she wanted, but he did write to say that he "released her, as he had earlier in their relationship."[55] Grateful for this, Anaïs wrote her last letter to Hugo, a paean of love, in which she told him, "I am proud to have loved you all of my life."[56] He treasured the sentiment for the rest of his own.

Anaïs grew steadily weaker throughout December 1976, but Rupert continued to care for her until her lungs filled with fluid and she lapsed into a coma. She died at the Cedars of Lebanon Hospital on January 14, 1977, at 11:55 P.M. Her death certificate cited as causes cardiorespiratory arrest, severe malnutrition, and widespread metastatic carcinoma.[57]

Early the next morning Rupert telephoned Joaquín, who then telephoned Hugo. When Anaïs Nin's obituaries appeared, *The New York Times* reported that she was survived by her husband, Hugh P. Guiler, and the *Los Angeles Times* by her husband Rupert Pole. Both men were exceedingly considerate of each other's feelings, and with Joaquín acting as intermediary, it was agreed by both that Hugo would allow her "friends" to take charge of her burial.

Anaïs Nin, the Pisces, influenced all her life by the sign "ruled by Neptune, the planet of illusion,"[58] asked to be buried at sea, so Rupert took her ashes aloft in a small plane over Santa Monica Bay.[59] Studying the navigation charts while the pilot flew, he noticed that all the markings were described by ordinary fish names except one: Mermaid Cove. He directed the pilot to fly there and dropped the bright pink blanket containing the ashes of Anaïs Nin just as a ray of sunlight broke through the overcast January sky. His eyes followed the blanket's descent to where it lay floating on top of the water for a very long time.

When Rupert returned to Silver Lake, he discovered that Mermaid Cove was directly over the hill from the house's living area, obscured from view by a willow tree. Several weeks later, for no discernible reason, the healthy tree died. Rupert believes it did not want to impede his view of Mermaid Cove. He never planted another.

Epilogue

HUGO LIVED IN Washington Square Village until his death at the age of eighty-six on January 7, 1985, his last decade made comfortable and secure by the terms of Anaïs's will. In the last years of his life he often described how the spirit of Anaïs visited him in the early morning, to sit comfortably on the edge of his bed and tell soothingly how she would guide him "over" or "across" when his time came.[1]

Ironically, the money came from the erotica that Anaïs Nin scorned, and which either embarrassed her or made her deeply ashamed (depending on her mood on any given day). *Delta of Venus,* followed by *Little Birds,* brought the financial security she craved throughout her lifetime to her two husbands after her death.[2]

In her last year of life, Anaïs Nin worried that medical expenses would deplete her assets, and subsequent sale of the diaries would not be enough to sustain Rupert and Hugo.[3] Rupert suggested that she sell the erotica, which she was reluctant to do because she feared it might adversely affect not only future sales of the diaries but also her reputation as a feminist icon. He persuaded Anaïs that it would be a sound financial move, and even though she agreed, she still did not want to see these writings in print. Eventually, she stipulated that if they were published, it must be with a firm other than Harcourt Brace Jovanovich in order to keep them from (in her mind) corrupting the reputation of the diaries.

When John Ferrone visited in 1975, Rupert brought up the subject of the erotica and Anaïs sheepishly told John her plan for the more-than-800-page manuscript. He urged her to let him publish it, but it still took another year before she was willing to let him read it, and not until his last visit in 1976 did she agree to part with the manuscript. By that time she was too weak to do anything but complete her work on the diary, so she agreed that Ferrone could cut and edit the erotica as he thought best. His work resulted first in *Delta of Venus,* and then in *Little Birds.*

Ferrone described the first book in a letter to the critic Herbert Mitgang: "I thought the erotica was extraordinary, and saw that, despite the injunctions of her client, she hadn't been able to 'leave out the poetry.' What was more, I was struck by the sensitive descriptions of women's sexual feelings, unlike anything I had ever read before . . . eventually I was able to convince her that it contained superb writing. . . . She conceded this only to a degree in the postscript to her preface."[4]

Anaïs Nin did not live to see her most successful writing in print—her first bestseller, actually—only the book's galleys and the jacket photograph of a kneeling young woman with a lifted skirt showing bare flesh above her gartered stocking.[5] In the years since, critics have agreed that her erotica represents one of the most striking expressions of the feminine sensibility and especially of female sexuality.[6] Both volumes have been translated into (at last count) twenty-six languages. All her writings, the diaries, novels, and erotica, have been published in approximately thirty languages and have sold something approaching 3 million copies.[7]

After Anaïs Nin died, Rupert Pole announced that it had been her last and strongest wish that the diaries be published a second time, in an unexpurgated version. Four volumes of "early diaries" appeared. The first two are translations of her adolescent writing in French and the latter two are about her young adulthood and marriage. Then came *Henry and June* and *Incest,* with material selected and edited primarily by Rupert Pole.

Rupert selects the passages from the original diaries (now housed at UCLA and available to qualified scholars only with his permission) and gives each volume its particular focus and shape. Gunther Stuhlmann then does the careful and precise editing that drove Anaïs Nin to tears in her lifetime. The two men argue their positions and points of view until both are satisfied with the text, then it is sent to a Harcourt Brace editor.[8]

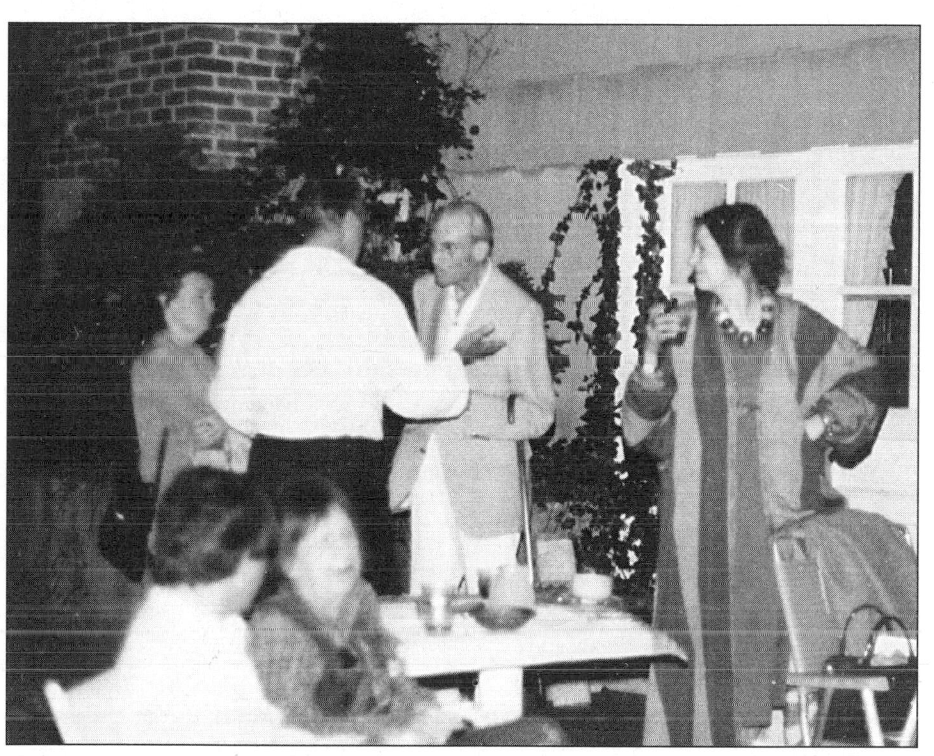

Hugo and Rupert at a party at Valerie Harms' Connecticut home after Anaïs's death.

All this shaping of AN's original text, from initial selection to correction of her grammar, punctuation, and spelling, and even in many instances of her actual language, has resulted in something different in many cases from what she actually wrote. John Ferrone described the process: *"Henry and June,* originally subtitled 'from the Unexpurgated Diary of Anaïs Nin,' was heavily edited to focus on the Anaïs-Henry-June relationship and to repeat as little as possible of already published material. Consisting of excerpts from Anaïs Nin's typed transcripts of the original journals with interpolations of a few passages from volume one of the published diary, it is undependable as a reference. Therefore, it is of questionable use to scholars."

In all fairness, Ferrone's working method duplicated Anaïs Nin's own editorial practices and was what most readers, scholars, and critics would call a continuation of her casuistic approach to both her life and her writing.

What, then, is Anaïs Nin's reputation since her death in 1977? The large initial interest in her work has dissipated into a small, dedicated band of scholars who still ask students to read *House of Incest* as a "representative" text of Surrealist literature. Some of Nin's novels appear in various Women's Studies courses, but professors tend to shun the diaries as "untruthful" or "unreliable." One wonders, however, why "truth" is the primary criterion for judging diaries, especially those such as Nin's, which were intended from the beginning to represent one woman's view of herself and her life.

Be that as it may, Nin, in the main, seems to be relegated to the literary rank and rung she strove all her life to avoid: that of a "cult," or coterie, writer. Part of this is due to the manner in which her original writings have been withheld from scholars, thus impeding, if not making impossible, legitimate critical inquiry.

The UCLA diaries, although owned by the University, remain under the control of the sole executor of Anaïs Nin's estate, Rupert Pole. He decides to whom they should be accessible, and for many years (until he agreed to cooperate with this biography), no one but Evelyn Hinz was permitted to read them. Anaïs Nin chose Hinz to be her official biographer in 1974; when Rupert Pole dies, the Canadian scholar will become the sole literary executor. Under such restriction, it is no wonder that the many scholars who were drawn to Nin's work soon abandoned interest in it, thus further marginalizing her writing within scholarship and literature.

However, as Rupert Pole finishes culling his selections for the

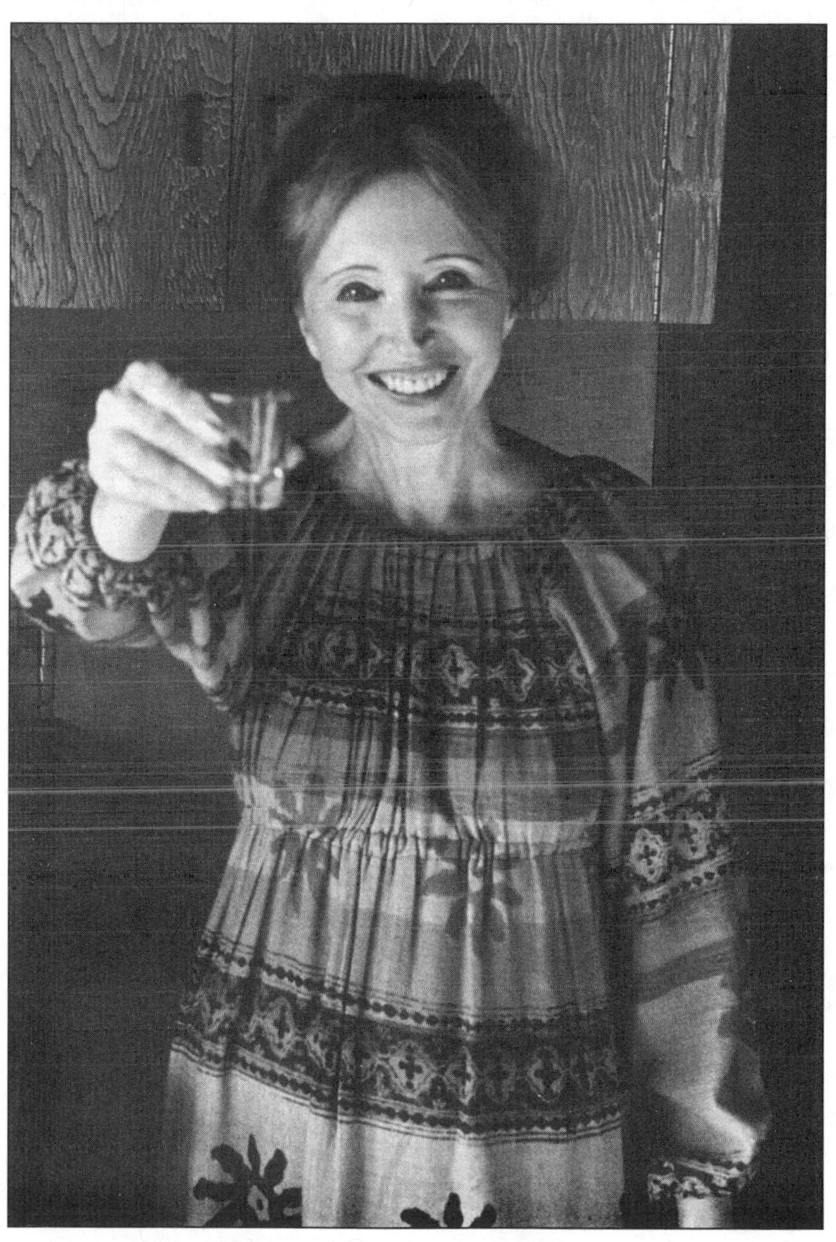

Anaïs Nin, toasting life.

second version of the diaries, which he calls unexpurgated, he makes the original diary volumes at UCLA available to scholars. Whether Evelyn Hinz will continue to honor his procedure remains to be seen. She has said that hers is the work of a lifetime; in 1994 she is a woman of middle age.[9]

Rupert Pole is seventy-five years old. He lives in the Silver Lake house with Pico, the third in the line of miniature white poodles Anaïs Nin loved. Each day he sits at the kitchen table where she was photographed in Robert Snyder's film *Anaïs Observed,* patiently sifting through the original diaries to select extracts for the next in his series of unexpurgated diaries. Rupert's adoration of Anaïs Nin has grown steadily since her death, and he has edited her diaries to include nearly every compliment anyone ever paid her. He has done all this out of his deep love, but that very love has sometimes distorted the text she actually wrote. It has, in many readers' views, and especially in opinions expressed by critics and scholars, presented Anaïs Nin in an unattractive light, as a monstrous narcissist if not a pathological personality. But Rupert is unfazed by negative criticism and remains so devoted to the memory of Anaïs Nin that he usually speaks of her in the present tense. He has also re-created his life with her, living half of each year with a woman whose circumstances are similar to hers.

Despite Anaïs's legacy, Hugo died bankrupt. He continued after her death to make bad investments and, following a series of financial reverses, died owing the United States government for unpaid taxes he did not know he had to pay, bilked by unscrupulous investment partners.

Eduardo Sánchez died in the mid-1980s in Dallas, where he had lived for many years, a victim of Alzheimer's disease. Thorvald Nin died of natural causes at his home in El Paso, Texas, on June 19, 1991.

The only surviving family member of Anaïs Nin's generation is her brother Joaquín Nin-Culmell, who continues his distinguished career in music.

KEY TO ABBREVIATIONS

AN	Anaïs Nin	JN	Joaquín Nin
AS	Alan Swallow	JNC	Joaquín Nin-Culmell
BC	Blanche Cooney	LD	Lawrence Durrell
CC	Caresse Crosby	LL	Lawrence Lipton
DB	Deirdre Bair	LW	Larry Wallrich
DN	Dorothy Norman	LR	Lila Rosenblum
ES	Eduardo Sánchez	MG	Maxwell Geismar
FSB	Frances Schiff Bolton	PO	Peter Owen
GM	Gonzalo Moré	RB	Roger Bloom
GNR	Gayle Nin Rosenkrantz	RC	Rosa Culmell
GS	Gunther Stuhlmann	RCA	Richard Centing Archives
GV	Gore Vidal	RD	Robert Duncan
HG	Hugh Guiler	RP	Rupert Pole
HM	Henry Miller	RW	Rebecca West
JF	John Ferrone	TN	Thorvald Nin
JLH	James Leo Herlihy	TS	Thurema Sokol
JMM	June Mansfield Miller	WB	William Burford

AN/KI: The Anaïs Nin archive at the Kinsey Institute for Research in Sex, Gender, and Reproduction, Indiana University, Bloomington
AN/LL: The Lilly Library, Indiana University at Bloomington
AN/NU: Anaïs Nin archive at Northwestern University
Anaïs: IJ: *Anaïs: An International Journal*
D (followed by number) indicates the published diaries
ED (followed by number) indicates the four volumes of the *Early Diaries*. Volume I is listed separately by name as *Linotte*
H & J: *Henry and June*
HRC: The Harry Ransom Humanities Research Center, the University of Texas at Austin
JNC/USF indicates Joaquín Nin-Culmell's archive at the Gleason Library, the University of San Francisco
LP: *A Literate Passion: Letters of AN and HM (1932–1953)*
OR/CU: The Otto Rank archive at Columbia University
RP/F and RP/Box (followed by number in both cases) is my terminology for file folders and boxes in possession of Rupert Pole
UD indicates unpublished diaries in the AN archive at UCLA

Anaïs Nin's Works cited in notes:

CA:	*Children of the Albatross*
DHL:	*D. H. Lawrence: An Unprofessional Study*
SIHOL:	*A Spy in the House of Love*
UAGB:	*Under a Glass Bell*

Notes

Introduction

1. Priscilla English, "New Woman Interviews a New Woman: Anaïs Nin," *New Woman,* Vol. 1, No. VII, Dec. 1971, 27.

2. Cynthia Ozick, "Alfred Chester's Wig," *New Yorker,* March 30, 1992, 79ff.

1. A Most Unlikely Marriage

1. I am grateful to Professor Joaquín Nin-Culmell (Anaïs Nin's younger brother) for information and documentation concerning the Nin and Culmell families and their history and genealogy; also to Gayle Nin Rosenkrantz, Esq., for information about the family of Thorvald Nin (her father and AN's elder brother), and to RP for his account of AN's description of her family and its background.

2. "The student's name was Ysolina, and years later, she still adored my father." —JNC, fax, 2/19/93. Cited here to show one of the first in a lifelong pattern of JN's relationships with women. In D-1, 103, AN gave a different version: that her father "had come from Barcelona to escape military service."

3. JNC, 2/11/93.

4. AN wrote a romanticized version of her parents' first meeting, subsequent courtship, and marriage in D-1, 103–104.

5. The eldest, Peter Emilius (1834–1914), ran an import-export business in the U.S. in the mid-19th century until he became aware of the need on Cuban sugar plantations for a constant infusion of laborers and became an importer of African slaves, whereby he made the greater part of his fortune. In the 1890s, he sold his businesses in the United States, severed his ties to Cuba, and bought an elegant château called La Volière, near Tours, France, frequently entertaining his two brothers and their families. The middle brother called himself Charles Culmell and was the first to drop the family surname when he bypassed Peter Emilius's two spheres of influence and went directly to Texas. He married there in 1860 and subsequently fathered three daughters. Some years later, he moved his wife and children back to Denmark and resumed his family surname. JNC (fax, 3/24/93) mentioned a "recently 'discovered' Culmell-Christensen [fourth brother] from Australia." No further information has since become available.

6. "I still remember tinned salted butter that came from Denmark, to say nothing of beer and cheeses." JNC, fax, 2/20/93.
7. Undated letter from Thorvald C. Culmell to Enrique Dupuy de Lome, diplomatic officer of the Royal Spanish Legation, Washington, D.C., in reply to his of 5/12/97. Courtesy JNC archives.
8. Pronounced "Ahna-ees," with the accent on the second syllable.
9. Her father, Pierre Théodore Vaurigaud, also kept a detailed diary, which he called *Journal,* c. 1822. JNC had copies made for his siblings and all the cousins who were Vaurigaud's descendants. GNR, citing the diary, confirms Anaïs Vaurigaud's birth in Havana on 11/27/1853. The diarist Pierre was born in Matanzas, Cuba, 4/24/1806 to a French general in Napoleon's army and his Creole wife, born in the West Indies. While she prepared the diary for publication, AN was obsessed with proving herself descended from nobility through both parents. Regarding the Vaurigaud family, JNC wrote: "In any case, you would not find the nobility business and certainly no castle. I made the trip [tracing genealogy] with Tío Enrique [Culmell] and [his wife] Tía Julia from Hendaye to Paris via the châteaux country . . . we saw everything but no family seat. We did find a small town called Anaïs." JNC/AN, 1/20/71, RP/Folder 1971; JNC/USF.
10. JNC/AN, 2/1/65, UD-65.1; JNC/USF: "Go easy on grandmother's 'many lovers.' I know this may sound 'romantic,' but. . . . AN/JNC, 4/30/65, ibid.: "Softened Grandmother's lovers. Mitigating circumstances."
11. Thorvald C continued to support Anaïs and her aged and impoverished father-in-law, Théodore Vaurigaud, until his (Thorvald C's) death in 1906. All of Anaïs Vaurigaud de Culmell's children took care of her, but Enrique Culmell saved his mother financially throughout her life. Beginning with Rosa, the children were Juana (Anaïs Nin's godmother), spinster; Anaïs, married Bernabé Sánchez (seven children: Ana María, Anaïs, Bernabé, Thorvald, Caridad, Eduardo, Graciella); Pedro Culmell (no issue); Téodoro (disappeared in the 1898 War, no issue); Enrique (no issue); Edelmira, married the American naval officer Gilbert Chase (two children: Gilbert, María Teresa); Antolina, married General Rafael de Cardenas (three children: Rafael, Antolina, Charles); and Thorvald (no issue).
12. Thorvald C made several trips to officials of the fledgling Cuban government, then in exile in New York. His mission was to convince the Cubans that Spain was prepared to decolonize Cuba but only if "its flag was respected," i.e., if political face were saved. This information and supporting documentation courtesy JNC archives. Much of it is taken from turn-of-the-century Cuban newspaper accounts, all undated, entitled *Documentos Cubanos Raros o Inéditos: Datos Históricos por Raimundo Cabrera.* Also, from Thorvald C. Culmell's correspondence with the Spanish envoy, Enrique Dupuy de Lome, and from official documents of the Spanish Legation in Washington, D.C
13. Pedro died young and Téodoro, who enlisted in the Spanish-American War without his father's permission, disappeared without a trace in 1898. Neither Enrique nor Thorvald had children of their own, so they took great delight in the many nieces and nephews of their sisters. JNC remem-

bers "the many kindnesses and much affection from [Enrique and Thorvald]." Both brothers lived in New York but finally settled in Cuba, and both died at a relatively young age.

14. JNC, 2/20/93.

15. At the end of their lives Juana and Edelmira needed financial assistance and Bernabé Sánchez came to their aid when "Tía Anaïs was too intimidated by her husband to suggest anything on her own." JNC.

16. Irene A. Wright, in the social history *Cuba* (New York: Macmillan, 1912), describes the phenomenon of "plantation" and "city" wives.

17. Gilbert Paul Chase was a member of the USNA class of 1893. He was stationed on the USS *Dixie* at Guantánamo Bay, Cuba, in 1903, and met his wife while on leave in Havana. He retired with the rank of temporary (later permanent) Commander, USN, in 1919. I am grateful to Rear Admiral Robert W. Schmitt, USN retd., for this information.

18. Eventually, Edelmira's marriage ended in separation, but not divorce. The illnesses of her early married life were probably "neurasthenic," quite possibly psychosomatic. Of all the sisters, she was the most fragile both mentally and physically, and the first among them to die, and at a relatively young age. María Teresa is called "Nuna" in Nin's early diaries. Gilbert Jr. ("Coquito") became a noted musicologist who specialized in Spanish and Latin-American music. He and his wife, Kathleen, were devoted to Anaïs Nin.

19. *Linotte,* 81.

20. The Brentwood Convent School later became an orphanage and has since ceased to exist. See *Linotte,* 30–32, for a description of AN's visit in 1920.

21. Expressed by a wealthy Cuban man, which, as Irene A. Wright noted in *Cuba,* 101, "realization of that fact forces many a Cuban girl into an uncongenial marriage."

22. She was "so motherly," recalls JNC, that "Tío Thorvald remembers how she used to warn him when he was a very young man to beware of homosexual predators, a subject Cuban sisters did not usually address with their brothers."

23. He introduced wall-mounted electric lights and the Christmas tree to Havana.

24. JNC, 2/19/93.

25. "When Juana went with her father to see the new-born Anaïs Nin and to be her godmother, she was the object of admiration from predatory males, including my Father."—JNC, 2/20/93. "When she was in Paris, she sat for Sunyer, who was having a hard time making a living. My father probably convinced Tía Juana to commission the work in 1905, but she never liked it, and gave it to my mother, with whom it traveled all over Europe and the United States. It now hangs in my living room." JNC, 3/4/93.

26. And also to separate himself from being confused with his uncle, the well known painter José Nin y Tudo. Joaquín Nin's son (AN's brother), who also became a pianist, composer and musicologist and wished also to avoid confusion, hyphenated his mother's and father's names and became Joaquín Nin-Culmell.

27. JNC/AN, 2/1/65; UD-65.1; JNC/USF.

28. Joaquín Nin-Culmell, telephone conversation, 2/11/93. Some of Joaquín Nin Tudo's writings included *Cartilla de moral para los niños, Cartilla económica* (1880), *Colección de autógrafos* (Havana, 1880), *Nociónes* *de Historia de España, Glorias de España, La mujer y el amor, Caridad y resignación, poesías y pensamientos* (Barcelona, 1885).

29. First in Salomo, where the Nin family originated, then in the close-by Vendrell, province of Tarragona, and finally in Barcelona, where his parents lived the rest of their lives.

30. It dated from great-great-grandfather Benet Nin's marriage to Carmen Guell in the mid-eighteenth century. "Father always maintained (and both Anaïs and Thorvald believed him) that the Guells (Guadí, etc.) were our Guells. Not so. Guell is a very common name in Barcelona."—JNC, 2/20/93. Nin is also a common name in Tarragona. Salomo has a mystery play given every year that involves a well-to-do merchant named Josep (José) Nin, who brings back to the village a miraculous Christ stolen by the Moors. Andrés Nin, Trotsky's secretary and the Spanish translator of Dostoyevsky, liquidated by the Stalinists in 1936 in the Spanish Civil War, was also from Vendrell but was not related to the Nin y Tudo family. In the last decade of her life, when she was preparing the final volumes of D, AN became obsessed with proving that she was descended from "THE Guells"—JNC/AN, 1/20/75. On 2/1/65, JNC wrote to AN: "I hate to disappoint you, but the Guells, the patrons of Gaudi, titled aristocrats, etc., were not our Guells. . . . I fear that Father embroidered the facts. We may have been related but in a very remote way. . . . The interesting thing about father's 'inventions' is that they are never entirely inventions. They might be called 'dreams that reality taught me.' " In a telephone conversation, 3/21/93, JNC added "one could say the same of Anaïs." On 9/8/58, JNC wrote to AN that their family was entitled to call themselves "de Nin: the de business was given to a Juan Nin and his descendants by Carlos II (el Hechizado) in 1679." They were also given a seal that was engraved on a ring passed down through the generations (JNC wears it now): "Meaning of the symbols on the ring: the child means nin, child in old Catalan; the T means Tarragona; the tree is an olive tree, typical of that region; and what looks like a globe is really a lamp (salomo in old Catalan) and stands for the birthplace of Juan Nin, Salomo."

31. Information about JN's career is from *Joaquín Nin: Pro arte e Ideas y Comentarios,* Primera Edición Especial, Julio 1974, Editado por Dirosa, Diputación 248, Barcelona. Also from JNC and Dr. Susan Shapiro, who graciously allowed me access to her mother, the late Prof. Elaine Brody's, music library and archives.

32. Joaquín Nin returned to Havana in 1939 when war broke out in Europe. As he was penniless, the Castellanos family supported him modestly until he died in 1949.

33. *See Linotte,* 223–224, for AN's early version of her parents' courtship and marriage.

34. D-1, 104. Also: "It is true that he told Gilbert Chase (my musicologist cousin) that he was more attracted to Edelmira (Gilbert's mother) than to Rosa. JNC, fax, 2/21/93.

35. They appeared with violinist Juan Torroella at the Sala López.

36. Thorvald C. Culmell's financial support continued until his death in 1906. The amount of the monthly stipend was deducted from Rosa's share of the inheritance at the request of two of his sons-in-law, Sánchez and de Cárdenas, so that the money she inherited was considerably reduced. **37.** JNC/AN, 2/1/65, UD-65/1; JNC/USF. "It was a losing battle to save Father. Didn't we all try?"

2. The Ugly Little Girl

1. As they were in France, her baptismal certificate reflected the country of her birth rather than her nationality: Angela Anaïs Juana Antolina Rosa Edelmira Nin *et* Culmell. In ED-2, 82, she gives the order of her names as Rosa Juana Anaïs Edelmira Antolina Angela.
2. "A boy would not have cried," she added. ED-2, 82.
3. At the Salle Aeolian, featuring works of Rameau, Bach, Couperin, and Kahnau.
4. His lectures on early music and derivation of musical forms were generally categorized as "Étude des formes musicales au piano." Historically, JN is said to have lacked "invention" and was "not a finder." When his period of greatest renown came, in the 1920s, it was as an interpreter of early Spanish keyboard music and "an active performing musicologist" rather than as a composer. He became the first pianist to play the music of Padre Soler in modern times and was also the first modern editor of Soler's works. —JNC, fax, 3/4/93.
5. "Thorvald, who is the least aristocratic in the family, was born in Grandfather's house, which was a palace!" ED-2, 83.
6. It was so slow to grow back that when she made her first Holy Communion at the age of seven, RC chose a veil that covered almost all of AN's head, and when photos were taken, posed the child so that the profile with the most hair was photographed. Quotes are by JNC, tel. conversation, 3/9/93.
7. D-1, 76.
8. *Linotte,* 326, 449.
9. D-1, 217.
10. In D-1, AN originally planned to write an account of how RC took her and Thorvald to Cuba for the funeral. JNC corrected the account in a letter of 2/1/65: "We did not go to Cuba for Papa To's illness and death. Mother went alone [with Juana]." AN replied on 4/30/65 (UD-65.1; JNC/USF): "Fixed chronology of trips to Cuba. Confused though, in my mind. As I knew I had been there very small. You mean we all went, saw Grandfather, I got typhoid, Thor was born, we returned to France and THEN Mother went again alone?"
11. *Incest,* 206. It should be noted that he made these and other vicious comments long after his marriage had ended and in the first flush of his incestuous involvement with his daughter. AN, who had been at odds with her mother since the beginning of her involvement with Henry Miller, was only too eager to record her father's scathing remarks.
12. Juan Manén remained a lifelong friend both to JN and to Rosa and her children. He visited them frequently in New York during the 1920s and is often mentioned in ED-2.
13. Just as his father had changed his name to avoid confusion with his painter uncle, JNC chose to hyphenate his maternal and paternal sur-

names to avoid confusion with his father. JNC became a distinguished concert pianist, composer, and professor of music, first at Williams and later at UC Berkeley, where he chaired the Music Department from 1951 to 1954. He holds the title of Professor Emeritus there now, and is also Correspondent Member of the Royal Academy of Fine Arts of San Fernando (Madrid). His compositions include over one hundred pieces for orchestra, piano, chamber music choir, and organ, as well as two ballets and one opera.

14. In ED-2, 84, AN writes of the Berlin years as "some of the happiest in Mother's life." JNC remembers just the opposite. After sifting much evidence in the UCLA archives, I conclude that his view seems more realistic.

15. ED-2, 85.

16. D-1, 211. The story AN tells has JN exaggerating his lineage and inventing the story of his family. See also 312.

17. *Linotte,* 414, 440.

18. Ibid., 297.

19. UD-56. JNC, fax 3/24/93. If Thorvald resented or was hurt by his father's remarks, no one in his family ever knew, for the silent little boy grew into a bitter, taciturn man who never spoke of his father, was estranged from his mother, resented his brother, and detested his sister.

20. *Linotte,* 478, 447.

21. The following information is taken from AN's writings in *Linotte,* 364–365; D-1, 72, ED-2, 84–89; UD 34–35. Also from interviews and conversations with JNC, 1990–1993.

22. ED-2, 84, and D-1, 95.

23. In ED-2, 86, AN remembers the weapon as a broom. In letter of 2/1/65, (JNC/USF, UD-65.1), JNC writes: "Our 'aristocratic' father would never have killed a mere rabid cat with a broom!!!" The incident made such an impression on AN that when she was preparing D-1, she wrote two separate accounts of it, TS pp. 144, 490.

24. ED-2, 86.

25. The questions are those AN asked herself in (among many others) UD 1933–1934, 35, 36, and 57; *Linotte,* D-1; and *Incest.* Information about the beatings is also from interviews and conversations with RP, JNC, and GNR. Among the works consulted for an understanding of AN's relationship to JN and how it affected so much of her later life were Alice Miller's *The Drama of the Gifted Child, The Untouched Key,* and *Banished Knowledge,* and Judith Lewis Herman's *Father-Daughter Incest.* See Miller's *Key,* 73 ff., for her account of how "the works of writers, poets, and painters tell the encoded story of childhood traumas no longer consciously remembered in adulthood." Also, Herman's chapter 2, "The Question of Harm," 30–35.

26. *Incest,* 105. Interviews and conversations with JNC and GNR. According to GNR, Thorvald still spoke of it with anger and resentment when he was an elderly man.

27. In *Linotte,* 184, she writes that it was "a family joke." It was actually a derogatory term first coined by her father.

28. JNC, fax, 3/24/93. AN wrote of this many times in both her published and unpublished diaries.

29. In what seems today a curious medical procedure, the doctors cleaned the infected area but left the ruptured appendix inside the child. AN discovered this years later in Los Angeles, during one of her several surgeries for cancer. This and the details that follow are taken in part from a letter to HG, 5/2/75, in RP/F-75, also JNC/USF.

30. This incision never healed properly, and for the rest of her life AN was bothered by adhesions. There are frequent references in her letters as well as diaries to various stomach pains, all located beneath the incision. A version of this illness appears in *Linotte,* 33, 37, 234.

31. D'Annunzio attended the last concert in Arcachon given by Joaquín and Rosa Nin and was so taken by her singing of the aria "O cessate di piagarmi" that he wrote about it in his novel *Notturno.* This was the only concert all three children attended together, having been warned beforehand by Joaquín not to "applaud like peasants." AN originally reports D'Annunzio telling Joaquinito (JNC) that he has "passionate" eyes (*Linotte* 113) but in D-1, 193, she writes that the remark was directed at her. JNC, fax, 3/3/93, says the earlier account is correct. In JNC/AN, 2/1/65, he writes that "The story was about your little brother." She replies 4/30/65: "Woman's vanity. I wanted D'Annunzio to notice my eyes. Yours were better! Honest."

32. For many years, AN believed that Les Ruines had been built for D'Annunzio and she planned to write that he loaned it to JN in PD-1 (TSS p. 382). JNC, 2/1/65, tells her it could not have been loaned "for the simple reason D'Annunzio and Father met in Arcachon." AN replied on 4/30/65 that "yes, Les Ruines was built for D'Annunzio. A few 'facts' like that, remember, were told to me by Father later. He talked a lot then."

33. ED-2, 88.

34. JNC, fax, 3/24/93.

35. Judith Lewis Herman's term for JN's behavior is "seductive father."

36. When Anaïs wrote about this period in ED-2, 88, some seven years after it happened, she still could not bring herself to admit that her father had abandoned his family and insisted, in a fantasy of denial, that Rosa had left the children in the care of the Rodríguez family.

37. In *Linotte,* 61, she wrote of Bouby: "I don't love him as much as I do my diary. Bouby is the only child I shall ever have, for I want to be free, always free."

38. ED-2, 89.

39. Carmen Karr (1865–1943) became an important writer and editor who celebrated the cause of Catalan women. Her origins were French.

40. From "proofs of 'Paper Womb' printed in *Booster,* December January 1938" (in AN's hand), UD-58, 102.

41. *Linotte,* 251–252. She wrote this passage when she was sixteen. I cite it here as the best example of her many musings on this subject throughout the early diaries.

3. The Indispensable Lifeline

1. "Proofs of 'Paper Womb' printed in Booster December-January 1938," UD-58, 102.

2. *Linotte,* 12. "The Nin family remained in our cabin. We didn't see anyone but ourselves until the storm was over." JNC, 7/91.

3. "Everyone in the family carried

what we cared most about and probably things that belonged to someone else as well. We simply picked up our belongings as best we could in order to leave the ship as quickly as possible." JNC, 7/91. AN gives several versions of arriving in New York: two in *Linotte,* 12–13, and Appendix, 501–502; and D-1, 218–219. See also Donald Newlove's *Painted Paragraphs: Inspired Description for Writers and Readers* (New York: Henry Holt, 1993), 112–115.

4. *Linotte,* 16, and JNC, 7/91. Emilia Quintero accompanied singers at the Met and also became JNC's first piano teacher. She was a friend of both Rosa and JN.

5. With the exception of RP, those persons who were closest to her (JNC, JF, etc.) always disputed this story. The very earliest diary writings themselves support the view that RC gave AN a notebook in Barcelona as a means to distract the child and improve her feelings about herself. AN wrote to and received letters from her father regularly when she lived in Barcelona, and continued to do so when she moved to New York. She told him everything that was happening within the family each day and was frequently scolded for her verbosity, as in ED-2, 346: "you say that my epistolary style puts you on edge. . . ." Thus, there was no need to keep a diary for him to read when and if he returned to the family, except perhaps to show off her personal musings. A second myth, created by the adult AN, was that RC interfered in the children's relationship with their father. JNC denies this, and AN's own diary evidence also belies it (see especially Vols. 1 and 2 of *The Early Diaries* and n.4 above). In most instances, she writes that she is "copying part of" various letters she has sent to JN, indicating that she has sent the original and merely wants a record of what she wrote. Curiously, none of JN's letters to her have survived in the voluminous archives she kept. After JN's death, JNC discovered that he had not kept any of AN's letters, while Rosa kept everything AN ever wrote to her. JNC has donated the AN/RC correspondence to the U. of SF Library, where it will eventually be available to qualified scholars.

6. ED-2, 132.

7. *Linotte,* 20.

8. It was published in *The Booster,* Dec.–Jan. 1938.

9. From a 1973 commencement address, quoted by JNC in *Linotte,* Preface, vii.

10. They lived at 166 W. 72nd St. and 219 W. 80th St. in one other apartment, and perhaps a second one as well, addresses not remembered by JNC. See also *Linotte,* 89.

11. She paid for a recital at Aeolian Hall, but no engagements resulted from it.

12. For a description of the house, see *Linotte,* 160–61. JNC, 7/91. "It was not a boarding house in the strict sense of the term because Mother never served meals to paying guests. Rather, she invited musicians she knew to live with us while they were studying or performing in New York."

13. UD-54. As an adult, when she was in constant conflict with her mother, AN frequently cited as an example of Rosa's extreme possessiveness that her mother made her sleep in the same bed until she was sixteen. JNC says, "It was simpler than that. We were poor in New York. Those were the beds and that was all the room we had."

14. There were two maids: Monserrat

(African–Puerto Rican) lived in and Dolly (Irish) came daily. JNC recalled that "She [Monserrat] and Anaïs were devoted to each other. Anaïs wrote a great deal about all the housework she had to do on W. 75th St., but mostly, this was her imagination. The two maids did it all."

15. Enrique followed Zayas, a rebel leader, in the Feb. 1917 rebellion against Pres. Mario García Menocal. When the rebels were defeated, he went into temporary exile and became one of RC's boarders. *Linotte,* 162, and JNC, 7/92.

16. She drew a picture in an early diary of a young girl's blackened face and figure, hunched over a desk beneath a high, barred window, and entitled it "School is a Prison."

17. ED-2, 16.

18. ED-2, 242.

19. Beginning with *Linotte,* 41, the remark is repeated throughout the UD.

20. *Linotte,* 210.

21. ED-2, 345–346.

22. Ibid., 126, 138. Also in UD. Ironically, her friends frequently used this expression to describe the adult AN.

23. There is a great deal of confusion about AN's citizenship, particularly after she married HG (discussed where appropriate later). In these years, RC was a Cuban citizen permanently residing in USA, as were her children. JNC and TN became U.S. citizens as young adults, but AN did not until much later.

24. *Linotte,* 286.

25. ED-2, 67.

26. In an interview, 7/15/93, Frances Schiff Bolton said she did not remember that they had elections at all, let alone that Anaïs Nin was elected president of her class several years in a row, as she wrote in *Linotte,* 211–212. AN refers to her as "Dick" in the correspondence quoted in the ED, a nickname she gave her because Bolton's younger sister was called "Nicky." FSB describes AN in those days as "beautiful, delicate, charming, a soul mate," and recalls how they walked each other home after school, back and forth, up and down Broadway, between their homes on 112th St. and W. 75th, reluctant to part because they were so engrossed in talking about art and literature.

27. Information from Frances Schiff Bolton and *Linotte,* 211–212. All diary quotes from this until noted otherwise. See also Eva Hoffman's *Lost in Translation: A Life in a New Language* (New York: Penguin Books, 1989), pp. 117–119, for interesting parallels to AN's high school experiences and how she came to write a diary in English, pp. 120–121.

28. Her early diaries are replete with letters in which she tells her father she is enclosing photographs of herself. She apologizes and equivocates for them, but the underlying message is that she wants him to reply that he thinks she is pretty. Apparently, he never did for she never thanks him for a compliment.

29. A version of this visit is in *Linotte,* 179–80. "We had many artistic people in our circle, and they were always saying they would paint, or compose, or write something about many of the women who were there. Often these remarks were merely a way of paying a compliment to an attractive woman. My sister, however, took all these remarks, whether sincere or superficial, to heart." JNC, 8/91.

30. *Linotte,* 258–259.

31. See *Linotte,* following 493, for the extraordinary list of the books she actually owned by 1920. The others she read in libraries or borrowed from friends demonstrate how much more advanced she was in literary studies than most of her classmates.

32. *Linotte,* 222.

33. Ibid., 261.

34. Throughout her life, AN directed animosity toward the Sánchez family. Some of it was warranted (her relationship with Eduardo, for example), but for the most part, she was always made to feel a part of it and the larger Cuban family created by all her aunts and uncles as well. "If anything, my aunts and uncles overcompensated so that we would not feel like 'the poor relations.' " JNC, 7/92.

35. AN gives a version of this in *Linotte,* 306. JNC provided details of his mother's financial maneuvers and name change.

36. ED-2, 480.

4. Miss Nin and Linotte

1. *Linotte,* 262.

2. Ibid., 262–263. The emphasis is AN's.

3. She gives one example of this in ED-2, 127. JNC verifies that it was a frequent occurrence from AN's sixteenth year onward.

4. This incident troubled her for the rest of her life. On 2/16/58, she made notes after a session with her psychiatrist, Dr. Inge Bogner, in which she wrote: "Image of myself inventing a big strike drama on the train to excuse my being late for Tía Anaïs (I was seventeen)." UD-58.1.

5. UD-58.1.

6. ED-2, 41–42.

7. These are actually her words for herself, but she puts them into the mouths of others in her diaries and letters throughout her life.

8. ED-2, 161.

9. All quotes until otherwise noted from ED-2, 440–441.

10. Ibid., 30. The literature of incest and childhood abuse is filled with examples of children who create separate identities as a means to deal with their trauma.

11. This material is found only in the UD.

12. See ED-2, 246–247, for her thoughts on Emerson and Stevenson.

13. Ibid., 30. All quotes from this until noted otherwise.

14. Ibid., 5. This is when she begins to think of it as a diary and the first time she writes in English. On p. 96 she writes that she did not expect to continue, "but I have discovered that I can express myself a thousand times better in English, and until I can teach myself some of my beloved French, I will continue in the language I have used in two volumes already."

15. Ibid., 340. This is an important passage for the development of her thinking in regard to diary writing.

16. Eugénie de Guérin, *Journal* (Paris: Librairie Lecoffre–J. Gabalda, 1934; Albi: Imprimerie Coopérative du Sud-Ouest, 1934). See also Maurice de Guérin, *Journal,* ed. G. S. Trebutien, trans. Jessie P. Frothingham (New York: Dodd, Mead, 1892).

17. ED-2, 290–291. All AN quotes from these pages until noted otherwise.

18. Journal of Marie Bashkirtseff, *Cahiers intimes inédits* (Paris: ed., P. Borel, 1925).
19. By this I mean specifically that even though she had switched to English, she still wrote with the stiffness and formality of 19th-century diary writing, and that in many crucial ways, the form and content of the diaries echoed 19th-century antecedents as well. I simply note this here, but will address it further when appropriate.
20. I am paraphrasing the definition in *Amazons, Bluestockings and Crones: A Feminist Dictionary,* Cheris Kramarae and Paula A. Treichler, eds., Pandora Press (London: HarperCollins, 1992), 77. The term "became associated with the women who held salons and who put their energies and emotions into work with each other, it became a term of abuse, with connotations of snob and misfit."
21. *Linotte,* 318–319. All AN quotes from these pages until noted otherwise.
22. This phrase and several variants are found throughout her writings, so I cite no particular example here. Also, most of her family and friends quoted it in one form or another throughout interviews, saying it was AN's "credo" or "dominant principle."
23. I am grateful to Blanche Cooney for sharing her impressions of Eduardo Sánchez in interviews and conversations from 1991 through 1993, and for information in her autobiography, *In My Own Sweet Time,* Ohio U. Press, 1993. Also, to Judith Hipskind, who in Aug. 1991 graciously showed me ES's archives, now in the collection of the Bridwell Library, Southern Methodist U., Dallas. Also to JNC for recollections of his cousin.
24. *Linotte,* 274. Linotte, a "little bird," or Linnet, was one of RC's nicknames for AN and is also the title of her first volume of ED. AN also referred to herself in the D as Linotte, Fifille ("little girl") and Miss Nin.
25. ED-2, 235.
26. Ibid., 67.
27. Ibid., 236.
28. *Linotte,* 232.
29. Ibid., 257.
30. Ibid., 277.
31. ED-2, 175.

5. "What to do with Anaïs"

1. Information that follows is from ED-2, 210, 273, 280; AN's undated letters to RC from Havana, 1922; UD-undated.
2. *Delineator,* 5/20, 42. Published by Butterick Publishing, New York.
3. ED-2, 15. The "Elegy" has not survived among AN's archives and was never printed. In late summer, the magazine published a "double issue," saying that due to "printers' strikes, the influenza epidemic, severe late spring snow storms, embargos on freight and express, and other reasons too numerous to express," they would not be able to publish the submissions of the "younger readers."
4. ED-2, 45–46. All quotes from this until noted otherwise.
5. Ibid., 123.
6. Ibid., 144–46. All quotes from this until noted otherwise.

7. "Probably dictated or written by her son. Angela was incapable of writing such a letter." JNC, conversation, 5/19/94.
8. ED-2, 98.
9. Ibid., 197.
10. Ibid., 156, 129.
11. Ibid., 208–209. All quotes from this until noted otherwise.
12. I have coined the term "major minor writer," which I think best describes AN's place in 20th-century arts and letters.
13. JNC, 8/92.
14. AN frequently used her "accent, peculiar inflections, gestures" to entertain her brothers and their friends. See ED-2, 229, for one example. Also, JNC, in 1991 conversations; RP, interviews 1991. Most persons I interviewed made this same comment, that her spoken English was so close to a lisp that people, men especially, frequently wanted to shelter and protect her when they heard the delicate lilt and trilled *r*.
15. AN gives a modified and softened version of Rosa's breakdown in ED-2, 229–230. I have also consulted UD-undated, and JNC, 1992 interviews and conversations.
16. ED-2, 367, AN's emphasis. All quotes from this until noted otherwise.
17. Ibid., 401.
18. *Saturday Evening Post,* 7/8/22.
19. ED-2, 407–408, 416, 460, and letters, n.d., AN to RC from Woodstock, 1922. All quotes from this until noted otherwise.
20. The editors have translated "fifille," RC's pet name for AN, into "little girl." It is not clear that Rosa meant this literally, for their correspondence shows clearly that she had now begun to address and confide in AN as an adult.
21. ED-2, 154–55. All quotes from this until noted otherwise.
22. For her first complete description of HG, see ED-2, 244–245.
23. JNC, "Hugo, My Brother-in-Law," *Anaïs: An International Journal* 4, p. 11.
24. Later in life, when he became a filmmaker known as Ian Hugo, Hugh Guiler used many of the images and memories he retained of his early years in Puerto Rico, particularly the huge ugly land crabs and the hideous masks and frightful costumes worn by the natives during Carnival.
25. Hugh P. Guiler, "Recollections," *Anaïs: IJ* 4, p. 27. All quotes from this until noted otherwise.
26. HG to AN, letter, n.d., c. 1960–1963. Until he met Anaïs, whose favorite color was violet, Hugo could not bear the violet or the scent of the flower because it reminded him of these two bitterly detested women. In an undated letter, c. 1960, HG said he had "quite gotten over" his childhood antipathy and that AN had given him "a different set of memories entirely."
27. Both boys initially resented their sisters because they had not also been sent away to school, until their parents told them it was because girls did not need to be educated as well as boys.
28. HG, "Recollections," 27.
29. Ibid., 28.
30. HG's correspondence with AN, a journal he kept briefly, and a collection of documents he prepared for his analyst, Dr. Inge Bogner (all JNC/USF), attest to how much this comment affected him and how he believed his relationship with his father was the root of his lifelong emotional distress.
31. ED-2, 266.
32. JNC, interview 7/25/91.

33. HG to AN, 10/2/22, JNC archives. Reprinted in ED-2, 492.
34. Ibid., 295.
35. Ibid., 248.
36. Ibid., 285.
37. Ibid., 341.
38. Ibid., 378.
39. Ibid., 430.
40. Ibid., 434.
41. Ibid., 438–439. All quotes from this until noted otherwise.
42. Ibid., 446–447. All quotes from this until noted otherwise.
43. Ibid., 449.
44. Ibid., 477.
45. RP, interview, 6/90; JNC, 7/91. See also ED-2, 484 ff. In undated letters to RC, AN writes of several wealthy Cuban men who pursued her. She encouraged one so strongly that he proposed and she kept him dangling until she heard from HG. When he finally proposed, she rejected her Cuban suitor. She hints of her less-than-honest behavior in ED-2, 524. JNC agrees that she had no intention of marrying anyone other than HG.
46. ED-2, 485.
47. HG to AN, undated letter c. Oct. 1922, partially copied in ED-2, 492.
48. Undated news clippings from Havana, UCLA Box 10, Journal 18.
49. AN to RC, 12/5/22. JNC/USF.
50. ED-2, 528.
51. Undated clippings from *El Mundo* and *Diario de la Marina,* Havana. UD, Box 10, Journal 18.

6. "Where shall this lead us?"

1. Information about the marriage and their sexuality is from ED-3, 29; UD-19, 24, 63, 65, 66; letters, n.d., from HG and AN to RC; interviews and conversations with JNC, RP, and JLH; tel. conversation with Caridad Sánchez Helm, 9/91, New York.
2. Throughout her life, AN always described the sexual act using a form of the verb "to be taken." Men always "took" her, and she always "responded."
3. Journal kept by both HG and AN, entitled (in AN's hand) Journal/ Hugh P. Guiler/ September 1927 to ——. In the beginning AN and HG note that it is meant to replace one they kept for the first three years of their marriage and which they lost. AN says all the writing duplicates their original entries. JNC/USF.
4. AN/HG *Journal,* n.d. JNC/USF. Later, after his family relented in the 1930s, HG wrote pontificating letters to his brother and sisters that AN proudly copied.
5. ED-3, 3.
6. JNC, 7/91, Berkeley. In ED-3, Preface, xv, JNC writes that "Hugo was extraordinarily attentive to my mother and acted as my own 'big brother' in many important and critical moments of my life."
7. He also kept extensive accounts of his dreams. After HG's death in 1985, his archives were cared for by JNC, who has graciously made them available to me. They will eventually be deposited in the Gleason Library of the U. of San Francisco.
8. Erskine based much of his fiction on retelling famous legends in what was then considered to be wry, "modern" (i.e., early 20th century) humor;

among these were such titles as *The Private Life of Helen of Troy* and *The Brief Hour of François Villon.* He also wrote novels based on writers' lives (*The Start of the Road,* about Walt Whitman) and historical figures (*Give Me Liberty,* about Patrick Henry). He was the coeditor of the *Cambridge History of American Literature* and the author of *A Musical Companion* and *What Is Music?*

9. Anna Crouse Murch (John Erskine's daughter), telephone interview 6/3/93. Unless otherwise noted, information about the Erskine family is from this interview.

10. All quotes from AN/HG *Journal,* JNC/USF, until noted otherwise.

11. Rereading this passage a decade later, Hugo thought it "curious to realize that [banking] was entered upon with little or no thought of acquiring power in business itself."

12. ED-3, JNC Preface, xv; also AN/HG *Journal,* JNC/USF; interviews and conversations, July, Aug. 1991, 1992. All quotes from these until noted otherwise.

13. HG to RC, autumn 1924, JNC/USF.

14. JNC's musical education occurred in Paris during the years 1924–1932 at the Schola Cantorum. He studied piano with Paul Braud and harmony, counterpoint, and fugue with the brothers Gallon. At the suggestion of Manuel de Falla (with whom he studied composition for three summers in Granada), he eventually enrolled in Paul Dukas' composition class at the Paris Conservatory. By the early 1930s, he had established a successful career as a concert pianist in Europe, the U.S., and Canada. During this time, he premiered several of his own compositions; others were performed by other prominent musicians and orchestras.

15. ED-3, 10. The play does not seem to have survived, for no dramatic writing can be identified among her papers either at UCLA or Northwestern, where a significant number of prose MSS is collected. She mentions this work in UD-19, Feb. 1923–April 1924, exactly as it appears in ED-3, but no follow-up reference exists nor does she describe it elsewhere.

16. She gives a brief description of the apartment in ED-3, 12.

17. ED-3, 26.

18. ED-2, 466 ff. All quotes from these pages until noted otherwise. These musings were occasioned after she read Carlyle's *Sartor Resartus.*

19. Henri-Frédéric Amiel (1821–1881) was a French Protestant diarist, critic, and professor of aesthetics and philosophy. AN liked two passages in particular: "I am not free because I do not have the strength to execute my free will," and "I am becoming more purely spirit. . . . Life is only a document to be interpreted, matter to be spiritualized. Such is the life of the thinker" [my translations]. AN read it first in French. When further fragments were published in 1927, HG bought a copy, enclosing a poem he wrote in the style of Amiel. Although HG expressed genuine admiration, he did not share AN's unqualified adoration.

20. A ten-volume, highly impressionistic account of a musical genius whose life and work unfold from the late nineteenth century and into the twentieth; a monumental collection of upheavals, crises, and sorrows, all of which the hero overcomes.

21. ED-2, 469.

22. The MS is at Northwestern U.

23. At one point he suggested that she use loose-leaf folders rather than bound volumes so that she could type, and thus write more, and faster and better. She was appalled at the suggestion, and continued to fill bound volumes in her flowing handwriting. In her hundreds of thousands of pages, there are almost no false starts, crossouts, or revisions. The diary writing flows in a way the other genres never did.

24. These sentences are from an undated diary entry, JNC/USF. However, a photocopy bearing the notation "From Hugo's Journal, 1932" in RP's hand (and in his archives) bears these same sentences followed by a long entry that begins: "I am so convinced of this that I am going to begin describing her life and the development of her mind and character which is I think something unique, more astonishing to me every day."

25. ED-3, 15. From that time on, she spoke of Eugene Graves only in thinly hidden sarcasm. She never showed him anything else she wrote, and when they went to Paris, persuaded HG first to diminish and soon after to end the correspondence and thus the friendship.

26. Although AN's diaries and correspondence with RC clearly indicate that TN was in France as I have written, GNR, in a fax of 11/13/94, said TN always claimed that he spent 1924–26 alone in New York while the family went to France: "He claimed that . . . he worked full time and sent half his salary to his mother, and that the second year he worked about 30 or more hours a week and attended Columbia . . . he did say that he went to live with Aunt Antolina in Havana after spending a year at Columbia, because living alone, working, and going to school was just too much for him. . . . When he talked to us, that seemed like an important time in his life . . . of suffering, loneliness, unhealthy living . . . I can understand better why he felt so resentful about this part of his life and why that pain never left him."

27. ED-3, 46.

28. Ibid., 57.

29. Ibid., 69.

30. Ibid., 72–73.

31. HG, misc. undated jottings made during analysis with Dr. Inge Bogner sometime after 1940. Private collection.

7. Battles of Interest

1. ED-3, 21, is only one example of the many to be found in her diaries and correspondence: "Each year I have felt more keenly the unimportance of time and dates. Solemnity on the occasion of the New Year appears to me more and more ridiculous." This view intensified throughout her life; the older she grew, the stronger she expressed it.

2. "There was never an official diagnosis. It was either that [TB] or something similar. . . . I was ill for a year." JNC, tel. conversation, 5/28/93. "Hugo made my recovery possible [by paying for it], just as he paid for all my musical studies from then on." JNC, interview, 5/11/90. Also from 5/11: "That was when my character changed. Until then I had been the physical equivalent of the Bubonic Plague. After that I calmed down." Throughout ED-3 and ED-4, AN notes the changes in their relationship, from older sister and mischievous little brother to two confidants and friends, which they remained for the rest of her life.

3. ED-3, 81–82. AN's version of Thorvald's response to JN differs from JNC's, which I have noted below.

4. JNC, telephone conversation, 5/28/93. All quotes from this until noted otherwise.

5. ED-3, 94–95.

6. Ibid., 84–85.

7. Ibid., 86–87. "That was Anaïs all over, yearning for the dream somewhere far away rather than the reality of where she was." JNC, 5/28/93. This tendency, of search and quest, became more pronounced in AN with every passing year.

8. He was the son of Count and Countess Guicciardi and "the first of Anaïs's *chevalier/servants.*" For many years he "unhappily measured his girl friends with Anaïs. It took him a long time to decide on an American [wife]." JNC, fax, 6/7/93. All three Guicciardis were responsible for introducing AN and HG to the highest strata of refined and rarefied Parisian society. When HG developed the estate-planning division of the National City Bank, he persuaded many of the persons he met at the Guicciardis' to invest their holdings with him. Until then this group had almost never trusted their money to any banks but the French. HG's standing in the French-American business community was of the highest because of his skill, sophistication, and diplomacy in handling vast fortunes, many of which came to him through Horace Guicciardi.

9. AN/HG *Journal,* JNC/USF. AN added this note on 4/12/28: "This picture does not fit me any longer. Too Bad!"

10. ED-3, 235.

11. Ibid., 114.

12. "I don't know for sure, I can only speculate, but given all we know now, in retrospect, that would seem to be the case." JNC, 5/28/93.

13. ED-3, 115.

14. Ibid., 90.

15. Ibid., 140.

16. A good example of this is in UD-24.

17. ED-3, 123. All quotes from this until noted otherwise. This ms has not yet been found in any university collection or among RP's archives.

18. Ibid., 144.

19. I discovered this curious coincidence accidentally, when JNC casually said, "When we lived on Schoelcher," during an interview. I do not believe SdB knew that AN once occupied her apartment; her attitude seemed to be that the apartment had no history until she bought it.

20. ED-4, 74.

21. AN to RC, 6/25/25. She says also that they will have to repay it at the rate of 500 fr. per month, so hiring a maid will be impossible. Nevertheless, they hired one, the first of a succession who, for various reasons, she could not manage. On 8/6/25, AN to RC, she says the rent for each apartment will be 800 francs per month, all inclusive.

22. AN to RC in Hendaye, 8/6/25. Following JNC's illness, RC and he returned to spend their summers in Hendaye for the next 5–6 years. To ease expenses, RC always sublet her apartment in Paris.

23. She may have incorporated parts of this play into the previous one—or vice versa, as no complete manuscript has yet been identified which incorporates the ideas and incidents she refers to from time to time in ED-3 and ED-4.

24. HG to RC, 4/16/24. He took the baptismal name of Theodore, in honor of RC's father, Thorvald C, whose original middle name it had been.

25. ED-3, 166. All quotes from this until noted otherwise.

26. AN/HG *Journal,* JNC/USF, ED-3, 264.

27. ED-3, 199. All quotes from this until noted otherwise.

28. UD-23. She gives a slightly different account of this in ED-3, 237. Shortly after, she changed her mind about Proust, and his writing became one of the lasting influences on her life.

29. ED-3, 203, AN/HG *Journal,* JNC/USF. In UD-27, she lists among her reading the following autobiographies, biographies, and biographically based writings: Édouard Herriot, *Vie de Madame Récamier;* Isadora Duncan, *Ma Vie;* Francisco Contreras, *Vie de Goya* and *Vie de Keats;* Virginia Woolf, *Orlando; Quelques lettres de Proust;* Princesse Bibesco, *Au bal avec Marcel Proust;* Jacques Lenormand, *Une vie secrète;* and Francis de Miomandre, *Vie amoureuse de Vénus.*

30. ED-3, 203.

31. Ibid., 208; UD-24. Several works have contributed to my own thinking about the concept of AN's "Self," and although I will refer to them specifically throughout this book, I wish to cite some here. Roland Barthes, *Image, Music, Text* (New York: Hill & Wang, 1977); Jerome Bruner, *Acts of Meaning* (Cambridge: Harvard U. Press, 1990); James Miller, *The Passion of Michel Foucault* (New York: Simon & Schuster, 1993); Donald Spence, *Narrative Truth and Historical Truth: Meaning and Interpretation in Psychoanalysis* (New York: Norton, 1982). The same is true of persons who discussed this issue with me and who will also be cited specifically later: Betty Berzon, Jerome Bruner, Edwin Fancher, Muriel Dimen, Carolyn Heilbrun, Lila Rosenblum, and Susan Shapiro.

32. ED-3, 241.

33. "Argentina was a great friend of my Father and Anaïs was never loath to use her father's name to get recognition. The legend that she tried out for a part in Argentina's productions at the Opéra-Comique is sheer nonsense. She may have *thought* that she had tried, and we all know that what Anaïs *thought* she did became factual truths." JNC, fax, 6/7/93.

34. Ibid.

35. In a letter to his brother, John Guiler, 11/1/27, HG wrote: "You could not understand the struggle Anaïs and I had just come through, how up to the year 1927 we were really very very poor . . . added to that I had come through a period of bad health lasting over a year." AN/HG *Journal,* JNC/USF.

8. Mediocre Unfaithfulness

1. Information that follows is from AN/HG *Journal,* JNC/USF. For a version of one of their many discussions about money, see ED-4, 77.

2. JNC, fax, 6/7/93.
3. John Erskine's daughter, Anna, then twelve, remembers being taken to these performances on the rue Schoelcher: "As Anaïs was very involved with Spanish dancing, poor Hugo had to go along with it. I would not say they 'stopped the show,' but they were fair dancers." Anna Crouse Murch, tel. interview, 6/3/93.
4. Miralles unwittingly gave her the name the first time she danced when he became flustered and called her "Niña Guilera." ED-4, 61; UD-25. HG always insisted that he had Spanish blood although it was never proven. He claimed that his family's name had been Aguilera, and that it had been corrupted into Guiler many generations previously.
5. The following account is based on UD, archival materials in JNC/USF, correspondence between HG and AN, and interviews and conversations with JNC, RP, and A. C. Murch.
6. UD-25, 26, 65. She fictionalized the Miralles encounter in *Children of the Albatross*, 6–10.
7. But as early as 3/28 she had begun to hide it. ED-4, 72; UD-25.
8. ED-4, 56. Further elaboration in UD-25. All quotes from this until noted otherwise.
9. In UD 24–28, AN appended a "Journal of Facts" to each diary listing all her activity for every single day. It is exhausting just to read it.
10. AN to RC, n.d., 1928.
11. AN/HG *Journal*, JNC/USF. This became a subject HG discussed with his analyst for many years.
12. ED-4, 95–97. All quotes from this until noted otherwise.
13. AN/HG *Journal*, JNC/USF.
14. "I don't think Hugo had any capital. Savings yes, but since they were in National City Bank stock you can well imagine what happened to them. Mother had no capital. Only the payments from [selling] Richmond Hill and eventually what she inherited from her mother, also small. We were dependent on Hugo's salary, which must have been considerable at that time in France." JNC, fax, 6/18/93.
15. "I gave her [piano classes] (at the instigation of Anaïs of course) on my way to the Schola Cantorum at the rue St.-Jacques, not far from the Erskine apartment on the rue du Val-de-Grâce." JNC, fax, 6/7/93. Information that follows is also from Anna Crouse Murch, 6/3/93; UD 26–29; AN/HG *Journal*, JNC/USF; also John Erskine, who gives a different account of the reason his family lived in Paris in his autobiography, *The Memory of Certain Persons* (Phil.: J. B. Lippincott, 1947), 370–371. When JF was preparing ED-4 for publication, he contacted the late John Erskine's children, Graham Erskine and Anna Crouse Murch, as a matter of courtesy. JF has graciously provided me with their correspondence and other documentation pertaining to this volume, such as the original of JNC's "Introduction," which contains much information that was omitted from the printed book. JF's description of AN's putative affair with Erskine is still the most apt: "This was her first transgression, but it is very significant, because it became the pattern for her life." JF to Graham Erskine, 3/22/84.
16. "[My mother's] New England background may have confused Anaïs, but she was intelligent and warm." Anna Crouse Murch to JF, 2/3/84, JF archives.
17. Most of these passages seem either not to have survived, or perhaps not to have been written at all. One

example that has survived, however, partially quoted here, is from UD-27, 250–251; ED-4, 197; and AN/HG *Journal,* JNC/USF. The latter two are much more effusive and flowery, whereas the former appears to have been somewhat changed and severely edited for publication.

18. RC and JNC were not in residence there: "I have no recollection of [having lived] on Port-Royal. We did all live together in between the rue Schoelcher and boulevard Suchet, but where? Sorry." JNC, fax, 6/18/93. Undated letters between AN and RC suggest that RC and JNC were on holiday in Hendaye during this Christmas season.

19. ED-4, 85–87, 194. All quotes from this until noted otherwise.

20. She inserted a photo of Madriguera from a concert program into UD-30, 402, under which she wrote "Premier Passion" ("First Love").

21. ED-4, 106. All quotes from this until noted otherwise.

22. Ibid., 79.

23. Ibid., 104.

24. AN to RC, n.d., probably 1932. In the letter AN asks RC to tell her brother Enrique (executor of her mother's estate) that she needs her inheritance in one lump sum "to buy a house," but in reality to loan it to AN: "We thought that if you could get that from Tío Enrique . . . then I could pay off Hugo's mother and slowly pay you back, at a lower amount . . . it would make our life so much easier. . . . We cannot antagonize Hugo's Mother because we still hope she will give us someday what Hugo's father promised him."

25. ED-4, 221.

26. Ibid., 288. "Anaïs was a rank amateur who never stood a chance as a dancer but who loved the momentary adulation and public acclaim. . . . [I]n spite of being the daughter of Joaquín Nin she didn't even make the chorus line of La Argentina's production of Falla's *El amor brujo* at the Opéra-Comique. Unpleasant reality but true." JNC/I, 11/25/92.

27. What follows is taken from AN/HG *Journal,* JNC/USF; ED-4, 189–193; UD-26, 27; and later diaries of the 1930s in which she refines earlier accounts. It should be noted that ED-4 is a highly edited and romanticized rendering of the original accounts.

28. AN and HG saw the Erskines only once after that, during their annual American vacation.

29. AN to RC, n.d., internal evidence suggests summer 1929.

30. These are listed in ED-4, 243, and the ones later published in *Waste of Timelessness and Other Early Stories* are marked.

31. ED-4, 247–248.

32. AN to RC, letter, n.d., early 1930. JNC/USF.

33. ED-4, 291.

9. An Unprofessional Study

1. Bald, author of the column "La Vie de Bohème" in the European edition of the *Chicago Tribune,* 1929–1933, often promised things he could not deliver and this was probably one of those times. AN and HG sometimes invited Bald and his wife to their home when they wanted to provide

"local color" for visiting bankers and investors.
2. ED-4, 203.
3. Ibid., 271–272.
4. Ibid., 277.
5. Ibid., 281, 303. It was the Spanish version of the heroine's name in Debussy's *Pelléas et Mélisande.* In the original typescript of his introduction to ED-4, JNC wrote: "Mélisande's words to Golaud provided [Anaïs] with one of her favorite lines during this time: 'Je ne suis pas heureuse ici' (I am not happy here)." Also JF archives.
6. An American woman named Kay Bryant, called "Kay B." in ED-4, whom she met on a holiday at Caux, gave her a letter of introduction.
7. UD-29. Two letters from Francis Arthur Jones, the first with date expunged, the second 5/20/30. For a detailed description of "practically all the manuscripts" of AN's fiction, see "The Manuscripts of Anaïs Nin at Northwestern," by Marie-Claire Van der Elst, in *The World of Anaïs Nin: Critical and Cultural Perspectives,* special issue of *Mosaic,* XI/2, (Winnipeg: U. of Manitoba Press, 1978), 59–63. Van der Elst notes that writings from this period consist mostly of "unpublished material including four novels, about sixteen short stories [later published by The Magic Circle Press as *Waste of Timelessness and Other Early Stories*] and many miscellaneous fragments," and of pages which are "not always numbered and terribly mixed up . . . [a] somewhat incoherent batch. Van der Elst concludes by saying "the extreme importance" of this archive cannot be denied. I agree that future scholarship about AN's literary development must begin with an annotated bibliography of all her unpublished writings. The study of her fiction, independent of her diary writing, has been greatly hindered by dispersion within several archives (to be noted within the text where appropriate) of her many fragmented as well as complete manuscripts. Also, whether or not any of these materials are still in RP's archives has, to the best of my knowledge, never been established.
8. There is some confusion of dates in the published ED-4. On p. 299, Nin tosses aside the rejection, but the date she supposedly wrote about it is 5/11/30. Jones's letter of rejection is clearly dated 5/20, and even if he mailed it promptly, she would not have received it for at least a week after that. "Three Old Countesses" and "Fear of Nice" were published in *Waste of Timelessness and Other Early Stories;* I have not been able to extract "Talkies" as a separate and complete entity from other MSS fragments at Northwestern.
9. She mentions these in one oblique reference in UD-29, but is not specific about either the journals themselves or the works she submitted. Jones tried to sell three stories entitled "Faithfulness," "The Idealist," and "A Dangerous Perfume." The first two stories were later published in *Waste of Timelessness.* Information from UD-29, second letter from Jones with date expunged, but as other writing in her hand on this page lists her activities for Sept. 1930, it was probably written about then. All quotes from this until noted otherwise. Jones's letter is also quoted in ED-4, 302, but probably dated incorrectly as 5/24/30.
10. UD-29 and 30.
11. HG wrote about Frank several times in AN/HG *Journal,* each time

fascinated that Frank wrote "from the inside of American life as seen by a socialist and a Jew." HG's comments about Jews were expressed in language that can be construed as anti-Semitic, but which should be interpreted in the context of the historical time in which he wrote it. In his friendships and business affairs, he was known all his life as eminently fair and without prejudice. This will be addressed and cited where appropriate throughout the text.

12. Kay Bryant, a friend of AN's, suggested she send it to a Toronto magazine, *The Canadian Forum,* where it was published in Vol. 11, no. 121, Oct. 1930, 15–17. Other information is from UD-27–32.

13. ED-4, 305; UD-29, 30.

14. Stephen Potter, *D. H. Lawrence, a First Study* (London: Jonathan Cape, 1930); F. R. Leavis, *D. H. Lawrence* (Cambridge, England: The Minority Press, 1930); ED-4, 305; UD-29, 30.

15. Harry T. Moore has melded these comments into a complete paragraph in his introduction to *DHL,* 10–11.

16. One of the most telling examples concerns *The Plumed Serpent,* which many scholars think is DHL's greatest work: AN does not even mention it in passing but chooses instead to lavish a chapter on a fairly insignificant story, "The Princess." A lighter example is her repeated misstatement of the title of *Studies in Classical American Literature,* which led to the charge that nothing in Nin's book could or should be regarded seriously because of such errors: "Its accuracy can best be exemplified by its three references . . . *Classical Studies in American Literature, Studies in American Classical Literature,* and *Studies in Classical American Literature.*" Review of *DHL, New Yorker* (5/30/64), 136.

17. From *Women in Love,* quoted in *DHL,* 79; D. H. Lawrence, *Women in Love* (New York: Penguin Books USA), 139 ff.

18. *D. H. Lawrence: An Unprofessional Study* (Denver: Alan Swallow, 1964), 12. Hereafter abbreviated as *DHL.*

19. This description was made by Harry T. Moore, the American professor of literature who was one of Lawrence's earliest and most respected champions, in the introduction to AN's Swallow edition of 1964.

20. Samuel Beckett, "Dante . . . Bruno. Vico . . . Joyce," in *Our Exagmination Round his Factification for Incamination of Work in Progress,* (London: Faber & Faber, 1972), 14.

21. AN/HG *Journal,* JNC/USF.

22. *DHL,* 14.

23. Ibid., 26. In ED-4, 200, while reading Hermann A. Keyserling, she notes "that the illness of our century is dissatisfaction."

24. Textual quotes from *DHL,* 27; AN's remarks from ED-4, 337.

25. All quotes from *DHL,* 34–35.

26. ED-4, 194. She first used this phrase in 1929, and it remained one of her most important for the rest of her life.

27. *DHL,* 50; UD-30, 343, 376–379, 389–390; ED-4, 200. She had read only *Pride and Prejudice,* which she did not like. She claimed to have read *Middlemarch,* but in truth never finished it. Conspicuously absent is Colette, whom she credited with "the most powerful descriptive style of all the women in literature."

28. Birkin, from *Women in Love,* quoted in *DHL,* 79.

29. All quotes from *DHL,* 85–86.
30. In a letter to JF, 8/2/81, ES gave permission "to include my name and material in relation to AN" in *Linotte* and ED 2-4. He had previously withheld permission from D 1–7. JF archives.
31. JNC, interview, 7/91.
32. AN to HG and JNC, occasional remarks in undated letters throughout the 1930s and early 1940s.
33. AN to RC, 8/18/30. All quotes from this until noted otherwise. I am also grateful to Lori A. Wood, founder and chairperson of the Louveciennes Project undertaken by the Anaïs Nin Institute, for providing detail about the house at 2 bis, rue Monbuisson. The Institute, according to Wood, "is an organization formed specifically to . . . restore the property to the magical state created by Nin in the 1930's and to administer an Artist in Residence program [on the premises]." The house is currently owned privately but in an advanced state of deterioration. The present owner is unwilling to cooperate with the Louveciennes Project and does not wish to alter either the ownership or the circumstances of the property in any way. RP and JNC have also provided me with information about the house during the time AN lived there. Published descriptions include those she wrote in the early 1960s for D-1 (1966) and "A House and a Garden," in *Anaïs: IJ* 8, pp. 32–46.
34. In ED-4, 328, she writes "The apartment is rented, at a profit to me, for my work, of 25,000 francs." This is later disproved in undated letters to RC in Hendaye, where she speaks of "the loss we incurred when renting Suchet."
35. ED-4, 321; UD, Vol. 29.
36. ED-4, 333.
37. The original passage is in UD-29; rewritten and changed in ED-4, 346; referred to in passing in later UD journals where she dwells briefly on Eduardo.
38. From various entries throughout UD–29-34.
39. ED-4, 334. AN elaborated upon the erotic feelings she had for ES in "Elena," a MS of some 200 pages in UCLA/AN. As I am leary of substituting fiction for the events of real life, and as there is no written evidence or verifiable oral testimony to support the contention that AN and ES ever consummated their relationship, I shall leave it to others who care to do so to read this MS and attribute factual correspondences of her life to it. Portions of this MS were later incorporated into *Delta of Venus,* the collection of erotica published in 1977.
40. JNC, interview, 7/91.
41. She bought it at the 1925 Arts Décoratifs exhibition in Paris and took it with her to every place she lived thereafter. Wood also notes that AN "identified so strongly [with the fishbowl] as a symbol of her inner life." She used one in her novel, *Winter of Artifice,* and gave one exactly like it to her father and another to Dr. René Allendy. Lori A. Wood, "Notes on Décor of 2 bis, rue Monbuisson," prepared for DB, unpublished as of 1993.
42. ED-4, 354–355. "Mother tried desperately to avoid the inevitable show-down with Hugo which, by the way, never came. . . . She was never against Anaïs but she was against (by withholding her approval) Anaïs's lies and deceits." JNC, commentary on *Incest* (here-

after JNC/I), prepared for DB, 11/29/92.

43. AN/HG *Journal,* JNC/USF. Poem (only partially quoted here) copied in AN's hand and dated Louveciennes 1930.

44. See ED-4, 316, for one such calculation.

45. AN's editor presents a coded version of this interlude in ED-4, 349. I have also relied on UD-30, 31; AN/HG *Journal,* JNC/USF; also, AN's undated letters and HG's from London, Biarritz, and Nice, all bearing 1930–1931 postmarks.

46. It will require the full attention of a textual scholar to sort out the many manuscripts that date from this period of AN's life; I can only list some of my observations here. The bulk of the more than 25 stories (partial as well as complete) that have thus far been identified are at Northwestern U. (hereafter AN/NU). Some were later rewritten entirely or else used partially in erotica composed during the 1940s and into the 1950s. Some of these are housed in The Kinsey Institute for Research in Sex, Gender, and Reproduction, Indiana U., Bloomington (hereafter AN/KI); the Lilly Library of Indiana U., Bloomington (hereafter AN/LL); and UCLA. Her first story on the subject of artists' models was "An Artist's Model," which became part of her first novel, *Aline* (1922, AN/NU). It was later changed and eroticized in "Artists & Models" (c. 1941, UCLA, Box 7, Folder 7). Other variations are in "Lilith" (AN/KI, published in *Delta of Venus*) and "Elena" (UCLA). Other stories were finally collected and published under the title of one of them, *Waste of Timelessness.*

47. Again, at Kay Bryant's suggestion.

48. ED-4, 361–362, 369; UD-30, 31.

49. An American woman whom AN met in Caux, and who professed to be a writer.

50. Edward Titus owned a bookstore, At the Sign of the Black Mannikin, on the rue Delambre in Paris and a publishing concern called The Black Mannikin Press. Among the writers he published was Djuna Barnes, but his most notorious case concerned *Lady Chatterley's Lover.* Titus successfully combated French suppression of the book with the help of several writers, including Louis Aragon. When Ernest Walsh died (he had founded *This Quarter* with Ethel Moorhead, Titus became publisher of the magazine. Information that follows is from UD-30, 31.

51. ED-4, 341–342, 395; UD-30, 31. In ED-4, 361–362, AN speaks of working with Robert Cole, who really was Titus's assistant at the time. "Working with Mr. Cole" appears in "Journal of Facts" for UD 30 and 31. "Mr. Drake" first appears in UD-31. RP (who edited ED-4 after AN's death) omits all information about Drake and AN's relationship with him. There is an account of their sexuality in *Henry & June,* 6–8, which gives an even more highly edited version than ED-4, as does *Incest.* A full account is in UD 30–38. All information is from these documents, mostly UD, unless noted otherwise.

52. Information about the loss of capital is from AN/HG, *Journal,* JNC/USF, dated 7/16/30, Caux. At the end of this passage, AN added: "(Here Hugh saw me lying naked on the verandah taking a sun bath and forgot all his worries with me for the rest of our vacation.)" Information about the salary advance he took to pay for her publication is from an undated

"Dream" manuscript HG prepared sometime after 1950, during his analysis. He mentions it in passing as one of the many ways he tried to further AN's career. There is an edited version in ED-4, 314, dated July 13.

10. "A man who makes life drunk"

1. I have selected UD-30 as an example. All quotes from it until further notice.

2. She made a list of her writings during this time. Her description is as follows: "Waste of Timelessness (story), Alchemy (story), Studio 28 (sur-realism, sketch), Play: Multiple Lives, Sequel to Woman No Man Could Hold (long story), Eduardo's Story (long story), Book: D. H. Lawrence—Study in Understanding [her temporary title], The Gypsy Dancer (story), Third and last part to Woman No Man Could Hold, 17 petit morceaux in prose—'Visions,' Partouze dans le Bois, Review of Murry's 'Son of Woman.' " Many of these (all or in part) are at AN/NU.

3. UD-31. All quotes from this until noted otherwise.

4. From UD-31 and ED-4, 372 ff. All quotes from this until noted otherwise.

5. "Had a terrible fright reading a eulogy of Dorothy Richardson, thinking someone had usurped my place, or rather, preceded me in literature. But it was a false alarm. Not me, not me, but it is very good." ED-4, 432.

6. She read Freud's *Beyond the Pleasure Principle, The Future of an Illusion, The Collected Papers of Volume 7,* and *Leonardo da Vinci;* Alfred Adler's *The Science of Living* and *Le Tempérament Nerveux* (probably the work translated as *The Neurotic Constitutional Outlines of a Comparative Individualistic Psychology and Psychotherapy*; W. B. Pillsbury's *The History of Psychology;* Elizabeth E. Goldsmith's *Life Symbols* (actual title is *Sacred Symbols in Art*); and Ramón Fernández's *De la Personnalité.*

7. ED-4, 440.

8. Ibid., 372. All quotes from this until noted otherwise.

9. C. G. Jung, "Psychology and Poetry," *transition,* 19–20, June 1930, 23–45.

10. From interviews and conversations with RP and many others.

11. ED-4, 418.

12. All descriptions of dreams are from UD-31.

13. ED-4, 431.

14. Many of these are in JNC/USF. AN wrote: "Love between women now appears possible to me, a mixture of fraternity and curiosity and perversity. I have only felt the curiosity so far. It is something new to explore—my feelings if I were a man novelist and powerfully desirous of stripping and devouring a woman. I should love a woman because I have never penetrated any woman but myself. It seems miserly of me." It was at this time that Eduardo began to try to persuade AN to indulge in orgies, both hetero- and homosexual.

15. She uses this expression in many undated letters to RC; internal evidence suggests 1929 through 1933. Much information that follows is from those of 1931 and interviews with JNC and Gayle Nin Rosenkrantz, 7/26/91.

16. Besides the annual visit to Hendaye, RC made frequent short visits to Mallorca during these years, and JNC was often in Spain either performing or attending master classes and special seminars. Much of what follows is based on undated letters, AN to RC.
17. Gayle Nin Rosenkrantz, 12/1/93.
18. AN to RC, 9/18/31, New York (AN and HG were on their annual leave). Teresa Castillo Nin gave birth to a daughter, Gayle, in 1932, and a son, Charles, in 1933. Teresa tried to mend the breach between brother and sister, but AN and Thorvald did not meet again until she and HG moved to New York during WW II and Thorvald was enrolled at Columbia.
19. In "Journal of Facts" for UD-31, she writes "July 23—Hugh's confession." Most of this appears in ED-4, 486–488. I have already incorporated much of what he said about his childhood and youth into earlier chapters.
20. The list is from UD-31, 251; her self-analysis from ED-4, 437–440. All quotes from the latter until noted otherwise.
21. AN/HG *Journal*, JNC/USF. All quotes from this until noted otherwise.
22. Here he was referring to her nervous tension and general irritability since Erskine's rebuff.
23. UD-31.
24. UD-32; with information edited for *Henry and June* (New York: Harcourt Brace Jovanovich, 1986), hereafter *H & J*, 2–4. All information from these until noted otherwise.
25. AN/HG *Journal*, JNC/USF.
26. The term first struck her fancy when she read Jung's 1930 essay in *transition* and grew in importance throughout her life. Around this time she began to make drawings of circles radiating out on spokes originating from a central circle. At the center was "Louveciennes," or herself, and in each separate circle were people, concepts, places, or activities that were important to her at the time. She was especially pleased with two events in the 1970s: Valerie Harms and Adele Aldridge, who operated the Magic Circle Press, organized a "Magic Circles Weekend" in AN's honor, April 28–30, 1972, in Rye, NY; Richard Centing published an independent "little magazine" called *The Widening Circle* (Vols. 1–4, Winter–Fall, 1973) and printed a selection from her writing in the first issue. Centing was also the editor of *Under the Sign of Pisces: The Anaïs Nin Newsletter*.
27. JNC, fax, 6/18/93.
28. UD-32; *H & J*, 6.
29. A published version of this conversation, heavily edited, appears in *H & J*, 10.

11. Those Millers

1. AN/HG *Journal*, JNC/USF. All quotes from this until noted otherwise.
2. The chronology of AN's first meetings with Henry Miller and his wife, June Mansfield, have been given as many different datings as there have been different writers on the subject. AN records these dates in the detailed chronology of the "Journal of Facts" for UD, Vol. 32. I think it is the most reliable source because she noted the

details of her developing relationship with HM every single day. After HM's first luncheon at Louveciennes, AN notes a second on Dec. 12 for HM and Osborn (without HG). On Dec. 23, she and HG dined alone with HM at Louveciennes. HG went to Holland on business on Dec. 27, returning early the 29th. AN and HG hosted a dinner at Louveciennes for HM and JM on Dec. 29. The four did not meet again, together or separately, until 1/2/32, when AN and HG took HM and JM to a restaurant and then to the Grand Guignol. AN met JM alone for the first time on Jan. 6 at the American Express office on rue Scribe, after which they went to lunch. She saw JM Jan. 11 ("4 h. June at home"); Jan. 12 ("lunch with June" [in Paris]); Jan. 14 ("June for lunch at home"); Jan. 16 ("9h. hair dyed black, 12 h. meet June for a few moments, afternoon rest with H[enry]"); Jan. 18 ("June for lunch" [in Paris]); Jan. 19. ("4h. Fierem Boyard [perhaps the ship on which she sailed] with June"). As June disappears from the daily entries after that, she must have sailed on the 19th. On Jan. 20 AN notes "4 h. Henry for overnight visit," and Jan. 21 "Henry at home—talks."

3. UD-33 (red), 12.

4. Henry Miller, *Letters to Emil* [Schnellock], ed. George Wickes (New York: New Directions, 1989). 71. All quotes from this until noted otherwise.

5. Ibid., 89.

6. For the text that follows concerning Henry Miller and June Mansfield Miller Corbett, I have consulted the following biographical sources: The Nin and Miller collections at UCLA, JNC/USF, several private archives, and various library holdings that will be cited where appropriate. Books include Mary Dearborn, *The Happiest Man Alive* (New York: Simon & Schuster, 1991), Robert Ferguson, *Henry Miller: A Life* (New York: W. W. Norton & Co., 1991), Jay Martin, *Always Merry and Bright: The Life of Henry Miller* (Santa Barbara: Capra Press, 1978), Wickes, op. cit., Henry Miller, *Letters to Anaïs Nin,* ed. Gunther Stuhlmann (New York: Paragon House, 1988), Henry Miller and Anaïs Nin, *A Literate Passion* (Letters 1932–1953), ed. Gunther Stuhlmann (New York: Harcourt Brace Jovanovich, 1987), Anaïs Nin, *Henry & June,* and *Incest,* both ed. Rupert Pole (New York: Harcourt Brace Jovanovich, 1986 and 1992). Also, numerous periodicals (especially *Anaïs: An International Journal*) and memoirs and interviews, all of which will be cited where appropriate. The account that follows is my own, based primarily on original documents and personal interviews. Many of the previously published works, whose authors did not have complete access to these materials, are replete with errors of fact. Rather than correct them, I have chosen to tell what I believe is the most accurate version until or unless new information or testimony comes to light. When archival material corresponds to the published record, I have given the published source.

7. *Letters to Emil,* 115.

8. UD, Vol. 32, "Journal of Facts."

9. *Letters to AN,* 3–4. The letter is dated simply "December, 1931," but internal evidence suggests it was sent just before AN invited him and June to dinner on the 29th. All quotes from this until noted otherwise.

10. Robert Osborn was, according to Ferguson (176), "an unstable man, an incipient alcoholic who suffered bouts of paranoid schizophrenia."

Ferguson believes "Miller's attitude towards Osborn demonstrates the pragmatism of which he was capable when choosing his friends." HM called Osborn his friend in public but privately "confessed that [they] had nothing in common" (both quotes 178–179).

11. Dearborn, 101.

12. ES became Anaïs's primary instructor about perversions. He gave her vol. 7 of Freud's writings, containing his three essays on sexuality: "The Sexual Aberrations," "Infantile Sexuality," and "The Transformations of Puberty."

13. Martin gives the fullest discussion of June's character and personality throughout her marriage to HM, but he does not give any details of her name or the circumstances of her birth. Born either 1/7/02 (Dearborn, galley 80), or 1/28 (Ferguson, 78) in Bukovina, Austria-Hungary. Her name at birth was either Juliet Edith Smerth (Dearborn) or June Smerth (Ferguson). Her parents came to Brooklyn in 1907 and changed the name to Smith (both biographers agree, using U.S. Immigration and Naturalization documents as their source). Dearborn says June Miller chose the name Mansfield "because of its elegance"; Ferguson says she changed June to Julia and chose Mansfield as her surname because Smerth in Polish meant "death," and Mansfield was as close to "cemetery" as she could get in the English language. HM called her "The June-Smith-Smerth-Mansfield-Miller woman," and various other combinations of her names in *Letters to Emil,* 123, 125, 126.

14. The description in general is from UD-33, red and green; the citation is from *Letters to Emil,* 72.

15. Wambly Bald, *On the Left Bank, 1929–33,* ed. Benjamin Franklin V (Athens: Ohio U. Press, 1987), 77–78. Bald's column is dated Wednesday, Oct. 14, 1931, and appears on p. 4.

16. *Linotte,* 319.

17. "Joyce": UD-31; "Albertine," UD-33 (green); "Lawrence" from *Letters to Emil,* 106. In UD-33, she quotes HM as telling her, "Your book is really beautiful. There are memorable pages in it. . . . It is above all a strong book—very intense. It is better than any other *woman's* book I have ever read." Emphasis mine. She seems to have taken this as a compliment, for she makes no comment but simply records his. See also Jay Martin, chapter XII, 285 ff., for a discussion of HM's changing attitudes toward Lawrence, Joyce, and Proust.

18. Information that follows is from UD-33 (green). All quotes from this until noted otherwise.

19. UD-32. As *H & J* has been heavily edited (by Rupert Pole), I will quote from this work only when it corresponds to the original diary. This remark appears on p. 14.

20. AN describes the pleasure she gets walking through Paris with "the Gang" in UD-33 (red and green).

21. Arthur Prager, tel. interview, 7/21/93. Prager knew June Mansfield Miller Corbett in the 1960s, when she worked in the NYC Department of Social Services: "She dressed like something out of . . . Greenwich Village in the '20s, in a cape and a snap-brimmed hat. The cape flew out behind her and she swished it very dramatically. 'Who is that?' I asked my secretary and she said, 'That's the Love Goddess herself, the wife of Henry Miller.' I introduced myself and we became friends, frequently lunching together. It was like dining with Lady Chatterley."

22. She had had it dyed especially

for June because Henry told her black was June's color, but June arrived in Paris that time with a very bad hair dye, somewhere between henna-red and strawberry blonde. During this time AN had cosmetic surgery and corrective dentistry. The tip of flesh on her nose was removed in Switzerland in March; a year later, she had a gap filled in between her front top teeth and wore braces for a short time to straighten them. Some years later, she had a second operation to make her nose smaller and less aquiline.

23. In *H & J,* 22, AN says she offered her extra pair of sandals to June but "They were too small for her," which is highly unlikely.

24. She was a Spanish woman RC found in Hendaye, and she lasted longer than any other maid they had in France. HM always called her "Amelia." Also, he always called AN "Annis," claiming he could not pronounce her name properly. So, too, did June. AN described how pleased she was with Emilia's ingenuity in converting the tablecloth into a sheet in a letter, n.d., to RC.

25. AN/HG *Journal,* JNC/USF; UD-33 (red).

26. UD-33 (red); *H & J,* 27.

27. HG sent HM to a Dr. Krans of the American University Union, a banking client. As a favor to HG, Dr. Krans arranged for HM to become a *répétiteur d'anglais* (assistant in English) at the Lycée Carnot.

28. AN to RC, n.d.; UD-33. HG speaks of "the Millers" in much the same way in AN/HG *Journal,* JNC/USF.

29. AN was flattered to be considered the object of ES's physical passion, even though she knew he was lying. She actually did go to a hotel with him in late Feb. 1932, but could not bring herself to engage in sexual relations. There is no evidence in any of her unpublished writings or in the few surviving letters they exchanged (hers are at UCLA, his at Southern Methodist U., Dallas) that they ever consummated their relationship sexually.

30. UD-33 (green); *H & J,* 58, 56.

31. UD-33 (red).

32. "I took Hugo to the Rue Blondel to incite him to infidelity to punish myself for my infidelity with John." Some pages later she writes that she had been confusing Erskine with HM for some time and had called him "John" several times as they made love. UD-33 (red).

33. All quotes until further notice are from UD-33 (red) and AN/HG *Journal,* JNC/USF. There is also an edited version in *H & J,* 70–72.

34. I am the first of Nin's biographers to have had access to her entire UCLA archive as well as to relevant holdings by and about her in other libraries. I have interviewed most of the persons still alive in whom she might possibly have confided details of her sexual activity, and I have been given access to privileged documents kept by several of her analysts. In all of this enormous mass of paper, there is no written evidence that AN ever masturbated. She seems to have preferred to wait for an encounter with a man.

35. In both, she wrote "Mon Journal & Notebook." The green has a photo of HM pasted on the front page and a photo of June on the next. In both she signs her name as "Anaïs Nin Guiler," and entitles them "The Possessed." In the red, the next line says "June & Henry—Eduardo," and the date is 2/2/32, to (nothing follows). In the green the names are omitted and the date is "From Feb. 12, 1932 [RP has added 'To May 25, 1932']." The addresses are the same in both: "Hôtel du Parc, Glion, Suisse, and 2 bis, rue Monbuisson, Louveciennes, Seine & Oise."

36. In *H & J*, 75–76, the editor has made it seem that she asked Hugo how did he know that she was telling the truth, that she was not lying, and that Hugo asked her to give him "realities to fight," for his imagination only made things worse. In reality, she had this conversation with HM: he gave her notes he had made on his life with June, and AN used the details in her "imaginary" (green) journal to persuade Hugo that her "adventures" did not include sex with HM. In exchange for his notes, she let HM read a letter she had written to June, and it was he who "found relief in knowing" and asked her to give him "realities to fight."

37. AN/HG *Journal*, JNC/USF; also in numerous letters throughout the period 1947–1966, JNC/USF. Repeated by AN in UD-66.

38. All quotations until further notice will be from the red diary, UD-33.

39. Paul Ekman would probably classify AN among the "Natural Liars," whom he differentiates from psychopaths, in *Telling Lies*, 56–57.

40. This phrase and the one that follows were told to me in these words or very similar ones by so many persons, from RP and JNC to so many others, that I cite only a few here: James Leo Herlihy, interviews 1991 and 1992; Lila Rosenblum, interviews, conversations, and correspondence, 1989–1993; Renate Druks, interview 1991 and telephone conversation 1992; Marguerite Young, interview 1990; conversations 1991–1992; Daisy Aldan, interview 1991; Harriet Zinnes, interview 1991, conversations 1992–1993; Sharon Spencer, interviews and conversations 1989–1993.

41. For this discussion and others that follow throughout this book, I am grateful to Professor Eugenia Zimmerman for bibliography and conversations. She led me to some of the earliest writings about lying: Plato's *Republic* and Aristotle's *Poetics*. Other texts I have consulted include: Sissela Bok, *Lying: Moral Choice in Public and Private Life* (New York: Vintage, 1989); Nicholas Denyer, *Language, Thought and Falsehood in Ancient Philosophy* (Boston: Routledge & Kegan Paul, 1990); Paul Ekman, *Telling Lies* (New York: Berkeley, 1985); S. Freud, *The Psychopathology of Everyday Life*, trans. & ed. James Strachey, vol. 6: *The Complete Psychological Works* (New York: W. W. Norton, 1976); Robert D. Hare, *Psychopathy: Theory and Research* (New York: John Wiley, 1970); Philip Kerr, ed., *The Penguin Book of Lies: An Anthology* (New York: Viking, 1990); Elizabeth Loftus and Katherine Ketcham, *Witness for the Defense* (New York: St. Martin's Press, 1991); Eva Sweetser, "The Definition of a Lie," in *Cultural Models in Language and Thought*, ed. Naomi Quinn and Dorothy Holland (Cambridge, England: Cambridge U. Press, 1990).

42. "Mother's excuse for our moving into Paris was that my program at the Conservatory was too time-consuming and exhausting for me to commute any longer. She never said anything to me about what Henry's relationship might have been with Anaïs. Somehow, possibly because I was so busy with my studies, Mother managed to shield me from all that." JNC, tel. conversation, 7/27/93.

NOTES

43. UD-33 (red).
44. Philip Jason, ***Anaïs Nin and Her Critics,*** 27. Root's review, "The Femininity of D. H. Lawrence Emphasized by Woman Writer," appeared in the European edition of the *Chicago Daily Tribune,* 3/28/32, and was reprinted as "Literary Sexism in Action," in *Anaïs: IJ* 6, pp. 75–76.
45. UD-33 (red).

12. The Well-kept Mistress

1. *Letters to Emil,* 96 (4/18/32), Clichy.
2. He used them as notebooks into which he made jottings that he incorporated later into his fiction. Many of these are in HM/UCLA.
3. HM, *Reflections,* 106. Jay Martin (266) writes that "Henry was still neurotically afraid of starving to death. But equally important was the aura of personal, psychic security which [AN's] complete acceptance of him conveyed when she gave him money for the rent or food."
4. These expressions and many others are found in UD-33 (red) to Vol. 36. She uses them for lovers other than HM as well.
5. Alfred Perlès, interview with Wendy Beckett, 1989, Wells, England. Perlès died before I could speak to him, so I am grateful to Wendy Beckett for allowing me to quote from her interviews.
6. UD-33 (red) to Vol. 36. In the last years of his life, Perlès insisted that AN slept with him several times in Clichy, refuting interviewer Beckett's contention that if true, AN did so out of pity. Perlès insisted that it was because Miller was not at home and AN wanted sex, no matter with whom. In all of AN's archives, I have found no evidence that this ever happened. AN always wrote about Perlès with thinly disguised disdain and frequently disparaged his physical appearance. Wendy Beckett, in an interview with me (8/8/90, Sydney, Australia), said she had no reason to disbelieve Perlès because she found him "an otherwise trustworthy commentator on his own life and the lives of his friends, Nin, Miller and [Lawrence] Durrell."
7. Perlès insisted it was neither novel, journal, nor diary, but simply a "book." Jay Martin (255) describes it as "a book of 'peripheral feelings,' a work about the fragments of his memory and the streams of associations flowing between memories." Going back to his childhood, they also included recent ones of HM, June, and AN. In D-1, 93, AN describes it as "delicate as a water color." For information that follows, I have also consulted the following: Henry Miller, *Reflections,* ed. Twinka Thiebaud (Santa Barbara: Capra Press, 1981), *Remember to Remember* (Norfolk: New Directions, 1947), *Quiet Days in Clichy* (New York: Grove Press, 1965); Alfred Perlès, *Sentiments Limitrophes, Le Quatuor en Ré-Majeur* (both Paris: Denoël), *Reunion in Big Sur,* and *My Friend Lawrence Durrell,* (both Village Press, London); Samuel Putnam, *Paris Was Our Mistress* (New York: Viking Press, 1947); Douglas Stone, *Alfred Perlès: Renegade & Writer* (London: Village Press, 1974); George Wickes, *Americans in Paris* (New York: Doubleday, 1969).
8. All quotes from his interviews with

Wendy Beckett until noted otherwise. Perlès offered this observation about the difference between AN's writing and his own: "She couldn't get outside herself. Her writing was not necessarily bad, but it is likened to self indulgence, to egomania, I think. It won't endure time. I create with a conscience, the soul always comes out in the writing no matter how diverse the topic."

9. Miller, *Remember to Remember,* 350.

10. The first appeared in *transition* 16/17, 1929; the second was published in The Hague, 1932. See also *Letters to Emil,* 96–97, 111. For an excellent history of the magazine, see Dougald McMillan, *transition 1927–38: The History of a Literary Era* (New York: George Braziller, 1975).

11. She writes of "Jolas and my beloved *transition"* in UD-33 (red). Each comment of Jolas's manifesto was followed by an aphorism from William Blake, added just for the fun of it by Stuart Gilbert, who later became AN's friend. ES had been studying Blake preparatory to writing a book. Under the pseudonym "Eduardo Santiago," he eventually wrote a privately printed pamphlet, *The Round* (see *Anaïs: IJ*) 9, p. 27. Because of ES, AN studied Blake sporadically, but HG made a more serious investigation and credited Blake for the technique he used as the engraver Ian Hugo..

12. UD-33 (green), dated 3/15 [32].

13. HM to AN; AN to HM, *A Literate Passion,* 6 and 10.

14. This discussion is based on information in UD-33, both red and green, for she wrote thoughtfully about her writing in each. All quotes from these until further noted.

15. It was probably the genesis of the novel she began several months later, *Alraune* (whether Alraune I or II is not clear from her comments in UD-33 [red]. In both novels June is called "Alraune," HM is "Rab," and AN is "Mandra."

16. UD-33 (red). If Allendy left any record of his analysis of AN, it has not yet been identified. I can only relate here what she wrote in the diary and said in various letters, which will be noted accordingly.

17. I am grateful to Elisabeth Roudinesco for her correspondence with me, and for her definitive histories: *La bataille de cent ans: Histoire de la psychanalyse en France,* Vol. I (Paris: Éditions Ramsay/Editions du Seuil, 1986), translated in part as *Jacques Lacan & Co., a History of Psychoanalysis in France, 1925–1985,* trans. Jeffrey Mehlman (U. of Chicago Press, 1990), hereafter Vol. II.

18. Roudinesco, Vol. I, 370. See pp. 370–376 for Allendy's biography and an account (based solely on the published diaries) of AN's analysis. An informal summary of his shorter writings yields more than 200 articles dealing with such diverse subjects as astrological influences on the psyche, nasal catarrh, the Emerald Table of Hermes Trismegistes, and the importance of dreams.

19. Roudinesco, Vol. II, 8. Allendy also analyzed the writer René Crevel, who wrote an account of it in *Le Clavecin de Diderot* (Diderot's Harpsichord) (originally published 1932, reprinted Paris: Pauvert, 1966). It includes a scathing account of Allendy's eccentric Socialist views expressed in his book *Capitalisme et sexualité,* particularly toward women.

20. Allendy also pointed out that Eduardo's mother and sister were named Anaïs. She used various forms of "conquest" and "to conquer" frequently during this time, all with a variety of meanings.

21. René Allendy, *Capitalisme et sexualité*. There, Allendy writes that "women have adapted to a role of social parasite and are bound to capital," and that "Woman is not only as in the symbolism of the poets, the cup which receives the seed and preserves it, she is also the cash-box that keeps the coins."

22. Roudinesco, I, part 4, chapter 1. In II, 30, she applies the "frivolity of" [Pierre Janet's] therapeutic practice, and applies it to Allendy as well, adding "Allendy did no better than Janet in his treatment of Artaud or Anaïs Nin; and yet he was perfectly aware of the former's genius and the latter's talent."

23. At this stage it is not clear which "novel" she is talking about. However, during this time, she began "Alraune I," a great portion of which she later used in *House of Incest*, and "Alraune II," which contains "Alraune," "Mandra," "Rab," and "Winter of Artifice." Some of this was included in her "Father Story"; some was later incorporated into the novels *Winter of Artifice* (the "Djuna" section) and *Ladders to Fire*. There are also passages in *Seduction of the Minotaur*. This period of her life provided her with almost all the material for her fiction. There is still much textual scholarship needed on these manuscripts, most of which are at AN/NU.

24. She had told him in the most general terms that as a child, she was aware that her father no longer found her mother sexually attractive.

25. In French, "dédoublement de la personnalité" is literally "splitting the personality."

26. In a very real sense, Allendy was right. After D-1 was published, she stopped writing anything but letters.

27. Here she digressed to insert a passage about what Eduardo found when he cast her horoscope (astrology was just becoming the passion that would dominate the rest of his life): she had the same "star" as all the great courtesans, of "superficiality, charm, aristocracy, luxuriousness, love of beauty, sensuality, etc. etc." It was all a form of "gigantic compensation," she decided, "because my father didn't love me."

13. The Banker Woman

1. There is a highly edited version of what follows in *H & J*, 156–159. Most of it does not appear in UD-33 (red), 34 and 35. I have based my account on those volumes, interviews, and conversations with JNC, several references in AN/HG *Journal*, JNC/USF, and AN/RC undated letters.

2. Information about the concert is from JNC, interview, 7/15/91; and fax, 4/20/94.

3. AN later insisted JNC seek Allendy's advice: "Allendy's socialism did not prevent him from charging her a double fee for my first and only visit. He spent the [hour] explaining how much he loved his wife and Anaïs, and how complicated all this was for him. I left in a complete daze and only told Anaïs about this years later when she was dying. We laughed and cried together like two idiots." JNC, fax, 4/20/94.

4. In UD-33 (red), she uses the expression "double-sided," which she translated literally from the French expression, "double-face."

5. In the last two decades of his life, HG had many friends younger than he, among them many homosexual men. The charge was frequently raised that he, himself, was homo- or bisexual. In interviews with these men, I asked if their friendship with HG had had a sexual component. Each vociferously denied it. In this instance my sources have asked to remain anonymous.

6. UD-33 (red), Vols. 35, 36.

7. The account that follows is from AN/HG *Journal,* JNC/USF. All quotes from this unless noted otherwise.

8. In 1947, HG made one other attempt to keep a journal of analysis for his new analyst, Dr. Inge Bogner. It was, however, brief. In it he returned to the subject of his relationship with his father and his life with AN.

9. AN to RC, Louveciennes-Hendaye, "Friday." Internal evidence suggests Aug. 1932.

10. UD, Vols. 33 (red), 34, 35. All quotes from these until noted otherwise.

11. Ibid., Vol. 36.

12. The natural pun evoked by contemporary slang is unfortunate: AN meant it in the sense of "creating" HM.

13. UD, Vol. 36.

14. The passage in question reads: "Only because you are a man who is always ahead of himself . . . and that it is this precursor of yourself whom I follow about obstinately and I never look backwards." (Underlined text is by HM and relates to comments quoted in text.) This is from AN/NU, "Rab," several pages of an unfinished TS, heavily annotated in HM's hand. Valerie Harms generously brought this MS to my attention.

15. HM was fond of underlining, doubly as well as singly, to emphasize the points he wished to make. I have followed his style here.

16. Oliver Evans defines "Alrunes" as "witches believed to be capable of reading the future in the blood of their prisoners. In Germanic mythology the word, with its several variants, has various occult meanings, all of them sinister. The name *Alraune* is somewhat misleading as applied to the character in *House of Incest,* who is not a consciously evil person." In *Anaïs Nin* (Carbondale: S. Illinois U. Press, 1968), 203 n. 6.

17. Self-published and printed by AN and Gonzalo Moré, calling themselves Siana (Anaïs backward) Editions, Paris, 1936. She dropped the article for the first American edition, published and printed by AN and GM in New York in 1947, calling themselves Gemor (G. More) Press. From then on, the title has been simply *House of Incest.*

18. I have based the following account on UD-33–37; HM/UCLA; AN/HM, *A Literate Passion;* Martin, *Always Merry and Bright;* John Ferrone, HBJ archives, MSS and letters connected with publication of *H & J;* interviews with RP, JNC, JF, SS; RCA archives; AN/HG *Journal,* JNC/USF; RC/AN correspondence, JNC/USF, and other sources that will be cited individually.

19. *Letters to Emil,* 107.

20. June may well have said it, but it is also an oft-used literary technique. AN used it to conclude several of her unpublished MSS, HM to conclude *Cancer.* It is also the time-honored technique of both the *Bildungsroman* and the *Künstleroman.*

21. UD-34–35.

22. *Letters to Emil,* 115.

NOTES

14. Lover of the World and Men

1. To write this chapter, I have consulted many analysts who adhere to differing theories. Some knew AN in varying degrees of friendship but did not see her professionally, among them Betty Berzon, Edwin Fancher, and Lila Rosenblum. There were others who did not know her personally but were generous enough to share their professional expertise in topics I wished to explore (childhood abuse, child and adult incest, narcissism, borderline personalities, and various forms of sexual pathology). Here I wish to thank Phyllis Grosskurth, Valerie Harms, Daniel Hill, Betty Jean Lifton, Paul Roazen, Elisabeth Roudinesco, and Peggy Reeves Sanday. The members of the seminar on Psychoanalysis at the New York Institute for the Humanities (co-directors Jessica Benjamin and Muriel Dimen) helped me to work through the most puzzling segments of AN's diaries, and I am deeply indebted for their friendship, writings, and continuing assistance. I especially wish to acknowledge Donna Bassin, Elsa First, Virginia Goldner, Adrienne Harris, Adria Schwartz, and Susan Shapiro. The works I consulted are many and they differ in allegiance to particular theory as well as identification and approach. I cite here only a portion of the texts I found most useful: Jessica Benjamin, *The Bonds of Love: Psychoanalysis, Feminism, and the Problem of Domination* (NY: Pantheon, 1991); Warren R. Brodey, "Image, Object, and Narcissistic Relationships," *American Journal of Orthopsychiatry* 31, 1961; S. Freud (all in the Standard Edition): "Screen Memories" 3:299–322, "Three Essays on the Theory of Sexuality" 7:125–243, "Family Romances" 9:235–241, "On Narcissism: An Introduction" 14:73–102; Peter Giovachinni, *Psychoanalysis of Character Disorders* (NY: Jason Aronson, 1975); Daniel Hill, "The Special Place of the Erotic Transference in Psychoanalysis: A Review of the Literature," in ms; Edith Jacobson, *The Self and the Object World* (NY: International Universities Press, 1964); Otto Kernberg, *Borderline Conditions and Pathological Narcissism* (NY: Jason Aronson, 1975); Heinz Kohut, *The Analysis of the Self. A Systematic Approach to the Psychoanalytic Treatment of Narcissistic Personality Disorders* (NY: International Universities Press, 1971); "The Recovery of Childhood Memories in Psychoanalysis," in *The Psychoanalytic Study of the Child* 11:54–88 (NY: International Universities Press, 1956); Christopher Lasch, *The Culture of Narcissism* (NY: W. W. Norton, 1979); Ethel Spector Person, "The Erotic Transference in Women and in Men: Differences and Consequences," *Journal of the American Academy of Psychoanalysis* 13: 159–180, and *Dreams of Love and Fateful Encounters: The Power of Romantic Passion* (NY: W. W. Norton, 1988); Theodore Roszak, *The Voice of the Earth* (NY: Simon & Schuster, 1992); W. Mackinley Runyan, *Life Histories and Psychobiography* (NY: Oxford U. Press, 1982); Roy Schafer, *The Analytic Attitude* (NY: Basic Books, 1983); J. Schimek, "The Interpretations of the Past: Childhood Trauma, Psychical Reality, and Historical Truth, *Journal of the American Psychoanalytic Association* 23: 845–865; Donald P. Spence, *Narrative Truth and Historical Truth: Meaning* *and Interpretation in Psychoanalysis* (NY: W. W. Norton, 1984).

2. There are few of the long daily passages of introspective self-absorption evoked by her reading. If her list of "books read" is complete, in 1933 she read only Dandieu's *Proust* and Céline's *Voyage au bout de la nuit.* UD-39, 108.

3. These are the titles of (respectively) UD-39 (Jan.–March 33), 40 (March–May 33), 42 (June–Aug. 33), and 41 (May–June 33). Each of these volumes is at least 200 pages of densely packed handwriting, a total of some 800 pages of intensely graphic sexuality. All citations are from these rather than from the published *Incest,* which consists of text that is heavily edited, chronologically rearranged, and contains pseudonymous names and disguised identities. Where I have written about these persons in this book, I have used their true names and identities and will indicate it in the appropriate places. See also Epilogue, 464, for John Ferrone's explanation of how *Incest* was edited.

4. UD-39. All quotes from this until noted otherwise.

5. AN's emphasis.

6. UD-42. AN's emphasis.

7. UD-39. She dated this entry "February 14, 1933."

8. At the end of UD-39, she has appended a long "liste d'amoureux," which in retrospect is both sad and pathetic because in many cases they were lovers only in her imagination: "Petite garçon in Berlin who wanted to run away with me when I was five. Henri in Brussels with whom I got married [she was nine]. Enrique Madriguera. A cousin of Charles [de Cárdenas]—Bermudez. John O'Connell in [grade] school. Eduardo Sánchez. Orces [boarder on 75th St.]. Waldo Sanford, Boris Hoppe, Edward King [high school infatuations]. Richard Maynard. Boy in Columbia carnival. Boy at Canterbury [preparatory school where she spent a weekend]. Jimmy Forgie [neighbor in Queens]. Hugh Guiler. Gerald Leake in Woodstock [artist who made a pass]. Charles [de Cárdenas]. Ramiro Collazo, Marquesito [Havana flirtations]. Alfred Belt [employer who made passes]. Three painters. Three Cubans. Eugene [HG's Columbia friend, who did not like her]. Gustavo Morales [homosexual]. John Erskine. Anna María Sánchez [ES's younger sister]. June Mansfield. Lawrence Drake. Ethel Guiler. Henry Miller. Gustavo Durán [her father's friend]. René Allendy. Nellie de Vogüé [comtesse, whom she met in 1933]."

9. I have reproduced AN's capricious spelling and punctuation. This is still UD-39, "February 14, 1933."

10. Mme. Allendy returned the invitation, and AN met Antonin Artaud at her home.

11. UD-41. All quotes from this until noted otherwise.

12. She is called "Dorothy," and described as "a friend of Eduardo's" in *Incest.*

13. A French cigarette company inserted photo cards into each packet as an enticement to buy their brand. These were not of athletes, but of writers, artists, and musicians. When AN told ES he should plot the horoscope of each person pictured, ES started his collection by smoking much more than he normally did and begging the cards from others. These cards are now pasted into several oversize scrapbooks with detailed horoscopes written in Eduardo's precise and careful handwriting. They are in possession of Judith Hipskind and are to be deposited in the ES archives, S. Methodist U., Dallas.

14. What impressed AN most was that she had not a single "earth sign" in her horoscope, "mostly water," saying it reinforced her feeling of rootlessness.

15. UD-40. All quotes from this until noted otherwise.

16. Dearborn, Ferguson, and Martin all write of it, as does Perlès. HM's *Letters to Emil* are filled with detailed descriptions of the food he ate and the wine he drank. AN writes much about the enormous meals of meat, potatoes, and bread that she cooked and served him.

17. The following is based on her account in UD-40, and is from her point of view. There is also an edited version of this in *Incest,* 147–149.

18. These and many more references to AN's financial dealings are in AN/RC, JNC/USF. The passages cited are undated, and, based on internal evidence, are from mid-1933 to early 1935. "Mother managed to keep this from me, and I really had no idea of the degree to which Anaïs manipulated our finances until much later, when I read these letters after Mother's death." JNC, interview, 7/27/91. Also from the document he prepared especially for this biography, "From a Commentary on Anaïs's Latest Publication" *(Incest),* hereafter cited as "Commentary."

19. "Hemingway wrote about Durán [who became a general in the Spanish Republican Army in 1936] in *For Whom the Bell Tolls.* He became the go-between for Anaïs and her father. He tried it on me but it didn't work. I tutored [Gustavo Durán] in counterpoint to no avail. Handsome, spoiled, self-centered, brilliant, superficial, but a good friend of my Father's." JNC "Commentaries."

20. UD, Vol. 40.

21. These are notes appended to the end of UD-30. She has used dashes throughout, for which I have substituted periods.

22. HM wrote it throughout 1933. See Jay Martin, chapter 14 for further detail. Lowenfels was then the author of *USA with Music* and *Apollinaire: An Elegy.* With Michael Fraenkel, he was co-founder of "The Death School" of writing. They were also founders of the publishing venture "Anonymous," in which they hoped to establish art, not the ego of the artist, as the ideal.

23. UD-40. All quotes from this unless noted otherwise.

24. This was a lifelong trait, as AN frequently developed infatuations for openly homosexual men. Several of her gay friends and three of HG's as well independently expressed the view that AN was "one of those women who think all she has to do to convert a gay man is to seduce him." Each of these five persons "marveled at her naïveté." One spoke of her "clumsy, blundering attempts to seduce [him]," calling them "laughable in their innocence."

25. My account is based primarily on UD-41–42; interviews with JNC, RP, Walter Lowenfels; AN/RC, JNC/USF; and correspondence with Kathleen Chase. There is a highly unreliable version of this that AN rewrote specifically for D-1, 230–235. An example: Artaud supposedly tells her she is "the plumed serpent" (231), using language from Lawrence's novel of the same name. It is more likely that she invented these remarks because Artaud could neither speak nor read English and the novel had not yet been translated into French.

26. Michiko Kakutani, "The Diary as an End Rather Than the Means," *NY Times,* 12/4/92, C27. "Perhaps it explains why Nin, for all her florid posturing, often seems so oddly detached from the consequences of her actions, why she so often seems like a prisoner of her own narcissism, transfixed by her own image in the mirror."

27. Her written French never advanced beyond that of a schoolgirl's vocabulary and syntax. In later years, she would frequently begin letters to French scholars and journalists by saying "I do not write French well and so I shall reply in English." I am grateful to JNC's "Commentaries" for pointing out the paucity of AN's knowledge of Spanish, even poorer than her French.

15. HIM

1. UD-42, "Incest." All quotes from this until noted otherwise.

2. Information that follows is based on AN's account in UD-43, dated Aug. 25.

3. Maruca and her parents, Sr. and Sra. Rodríguez, joined them there. It is also where AN dined with the pianist Ignacy Paderewski. A different version of this trip from the one given in UD-43 appears in D-2, 248–249, and in *Incest,* 247–254.

4. It is not clear if she meant "Mother" (Rosa) or Maruca, for in earlier passages she uses the initial to refer to them both.

5. She also copied her letters to him, so a complete exchange of most of the correspondence exists in UD-42, 43, 44. When JN died in Havana in 1949, JNC was responsible for settling his estate and cleaning out his apartment. JN had not kept a single page of writing from AN, letter or otherwise.

6. In these early drafts, June's name has been changed from "Mona" to "Alraune," but there are actually three separate "Alraune" characters, delineated as I, II, and III. The manuscripts are AN/NU. For critical explication, see Valerie Harms, "Interaction and Cross-Fertilization: Miller and Nin," *Anaïs: IJ* 4, pp. 109–15; and "The Dream Is the Key: The Drafts That Became *House of Incest,*" *Anaïs: IJ* 5, pp. 102–110. Also in *Anaïs: IJ* 5: Henry Miller, "On *House of Incest,* a 'Foreword' and a 'Review,' " 111–114; Gunther Stuhlmann, "The Genesis of 'Alraune': Some notes on the making of *House of Incest,*" 115–123.

7. The first quote is from Stuhlmann, op. cit., 120; the second AN/HM in *Literate Passion,* 4/24/33.

8. The June who was initially the character Alraune I eventually gave way to one called Sabina. Alraune II eventually coalesced into the character of Jeanne, based on the real-life Louise de Vilmorin, and Alraune III became the voice of the narrator.

9. Erskine (Bradley's Columbia classmate) recommended that AN take chapters of her childhood diaries to Bradley as early as 1929, but she did not have the courage until HM insisted. (See *Literate Passion,* 152–153, 215–216 in particular, although there are many other pertinent references to Bradley throughout.) See also Erskine's *The Memory of Certain Persons,* 66, 321, 361.

10. Gunther Stuhlmann provided the following editorial note in *Literate Passion,* 215–216: "In an effort to make some material from the diary publishable without revealing the actual persons involved, AN, at various times, had 'adapted' sections by changing names . . . or by recasting diary material as fiction." All quotes from these pages until noted otherwise.

11. *Literate Passion,* 217–218.

12. UD-44. All quotes from this until noted otherwise.

13. Turning to sex as a way to mute his criticisms seems to have worked more than once, for AN repeats HM's method of "calming her down" in several other instances in UD-44, 47, 48.

16 "An emotional love tapeworm"

1. See Jay Martin, 278–279, for details concerning HM's writing. HM saw Rank once only, on 3/7/33 (see HM/AN in *Letters to AN,* 80–86, and *Literate Passion,* 136n.). AN was in analysis with Allendy throughout 1933, visiting Rank for the first time as noted on Nov. 7 (not Nov. 8, as Lieberman writes in *Rank,* 332, reprinted in *Anaïs: IJ* 3, p. 56). Nov. 8 was the date she began "to live without the diary." Discussed later in this chapter.

2. *Letters to AN,* 80 (the first quotation) and 81 (the second). All subsequent quotes are from HM's letter of 3/7/33, 81–86, until noted otherwise.

3. *Art and Artist* (New York: Alfred A. Knopf, 1932). The original unpublished German Ms is now in the Rank Collection, Manuscript and Rare Book Room, Butler Library, Columbia (hereafter OR/CU). AN wrote an article for *Journal of the Otto Rank Association* (hereafter *JORA*), which was reprinted as a preface for the 1989 Norton paperback edition. At the request of her French publisher, Éditions Stock, AN also wrote a preface to a reprinting of *La Volonté du Bonheur,* the French translation of Rank's *Wahrheit und Wirklichkeit* (Truth and Reality), reprinted in *JORA* 6, no. 2, Dec. 1971.

4. Roudinesco, Vol. I, 346, my translation. Other works I have consulted to write about Rank include: Frederick H. Allen, "Otto Rank: An Appreciation," *American Journal of Orthopsychiatry* 10, 1940, 186–187; S. Freud, *The Letters of Sigmund Freud,* ed. Ernst L. Freud (New York: Basic Books, 1975); *Freud/Jung Letters,* ed. William McGuire (Princeton U. Press, 1974); James Hillman, *The Myth of Analysis* (Evanston: Northwestern U. Press, 1972); Phyllis Grosskurth, *The Secret Ring: Freud's Inner Circle and the Politics of Psychoanalysis* (New York: Addison Wesley, 1991); Jack Jones, "Otto Rank: A Forgotten Heresy," *Commentary* 30, 219–29, 1960; Lieberman, *Acts of Will;* Paul Roazen, *Freud and His Followers* (New York: Alfred A. Knopf, 1974), and "Tola Rank" *Journal of the American Academy of Psychoanalysis* 18 (2), 1990, 247–259; Gunther Stuhlmann, "Remembering Dr. Rank," *Anaïs: IJ* 2, pp. 101–112,

1984; Keith Sward, "Self-actualization and Women: Rank and Freud Contrasted," *Journal of Humanistic Psychology* 20, 2: 5–26, 1980; Jessie Taft, *Otto Rank* (New York: Julian Press, 1958); Sherry Turkle, *Psychoanalytic Politics* (New York: Basic Books, 1978).

5. Besides Rank, they were Sandor Ferenczi, Hanns Sachs, Karl Abraham, Max Eitingon, and Ernest Jones. Their main target of attack was C. G. Jung, once Freud's heir apparent but with whom he had broken in a protracted battle of wills that took place throughout 1912–1914.

6. See Roazen, "Tola Rank." Hélène Rank Veltfort is a practicing analyst in San Francisco.

7. Roudinesco, Vol. I, 347, my trans.

8. UD-45. The dates of this volume are Feb. 1934–July 6, 1934, but inside the front cover she inserted enough loose pages of writing to make one doubt that she followed Rank's order. Some of these are dated 1/14/34, when she checked herself into the hotel, but the greater part is undated. All diary quotes are from this volume until noted otherwise.

9. AN's emphasis.

10. This contradicts Rank's writings about incest. Perhaps he told her what she wanted to hear, or perhaps she told herself what she wanted to hear and transposed it into the diary as Rank's advice. What she wrote parallels the Nin family motto, engraved on the signet ring Joaquín Nin wore proudly: "If hurt, forgive. If humiliated, don't forgive." In UD-43, AN describes how she and JN talked about the ring and the Nin family history one afternoon after coitus in Valescure. The ring is now in possession of JNC, who provided me with the Spanish translation of the motto.

11. AN's emphasis.

12. HG paid Moricand for lessons; within the year, AN elevated him to one of her "children," and like HM, gave him a monthly stipend as well.

13. A family scandal erupted when HG and AN's wedding gift, an expensive crystal bowl purchased to show the Sánchez family wealth they did not have, was returned. Ana María wrote a letter dictated by her husband, saying they would not accept something so valuable from a person whose "moral and spiritual values" were so shockingly different from theirs. "End of the Ana Maria episode," AN wrote after pasting the undated letter into the diary. Frequently she made some comment as she did with a headline clipped from a New York newspaper: "NY girl ends life over man." "Tell him not to boast of it," AN wrote.

14. AN's emphasis.

15. Tola Rank was sensitive to the nuances of her husband's feelings and was probably aware by this time that AN was trying to seduce him and he was on the verge of responding.

16. These letters of AN/RW are in the Harry Ransom Library, Humanities Research Center, U. of Texas, Austin (hereafter AN/RW, HRC). I am grateful to West's biographer, Carl Rollyson, for making them known to me, and also additional letters by RW in other collections, which I shall cite accordingly.

17. AN wrote about RW in D-3, 31–32 and 52, and in UD-45–48. RW's letter to Gordon N. Ray is in the Pierpont Morgan Library, New York.

18. In her letter to Ray, West said Nin's accounts "outdid Anthony [West, her estranged son]."

19. The account that follows is based primarily on RW's letter to Ray and UD-45.
20. The phrase is the title of Donald Spence's book, cited elsewhere in this text, and a useful source in this context. I am also grateful to Lila Rosenblum for her insights on this matter.
21. RW/GNR, Pierpont Morgan Library. All quotes from this until noted otherwise.
22. At this time, RW told Ray she had only a cook and one housemaid. All subsequent quotes from UD-45, until noted otherwise.
23. RW says it was dinner. AN says she brought *Black Spring* to RW's attention; in D-3, 31–32, she says it was *Tropic of Cancer*. RW, in her letter to Gordon N. Ray, denies ever seeing either of these, in book or ms. However, in an exchange of letters with Peter Green, West's literary agent, (AN's n.d., Green's reply 5/8/34, RW/HRC), West clearly gave the Ms of *Black Spring* to Green in hopes that he could place it.
24. RW's version is correct: Laughton appeared that season in *Othello*.
25. When Hinz alluded to passages in UD that AN wrote about RW's alleged sexual abuse by her father, RW counseled Gordon N. Ray to "Pause, I think, for a stiff drink." RW admitted to the established fact that her father left home forever when she was almost nine, but not to sexual abuse. She claimed that AN distorted an analytic memory from "the dawn of consciousness" of "a latent, highly disguised sexual fantasy" about her father, which RW recognized as such and discussed in her analysis and subsequently with AN. She asked Ray: "What do I do about this? Where should I park a disclaimer of all this nonsense?" RW/GNR, Pierpont Morgan Library.
26. N.d., on stationery of Joaquín Nin, 27, rue Henri-Heine, Paris 16, HRC.
27. RW to AN, copied into UD-45. AN has dated it 5/18/34.
28. AN may have succumbed to HM's entreaties not to upbraid Waverly Root for his condescending review of her DHL book, but from then on, she did not hesitate to write scathing letters lambasting reviewers for unfavorable reviews. (All these letters are in the UCLA archives.) In this instance, she wrote a fairly restrained letter to Peter Green, simply asking him to return HM's Mss, as the publisher Jonathan Cape was interested (he was not). Green replied that the Ms was with RW, that he did not accept "isolated works" for negotiation, and that "Mr. Miller's work in general is not likely to appeal to me." These two letters are in RW/HRC.

17. Birth

1. UD-45. All quotations from this until noted otherwise.
2. I asked three obstetricians in France to read AN's original account and all agreed that "she must have made this up, she must not have wanted an abortion. All three have performed legal abortions and believe in their efficacy. They agree that AN's mental state had a great deal to do with

her hesitation, and that the doctor who aborted her in her third trimester was guilty of "gross negligence."

3. Hélène Rank Veltfort, the Ranks' only child, said "Both my parents were so European and so civilized about it." Tel. interview, 3/13/93.

4. UD-46. All quotes from this until noted otherwise.

5. One of the physicians I spoke to noted that there were already many refugee doctors in France who had to resort to "less than legal" treatment to survive, and this doctor may have been one of them.

6. HG still held the lease but the tenant had departed. The account that follows is based primarily on UD-46. All quotes are from this unless noted otherwise. HG never wrote about the birth except for occasional fleeting references in AN/HG *Journal.* A heavily edited and substantially rewritten account is in *Incest,* 372–385. AN converted her experience into the story "Birth," published in *Under a Glass Bell* (Swallow, 1948) 96–101, reprinted in *Anaïs Nin Reader,* ed. Philip K. Jason (New York: Avon Books, 1973), 130–134.

7. RC returned to Paris the day after receiving a cable announcing the stillbirth. Her attempts to comfort AN by telling her she must try again as soon as possible to have another child were misinterpreted as uncaring and unsympathetic.

8. There is an edited version of her affair with Andard in *Incest* and a biographical note that describes him as a "French politician and publisher of popular authors." The note says he also "expressed interest" in publishing AN, HM, and Perlès. His only interest was in the affair with AN.

9. Most of the participants in Rank's program were American psychiatric social workers, others were mainly Parisians interested in Rank's ideas, among them Hilaire Hiler, an American journeyman artist who briefly owned and managed the celebrated Jockey bar, and whom HM recruited into giving him art lessons. Like so many others whom Anaïs Nin met briefly, Hiler provided material for a portrait that allowed her to use someone else's name to reflect back upon herself in the published diaries (D-2, 67–68, 107).

10. Many years later he was still upset to remember how he had been taken in: "She never realized how painful it was for me to go behind Hugo's back. Hugo, whom I loved. She tried the 'Rank trick' many times after that, but was always turned down as soon as I realized what she was trying to have me do. Lies, lies, lies. What a plague." JNC, "Commentary," 11/27/92.

11. Otto Rank's letters and clippings are pasted into UD-46 and 47.

12. See Grosskurth, *Secret Ring.*

13. Joaquín Nin-Culmell has had "a life-time devotion to St. Ignatius." From Newsletter of the Gleason Library Associates, No. 24, p. 5, Summer 1993, U. of SF. This was a period of particularly devout religiosity in JNC's life and AN felt it was her responsibility to keep him from entering a religious order. JNC fax, 8/22/93.

14. "Your soul is being fought over." Altermann's phrase has more to do with the dispute between good and evil than with Anaïs's inner combats. For Altermann, Allendy and Rank "were not on the side of the angels." JNC, fax, 9/8/93.

15. UD-47.

16. UD-48.

17. UD-46, OR to AN, 10/26/34.

18. She has appended a list of these

nightclubs, shows, and restaurants to the end of UD-48.

19. Information that follows is from UD-46, until noted otherwise.

20. "Canalize" was one of her invented locutions, coming from her faulty familiarity with three languages. At times she uses this word to mean other invented locutions: "cannibalize" and "channelize." In this instance, either meaning fits her intention.

21. UD-47. All quotes from this until noted otherwise.

22. She copied the long list into UD-47.

23. All quotations from UD-48 until noted otherwise.

24. UD-47.

25. One of these women, although quite elderly, is still alive and granted me an interview. I spoke to the daughter of another, who as a teenager remembered a weekend visit by AN and HG. As they are private persons who have never been in the public eye, I see no reason to divulge their identities here.

26. She wrote to several of them, and some of her letters have survived and been sold to libraries and private collectors. Dr. E. James Lieberman has made one of them available to me; I have been shown others by one former patient and the daughter of the other. As these persons are all private citizens, I will paraphrase the contents but will not reveal their names.

27. She found Nin "soothing but scary: there was just something about her that kept sucking me in, like an undertow. She was too needy. After a while I was frightened and never went back or answered her letters or phone calls." Anonymous—interview, Greenwich, CT, May 1992.

28. *Reflections,* 118.

29. UD-48. All quotes from this until noted otherwise.

30. In notes Hugo made for his analysis with Bogner in the 1960s, he alluded to "one or two brief flings" during this time.

31. Information that follows is from RW to Gordon N. Ray, n.d., Pierpont Morgan Library, and UD-48.

32. Arthur T. Polos, *A History of Industrial Design* (Cambridge, MIT Press, 1983), 288. Norman Bel Geddes (1893–1958) was considered a Renaissance man, successful in advertising, theater design, painting, illustration, and graphic design. He conceived bold window displays, mounted design exhibits, and staged extravaganzas. He was an inventor and architect, product planner and industrial designer. He believed in "the drawing power of grand spectacles and soaring design concepts" and held a lifelong conviction that "the worlds of fact and fancy are often inseparable" (Polos, 289). This may be why he and AN were initially attracted to each other. RW accused AN of writing "quite obscene letters which caused [Bel Geddes] embarrassment." More likely, they were AN's usual effusive declarations of undying passion, even when what she truly felt was the opposite. RW also told Ray she never saw AN again after this period in New York, but that AN pursued her for the rest of her life, hoping to persuade RW to write blurbs or review her books. RW was mistaken about not seeing AN again, as chapter 19 will show, for she visited Louveciennes in Oct. 1935. I am grateful to Katney Bair and Niko Courtelis for research assistance about Bel Geddes.

33. UD-48.

18. Friendships with Women

1. UD-48. All AN's diary quotes from this until noted otherwise.
2. I am grateful to Tom Thompson, owner of Carrefour Press, for making the AN–Michael Fraenkel (hereafter Carrefour) correspondence available to me.
3. UD-48 and undated AN/Carrefour, c. 1935–1936.
4. She held on to this title until 1938, when she wrote Fraenkel (Carrefour, n.d.) that her new novel would not be called "Chaotica" after all, but *Winter of Artifice*.
5. RW to Gordon N. Ray, Pierpont Morgan Library. RW later remembered (interview with Julie Davidson, *The Scotsman,* Aug. 18, 1982, p. 1) saving HM from drowning during a house party at AN's: "HM got very drunk as usual. He tried to take a bath half-dressed and AN and I discovered him under the water blowing bubbles. We pulled him out and . . . the rest of his clothes came off. I may say that HM without clothes was even less appealing than HM with clothes." Of AN, RW said, "She's the only person I know who committed bigamy quite calmly and got away with it. She also falsified her memoirs." RW's biographer, Carl Rollyson, graciously called this to my attention.
6. AN writes that RW told her in some detail of a new lover she wished to take.
7. Her capitalization.
8. HG's calling card is pasted into UD-48.
9. The original of this letter has disappeared. AN copied its contents into UD-48.
10. UD-48. At various times she writes his name as "Ferri" and "Feri," but in the Carrefour letters, he is always "The Boy."
11. UD-49.
12. Letter, n.d., on Barbizon Plaza Hotel stationery, in UD-48. I think it is misfiled, as contents bear more relevance to UD-50, post-Jan. 1936.
13. AN/RC, n.d.
14. As the woman is a private citizen, I shall not reveal her full identity here. A thorough check in the archives of *Time* shows that the woman's husband did not hold a significant enough position to be listed on any of the mastheads from 1923 to 1940, so it is unlikely that he worked there in anything other than a minor position.
15. UD-50.
16. According to UD-49, the three participants in the orgy met for others several times afterward.
17. A harpist and graduate of the Conservatory of Music in Mexico City, TS was a member of the Salzédo Harp Ensemble and the Lawrence Harp Quintet as well as a talented solo recitalist.
18. An expression used repeatedly throughout her diaries, so I shall cite no particular instance here.
19. Information that follows is from UD-50; and interviews and conversations with JNC. GNR (fax, 11/14/94) wrote that TR told her that "*his* father told *him* that Anaïs had invited her father to have sex with her, but that the father had refused her. . . . As far as I know, my father always thought that they had *not* had sex, and he seemed horrified that she had proposed it." I am grateful to the following members of the seminar on Psychoanalysis and Feminism at New York Institute for the Humanities who devoted a session to this subject and

have been generous with their time, friendship, and suggestions for further research ever since: Donna Bassin, Jessica Benjamin, Muriel Dimen, Elsa First, Virginia Goldner, Adrienne Harris, Adria Schwartz, and Susan Shapiro. Other mental health professionals I have consulted include Patricia Louis, Linda Rankin, and Phyllis O. Ziman Tobin.

20. Martin, *Always Merry and Bright,* 313, 314; AN/HG undated correspondence, UCLA; UD-49, 50. In *Anaïs Nin: A Bibliography,* Benjamin Franklin V writes that *The Winter of Artifice* (1939) is "the third and last volume" published in Henry Miller's "Villa Seurat" series. The others were Lawrence Durrell's *Black Book* and Miller's *Max and the White Phagocytes* (both 1938). Mike Harris, former owner of Carrefour Press, has annotated the AN/MF correspondence. In a letter to MF on Barbizon Plaza stationery (n.d. but definitely 1936), AN says she agrees to anything he plans for publication of *House of Incest;* Harris interprets this as MF's not only organizing the publication but also paying for it. It was actually paid for by HG, who also helped MF financially the following year when he suffered reversals after the death of his partner and Walter Lowenfels allegedly cheated him out of other money.

21. Thorvald's daughter, Gayle Nin Rosenkrantz, remembers that the story of her father's detention at Ellis Island became a happy, oft-repeated part of her family's history. In it, TN entertained his children with tales of the Island's spookiness and gloom and how eagerly he greeted daylight and the opening of the Office of Immigration and Naturalization.

22. Officials at the several shipping lines I consulted think it highly unlikely that a ship just completing an Atlantic crossing would not only take responsibility for feeding anything other than the most rudimentary meal to a detained passenger, let alone his guest, but also that a cabin would be prepared for the nonpaying guest to spend the night. The only semilogical explanation they offer is that she stayed on board so long that no taxi could be found on the deserted piers and so the ship's duty officer was forced to let her remain on board. Members of the Psychoanalysis and Feminism seminar think it likely that the incident took place because of the "characteristic" language of incest that AN uses to describe it, but they also caution that it may be in large part a "screen memory" of an incident that happened in her past and which she is transposing to this particular situation.

19. *Nanankepichu*

1. UD-49.

2. UD-50.

3. There is a long, detailed account of the trip in UD-50, complete with many photographs; repeated virtually verbatim in D-2, 71–81.

4. For the most recent and most complete account of this novel's publishing history and critical reception in the years since, see Philip Jason, *Anaïs Nin and Her Critics,* 32–39.

5. UD-50. All diary quotations from this until noted otherwise.
6. Louveciennes was unrented and HG was responsible for the lease for the next year. In D-2, 138–139, she describes her sorrow at the dismantling of Louveciennes. There is a brief mention of dismantling Louveciennes in UD-49–53, but her sadness at its dismantling is secondary to her joy at taking the Passy apartment. In *Anaïs: IJ* 7, p. 32, the editor's note reads that the text there is "drawn from the *typed* [my emphasis] transcripts of the original diaries," which "varies, at times, from the published edited version, and includes much previously unpublished material." This is another instance in which AN rewrote substantially when she typed the original diaries in their many manifestations before they were finally published.
7. AN/RC, undated, JNC/USF. RC was spending most of her time in these years in Mallorca. After JNC received his diploma at the Schola Cantorum in Paris, he entered Paul Dukas's composition class at the Paris Conservatory in 1932. The apartment at 18 bis, avenue de Versailles, was still their main residence and they lived there until World War II, when they relocated to New York. JNC concertized extensively in those years: 1934–1935, he went alone to Havana while RC remained in Mallorca; 1936, they returned to Havana together; 1936, after the beginning of the Spanish Civil War, they went together to Milan, Rome, and Venice on an Italian tour. In 1938, JNC assumed full financial responsibility for himself and his mother.
8. Gunther Stuhlmann has completed scholarship proving that Gonzalo's surname contains an accent: Moré. He will publish detailed accounts in forthcoming issues of *Anaïs: An International Journal,* starting in 1995.
9. AN writes briefly of this in UD-52.
10. UD-50 and 51.
11. UD-53.
12. UD-51.
13. The account in D-2, 118–119, was created specifically for publication, melding the two houseboats she rented. There, she writes of the second boat, owned by the actor Michel Simon. "René" is fictionalized as a worker who lives on the boat in exchange for taking care of it, but he was a character connected with the first boat. My account is based primarily on UD-51, 52.
14. Some of these passages are an early version of the childbirth story and one about ragpickers, inspired by the chaos of the Huara-Moré apartment. "Birth" was first published in *Twice a Year* (New York), no. 1, Fall-Winter 1938, 132–137; "Ragtime" is part of *Under a Glass Bell* (New York and Harmondsworth: Penguin Books, 1978), 60–64. There is also one page about sitting on a roof in China, which in and of itself never became a finished entity, but various phrases appear later in *Winter of Artifice.*
15. UD-51.
16. UD-52. All quotes from this until noted otherwise.
17. AN's emphasis.
18. Published in 1954 by Newstory Books, British Book Centre, Paris and New York. The quotation is from UD-52, 2/4/37. (She had begun occasionally to date her entries.) All quotes from this until noted otherwise.
19. UD-53.
20. Ibid.
21. Ibid.
22. Ibid.
23. UD-52.

NOTES

20. The Three Musqueteers

1. Martin, *Always Merry and Bright,* 326.

2. A copy of the 4 p. typed letter is in UD-55, which covers the period Sept.–Nov. 1937 and is reproduced in *A Literate Passion,* 306. There, Gunther Stuhlmann (ed.) dated AN's letter [March 1937] and HM's reply "Sunday" [March 1937]. I believe the letter was written in Sept. because of its placement in Vol. 55 and because there are similar corresponding outbursts in other UD diaries of the time, Vols. 54 and 56. In Vol. 55, AN writes "this letter to H. I never showed him. I wrote it a few days ago and when I saw he was sick, I put it away." Several days later, her anger revived, she typed another copy and sent it to him.

3. Stuart Gilbert's foreword to *House of Incest* is reprinted in Zaller, *Casebook,* 1. In UD-53, AN quotes a letter Gilbert supposedly wrote to her: "I have never read anything like it. The lucidity is amazing. You let yourself go and at the same time you are seeing your self. It is a dédoublement. You are at once the warmest bloodest person I know and the coldest. At times you are absolutely ruthless." Perhaps he actually made comments such as these, but it is highly unlikely: the language is entirely AN's own and his original letter is missing. Gilbert was renowned for his meticulous phrasing, proper diction, and elegant vocabulary. He was also noted for his reticence to make any sort of personal remark, especially compliments.

4. Letter from Faber & Faber to Denise Clairouin, inserted into UD-53.

5. UD-54. This entry is c. late Aug. 1937 and strengthens my assertion that the letters were exchanged later in the year than March.

6. For the Miller-Durrell correspondence, see *The Durrell-Miller Letters: 1935–80* (Faber & Faber: London and Boston, 1988), ed. Ian S. MacNiven; and *Lawrence Durrell and Henry Miller: A Private Correspondence* (New York: E. P. Dutton, 1963).

7. He chose Charles Norden for his second novel, *Panic Spring,* published in 1937.

8. MacNiven, op. cit., 2–3.

9. Later published as "Asylum in the Snow" in *Seven.* In D-2, 150, AN writes that the story was dedicated to her, and the editor's note on this page says the story was reprinted in 1947 "without the dedication."

10. UD-54. All quotes from this until noted otherwise.

11. MacNiven, op. cit., 38, dates this letter [end Dec.? 1936]. In UD-52, AN writes sometime in mid-Jan. 1937 that she liked his "Christmas Carol" and was sending *House of Incest.* As both HM and LD complain frequently about how long it took mail to arrive in either Paris or Corfu, it is quite likely that LD did not write this letter until mid-Feb. 1937, at the earliest.

12. UD-54. See also D-2, 223, for AN's revised version. For the following account, I have also consulted Alfred Perlès's *My Friend Lawrence Durrell* (London, Village Press, 1961), and Douglas Stone, *Alfred Perlès: Renegade and Writer* (London: Village Press, 1974).

13. Perlès, *Lawrence Durrell* (London: The Village Press, 1973), 11.

14. On 4/1/69, Folder 70, AN asked rhetorically why HM stopped writing after the trilogy: "Did he say all he wanted to say? Or was it the devastating criticism by Durrell at the end of their correspondence: 'When will you stop lavatory writing?' Durrell really killed the father. Nobody noticed the assassination, not even Henry."

15. The account of the conversation that follows is taken from UD-54. She rewrote it significantly for D-2, 231–236, and in the process rendered it ordinary and did not convey the excitement she felt in the original text.

16. For fuller discussion, see Martin, *Always Merry,* 312–313. It began on 11/1/35, when the three men decided to write a 1,000-page "correspondence" using the play as their point of departure for a "kind of artists' cathedral, a vast outline of the themes, plots, myths, fables, fictions, and characters which future artists would employ." The real subject, according to Martin, was "reality—super-reality, surreality, dream reality—and the art based on the multiple conception of reality." AN invited herself to participate in the written correspondence by sending letters to Fraenkel (in the Carrefour correspondence), but he quickly eliminated her contributions. After this, her only comments in the diaries are disparaging ones.

17. Elaine Feinstein, in *Lawrence and the Women: The Intimate Life of D. H. Lawrence* (New York: HarperCollins, 1993), points to recent feminist scholarship that faults his fiction "because he increasingly came to see liberation for women entirely in terms of a saving sexual relationship, and his writings show a mounting rage against women's desires to use their minds and express their individuality." It is my contention that this is the time in AN's life when she began to give up on the idea of such a relationship and began to consider her own intellectual concerns as separate and individual from her sexual needs.

18. UD-55. All quotes from this until noted otherwise.

19. The book was for many years considered to be one of the best studies of the female psyche. Dr. Harding was a leader of the Jungian school of analysis and taught at the Institute of Analytical Psychology in New York, where she also had a private practice.

20. In UD-56, she writes of working concurrently on three novels and of "do[ing] Louise [de Vilmorin] and her brothers better than Cocteau's Enfants Terrible . . . June better than Djuna Barnes' Nightwood . . . Artaud better than Carl Suarez Procession enchainé. I want to do my father, Eduardo. It is Rank I am doing now—fully."

21. In the last years of her life, AN refused to let a fan letter go unanswered, saying she had vowed at the time of her "humiliation" by Barnes that she would never be guilty of such rudeness. RP, interview, 7/91.

22. Copy of letter, n.d., to Thurema Sokol, inserted into UD-54, and UD-56.

23. RC was in Italy with JNC. When her mother was away, AN often used the apartment for her own purposes. She had several assignations "on Joaquín's bed" before meeting Gonzalo, whom she also allowed to stay there with Helba when they were between apartments. She kept all this secret from her mother and brother. UD-51, 54, 55; also JNC interview 1991, and fax 1993.

24. UD-55. All quotes from this until noted otherwise.

25. UD-57.

26. Henry Miller, *Scenario* (A Film

with Sound) (Paris: Obelisk Press, 1937).

27. UD-55, 56, 57. All quotes from these diaries, all emphasis AN's until noted otherwise.

28. Printed first in *The Criterion,* Vol. XVII, No. 66, reprinted in *The Booster,* Dec.–Jan. 1938.

29. UD-55. Inserted into this volume is AN's letter to Jean Paulhan describing the diary, showing "that it is not, as so many diaries are, a static, reflective or meditative, or analytical symphony. Each volume contains . . . a novel, an incident, a drama," all of which she presented in outline form. Even at this early stage, the exaggeration and outright fictionalizing of her life are in evidence.

30. I have chosen not to reveal her patient's name, so I will not cite this passage.

31. Letter from the editor, T. Rokotov, Moscow, 11/10/37, inserted into Vol. 56, which covers the period ending Jan. 1938. As she writes about this letter in that volume, it appears she did not receive it until early 1938.

32. From a flyer in French and English that HM circulated for "subscriptions," which AN called "another begging letter." Inserted into UD-55. HM announced that he planned to publish "all 54 volumes," leading to André Maurois's reply that he wanted only one as he already had too many books and nowhere to store them. A refusal to subscribe came from "book collector Abramson," who gave as his reason "H. of I. means absolutely nothing, it's Joyce without passion and Gertrude Stein without ancestry." UD-56.

33. I wish to thank Dorothy Norman for personally granting me access to her archives, especially her correspondence with AN, which is in the Beinecke Library, Yale U. (hereafter DN/Yale). Judith Mara Gutman made other pertinent materials known to me. I have also relied on UD-56, 57, for the account that follows, and Dorothy Norman to AN, 2/7/38. DN/Yale. AN was eventually published in *Twice a Year,* no. 5/6 (Fall-Winter 1940, Spring-Summer 1941), 413–422, and revised and included in *Ladders to Fire,* 69–77 of the Swallow ed. "From: Diary—Volume One (Age 11–12)" was published in *Twice a Year,* no. 7 (Fall-Winter 1941), 48–56.

34. AN to Dorothy Norman, n.d., Hôtel Acropolis, Paris. DN/Yale.

35. "From: Diary—Volume One."

36. UD-57, entitled "Les Mots Flottants." She also listed the places where she lived between Jan. and March 1938. "30 Quai de Passy; Hôtel Acropolis, 31 rue de Buci; Péniche 'La Belle Aurore,' Quai des Tuilleries entre Pont Royal et Pont Solferino."

37. UD-57.

38. UD-58: "The day of Gonzalo's mad outburst I had been pregnant and had taken an injection which unnerved me. The shock was tremendous." This is her only comment.

39. Information that follows is from UD-57 and 58, and letters, n.d., AN/RC, JNC/USF.

40. These appear throughout her diaries from her teenage years until her late adulthood.

41. These thoughts are confided to a loose sheaf of undated papers Hugo wrote for his analyst, Dr. Inge Bogner, sometime after 1952 and probably before 1962 (based on internal evidence).

42. Around this time, JNC received his first royalty payment, from the Oxford U. Press, for his piano sonata subsequently known as "Sonata Breve" (now published by Broude Int. Editions). He sent the royalty payment to HG, offering to begin a systematic repayment of all the money HG had provided for his education and his and RC's living expenses, but HG declined to accept it. JNC, fax, 9/8/93, and interviews 1991, 1992. GNR said (tel. conversation, Dec. 1993) that her father also contributed to RC's expenses throughout the 1930s and 1940s.

43. UD-58 (March–Sept. 1938), "Nearer the Moon," written at "Péniche de la Belle Aurore, Quai des Tuileries, Paris 1er; Bad Ragaz, Suisse; Hôtel Acropolis, 160 Blvd. St.-Germain."

44. They were found among his papers and are now in the JNC archives at USF. Even after AN's death, HG continued to amass them, as one by Ruth Adam entitled *A Woman's Place, 1910–1975,* shows.

45. AN to RC, undated second page of a letter (first page is missing). JNC/USF.

46. AN to RC, n.d., but internal evidence suggests end of July 1938. JNC/USF. My emphasis in both cases.

47. The account that follows is based on UD-58–61; JNC interviews 1991, 1992, faxes, conversations; AN/RC undated letters, JNC/USF. There is also an account in D-2, 297–302, which is basically similar to the UCLA diaries.

48. UD-61 (Jan. 1939–April 1939).

49. "The concert scene was beginning to close down, there were more opportunities in the US, and I was asked to go back to Middlebury. After that, I received an appointment to teach at Williams College . . . and I went there in the fall of 1940. My sister and I were pretty much estranged in those years, so she and Mother mostly communicated by letter. We did see each other on the rare occasion when we went to New York." JNC, interview, 7/26/91.

50. UD-59. All quotes from this until noted otherwise.

51. AN to LD, undated first page of letter inserted in UD-60.

52. Ibid. (Jan. 1939–April 1939). All quotes from this until noted otherwise.

53. His most famous and endearing is *Mr. Hulot's Holiday.*

54. AN to RC, n.d., JNC/USF.

55. AN to RC, 11/15/38, JNC/USF.

56. HM's letters are inserted into UD-61, from which these quotes are taken.

57. HG to AN, Aug. 1939, inserted into UD-61. Also, a second partial letter (she has ripped off the top half of the page and kept only the bottom half) states that she will find $400 in the bank and each month thereafter will deposit another $200. In her own curious arithmetic, she figures that Lantelme will require 2,000 francs, and Helba and Gonzalo 3,000, which equals $125, thus leaving her approximately $300 to do with as she pleases.

58. HM to AN, Sept. 25 and Oct. 2, both from Corfu, also Sept. 20 to Obelisk Press. All letters inserted into UD-61.

59. Dated 9/20/39, inserted into UD-61. Kahane had died and his son, Maurice Girodias, had been drafted into the French army. Vol. 62 (Oct. 1939–Nov. 1940).

60. UD-62.

NOTES

21. The Literary Madam

1. UD-62. All diary quotes from this until noted otherwise.

2. Miss Frances Steloff owned the Gotham Book Mart. For more than half a century, she was one of the most beloved figures in the New York literary world for her unstinting efforts to promote contemporary literature. She was dedicated to furthering AN's work throughout her long life and always did her best to sell each book as it appeared. To this day, there is an "Anaïs Nin shelf" in the bookstore. Dorothy Norman was married to an heir of the Philadelphia family that owned Sears, Roebuck. She used his money to support liberal causes and to advance contemporary literature. I have relied in part on her correspondence (DN/Yale) and her memoir, *Encounters* (Harcourt Brace Jovanovich, 1987).

3. AN eventually came to address Frances Steloff by her first name in person or in correspondence, but when speaking of her to others, she was always "Miss Steloff." Undated letters to Lila Rosenblum (privately held) and Gore Vidal (Vidal archives, U. Wisconsin, Madison).

4. They were living in Maverick, the colony of artists and writers founded by Hervey White.

5. HM's "Universe of Death" section of the DHL MS appeared in the first issue of *The Phoenix.*

6. Cooney attacked HM as one of the writers "merely seeking to further their own names and fame." *Phoenix,* Vol. 2, no. 1 (Spring 1939), 118.

7. A version of this weekend appears in D-2, in which AN makes it appear that Robert (Symmes) Duncan was in residence, but according to Blanche Cooney, he was not yet there. In UD-62, AN says they met in her hotel room in mid-Feb. after he wrote to her from Berkeley and Woodstock. This version was also confirmed by Virginia Admiral in tel. conversations 4/22/92 and 4/29/92 and in interviews with her and Marjorie McKee, 4/30/92.

8. B. Cooney, *In My Own Sweet Time,* 101.

9. Ekbert Faas, Duncan's biographer, cites D-3, 18, 82, 100, and says they met first on Christmas Day, 1939, at the Cooneys' in Woodstock, but AN and HG did not go to Woodstock until the second weekend in Jan. 1940. AN compressed a great deal of information to create the account in D-3, which is factually incorrect. In UD-64, she sets the first meeting with Duncan in Feb. 1940, in the George Washington Hotel, where she was then living. Her letters to Duncan in the Bancroft Library, UC Berkeley, corroborate the UCLA diary.

10. For the account that follows, I have relied upon UD-62, 63, 64; Ekbert Faas, *Young Robert Duncan, Portrait of the Poet as Homosexual in Society* (Santa Barbara: Black Sparrow Press, 1983), and "The Barbaric Friendship with Robert: A Biographical Palimpsest," *Mosaic* XI/2 (Winnipeg: U. of Manitoba Press, 1978), Evelyn J. Hinz, guest ed., 141–152; RD/Bancroft; and interviews with Marjorie McKee (formerly Mrs. Robert Duncan) and Virginia Admiral, 4/30/92.

11. *The Phoenix,* Vol. 2, no. 3 (Easter, 1940), 157. This was the same issue in which AN's diary fragment was published.

12. From the announcement in *Phoenix.*

13. Comment about *Twice a Year* from *Time,* 12/25/39. *The Phoenix* was founded by two Yale undergraduates, the poet Reed Wittemore and James Jesus Angleton, who later became known as the CIA's "master spy hunter" (from the title of Tom Mangold's book, *James Jesus Angleton: the C.I.A.'s Master Spy Hunter* (New York: Simon & Schuster, 1991). 35. In a letter, n.d., RD/Bancroft, she tells him to send his writings to LD in Athens and also to "J. Angleton, 1456 Yale Station, New Haven."

14. A version of this story later appeared as "I Shall Never Forgive the King of England," in *Matrix,* Vol. III, no. 3 (Phil., 1941), 28–33. It was rewritten as "Houseboat" and collected in all editions of *Under a Glass Bell* (1944).

15. The reprinted portion was given the title of the book and appeared in *Ritual,* Vol. 1, no. 1 (Annapolis, Spring 1940), 12–16. Duncan published a second installment from the novel in his third magazine, *Experimental Review,* no. 2, (Woodstock, NY, Nov. 1940), 33–37. In an undated letter, RD/Bancroft, she tells him to use whatever he likes as she has no other writings and cannot get the diaries out of France.

16. AN to RD, undated letter, RD/Bancroft.

17. These are collected as "Notebooks" and are in RD/Bancroft.

18. Between Feb. and Sep. she lived in a studio at 249½ W. 20th St., in a furnished apartment at 33 Washington Sq. West, in another studio "across from the Provincetown Playhouse" in Greenwich Village, and when HM was in New York, in various hotels on Lexington Ave., in the 60s, to be near him. For most of this time HG was traveling between London and New York on bank business.

19. "We sent him to a [bank] vice president who then arranged his transfer to America." UD-62.

20. Virginia Admiral confirmed that AN resented Patchen's demands for support because "he did not properly act like her supplicant." Interview, 4/30/92.

21. The "Elena" story appeared in *Twice a Year* as "Woman in the Myth," No. 5/6 (Fall-Winter 1940/ Spring-Summer 1941), 413–422. AN was paid $35, which she gave to HM.

22. Although she wrote that Leaf wanted to be her lover, she did not write that she had sex with him as well. She did write, however, that they wanted her to support them in New York and that she refused. Her many other financial responsibilities were so great, she wrote, that she was "able to rebel against them." UD-62.

23. The passage quoted earlier about her financial responsibilities is filled with contradictions that make one doubt the entire account. For example, she writes there that *she* was burdened by the "heavy expenses of the abortion." If Hugo accompanied her, he surely paid for it and it would not have come from her household expenses. Hugo was a willing accomplice in helping her to end her pregnancies because he knew (even if he could not admit it to himself) the odds were strong that any child she carried would not be his. Interviews with Virginia Admiral, 4/30/92; Lila Rosenblum, 10/4/90; James Leo Herlihy, 7/17/91; Anne Geismar, 7/15/91; Bebe Barron, 7/31/91; and others who will be cited where appropriate.

24. In another example of convoluted reasoning, she conveniently forgot that the Lawrence book was already published when she met Henry, and gave him credit for it; said only after the affair with Gonzalo began was she able to write *House of Incest* (which was already finished), and she credited John Dudley with *Winter of Artifice* although it had been published long before they met.

25. Virginia Admiral also admitted (interview, 4/30/92) that she was not above using Anaïs herself: "My role was to string along with Anaïs as long as Robert felt as he did about her. We were just two kids from Berkeley and as she took us to parties and fed us, well . . ."

26. Ibid. AN admits this in UD-63, where she writes disparagingly of the physical relationship of RD and ES.

27. VA, interview, 4/30/92.

28. This is the same HM who wrote to AN from Greece, 12/4/39: "Don't you realize that you have put yourself into the situation you are in? . . . The money problem is only an excuse you give yourself. Everybody—myself included—would manage somehow to exist if you stopped payments. Supposing you died, do you ever think of that?" Letter inserted into UD-62.

29. Millicent Rogers remained in AN's employ until the late 1960s and was her friend and confidante until AN's death in 1977.

30. UD-63 (Dec. 1940–June 1941). All diary quotes from this until noted otherwise.

31. Both qualities were highly praised and put her on worldwide bestseller lists when they were collected and published as *Delta of Venus* and *Little Birds* in the 1970s.

32. For further information see Blanche Cooney, "Eduardo—A Memoir," *Anaïs: IJ* 9, p. 17; and Faas, *Young Robert Duncan,* where ES is called "Paul."

33. There is a card from HG inserted into UD-63 that accompanied the fountain pen he bought for AN to replace the one AN claimed was stolen by RD.

34. Two undated letters, RD/Bancroft, the second bearing Gonzalo's address, 249½ W. 20th St.

35. Information that follows is from UD-63.1; interview with DN, 3/29/90; and correspondence, DN/Yale.

36. I interviewed a number of these persons, all eager to "tell" whether or not they had actually "kissed" AN. This appellation is among the kinder ones they offered. As much of their testimony was untrustworthy, and as I have not otherwise used it in forming my views of AN, I see no reason to dignify their remarks by citing their names here.

37. UD-63.

38. DN/Yale, n.d., no. 70.

39. UD-63. Interestingly, Luise Rainer is not mentioned in DN's memoir, *Encounters.*

40. AN incorporated her few pages of dialogue into fiction, and the character of Stella in her story of the same name is based on Rainer. "Stella" was first published in *Harper's Bazaar,* Aug. 1946, and later recycled in *This Hunger, Ladders to Fire,* and *Winter of Artifice.* See Franklin, *Bibliography,* 81, for further information. Information is also from UD-63, 64, 65.

41. UD-63.

42. Ibid.

43. RD/Bancroft, n.d.

44. UD-64. She calls this brief diary, which includes July–Aug. 30, 1941, "Intermezzo."

45. AN/RC, n.d., JNC/USF.

46. Virginia Admiral (interview, 4/30/92): "That summer it seemed to me that she was running out of [long pause] something. I got the impression that he [Graeffe] wasn't interested, that he wasn't responding." AN's account in UD-64 is replete with details of many passionate encounters with a genuinely affectionate man. As she and Graeffe continued their affair until she met RP and ended it, her account seems closer to the truth. Warm and affectionate letters from Edward Graeffe are inserted into diary Vols. 64 through 67 and in some of the folders she used when she stopped writing in actual blank books. Graeffe later became the lifelong companion of Alice Tully.

47. Helba insisted that AN rent an apartment for her and Gonzalo in Provincetown. Unlike AN and HG, who sublet their New York apartment, H and G did not, thus saddling AN with their two rents to pay as well as her own.

22. Changes

1. Virginia Admiral insists that Helba, not Gonzalo, destroyed the studio (interview, 4/30/92). AN speaks euphemistically of "Gonzalo's anger" in UD-66. It is unlikely that the obese Helba, who was then recovering from an unspecified "surgery," would have had the energy to get herself down four flights of stairs at W. 20th St., over to W. 13th, up five long flights, and then wreak so much havoc.

2. AN described Duncan's account in UD-66. VA told this story in an interview, 4/30/92, as an example of Duncan's perversity and how he constantly strove to destroy relationships by putting himself in the middle of any couple. However, she insisted that she was not personally involved and said "the couple was one I knew."

3. The article is inserted into UD-63.

4. *A Spy in the House of Love* was published in 1954 by the British Book Centre, a "vanity" press, with all costs met by HG. Eventually it was collected as one of a series of novels in the *roman fleuve, Cities of the Interior.* For the developmental history of AN's career as a novelist, see Jason, *AN and Her Critics,* Chapter 5, 55 ff.

5. UD-64.

6. UD-63.

7. AN alludes obliquely to this in UD-65, saying he used "all his knowledge of my intimate life, my weakness, to attack." JNC verifies this incident, adding, "Duncan was not the only one to be cruel to Hugo." Fax, 4/21/94. Virginia Admiral confirms that Robert did tell HG all that he knew of AN's erotic life, but that HG refused to be baited and ignored him. HG alludes to "those who were cruel" in documents prepared in the 1960s for Dr. Inge Bogner (JNC/USF).

8. UD-65. There is a sizable exchange of correspondence inserted into Vols. 65 and 66 concerning her rupture with DN that is not in the DN/Yale archives. Carbons of AN's letters to DN, especially one of 11/20/42, show a very different portrait of their friendship than one would have if only the

Yale archive is consulted. AN is sharply, bluntly critical. DN replies, trying to rebut AN's criticisms and imploring her to remain on good terms, but AN stands fast and insists that they end the friendship.

9. Some of the correspondence from this period is collected in *Literate Passion,* 329 ff. Most of the important letters pertaining to their eventual breakup are not included; what is there is usually rewritten or highly edited to disguise the truth of the relationship.

10. Until otherwise noted, quotations are from two undated letters, AN to HM, inserted into the front cover of UD-66. Internal evidence suggests the end of Nov. or sometime in Dec. 1942. Both may be her replies to HM's letter of 11/9/42, edited and partially reproduced in *Literate Passion,* 351–352.

11. UD-65.

12. HM's letter is inserted into UD-66, after p. 236. It is not included in *LP.*

13. An untranslatable Spanish term of endearment, according to Carmen and Jairo Hinestroza and JNC.

14. HG (and AN) were led to Blake's entire *oeuvre* by ES, to whom Blake was of lifelong importance. Quotation is from Mary Ryan, "The Heritage of Atelier 17," *Anaïs: IJ* 4, p. 19. See also Ian Hugo (pseudonym of HG), "On the Art of Engraving," *Anaïs: IJ* 1, pp. 42–51.

15. Robert Tauber, director of Logan Elm Press at Ohio State U., described Blake as "the phenomenal forerunner of processes we are not sure about even today." Tauber also spoke of Hayter's invention of "viscosity printing," which has antecedents in Blake, and raised the possibility that HG's work was an amalgam of Blake's and Hayter's.

16. In his 1983 essay ("On the Art of Engraving," 51), written six years after AN's death and two years before his own, HG summed up his vision with the following paragraph: "Every artist owes it as a duty to himself and to the world to know what messages he is conveying. Above all he should know when he is a free agent and when he is a prisoner of his own obsessions or of anything else. For the power of an image-maker is the power of a god or a goddess and with that power go responsibilities."

17. *NY Times,* 11/16/41, 10X, "A Reviewer's Notebook." AN inserted a copy in UD-65. Ruder bought two, but according to Anaïs only because he "wanted to do something" for her and she wanted "to make [Hugo] feel successful." UD-65. All diary quotes from this volume until noted otherwise.

18. UD-65; second diary quote is from UD-54; comment from JLH is from 7/17/91 interview, L.A. She also inserted a passage similar to UD-65 in Ruder's Erotica.

19. All quotes that follow are from UD-65, until noted otherwise.

20. She came to this conclusion after she began to consult Dr. Martha Jaeger in mid-Dec. 1942. Information concerning this discovery is from UCLA/UD, Vol. 66 (Oct. 27, 1942–Oct. 3, 1943).

21. In D-3 she is called "Gibbens," but in UD-65, Anaïs calls her Givens, which is also the name on correspondence enclosed in that volume. "Beamish" has no other name, is mentioned only once in UD-65; not at all in D-3 and 4.

22. UD-65. All quotes from this until noted otherwise.

23. In D-4, she dates the naming as April 1944, but in UD-65, the name was chosen sometime between Jan. 20 and April 1942.

24. He and Blanche lost the first farm they tried to buy in Mass. and were now spending the winter with his mother in Queens as an economy move. Each morning he dressed and departed for what he said was a publishing job, but in reality he came to Anaïs's studio and wrote erotica for Ruder. UD-65; Blanche Cooney, interview with DB and *In My Own Sweet Time,* Chapter 10.

25. See Franklin, *Bibliography,* 9–10, for full information. Franklin is correct when he dates the printing as 5/42, which UD-65 verifies. For the history of the several different versions of this novel, see also Jason, *AN and Her Critics,* 39–41.

26. I have not been able to ascertain where the hand-rewritten diaries are now—probably in RP's archives in the Silver Lake house.

27. Anne Geismar, the widow of critic Maxwell Geismar who denounced AN as a liar after her death, was shocked when I explained all these various versions to her during an interview, 7/15/91. It was the first time Mrs. Geismar realized that she and her husband had never seen the originals, only typed copies. Also, it is quite likely that she saw yet another version further removed from the originals, for the ones she remembered storing in her house for AN were not typed on the thin rice paper but on a regular medium-weight typing paper.

28. AN copied this much of the letter into UD-65. She did not date it, nor did she supply a signature.

29. This and information that follows is until noted otherwise from UD-65.

30. Roditi never wrote his review. Harvey Breit tried to have his published in *New Republic* but "the editor who accepts his work is deposed and the new one does not like him." UD-65.

31. Lucia Cristofanetti was a designer and jewelry maker whose creations were featured in such stores as Bonwit Teller and Rodier de Paris. For a time AN tried to work with her on jewelry. The collaboration quickly ended because of AN's clumsiness and inability even to glue various simple pieces together. AN met Frances Brown Field through Blanche Cooney. She remained one of AN's closest friends until her death, within days of AN's, in Jan. 1977.

32. Paul Rosenfeld, "Refinements on a Journal: *Winter of Artifice* by AN," *Nation,* 9/26/42, 276–77. AN's opinions of her critics are taken from UD-65.

33. William Carlos Williams, " 'Men... Have No Tenderness': AN's *Winter of Artifice,*" *New Directions* 7, 1942, 429–436. See also *The Last Word,* letters between Marcia Nardi and WCW, ed. Elizabeth Murrie O'Neil (Iowa City: U. of Iowa Press, 1994).

34. Sharon (Bobby) Vail, "Four Poems" (New York: Gemor Press, 1942), 100 copies with heavy green paper cover and red paper. A copy of this volume is in Kay Boyle's papers at Southern Illinois U. Library. I am grateful to Boyle's biographer, Joan Mellen, for calling it to my attention.

35. She has inserted one single page of this undated letter from HM into UD-66. No part of it is included in *Literate Passion.*

36. This is AN's transcription, inserted into UD-66. Rosemary Sullivan, biographer of Elizabeth Smart, with whom Barker had a long relationship and fathered several children, tells me that Barker left no archival materials relating to AN.

37. Interview with Frances Schiff Bolton, 10/15/93. Information that follows is from UD-66 and from a pocket diary AN used during this time to keep track of her appointments. It was found among the archives of the late Louis Schaeffer by his niece and executor, Michele Slung, who graciously made it available to me.

23. The Hurt Self

1. Verified through AN's appointment book in the Schaeffer archives. Also UD-66. All diary quotes from this volume until noted otherwise.

2. Bernard Reis was an art dealer and collector. Rebecca Reis was noted for the elegant gatherings of artists and intellectuals in her Upper East Side town house.

3. *UAGB* was "printed in an edition of 300 copies, hand set by the author in Bernhard Gothic Light 10 point type, printed on water-marked Zurich plate paper, typography and printing by the Gemor Press. Seventeen engravings by Ian Hugo have been printed in relief directly from the original copper plates, February, 1944." From the information page in the book.

4. UD-67 (Oct. 1943–March 1944). All diary quotes from this volume until noted otherwise.

5. Two friends who asked not to be named volunteered this information.

6. GM is correct. Even her bibliographer, Franklin, was struck by the "many typographical errors" (*Anaïs Nin: A Bibliography*. Kent State U. Press, 14–15).

7. Rosa lived in Williamstown while Joaquín was in the Cuban army. He was about to be discharged and she was on her way to Havana, both to stay with him until he returned to Williams and to attend to the estate of her sister Juana (Anaïs's godmother), who had just died. In Havana, JNC and RC lived as paying guests at the Edificio América, owned by the Sánchez family and managed by RC's brother Thorvald Culmell. JNC remembers that after RC's visit to AN there were "no comments from Mother but what she didn't say was most revealing." Fax, 10/18/93.

8. These comments, until further notice, are from the appointment book in the Schaeffer archives.

9. "Berthier" has no other name in the appointment book, Schaeffer archives. Notation for Sunday, Dec. 9, includes "writing pages on sewing and taxi drive," and on Dec. 18 "writing pages on Frances's eyes." She printed cards for Martha Jaeger and Valeska Imbs (among others), and matted some of Hugo's engravings for friends who bought them for Christmas presents (Valeska Imbs is noted on Dec. 18).

10. Appointment book in the Schaeffer archives.

11. This information is from UD-67. An article with two photos (one of her at the new press) appeared in *Town & Country,* June 1944.

12. This and the information that follows is from UD-67 and notes inserted into that volume.

13. UD-67; also appointment book in

Schaeffer archives. Information that follows is from both until noted otherwise.

14. UD-67. Several letters to/from AN and Wallace Stevens are also in later volumes of UD.

15. AN's emphasis.

16. AN, HG, RC, and JNC were all friends of Dollie Chareau and her husband, Pierre (the designer of the famed glass house in Paris), before the war and continued the friendship in New York. AN writes of them occasionally in various UD volumes and in D-3, 109–110. JNC discussed his and RC's friendship with the Chareau family in conversation, April 1994.

17. All three are in UD-67. A separate fragment makes it possible that she at least began a fourth.

18. UD-68 (April 15, 1944 to May 1944 to Nov. 1945).

24. "Begin anywhere and flow along"

1. UD-68 contains the program for "Ian Hugo: Engraved Copper Plates and Prints," April 2–14, G Place Gallery, Washington, D.C.

2. UD-68. Barbara Reis Poe is the daughter of Rebecca and Bernard Reis. In an interview, 9/17/91, BP said "that black lace blouse was one of my favorites. She borrowed it and never gave it back." The *New Yorker* review appeared 4/1/44, a review by Jon Stroup and the photos appeared in the June 1944 *Town & Country*. There was a brief note about the book with emphasis on HG's engravings in *Mademoiselle,* May 1944.

3. When AN became a feminist icon in the 1970s, she cannily changed her attitude toward Woolf and always spoke respectfully of her. This was not always the case. Her response to VW's suicide was typical of her response to the fiction: "reaction negative." AN's comment on VW's obituary in the *NY Times,* 4/2/41, pasted into UD-63. In a letter to Gore Vidal, 10/1/52 (Vidal archives, U. Wisconsin, Madison), the passage of time brought reflection and reappraisal: AN spoke disparagingly of a New York editor, "Aldridge," who dismissed VW and Joyce as "some brilliant acrobatic feat, forgetting all the descendents fecundated by them, and overlooking the deep meaning of that trend." She called this editor "one of the descendants of Hemingway," a school of writing for which she had no liking.

4. HM, "Another Open Letter," *New Republic,* 12/6/43.

5. According to the editor's note in *Literate Passion,* 360, "a benefactor hiding behind the name Harry Koverr" agreed to pay HM a total of $2,500 in monthly installments of $200 each, to be repaid only if and when he could afford to do so. His intentions to share it with AN may have been good, but I have found no evidence that he did so for more than three months. IN UD-68, she cites the sum HM offered initially as $1,000, but there is enough other documentation that I believe she added one zero too many. Most of this information and the subsequent AN/HM exchange has not been included in the published letters, but it is in UD-67, 68, 69.

6. In a letter to RC (n.d., JNC/USF), AN talks about appearing in Maya

Deren's films in 1945, and ends somewhat acerbically by saying that Deren had just received a Guggenheim Fellowship. Her Proposal is inserted into UD-68. All quotes from this until noted otherwise.

7. HM to AN, April 1944, Big Sur. Inserted into UD-68.

8. AN to RC, n.d., JNC/USF.

9. All three of Miller's biographers have detailed versions of the Hershkowitz affair based on AN's D-4, where he is called Harry Herkovitz. My version is based primarily on UD-68.

10. See Jason, *AN and Her Critics,* 55–56, for the history of how AN rewrote and reshaped the novel.

11. Which of course became the title of her authorized biographer, Evelyn Hinz's, book about AN's writing, *The Mirror and the Garden.*

12. She calls him "Leonard" in D-4, 45 ff.

13. This compulsion to answer letters originated when Djuna Barnes ignored AN's fan letter for *Nightwood.* Not content with a polite reply, AN's letters were voluminous, such as those during 1945, when she boasted in the diary about conducting an entire analysis by mail with a woman who wrote to her (some of their letters are in UD-68 and 69, but I will protect the woman's privacy): "I achieved a complete psychoanalysis of a young woman, incredible effectiveness. I made her confess."

14. Immediately after this she wrote to RC: "Am having trouble with my passport. Have to write to Paris for a birth certificate." AN/RC, n.d., JNC/USF.

15. Ibid.

16. To write about AN and Wilson, I have consulted their correspondence in UD and in the Wilson archives of the Beinecke Library, Yale; also three volumes of his memoirs, *The Forties, The Fifties,* and *The Sixties.*

17. "Without reviews or advertisements I've sold 150 in two weeks. Another book shop gave me a window, with copper plates, photos etc. Every day I get letters. And best of all three or four poets want their books done and I am sure I will get one real order." AN/RC, n.d., JNC/USF.

18. Because she owed Dr. Jacobson so much money, she was embarrassed to go to him, so she had RC write for medicine, then send it to her: "and then I get a nurse to inject me and I only spend $2 instead of $5." AN/RC, n.d., JNC/USF.

19. UD, Folder 1946.1. AN ceased writing in actual diary volumes in 11/46. From this time on, she wrote on whatever paper came to hand, and included everything from correspondence to playbills and newspaper clippings in boxes or folders that she labeled sometimes by the entire year, at other times by several months at a time. When there are more than one folder per year, I indicate it directly after the year itself. The reviews to which she refers here are Wilson, *New Yorker,* 11/10/45, 97–101; Trilling, *Nation,* 1/26/46, 105–107; Lerman, *Mademoiselle,* 5/44; Isaac Rosenfeld, *New Republic,* 12/17/45, 844–845.

20. A three-page typed statement in UD-68 describes research paid for by the Hoffmann–La Roche drug company on a "compound" to combat battlefield fatigue, in which "an amino acid and a vitamin B complex group" were combined. All further information is from this diary until noted otherwise.

21. In a letter, n.d., to RC (JNC/USF), AN describes a "fibrone" and says the doctor was confident that it would "dissolve." She also writes of the tumor in UD-68. This marked the start of her gynecological problems and may well have been the incipient cancer that eventually killed her.

22. UD-69 (Nov. 1945–May 1946). She shared the program with Charles Parker Tyler.

23. AN acted in one of Deren's films shot in Central Park during the summer of 1945.

24. UD-69; HG's papers prepared for Dr. Inge Bogner, JNC/USF.

25. There are notations of his (and later her) appointments with Pascal Covici at Viking Press and unnamed editors at Charles Scribner & Sons in UD-68 and 69.

25. Colette and Chéri

1. To write about Gore Vidal, I have consulted UD-69; Folders 46 ff. Correspondence: GV's letters to AN are inserted in the UCLA sources quoted here; AN's to GV are in the Vidal archives, U. Wisconsin, Madison (I am grateful to Mr. Vidal for allowing me to use them); GV to DB, 2/2/92 and 3/4/92; Nina Gore Olds to *Time,* 4/5/76. Interviews: Gore Vidal (by tel., 4/28/92); Rupert Pole, July, and Sept. 1991, July–Aug. 1992; Walter Clemmons; Charles Ruas; Marguerite Young. Books and articles (general): Charles Ruas, *Conversations with American Writers* (NY: Alfred Knopf, 1984); John Guare's introduction to Dawn Powell's *The Locusts Have No King* (NY: Yarrow Press, 1990). By Gore Vidal: *Live from Golgotha* (NY: Random House, 1992); *Two Sisters* (NY: Ballantine Books, 1987); *Williwaw* (NY: Ballantine Books, 1986); GV's 1987 *NY Review of Books* essay; "Taking a Grand Tour of AN's High Bohemia Via the Time Machine," *L.A. Times Book Review,* 9/26/71; "Pen Pals: Henry Miller and Lawrence Durrell," in *A View from the Diners Club* (London: Andre Deutsch, 1991). About GV: Arthur Lubow, "Gore's Lore," *Vanity Fair,* Sept. 1992, 126 ff.

2. There are casual comments throughout UD-69, Folder 1946.1, and her correspondence for this period, such as "The Lesbians seek me out," or "I ensorcell the young homosexuals."

3. Gore Vidal was born Eugene Luther Vidal, Jr. His mother's maiden name was added at his christening. When he was fourteen and began to publish stories at Exeter, he decided he did not want to be "junior to anybody," and took his mother's maiden name as his first.

4. GV was taught to fly by his father and piloted his first plane at the age of ten, a feat filmed and photographed in *Life.*

5. Nina Gore was married to Hugh Auchincloss, who later married Janet Lee Bouvier, the mother of Jacqueline Kennedy Onassis, thus giving Gore Vidal and Ms. Onassis a distant quasi-sibling relationship.

6. UD-69. All diary quotes from this until noted otherwise.

7. JLH spoke repeatedly throughout interviews of Hugo's "extreme discretion" and "exaggerated politeness and distance." He said it was a topic of conversation among his and AN's other friends, "How Hugo could just pretend there was nothing going on at all, even when it was right under his nose." Gore Vidal (interview, 4/28/92) said, "I think Hugo was totally indifferent to her by the time I met them. He had relationships by then and didn't really try to hide them. I truly believe that by 1946 he no longer had any interest in AN." When I questioned this, GV retorted: "Well, you have to remember that she was a megalomaniac with a program, and she needed to believe that this man still adored her." William Burford (tel. interview, 10/27/93) described Hugo as "a sad, wan person; a household superfluity; always there, but absent at the same time. He was devoted to her but she didn't treat him right and he got the raw end of the stick."

8. GV refers to this as "the red diary" and swears that he never read it. When she pestered him, he returned it to her so he would not have to do so. RP calls it "the Gore" or "the green" diary. In 1992 I asked RP to let me read "The Gore Diary." He said he had lost it. It is the one document in AN's archives that I know of to which I have not had access. However, I think it probably consists of all the voluminous passages that began in UD-69 and continued for the next several years, probably recopied and enlarged upon, and perhaps containing some new insights.

9. First quote is paraphrased from GV's dedication to AN in her copy of *Williwaw,* second is from *Two Sisters,* third from *Live from Golgotha.* In "Pen Pals: Henry Miller and Lawrence Durrell," *TLS,* Sept. 9–15, 1988, reprinted in *A View from the Diners Club: Essays 1987–1991* (London: Andre Deutsch, 1991), 18, GV writes: "AN . . . has begun to publish her diaries; she is also rewriting them as she goes along, paying off new as well as old scores."

10. When they were in the company of others, it was usually in literary gatherings that included many persons who have since died, among them Tennessee Williams, Truman Capote, Carson McCullers, and James Leo Herlihy.

11. UD Folder. 1946.

12. GV/DB, interview, 4/28/92.

13. GV, interview, 4/28/92, confused the Pinckard affair in the winter of 1946 with one she had in East Hampton that summer with John Paanicker (as AN spells his name in the diary; GV says Pannicher is correct).

14. UD Folder 1946.1.

15. Lubow's *Vanity Fair* article gives a succinct account of this troubled relationship. For Nina Gore Olds' account, see "Letters," *Time,* 4/5/76.

16. GV, interview, 4/28/92: "You do know that she called me 'Chéri' and I was instructed to call her 'Colette,' which meant she not only knew the way things were, she knew the way things would have to end." In their letters, however, he addressed her as "Chérie."

17. Both denied that they were ever intimate: she in her diaries, he in several interviews.

18. GV, in interview, 4/29/92, said AN frequently referred to herself as "Dona Giovanna, a woman who could fuck men the way they fucked women."

19. UD Folder 1946.1.

20. A letter to HG from the Community Service Society of New York, 2/10/47 (mistakenly placed in UD-67), states that Gonzalo understood his assistance had run its course and was being terminated. He refused to apply for welfare because he feared deportation. By this time he had disappeared from AN's and HG's daily life. He paid one last visit to AN in Jan.

1947, asking her for money to pay his and Helba's passage to France, where her daughter, Elsa (now married to a Frenchman), would take over their support. As AN does not write of giving him money, it is unlikely that she did. Later AN learned that he and Helba returned to Paris, where both died in the 1970s.

21. UD Folder 1947.1.

22. I have talked to students who were in these audiences between 1947 and 1970, at (among others) Harvard, Amherst, Smith, Bennington. Their recollections present a much more realistic account of student reaction and audience size. Also, as to her claim that F. O. Matthiessen praised her: there is a letter, n.d., from him in UD Folder 1946.1 in which he thanks her for having written to him *after* her talk at Harvard, and says he is sorry that he was unable to meet her while she was there.

23. She wrote many times in the coming years to ask for copies of the tape for her personal publicity purposes. The Film Service refused politely at first, saying they would send a few as a favor for her personal collection. When she continued to pester them, they sent a strong letter saying that the recording had been made for their archives only and they could not get into the business of serving as her publicity agent. Correspondence, various UCLA folders, starting 1946.

24. I base what follows partially on interviews with James Merrill (10/14/91) and William Burford (10/27/93). Also, UD-69 and Folder 1946. Some of the AN/WB letters are inserted into these diaries, others are at HRC, Texas.

25. Barnes was irritated by AN's genuine adulation. She did not like her personally and resented AN's appropriation of her first name for various fictional characters.

26. Within the year, Friar left Amherst, dismissed by the English Dept. because of his relationship with Merrill. Although he does not mention AN in his memoir, *A Different Person* (New York: Knopf, 1993), Merrill writes of this period in his life.

27. Burford says his favorite reading in those years was "Plutarch, not *Nightwood,*" and he insists that he does not know where AN got the idea that he wanted to be "the second Rimbaud," as she wrote to Durrell, undated letter, c. 1946, Morris Library, Southern Illinois U., Carbondale. AN may have been prescient, however, for WB did become a poet and professor of literature. See also: Sylvia Plath, "Poets on Campus," *Mademoiselle,* Aug. 1954, 291; *Contemporary Poets* (3rd ed.), ed. James Vinson (New York: St. Martin's Press, 1980), 213–214.

28. Merrill's comments about AN are the soul of discretion, but he made it clear that he consciously avoided becoming drawn into her orbit. However, in a letter of 11/13/46, he tells AN that Burford is dangerous and to beware of his sadism and cruelty.

29. In an interview, 10/27/93, WB said he burned all AN's letters. In a letter to Richard Centing, 7/28/72, WB wrote that in searching through some of his old papers, he came across seventeen letters and a postcard from AN that he had forgotten to burn, and which he sent to RC and are now in the Richard Centing archives.

30. To write about AN and WB, I have consulted their correspondence (noted earlier), and WB's letters to Richard Centing, 9/5/71 through 7/28/72, in Centing Archives.

31. AN learned of Hauser through a

novel by Jakob Wassermann. There are references to Hauser in her letters and Pinckard's, so they must have discussed him. Burford (interview, 10/27/93) remembered her talking of Hauser: "Her interests were very narrow and she was always psychologizing. She was always interested in demented people."

32. In 3/46, HG wrote that he had Cuba "in my hands," and was pleased that he had persuaded her wealthy Sánchez relatives to invest in his bank. Copy in UD Folder 1946, orig. JNC/USF.

33. GV, interview, 4/28/92. He added that she was "not intelligent," and that "she was her subject, so she could not stop honking on the subject."

34. This was one of her favorite words, and she chose it to be the name of the newsletter founded by Richard Centing and dedicated to her work, *The Magic Circle.* From the first years of diary writing, she created drawings in which her name was at the center and the names of others radiated out from hers in spokes or radii. Many of these names belonged to persons she did not know well and, in some cases, did not know at all; they were simply people whose paths crossed hers in New York and to whom she gave greater prominence in her life than was accurate.

35. WB, interview, 10/27/93. All quotes from this until noted otherwise. Mme. de Staël and Constant had a tempestuous love affair based on strong intellectual sympathy that lasted from 1794 to 1811.

36. WB became "Kendall" in D-4. In a letter to Richard Centing, 7/19/72, WB stated that "the 'letters' and the 'fragment of the poem' are phoney," and "some kind of curious transposition (or did she have a quite conscious intention which was a psychological necessity for her) took place in her rearrangement of the material." In an interview, 10/27/93, WB denied knowing of AN's tendency to create "twins" out of others, so it is interesting to see his 1972 comment: "In effect, she has created a half-fictional character, a sort of Siamese twin, out of the two of us! Surely she knows this, and it was for this reason that she used the pseudonym."

37. Information that follows is from UD-69 and Folders 1946 and 1947; AN to WB, undated letters and AN/HM, partial undated letters, both inserted into these volumes; Philip K. Jason, "Oscar Baradinsky's 'Outcasts,' " *Anaïs: IJ* 3, pp. 109 ff.

38. Fraenkel's *Land of the Quetzal,* AN's *Realism and Reality,* Ian Hugo's (HG's) *New Eyes on the Art of Engraving.*

39. Jason *(AN and Her Critics)* describes this 1946 pamphlet and the 1947 essay *On Writing* as "interim" and "slight." It is a view most AN scholars and critics share (I among them). Generally, they are considered AN's first attempts to formulate the literary credo that became *The Novel of the Future* (1968).

40. This is verified by partial manuscripts in Folder 1947 and exchanges in their letters, Folders 1946 and 1947. Comments that follow are from WB, interview, 10/27/93.

41. Quotations from this letter and those which follow are all n.d., but internal evidence attests to 1946. AN/RC, JNC/USF.

42. All quotes from GV, interview, 4/28/92.

43. To supplement the greatly reduced material concerning Djuna and Sabina from *This Hunger,* she added a second part to the new work, which she called "Bread and the Wafer." Another major change was to give Djuna a clutch of young boys who surrounded her. Jason *(AN and Her Critics)* gives some information about the development of these novels and their subsequent incorporation into *Cities of the Interior.* Sharon Spencer, in *Collage of Dreams: The Writings of AN* (expanded edition) (New York: Harcourt Brace Jovanovich, Harvest Edition, 1981), has the most extensive discussion.

44. Copies in Folder 1946. None were printed in the *NY Times.*

45. Their letters are in Folder 1946.

46. AN/RC, n.d., JNC/USF.

47. Folder 1947.1. All diary quotes from this until noted otherwise.

48. Ibid. The emphasis is mine, for she is describing these boys as girls.

26. "Life again, life!"

1. There is no mention of the ink-stained hands by AN in Folders 1947.1 or 2. RP first told me this story in 9/89, and repeated it for me and others many times since.

2. Folder 1947.1. All diary quotes from this until noted otherwise.

3. Information is from Rupert Pole, in interviews beginning in 1989 and taking place several times each week after that during May–June 1990; July and Sept. 1991; July, Aug., Sept. 1992, and in many tel. conversations from 1989 to 1993. I am grateful to RP for his friendship and courtesy and for his generosity in permitting me full access to AN's archives in his possession and for granting access to the UCLA archives.

4. His mother, Helen, was married to Lloyd Wright, FLW's architect son. Together they had one child, Eric, also an architect. RP's father was Reginald Pole, an English classical actor who had a long stage career. He named RP after his Cambridge U. roommate, the poet Rupert Brooke.

5. Jane Lloyd-Jones (1922–1969) later married Heywood Hale Broun and had a long career as a stage actress.

6. In separate interviews, the comparison was made by James Leo Herlihy, Lila Rosenblum, Betty Berzon, Daisy Aldan, Sharon Spencer, and many others.

7. Several years later she told Rosenblum, Herlihy, and Miriam Preiselman Slater, all in separate conversations, that RP had given her her "first real orgasm," an unbelievable statement that contradicts the sixteen years of diary writing since she began her affair with HM.

8. She kept her age secret for many years after their relationship began in earnest. Surprising as it seems, RP swears he did not care to know her true age and never asked.

9. If most of the information that follows sounds familiar to readers of an article in *Angeles* magazine, it is because I was the original author. When the editors insisted on inserting material from the published diaries and other sources that I knew was factually incorrect, I made them remove my name.

10. Information that follows is from interviews with Lila Rosenblum, May 22 and Oct. 5, 1990, from many conversations since then, and from the

AN/LR correspondence (1947–1972), which LR has graciously made available to me. Also, from Folders 1947.1 and 2, and from other folders that follow, which will be cited individually as their provenance occurs in the text.
11. Lila Rosenblum, interview, 10/5/90.
12. JNC, tel. conversation, 6/93. Others include the following, who used the phrase in separate interviews: James Leo Herlihy, Lila Rosenblum, Daisy Aldan, Anne Geismar, Betty Berzon, Marguerite Young, Harriet Zinnes, Bebe Barron, Blanche Cooney, and many, many others.
13. AN to Leo Lehrman, letter, n.d., inserted into Folder 1947.1.
14. Anne Geismar, for example, was shocked when I explained that the typed copies she and her husband kept for AN in their house were not the originals but merely copies of copies.
15. Folders 1947.1 and 2.
16. AN's emphasis in Folder 1947.1.
17. Information that follows is from Folder 1947.2 and loose papers prepared by HG during analysis with Dr. Inge Bogner, probably dating from the late 1950s, early 1960s.
18. AN had her first inkling of it when RP dipped into Henry's novels, intuited their relationship, and was outraged and offended.
19. Information about the trip from Folders 1947.2, 1948.1 and 2, and interviews with Rupert Pole, Lila Rosenblum, and JNC. Also, AN's correspondence with GV in Folder 1947.2 and U. Wisconsin, Madison, LR archives, and AN/RC, JNC/USF.
20. "Insist" is AN's word. In her last diary, 1974, she wrote that RP was distressed to read the 1948 passage, saying he would have put the top up at once had she only asked him.
21. A remark I heard repeatedly in interviews, among them Curtis Harrington, Samson De Brier, Kenneth Anger, and many others, was that GV accused his "best girl" of stealing his "best boy." Both GV and RP strongly deny this, saying they met only briefly once or twice, 1947–1977, and then only in social situations.
22. AN/GV, copy inserted in Folder 1947.1.
23. LR was in fragile health and her physician ordered her to move away before another New York winter. She also served as a mail drop for AN on this trip.
24. Itinerary inserted into Folder 1947.2.
25. Confirmed by Sherry Donati Martinelli, tel. interview, 5/10/94.
26. She still had difficulty using RP's name to others, as this and other correspondence attests. Also, she still avoided using his name in her sessions with Dr. Staff.
27. Herlihy's comments are from interviews, July and Sept. 1991 and July–August 1992, and from correspondence that will be cited where appropriate.
28. Later, she perfected this contention in "Proceed from the Dream," chapter V of *A Woman Speaks,* 115–147.
29. Undated letter in Folder 1947.2. He tells her to "keep the money" he gave her to pay for the flight.
30. All these comments are in her undated letters to RP, inserted into Folders 1947.1 and 2.
31. Information that follows is from HG to AN, Dec. 11, 22, 24, all from New York; Dec. 25 from Hotel Nacional, Havana; undated mss prepared for Dr. Inge Bogner, late 1950s or early 1960s.
32. *Children of the Albatross,* 18.

33. Elizabeth Hardwick, "Fiction Chronicle," *Partisan Review,* June 1948, 705–708, wrote: "No writer I can think of has more passionately embraced thin air. Still she has nerve and goes on her way with a fierce foolishness that is not without beauty as an act, though it is too bad her performance is never equal to her intentions."

34. One of the women whom AN analyzed in the 1930s was the wife of one of HG's superior officers in the bank. She told me that, contrary to popular rumor, HG was not ever under threat of being fired. His job was secure for as long as he wanted it, and the woman's husband and his colleagues were surprised by HG's decision and tried to talk him out of it.

35. HG to AN, 12/11/47. Copies of this letter and those that follow in this chapter are in Folder 1947.2; originals are in JNC/USF.

27. An Edifice of Lies

1. HG/AN, 3/28/49. Copy in Folder 1949.1, original JNC/USF.

2. AN/GV, n.d., U. Wisconsin, Madison.

3. HG/AN, 11/6/48, copy in Folder 1948.2, original JNC/USF.

4. AN to RP, n.d., Folder 1948, and interview with Gayle Nin Rosenkrantz. In a fax of 11/14/94, GNR confirmed that AN re-created chronology to suit her needs: TN's third child was not born until March 1949; GNR was about to enter Stanford and Charles "was almost 16, driving a car, hardly in need of child care." In a curious twist, TN did need back surgery, but not until the winter of 1950.

5. Kenneth Anger, interview, 9/17/91. AN also notes this meeting in Folder 1947.1.

6. Undated letters to Gore Vidal, AN/GV, U. Wisconsin, Madison; to HG, RC, and JNC, all JNC/USF. Interviews with GV, James Leo Herlihy, Lila Rosenblum, Betty Berzon, Don Bachardy, Curtis Harrington, Kenneth Anger, and Samson De Brier, among many others.

7. A highly romanticized version is in D-5, 37.

8. She met Varda by mail several years earlier when HM introduced him. HM was living in Big Sur at the time, but she made no effort to see him, nor did she write to him.

9. Leite published AN's "Hedja" in 1946. Robert Duncan was associated with Leite and resented AN's very presence in the Bay Area. In later years, Porter boasted of an affair with AN. She says nothing in the diary about it, and as she recorded even the most casual assignation there, I am cautious about accepting his testimony.

10. Folder 1949.1. All diary quotes from this volume until noted otherwise.

11. HG/AN, n.d., copy in Folder 1949, orig. JNC/USF. AN/HG, typed copy in Folder 1949. I should note here that space and the exigencies of biography have not permitted me to write of AN's interaction with her Cuban aunts and cousins, which was constant and ongoing throughout her life.

12. Folder 1949.1.

13. James Leo Herlihy, who lived in the apartment on W. 9th St. at various times in the next few years, was appalled by the vast number of prescription drugs AN had in her medicine cabinet and the seemingly random way she took them.

14. Information that follows is from letters to/from AN/RP, inserted into Folder 1949.1; and correspondence between AN/GV, AN/LR, AN/JLH.

15. In reality, Thorvald and Kay were living in Chihuahua and Charles and Gayle were attending Choate and Westover.

16. AN in Folder 1949.2, JNC/AN, letter of 10/29/49, inserted into Folder 1949.2; conversation with JNC, 7/92. AN noted in 12/49: "when all the details of father's death were settled (his assets consisting of books, barometer, music and letter files etc.), death, funeral, J's round trip air ticket, were added up, $314.45 was left. We each got $104.82."

17. HG/AN, 12/4/49, copy in Folder 1949.2; orig. JNC/USF.

18. This word appears in her diary beginning with Folder 1949.2 and continues until the early 1970s. It was also the expression she used in correspondence with GV and JLH.

19. AN/RP, postmarked 2/7/50, Folder 1950.

20. Information about this incident is from several undated letters, 1949–1950, AN to Gore Vidal, U. Wisconsin, Madison; also from Folder 1950.

21. AN/GV, n.d.

22. Hayden Carruth, in the *Providence Sunday Journal,* 1/29/50, 10; Charles Rollo, "The Life of the Heart," *Atlantic Monthly,* Feb. 1950, 86–87.

23. Interview with RP, disparaging remarks by AN in various folders beginning 1948.

24. From Folders 1950 and 1951.1; also letter, n.d., to GV, U. Wisconsin, Madison.

25. These programs, flyers, posters, and letters of invitation and acceptance fill the diary folders from 1948 to the late 1960s. As they are so many, and as the exigencies of biography are incapable of dealing with them, I will only mention some specifically where appropriate. As of 1994, neither AN as writer nor Ian Hugo as artist has a complete bibliography of publications, recordings, films, and performances.

26. JLH was working at the Satyr Bookshop in Hollywood while attending the Pasadena Playhouse; LR was a student at UCLA. In interviews, both recalled the delicate task of trying to persuade AN that her novels were very different from the usual Hollywood fare.

27. Irene M. Selznick to AN, 6/2/50, in Folder 1950.

28. Lila Rosenblum, interview, 10/5/90. LR referred specifically to the time AN decided to invite Tennessee Williams to tea after seeing *Streetcar Named Desire.* She asked him to bring a friend and said she would also invite one. Williams brought Oliver Evans, who went on to write a critical study of AN. AN's guest was LR, who was one of several persons who noted how much AN identified with Williams's character, Blanche DuBois.

29. Isherwood to AN, 10/9/50, in Folder 1950.

30. Folder 1951.2. All diary quotes from this until noted otherwise.

31. She had two passports, the Cuban of her birth and the U.S. because of her marriage, and was always careful to travel on the Cuban when they went to Mexico. In a 1952 letter, n.d., to GV, AN tells him she has finally taken full U.S. citizenship and asks him to keep it secret.

NOTES

28. The Trapeze

1. Folder 1951.2. All diary quotes from this until noted otherwise.
2. These included James Leo Herlihy, Lila Rosenblum, Gore Vidal, Ruth Witt Diamant, Betty Berzon, Stanley Haggert, and Woody Parish Martin.
3. Continuing complaints about *Time* and "the commentators" begin in Folder 1951 and continue until the 1970s.
4. Information that follows is from Folders 1951 through 1954.
5. Information that follows is from Daisy Aldan and Marguerite Young. Also Lila Rosenblum and James Leo Herlihy, who were involved in similar schemes.
6. Herlihy and Rosenblum confirmed this story, which AN alludes to in Folder 1954.
7. Information that follows is from separate interviews with Rupert Pole, Kenneth Anger, Curtis Harrington, and Samson DeBrier, who were all guests at the party; James Leo Herlihy was staying in the West 9th St. apt.; Lila Rosenblum, Betty Berzon, Renate Druks, Daisy Aldan, Marguerite Young, and others were later told a similar story by AN. I have based my account on the testimony of all those listed above, and from diary entries in Folder 1952.2 and brief mentions in 1953 and 1956.
8. The expression is one they used to address each other in letters and in conversation. JLH's letters are in Folders 1951 through 1954.
9. I have not been able to discern exactly what this was, for she mentioned it only once in Folder 1954, saying it caused her great pain and she was sure it only made matters worse. Physicians I have consulted think it was probably "worthless mumbo-jumbo," but one also pointed out that in some quarters, Jacobson was respected during these years for endocrine research, specifically as it related to aging.
10. Folder 1954.
11. I have based this profile of Inge Bogner on the testimony of her five former patients, who have asked to remain anonymous, and an interview with her widower, Martin Sameth, 4/14/92. Also, on HG's diary writings prepared for Dr. Bogner (JNC/USF) and folders beginning in 1951, cited specifically where appropriate. Also, on an article by AN, "Women of New York," translated into German and printed in *Merian,* 9/9/70, p. 82.
12. I have spoken to five of Dr. Bogner's former patients, all of whom insist she kept no written records. Her husband concurs. When Inge Bogner was in her last and fatal illness, she collected all the letters AN and HG wrote to her, as well as the documents HG prepared during his treatment, and sent them to JNC, whom HG named as his executor. It would seem that Dr. Bogner knew how valuable they would be for critics and scholars who studied both AN and HG, and by her action ensured that they would be used. JNC has graciously made them available to me and I have used them throughout this book where appropriate. He has also arranged for them to be deposited in the Gleason Library, U. of San Francisco, where they will be available at a future date to qualified scholars.
13. All that follow are from Folders 1951 through 1955.
14. AN's undated letters to GV are in U. Wisconsin, Madison; her carbons

and his replies are in Folders 1951 through 1956.

15. Information is from personal interviews with both as well as AN/LR, LR archives, with carbons in Folders 1953 through 1957; AN/JLH, Folders 1950 through 1955.

16. This expression occurs from 1953 onward, and in letters to JLH and Gunther Stuhlmann, who were the only two persons to whom she entrusted duplicate keys.

17. Telegram and diary account are in Folder 1952.2; verification and elaboration of details from RP, interview, 1991, and JLH and LR.

18. AN's emphasis, Folder 1952.2.

19. Information that follows, ibid.

20. AN's emphasis, Folders 1952.2 and 1953.

21. HG/AN, 11/14/51; original JNC/USF, copy in Folder 1951.

22. Among the many persons to whom she used this expression are James Leo Herlihy and Kenneth Anger. I cite them specifically because they provided the most accurate physical description of it.

23. This is a frequent remark that appears from the earliest diaries to the last, as she exhorts herself to tell the truth about herself on the written pages, no matter how wounding it might be.

24. RP insists that AN never kept anything locked in their domiciles, first in Sierra Madre or later in the Effie St. apt. and the Silver Lake house. AN herself writes of various locked hiding places in Folders 1951 through 1959, and undated letters to JLH and JNC attest to this as well.

25. Folder 1952.1.

29. Literature's Invisible Woman

1. These letters begin in the winter of 1951 and continue throughout 1954, and are in the appropriate diary folders.

2. Undated letters from HG and Curtis Harrington in Folders 1952 and 1953. AN writes of it as well in Folder 1953.

3. Mentioned repeatedly in Folders 1951 through 1954.

4. Folder 1952.1.

5. Folder 1952.2. She might have added, but did not, that JLH had a certain degree of input into the production and was responsible for the title. His original suggestion was "Bells of Atlantyde," which HG changed to "Bells of Atlantis."

6. Ibid.

7. Two distinguished authors whose work Haydn rejected told me this anecdote in separate conversations; both have asked me to respect their privacy.

8. 12/28/51, Folder 1951.

9. 11/26/51, ibid.

10. 8/30/52, Folder 1952.2.

11. 9/9/52, ibid.

12. 3/10/52, ibid.

13. Covici's letter is 11/26/51; Purdy's 12/4/51. Both are in Folder 1951; others expressing similar reservations are in Folders 1952.1 and 2.

14. Folder 1952.2.

15. AN to JLH, n.d., in Folder 1952.2. She added that she no longer gave in automatically because if she really wanted something, throwing a tantrum would always get it for her.

16. AN's comments are from Folder 1952.1. All diary quotations from this until noted otherwise. Her emphasis here.
17. AN to René de Chochor, 7/22/52, copy in Folder 1952.1. For an excellent discussion of the Lie Detector, see Spencer, *Collage of Dreams,* 52–53.
18. Folder 1952.1.
19. AN to Stuart Gilbert, n.d., but internal evidence suggests 6/52; copy in Folder 1952.1.
20. Folder 1952.2.
21. Folder 1952.2. In correspondence JLH called himself "The Spy Ring," and AN referred to him as "The Intelligence Service."
22. Apparently she managed to retain her Cuban passport, and continued to use it on their trips to Mexico, for RP complained several times in 1991 interviews of standing in long U.S. Customs lines every time they returned while her documentation was checked.
23. AN to GV, n.d., internal evidence suggests mid-1952; U. Wisconsin, Madison.
24. GV to AN, n.d., Folder 1952.1.
25. Robert F. Burford to AN, 9/22/52, Folder 1952.2. Eric Protter, in a tel. interview, 12/14/93, said HG and de Chochor sent "pressure letters, that's all. We gave them the wrong estimate on how much it would cost to print her. We were a magazine, not a book." He did admit that he and Burford "used the money to pay some bills."
26. Betty Berzon, interview, 7/91. I am grateful to Dr. Berzon for granting me access to the chapter of her forthcoming memoir, which deals with the affair with RP. RP confirmed the relationship in an interview, 7/91. Rosenblum and Herlihy also confirmed details of AN's reaction when she discovered this relationship and some of the others.
27. In interviews with many of her accusers, I have been able to verify that she was not even in the city at the time the pursuit was purported to take place. No one has been able to provide documentation or evidence that withstands rigorous scrutiny, and until someone does, I believe what I have written here is the truth.
28. AN's emphasis. Folder 1952.2.
29. AN/RC, Mon. 2/9/53, JNC/USF.
30. Information that follows, ibid.; official medical report and diary notations in Folders 1953.1 and 2; interviews with RP, July and Sept. 1991, and Aug. 1992; JNC interviews and faxes, 1991–1993; JLH, July 1991.
31. Folder 1953.2. The rheumatic fever is something an unnamed California doctor told her she "probably" had as a child, and the enlarged heart and heart murmur are conditions she first speculated about as early as 1935 but afterward convinced herself were true. The other conditions were indeed true and did plague her until the end of her life.
32. On a batch of diary papers she calls "Vol. 75" and dates as April–Aug. 1952, she has written on what serves as a title page: "On one end of the trapeze there was a tree. On the other end a pillar."
33. René de Chochor to Eric Protter, 6/5/53, copy in Folder 1953.1.
34. Letters to/from K. Winslow are in Folders 1951 through 1955.
35. JLH to AN, n.d., Folder 1952.2.
36. Information that follows is from Folder 1955; interview with RP, July 1991; JNC, 1991–1992; JLH, July 1991. I am grateful to Vincent J. Bartolotta, Esq., and Dan Cassell for providing me with a copy of the official

marriage license issued by the State of Arizona.
37. The name of the justice of the peace on the marriage license is George Hagely, and witnesses were Floyd and Marie Truitt.

30. Acting Out the Dream

1. Although this notation appears in Folder 1953.2, and the movie was first shown in 1953, the discussion of her bigamous marriage that follows clearly indicates that she did not see it until 1955. When AN entrusted her friend Tristine Rainer with the secret of her dual life in the late 1970s, Rainer wrote a screenplay for a tv movie based on it. Interview with TR, L.A., 7/91.
2. Lila Rosenblum, interview, 10/4/90.
3. Folder 1955.1. These two words take on increasing importance in AN's vocabulary from this time until the end of her life, when her quest for "absolution" became paramount. All quotes from this Folder until noted otherwise.
4. Folder 1955.1 and 2; HG/AN; JNC/USF.
5. I discussed this with JLH, and he said it made him feel "very sad. There is no question that my primary loyalty was always to Anaïs, but I was extremely fond of Hugo and would never have done anything to cause him to be hurt."
6. AN eventually transported all the originals as part of her airline baggage to a storage vault at First National Bank, 181 Montague St., Brooklyn. Copies were redeposited in Bekins Storage, Arcadia. Originals from the 1960s were deposited in a local branch bank in Silver Lake once AN and RP moved into the house on Hidalgo Ave. Shortly before her death, they were all gathered by RP and housed in the Silver Lake Bank until they were purchased by UCLA. AN sometimes offered a "special treat" to her admirers and scholars whose writings met with her approval by taking them to view (but not read) the originals in Brooklyn. Among these were Richard Centing (interview, 1/92, Columbus).
7. AN's emphasis.
8. Repeated references to HG's difficulties with "Mr. de St. P." are found in AN and HG letters dating from 1955–1961, JNC/USF.
9. When the British Book Centre refused to pay HG money owed, AN marched "daringly" into their offices and loaded 200 copies of *Spy* into a taxi without incident or opposition. In Folder 1955.1. Eric Protter verified that AN did this, in interview 12/14/93.
10. I base this estimate on figures taken from HG's and AN's letters about finances, JNC/USF, and AN's comments in Folders 1955.1 and 2.
11. Sylvia Ruggles, who worked for the U.N., and her husband, Ted, who according to AN, "used to be a writer." 35 W. 9th boasted another illustrious tenant, the novelist Dawn Powell, whose penthouse shared the top floor with AN's and HG's. I am grateful to Gail Woodley-Atella for introducing me to Claire and Benjamin Shapiro, neighbors of HG and AN,

who shared their memories of 35 W. 9th St.

12. Various lists begin to show up in Folders 1953 ff. As they differ, it seems likely that she changed her "pitch" for specific library collections.

13. She still looked much younger than her years, as an incident with filmmaker Willard Maas indicates. He told her she looked marvelous for her age: "You must be about 40 and you still look 30." She thought to herself, "Blessed be Jacobson, Bogner, and Elizabeth Arden—once more I escape illness, old age, tragedy, and neurosis. The race horse is running again!" In Folder 1955.2.

14. In a letter, 6/13/55, James Brown politely tells AN that with the departure of René de Chochor from his agency, he (Brown) is unable to give her the attention a writer of her "distinction" needs. He suggests that she contact Georges Borchardt, which she did, but Borchardt apparently declined to represent her.

15. Folder 1955.2. Among those whom she met between 1953 and 1957 and who figured with varying degrees of significance in years to come were Renate Druks and her son Peter, Paul Mathiesen, Curtis Harrington, Gavin Lambert, Samson DeBrier, Kenneth Anger, Olivia and Gil Henderson, Cornelia Runyon, Leslie Blanche and her then-husband Romain Gary. She also renewed her acquaintance with Laura Archera, who was now married to Aldous Huxley.

16. Interview with Anne Geismar, 7/91; undated note from Maxwell Geismar, Folder 1955.1; AN's comments about their response in Folders 1955.1 and 2.

17. AN notes in Folder 1955.1 that Anne feared her influence on Max, always answering the telephone and saying that Max "was busy." In Folders 1956 and 1957, AN makes occasional reference to the fact that she never desired anything but an intellectual relationship with MG; from his letters to AN, there is an occasional warm compliment, but no indication that he did either.

18. The following account is based on correspondence between AN and MG found in various folders from 1955.1 and 2 through 1972, all of which will be noted more specifically as they occur in the text. At various times, MG arranged introductions to his publishers and even tried to repair the breach between AN and Edmund Wilson. He was unsuccessful because AN was violently opposed to seeing Wilson. She notes in Folders 1955.1 and 2 that EW offered several invitations to dinner, all of which she refused rudely. It makes me call into question his diary accounts of dining with her in the 1960s, for AN makes no mention of ever being alone with him again.

19. AN/MG, n.d., in Folder 1955.1. All quotes from this until noted otherwise.

20. AN/MG, n.d., 2 pp. typed, Folder 1955.2.

21. *Solar Barque* was first published by Edwards Brothers, Ann Arbor, MI, 1958, in an edition paid for by HG. It was incorporated into *Cities of the Interior* in 1959 and published by Alan Swallow, Denver.

22. The following account is taken primarily from Folder 1955.2, but I have drawn upon conversations with JNC, RP, and Gayle Nin Rosenkrantz as well.

23. MG/AN, card, n.d., in Folder

1955.2; AN's comments from ½ page of loose text.

24. Letter, n.d., in Folder 1955.2. All quotes from this until noted otherwise.

25. Pollack was to remain one of AN's most dedicated admirers and boosters of her work. He was responsible for the purchase by Northwestern of her early mss, and he tried heroically but unsuccessfully to see that the diaries found a home at Northwestern. He sponsored lectures and readings in the next decade, was a devoted correspondent, and finally expressed warm personal feelings for AN, which she gently but firmly rejected.

26. Brief note from Mme. Simenon in Folder 1955.2.

27. Information that follows is from Folders 1954.1 and 2, 1955.1 and 2, and interviews and conversations with JNC.

28. For almost a decade, AN had taken up rug-making as a kind of therapy to keep herself emotionally calm and stable. References to her rugs are found throughout the last several diary volumes and into the folders until the early 1960s. She took great pride and pleasure in her achievement.

29. "Mother was buried in the Culmell plot in Havana, but not next to father. Same cemetery, very different plots." JNC, fax, 4/23/94.

30. Although they maintained separate bedrooms from this time until the end of their marriage, they still had occasional conjugal relations when in New York. In Europe, where they went frequently during the next decade, they always slept in the same bedroom, if not the same bed.

31. Folder 1955.2. All quotes from this until noted otherwise. In undated letters to Lila Rosenblum, AN seeks to persuade LR that destruction of the diary is the best course, while LR sought to persuade her otherwise. In interviews, LR recalled how tortured AN seemed about destroying the diaries but how firmly she insisted she would do so.

32. Brown's letter is dated 6/3/55; Armstrong's reply 6/9/55. Copies are in Folder 1955.2.

33. AN to Neville Armstrong, n.d., in Folder 1955.2. AN's emphasis.

34. In a letter of 5/26/55, Armstrong suggested that AN extract "suitable portions" to make one volume of 70–80,000 words. He urged AN "most earnestly" to consider his suggestion, but she refused.

35. Margaret Crosland to AN, 11/22/55.

36. A friendship of sorts was formed between the two women, as they exchanged letters well into the 1960s, but Crosland was never responsible for a single translation or sale.

37. Copies of legal agreements from Montgomery & Marcus and letter dated 11/25/55 are in Folder 1955.2, as is JLH's letter of 12/8/55, quoted below.

38. In Folder 1955.2 she notes "in seven years only a few lapses, when Bill returned from Korea, when Carter Harman sought to retrieve a lost opportunity, once with Chinchilito [Graeffe]."

39. Folder 1955.2, AN's emphasis.

40. AN quotes Bebe Barron as saying this in Folder 1955.2. BB confirmed it in an interview, 7/91.

41. Folder 1955.2, a habit that RP said (in 1991 conversations) AN continued for many years thereafter.

31. Wider Perspectives

1. HG did not tell AN that he lost because she had earlier advised him to relinquish control over his siblings' funds and "he scorned [the advice] as coming from ignorance." Folder 1956.1.
2. HG made the first of several gestures to return to the bank as early as 6/53 (noted in Folder 1954.2), and others are mentioned in passing in undated letters, JNC/USF.
3. Folder 1956.1, typed.
4. There are references to the ulcer in AN's undated letters to James Leo Herlihy, and her brother JNC, with whom she renewed both closeness and correspondence since their mother's death. Also in Folders 1955.2, 1956.1 and 2, and 1957.
5. Harold E. B. Pardee, M.D., to AN, 2/17/56, in Folder 1956.1. All quotes from this until noted otherwise.
6. AN to JLH, 7/21/56, ibid.
7. Gary sent a letter thanking AN "for all the nice things you say about my last book. coming from such a distinguished writer as you. . . ." Folder 1956.2.
8. HG/AN, 11/11/56: "I am glad to hear you are comfortable in Isherwood's apartment. It sounds less isolated and more convenient." Copy in Folder 1956.2, orig. JNC/USF.
9. Folder 1956.1.
10. HG never told AN the woman's name.
11. Folder 1956.1. The date of this diary entry is 7/27/56. All quotes are from this entry until noted otherwise.
12. AN quotes him as saying this in Folder 1956.1. HG did not write specifically about this incident in the many papers he prepared for Dr. Bogner. If he did, the account has not survived.

32. The Meaning of Freedom

1. The title came from a newspaper article AN read about the discovery of an Egyptian funerary cave in which a boat was found, ostensibly to transport the dead person's soul to the heavens. Throughout the novel's gestation, AN always wrote the name as "Solar Bark." She learned the correct spelling only when it was ready for publication in 1958. For the complex history of this novel, see B. Franklin V, "AN: A Bibliographical Essay," 32, and 33, n. 5; also Sharon Spencer, "AN's 'Continuous Novel' *Cities of the Interior,*" note, 65; both in Zaller, ed., *A Casebook on AN.*
2. In his review "Temperament vs. Conscience," *Nation* 179 (7/24/54), 75–76. Geismar's portion of their correspondence consists of undated small file cards that he filled with closely typed text on both sides and sometimes around the margins. They are in Folders 1954 and 1955.1. In both folders, AN expresses her anger at Geismar's refusal to give her unequivocal praise.
3. Robert Hatch to AN, 10/31/56, Folder 1956.1.
4. AN to MG, n.d., probably late Oct. 1956, copy in Folder 1956.1.
5. In Folder 1956.1, she wrote, "I like

to slip into black tights and a beige car coat, hair down on my back, a black velvet circlet to keep the front in place. I like the way [beatniks] dress, flannel shirts and berets, girls in ski clothes with cloche hats. I don't know what they read but I share their love of jazz."

6. HM's literary idols of the time—Nietzsche, Spengler, Hegel—had little influence, if any, upon the development of AN's writing and thinking. Despite accepting the role of *femme inspiratrice* to a male writer, she still followed her own unique vision.

7. Letter, n.d., to "Steve" (Ruth Witt Diamant's son, Stephen), in Folder 1956.1.

8. Barney Rosset had recently published Beckett's English translation of the play. He took advantage of the informal discussions, sometimes arguments, that sprang up spontaneously in the lobby after each performance to sell books, and HG was among the many who bought a copy.

9. In Folder 1956.1. All quotes from this until noted otherwise.

10. The main characters, Pierre and Françoise, are not married, only lovers. They invite the young girl, Xavière, to share their relationship.

11. I base this view on their correspondence throughout 1956–1957, most of it undated, some copies in Folders 1956.1 and 2 and 1957, originals all in JNC/USF.

12. And also to cure her of drinking too much gin, for HG feared she was becoming addicted to martinis.

13. AN quotes Inge Bogner as asking this in Folder 1956.1.

14. RWD to AN, 10/19/56, Folder 1956.2. All quotes from this until noted otherwise.

15. AN/HG, n.d., Folder 1956.2, AN's ellipses in both instances. All quotes from this until noted otherwise.

16. She began using the term in 1956 and did not stop until 1961, in letters to RP, all UCLA; and AN/HG, JNC/USF.

17. All information about literary influences upon AN and her reading during this time come from Folders 1956.1 and 2 and Folder 1957.1, from letters to JNC, JLH, HG, and RP, among others, and from notes toward a possible article that was never completed on Beckett and the Beat Generation.

18. Folder 1956.1. All quotes from this until noted otherwise.

19. Beginning in Folders 1956.1 and 2, there are extensive passages written about why and how she made the changes that eventually resulted in the text of the published diaries. Some will be cited specifically where appropriate.

20. Later incorporated into *Seduction of the Minotaur.* The portion that was originally *Solar Barque* roughly comprises pp. 5–95 of the 1959 ed. published by Alan Swallow.

21. Folder 1956.1. All quotes from this until noted otherwise.

22. Folder 1956.2.

23. Spencer, *Collage of Dreams,* 62–63.

24. Book jacket of this edition is in Folder 1956.1. All quotes from this until noted otherwise. As a gift to James Leo Herlihy, the French artist Claude Michel Seren painted a portrait from the photo of AN on the back cover: *Portrait of Anaïs Nin,* 1977, oil on Masonite (48 × 33 inches). Collection JLH, L.A.

25. Undated letter to Neville Armstrong, Folder 1956.1.

26. In Folder 1957.1, AN thanks FP

for his "thoughtfulness in sending [Christmas] cards to both lives. You are the only one who thought of doing that." Also, letter to Felix Pollack, n.d., 3 pp. typed, in Folder 1956.2. All quotes from this until noted otherwise.

27. I base this statement and the brief profiles that follow on AN's writing in Folders 1953–1959; AN/HG, letters from 1953–1960, JNC/USF; AN/RP, in Folders 1953–1959; AN/LR, LR personal archives; AN/JLH, JHL personal archives with some copies in various UCLA folders; AN/GV, U. Wisconsin, Madison; and other sources that will be noted individually where appropriate.

28. Among the last are two women, one in each city, who believed themselves lesbians at the time but have since married, had children, and consider themselves now to be heterosexual. They have contributed to the discussion that follows but have asked not to be identified here.

29. Information from Folder 1954.1.

30. Barbara Reis Poe is among the late Cornelia Runyon's many friends who told me this.

31. She started to use notebooks in which carbon and second sheets were attached around 1951, and frequently complained that she had to use pencil and press too hard for an impression to come through, and that she could not easily tear the sheets from the folder. Nevertheless, it was a system she used until the end of her life.

32. AN/HG, n.d., 1958, JNC/USF.

33. RP, interviews, 1991.

34. In Folder 1953.1, AN states that Paul Mathiesen was the originator of the party, which was held in late Oct. 1953, and gives Renate Druks credit only for allowing it to be held at her house.

35. D-5, 133–135. AN claimed Anger told her she would be the star, but Anger became entranced by the painter who uses only one name, Cameron, and devoted more of the film to her. Anger said (interview, 9/17/91) AN knew from the beginning that her role would be limited but that she behaved "like a prima donna" and "would have taken over the entire film" had he not remained "firmly in control." Many years later, Cameron had nothing negative to say to me about AN, "with whom I really had very little contact throughout the filming and did not see after that" (interview, 9/25/91).

36. Folder 1953.1; confirmed by RP in interviews, 7/91.

37. Age is, of course, a relative concept closely related to the historical time in which it is considered. A fifty-year-old woman in 1953 was considered to be much older than a woman of the same age in 1993. AN kept her body firm and supple with daily massage, swims, and long walks. Many of her friends have remarked about how her body seemed more that of an adolescent than an adult, and many of those who were at this party were astonished at her youthfulness, for she was naked to her waist and wearing only a body stocking on the bottom half of her body.

38. In an interview, 7/91, Curtis Harrington said he was delighted to be given credit for such a striking phrase, but cannot truthfully remember ever saying it. He thinks AN invented it herself.

39. Folder 1957.1.

NOTES

33. The Black Children

1. Although they had not seen each other, as she notes in Folder 1957.1, they had been in sporadic correspondence, each pretending there was nothing amiss with Vidal's devastating depiction of AN as Marietta Donegal in *Two Sisters.* Throughout Folders 1949–57, AN worried that GV might be angry enough to tell both HG and RP about her bigamy, thus causing her to lose both men.

2. Folder 1953.1.

3. GV, interview, 4/29/92; Bebe Barron, interview, 7/31/91; AN, Folder 1957.1.

4. This and all quotes that follow from Folders 1957.1 and 2 until noted otherwise.

5. Folder 1957.1. AN described "fever, chills, swollen glands, painful breasts, swollen clitoris" and the usual "hot flashes" that had plagued her since she ceased menstruation at the age of 42. Now there was occasional spotting or bleeding as well, but it does not seem that she was alarmed by any or all of these symptoms. Dr. Jacobson then prescribed "sulfa" and several vitamin injections and most of her symptoms disappeared. However, from this time on she was plagued with unexplained, undiagnosed pain, and when she had her first operation to remove a tumor in 1969, she wondered if all these symptoms were related to it.

6. GV hinted to gossip columnists that they would soon marry, but "it was all a ruse to get Paul [Newman] to propose to her." He also said that he and JW have "remained devoted friends," and that AN was jealous of the friendship and did not understand it. Interview, 4/29/92. AN makes only a passing reference to "an actress Woodward whom he 'nearly married (it cost me $300 not to have a child)' but this I do not believe because I remember how he talked to everyone about my being his mistress." Folder 1957.1.

7. AN writes of this, ibid. GV (interview, 4/29/92) denies the conversation ever took place. I leave it for the reader to decide.

8. Folder 1957.1.

9. GS to AN, 10/28/57, original, ibid.

10. A Haitian diplomat whom she met at Lucas Premice's parties in the 1940s and with whom she had a sporadic relationship.

11. Folder 1957.1.

12. Folder 1957.2. All quotes from this until noted otherwise.

13. In the summer of 1959, in Paris, AN and HG accidentally encountered their W. 9th St. neighbors, Claire and Benjamin Shapiro, and invited them to lunch. In a letter to me, 10/20/92, Mrs. Shapiro wrote: "We discussed Lawrence Durrell's *Alexandria Quartet* which was a best seller at the time. AN dismissed him with some disdain saying 'He never would have made it without my help. I taught him what he knows about writing.' "

14. The others became *Balthazar, Mountolive,* and *Clea.* Information that follows is from three letters, n.d., LD/AN, and two AN/LD, n.d., all in Folder 1957.2.

15. Apparently AN was not content to let the matter rest, for he wrote again, 1/58, to tell her once again politely but also very firmly that Dutton would publish all his work in the United States, that *The Black Book* was "so full of errors it would be quite impossible to photoprint from it," and that he "never kept a diary; always felt it would swallow me."

16. It seems to have been Lipton who taught her the correct spelling, for she changed the title after their first exchange of letters.

17. From the letterhead, which also included the names of Elaine Bond, Publisher; Lawrence Lipton, Assistant to the Publisher; and Jane [Molson] Morrison, Editor; a publication of Enthusiasts Publications, Inc. (*Road and Track* magazine), Playa del Rey, CA.

18. In his letter of 11/17/57, Lipton makes it very clear that AN will be writing on speculation and that only Elaine Bond can make "any definite commitment." It seems she never did, but AN attacked the job as if she were a full-time salaried employer, as will be shown in this chapter.

19. LL/AN, 11/14/57, in Folder 1957.1.

20. AN/LL, n.d., ibid.

21. These lists are included in Folders 1957.1 and 2; Folders 1958.1 and 2. Of the proposals named above, Mead declined through her agents, Fromm did not reply, Santha Rama Rau said she was too busy filming in London, and Geismar said he was interested "in principle" but did not make a commitment. Herlihy sent the story, "Pretty on the Bus," which later appeared in *The Sleep of Baby Filbertson & Other Stories* (New York: E. P. Dutton, 1959).

22. LL/AN, 11/21/57.

23. Folder 1957.1. All quotes from this until noted otherwise.

24. AN's emphasis. I have been told by persons who are professionals in the field of mental health—psychiatrists, psychoanalysts, psychologists, and clinical social workers—that this passage represents a classic definition of a Narcissistic Borderline personality. Among those who discussed this with me, I wish to thank the members of the Psychoanalysis Seminar at the New York Institute for the Humanities and Drs. E. James Lieberman, Edwin Fancher, and Lila Rosenblum.

25. Elaine Bond and the members of her family who owned Enthusiasts Publications decided to stop publishing *Eve* in order to double the size of *Road and Track,* their most profitable publication. Jane Morrison Molson to AN, 5/5/58.

26. The first quote is AN's description of CC from Folder 1957.1, the second from CC/AN, letter of 6/13/58, in Folder 1958.1.

27. Ibid. All quotes from this until noted otherwise.

34. "Why not me?"

1. Information about this friendship is from Folders 1958.1–4. When the diary was published, Lesley Blanch was one of several persons who insisted AN remove all discussion of her life or else face legal consequences.

2. The actress Tracey Roberts was one; producer and director Henry Jaglom another. For a shorter time, UCLA professor and writer Jascha Kessler also tried to satisfy AN's demands for a screenplay of *Spy.* They figure in the 1960s and will be cited accordingly in later chapters.

3. Cecil Smith, "TV Story Producer Kozlenko Bursting with New Project," *L.A. Times,* 10/58, photocopy in Folder 1958.4.

4. He had just become affiliated with Revue Productions, whose main purpose was to hustle up stories and turn them into quick scripts for what was then the *crème de la crème* of television drama such as "Schlitz Playhouse" or "GE Theater."
5. AN to GS, undated but probably 2/58, as it refers to her first dinner with Kozlenko, which took place then. In folder 1958.2.
6. Ibid.
7. WW/AN, 2/17/59, in Folder 1959.1.
8. AN/HG, 3/5/58, JNC/USF, copy in Folder 1958.1. For a brief time, AN dated her letters because HG gave her a wristwatch for Christmas that had day and date on its face. Huxley's wife, the Italian violinist Laura Archera, was AN's patient many years before during AN's putative career as an analyst, both in Paris and New York.
9. AN to Milly Johnstone, n.d., copy in Folder 1958.1. As the drug counterculture of the 1960s–1970s accelerated, and "tripping" became the in thing to do, AN magnified both the effect and the importance of her single experience.
10. Uncharacteristically, she dated this entry: 3/29/58. Ibid.
11. Maschler later became director of Jonathan Cape and one of the most influential shapers of literary taste in the British publishing community.
12. She pursued Peter Owen in his capacity as publisher, not, as Owen has stated several times since AN's death, because she was in sexual pursuit. In all her correspondence with Owen, and in all her diary accounts, her only personal comments about him concern his manners and treatment of his staff.
13. In a letter of 6/29/58, on Penguin stationery, TM asked AN to give him "a little more time to get Heineman working on it." Folder 1958.2.
14. They paid heavy consequences as many of their assets were seized and confiscated. Most of the family managed to flee, but many were marooned there, and within certain families some were not able to join spouses and children who did manage to escape.
15. According to what Hugo wrote in letters to AN, Antolina de Cárdenas lost everything and died destitute, but a firm believer to the end in Castro. JNC, fax, 4/23/94, said, "As to her undying belief in Castro, that is another matter. . . . Anything having to do with Anaïs's Cuban family should be viewed with skepticism if coming from [her]."
16. HG/AN, 6/9/58, copy in Folder 1958.1, orig. JNC/USF.
17. AN/GV, n.d., U. Wisconsin, Madison, copy in Folder 1958.1.
18. AN/RP, air letter postmarked Sat., May 3, Paris. Folder 1958.2.
19. Folder 1958.1. All quotes from this until noted otherwise.
20. AN's emphasis.
21. RP/AN, Friday, 7/4/58, in Folder 1958.2. All quotes from this until noted otherwise.
22. CC/AN, 6/27/58, ibid.
23. RP/AN, 7/7/58, L.A., ibid.
24. Folders 1958.3 and 4. All quotes from these until noted otherwise.
25. Telegram, n.d., in Folder 1958.4; RP/AN, letter, 9/9/58, L.A., in Folder 1958.3.
26. AN/JNC, n.d., JNC/USF.
27. "Bohemia on the Waterfront: Serious writers and painters are creating new Shangri-La at the East River's edge near the tip of Manhattan," by Faye Hammel, *Cue,* 3/22/58, 16–17; copy in Folder 1958.3.

28. Information that follows is from Folder 1958.2 and 3; and interview with Lenore Tawney, 10/22/90.
29. When good friends gave birth to a daughter and asked to christen the child after Tawney, she suggested "Tristine" as a first name. In the 1970s, that same child, Tristine Rainer, became a friend and disciple of AN, and wrote *The New Diary* (L.A.: Jeremy Tarcher; distributed by St. Martin's Press, NY, 1978). Rainer dedicated it to three mothers: her birth mother, "Anaïs, through whom I found the second birth," and "Tawney, a true godmother." AN wrote the preface.
30. As late as 10/2/68 (in a letter to Natalie Barney, Bibliothèque Ste. Geneviève, Paris), Djuna Barnes still resented AN: "—and Miss Nin (something of a pathological 'little girl lost')! . . . It is intolerable!" I am grateful to Frances McCullogh for calling this letter to my attention.
31. Folder 1958.3. All quotes from this until noted otherwise.
32. LT, interview, 10/22/90. "I still have the books," Tawney said, having moved them to a succession of lofts over the years.
33. GV/AN, n.d.; AN/JLH, n.d.; AN/HG, n.d.; also diary writings, all Folders 1958.3 and 4.
34. AN/JNC, copy in Folder 1958.4. No matter what she thought of Nabokov's novel, she still bought boxes of the Olympia Press edition for $1.50, had them shipped to New York and L.A., and sold them for $15–$20 each. She did the same with some of HM's novels. Folder 1958.3.
35. AN writes of being unable to extend a compliment or to make any remark at all. JLH remembers this as "the time of my cardinal sin: I got famous and made money." Interview, 7/91.
36. Folder 1958.1.
37. Neville Armstrong, 10/7/58, London, in Folder 1958.3.
38. Information that follows is from MP/AN, 11/3/58, in Folder 1958.4.
39. AN/HG, n.d., JNC/USF.
40. Information that follows is from letters, n.d., AN/LD/AN, in Folders 1958.1–4.
41. Folder 1958.2.
42. All quotes from LD/AN, n.d., in Folder 1959.1.
43. AN/HG, 12/18/58, JNC/USF, copy in Folder 1958.4.
44. Ibid.
45. LD/AN, n.d., in Folder 1959.1.
46. JF/AN, 1/10/59, ibid.
47. Ibid. All quotes from this until noted otherwise.

35. "Too much to say"

1. They were using Hugo's insomnia as the excuse to maintain separate rooms, but each morning he or she would go into the other's bed and they would lie together and talk. AN claimed they were no longer having conjugal relations; in the few instances HG mentions these times (in the Bogner papers), he does not specify whether or not this is true. Information that follows is from Folder 1959.2, 1960.1; AN/JLH, 12/19/59; HG diary writings for Inge Bogner, JNC/USF; and RP interviews, 1991.

2. He does not mention sex specifically in his Bogner writings, but he does mention a new gentleness and tranquillity in their rapport.
3. RP/AN, n.d., in Folder 60.1.
4. Information that follows, ibid.
5. Wardell B. Pomeroy, Director of Field Research, to AN, 6/18/59, in Folder 1959.2. AN's mss included *Erotica One, Two,* and *Three, Brazil Erotica, Life in Provincetown, Marcel, Novel,* and *Second Novel.*
6. Owen told her he would not use her photo on the dust jacket because she would not permit any biographical information to accompany it; by the time she changed her mind, it was too late, for the jacket was already printed. PO/AN, 1/22/59, Folder 1959.2.
7. The AN/RB correspondence is in the Lilly Library, Indiana U. AN began her correspondence when HM asked her to write to a prisoner who had written to him, as he did not have time to continue the exchange. AN's letters and Bloom's replies begin in Folders 1959.2 and continue through the early 1970s, when he was released after serving his sentence. She also corresponded with inmates of mental hospitals in Calif. and Texas and a prisoner at Joliet called only "Duke." The exchanges did not last long and are found scattered in folders from 1961–1974.
8. AN/Eve Miller, n.d., in Folder 1959.2.
9. Her letter is n.d.; Vincent Crapanzano's is 4/11/60.
10. PO/AN, 10/19/60, in Folder 1960.1.
11. AN/PO, n.d., in Folder 1960.1.
12. Undated letters to HG, JLH, and RP contain comments about the difficulty of finding a title. In Folders 1959, 1960, and 1961, JLH private archives, and AN/HG, JNC/USF.
13. PO/AN, 10/19/60, in Folder 1960.1.
14. GS sent several letters to AN, among them 11/14/60 and 12/6/60, sympathizing with her and complaining about PO's intransigence. He urges AN to stop corresponding with PO, for "it is too much aggravation for you to be subjected to all this straddling. . . ."
15. AN/HG, Monday, 12/5/60, orig. JNC/USF, copy Folder 1960.1.
16. Quote from JLH, interview, 7/91. For a complete description and photos of the house, see Barbara Kraft's article in *Architectural Digest.*
17. AN/JLH, n.d., orig. JLH archives, copy in Folder 1960.1. All quotes from this until noted otherwise.
18. AN/JLH, orig. JLH archives, copy, ibid.
19. AN/JLH/AN, n.d., Folders 1960–1961; AN/HG, n.d., JNC/USF.
20. Correspondence and diary commentary begin in Folder 1961.1 and continue to the early 1970s.
21. However, she wrote to her brother Thorvald that the new apt. offered "fine view of the sky and skyline, space and comfort." 3/1/60, copy in Folder 1960.1. TN was then living in Chihuahua, where he was part owner of a plywood-processing corporation.
22. The following account is from diary writing dated 8/8/62, in Folder 1962.2.
23. Anne Baxter was well known in Hollywood for her white miniature poodles, and she helped AN to select her pup. Diary writings, n.d., in Folders 1961–1963, also confirmed by RP.
24. It was precisely this behavior that both infuriated AN and gave her the

excuse to postpone her parting from HG indefinitely. Their correspondence is filled with his comments that he could make no decision until he discussed it with Bogner, and hers that he must learn to take action and make choices without the analyst's prior approval.

25. AN/HG, n.d., copy in Folder 1960.1, orig. JNC/USF.

26. On the initial announcement, anyone who wanted to subscribe was directed to send money to Miss Anaïs Nin at 39 W. 9th St. She spent long angry hours hand-correcting her misprinted address.

27. The following is based on AN/JF/AN, Folders 1959.2 through 1963; AN's occasional diary commentary in the same folders; AN/HG/AN, JNC/USF, AN/LD/AN, Folders 1962–1963, AN/Daisy Aldan/AN, Folders 1961–1964, and interviews with RP, Daisy Aldan, Marguerite Young, and Harriet Zinnes.

28. Marguerite Young "could not get around to [writing about AN] in time"; Interview, 11/3/90. Kathleen Chase's original article was revised and submitted by AN. Edwin Fancher, "Anaïs Nin: Avant-Gardist with a Loyal Underground," *Village Voice,* 5/27/59, 4–5. Fancher called her "a major figure in the avant-garde literary movement of the past twenty-five years," and praised her work even though it was not well known by the general reader. AN's letters to EF are in Folders 1959.2 and 1961.1. In an interview, 4/29/92, EF did not remember a specific request to write about her for *Two Cities,* but did remember that she contacted him from then on whenever she published something, always hoping *VV* would write about it.

29. Jean Fanchette, "Notes pour une Préface," *Two Cities: La Revue Bilingue de Paris,* 4/15/59, 56–60. See also Cutting, *Reference Guide,* 21.

30. This topic came up one night in 1991 at a dinner party in Pasadena, when several of the guests remembered such an incident and joked about AN's "total lack of humor" and "how seriously she took herself." Several weeks later, one of the guests (who has asked not to be named) sent me the article AN insisted he take, which he found when sorting through an archive dating from 1960.

31. Information that follows is from diary writings in Folder 1961.1; interviews with LR, 1990; AN/LR/AN, private LR archives, and interviews with RP, 1991.

32. AN/LR, 2/27/61. All quotes from this until noted otherwise.

33. AN/LR, 5/61, original LR archives, copy in Folder 1961.2.

34. I asked RP repeatedly during the several years of our interviews and conversations to discuss many other matters relating to AN's taxes and medical expenses. I received so many confusing and contradictory replies to my questions that I have decided within this book not to speculate, but only to write what can be legally proven.

35. I am grateful to LR for making this card, still in her possession, available to me.

36. AN/MG, 5/61, copy in Folder 1961.2. Of all the women writing in the 1960s, Anaïs believed that only Simone de Beauvoir was taken seriously, and then because "she has the mind of a man (and an old fashioned one at that!)."

37. D-6. 257–258; the story appears in *Collages,* Swallow edition, 100–105. Lila never told AN how deeply

wounding both were: "It was my dream, and she was superficial and flippant about it."
38. AN/LR, 7/7/61, LR archives.
39. AN/LR, 7/7/61, ibid.
40. AN/LR, 1961, LR archives. LR's dating is "October (?), 1961."

36. "Nin Rediscovered in Denver"

1. AN/LR, 9/15/61. All quotes from this until noted otherwise. In a separate letter to "Dr. Greenwood" of L.A. (Folder 1961.1, n.d.), AN says he prescribed "entero-vioform" for her "fits of extreme nervousness." She reminds Greenwood to call Bogner, "who would like to know about my physical condition." AN also asks him to "send the bill to my husband, Hugh Guiler . . . and it will be paid."
2. His distinguished list included Yvor Winters (who just that year won the Bollingen Prize), poet and critic Allen Tate, and novelist Vardis Fisher. His enterprise was varied, as he also published Renaissance poetry, bibliographies, periodical indices, and a journal devoted to contemporary literature. Information from Richard Ellmann, "A Publisher for Poets," *Saturday Review of Literature*, 7/22/61, 33–34.
3. AN/AS, 2/61, copy in Folder 1961.1. All quotes from this until noted otherwise.
4. AS/AN, 3/6/61, ibid. All quotes from this until noted otherwise.
5. *Publishers Weekly,* announcement and review/article by Alex Rode, 7/10/61; copy, ibid.
6. Cutting's *Reference Guide* provides only a partial listing. After almost two decades of scant publicity, the period 1961–1977 (the year of AN's death) is marked by frenetic publishing activity, both AN's on behalf of herself and others and the writings of others about her. A complete bibliography is long overdue and much needed.
7. Royalty statement dated 3/31/62. A letter from GS, 6/18/62, had slightly better news, as he had just deposited $270 in further Swallow royalties to AN's account. Both documents in Folder 1962.3.
8. "The Seal Friends," *Vogue,* CXXXVIII, no. 2, Aug. 1, 1961, 20, 32. The article comprised pp. 44–47 of the Swallow edition of *Collages.* In a letter to B. Franklin V, 10/20/71, AN said she intended the story to be entitled "Death of a Seal," and that the magazine changed it without her permission.
9. The following is based on AN's diary account in Folder 1962.2; AN/HG/AN, n.d., but from the first six months of 1962, JNC/USF; and AN/HM/AN, UCLA Nin and Miller collections.
10. Joseph Kaye, "Woman Sues to Import Banned Books," *Kansas City Star,* 5/21/61. The headline referred to Dorothy Upham, an artist in New York, whose copies were seized at customs and was now suing for their return. All quotes from this article until noted otherwise.
11. In the late 1960s, Edwin Fancher was walking down a Greenwich Village street behind a comely young woman—so he thought—when she turned and he discovered it was AN, then in her early 60s. He remembers

thinking what marvelous care she must have taken of herself to have retained the body of a much younger woman. Interview, 4/29/92. AN's diary writings are filled with notations of her daily schedule that frequently included "one hour taking care of myself."

12. In almost every interview I conducted with persons who met her between 1960 and 1972, when she still lived part of the time in New York, the same comment was made time and again. All referred to how cleverly AN suffused HG's apartment with soft pink lighting and of how, even on sunny days, she drew the thick draperies and suffused the setting in the more flattering artificial light. She also decorated the apartment in shades of mauve, lavender, and pink, all of which showed off her porcelain complexion. As she aged, she began to pile on cosmetics, especially the white face power so favored in the late 60s and early 70s, so the effect was sometimes more ghoulish than enhancing.

13. George Wickes was then editing the Durrell-Miller correspondence for publication.

14. HM first gave his archives to librarian Lawrence Powell, who volunteered to store them "for safety purposes." This eventually led to their sale and UCLA remained the permanent repository of all the papers in HM's possession.

15. Larry Wallrich arranged for Phil Kaplan to appraise the letters. Kaplan offered $1,000 "for the collection," which included 150 autograph letters and 50 typed letters signed, plus their carbons "which have no real value but add interest." Kaplan conceded that the collection was probably worth between $2,000 and $2,500, but he offered to buy them himself for $1,000. LW/AN, 11/14/60. In her reply, AN said she had to accept the offer "as I need the money now." She asked if Kaplan could be persuaded to "offer a little more if I included . . . the love letters, of which there are about as many as of the others, and I could sign a contract that they are to go to him after Hugo's death." She either decided not to sell the love letters or he did not agree to buy them, for she retained them. "In any case, I have to sell the first batch as I cannot wait. I am in difficulties on this end." AN/LW, n.d., in Folder 1960.1.

16. AN was wrong in this matter: United States law states that letters are the physical property of the recipient; the writer owns only the content, not the paper on which his/her words are written. Legally, HM had no obligation to return the physical property to AN.

17. HM/AN, 7/19/62, orig. HM/UCLA; copy in Folder 1962.2. All quotes from this until noted otherwise.

18. HM/AN, 7/25/62, HM/UCLA; copy, ibid.

19. Wilbur J. Smith/AN, 8/16/62, ibid.

20. JLH/AN, Folders 1961.2 and 1962.1.

21. This and information that follows is from diary writings in Folder 1963.1.

22. Diary entry, 8/8/62, in Folder 1962.2.

23. AN made several trusts during her lifetime: In 7/92 she named Inge Bogner and Gunther Stuhlmann as Trustees. It was revoked and re-executed on 11/10/75, when AN named RP sole trustee, was further amended on 4/20/76, and again on 6/21/76. RP is to be succeeded by Evelyn Hinz and

Phyllis Deutsch (RP's attorney) as co-trustees; the survivor to be sole trustee. However, successor trustees may be appointed by mutual consent of the beneficiaries or by court order. The assets transferred to the 1975 trust consist of all of AN's literary property. The income beneficiaries were HG and RP, or the survivor. As of HG's death, RP became the sole beneficiary of the income for his life. Upon his death, the income is to be shared equally by Eric Wright and JNC, or the survivor. The balance of the trust estate was to be distributed to the Los Angeles Center for Group Psychotherapy, but the amendment of 6/21/76 created the Anaïs Nin Foundation, to help "creative young people in need of aid in their respective fields." Information provided by Gayle Nin Rosenkrantz, Esq., letter to DB, 12/2/93.

24. Diary account, 8/8/62, verified by RP, interview, 7/91.

25. Both Gunther Stuhlmann and Larry Wallrich were trying to help her. Wallrich consulted a lawyer because of the possibly pornographic content of some of the diaries, but nothing came of it. He also was unsuccessful with a "Dr. Hammerschlag," who was "qualified in literary as well as psychiatric matters." LW/AN, 11/14/60, in Folder 1960.1.

26. AN/RW-D, n.d., ibid. All quotes from this until noted otherwise. AN also said she read "The Party" with an actor at The Living Theatre and that "Julian [Beck] and Judith [Malina] who are hard to please" gave her warm praise. She added that it was not a play, that it lasted 40–45 minutes, and that she added three descriptive passages from the novels that introduced her three female characters and made them more accessible to the audience.

27. GS/AN, 6/18/62, copy in Folder 1962.3. All information from this until noted otherwise.

28. George Wickes edited this volume. In a letter to AN, 6/28/62, Wickes asked her to consider writing something for a "critical miscellany" he was assembling. Innocently, Wickes wrote that "the book needs something from you to give a complete account of Henry Miller's biographia literaria, especially in the thirties." It threw her into a panic and made her more determined than ever to control her correspondence with HM.

29. In a tel. conversation, 1/19/94, GS said of all AN's efforts to get a screenplay that "no money ever changed hands, even though from time to time there was a lot of enthusiasm for the project. Most of the enthusiasm was hers, however. She had an iron constitution despite her protestations that she suffered all the time, and she worked very, very hard to get someone to film something. But all the agreements she made were only drafts, agreements that were supposed to lead to formal contracts. They were never signed and no money ever changed hands. I have a folder in my files, a thick one, full of 'drafts of agreements,' but no one ever went beyond that."

30. In a letter to HG, 1/23/62, JNC/USF, copy in Folder 1962.1, AN asks him to consider "if you don't wish to tackle the whole film, at least [directing] such sequence as the end."

31. Copy of "Translation of Contract" with Albicocco and Jacques Lanzman, Paris, 3/19/62. In Folder 1962.2.

32. Although there was almost a year of negotiation and correspondence flew back and forth, no money changed hands and no treatment was written.

33. Tracey Roberts also worked with Jerry Bick of the Bick and Siegel Agency. For several years she held an unpaid option on *Spy*. When she learned that AN engaged Jascha Kessler to write a screenplay, she hurriedly gave AN a check for $1,000 to secure an option, but it bounced and AN was forced to ask HM to lend her the money to make it good. AN wrote to HG that TR gave her several other checks to secure an option but they all bounced, too. Whether this is true or simply something she told HG is not known. Despite this history, AN pursued TR and JB for the next several years in the hope that a film would eventually be made.

34. Folder 1962.2 contains a draft of a letter she sent to most of these scriptwriters, in which she tries to convince them to stress Sabina and not Djuna, saying "with your help [Sabina] could be marvellously alive." AN insists Sabina's story is "more universal," and that "she belongs to our time of anxiety."

35. To seal the contract, AN borrowed $1,000 from HM to pay him the first installment (and the only payment he ever received). In a letter to HG, 1/17/63, original JNC/USF, copy in Folder 1963.1, AN said she had no qualms about borrowing from HM because "after all he is paying an old debt and was glad to do it." Information that follows is from Folders 1962.2, 1963.1; Jascha Kessler to AN, 4/30/62, in Folder 62.1; interviews and conversations with Jascha Kessler and Julia Braun Kessler, July 1991, July–Aug., 1992; interviews with RP, 1991 and 1992.

36. Correspondence, n.d., between AN/HG, probably early 1970s.

37. Correspondence and diary accounts in folders for the years 1963–1964 mention this elusive woman who seems to have had emotional difficulties and probably was not the heiress she pretended to be.

38. RP, interview, 7/91.

39. From Folders 1962.2 and 3; AN/HG/AN, n.d., but 1962–1963; RP interviews, 7/91.

40. AN/HG, 8/29/62 and 8/31/62, JNC/USF, copies in Folder 1962.2.

41. Diary writing for 8/8/62, in Folder 1962.2. All quotes from this until noted otherwise.

42. Information that follows is from diary writings in Folder 1963.1. All quotes from this until noted otherwise.

37. "Story of the Diary"

1. Swallow published the first American edition of *DHL: An Unprofessional Study* in 1964. Neville Spearman published the British reissue in 1961. That edition sold respectably and garnered few, but cautiously positive reviews.

2. From a diary segment in Folder 1964.1. She never names this librarian. All quotations are from these pages until noted otherwise.

3. It was the first critical study of AN, published in 1968 as *Anaïs Nin* by Southern Illinois Press.

4. The following is from three letters, n.d., to Oliver Evans, all in Folder 1962.2. All quotes from these until noted otherwise.

5. Oliver Evans, "Anaïs Nin and the Discovery of Inner Space," *Prairie Schooner* 36, Fall 1962, 217–231. During the time Evans wrote the article, AN initiated a correspondence with the journal editor, Karl Shapiro. In reply to several modest statements about how exciting her life must have been in Paris, AN confided all the details of her "secret" double life to him, and thus ensured that he would not permit Evans to publish anything that might give it away. This correspondence is in Folders 1961.1 and 1962.2.

6. AN/HG, n.d., JNC/USF; copy in Folder 1963.1.

7. HG/AN, 3/28/64, JNC/USF, copy in Folder 1964.1.

8. From the vagueness of her remarks to HG, this may just have been idle chatter on her part, for in their ensuing contact, AN remarks frequently about MD's "vagueness," her inability to grasp the essence of what is important in *Spy*, and questions her "concentration" on the project.

9. Jerry Bick to Georges Borchardt, 4/19/64, in Folder 1964.1.

10. AN/HG, 4/2/64, ibid.

11. Whether HG paid her all or part of the $4,000 is not known, but she was paid by someone other than Wise or Bick, so by a process of omission he is the only logical participant left.

12. Published by Cahiers de l'Herne, whom she said wanted "to do all the books [André] Bay [of Stock] does not do." Letter to Anne [Metzger, French translator of *Ladders to Fire*], n.d., copy in Folder 1964.1. AN also told Metzger that she was "particularly unhappy" with Bay and "I dream of escaping from him." This was because he made decisions concerning her work that made publishing sense but did not correspond to the overinflated view she had of the reception for her work in France.

13. Edgard Varèse, *Nocturnal* (1961). 1968 version including text from AN's *House of Incest* recorded by Vanguard Classics, # OVC 4031.

14. GS/AN, 3/23/64, in Folder 1964.1. In this letter GS says the money came from Random House, but in a telephone interview, 1/27/94, GS said he did not remember any option money coming from RH and does not remember why he wrote this letter or what the money represented. He could not remember specifically dealing with Peter Israel, and said when the letters were eventually published by Putnam, William Targ was the editor.

15. HG/AN, 6/5/64, JNC/USF; Folder 64.1.

16. AN/HG, 6/18/64, JNC/USF; copy, ibid. All quotes from this until noted otherwise.

17. Eventually, that is exactly what happened. Wise's option expired in 11/64 and he went on to other projects. Bick took the script he and AN wrote and tried to interest Joseph Losey in producing it. He was not interested. By 1965, when AN was under contract to publish the diaries, she remained interested in a film, but no longer gave it her full attention.

18. HG/AN, 6/13/64, JNC/USF; copy in Folder 1964.1.

19. She chose the title in honor of her friend Jean Varda's chosen form of artistic expression. Varda presented AN and RP with a collage as a gift for their new home.

20. AS/AN, 12/2/64, in Folder 1964.1.

21. The following information is from AS/AN, 12/2/64, ibid.

22. AN/GS, 12/31/64, copy, ibid.

23. Internal memo from Peter Israel,

specifically concerning the story "Count Laundromat and the Flying Carpet," but dealing with other parts (later revised) of *Collages* as well, 9/19/63, copy, ibid.

24. It also helped when William Goyen gave a favorable review in the *The NY Times Book Review*, engineered by Nona Balakian, one of the editors and a new friend of AN.

25. The letters to Bogner have not survived, but there are repeated references to them in her undated letters to HG, most of which are JNC/USF, some of which are in various UCLA folders for 1964–1966.

26. HG's initial letter is dated 8/22/64. Although I base the account that follows on several other letters, uncharacteristically n.d., all quotes are from the 8/22 letter unless noted otherwise.

27. HG/AN, 8/22/64, JNC/USF, copy in Folder 64.1.

28. Information that follows is from AN's letters, n.d., to HG and JNC, all JNC/USF.

29. AN/GS, 11/5/64, copy in Folder 1964.1.

30. In D-6, 382, AN quotes a letter supposedly written by Peter Israel rejecting the diaries. GS, in a tel. conversation, 1/27/94, said he remembered asking PI for permission to quote from this letter, which is not included in the UCLA files. As AN saved every other communication pertaining to the publication of the diaries, I find it odd that the original of this letter is not among them. All that exists is AN's letter, n.d., to HG, in which she not only inserts the passage purportedly by PI reprinted in D-6, but also her own commentary that follows in the text there.

31. AN/HG, 2/8/65, JNC/USF, copy in Folder 65.1. Bay's demands were answered: Éditions Stock published all three.

32. This is taken from the only portion of James Silberman's letter of rejection, sent to Gunther Stuhlmann, that GS thought appropriate for AN to see. She quotes the passage in its entirety in a letter to HG, 11/16/64. Copy in Folder 1964.1. All quotes from JS are from this letter unless noted otherwise.

33. GS/AN, 11/6/64, copy, ibid.

34. AN/GS, 11/9/64, copy, ibid. All quotes from this until noted otherwise.

35. JS/GS, passage quoted in AN/HG, 11/14/64.

36. In Folder 1965.1. All quotes from this until noted otherwise. It is also strange that the woman who not only kept but filed meticulously every scrap of paper that came her way kept almost no letters or other supporting documentation pertaining to Hiram Haydn.

37. In "Story of the Diary," she wrote that HM was "concerned over June and his first wife. And in his letter to me he protected his first daughter."

38. JNC, interview, 7/91.

39. AN/ JNC, 4/30/65, Folder 1965.1.

40. Gayle Nin Rosenkrantz, tel. conversation, 12/1/93. In a fax (11/15/94), GNR said, "In talking to Charlie de Cardenas about his investments, his motive was not lack of compassion, but an honest desire to help. . . . OK, maybe bragging too [about his own sound business acumen]."

41. Information that follows is from AN/Dr. Inge Bogner, n.d. (internal evidence suggests summer 1965), copy in Folder 1965.1. Also, interviews with JNC, 7/92, tel. conversation with Gayle Nin Rosenkrantz, 12/1/93.

42. AN/Inge Bogner, n.d. Folder

1965.1. All quotes from this until noted otherwise.
43. Lesley Blanch broke off all contact with AN once *Collages* was published. She left L.A. and moved to France after her divorce. Undeterred, AN wrote to ask LB to sign a release when she was preparing D-5 and 6. Blanch repeated her threats of legal action. AN wrote about her anyway.
44. RW/AN, 11/18/65, copy in Folder 1965.1. RW signed the letter "All my blessings, yours ever, with love." In the 1965 letter, RW objected to AN's "reference to Miller," which "isn't fair to me, in its brief state." AN did eliminate RW in D-1, but she wrote her version of their encounters in D-2, thus provoking RW's outrage at being so treated and inspiring her angry letter to Gordon Ray, quoted earlier.
45. AN/JNC, 4/30/65, Folder 1965.1. All quotes are from this unless noted otherwise. I have also relied upon interviews with RP, GS, JNC, JF, and others who were familiar with AN's adaptation of the diaries and who will be cited individually where appropriate. There are others whose identity AN disguised, particularly her analytical patients. One to whom I spoke said she was mortified when friends who did not know of her analysis with AN said descriptions of some invented characters "fit me to a T." In some cases, as with Antonia Brico and her all-woman orchestra, AN telescoped several persons into one. In other cases, with persons who have asked me not to identify them, she simply changed gender or sexual preference to suit her version of the other person's self.
46. "Story of the Diary."
47. Such thinking is, of course, subjective. What did not seem destructive to AN caused emotional anguish in two cases in which I have been asked to respect confidentiality. In another instance, someone's professional reputation suffered damage, and still another person complained of suffering familial distress because of AN's version of what he believed was "mere casual acquaintance." My judgment as an objective observer of the case presented by both sides is that each had some merit: AN to write as she did, the others to respond as they did.
48. Whether or not AN reverted to the Catholicism of her girlhood is a point that has been argued by many of the persons closest to her who were generous with their support and assistance for this book, among them Rupert Pole, Joaquín Nin-Culmell, and John Ferrone. Although there is a wide range of disagreement in their beliefs, and in mine as well, the Catholic conception of absolution is the one AN demonstrated in her dealings with those closest to her, HG in particular, for the rest of her life. Absolution became an important concept in her life's last decade.

38. Being Famous

1. From a random collection of jottings by AN dated 4/1/69, in Folder 1970.
2. Jean Garrigue, "The Self Behind the Selves," *NY Times Book Review,* 4/24/66, Section 7, 1. Professor Aileen Ward, Garrigue's literary executor, told me (tel. conversation, 12/93)

that AN cultivated Garrigue's friendship before and after this review appeared, and that JG frequently complained of AN's excessive and blatant attempts to influence what she wrote about her. For some reason, AN did not entirely approve of this flattering review. She complained about it directly to JG and then spoke disparagingly of her to others, who relayed the stories to the bewildered reviewer, who had no idea of what exactly she had written to offend AN.

3. For several years in the early 1970s, Nan Fuchs, whom AN called "the Herb Lady," drove her each day to the Silver Lake Post Office, where she always kept a box, to collect her mail. Fuchs remembers being stunned by the "several sacks, cartons," which AN collected on a daily basis and also by the equally large number of letters she sent each day. Interview, 7/92, Santa Monica.

4. Once she became famous, AN's preferred form of address became her full name. In a letter to Sharon Spencer, 9/19/63, AN wrote "Please call me Anaïs Nin (like Virginia Woolf, Rebecca West, etc.)." I shall respect her wishes and do the same here.

5. AN/Marguerite Rebois, 12/13/69, in a box of letters, otherwise untitled, in possession of Rupert Pole, hereafter referred to as Box/RP.

6. The following account is based on documentation in Folders 1966–1972 and an interview with the person in question, who has asked not to be identified. I was alerted to this situation by the person's analyst, whom I met socially. I initiated the discussion by telling him that I was writing this book and that I had read his letter to AN. He suggested (without otherwise commenting or breaching confidentiality) that I pay careful attention to AN's "meddling in doctor-patient relationships after she became famous."

7. For obvious reasons I have not identified the parties in question. AN continued to write to the patient for several years, each time insisting the letter would be her last, but always unable to extricate herself from the relationship.

8. Quote is from AN/HG, 6/3/66. Among the negative letters is one in Folder 1970 to Leon Edel, objecting to his "Life Without Father," in *Saturday Review of Literature,* 5/7/66, 91. She objected to two of Edel's judgments: "Literary history will probably place her with that last backwater of Romanticism [i.e., Surrealism] before World War II," and "Her diaries . . . should be quarried, it might be suggested, with caution, lest they become like Frankenstein monsters, too large for Miss Nin's own child-like lotus-flower existence." Robert Kirsch, the chief book reviewer of the *L.A. Times,* was not safe even in London, where he was on sabbatical. AN accused him of deliberately giving her books to "incompetant reviewers." In his reply, he wrote, "I hardly know how to answer it." When she threatened him with an unflattering portrait in the forthcoming D-3, he wrote, "I cannot help the aura I give off . . . I am simply myself and I cannot take any roles. What you write in your diary about me must be what you think . . . I cannot influence that."

9. AN's undated letter is in Folder 1966.2. Most of her complaints can be summed up in one of her phrases: "Our first disagreement was based not on evaluation . . . but on your biographical assertions, or interpretations . . . you think I expect praise, and all the time what I am struggling to get is interpretation, not evaluation." Throughout the writing of the book, as their correspondence attests, Evans made almost every change or deletion she wanted and followed nearly all her suggestions. His final reply, dated 8/3/66, seems to sum up his dilemma: "it seems incomprehensible that you should not have found [the book] pleasing."

10. Knapp's review of *The Novel of the Future* appeared in *The Village Voice,* 4/10/69, 6–7.

11. Knapp's undated note is attached to a review of *Novel of the Future* prepared for *VV,* which AN was instrumental in securing for her to write. In the first of five files of 1969 correspondence, this one dated in AN's hand, Jan.–Feb. AN's reply is dated 4/26/69.

12. There are several letters exchanged between Nona Balakian and AN that show how NB may have bent, if not actually have broken, some of the *Times*'s stringent rules to please and pacify AN when the diaries were reviewed there.

13. Anna Balakian, review of *Anaïs Nin,* by Oliver Evans, in *American Literature* 41, March 1969, 130–133.

14. AN/AB, n.d., in first of five correspondence folders for 1969, Jan.–Feb.

15. Information is from misc. letters enclosed in Folders 1966–1973, interviews with RP, undated letters to HG and JNC, both JNC/USF. The page numbers are among the many that dot her random diary jottings 1968–1974.

16. AN/AS, Folder 1966.1.

17. Not everyone shared this view. Maureen Howard, in a comment made after a lecture I gave to the New York Institute for the Humanities, 3/27/92, said AN was "truly an embarrassment, a horror, a frightening sight to come upon in Greenwich Village with that mask of makeup."

18. When the diaries began to pay royalties, she splurged on several cosmetic enhancements, including one full face-lift. RP, interviews, 9/91.

19. Many of these lectures were collected in two separate volumes, *Anaïs Nin: A Woman Speaks,* ed. Evelyn J. Hinz (Chicago: The Swallow Press, 1975), and Anaïs Nin, *In Favor of the Sensitive Man and Other Essays* (New York: Harcourt Brace Jovanovich, 1976).

20. Letter signed by "Beatrice" on W. Colston Leigh letterhead, 6/14/66, telling her she has been confirmed to speak at the Library of Congress on 3/13/67, for $750. Also that the agency was working on a tour to encompass the East and West coasts as well as the Midwest. All these lectures were in addition to the ones AN accepted on her own to speak at various colleges and universities. Just as she had ignored Gunther Stuhlmann's representation to make her own publishing arrangements, she now did the same with the W. Colston Leigh Agency, causing frequent scheduling conflicts that eventually led to their dropping her from their roster of speakers. From 1966 to 1973 she toured almost constantly and insisted to both RP and HG that these lectures provided a considerable segment of her income, which they did not. Also, to make sure that John Ferrone (her ed. at HBJ) and Richard Centing (founder and ed. of the AN newsletter, *Under the Sign of Pisces*) always knew where she could be reached, AN would send them photocopies of her Month-At-A-Glance calendar with engagements duly noted. The schedule was indeed grueling.

21. AN/AS, 5/9/66, Folder 1966.1.

22. She did have a separate bedroom and bath, but her letters and diary jottings continue to mention how each got into the other's bed in the morning for cuddling and conversation. As Hugo was sexually active with other women, one can infer that he may have had occasional relations with his wife.

23. Phyllis Deutsch practiced in L.A. In New York, AN was represented by George C. Shively, of the firm Satterlee, Warfield & Stephens. Shively drew up the first of several trusts in 5/66 (his correspondence begins in Folder 1966.2), which Deutsch later annulled when she prepared new trusts in accordance with California laws.

24. Phyllis Ziffren Deutsch/AN, 6/24/66, Folder 1966.2; a copy of the Judgment of Annulment dated 6/16/66, between Rupert Pole and Anaïs Nin, is on file in the Court, County of Los Angeles, State of California. Deutsch advised AN not to sign quitclaim deeds on the house, to change passport statements, or to settle any taxes.

25. AN/HG, 11/4/64, JNC/USF, copy in Folder 1966.1. AN used the excuse of preparing vol. 1 for publication to spend most of 1964–1965 in the Silver Lake house, which she grew to love more and more as time passed.

26. It is a question I raised myself the first time I read the published diaries, and also by so many persons I encountered throughout the writing of this book that I have singled none out for attribution here.

27. HG/ Irina Aleksander, 10/15/71, copy in Folder 1966.2. Emphasis HG's. All quotes from this until noted otherwise. In the preface, D-1, xi, Gunther Stuhlmann does state that "Several persons, when faced with the question of whether they wanted to remain in the diary 'as is'—since Miss Nin did not want to change the essential nature of her presentation—chose to be deleted altogether from the manuscript (including her husband and some members of her family)." GS also added to the controversy when he innocently admitted that AN changed "the names of some incidental figures, since . . . the factual identity of a person is basically unimportant within the context of the diary. Miss Nin's truth, as we have seen, is psychological."

28. JNC/USF. Pencil, very faint, on pages torn from a stenographer's notebook.

29. Diary passage dated Sunday, 8/17/69. JNC (tel. conversation, 1993) recalls that the surgery was neither alarming nor life threatening. HG had a detached retina that he claimed threatened his vision and necessitated emergency surgery. AN was in NY at the time and she remained there until he was well. All quotes are from Folders 1969 and 1970 and JNC conversation until noted otherwise.

30. AN/GS, Paris, Monday, 10/20/69, copy in Folder 1970.

31. The original diaries were still in the Brooklyn vault. She prepared all seven volumes working from typed copies made by Virginia Admiral, Lila Rosenblum, and several other typists she engaged over the years. A screenplay of "SIHOL" was supposedly being written by Barbara Turner, but AN rejected it shortly after. AN and HG decided together not to proceed with Tom O'Horgan and Jean Reavey, then working with Ellen Stewart at LaMama in New York and who were all interested in adapting the novel, because HG was affronted by the strong language, nudity, and crude surrealism of their work when he saw it staged. He thought it "too déclassé" for AN and urged her not to associate her work with "hippie" drama. Undated letters in Folders 1966, 1968, 1970.

32. I base this and the following discussion on my interviews with her family, devoted friends, and mortal enemies. My interpretations are based on several hundred conversations over a three-year period.

33. One of Inge Bogner's patients, then in her twenties, recalled seeing "this apparition walk into the waiting room. She sees me and immediately starts talking as if we're old and good friends. I was shocked and scared—who was she, to invade my space that way. Later, when I found out it was Anaïs Nin, and I put together what friends told me about her, I knew why she acted that way. Everybody had to love her." This was the woman's only meeting with AN. She has asked not to be identified.

34. One of these women, who has asked not to be named, said that "after so many gross guys, it was amazing to find someone whose idea of an old lady was not just a punching bag and coffee maker."

35. What follows was selected as representative from a handwritten calendar for 1969–1970, Folder 1970.

36. From diary jottings for 11/69 and correspondence with "Professor Newcomb," in Folders 1970 and 1971.

37. AN and SS were the same size and wore the same sort of ethnic clothing, which they sometimes exchanged.

38. She also noted proudly in an undated letter to HG, probably 1971, that her "Paris Diary" was to be published there and she would be paid $1,700 for it. JNC/USF.

39. A full listing of their publications can be found in Cutting's *Reference Guide* and Jason's *AN and Her Critics.*

40. Not everyone was privy to AN's double life. In a 1990 interview, Lila Bita and Robert Zaller recalled how shocked they were to learn after AN's death that she had a husband in New York throughout the entire time they knew her, 1969–1977. Another woman, who lived in L.A. and met AN during this time, Barbara Kraft, was also shocked when Sharon Spencer assumed she knew about HG and took her to a party at his apartment when she visited New York. In an interview, 9/89, Kraft said it was "one of several things" for which she "never forgave" AN.

41. *The Mirror and the Garden: Realism and Reality in the Writings of Anaïs Nin* (Columbus, Ohio State U. Libraries Publications Committee, 1971), revised ed. (New York: Harcourt Brace Jovanovich, 1973). In 1974, AN chose Hinz to be her authorized biographer, but as of 1994, she has not published the book.

42. Holt and her then-husband established Ragnarock Press; Harms and Aldrich called theirs Magic Circle Press. Harms and Aldrich were also co-sponsors of the Magic Circles Weekend, 4/92.

43. I am grateful to Richard Centing for granting me permission to use his considerable archives, which will be referred to as RCA.

44. This became AN's favorite phrase and semiofficial title for what was officially entitled *Under the Sign of Pisces,* a term Centing thought more appropriate for a publication sponsored by a university library's publications committee.

45. AN/RC, 1/29/70 and 4/16/70, both RCA.

46. From a 1969 list prepared for RC, RCA.

47. D-7, 268. In AN's defenses, I cite

RP's letter to RC, 8/1/76, in which he spoke of AN's continuous pain during her final illness: "she has had more physical and emotional problems in the last two years than most have in two lifetimes. This is why she has been particularly touchy about what she saw (and didn't see) in Pisces. In her time she has seen a lot of long, dumb, anti-Nin diatribes, but when she read one in Pisces on top of the illness, it upset her terribly. I know you will understand and be extra careful of Pisces contents during this horrible period." RP was responsible for the final decision on content of D-7, which was published in 1980.

48. In his initial letter, BF/AN, 9/29/69, he said he envisioned the newsletter as "a source for reminiscences, critical articles, bibliographic data, news about your current activities, etc." She found this acceptable and welcomed him until he insisted on fulfilling his mission.

49. D-7, 289; undated correspondence, RCA; random diary jottings in Folder 1971 and Box/RP.

50. Meryle Secrest, "Economics and the Need for Revenge," *Anaïs: IJ* 6, pp. 33–35. Secrest's article is one of three views of the then-just-published *Henry and June,* but it is also one of the most astute and perceptive analyses.

51. D-7, 290. Nancy Scholar Zee published *Anaïs Nin* (Boston: Twayne, 1984) and articles in *Pisces* and several other scholarly journals.

52. Millet's article originally appeared in *Le Monde* as "Portrait de l'Artiste en Femme: Nous sommes toutes des Anaïs," 1976. It was translated and reprinted in slightly different form after Nin's death in *Anaïs IJ* 9, pp. 3/8. Quote is from AN/RC, 8/1/70, RCA.

53. Mostly in undated letters beginning in 1971 and lasting for the rest of her life. Mostly in JNC/USF, some copies in various UCLA folders and Box/RP.

54. AN/RC, n.d., postmarked 10/30/70, RCA.

55. AN/DS, undated, probably 1967. I am grateful to Dan Stern for making his letters from AN available to me.

56. William McBrien, conversation, 1991.

57. This phrase is repeated time and again, mostly in letters she did not date, all RCA.

58. HZ/AN, 11/3/69, Geneva, Switz., in Box/RP.

59. She persuaded Claire to devote a special issue to the novels of Hiram Haydn, hoping it would help her to penetrate his implacable reserve toward her and her work. Haydn remained impervious to the considerable charm she lavished upon him. Her correspondence with (among many others) Daisy Aldan and Daniel Stern is full of references to their contributions, real or proposed.

60. AN/HH, 6/14/69, copy in Folder 1970.

61. AN/Roger Boulogne, 11/10/69.

62. GS/AN, 4/28/69, Box/RP.

63. AN/GS, 5/1/69, ibid.

64. AN/GS, 2/4/69, ibid.

65. These letters are in Box/RP. It does not seem necessary to single out some of the many here.

66. Gore Vidal, "Taking a Grand Tour of Anaïs Nin's High Bohemia via the Time Machine," *L.A. Times Book Review,* 9/26/71, 1.

67. AN repeats his word in a letter of 2/69, in Folder 1970.

68. Shortly thereafter, when Hiram Haydn retired, JF became her official editor at HBJ. He also became one of her closest friends and confidants for the remaining years of her life.

69. John Ferrone, interview, 7/90. AN

also writes of this in diary jottings in Folder 1970.

70. Marlis Schweieger took the photograph.

71. Her letter, n.d., to Roger Boulogne and a list of her itemized expenses for the year are in Folder 1970. All quotes from this until noted otherwise.

72. AN/HG, n.d., JNC/USF.

73. From a jotting in Folder 1970.

74. AN/GS, 11/18/69. All quotes from this until noted otherwise.

75. AN/HM, 11/17/69, Box/RP.

76. From random jottings, 6/10/69, in Folder 1970.

77. AN/BC, 7/7/71, copy in Box/RP. AN is referring to "An Evening with Anaïs Nin," sponsored by *Second Wave* and *Female Liberation,* 5/28/71, at Old Cambridge Baptist Church, Harvard Square. A reporter estimated the crowd at 1,100. All quotes from this until noted otherwise.

78. Gore Vidal, interview, 4/29/92, said AN spoke disparagingly to him when they met in Paris in 1970 of "Kotex Congresses" and claimed she did not understand the younger generation of women and what they wanted from her. Many of her women friends, among them Deena Metzger, Sharon Spencer, Tristine Rainer, believed AN thought of herself as a feminist, but in her own individual way. Too many persons to cite here told me in interviews how puzzled AN was by women who would not accept her version of female liberation.

79. Word used by several graduates of Bennington, class of 1971, where AN was the commencement speaker.

80. Bertha Harris, "Who Chose These Women, and Why?" *Village Voice,* 11/30/72, 71, a review of *Four Chosen Women: Anaïs Nin, Suzanne Benton, Joan Stone, and Vinie Burrows,* in a "celebration of the rebirth of women," Edison Theatre, New York, 11/20/72. All quotes from this until noted otherwise.

81. To cite just one of many feminist forums honoring AN, the Woman's Salon presented "A Tribute to AN," in celebration of the publication of D-6. Speakers and readers included Daisy Aldan, Nona Balakian, Erika Duncan, Valerie Harms, Gloria Orenstein, Sharon Spencer, Frances Steloff, Karen Malpede, and Alice Walker.

82. I am grateful to John Ferrone for this information.

83. For a long time it seemed as if Dartmouth would purchase the diaries because of the efforts of Barry Jones during his undergraduate years there. He was a Nin scholar who also nominated her for the honorary degree the college granted her in 1974. Correspondence attesting to this, and to his interest in her writing, is in Folders 1973 and 1974. Besides Dartmouth, among the colleges that expressed interest were the University of Texas, Northwestern, and several in the California state system. There were several cautious letters of inquiry from Harvard, but interest there was brief and probably not serious.

39. "The Book of Pain"

1. This is one of the final entries in a volume she entitled in the style of her earlier formal diary volumes, "Mon Journal/ Anaïs Nin." Informally, she and RP referred to it as "The Book of Music" (hereafter BM). On the inside cover, in RP's hand, is written, "May this diary bring life and love to the love of my life." It is signed simply "Rupert" and dated 11/1/75. The quotation cited here is from entries dictated by AN in the last weeks of her life, between Nov. 26 and Dec. 6, 1976, and written in this diary by RP when she was no longer able to write. She died 1/14/77. AN named the first volume of diary writing, which covers most of the year 1974, "The Book of Pain" (hereafter BP).

2. Physicians I have consulted tell me it is likely that she had venereal warts, but whether she had this or some other manifestation is not entirely clear. To this day, Rupert Pole cannot bring himself to discuss the physical manifestations of AN's terminal illness. Nor will he permit those physicians who are still alive among the many who treated her to discuss it or to release her medical records. His reaction is eminently comprehensible, and I fully appreciate that discussing AN's decline and death brings him more pain than he wishes to bear. He already knows how sincerely apologetic I was when I asked him to discuss it in the many generous interviews he granted me. But this situation proposes a dilemma for AN's biographer: I would have simply stated in this chapter that Anaïs Nin died of cancer had she herself not left such detailed reports of her condition. Because these diaries will most likely be published someday, and because this biography seems likely to remain the one of record for a long time to come, I felt it imperative to consult medical experts and ask for their help in interpreting the passages AN wrote describing the symptoms and treatment of her cancer. Although my analysis is based on their expert testimony, I nevertheless take full responsibility for the account that follows.

3. I am aware that AN wrote a different version in D-7 than what I am about to write here. The unpublished diaries and her correspondence do not support the published version, so I must dispute it. During the years she and RP worked on D-7, there are many references to permissions and legalities, and possibly libelous statements that had to be corrected. I cannot help but wonder if the details of her illness were not among those that had to be changed accordingly. The account that follows is from the first diary, which covered 1974 and that AN called "The Book of Pain." All quotes from it until noted otherwise. I have also relied here on AN/HG, 7/14/71, misfiled in Folder 1966.3; undated letters to HG, JNC/USF; and interviews with RP, JNC, and JF.

4. Physicians I have consulted say that if this were true, she would have experienced difficulties long before this.

5. She had been diagnosed earlier as having a "fibrone tumor," which the doctor told her would eventually dissolve. She left no writing to indicate that it did.

6. In D-7 she refers to it as a "radium implant." It may have been one of a number of things.

7. The activity was so intense and there was so much of it that I will simply refer interested scholars to *Pisces* for a full and accurate account.

8. Conversation with Nancy Milford, 12/90. AN/JNC, n.d., in Folder 1971. In a loose collection of diary jottings in possesson of RP (hereafter BoxDL/RP), AN wrote the following: "I wanted to discuss the possibilities of Zelda having been able to publish her diary . . . if she had not been surpressed as a writer might not have gone mad. We almost got into [theme of] retaliation. I would have suffered if I had been explicit about sex. Many themes occurred to me which Milford snuffed out. I asked her if she did not think we should eliminate all taboos. She hesitated. It was not an in-depth talk and not cohesive." I am grateful to Honor Moore for making her diary account of this program available to me. It corroborates both Milford's and AN's account.

9. This information is from an undated letter to HG. Internal evidence sets it at the end of 1970, the beginning of 1971. All quotes from it until noted otherwise.

10. AN/RCA, 3/14/70, RCA; also, a collection of undated pages of letter writing without a greeting, but which are obviously to Hugo. Internal evidence shows they date from April–June 1970.

11. AN/RC, 5/70, RCA.

12. AN/Inge Bogner, 1/4/74, copy in Folder 1974.

13. All of these comments and many more unflattering appellations are found in BP and BM.

14. AN/HG, 7/14/71, misfiled in Folder 1966.3. She also refers to increasingly cloudy vision diagnosed as a cataract in 1975. By that time she was so ill that no surgery was performed.

15. Bogner's initial training was in internal medicine, and from the beginning, AN asked all her physicians to explain her condition fully to Bogner so that she might translate it into lay terms and explain it in language AN could understand.

16. Letters, n.d., to her accountant, Roger Boulogne, and to HG. All folder 1973, with occasional originals to HG in JNC/USF.

17. Announcement to "Friends of Anaïs Nin" from Linden G. Leavitt, Dean of the College. AN explains her methodology and discusses how she taught one of her seven students in D-7, 277–278 and 320–322.

18. She used this term in an undated letter to James Leo Herlihy, which he read to me during an interview, 7/91. It appears in a slightly different form in D-7, 278–279.

19. JNC, interview, 7/91; AN/Inge Bogner, 11/29/71, misfiled in Folder 1973; HG/AN, 11/73. All quotes from these until noted otherwise.

20. This remark and many similar ones are from her letters to HG in various UCLA folders starting in 1972, others JNC/USF.

21. The following information is from a letter, n.d., to Gunther Stuhlmann, in which AN makes a drawing of the interior and explains what he must do to get the panel to open and shut. Copy in Folder 1971.

22. AN/HG, 9/18/73, copy in Folder 1973. These pleas start in the 9/3/73 letter and continue until the end of the year.

23. AN/HG, 11/6/73, original marked in AN's hand "please return," is in Folder 1973. I chose this letter to cite here because it represents the most clearly written statement of sentiments she expressed as early as 9/3/73.

24. HG/AN, 11/22/73.

25. This was how she explained the background and setting of Snyder's film to Hugo and all the others whom she did not tell about her double life.

26. AN/HG, 10/3/73, original in Folder 1973.

27. AN/Inge Bogner, 10/3/73, copy in Folder 1973.

28. BoxDL/RP. All quotes from this until noted otherwise.

29. These jottings begin on 1/9 and end on 2/2/74, when she returned to L.A. All quotes from BoxDL/RP until noted otherwise.

30. D-7, 302, gives a slightly different version of this remark.

31. Both in possession of RP. He did not include them with the others sold to UCLA.

32. BP. All quotes from this until noted otherwise.

33. I refer to all such letters, both originals and copies, in Folders 1975, BoxDL/RP, and JNC/USF. Because this letter is so filled with errors due to the medication that dulled her thinking and made her write in a scribble, I have taken the liberty in this one instance of correcting some of her words, occasionally inserting correct terminology in brackets, and also correcting her spelling. I have not, however, changed the content of the letter, which is exactly as I have quoted it here. The procedure she describes is probably an ileostomy.

34. BM, 4/24/76.

35. JNC/AN, 2/6/76, copy in Folder 1976, orig. JNC/USF. Unfortunately, Thorvald Nin did not express the same sentiments. In a letter addressed simply to Harcourt Brace & World, 5/13/71, TN said that "in spite of my wishes for absolute privacy," he discovered that "Mrs. Guiler" had "made references" to him in the published diaries. He instructed them to remove his name from any further diary volumes and "later on, we shall have to consider the damage done to date by the publication of the first three 'Diaries' and as a result of the extraordinary actions of Mrs. Guiler." He added that he was sending a copy "to Mrs. Guiler . . . requesting that she also acknowledge my requests." TN's letter was written shortly before the last reunion of the three children of Joaquín Nin and Rosa Culmell, to celebrate the playing of JNC's "Dedication Mass" at the dedication of the Cathedral of St. Mary of the Assumption in San Francisco. JNC and Gayle Nin Rosenkrantz describe encounters between TN and AN as "strained," "fractious," and "putting a damper on the festivities."

36. JNC, conversation, 5/20/94.

37. BP, April–May 1975. All information from this until noted otherwise. She wrote nothing in any of the diaries to indicate that she actually took this drug, Maruyama cancer vaccine. But in D-7, 339, RP wrote that she took it for two years "under a special dispensation of the U.S. Food and Drug Administration."

38. BM, 6/25/76. All information from this until noted otherwise.

39. Phrase she uses in letter to Inge Bogner inserted into BP, 5/4/75.

40. This is her first long meditation on death, in BM, 8/1/76.

41. AN's emphasis.

42. BM, 10/27/76.

43. The following account is from AN/Inge Bogner, 5/5/75, and repeated retellings of this incident throughout BM in 1976.

44. BM, 8/76.

45. BM, 8/20/76.

46. After her death, RP assumed editorial responsibility for D-7 and the other unexpurgated volumes that have since appeared.

47. From documents re: *Estate and Trust of Anaïs Nin,* Last Will of AN dated 4/20/76, Trust Agreement between AN as Trustor and RP as Trustee executed 11/10/75, amended 4/20/76, amended again 6/21/76. All prepared by Phyllis Z. Deutsch. I am grateful to JNC and Gayle Nin Rosenkrantz for making copies available to me, also to GNR for her letter of 12/2/93, explaining the legal history of AN's estate.

48. In a letter dated 2/16/76, Boston, Corita Kent said, "it's hard to believe I've never seen you face to face." AN had earlier written to offer to go to Boston to take care of her. She meant the offer sincerely, but of course it was impossible.

49. Ronald de Leeuw, "Anaïs Nin et son édifice Proustien," *Bulletin de la Société Neérlandaise de la Société des amis du Proust.*

50. Joan Palevsky, interview, 10/4/91.

51. One of the first is in his letter of 4/15/76. Hers to him are mostly undated. All are JNC/USF.

52. As told by AN to JNC, RP, and many, many others. John Ferrone, in a letter to DB, 10/12/92, believes that AN never told HG directly not to visit her, and that "It was [Evelyn] Hinz who told Hugo that Anaïs did not want him to visit her in L.A. because she wanted one person to remember her as she was."

53. These letters begin as early as 1955 and are in the appropriate folders, ending in 1975.

54. The following account is taken from conversations with JNC and JF; from JF/DB, 10/12/92, and JF's journal entry for 9/8/77, written after a visit to HG in his apartment in Washington Square Village.

55. JF, journal entry, 9/8/77.

56. JNC/USF, n.d.

57. On file in the office of the Registrar-Recorder/County Clerk, County of Los Angeles.

58. Robert Snyder, *Anaïs Observed,* 112.

59. The following account is taken from the original ending of an article I wrote for *Angeles* magazine in 1990.

Epilogue

1. Tel. conversations with Raymonde Olivier, 2/28 and 3/9/92; interviews with JNC, Victor Lipari, 5/7/92; Frank Alberti, 7/91; Alexandra Souteriou, 4/12/93. Ms. Olivier told me she often heard HG talking and chuckling, and he would tell her later how "amusing" AN had been that morning.

2. Information that follows is from John Ferrone, "The Making of *Delta of Venus,"* in *Anaïs Nin, Art and Artists,* Modern Literatures Annual, vol. 2, ed. Sharon Spencer (Greenwood, FL, Penkevill Publishing Company, 1986); interviews with JF, RP, JNC, Spencer.

3. RP, in interviews, has said that it was AN's wish to publish the erotica because she was afraid there was not enough money to pay her medical bills. He has also said repeatedly that as his wife, AN's medical bills were paid by his health plan, Kaiser Permanente. They were actually paid by HG through his Blue Cross, Blue Shield, and Guardian health insurance, and by Medicare in the last years of AN's illness. All her medical bills were tendered in the name of Anaïs Nin Guiler and delivered to HG in New York.

4. JF/HG, 8/11/77. From his archives and graciously made available to me by JF.

5. The jacket was designed by Harris Lewine of HBJ and the graphic artist

Milton Glaser, using a photo from the Richard Merkin Collection of Erotic Art. It is not, as has so often been reported, a photograph of AN, whose reaction to it was negative until friends persuaded her to withdraw her reservations.

6. Sharon Spencer noted this in a review, "Delta of Venus: Erotica," *The American Book Review,* Vol. 1, no. 1, 12/77.

7. This is an informal count prepared by Gunther Stuhlmann for this book in 1/94. As it changes monthly, I have settled here for approximation.

8. John Ferrone retired after the publication of *Henry and June;* the publishing house resumed its original name when William Jovanovich sold it.

9. Evelyn Hinz to DB, RP, and JNC, all 12/8/92.

Index

Figures in italics indicate illustrations

INDEX

INDEX

INDEX

INDEX

INDEX

INDEX

INDEX

INDEX